Adobe® InDesign® CS4
The Professional Portfolio

AGAINST THE CLOCK
mastering graphic technology

Managing Editor: Ellenn Behoriam
Cover & Interior Design: Erika Kendra
Copy Editor: Laurel Nelson-Cucchiara
Proofreader: Angelina Kendra

Copyright © 2009 Against The Clock, Inc. All rights reserved. Printed in the United States of America. This publication is protected by copyright, and permission should be obtained in writing from the publisher prior to any prohibited reproduction, storage in a retrieval system, or transmission in any form or by any means, electronic, mechanical, photocopying, recording, or likewise.

The fonts utilized in these training materials are the property of Against The Clock, Inc., and are supplied to the legitimate buyers of the Against The Clock training materials solely for use with the exercises and projects provided in the body of the materials. They may not be used for any other purpose, and under no circumstances may they be transferred to another individual, nor copied or distributed by any means whatsoever.

A portion of the images supplied in this book are copyright © PhotoDisc, Inc., 201 Fourth Ave., Seattle, WA 98121, or copyright ©PhotoSpin, 4030 Palos Verdes Dr. N., Suite 200, Rollings Hills Estates, CA. These images are the sole property of PhotoDisc or PhotoSpin and are used by Against The Clock with the permission of the owners. They may not be distributed, copied, transferred, or reproduced by any means whatsoever, other than for the completion of the exercises and projects contained in this Against The Clock training material.

Against The Clock and the Against The Clock logo are trademarks of Against The Clock, Inc., registered in the United States and elsewhere. References to and instructional materials provided for any particular application program, operating system, hardware platform, or other commercially available product or products do not represent an endorsement of such product or products by Against The Clock, Inc.

Photoshop, Acrobat, Illustrator, InDesign, PageMaker, Flash, Dreamweaver, Premiere, and PostScript are trademarks of Adobe Systems Incorporated. Macintosh is a trademark of Apple Computer, Inc. QuarkXPress is a registered trademark of Quark, Inc. FrontPage, Publisher, PowerPoint, Word, Excel, Office, Microsoft, MS-DOS, and Windows are either registered trademarks or trademarks of Microsoft Corporation.

Other product and company names mentioned herein may be the trademarks of their respective owners.

10 9 8 7 6 5 4 3 2

978-0-9815216-6-4

AGAINST THE CLOCK
mastering graphic technology

4710 28th Street North, Saint Petersburg, FL 33714
800-256-4ATC • www.againsttheclock.com

Acknowledgements

About Against The Clock

Against The Clock has been publishing graphic communications educational materials for more than 17 years, starting out as a Tampa, Florida-based systems integration firm whose primary focus was on skills development in high-volume, demanding commercial environments. Among the company's clients were LL Bean, The New England Journal of Medicine, the Smithsonian, and many others. Over the years, Against The Clock has developed a solid and widely-respected approach to teaching people how to effectively utilize graphics applications while maintaining a disciplined approach to real-world problems.

Against The Clock has been recognized as one of the nation's leaders in courseware development. Having developed the *Against The Clock* and the *Essentials for Design* series with Prentice Hall/Pearson Education, the firm works closely with all major software developers to ensure timely release of educational products aimed at new version releases.

About the Authors

Erika Kendra holds a BA in History and a BA in English Literature from the University of Pittsburgh. She began her career in the graphic communications industry as an editor at Graphic Arts Technical Foundation before moving to Los Angeles in 2000. Erika is the author or co-author of more than fifteen books about graphic design software, including QuarkXPress, Adobe Photoshop, Adobe InDesign, and Adobe PageMaker. She has also written several books about graphic design concepts such as color reproduction and preflighting, and dozens of articles for online and print journals in the graphics industry. Working with Against The Clock for more than seven years, Erika was a key partner in developing the new Portfolio Series of software training books.

Gary Poyssick, co-owner of Against The Clock, is a well-known and often controversial speaker, writer, and industry consultant who has been involved in professional graphics and communications for more than twenty years. He wrote the highly popular *Workflow Reengineering* (Adobe Press), *Teams and the Graphic Arts Service Provider* (Prentice Hall), *Creative Techniques: Adobe Illustrator*, and *Creative Techniques: Adobe Photoshop* (Hayden Books), and was the author or co-author of many application-specific training books from Against The Clock.

Contributing Authors, Artists, and Editors

A big thank you to the people whose artwork, comments, and expertise contributed to the success of these books:

- **Doris Anton,** Wichita State University
- **Carin Murphy,** Des Moines Area Community College
- **Michael Wills,** Art Institute of Pittsburgh
- **Robin McAllister,** Against The Clock, Inc.
- **Debbie Davidson**, Sweet Dreams Design
- **Dean Bagley**, Against The Clock, Inc.

Thanks also to **Laurel Nelson-Cucchiara**, editor, and **Angelina Kendra**, proofreader, for their help in making sure that we all said what we meant to say.

Walk-Through

Project Goals
Each project begins with a clear description of the overall concepts that are explained in the project; these goals closely match the different "stages" of the project workflow.

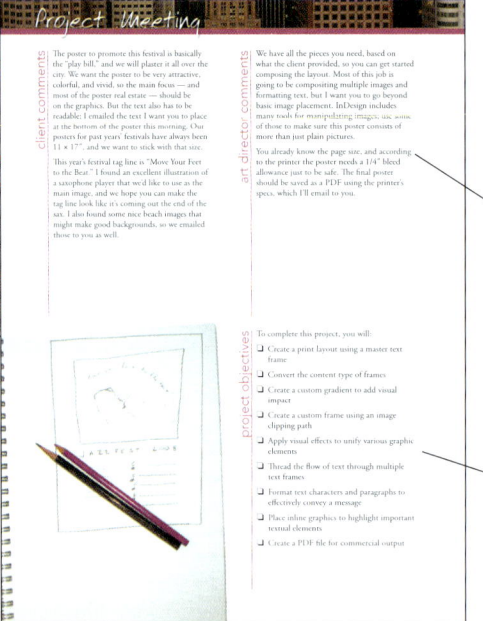

The Project Meeting
Each project includes the client's initial comments, which provide valuable information about the job. The Project Art Director, a vital part of any design workflow, also provides fundamental advice and production requirements.

Project Objectives
Each Project Meeting includes a summary of the specific skills required to complete the project.

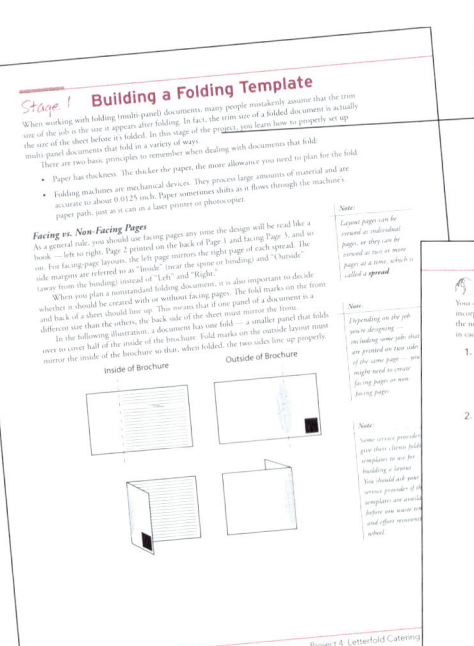

Real-World Workflow
Projects are broken into logical lessons or "stages" of the workflow. Brief introductions at the beginning of each stage provide vital foundational material required to complete the task.

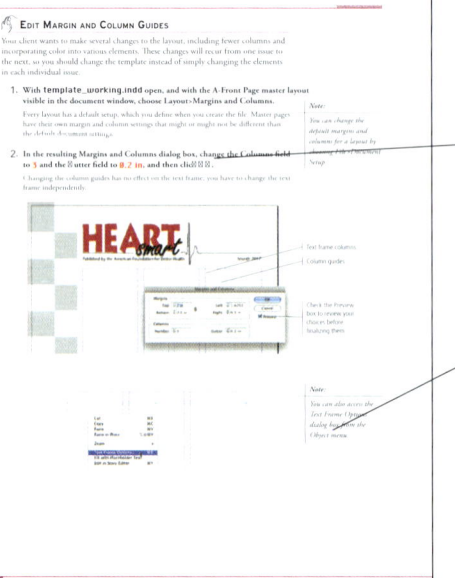

Step-By-Step Exercises
Every stage of the workflow is broken into multiple hands-on, step-by-step exercises.

Visual Explanations
Wherever possible, screen shots are annotated so students can quickly identify important information.

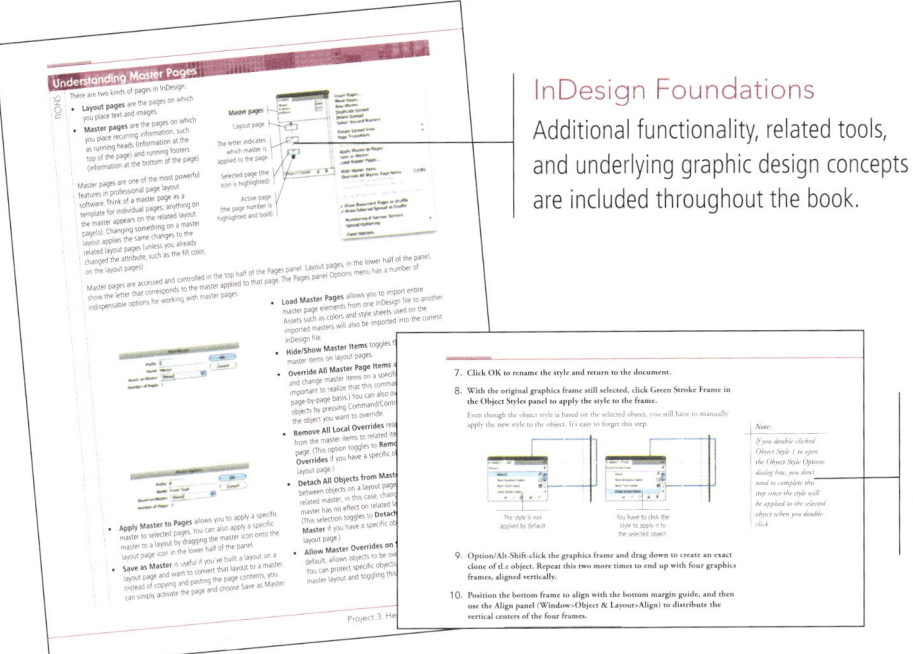

InDesign Foundations
Additional functionality, related tools, and underlying graphic design concepts are included throughout the book.

Advice and Warnings
Where appropriate, sidebars provide shortcuts, warnings, or tips about the topic at hand.

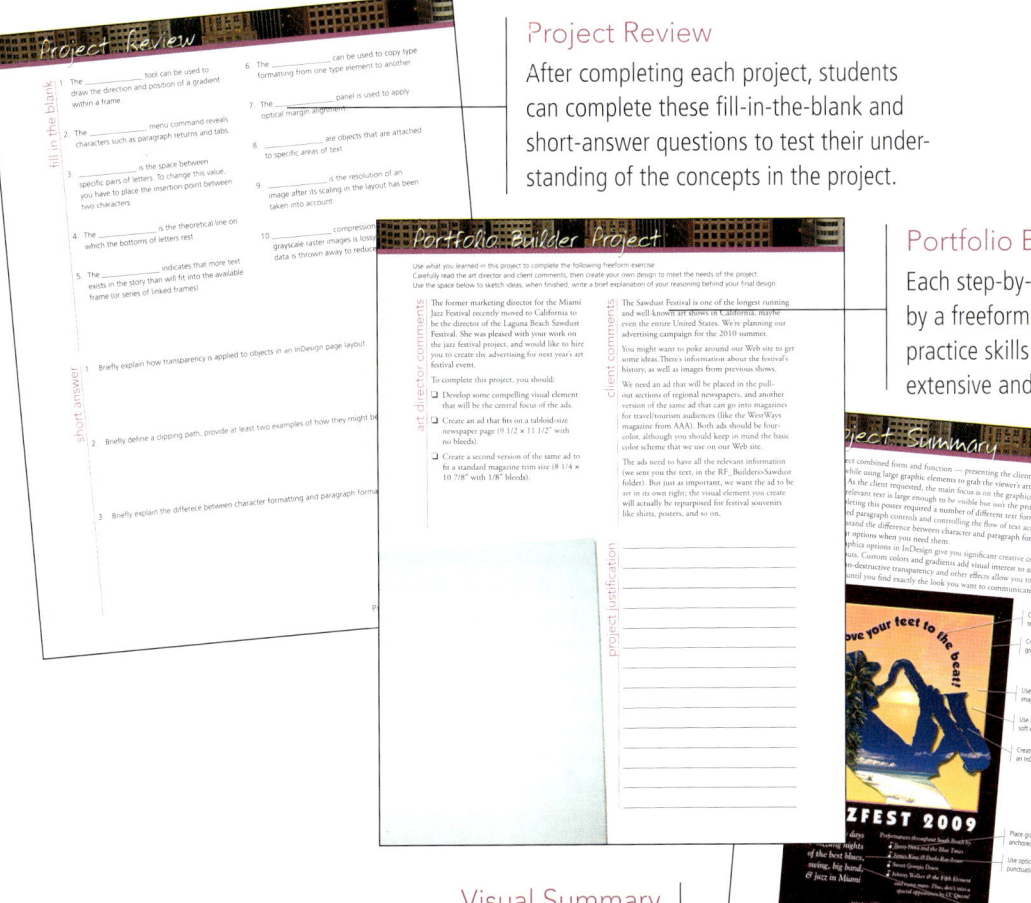

Project Review
After completing each project, students can complete these fill-in-the-blank and short-answer questions to test their understanding of the concepts in the project.

Portfolio Builder Projects
Each step-by-step project is accompanied by a freeform project, allowing students to practice skills and creativity, resulting in an extensive and diverse portfolio of work.

Visual Summary
Using an annotated version of the finished project, students can quickly identify the skills used to complete different aspects of the job.

Projects at a Glance

The Against The Clock *Portfolio Series* teaches graphic design software tools and techniques entirely within the framework of real-world projects; we introduce and explain skills where they would naturally fall into a real project workflow. For example, rather than offering an entire chapter about printing (which most students find boring), we teach printing where you naturally need to do so — when you complete a print-based project.

The project-based approach in the *Portfolio Series* allows you to get in depth with the software beginning in Project 1 — you don't have to read several chapters of introductory material before you can start creating finished artwork.

The project-based approach of the *Portfolio Series* also prevents "topic tedium" — in other words, we don't require you to read pages and pages of information about text (for example); instead, we explain text tools and options as part of larger projects (in this case, beginning with placing text on corporate identity pieces).

Clear, easy-to-read, step-by-step instructions walk you through every phase of each job, from creating a new file to saving the finished piece. Wherever logical, we also offer practical advice and tips about underlying concepts and graphic design practices that will benefit students as they enter the job market.

The projects in this book reflect a range of different types of InDesign jobs, from creating a corporate identity package to implementing a newsletter template to compiling a multi-chapter book. When you finish the eight projects in this book (and the accompanying Portfolio Builder exercises), you will have a substantial body of work that should impress any potential employer.

The eight InDesign CS4 projects are described briefly here; more detail is provided in the full table of contents (beginning on Page viii).

project 1: *Identity Package*

- ❏ Setting up the Workspace
- ❏ Drawing in InDesign
- ❏ Create and Format Basic Text
- ❏ Creating a Cohesive Layout
- ❏ Printing InDesign Files

project 2: *Festival Poster*

- ❏ Building Graphic Interest
- ❏ Importing and Formatting Text
- ❏ Graphics as Text and Text as Graphics
- ❏ Outputting the File

project 3: *HeartSmart Newsletter*

- ❏ Working with Templates
- ❏ Working with Styles
- ❏ Working with Tables
- ❏ Preflighting and Packaging the Job

project 4: Letterfold Catering Menu

❏ Building a Folding Template
❏ Working with Imported Text
❏ Editing Advanced Frame Options

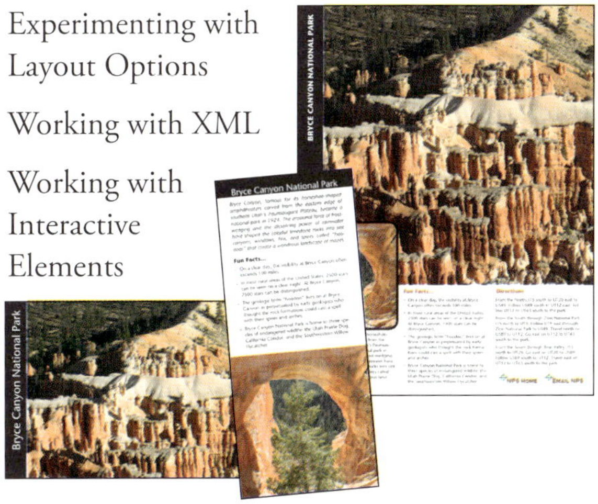

project 5: Realtor Collateral Booklet

❏ Working with Master Pages
❏ Controlling Text Flow
❏ Outputting Variations of Files

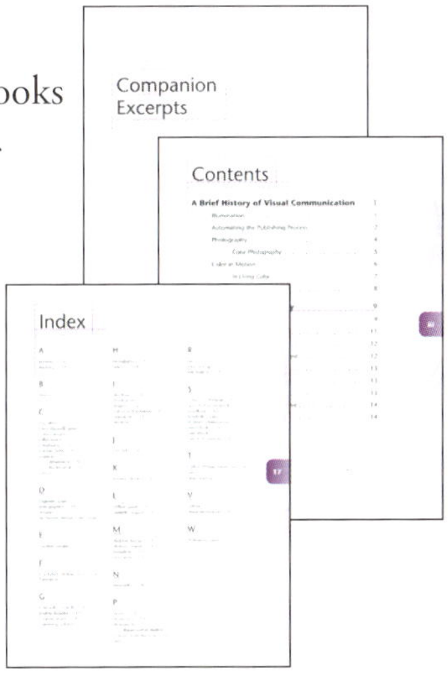

project 6: Versioned Brochure

❏ Controlling Color for Output
❏ Placing and Controlling Images
❏ Controlling and Checking Text
❏ Creating Multiple Layers

project 7: National Parks Info Pieces

❏ Experimenting with Layout Options
❏ Working with XML
❏ Working with Interactive Elements

project 8: Multi-Chapter Booklet

❏ Combining Documents into Books
❏ Building a Table of Contents
❏ Building an Index
❏ Exporting Book Files
❏ Merging Data into an InDesign Layout

Some experts claim most people use only a small fraction — maybe 10% — of their software's capabilities; this is likely because many people don't know what is available. As you complete the projects in this book, our goal is to familiarize you with the entire tool set so you can be more productive and more marketable in your career as a graphic designer.

It is important to keep in mind that InDesign is an extremely versatile and powerful application. The sheer volume of available tools, panels, and features can seem intimidating when you first look at the software interface. Most of these tools, however, are fairly simple to use with a bit of background information and a little practice.

Wherever necessary, we explain the underlying concepts and terms that are required for understanding the software. And we're confident that these projects provide the practice you need to be able to create sophisticated artwork by the end of the very first project.

vii

Contents

Acknowledgements III

Walk-Through IV

Projects at a Glance VI

The InDesign User Interface 1
InDesign Menus 1
The Macintosh Application Frame 3
Identifying and Accessing Tools in InDesign 6
Explore the Arrangement of InDesign Panels 7
Create a Saved Workspace 10
Customizing Keyboard Shortcuts and Menus 11
Customizing InDesign Preferences 12
Explore the InDesign Document Views 12
Explore the Arrangement of Multiple Documents 18
Summing up the InDesign View Options 19

Project 1 Identity Package 23
Stage 1 Setting up the Workspace 25
Create and Save a Basic InDesign File 25
Create the Letterhead Document 28
Create the Business Card Document 31
Managing Document Presets 33
Create the Envelope Document 34

Stage 2 Drawing in InDesign 35
Vector Graphics vs. Raster Images 35
Understanding Resolution 36
Create and Transform Basic Shapes 37
Understanding the Control Panel 40
Using InDesign Smart Guides 43
Aligning and Distributing Objects 44
Create and Edit Anchor Points and Curves 45
Understanding Anchor Points and Handles 48
Apply Color to Page Elements 49
Create and Control Lines 51
The Stroke Panel in Depth 56
Create Irregular Shapes with the Polygon Tool 56
Use the Pathfinder Panel to Create Complex Objects 59
The Pathfinder Panel in Depth 61

Stage 3 Create and Format Basic Text 62
Create a Simple Text Frame 62
Selecting Text 63
Export EPS Files 67
Why CMYK? 67
Export EPS Options 68

viii

Stage 4	**Creating a Cohesive Layout**	71
	Place External Graphics Files	71
	Place an External Text File	75
	Control Paragraph Formatting	79
	Copy Objects and Import Spot Colors	81
	Design the Business Card	85
Stage 5	**Printing InDesign Files**	85
	Print Desktop Proofs	85
	Project Review	88
	Portfolio Builder Project	89

Project 2 FESTIVAL POSTER   91

Stage 1	**Building Graphic Interest**	93
	Define Color Swatches	93
	Color by Numbers	95
	Define and Apply a Gradient	97
	The Gradient Tools	100
	Create Visual Impact with Transparency	101
	Blending Modes	104
	Applying Effects	107
	Create an Irregular Graphics Frame	109
Stage 2	**Importing and Formatting Text**	113
	Control Text Threading	113
	Clipping Path Options	113
	Define Manual Frame Breaks	116
	Apply Character Formatting	118
	Apply Paragraph Formatting	122
	Understanding the Baseline Grid	123
	Use Optical Margin Alignment	126
	Copying Type Attributes with the Eyedropper Tool	127
Stage 3	**Graphics as Text and Text as Graphics**	128
	Place Inline Graphics	128
	Working with Anchored Objects	129
	Anchored Object Size and Text Position	130
	Custom Anchor Options	131
	Create Type on a Path	132
	Text Path Options	134
	Flattener Presets	136
Stage 4	**Outputting the File**	136
	Export a PDF File for Print	137
	Using the Flattener Preview Panel	137
	Resolution Options for PDF	139
	Project Review	141
	Portfolio Builder Project	142

Contents

Project 3   HeartSmart Newsletter **145**

Stage 1   Working with Templates 147
- Manage Missing Fonts and Images 147
- Replace Missing Graphics 150
- The Links Panel in Depth 151
- Edit Margin and Column Guides 152
- Change Repeating Template and Master Page Elements 154
- Understanding Master Pages 155
- Save a New Template 158
- Create a New File Based on the Template 159
- Implement the Newsletter Template 162

Stage 2   Working with Styles 165
- Apply Template Styles 165
- Working with Microsoft Word Files 171
- Text Frame Options 172
- Create a Sidebar Box 173
- Text Wrap Options 176

Stage 3   Working with Tables 177
- Place a Microsoft Excel Table 177
- Format Cell Contents 179
- Format Cell Attributes 181
- Controlling Cell Attributes 183
- Strokes and Fills in Tables 184
- Define Table Fills and Strokes 184
- Managing Table Setup 186
- Creating Table Headers and Footers 189
- Table Styles 190

Stage 4   Preflighting and Packaging the Job 191
- Define a Preflight Profile 191
- What's in a Preflight Profile? 195
- Evaluate the Layout 197
- Create the Job Package 199

Project Review 201

Portfolio Builder Project 202

Project 4 LETTERFOLD CATERING MENU — 205

Stage 1 Building a Folding Template 207
    Basic Types of Folds 208
    Set up Folding Guides 209
    Add Slug Information and Placeholders 212
    Save a Template 215
    Pages Panel Options 216

Stage 2 Working with Imported Text 217
    Import and Thread Text across Frames 217
    Import Styles from Microsoft Word 219
    Import and Replace InDesign Styles 222
    What's in a Paragraph Style? 225
    Edit Style Definitions 226
    Cut and Delete Text 230
    Create a Style for Pull Quotes 231
    Understanding Nested Styles 232
    Building Complex Nested Styles 233
    Nested Style Character Options 236
    Control Tab Formatting 237

Stage 3 Editing Advanced Frame Options 239
    Define an Object Style 239
    What's in an Object Style? 240
    Edit the Basic Graphics Frame Style 243
    Access Embedded Clipping Paths and Alpha Channels 244
    Import Object Styles 248
    Add the Logo and Address Information 250
    Create an InDesign Library 251
    Managing Libraries 253

    Project Review 254
    Portfolio Builder Project 255

Project 5 REALTOR COLLATERAL BOOKLET — 257

Stage 1 Working with Master Pages 259
    Create the Booklet File 259
    Create Master Pages from Layout Pages 260
    Understanding Master Page Icons 261
    Import Master Pages 263
    Edit the Default Master Page 266
    Understanding Relative Object Positioning 268
    Add Common Elements to a Master Page Layout 271
    Special Characters and White Space 274
    Place Automatic Page Number Markers 274
    Keyboard Shortcuts for Special Characters 276
    Create Text Variables 278
    Custom Text Variable Options 281

Contents

Stage 2 Controlling Text Flow 283
    Change the Custom Text Variable 283
    Import and Auto-Flow Client Text 284
    Review, Replace, and Edit Imported Styles 286
    Define Parent-Child Style Relationships 290
    Define Bullets and Numbering Options 294
    The Glyphs Panel 297
    Control Page and Frame Breaks 298
    Control Automatic Hyphenation 303
    Overriding Automatic Hyphenation 305
    Paragraph Composition Options 306
    Redefine Styles Based on Local Formatting Overrides 306
    Finalize the File 309

Stage 3 Outputting Variations of Files 312
    Create a Folding Dummy 312
    Print a Booklet Proof 313
    Understanding Imposition 314
    Create a PDF with Page Transitions 316
    Create Variations with Conditional Text 319

    Project Review 322
    Portfolio Builder Project 323

Project 6 Versioned Brochure 325

Stage 1 Controlling Color for Output 327
    Color Management in Theory and Practice 329
    Define Color Settings 330
    Understanding Rendering Intents 331
    Assigning and Converting Color Profiles 332

Stage 2 Placing and Controlling Images 333
    Replace a Native Illustrator File 333
    Place a Native Photoshop File 336
    Reviewing Image Color Settings 338
    Place an EPS File 340
    Controlling Display Performance 342
    Place a TIFF File 343
    Place a PDF File 344
    Place an InDesign File 346
    Edit a Linked File 347
    Place Multiple JPEG Images 350
    Content Fitting Options 352

Stage 3	**Controlling and Checking Text**	355
	Place and Cut Text	355
	Find and Change Layout Text	358
	Entering Special Characters in Dialog Boxes	360
	Find and Change Formatting Attributes	361
	The Find/Change Dialog Box in Depth	367
	Check Document Spelling	368
	Using Dynamic Spelling	372
Stage 4	**Creating Multiple Layers**	373
	Create a New Layer	373
	Controlling Text Wrap on Different Layers	374
	Control Objects and Layers	375
	Use a Duplicate Layer to Create Different Versions	378
	Preview Separations	379
	Monitoring Ink Limits	380
	Export Color-Managed PDF Files	383
	Using the Ink Manager	385
	Understanding Trapping for Color Printing	386
	Controlling Trapping in InDesign	388
	Project Review	389
	Portfolio Builder Project	390

Project 7   NATIONAL PARKS INFO PIECES   393

Stage 1	**Experimenting with Layout Options**	395
	Use Text Placeholders to Structure a Layout	395
	Experiment with Text Formatting	399
	Navigating and Selecting Text with Keyboard Shortcuts	400
	Formatting Text with Keyboard Shortcuts	402
	Experiment with Glyphs	403
	Using OpenType Attributes	406
	Create Styles from Experimental Formatting	407
	Experiment with Graphic Placeholders	409
	Save the Final Template	412
	Adjust the Layout to Supplied Content	414
	Create Swatches from Sampled Colors	417
Stage 2	**Working with XML**	419
	Tag Frames for XML	419
	Review Document Structure	422
	Review XML Structure and Attributes	424
	Identifying Structure Pane Icons	425
	Place Unstructured XML Content	427
	Options for Exporting XML	427
	Import XML Options	429
	Update Linked XML Data	432
	Import Structured XML	434
	Validating Structure with a DTD	439

Contents

Stage 3	**Working with Interactive Elements**	440
	Define Hyperlinks	440
	Create Button States	442
	Define Button Behavior	444
	Export Multiple PDF Files	447
	Project Review	449
	Portfolio Builder Project	450

Project 8   MULTI-CHAPTER BOOKLET   453

Stage 1	**Combining Documents into Books**	455
	Build an InDesign Book	455
	Add Book Chapters	457
	Managing Book Chapters	459
	Control Section and Page Numbering	460
	Understanding Book Page Numbering	461
	Section and Chapter Numbering in Depth	464
	Synchronize Book Files	466
	Smart Matching Style Groups	468
Stage 2	**Building a Table of Contents**	470
	Define a Table of Contents Style	470
	Build and Update a Table of Contents	474
Stage 3	**Building an Index**	476
	Tag Basic and Reversed Index Topics	477
	Changing Topic Sort Order	479
	Add Multiple Page References	481
	Add Page-Range References	483
	Adding Cross-References in an Index	486
	Add Multiple-Level References	486
	Build the Book's Index	487
	Options for Generating an Index	489
Stage 4	**Exporting Book Files**	490
	Export PDF Files for Print and Digital Distribution	490
	The Data Source File	492
Stage 5	**Merging Data into an InDesign Layout**	492
	Create the Merged Document and Load the Source Data	493
	Cleaning up Data	494
	Incorporating Images in a Data Merge	496
	Complete the Merged Document	497
	Managing Empty Data Fields	498
	Working with Long Text Fields	499
	Merging Multiple Records on a Single Page	500
	Project Review	501
	Portfolio Builder Project	502

Getting Started

Prerequisites

The entire Portfolio Series is based on the assumption that you have a basic understanding of how to use your computer. You should know how to use your mouse to point and click, as well as how to drag items around the screen. You should be able to resize and arrange windows on your desktop to maximize your available space. You should know how to access drop-down menus, and understand how check boxes and radio buttons work. It also doesn't hurt to have a good understanding of how your operating system organizes files and folders, and how to navigate your way around them. If you're familiar with these fundamental skills, then you know all that's necessary to use the Portfolio Series.

Resource Files

All of the files that you need to complete the projects in this book are on the provided Resource CD in the **RF_InDesign** folder. This folder contains nine subfolders, one for each project in the book (including the Interface); you will be directed to the appropriate folder whenever you need to access a specific file. Files required for the related Portfolio Builder exercises are in the **RF_Builders** folder.

The Resource CD also includes a **WIP** folder, which also contains (mostly empty) subfolders for each project in the book. This is where you will save your work as you complete the various projects. In some cases, the location of a file will be extremely important for later steps in a project to work properly; that's why we've provided a specific set of folders with known file names.

Before you begin working on the projects in this book, you should copy the entire WIP folder to your hard drive or some other recordable media such as a flash drive; when we tell you to save a file, you should save it to the appropriate folder on the drive where you put that WIP folder.

ATC Fonts

You must install the ATC fonts from the Resource CD to ensure that your exercises and projects will work as described in the book; these fonts are provided on the Resource CD in the **ATC Fonts** folder. Specific instructions for installing fonts are provided in the documentation that came with your computer. You should replace older (pre-2004) ATC fonts with the ones on your Resource CD.

System Requirements

As software technology continues to mature, the differences in functionality from one platform to another continue to diminish. The Portfolio Series was designed to work on both Macintosh or Windows computers; where differences exist from one platform to another, we include specific instructions relative to each platform.

One issue that remains different from Macintosh to Windows is the use of different modifier keys (Control, Shift, etc.) to accomplish the same task. When we present key commands, we always follow the same Macintosh/Windows format — Macintosh keys are listed first, then a slash, followed by the Windows key command.

Minimum System Requirements for Adobe InDesign CS4:

Windows
- 1.5GHz or faster processor
- Microsoft® Windows® XP with Service Pack 2 or Windows Vista® with Service Pack 1
- 512 MB of RAM (1 GB recommended)
- 1.8 GB of available hard-disk space for installation
- 1,024×768 display with 16-bit video card
- DVD-ROM drive
- QuickTime 7 required for multimedia features

Macintosh
- PowerPC® G5 or multicore Intel® processor
- Mac OS X v10.4.11–10.5.4
- 512 MB of RAM (1 GB recommended)
- 1.6 GB of available hard-disk space for installation
- 1,024×768 display with 16-bit video card
- DVD-ROM drive
- QuickTime 7.2 required for multimedia features

The InDesign User Interface

Adobe InDesign is a robust desktop-publishing application that — together with Illustrator, Photoshop, and Acrobat — rounds out Adobe's Creative Suite for print applications. InDesign provides the tools you need to design and create effective pages. It allows you to integrate text and graphics — prepared in the program or imported from other sources — produce files that can be printed to a local or networked printer, taken to a commercial printer or other graphic arts service provider, or published to the World Wide Web.

Since its initial release, InDesign has offered designers the tools they need to exercise precise control over every element on a document page. This book is designed to teach you how the tools and features of InDesign can be used to complete any project, from a 1-page flyer to a 500-page book. We also teach you how to produce professional layouts quickly and easily, including shortcuts and tips that help you produce the same high-quality results with far less repetition.

The sheer volume of available options in InDesign means there are numerous tools, panels, and other elements you need to learn to make the most of the application. The simple exercises in this introduction are designed to let you explore the InDesign user interface. Whether you are new to the application or upgrading from a previous version, we highly recommend you follow these steps to click around and become familiar with the basic workspace. When you get to Project 1, you will be better prepared to jump right in and start building pages.

Explore the InDesign Interface

The user interface (UI) is what you see when you launch the application. The specific elements you see — including which panels are open and where they appear on the screen — depend on what was done the last time the application was open. The first time you launch InDesign, you see the default workspace settings defined by Adobe. When you relaunch the application after you or another user has quit, the workspace defaults to the last-used settings — including specific open panels and the position of those panels on your screen.

InDesign Menus

InDesign Foundations

Like most applications, InDesign has a Menu bar across the top of the workspace; nine menus provide access to virtually all available options. (Macintosh users have two extra menus. The Apple menu provides access to system-specific commands. The InDesign menu follows the Macintosh system-standard format for all applications; this menu controls basic application operations such as About, Hide, Preferences, and Quit.) Although you will explore most of the specific menu options as you complete the projects in this book, you should understand what different indicators mean within the application menus.

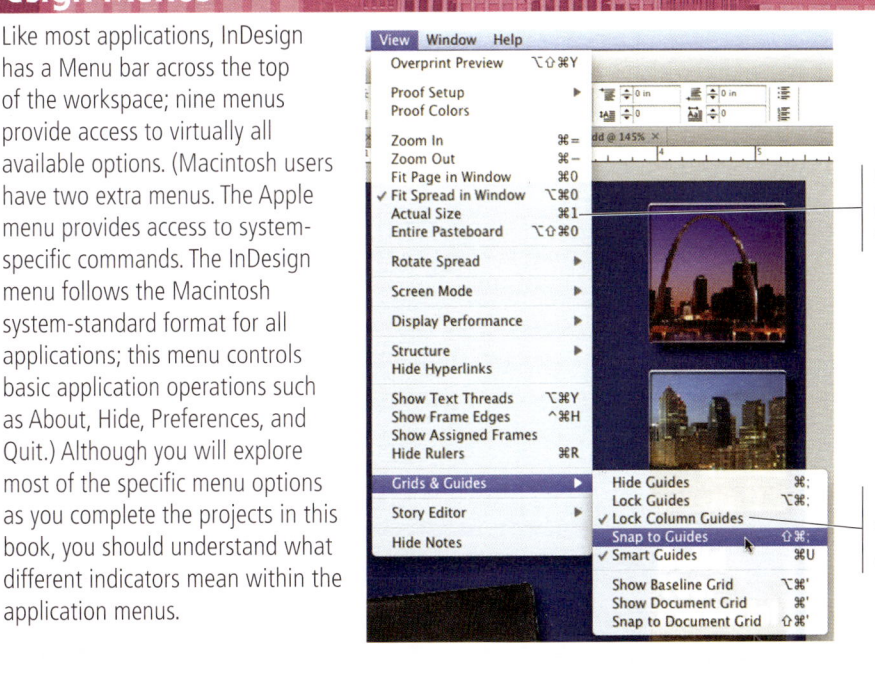

Keyboard shortcuts (if available) are listed on the right side of the menu.

Many menu commands are toggles; the checkmark indicates that an option is visible or toggled on.

1

1. **Launch InDesign.**

2. **Macintosh users: Open the Window menu. If Application Frame is not checked (active), choose that command in the menu.**

Note:

Most screen shots in this book show floating panels so we can focus on the most important issue in a particular image. In our production workflow, however, we make heavy use of docked and iconized panels and take full advantage of saved custom workspaces.

3. **Choose Window>Workspace>Reset Essentials.**

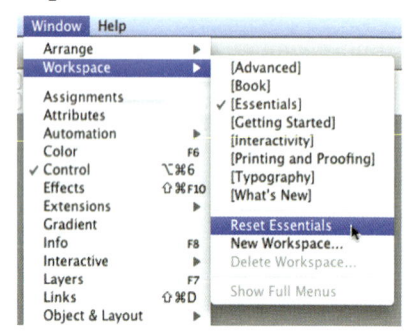

This step might not do anything, depending on what was done in InDesign before you started this project. If you or someone else changes anything and quits the application, those changes are remembered even when InDesign is relaunched. Because we can't be sure what your default settings show, by completing this step you reset the user interface to one of the default Essentials workspaces so your screen shots will match ours.

Saved **workspaces** (accessed in the Window>Workspace menu, or in the Workspace switcher on the Application/Menu bar) provide one-click access to a defined group of tools that might take ten or more clicks to create each time you need the same toolset.

The Essentials workspace includes the Tools panel on the left side of the screen, the Control panel at the top of the screen, and a set of panels attached to the right side of the screen. (The area where the panels are stored is called the **panel dock**.)

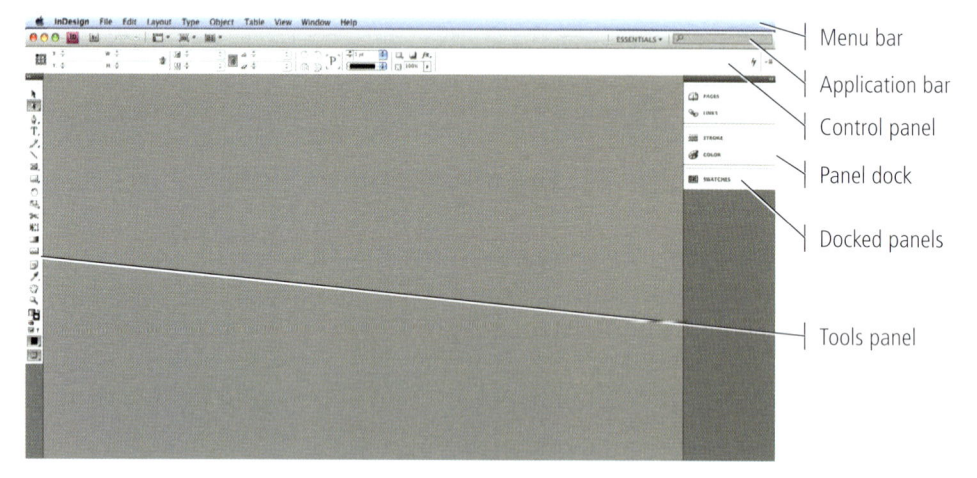

Note:

On Macintosh systems, the Application bar includes a number of buttons for accessing different view options. On Windows systems, those same options are available on the right side of the Menu bar. (We'll come back to these specific options later in this chapter.)

Menu bar
Application bar
Control panel
Panel dock
Docked panels
Tools panel

On Windows, the right side of the Menu bar provides access to the same options that are in the Macintosh Application bar.

Menu bar
Control panel

2 The InDesign User Interface

4. **Click the title bar above the column of docked panels.**

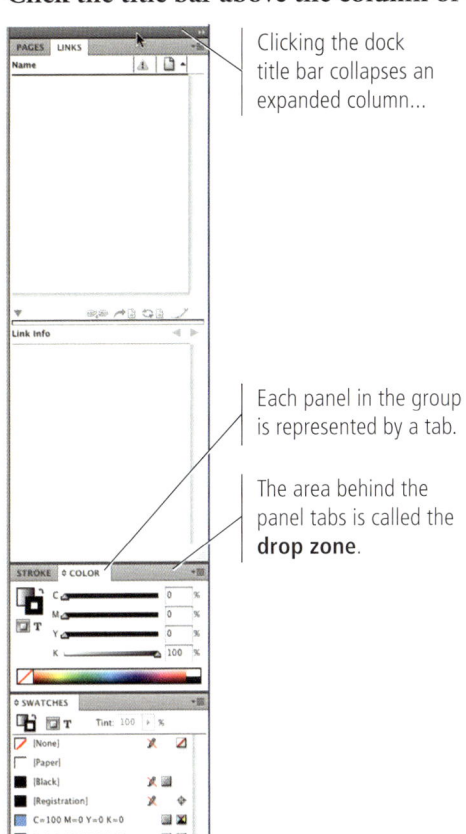

Clicking the dock title bar collapses an expanded column...

...or expands a collapsed column.

Each panel in the group is represented by a tab.

The area behind the panel tabs is called the **drop zone**.

Note:

You can create multiple columns of panels in the dock. Each column, technically considered a separate dock, can be expanded or collapsed independently of other columns.

The Macintosh Application Frame

On Windows, each running application is contained within its own frame; all elements of the application — including the Menu bar, panels, tools, and open documents — are contained within that Application frame.

In CS4, Adobe introduced the Application frame concept to Macintosh users as an option for controlling the workspace. When you activate the Application frame, the entire workspace shifts into a self-contained area that can be moved around the screen; all elements of the workspace (excluding the Menu bar) move with the Application frame. The Application frame is active by default, and it can be toggled on or off in the Window menu.

Using the Application frame is purely a matter of personal preference; it can be particularly useful for Windows users who recently made the switch to Macintosh, because the Application frame closely resembles the appearance of a Windows system. The screen shots throughout this book show the Application frame in use.

When the Application frame is not active, the Application bar appears below the menu bar; in this case, the Application bar can be moved or turned off.

When the Application frame is not active, the desktop is visible behind the workspace elements.

The InDesign User Interface

5. **In the panel dock, click the Stroke button.**

   Most InDesign functionality is accessed in one of more than 40 **panels**. Virtually everything you do in InDesign requires interacting with at least one panel; more often than not, you use multiple panels to complete any given project.

   - Clicking a panel icon expands that panel to the left of the icon.
   - The icon you clicked is the active panel in the expanded group.
   - When you expand a panel that is part of a panel group, the entire group expands.
   - Dock title bar
   - Icons that are grouped together in the dock represent a panel group.
   - Panel group title bar

   Note:

   *Collapsed panels are referred to as **iconized** or **iconic**.*

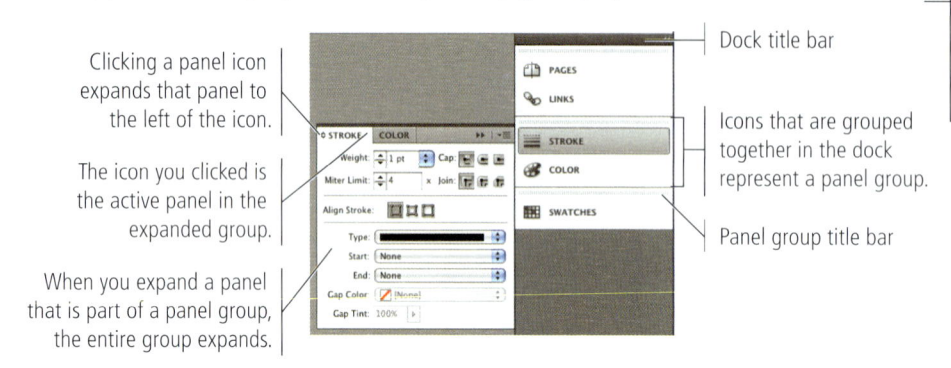

6. **Click away from the expanded panel, anywhere in the application workspace.**

   By default, expanded panels remain open until you manually close them or expand another panel in the dock.

   Note:

   The Auto-Collapse Iconic Panels option is also available in the User Interface pane of the Preferences dialog box, which you can open directly from the dock contextual menu.

7. **Control/right-click the title bar above the docked panel icons. Choose Auto-Collapse Iconic Panels in the contextual menu to toggle on that option.**

   Control/right-clicking a dock title bar opens the dock contextual menu, where you can change the default panel behavior. If you toggle on the Auto-Collapse Iconic Panels option (which is inactive by default), an open panel collapses as soon as you click away from it.

   - Dock title bar
   - This option should be checked (active) after you select it.

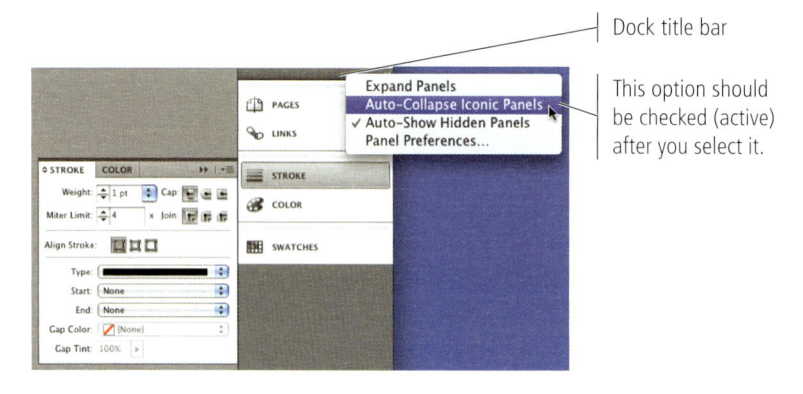

   Note:

   If you're using a Macintosh and don't have a mouse with right-click capability, we highly recommend that you purchase one. They're inexpensive, they're available at almost any retail store, and they save significant amounts of time accessing contextual options.

8. **In the panel dock, click the Swatches button to expand the panel, and then click away from the expanded panel.**

   When Auto-Collapse Iconic Panels is toggled on, the expanded panel collapses as soon as you click away from it.

   - Clicking the panel icon expands the panel.
   - When Auto-Collapse Iconic Panels is active, the expanded panel collapses back to an icon when you click away from the panel.

   The InDesign User Interface

9. **Click the left edge of the docked panels and drag right.**

   When panels are iconized, you can reduce the panel buttons to icons only. Doing so can be particularly useful once you are more familiar with the application and the icons used to symbolize the different panels.

   Click here...   ...and drag right to hide the panel names.

   Note:

   Throughout this book, our screen shots show the Tools panel in the one-column format. Feel free to work with the panel in two columns if you prefer.

10. **On the left side of the workspace, click the title bar of the Tools panel.**

    The Tools panel can't expand, but it can display as either one or two columns; clicking the Tools panel title bar toggles between the two modes.

    Using the one- or two-column format is a purely personal choice. The one-column layout takes up less horizontal space on the screen, which can be useful if you have a small monitor; the two-column format fits in a smaller vertical space, which can be especially useful if you have a laptop with a widescreen monitor.

    Note:

    If the Tools panel is floating instead of docked, you can toggle through three different modes — one-column vertical, one-row horizontal, and two-column vertical.

    Click the Tools panel title bar to toggle between the one-column and two-column layouts.

    Note:

    The Tools panel can also be floated by clicking its title bar and dragging away from the edge of the screen. To re-dock the floating Tools panel, simply click the panel's title bar and drag back to the left edge of the screen; when the blue line highlights the edge of the workspace, releasing the mouse button places the Tools panel back in the dock.

11. **Continue to the next exercise.**

The InDesign User Interface

Identifying and Accessing Tools in InDesign

InDesign CS4 includes more than 30 tools — a large number that indicates the real power of the application. In addition to the basic tool set, the bottom of the Tools panel includes options that control the foreground and background colors, as well as the preview mode you're using. You will learn how to use all these tools as you complete the projects in this book. For now, you should simply take the opportunity to identify the tools.

Nested Tools and Keyboard Shortcuts

Any tool with an arrow in the bottom-right corner includes related tools below it. When you click a tool and hold down the mouse button (or Control/right-click a tool), the **nested tools** appear in a pop-up menu. When you choose one of the nested tools, that variation becomes the default choice in the Tools panel.

This arrow means the tool has other nested tools.

When you hover the mouse cursor over the tool, a tool tip shows the name of the tool.

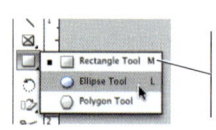

Click and hold down the mouse button (or Control/right-click a tool) to show the nested tools.

Selection tool
Direct Selection tool
Pen tool
Type tool
Pencil tool
Line tool
Rectangle Frame tool
Rectangle tool
Rotate tool
Scale tool
Scissors tool
Free Transform tool
Gradient Swatch tool
Gradient Feather tool
Note tool
Eyedropper tool
Hand tool
Zoom tool
Fill color
Default Fill and Stroke
Formatting Affects Container
Stroke color
Formatting Affects Text
Apply Color/Gradient/None
Preview menu

Most of the default InDesign tools can be accessed with a keyboard shortcut. When you hover the mouse cursor over a tool, the pop-up **tool tip** shows the name of the tool and a letter in parentheses. Pressing that letter on the keyboard activates the associated tool (unless you're working with type, in which case pressing a key adds that letter to your text). If you don't see tool tips, check the Interface pane of the Preferences dialog box; the Show Tool Tips check box should be active.

The following chart offers a quick reference of nested tools, as well as the keyboard shortcut for each tool (if any).

Selection tool (V)	Line tool (\\)	Scissors tool (C)
Direct Selection tool (A)	Rectangle Frame tool (F)	Free Transform tool (E)
Position tool (Shift-A)	*Ellipse Frame tool*	Gradient Swatch tool (G)
	Polygon Frame tool	Gradient Feather tool (Shift-G)
Pen tool (P)	Rectangle tool (M)	Note tool
Add Anchor Point tool (=)	*Ellipse tool (L)*	Eyedropper tool (I)
Delete Anchor Point tool (-)	*Polygon tool*	*Measure tool (K)*
Convert Direction Point tool (Shift-C)	Rotate tool (R)	
Type tool (T)	Scale tool (S)	Hand tool (H)
Type on a Path tool (Shift-T)	*Shear tool (O)*	Zoom tool (Z)
Pencil tool (N)		
Smooth tool		
Erase tool		

The InDesign User Interface

Explore the Arrangement of InDesign Panels

As you gain experience and familiarity with InDesign, you will develop personal artistic and working styles. You will also find that different types of InDesign jobs often require different but specific sets of tools. Adobe recognizes this wide range of needs and preferences among users; InDesign includes a number of options for arranging and managing the numerous panels so you can customize and personalize the workspace to suit your specific needs.

We designed the following exercise to give you an opportunity to explore different ways of controlling panels in the InDesign user interface. Because workspace preferences are largely a matter of personal taste, the projects in this book instruct you to use certain tools and panels, but where you place those elements within the interface is up to you.

1. **With InDesign open, choose Window>Color.**

   All panels can be toggled on and off from the Window menu.

   - If you choose a panel that's already open but iconized, the panel expands to the left of its icon.

   - If you choose a panel that's already open in an expanded group, that panel comes to the front of the group.

   - If you choose a panel that isn't currently open, it opens in the same position as when it was last closed.

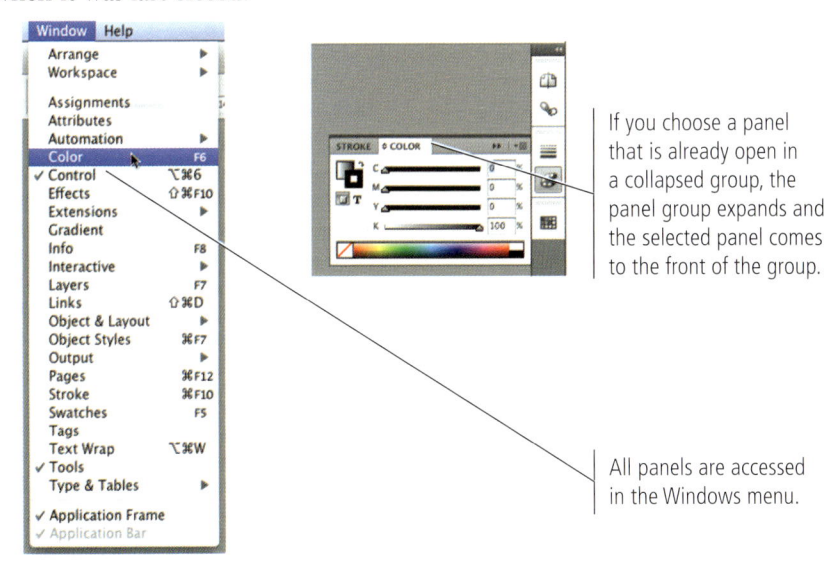

   If you choose a panel that is already open in a collapsed group, the panel group expands and the selected panel comes to the front of the group.

   All panels are accessed in the Windows menu.

2. **Control/right-click the panel group drop zone (to the right of the panel tabs) and choose Close Tab Group from the contextual menu.**

   You can also Control/right-click a panel tab and choose Close to close only one panel in a group.

   Control/right-click the panel group's drop zone to access the contextual menu.

   The closed panel group is removed from the panel dock.

The InDesign User Interface

3. **Click the title bar of the panel dock to expand the dock column.**

4. **Click the Links panel tab in the top panel group and drag away from the panel dock.**

   Panels can be **floated** by clicking a panel tab and dragging away from the dock.

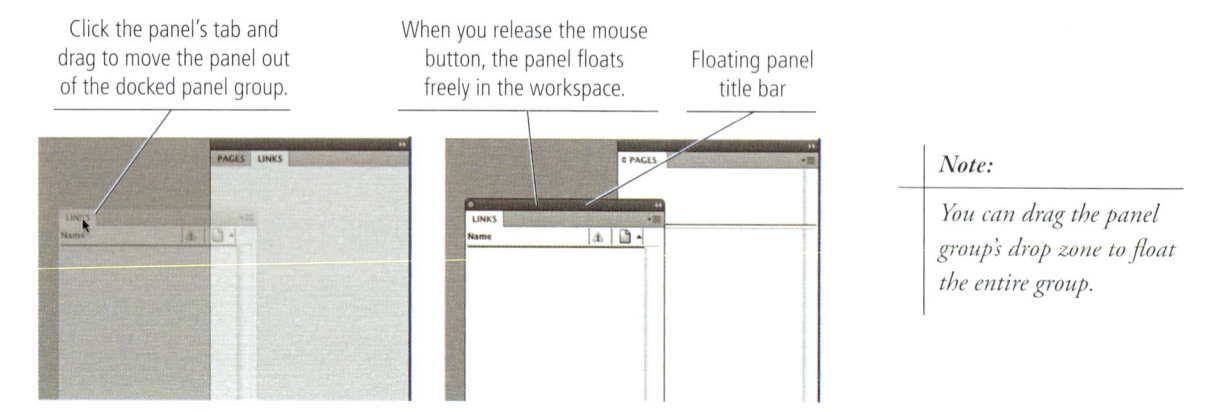

   Click the panel's tab and drag to move the panel out of the docked panel group.

   When you release the mouse button, the panel floats freely in the workspace.

   Floating panel title bar

   Note:

   You can drag the panel group's drop zone to float the entire group.

5. **Click the drop zone of the floating panel (behind the Links panel tab) and drag to the dock, between the Pages and Swatches panels. When you see a blue line between the two docked panels, release the mouse button.**

   Individual panels can be dragged to different locations (including into different groups) by dragging the panel's tab; the target location — where the panel will reside when you release the mouse button — is identified by the blue highlight.

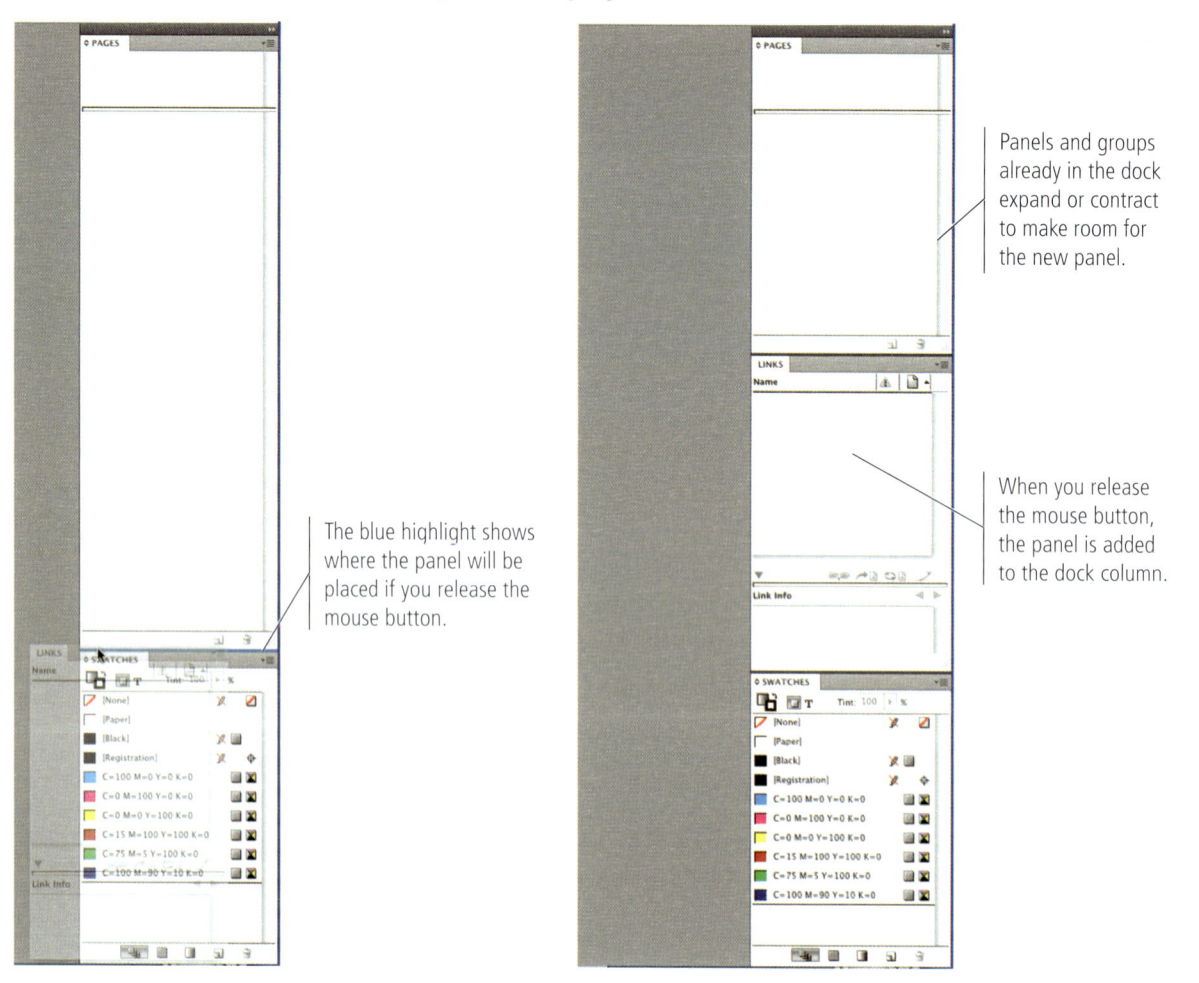

   The blue highlight shows where the panel will be placed if you release the mouse button.

   Panels and groups already in the dock expand or contract to make room for the new panel.

   When you release the mouse button, the panel is added to the dock column.

   The InDesign User Interface

6. **Click the Swatches panel tab and drag left until the blue highlight shows a second column added to the dock.**

    As we mentioned earlier, you can create multiple columns of panels in the dock. This can be very useful if you need easy access to a large number of panels and have a monitor with enough available screen space.

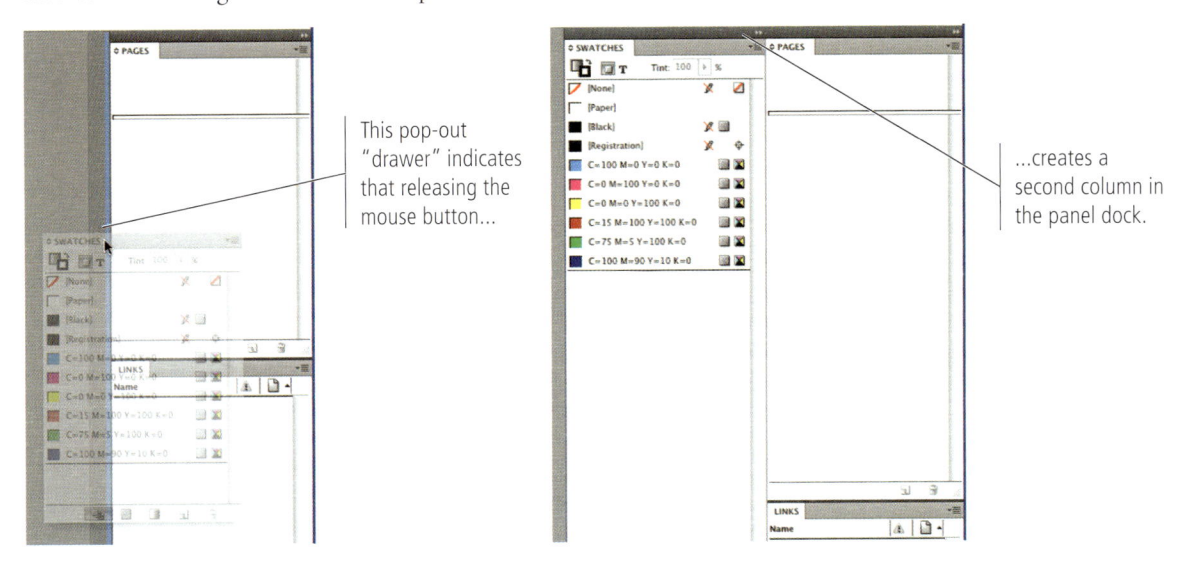

    This pop-out "drawer" indicates that releasing the mouse button...

    ...creates a second column in the panel dock.

7. **Click the title bar of the left dock column to iconize that column.**

    You can independently iconize or expand each column of docked panels and each floating panel (group).

8. **Click the bottom edge of the first panel group in the right column of the dock and drag up.**

    When you drag the bottom edge of a docked group, other panels in the same column expand or contract to fit the available space.

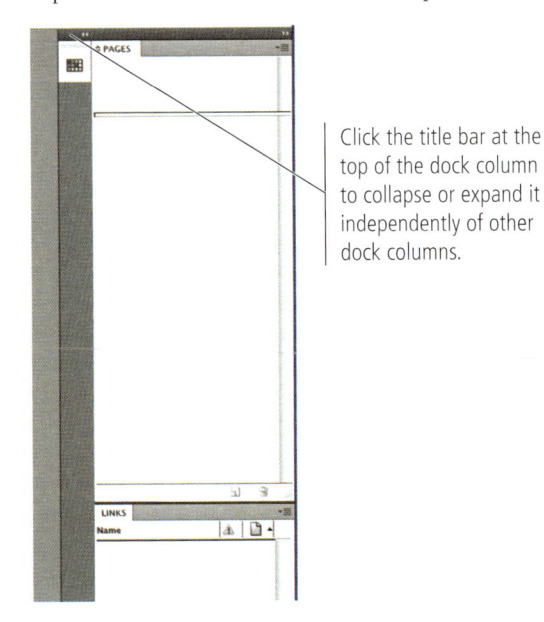

    Click the title bar at the top of the dock column to collapse or expand it independently of other dock columns.

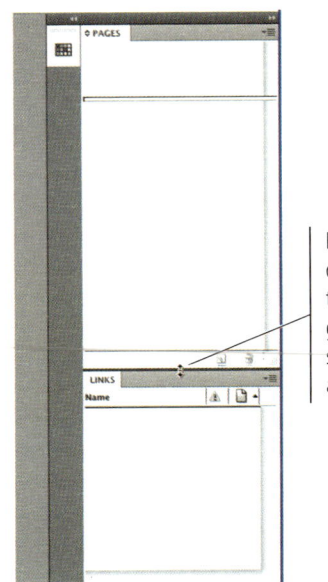

    Dragging the bottom edge of a docked panel (group) changes the height of that panel (or group). Other panels in the same column expand or shrink as necessary to fit the column.

    The InDesign User Interface

9. **Click the left edge of the right dock column and drag left.**

   Each column of the dock can be made wider or narrower by dragging the left edge of the column.

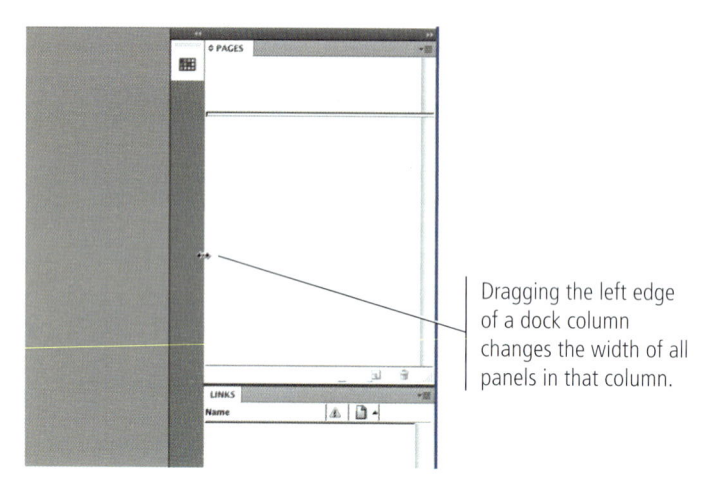

   Dragging the left edge of a dock column changes the width of all panels in that column.

10. **Continue to the next exercise.**

Create a Saved Workspace

By now you should understand that you have extensive control over the appearance of your InDesign workspace — what panels are visible, where and how they appear, and even the size of individual panels or panel groups.

Over time you will develop personal preferences — the Colors panel always appears at the top, etc. — based on your work habits and project needs. Rather than re-establishing every workspace element each time you return to InDesign, you can save your custom workspace settings so you can recall them with a single click.

1. **Click the Workspace switcher in the Application/Menu bar and choose New Workspace.**

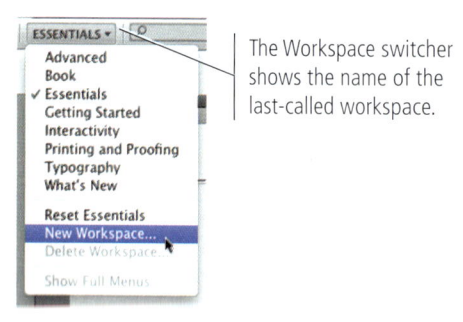

   The Workspace switcher shows the name of the last-called workspace.

   Note:

   The Delete Workspace option opens a dialog box where you can choose a specific user-defined workspace to delete. You can't delete the default workspaces that come with the application.

2. **In the New Workspace dialog box, type Portfolio. Make sure the Panel Locations option is checked and click OK.**

   You didn't define custom menus, so that option is not relevant in this exercise.

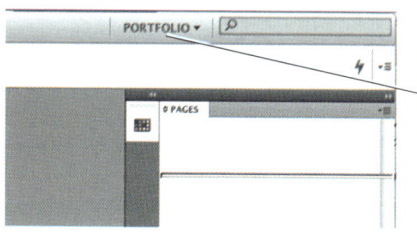

   After saving the current workspace, the Workspace switcher shows the name of the new saved workspace.

The InDesign User Interface

3. **Click the Workspace switcher and choose Getting Started from the list of available workspaces.**

   As we explained earlier, saved workspaces — whether part of the default set or ones you create — call specific sets of panels in specific places. This step calls one of the built-in workspaces defined by Adobe.

   Custom workspaces are listed at the top of the Workspace switcher.

4. **Continue to the next exercise.**

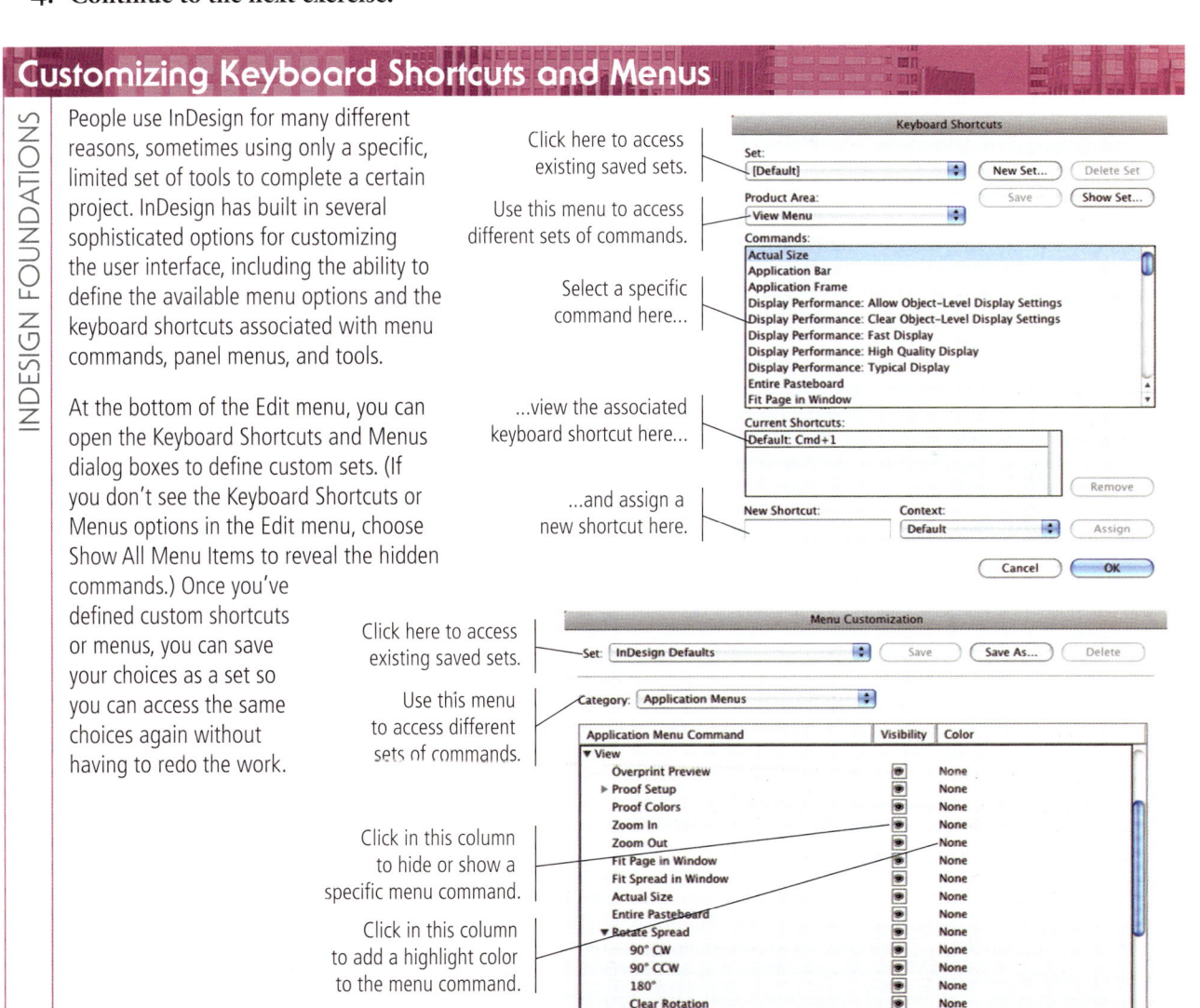

Customizing Keyboard Shortcuts and Menus

INDESIGN FOUNDATIONS

People use InDesign for many different reasons, sometimes using only a specific, limited set of tools to complete a certain project. InDesign has built in several sophisticated options for customizing the user interface, including the ability to define the available menu options and the keyboard shortcuts associated with menu commands, panel menus, and tools.

At the bottom of the Edit menu, you can open the Keyboard Shortcuts and Menus dialog boxes to define custom sets. (If you don't see the Keyboard Shortcuts or Menus options in the Edit menu, choose Show All Menu Items to reveal the hidden commands.) Once you've defined custom shortcuts or menus, you can save your choices as a set so you can access the same choices again without having to redo the work.

Click here to access existing saved sets.

Use this menu to access different sets of commands.

Select a specific command here...

...view the associated keyboard shortcut here...

...and assign a new shortcut here.

Click here to access existing saved sets.

Use this menu to access different sets of commands.

Click in this column to hide or show a specific menu command.

Click in this column to add a highlight color to the menu command.

The InDesign User Interface | 11

Customizing InDesign Preferences

INDESIGN FOUNDATIONS

You can also customize the way many of the program's tools and options function. On Macintosh, the Preferences dialog box is accessed in the InDesign menu. Windows users access the Preferences dialog box in the Edit menu.

The right side of the Preferences dialog box (InDesign>Preferences on Macintosh or Edit>Preferences on Windows) allows you to display the various sets of preferences available in InDesign). As you work your way through the projects in this book, you'll learn not only what you can do with these different collections of preferences, but also *why* and *when* you might want to use them.

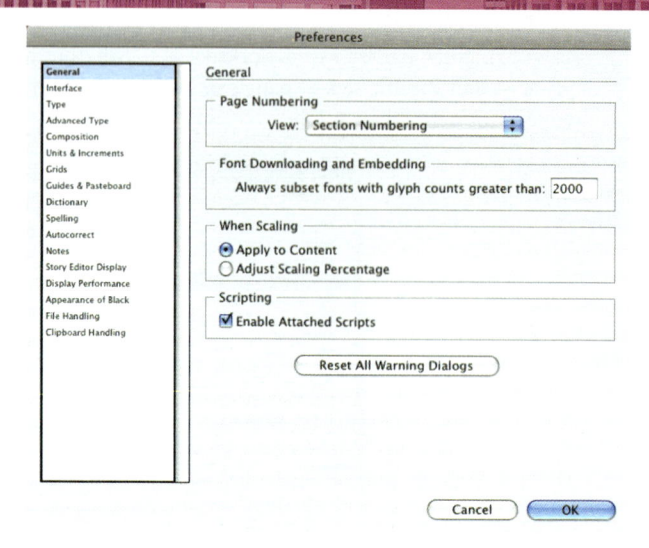

Explore the InDesign Document Views

There is far more to using InDesign than arranging panels around the workspace. What you do with those panels — and even which panels you need — depends on the type of work you are doing in a particular file. In this exercise, you open an InDesign file and explore the interface elements you'll use to create documents.

1. **In InDesign, choose File>Open.**

2. **Navigate to the RF_InDesign>Interface folder on your Resource CD and select career.indd in the list of available files.**

   The Open dialog box is a system-standard navigation dialog box. This dialog box is one area of significant difference between Macintosh and Windows users.

3. **Press Shift, and then click experience.indd in the list of files.**

   Pressing Shift allows you to select multiple contiguous (consecutive) files in the list.

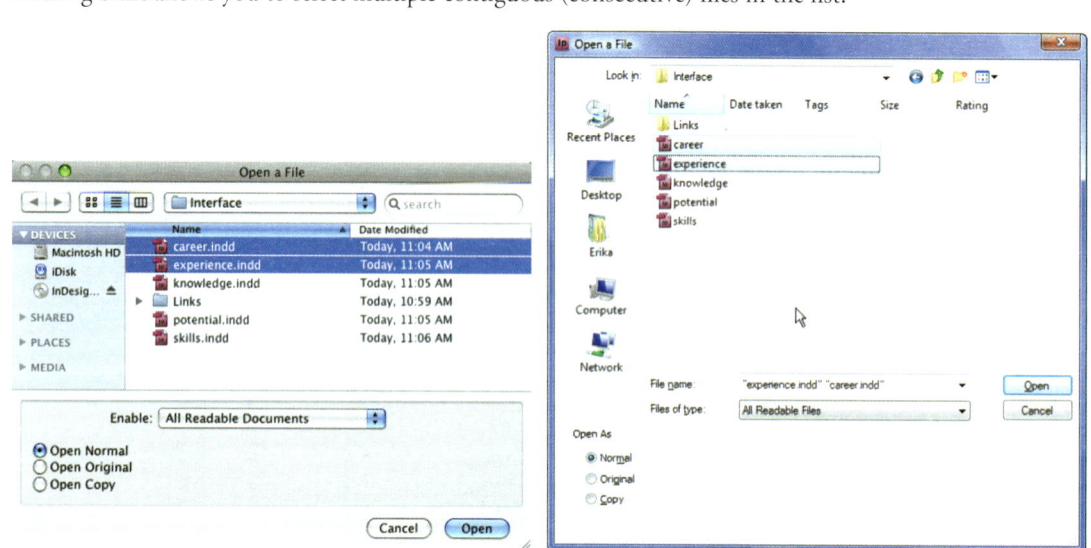

Note:

Press Command/ Control-O to access the Open dialog box.

The InDesign User Interface

4. **Click Open.**

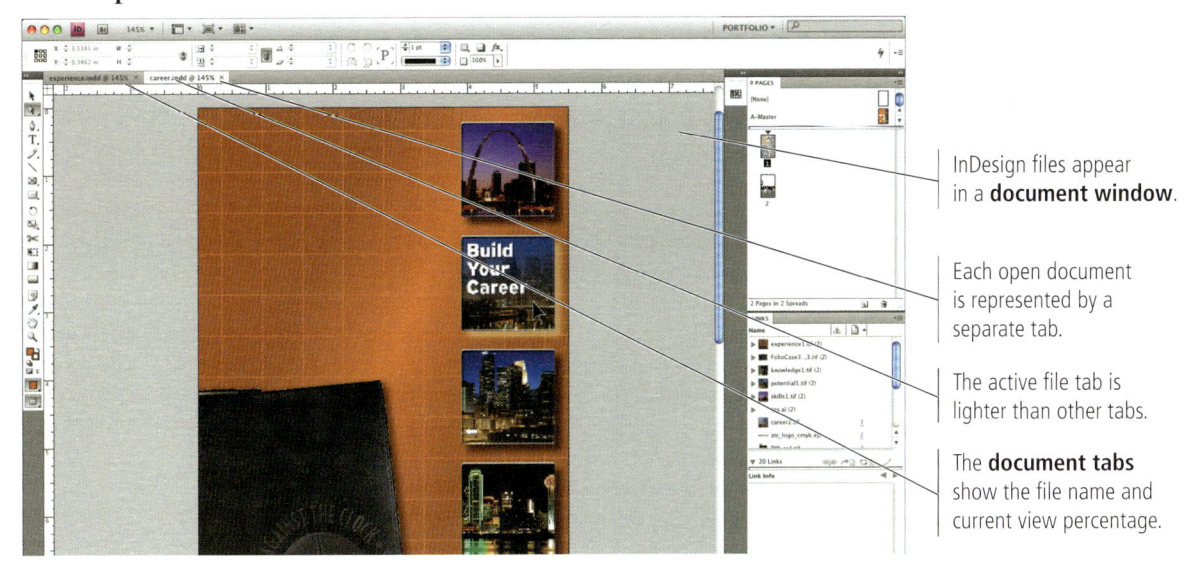

   *InDesign files appear in a **document window**.*

   Each open document is represented by a separate tab.

   The active file tab is lighter than other tabs.

   *The **document tabs** show the file name and current view percentage.*

5. **Click the experience.indd tab to make that document active.**

6. **Click the Zoom Level field in the Application/Menu bar and change the view percentage to 200.**

   Different people prefer larger or smaller view percentages, depending on a number of factors (eyesight, monitor size, and so on). As you complete the projects in this book, you'll see our screen shots zoom in or out as necessary to show you the most relevant part of a particular file. In most cases we do not tell you what specific view percentage to use for a particular exercise, unless it is specifically required for the work being done.

   Note:

   Macintosh users: If you turn off the Application frame, the new document will have its own title bar.

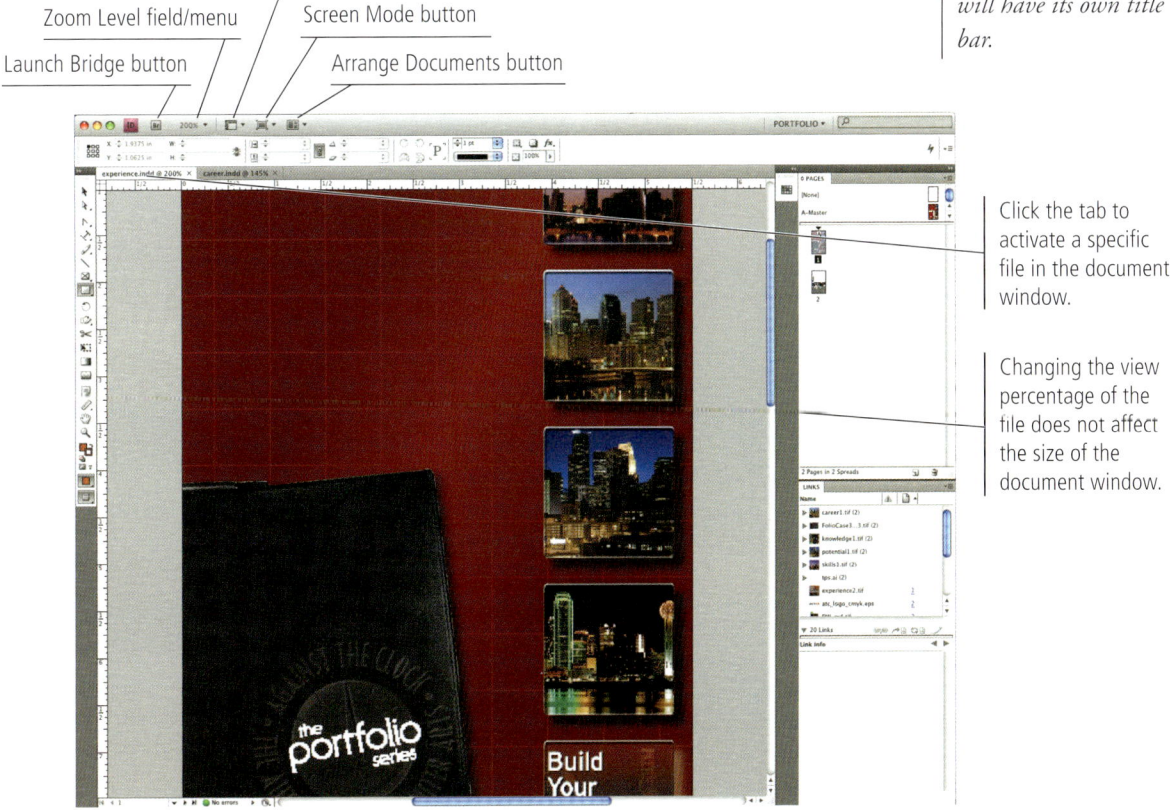

   View Options button
   Zoom Level field/menu
   Screen Mode button
   Launch Bridge button
   Arrange Documents button

   Click the tab to activate a specific file in the document window.

   Changing the view percentage of the file does not affect the size of the document window.

   The InDesign User Interface | 13

7. **Choose View>Fit Page in Window.**

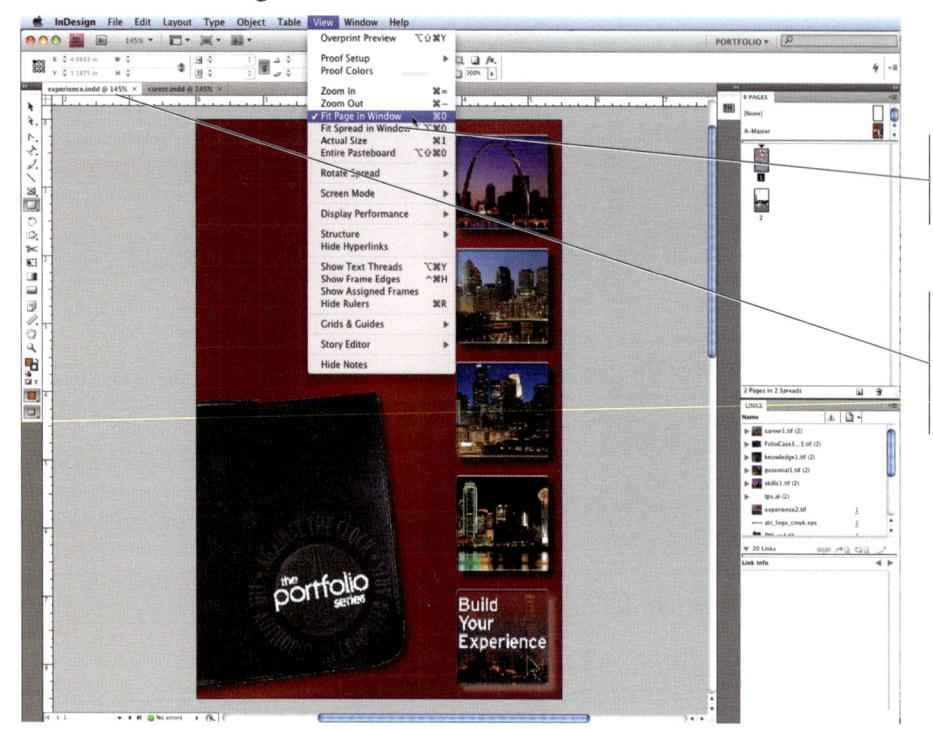

These six options affect the view percentage of a file.

The Fit Page in Window command automatically calculates view percentage based on the size of the document window.

Note:

The Fit Spread in Window option relates to documents that have left- and right-facing pages, such as a book. You build this kind of document in Project 5.

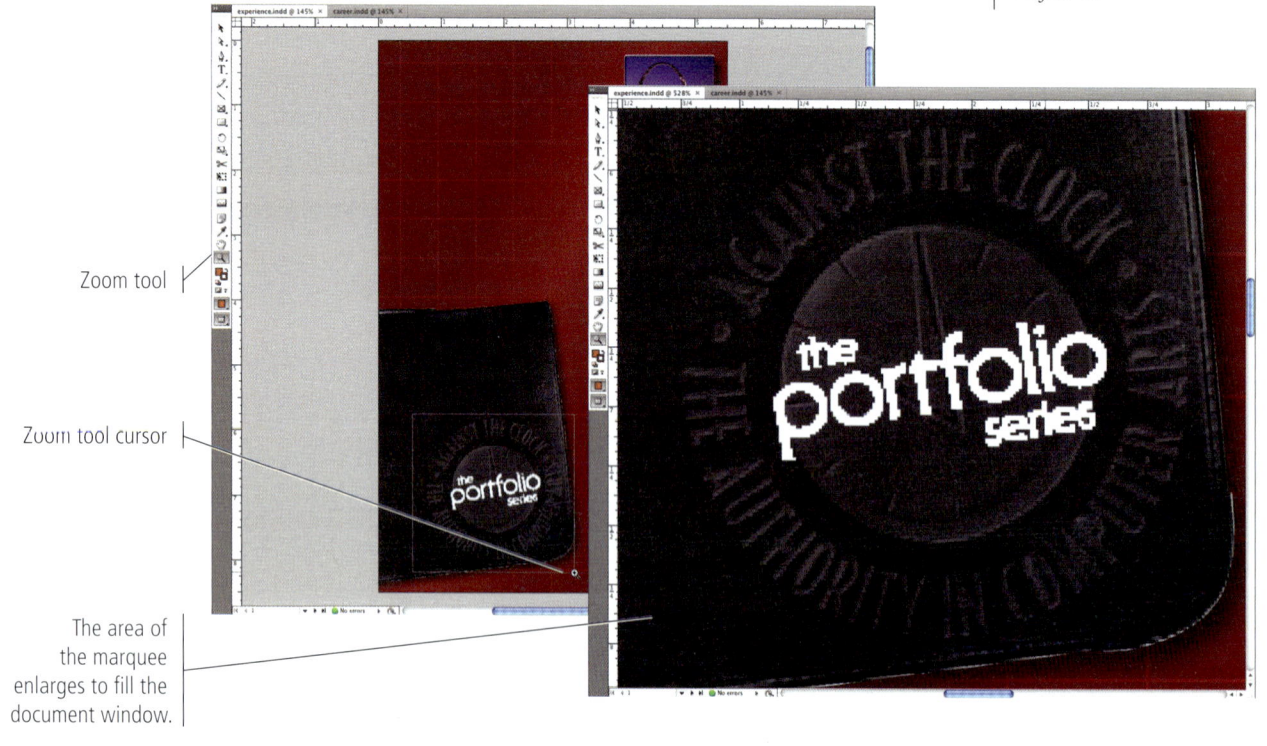

8. **Click the Zoom tool in the Tools panel. Click in the document window and drag a marquee around the logo on the portfolio.**

   Dragging a marquee with the Zoom tool enlarges the selected area to fill the document window.

   Zoom tool

   Zoom tool cursor

   The area of the marquee enlarges to fill the document window.

14 The InDesign User Interface

9. **With the Zoom tool selected, Option/Alt-click in the document window.**

    Clicking with the Zoom tool enlarges the view percentage in specific, predefined steps. Pressing Option/Alt while clicking with the Zoom tool reduces the view percentage in the reverse sequence of the same percentages.

    Note:

    You can set the viewing percentage of an InDesign document to anything from 5% to 4000%.

    Option/Alt-clicking with the Zoom tool reduces the view percent in the predefined sequence of percentages.

    With the Zoom tool active, pressing Option/Alt changes the cursor to the Zoom Out icon.

10. **Click the Hand tool near the bottom of the Tools panel.**

11. **Click in the document window, hold down the mouse button, and drag around.**

    The Hand tool is a very easy and convenient option for changing the visible area of an image in the document window.

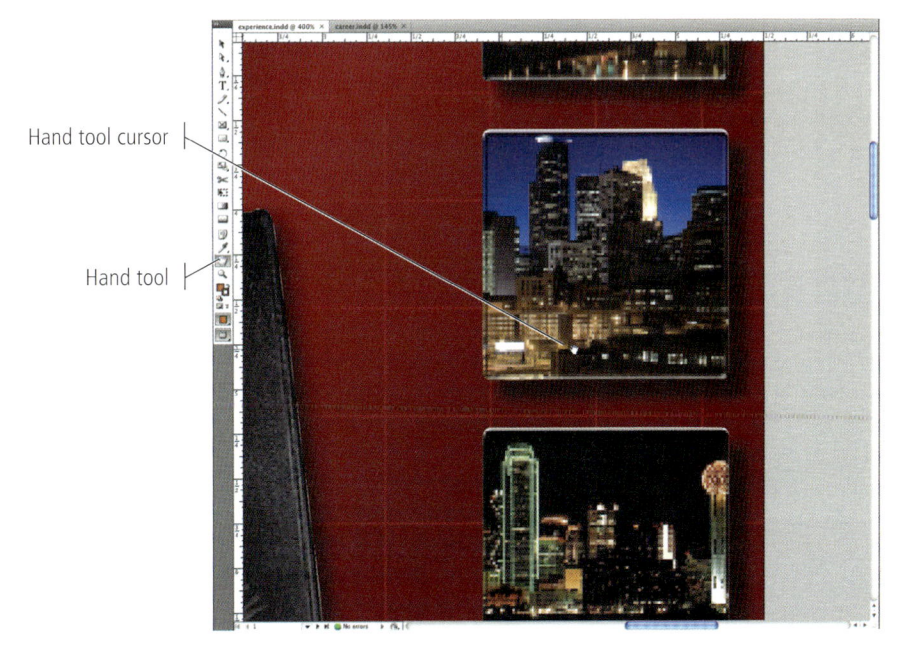

    Hand tool cursor

    Hand tool

    Note:

    Press the Z key to access the Zoom tool.

    Press the H key to access the Hand tool.

12. **Choose View>Fit Page in Window to see the entire page.**

    You might have noticed that the images in this file look very bad (they are badly bitmapped). This is even more evident when you zoomed in to a high view percentage. By default, InDesign displays a low-resolution preview of placed images to save time when the screen redraws (i.e., every time you change something). Fortunately, however, you have the option to preview the full-resolution images placed in a file.

The InDesign User Interface

13. **Choose View>Display Performance>High Quality Display.**

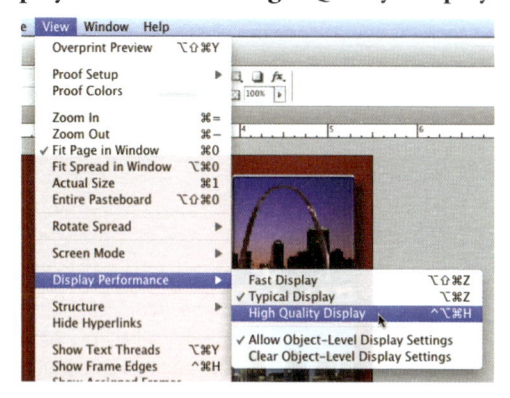

Note:

The Fast Display option replaces all placed images with a solid medium gray (in other words, no preview image displays).

Using the High Quality Display, images do not display the bitmapping of the default low-resolution previews.

14. **Control/right-click the bottom button image (the one with the text) and choose Display Performance>Typical Display from the contextual menu.**

Because the Allow Object-Level Display Settings option is active, you can change the display of individual objects on the page.

High-Quality Display is especially evident where sharp lines exist.

Typical Display uses a low-resolution preview of placed images.

15. **In the Pages panel, double-click the Page 2 icon to show that page in the document window.**

    The Pages panel is the easiest way to move from one page to another in a multi-page document. You will use this panel extensively as you complete the projects in this book.

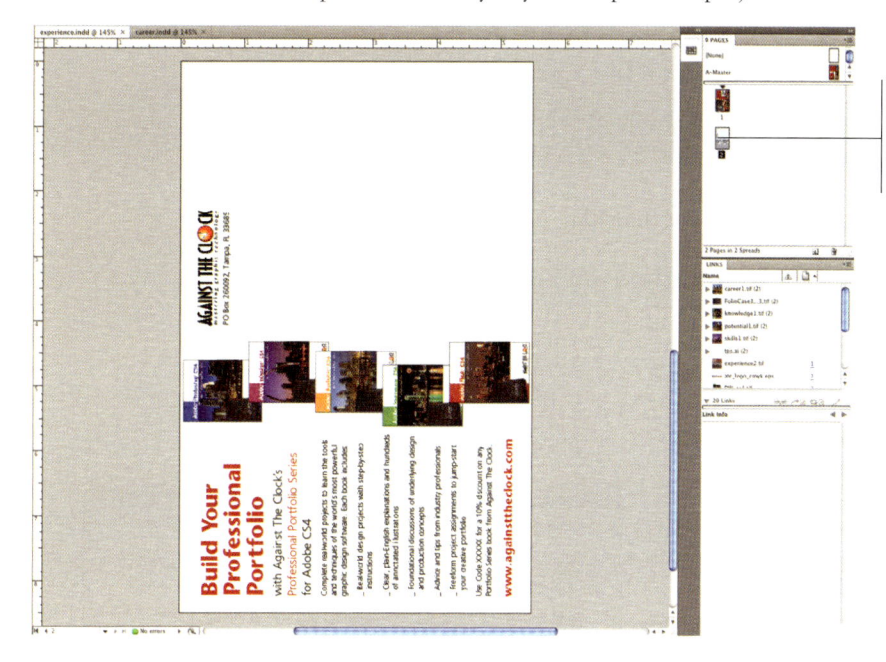

    Double-click a page icon to display that page in the document window.

16. **Control/right-click the Page 2 icon in the Pages panel and choose Rotate Spread View>Rotate 90° CW from the contextual menu.**

    Rotating the view only changes the display of the page; the actual page remains unchanged in the file. This option allows you to more easily work on objects or pages that are oriented in a different plane as the overall document. For example, the front side of the postcard has portrait orientation, but the mailer side has landscape orientation.

    Note:

    You can also rotate page views using the options in the View>Rotate Spread menu.

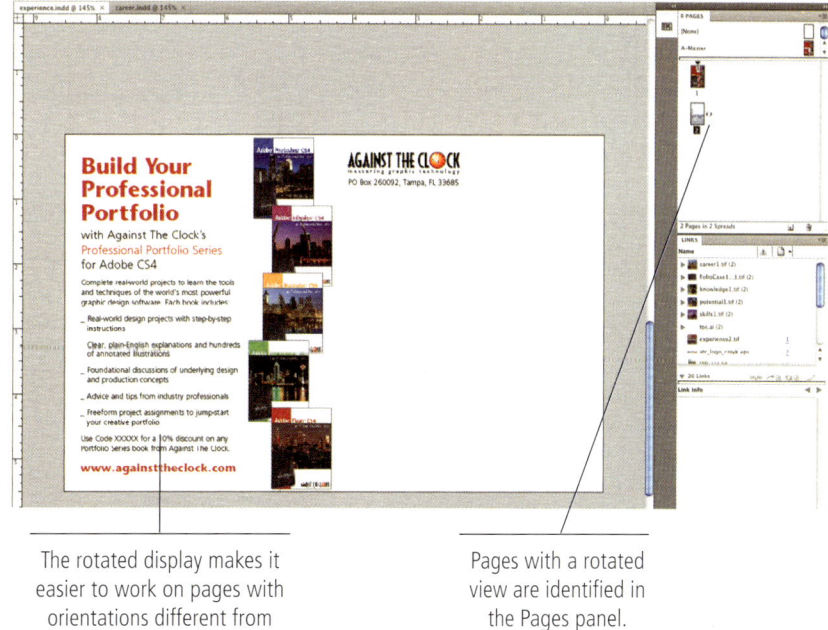

    The rotated display makes it easier to work on pages with orientations different from the document definition.

    Pages with a rotated view are identified in the Pages panel.

17. **Continue to the next exercise.**

The InDesign User Interface

☞ EXPLORE THE ARRANGEMENT OF MULTIPLE DOCUMENTS

In many cases, you will need to work with more than one InDesign file at the same time. InDesign CS4 incorporates a number of options for arranging multiple documents. We designed the following simple exercise so that you can explore these options.

1. **With the `career.indd` and `experience.indd` files open, choose File>Open.**

   The Open dialog box defaults to the last-used location, so you should not have to navigate back to the RF_InDesign>Interface folder.

2. **Click `knowledge.indd` in the list to select that file.**

3. **Press Command/Control and click `potential.indd` and `skills.indd` to add those files to the active selection.**

   Pressing Command/Control allows you to select and open non-contiguous files.

   (On Windows, folders might be listed before other files, as shown in our screen shot. If that's the case on your system, you can press Shift or Control to select all three files.)

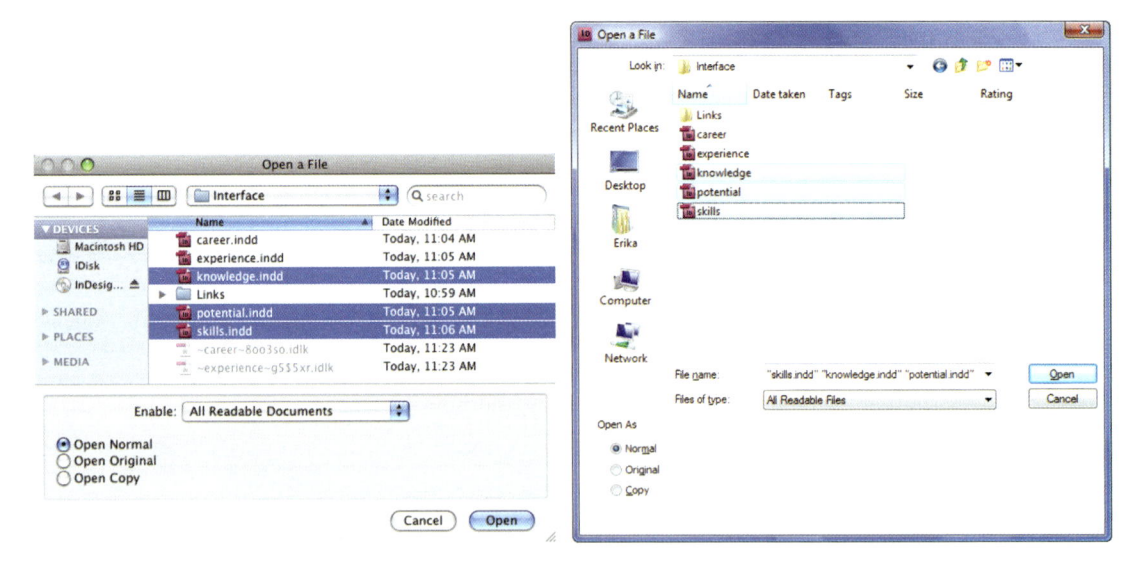

4. **Click Open to open all three selected files.**

5. **Open the Window menu and choose potential.indd at the bottom of the menu.**

   All open files can be activated using the file names at the bottom of the Window menu.

18 The InDesign User Interface

6. **Choose Window>Arrange>Float in Window.**

Note:

You can separate all open files by choosing Window>Arrange>Float All In Windows.

Floating a document separates the file into its own document window.

The title bar of the separate document window shows the same information that was in the document tab.

Summing Up the InDesign View Options

Most InDesign projects require some amount of zooming in and out to various view percentages, as well as navigating around the document within its window. As we show you how to complete various stages of the workflow, we usually won't tell you when to change your view percentage because that's largely a matter of personal preference. But you should understand the different options for navigating around an InDesign file so you can easily and efficiently get to what you want, when you want to get there.

View Menu

The View menu provides options for changing view percentage, and lists the associated keyboard shortcuts. (Zoom In and Zoom Out step through the same predefined view percentages you see by clicking with the Zoom tool.)

Zoom In	Command/Control-equals (=)
Zoom Out	Command/Control-minus (-)
Fit Page in Window	Command/Control-0 (zero)
Fit Spread in Window	Command-Option-0/Control-Alt-0
Actual Size (100%)	Command/Control-1
Entire Pasteboard	Command-Option-Shift-0/Control-Alt-Shift-0

Zoom Level Field/Menu

You can use the Zoom Level field in the Application/Menu bar to type a specific view percentage, or you can use the attached menu to choose from the predefined view percentage steps.

Zoom Tool

You can click with the **Zoom tool** to increase the view percentage in specific, predefined intervals (the same intervals you see in the View Percentage menu in the bottom-left corner of the document window). Pressing Option/Alt with the Zoom tool allows you to zoom out in the same predefined percentages. If you drag a marquee with the Zoom tool, you can zoom into a specific location; the area surrounded by the marquee fills the available space in the document window.

Hand Tool

Whatever your view percentage, you can use the **Hand tool** to drag the file around in the document window, including scrolling from one page to another. The Hand tool only changes what is visible in the window; it has no effect on the actual pixels in the image.

The InDesign User Interface   19

7. **In the Application/Menu bar, click the Arrange Documents button to open the panel of defined arrangements.**

8. **Click the 2 Up button in the Arrange Documents panel.**

   The defined arrangements provide a number of options for tiling multiple open files within the available workspace; these arrangements manage all open files, include those in floating windows.

   Note:

   On Macintosh, the Application bar must be visible to access the Arrange Documents button.

   The Arrange Documents panel includes a number of tiling options for arranging multiple open files in the workspace.

   The appearance of each icon suggests the result of each option.

   Rolling your mouse cursor over an icon shows the arrangement name in a tool tip.

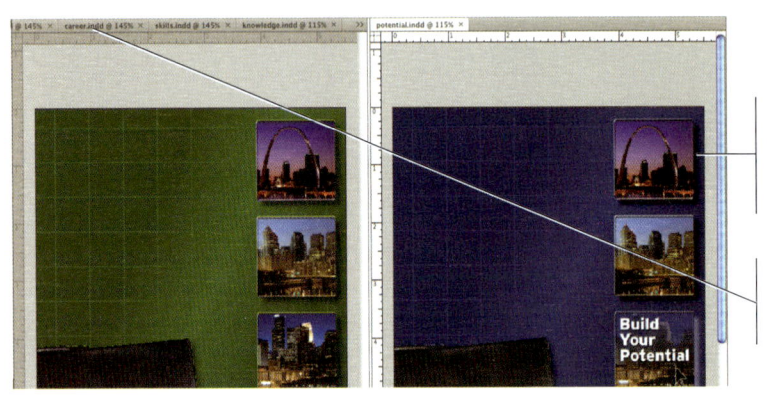

   The 2-Up arrangement divides the document window in half, as indicated by the button icon.

   Extra documents remain as tabs in the left document window.

9. **Open the Arrange Documents panel again and click the Consolidate All button.**

   The Consolidate All button (and the Consolidate All to Tabs command in the Window>Arrange menu) restores all floating documents into a single tabbed document window (the same as you see in the default arrangement).

   The remaining buttons in the top row separate all open files into separate document windows and then arrange the different windows as indicated.

   The lower options use a specific number of floating documents (2-Up, 3-Up, etc.); if more files are open than an option indicates, the extra files are consolidated as tabs in the first document window.

   Note:

   When multiple document windows are open, two options in the Window>Arrange menu allow you to cascade or tile the document windows.

   The consolidated document window snaps to fill the available monitor space (within the boundaries of docked panels).

   The Consolidate All arrangement restores all open documents into a single document window.

20 The InDesign User Interface

10. **Click the Close button on the active document tab.**

   When multiple files are open, clicking the close button on a document tab closes only that file.

11. **Macintosh users: Click the Close button in the top-left corner of the Application bar. Click Don't Save when asked if you want to save changes to experience.indd.**

   Closing the Macintosh Application frame does not quit the application.

   On Macintosh, closing the Application frame closes all files open in that frame.

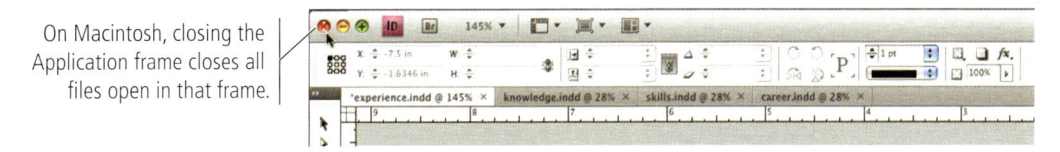

   Windows users: Click the Close button on each open document tab to close the remaining files. Click Don't Save when asked if you want to save changes to experience.indd.

   Clicking the Close button on the Windows Menu bar closes all open files *and* quits the application. To close open files *without* quitting, you have to manually close each open file.

   Click the Close button on each document tab to close the open files.

   Clicking the Menu bar Close button closes all open files, and also quits the application.

The InDesign User Interface

project 1

Identity Package

Your client, Tracey Dillon, is a local architect. She hired you to create a corporate identity package so she can begin marketing her services to local land development companies. She asked you to first develop a logo, and then create the standard identity pieces (business card and letterhead) that she can use for business promotion and correspondence.

This project incorporates the following skills:

❏ Creating new files in various sizes to meet the project needs
❏ Using the basic InDesign drawing tools to develop a logo
❏ Creating and formatting text
❏ Placing and manipulating external graphics files
❏ Incorporating color into the various design elements

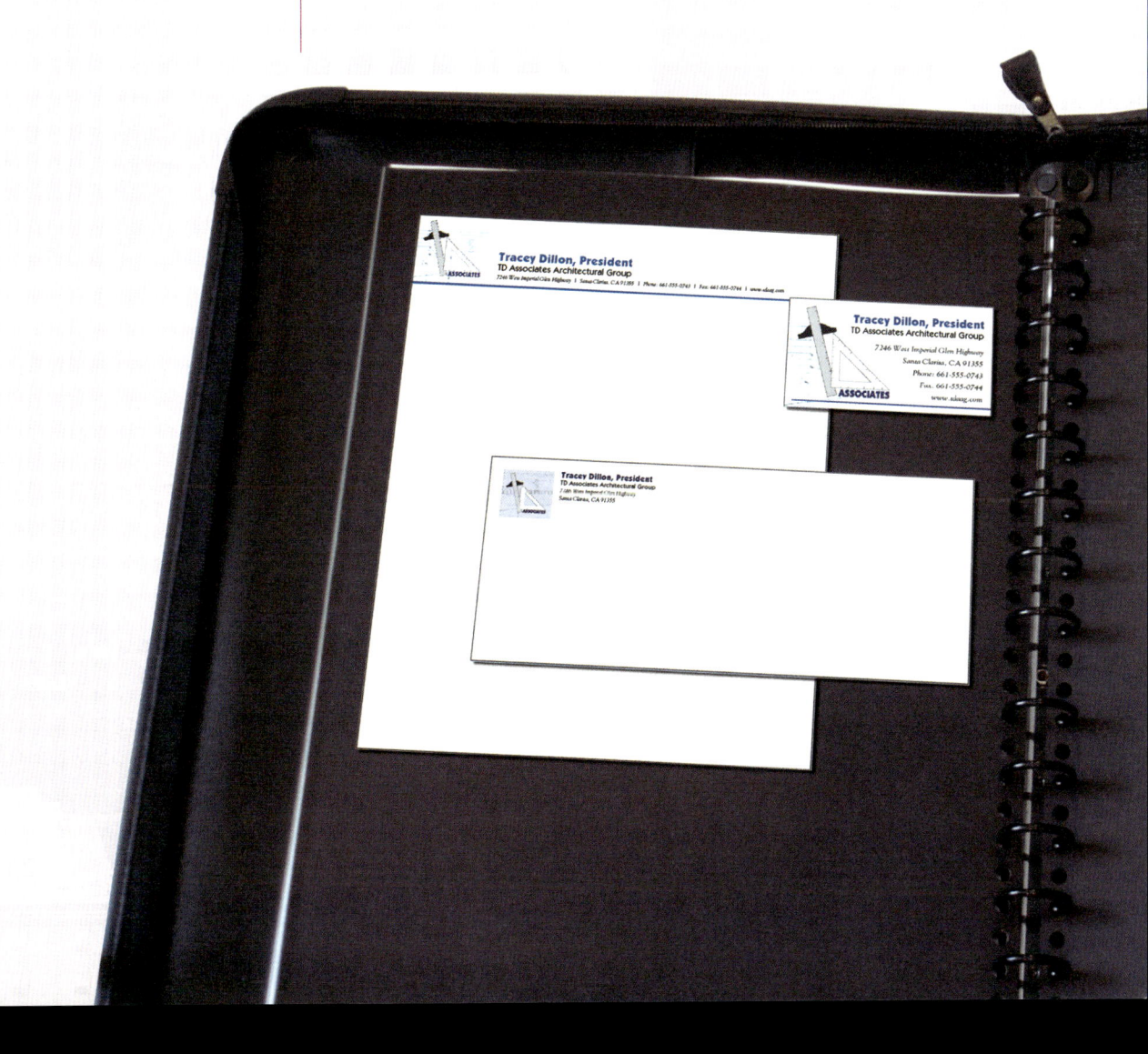

Project Meeting

client comments

I've decided to open my own architectural services firm, and I need to start advertising. That means I need to brand my business so companies who need an architect will recognize and remember my name. I'm calling my business TD Associates.

I want a logo that really says "architect." Then I want you to use the logo on business cards, letterhead, and envelopes that I will have preprinted; I want a more professional feel than I can create using my laser printer. The printer I spoke with said I could do this for less money if I go "4-color" for the business card and letterhead, but "2-color" for the envelope; I really don't know what that means — I'm hoping you do.

art director comments

I want you to create the logo first because you'll use it on the other three pieces. I have an idea that I think will meet the client's needs. Fortunately, Tracey is going to call her business "TD"; two tools that people associate with architecture are a T-square and a measuring triangle. The T is obvious, and if you rotate the triangle — instant D!

Since logos are used on far more than just these three jobs in this one application, you'll save the final logo in a file format that can be used in different ways, and then place that file into the other three pieces. Tracey wants to print the card and letterhead in 4-color and the envelope in 2-color, so you'll have to create two different versions of the logo.

One of the colors will be black in this case, because most of the text on the letterhead and envelope should be black. We have to pick one other spot ink color; I think we should use some kind of blue since architects create blueprints.

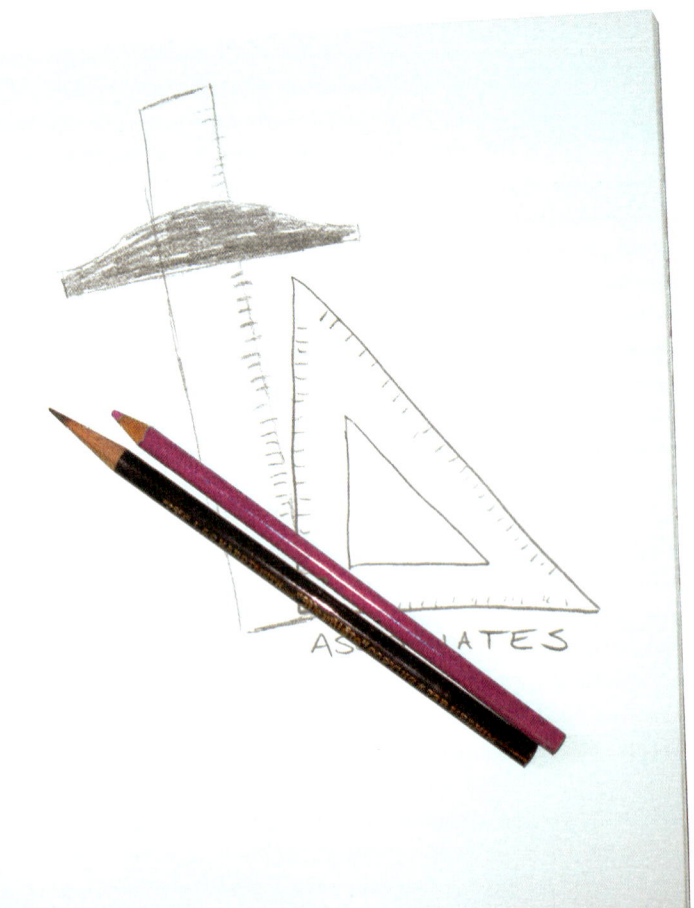

project objectives

To complete this project, you will:

❏ Create and save several versions of the same document to meet different requirements for commercial printing.

❏ Create a document preset to access common job settings

❏ Draw basic shapes using native InDesign tools

❏ Work with Bézier paths to create complex shapes

❏ Edit shapes using the Pathfinder, Align, and Transform panels

❏ Apply color to fills and strokes

❏ Create and format basic text elements

❏ Import external text and graphics files

❏ Export an EPS file

❏ Print desktop proofs

Stage 1 Setting up the Workspace

The best way to start any new project is to prepare your workspace — just as any good chef sharpens his or her knives and locates all the necessary ingredients before starting to cook. As you learned in the Interface chapter, InDesign allows you to save custom workspaces that can be called whenever you need them — a very useful function if you're working on a shared computer or if you move back and forth from one job to another on your own computer. We start each project from the default Essentials workspace and access other panels in the Window menu as neessary.

CREATE AND SAVE A BASIC INDESIGN FILE

This project ultimately requires four files: one for creating the logo, one for the business card, one for the letterhead, and one for the envelope. The logo file is basically freeform, since it's essentially an artboard on which to draw. The other three files have specific size and output requirements, which you can define when you create the files.

1. **Copy the Identity folder from the WIP folder on your Resource CD to the WIP folder where you're saving your work.**

   Use this folder to save all files for this project.

2. **Choose File>New>Document.**

   InDesign uses picas as the default unit of measurement when you first install the application. All the measurements in this dialog box are shown in picas, using the "ApB" notation (for A picas and B points).

   Note:

   You can create a new file by pressing Command/Control-N.

   Note:

   Picas are the measuring system traditionally used in typography, and they are still used by many people in the graphic communications industry.

   1 point = 1/72 inch

   12 points = 1 pica

   1 pica = 1/6 inch

   6 picas = 1 inch

3. **Highlight the Width field and type 3".**

Project 1: Identity Package 25

4. **Press Tab to move to the Height field.**

   You can work with units other than the default; InDesign makes the necessary conversion for you. When you enter a value in a unit other than the default, you have to include the alternate unit.

   This technique works in dialog boxes and panels — basically anywhere you can enter a measurement.

   When you enter a different value into the Width or Height field, the Page Size menu changes to Custom.

   Note:

   InDesign recognizes measurements in points, picas, inches, inches decimal, millimeters, centimeters, ciceros, and agates.

   Note:

   You can tab through the fields of most dialog boxes and panels in InDesign. Press Shift-Tab to move the highlight to the previous field in the tab order.

5. **Change the Height field to 3".**

6. **In the Margins area, make sure the chain icon is active.**

   When the chain icon is active (dark gray), all four margin fields will be the same; changing one field changes all margin values to the same value.

7. **Highlight the first Margins field (Top) and type 0.**

   You don't need to type the full "0p0" notation when you change measurements using the default units. Zero pica is still zero, so you don't need to worry about converting units.

8. **Press Tab to move the highlight to the next Margins field (Bottom).**

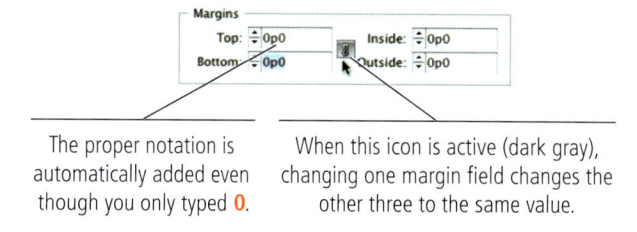

   The proper notation is automatically added even though you only typed 0.

   When this icon is active (dark gray), changing one margin field changes the other three to the same value.

9. **Click OK to create the new document.**

   The document window appears, with the file filling the available space. If you look in the bottom-left corner, you probably see that your file is displayed far larger than 100%.

10. **If you don't see rulers at the top and left edges of the document window, choose View>Show Rulers.**

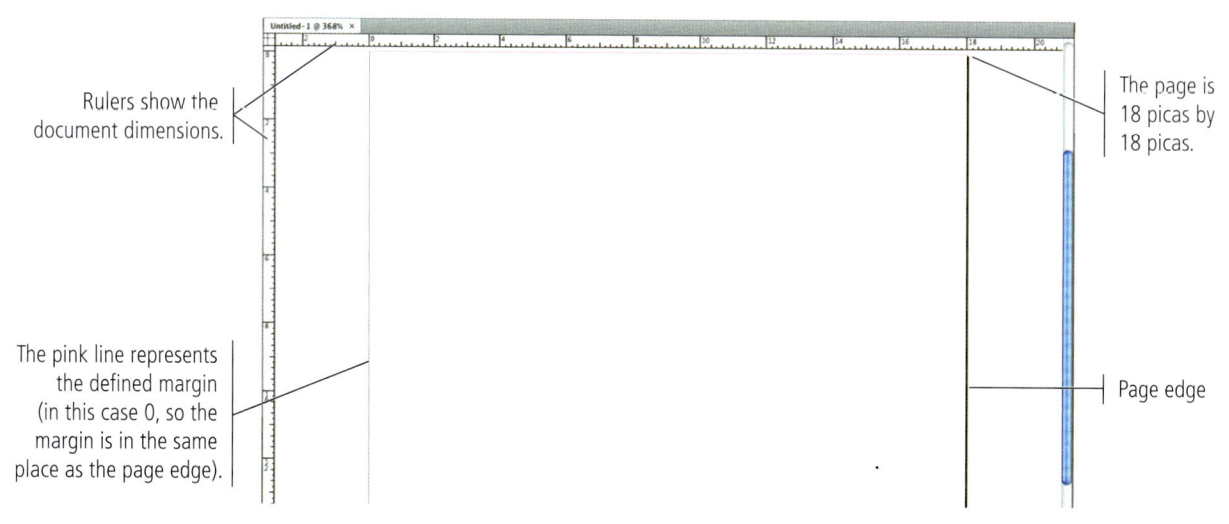

    Rulers show the document dimensions.

    The pink line represents the defined margin (in this case 0, so the margin is in the same place as the page edge).

    The page is 18 picas by 18 picas.

    Page edge

    Since most people (in the United States, at least) think in term of inches, we use inches throughout the projects in this book.

26   Project 1: Identity Package

11. Open the Preferences>Units & Increments dialog box (in the InDesign menu on Macintosh or the Edit menu on Windows).

12. In the Ruler Units area, choose Inches in the Horizontal and Vertical menus, and then click OK.

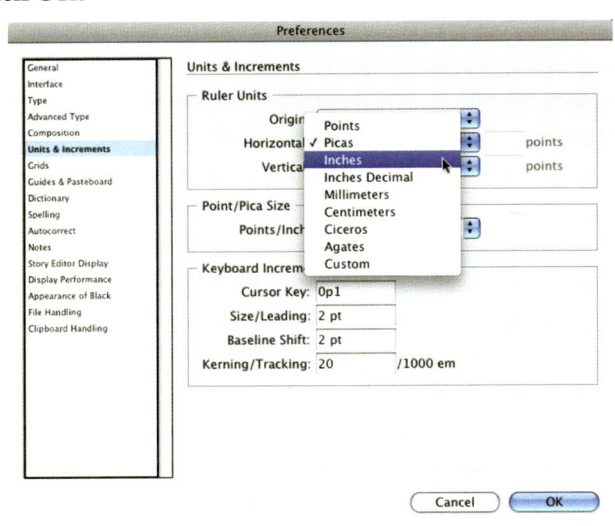

When you return to the document window, you see the rulers now display in inches.

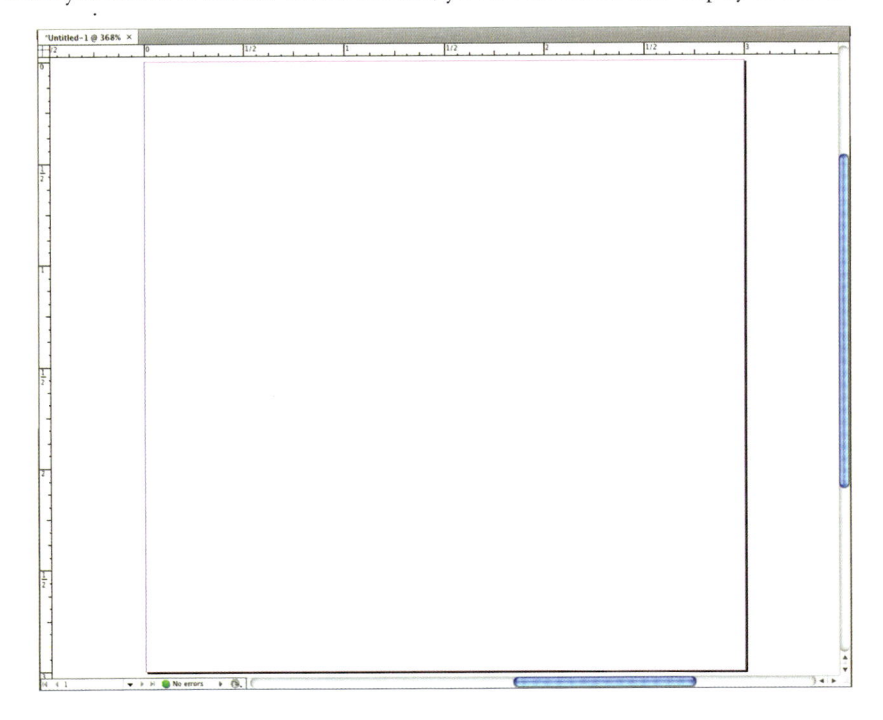

13. Choose File>Save As.

Note:

The first time you save a file, the Save command opens the same dialog box for the File>Save As command. After saving the file once, you can use Save to save changes to the existing file, or use Save As to create an additional file under a new file name.

Project 1: Identity Package 27

14. **In the Save As dialog box, navigate to your WIP>Identity folder as the target location for saving the file.**

    The Save As dialog box follows a system-standard format. Macintosh and Windows users see slightly different options, but the basic InDesign functionality is the same.

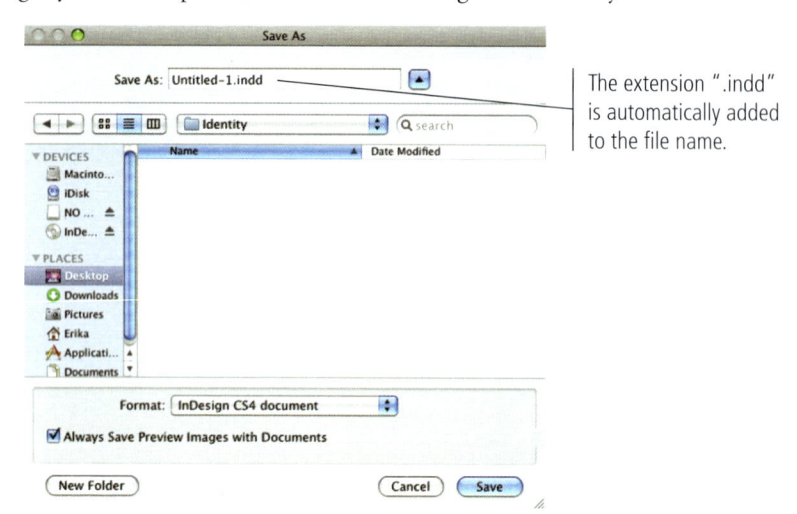

    The extension ".indd" is automatically added to the file name.

    Note:

    You can use the Format menu to save a file as a document or a template (you begin working with templates in Project 3).

15. **Change the file name (in the Save As field) to logo.indd and click Save.**

16. **Close the open document and continue to the next exercise.**

CREATE THE LETTERHEAD DOCUMENT

The most important aspect of a letterhead is to clearly and unobtrusively present the sender's contact information. The content on the letterhead — meaning the actual letter being sent — should be the main focus when someone receives a piece of your client's (or your) letterhead. This doesn't mean you can't be creative in the design, but it does mean that you shouldn't get carried away with huge, overbearing design elements that detract from the contents of the letter.

Some production-related concerns will dictate how you design letterhead. In general, there are two ways to print letterhead: commercially in large quantities, or one-offs on your desktop laser or inkjet printer. (The second method involves creating a letterhead template, which enables you to write and print letters from directly within InDesign; this method is quite common among designers.)

If letterhead is being printed commercially, it's probably being printed with multiple copies on a large press sheet, from which the individual letterhead sheets will be cut. (Most commercial printing happens this way.) This type of printing typically means that design elements can run right off the edge of the sheet, called **bleeding**.

If you're designing for a printer that can only run letter-size paper, you have to allow enough of a margin area for your printer to hold the paper as it moves through the device (called the **gripper margin**); in this case, you can't design with bleeds.

The letterhead for this project will be printed commercially. The printer said the design can safely bleed on all four sides, and their equipment requires a 1/8" bleed allowance.

Note:

These are only general rules. If you're using a commercial printer, always ask the output provider whether it's safe (and cost-effective) to design with bleeds, and find out how much bleed allowance to include.

Note:

Older desktop printers typically have a minimum margin at the page edges; you're usually safe with 3/8". Newer inkjet printers often have the capability to print 8.5 × 11" with full bleed. Consult your printer documentation to be sure.

28 Project 1: Identity Package

1. **With no file open in InDesign, open the Units & Increments Preferences dialog box (in the InDesign menu on Macintosh or the Edit menu on Windows).**

2. **Change both Ruler Units menus to Inches and click OK.**

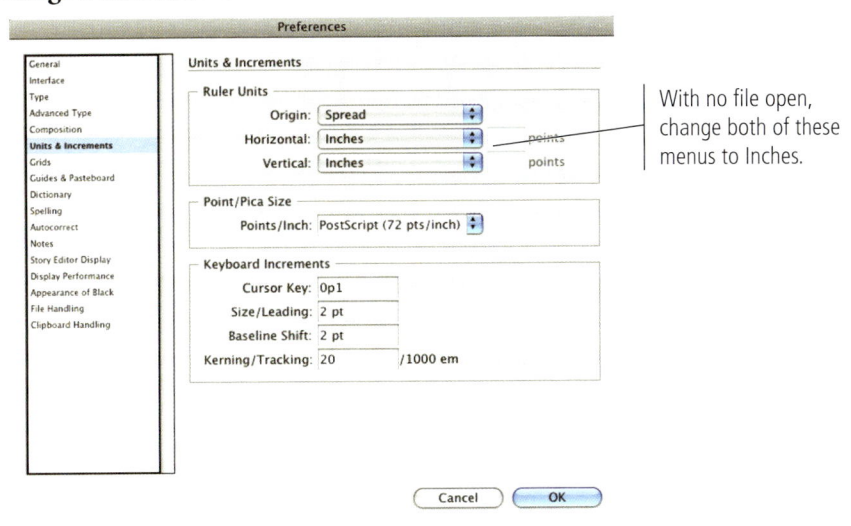

   With no file open, change both of these menus to Inches.

3. **Choose File>New>Document.**

   By changing the preferences with no file open, you're changing the application default preferences. Your changes will be applied in any new file you create, but not to already-existing files.

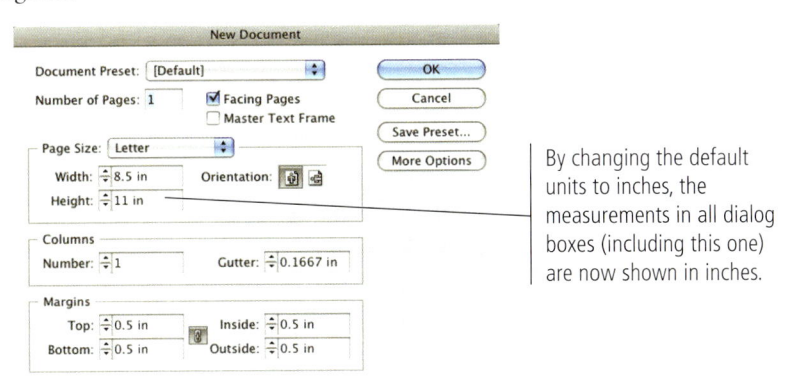

   By changing the default units to inches, the measurements in all dialog boxes (including this one) are now shown in inches.

4. **Make sure the Page Size menu is set to Letter.**

   You can use this menu to create a number of standard page sizes.

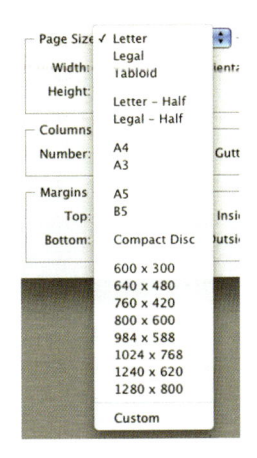

   Note:

   Choosing Custom in the Page Size menu has no real effect. This setting is automatically reflected as soon as you change the Width or Height field from the standard measurements.

   Project 1: Identity Package   29

5. **With the chain icon active in the Margins area, change the Top field to 0.75 in and then press Tab to move to the next field.**

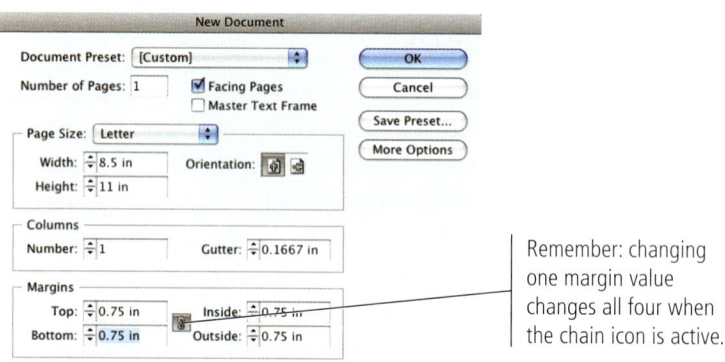

   Remember: changing one margin value changes all four when the chain icon is active.

   > *Note:*
   >
   > *You should become familiar with the common fraction-to-decimal equivalents:*
   >
   > *1/8 = 0.125*
   > *1/4 = 0.25*
   > *3/8 = 0.375*
   > *1/2 = 0.5*
   > *5/8 = 0.625*
   > *3/4 = 0.75*
   > *7/8 = 0.875*

6. **At the top of the dialog box, uncheck the Facing Pages check box.**

   Facing pages are used when a printed job will be read left to right like a book — with Page 1 starting on the right, then Page 2 facing Page 3, and so on. Facing-page layouts are based on **spreads**, which are pairs of left-right pages as you flip through a book (e.g., Page 6 facing Page 7).

   When you work with non-facing pages, the Inside and Outside margin fields change to Left and Right respectively. Technically, non-facing pages do not have an inside (spine edge) or outside (face or trim edge), so there are only left and right sides.

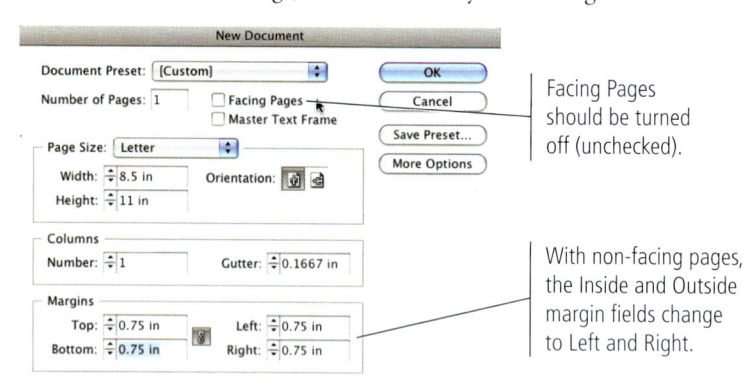

   Facing Pages should be turned off (unchecked).

   With non-facing pages, the Inside and Outside margin fields change to Left and Right.

   > *Note:*
   >
   > *You work extensively with facing pages starting in Project 4.*

7. **Click the More Options button.**

   The printer for this job says you need to include at least 1/8″ bleed allowance. In the Bleed and Slug area, you can specify that requirement so you'll see the appropriate marks later when you add design elements to the page.

8. **To the right of the Bleed fields, make sure the chain icon is active (dark gray), and then change the first Bleed field to 0.125 (the decimal equivalent of 1/8).**

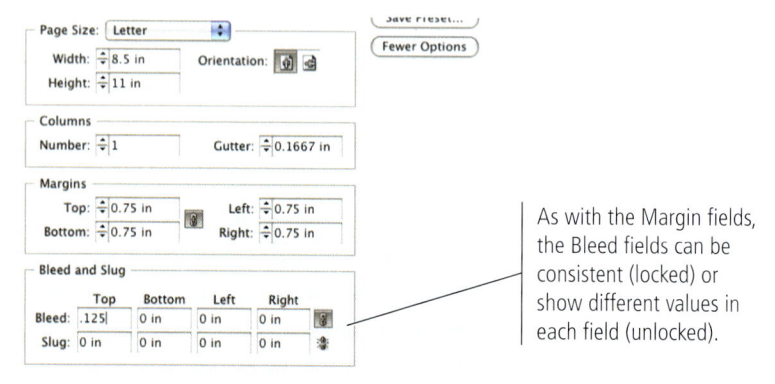

   As with the Margin fields, the Bleed fields can be consistent (locked) or show different values in each field (unlocked).

   > *Note:*
   >
   > *A **slug** is an element entirely outside the page area, but included in the final output. The slug area can be used for file/plate information, special registration marks, color bars, and/or other elements.*

   > *Note:*
   >
   > *Your default units are now inches, so you don't have to type the units. You also don't have to type the leading "0" before the decimal point.*

Project 1: Identity Package

9. **Press Tab to apply the new Bleed value to all four sides.**

10. **Click OK to create the new file.**

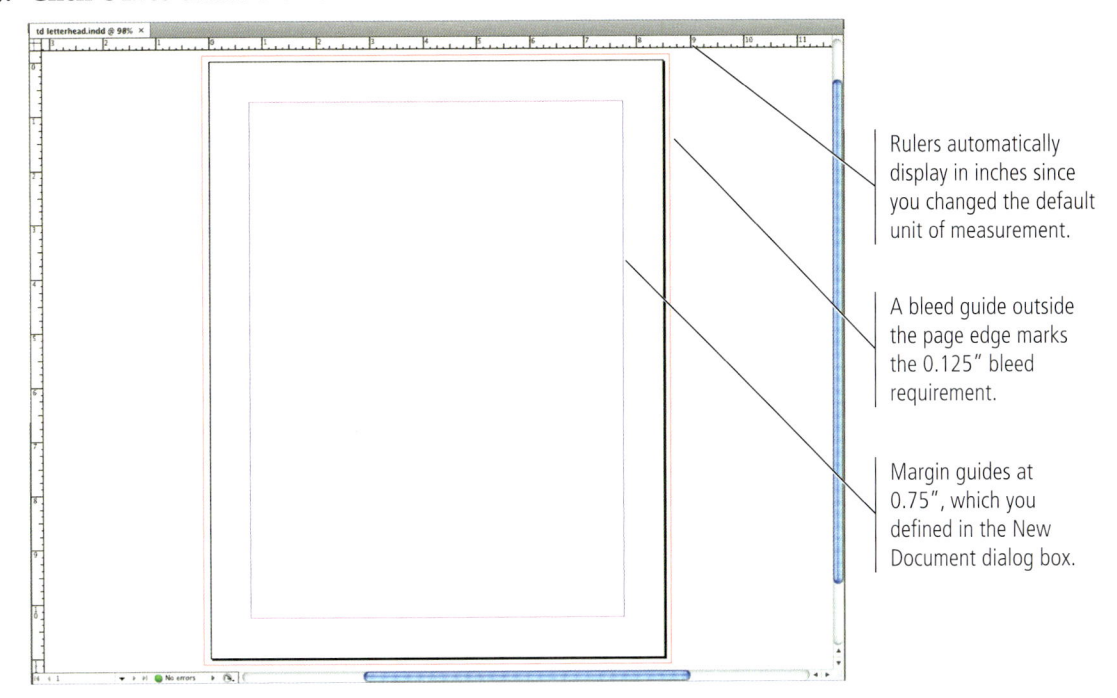

   - Rulers automatically display in inches since you changed the default unit of measurement.
   - A bleed guide outside the page edge marks the 0.125″ bleed requirement.
   - Margin guides at 0.75″, which you defined in the New Document dialog box.

11. **Save the file as td letterhead.indd in the WIP>Identity folder, and then close the file.**

CREATE THE BUSINESS CARD DOCUMENT

When business cards are printed, they are almost always printed as multiple copies on a single sheet, and then trimmed from the sheet to the standard 3.5 × 2″ size. Not long ago, printers asked for business cards to be submitted already **imposed multiple-up** (the term for printing more than one copy of an item on the same page). This practice has largely fallen out of use, partly because software makes it easier for the printer to impose the cards, and partly because the small cards are often **ganged** on a press sheet with other jobs (printed on the sheet outside the main job margins, making efficient use of what would otherwise be wasted paper).

According to the printer, the TD business cards for this project will be printed on their own press sheets; the design can safely bleed on the left, top, and bottom, and it requires a 1/8″ bleed allowance. The printer also said you should allow a 1/8″ margin to avoid important elements being cut off when the cards are cut from the press sheet.

1. **Choose File>New>Document.**

   The New Document dialog box always defaults to the last-used document preset.

Note:

*The **live area** is the "safe" area inside the page edge, where important design elements should reside. Because printing and trimming are mechanical processes, there will always be some variation — however slight. Elements placed too close to the page edge run the risk of being accidentally trimmed off.*

Project 1: Identity Package

2. **In the Page Size area, change the Width to 3.5 in and the Height to 2 in.**

   By typing values that are wider than high, InDesign automatically recognizes that you're creating a landscape document. The Landscape orientation button becomes active.

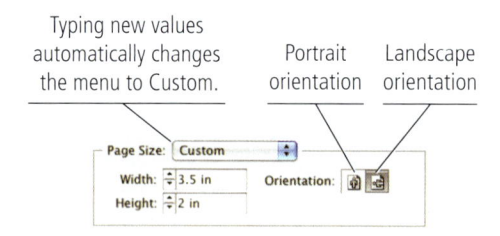

   Note:

   Portrait orientation is taller than wide; landscape orientation is wider than tall. Clicking the opposite button reverses the values in the Width and Height fields.

3. **Uncheck the Facing Pages option, and then define 0.125″ margins and bleeds for all four sides.**

4. **Click the Save Preset button.**

   A **preset** stores groups of common settings; you define a preset once, and then you can access the same group of settings later with a single click. You'll often use this concept while creating documents InDesign —when you use style sheets, table styles, object styles, and output documents for printing.

5. **In the Save Preset dialog box, type Bleed Business Card in the Save Preset As field and click OK.**

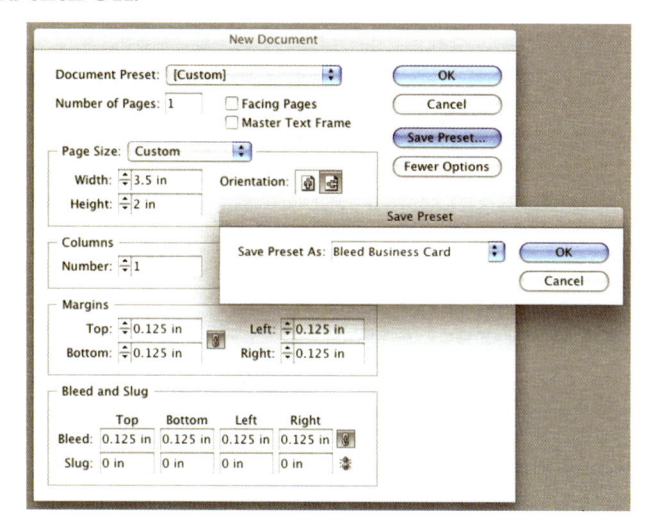

   When you return to the New Document dialog box, your new preset appears as the selection in the Document Preset menu. Any time you need to create a business card with the same bleed and live areas, you can choose Bleed Business Card from this menu.

Project 1: Identity Package

6. **Click OK to create your new document.**

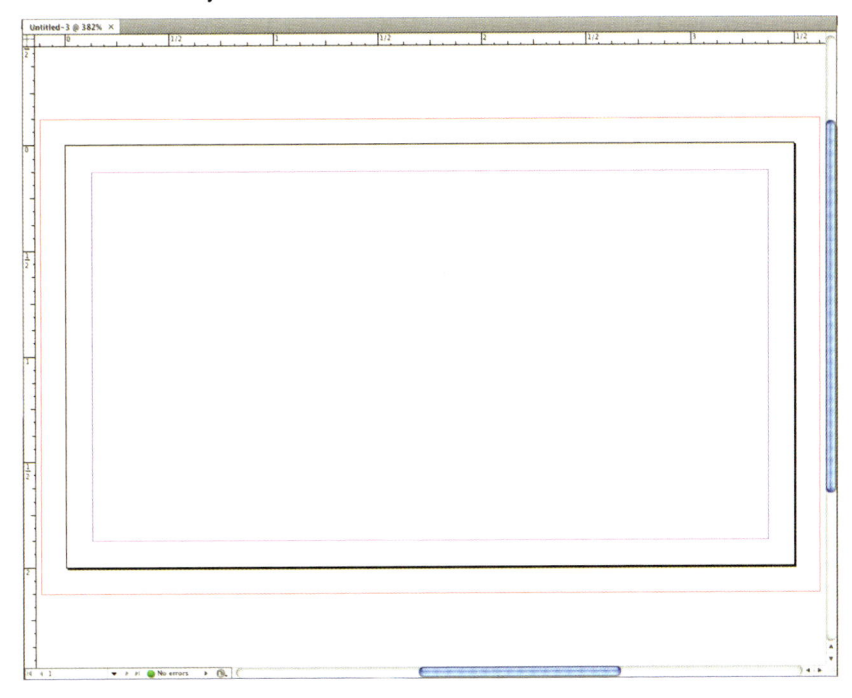

7. **Save the file as `td card.indd` in your WIP>Identity folder, and then close the file.**

Managing Document Presets

You can access and manage document presets in the File menu. If you choose one of the existing presets in the menu, the New Document dialog box opens, defaulting to the values in the preset you call (instead of defaulting to the application-default letter-size page). All the settings you saved in the preset automatically reflect in the dialog box.

You can also create, edit, and manage presets by choosing Define in the Document Presets submenu. This command opens a dialog box that lists the existing presets.

- Select a preset and click Edit to change the preset's associated options.
- Select a preset and click Delete to remove the preset from the application.
- Click New to open the New Document Preset dialog box, which is basically the same as the New Document dialog box, except the Preset menu is replaced with a field where you can type the preset name instead of clicking the Save Preset button.
- Click Save to save a preset (with the extension ".dcst") so it can be sent to and used on another computer.
- Click Load to import presets created on another computer.

Project 1: Identity Package   33

☞ CREATE THE ENVELOPE DOCUMENT

In general, printed envelopes can be created in two ways. You can create and print the design on a flat sheet, which will be specially **die cut** (stamped out of the press sheet), and then folded and glued into the shape of the finished envelope. Alternatively (and usually at less expense), you can print on pre-folded and -glued envelopes.

Both of these methods for envelope design have special printing requirements, such as not putting ink where glue will be applied (if you're printing on flat sheets), or not printing within a certain distance from the edge (if you're printing on pre-formed envelopes). Whenever you design an envelope, consult with the output provider who will print the job before you get too far into the project.

In this case, the design will be output on pre-folded #10 business-size envelopes (9.5 × 4.125″). The printer requires a 0.25″ gripper margin around the edge of the envelope where you cannot include any ink coverage.

1. **Choose File>New>Document.**

2. **Create a document preset named Prefolded Envelope, using the following settings:**

Size (W × H):	9.5 × 4.125″, without facing pages
Margins:	0.25″
Bleed:	0″

3. **Create a new file from the Prefolded Envelope preset.**

4. **Save the new file as td envelope.indd, and then close the file. Proceed to the next stage of the project.**

Stage 2 Drawing in InDesign

Now that you have the basic files you need, the next part of this project is to create the client's logo. When designing a logo, keep these important points in mind. First, logos should be representational; in other words, they are visual devices that suggest a concept without spelling out every detail. There are many schools of thought on this subject, but we believe that as a general rule logos should be relatively simplistic — suggesting an idea rather than being a photographic representation.

Second, logos need to be scalable. A company might place its logo on the head of a golf tee or the side of a building. (This creates a strong argument for the simpler line-art approach instead of photography.) Vector graphics — the kind you can create in InDesign — can be scaled as large or small as necessary without losing quality; photographs are raster images, which means they can't be greatly enlarged or reduced without losing quality.

Third, you will almost certainly need more than one version of any given logo — and possibly in more than one file format. Different kinds of output require different formats (specifically, one set of files for print and one for the Web), and some types of jobs might require special options saved in the files (such as the 4-color and 2-color versions of the TD logo you need to create in this project).

Vector Graphics vs. Raster Images

INDESIGN FOUNDATIONS

Vector graphics are composed of mathematical descriptions of a series of lines and shapes. These files are commonly created in illustration ("drawing") applications such as Adobe Illustrator or in page-layout applications such as Adobe InDesign. Vector graphics are **resolution independent**; they can be freely scaled, and they are automatically output at the resolution of the output device.

Raster images are made up of a grid of independent pixels (rasters or bits) in rows and columns (called a **bitmap**). Raster files are **resolution dependent** — their resolution is determined when you scan, photograph, or otherwise create the file. (You can typically reduce raster images, but not enlarge them without losing image quality.)

Line art is a raster image made up entirely of 100% solid areas. The pixels in a line-art image have only two options: they can be all black or all white. Examples of line art are UPC bar codes or pen-and-ink drawings. The rule for line-art reproduction is to scan the image at the same resolution as the output device. Think about it like this: a 600 dpi printer can create a maximum of 600 × 600 (360,000) dots in one square inch. With line art, we want to give the printer the most information available, which in this case would be 600 pixels per inch. If the art is created and printed at only 300 ppi, then the printer would have to skip to every other possible space to place a dot. The result is known as "stair-stepping" or "bitmapping."

A bitmap or line-art image has only two colors — black and white. There are no shades of gray or color.

Most laser printers today image at 600 to 1200 dpi, but film on an imagesetter is typically produced at a much higher resolution, possibly 2400 dpi or more. Fortunately, the human eye is not sensitive enough to discern bitmapping beyond 1200 dpi, so you can be fairly safe capturing line art at 1200 ppi.

Project 1: Identity Package 35

Understanding Resolution

Raster image quality depends directly on the file's resolution; when you work with raster image files, you need to understand the resolution requirements from the very beginning of the process:

- **Pixels per inch (ppi)** is the number of pixels in one horizontal or vertical inch of a digital raster file.
- **Lines per inch (lpi)** is the number of halftone dots produced in a horizontal or vertical linear inch by a high-resolution imagesetter in order to simulate the appearance of continuous-tone color.
- **Dots per inch (dpi)** or **spots per inch (spi)** is the number of dots produced by an output device in a single line of output. Dpi is sometimes used interchangeably (although incorrectly) with pixels per inch.

When reproducing a photograph on a printing press, the image must be converted into a set of different-size dots that fool the eye into believing it sees continuous tones. The result of this conversion process is a halftone image; the dots used to simulate continuous tone are called **halftone dots**. Light tones in a photograph are represented as small halftone dots; dark tones are represented as large halftone dots. Prior to image-editing software, photos were converted to halftones with a large graphic-arts camera and screens. The picture was photographed through the screen to create halftone dots, and different screens produced different numbers of dots in an inch, hence the term "dots per inch."

Image Resolution

When a printer creates halftone dots, it calculates the average value of a group of pixels and generates a spot of appropriate size. An image's resolution controls the quantity of pixel data that the printer can read. Regardless of the source — camera, scanner, or files you create from scratch in a program such as Photoshop — images need to have sufficient resolution for the output device to generate enough halftone dots to create the appearance of continuous tone.

Ideally, the printer has four pixels for each halftone dot created. The relationship between pixels and halftone dots defines the rule of resolution for all raster-based images — the resolution of an image should be two times the screen ruling (lpi) that will be used for printing.

Screen Ruling

The screens used with old graphic-arts cameras had a finite number of available dots in a horizontal or vertical inch. That number was the **screen ruling**, or lines per inch of the halftone. A screen ruling of 133 lpi means that in a square inch there are 133 × 133 (17,689) possible locations for a halftone dot. If the screen ruling is decreased, there are fewer total halftone dots, producing a grainier image; if the screen ruling is increased, there are more halftone dots, producing a clearer image.

Line screen is a finite number based on a combination of the intended output device and paper. You can't randomly select a line screen. Ask your printer what line screen will be used before you begin creating your images. If you can't find out ahead of time or are unsure, follow these general guidelines:

- Newspaper or newsprint: 85–100 lpi
- Magazine or general commercial printing: 133–150 lpi
- Premium-quality-paper jobs (such as art books): 150–175 lpi (some specialty jobs use 200 lpi or more)

If you find this information a bit confusing, don't worry. As a general rule for preparing a document for commercial printing, most raster images should have about twice the pixel resolution as the line screen that will be output.

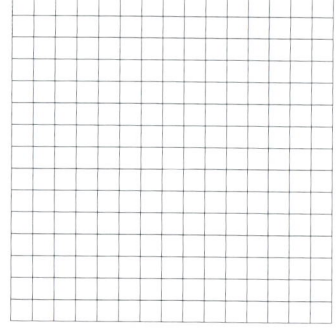

72 ppi 300 ppi

Each white square represents a pixel. The highlighted area shows the pixel information used to generate a halftone dot. If an image only has 72 pixels per inch, the output device has to generate four halftone dots per pixel, resulting in poor printed quality.

The same raster image is reproduced here at 300 ppi (left) and 72 ppi (right). Notice the obvious degradation in quality when the resolution is set to 72 ppi.

Project 1: Identity Package

CREATE AND TRANSFORM BASIC SHAPES

Although much drawing and illustration work — including creating logos — is done in a dedicated illustration program such as Adobe Illustrator, you can use the drawing tools in InDesign to create some types of artwork.

InDesign and Illustrator are both Adobe products; the drawing tools in InDesign are actually a limited subset of the more comprehensive Illustrator toolset, which means you can create fairly sophisticated artwork entirely within the layout application.

1. **Choose File>Open.**

2. **Navigate to the WIP>Identity folder and select the logo.indd file that you created earlier. Click Open.**

   Note:

   You can access the Open dialog box by pressing Command/Control-O.

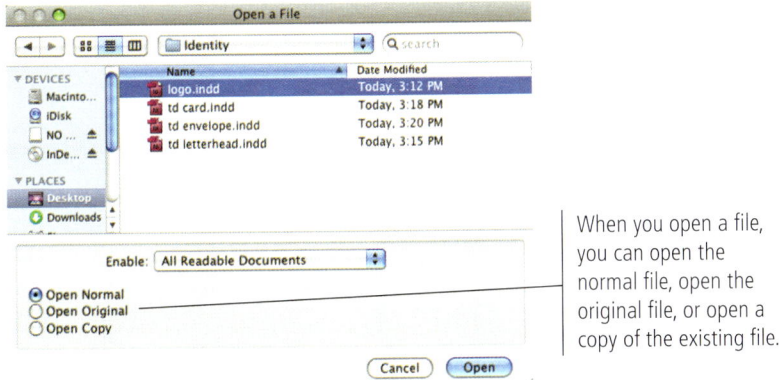

   When you open a file, you can open the normal file, open the original file, or open a copy of the existing file.

   When you open a file, the document window defaults to fill the available space on the screen. In this case, you're using the document as a drawing space, so a view percentage higher than 100% will be useful (remember, the actual document is only 3 × 3″).

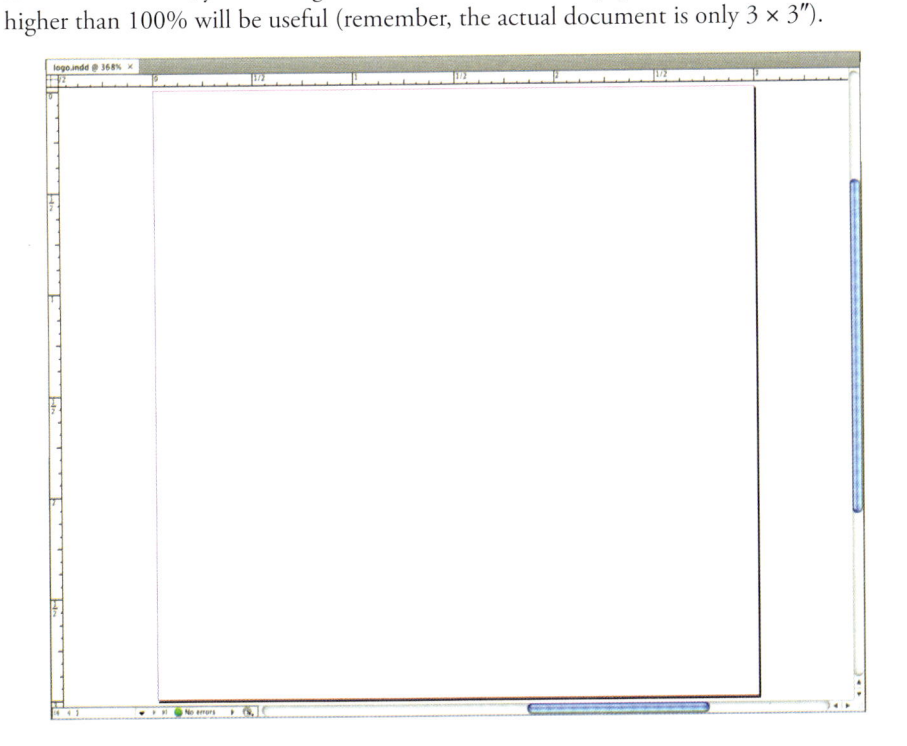

Project 1: Identity Package   37

3. **In the Tools panel, click the Rectangle tool to select it.**

   If you don't see the Rectangle tool, click and hold the default shape tool until the nested tools appear; slide over and down to select the Rectangle tool.

4. **Click the Default Fill and Stroke button at the bottom of the Tools panel.**

   In InDesign, the default fill is None, and the default stroke is 1-pt black.

5. **Click near the left page edge and drag down and right to draw a rectangle. Stay within the page edge as you drag.**

   For now, the size of the rectangle isn't really important; you change it to a specific size shortly. As you draw, cursor feedback shows the size of the shape you are creating. If you don't see the cursor feedback, choose View>Grids & Guides>Smart Guides to activate that feature.

Note:

Tools with nested options default to show the last-used variation in the main Tools panel.

Note:

Press Shift while drawing a shape (or frame) to constrain the horizontal and vertical dimensions of the shape — in other words, to create a perfect square or circle.

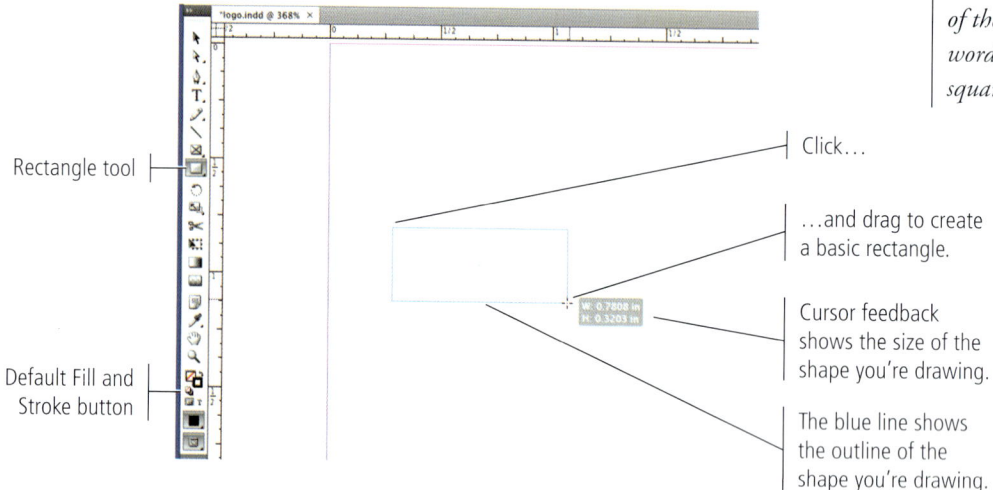

- Rectangle tool
- Default Fill and Stroke button
- Click…
- …and drag to create a basic rectangle.
- Cursor feedback shows the size of the shape you're drawing.
- The blue line shows the outline of the shape you're drawing.

6. **Release the mouse button to create the rectangle.**

   Every shape you create in an InDesign document has a **bounding box**, which is a non-printing rectangle that marks the outer dimensions of the shape. (Even a circle has a square bounding box, marking the largest height and width of the object.) The bounding box has eight handles, which you can drag to change the size of the rectangle. If you can see an object's bounding box handles, that object is selected.

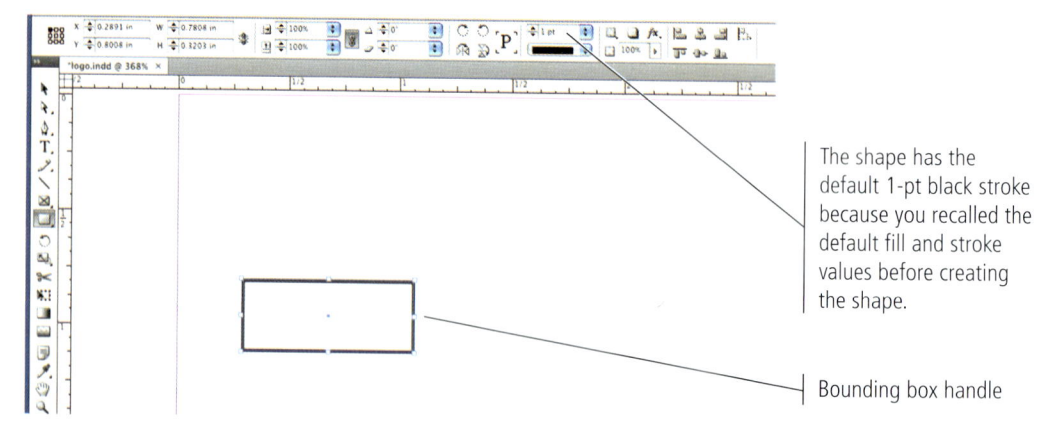

- The shape has the default 1-pt black stroke because you recalled the default fill and stroke values before creating the shape.
- Bounding box handle

7. **With the object selected, look at the bottom of the Tools panel.**

   Every object you create with the InDesign drawing tools has a stroke (border) and a fill (background) color — even if one or both of those is colored "None."

Project 1: Identity Package

8. **Click the Swap Fill and Stroke button.**

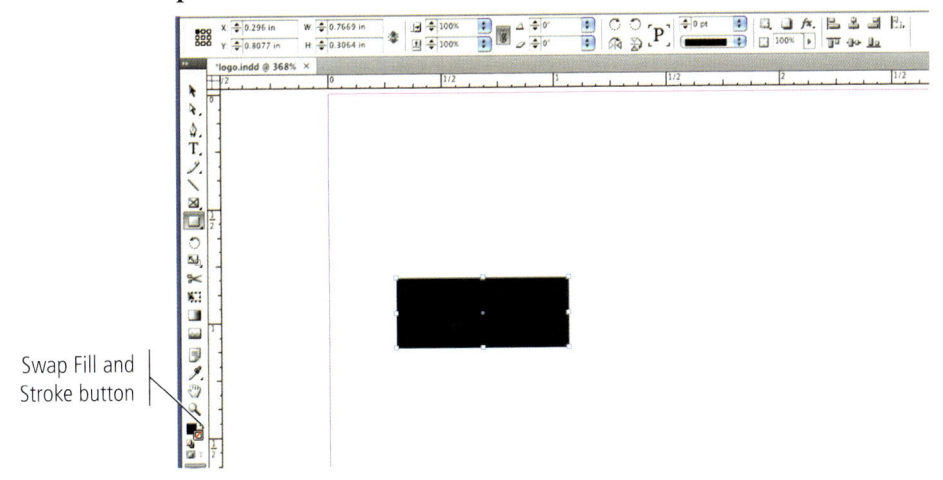

   Swap Fill and Stroke button

9. **At the left end of the Control panel, select the top-left reference point.**

   The Control panel is context-sensitive, which means different options are available depending on what is selected in the document. This panel consolidates the most common options from multiple InDesign panels.

   The **reference point** determines how transformations will occur (in other words, which point of the object will remain in place if you change one of the position or dimension values). These points correspond to the object's bounding box handles, as well as to the object's exact center point.

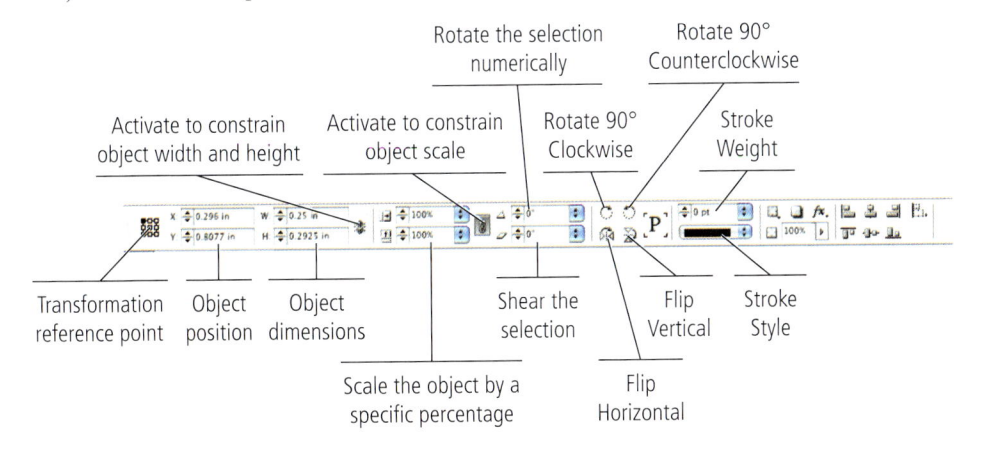

   - Activate to constrain object width and height
   - Activate to constrain object scale
   - Rotate the selection numerically
   - Rotate 90° Clockwise
   - Rotate 90° Counterclockwise
   - Stroke Weight
   - Transformation reference point
   - Object position
   - Object dimensions
   - Shear the selection
   - Flip Vertical
   - Stroke Style
   - Scale the object by a specific percentage
   - Flip Horizontal

10. **Make sure the chain icon for the W and H fields is inactive (not checked), change the W (width) field to 0.25 in, and then press Return/Enter.**

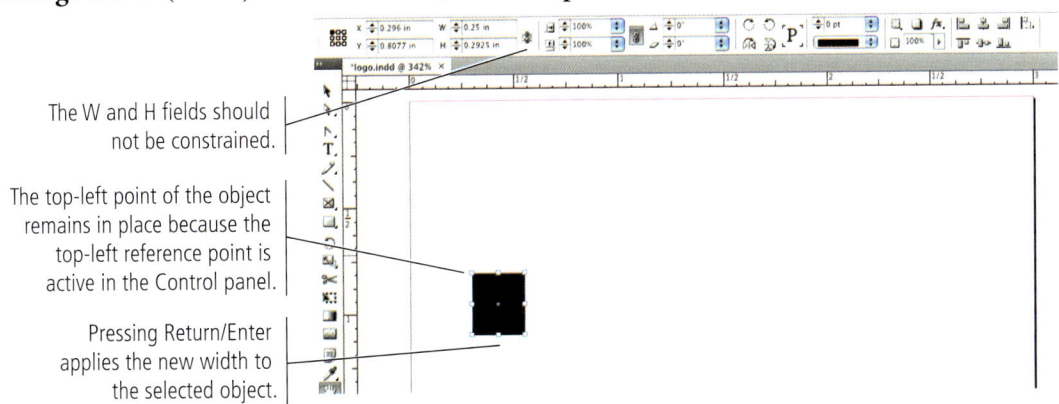

    The W and H fields should not be constrained.

    The top-left point of the object remains in place because the top-left reference point is active in the Control panel.

    Pressing Return/Enter applies the new width to the selected object.

Project 1: Identity Package

Understanding the Control Panel

The Control panel is one of the most versatile, productive tools in the InDesign workspace, combining all the most common formatting options into a single, compact format across the top of the workspace. It is context sensitive, which means different options are available depending on what is selected in the layout. Finally, it is customizable, which means you can change the options that are available in the panel.

If you start with the built-in Essentials workspace, the Control panel presents an abbreviated set of options. If you have a wide enough monitor, the Advanced workspace includes all the available options.

Essentials Control panel when a frame is selected (top) and when text is selected (bottom).

Advanced Control panel when a frame is selected (top) and when text is selected (bottom).

The panel Options menu includes options for controlling the position of the panel (top, bottom, or floating), as well as how transformations affect selected objects:

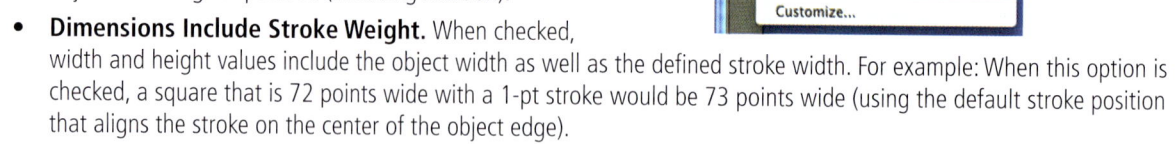

- **Stroke Styles.** This opens a dialog box where you can edit or define custom styles for lines and object strokes.
- **Clear Transformations.** Choosing this option resets an object to its original position (including rotation).
- **Dimensions Include Stroke Weight.** When checked, width and height values include the object width as well as the defined stroke width. For example: When this option is checked, a square that is 72 points wide with a 1-pt stroke would be 73 points wide (using the default stroke position that aligns the stroke on the center of the object edge).
- **Transformations are Totals.** When checked, transformations to an object's contents reflect the object's transformations plus transformations applied to the content within the frame. For example: If an object is rotated 10°, and the graphic within the object is rotated 5°, the object's rotation displays as 15° when this option is checked.
- **Show Content Offset.** When checked, the Control panel shows X+ and Y+ values for the graphic placed within a frame when the object is selected with the Direct Selection tool.
- **Adjust Stroke Weight when Scaling.** When checked, resizing an object changes the stroke weight proportionally. For example: Resizing an object with a 1-pt stroke to 50% results in a 0.5-pt stroke.
- **Dock at Top**, **Dock at Bottom**, and **Float**. These control the position of the Control panel within the workspace.

Choosing Customize in the panel Options menu opens a dialog box where you can define the available options in the panel; anything with a checkmark will be available when it's relevant to the selection in the document.

Clicking the Quick Apply button opens a special navigation dialog box. This feature enables you to easily find and apply what you want — menu commands, user-defined styles, and so on — by typing a few characters in the text entry field, and then clicking the related item in the list.

Project 1: Identity Package

11. **Highlight the H field and type 2 in. Press Return/Enter to apply the change.**

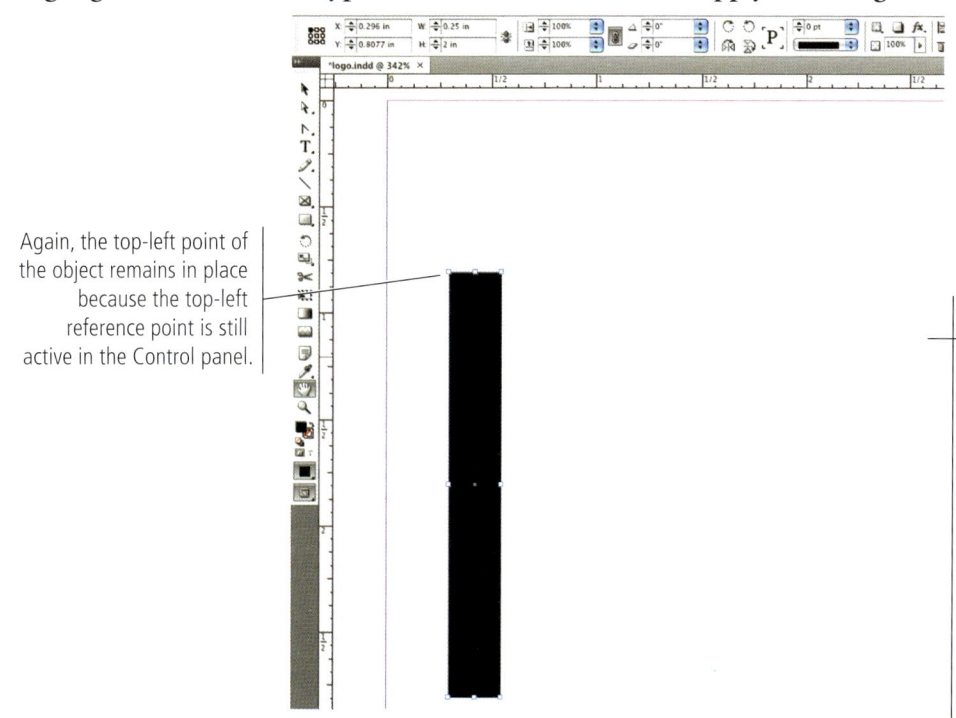

   Again, the top-left point of the object remains in place because the top-left reference point is still active in the Control panel.

   Note:

   The Transform panel (Window>Object & Layout>Transform) includes the same options that are available in the Control panel when an object is selected with the Selection tool. You can change an object's position or dimensions, scale an object to a specific percentage, and apply rotation or shear to the selected object. The panel Options menu includes the same options that are available in the Control panel Options menu, as well as commands to rotate and flip the selected object.

12. **Choose the Selection tool, then click away from the rectangle to deselect it.**

13. **Select the Rectangle tool, click the Default Fill and Stroke button in the Tools panel, and then click once near the middle of the page.**

    Single-clicking with a shape tool opens a dialog box where you can define specific measurements for the new shape.

14. **In the Rectangle dialog box, set the Width to 1 in and the Height to 0.25 in, and then click OK.**

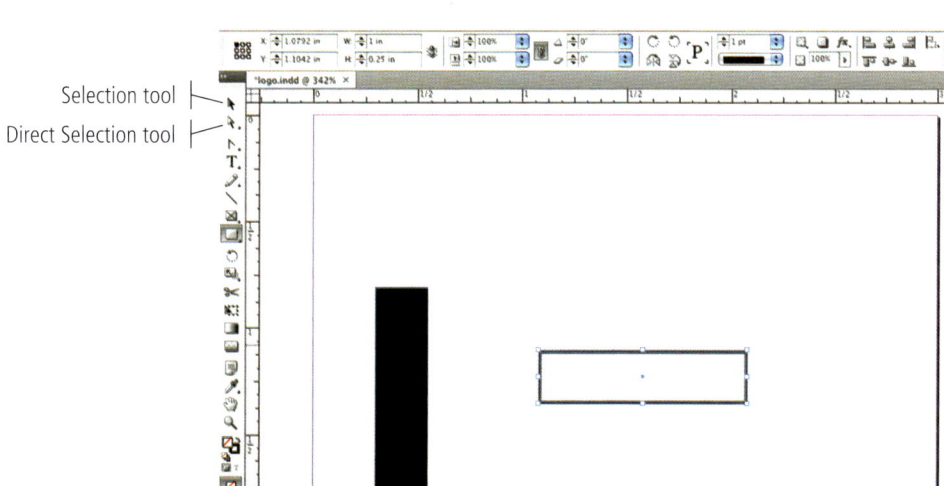

    Selection tool
    Direct Selection tool

15. **Swap the fill and stroke colors in the second rectangle.**

Project 1: Identity Package   41

16. **Choose the Selection tool (solid arrow) in the Tools panel.**

    The Selection tool is used to select entire objects; the Direct Selection tool (hollow arrow) is used to select parts of objects.

17. **Click the vertical rectangle and drag right until a green line identifies the center of the horizontal rectangle.**

    The green line is a function of InDesign's Smart Guides, which make it easy to align objects to each other by simply dragging.

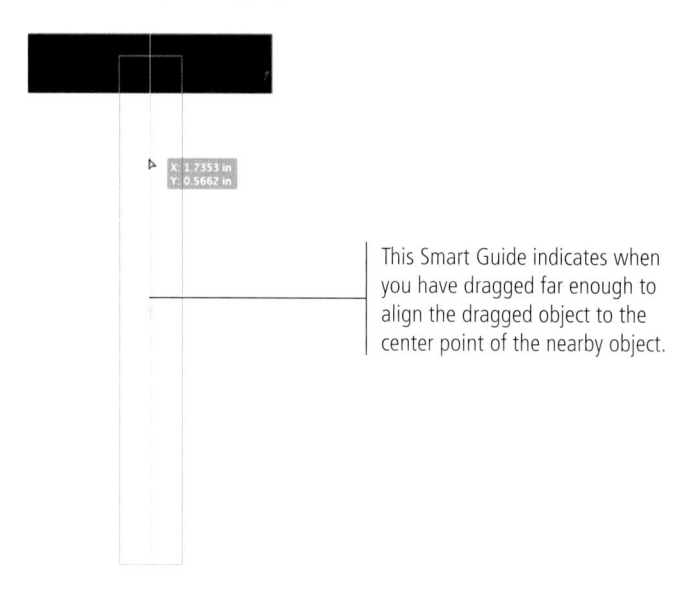

    This Smart Guide indicates when you have dragged far enough to align the dragged object to the center point of the nearby object.

18. **Select the horizontal rectangle and drag down until a horizontal Smart Guide appears.**

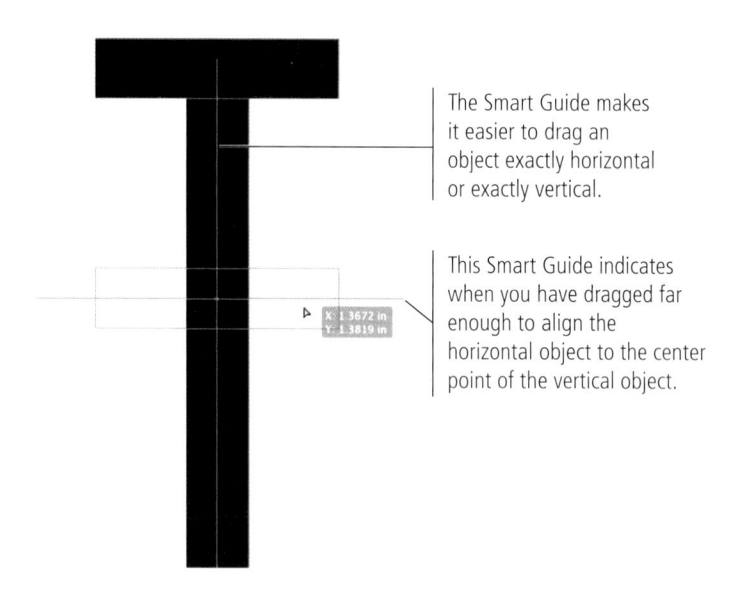

    The Smart Guide makes it easier to drag an object exactly horizontal or exactly vertical.

    This Smart Guide indicates when you have dragged far enough to align the horizontal object to the center point of the vertical object.

    Note:

    You can also press the Shift key and drag to constrain movement to exactly horizontal or exactly vertical.

19. **With the horizontal rectangle selected, click in the Y field of the Control panel to place the insertion point at the end of the existing value.**

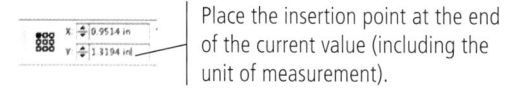

    Place the insertion point at the end of the current value (including the unit of measurement).

Project 1: Identity Package

20. **Type -.5 and press Return/Enter to apply the change.**

   You can use mathematical functions to add (+), subtract (-), divide (/), or multiply (*) existing values in the Control panel. This is useful when you want to move or change a value by a specific amount.

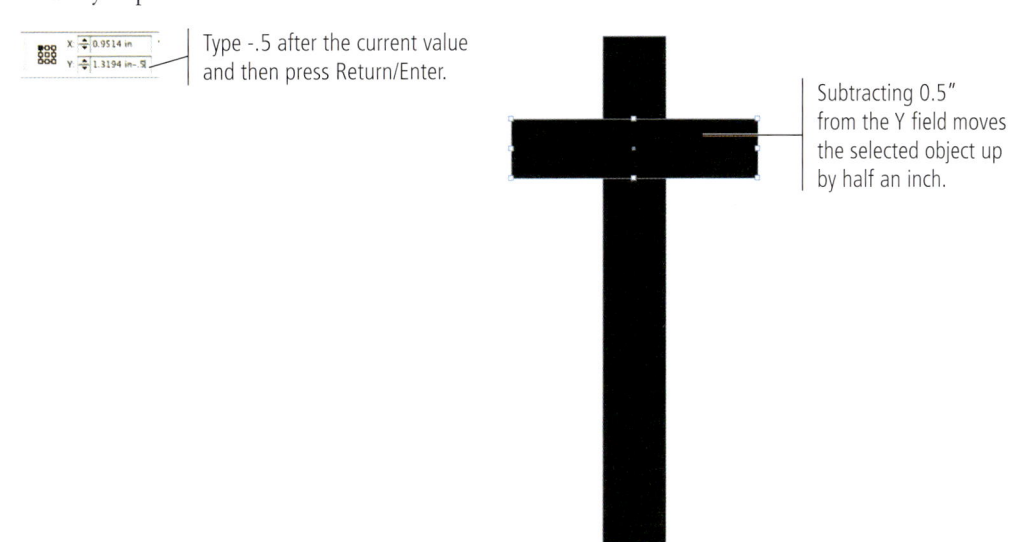

   Type -.5 after the current value and then press Return/Enter.

   Subtracting 0.5" from the Y field moves the selected object up by half an inch.

21. **If any part of the two rectangles is outside of the page area, select both objects with the Selection tool and drag them to the middle of the page area.**

22. **Save the file and continue to the next exercise.**

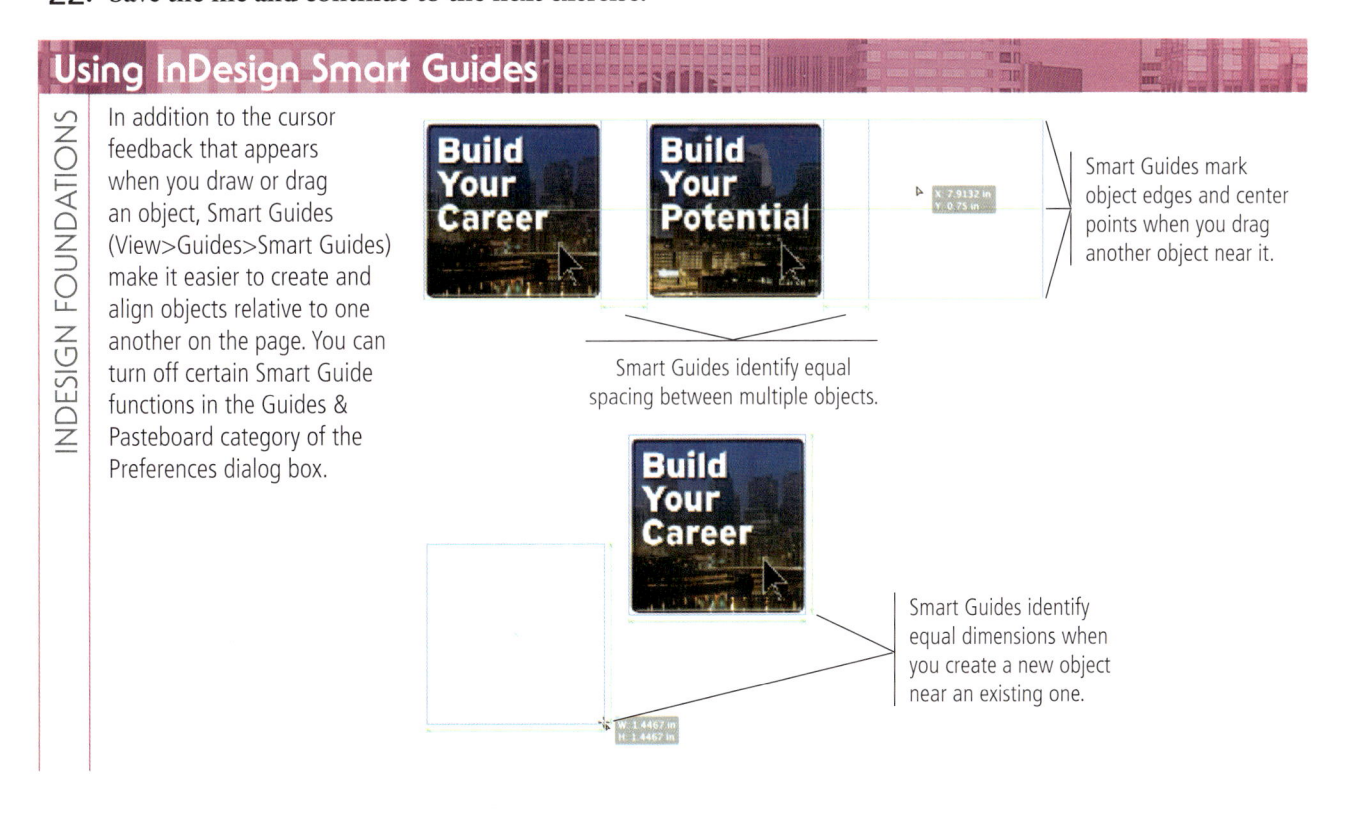

Using InDesign Smart Guides

INDESIGN FOUNDATIONS

In addition to the cursor feedback that appears when you draw or drag an object, Smart Guides (View>Guides>Smart Guides) make it easier to create and align objects relative to one another on the page. You can turn off certain Smart Guide functions in the Guides & Pasteboard category of the Preferences dialog box.

Smart Guides mark object edges and center points when you drag another object near it.

Smart Guides identify equal spacing between multiple objects.

Smart Guides identify equal dimensions when you create a new object near an existing one.

Project 1: Identity Package   43

Aligning and Distributing Objects

In addition to aligning objects with the assistance of Smart Guides, you can also use the Align panel to align multiple objects relative to one another, to the page margins, to the page, or to the spread.

The Align Objects options are fairly self explanatory; when multiple objects are selected, the objects align based on the edge(s) or center(s) you click.

The Distribute Objects options enable you to control the positions of multiple objects relative to each other. By default, objects are equally distributed within the dimensions of the overall selection; you can check the Use Spacing option to space edges or centers by a specific amount.

The Distribute Spacing options place equal space between the overall selected objects. You can also check the Use Spacing option to add a specific amount of space between the selected objects.

Below the Distribute Objects option, you can choose from the menu to determine how objects will align. (Because you can align objects relative to the document, the align buttons are also available when only one object is selected, allowing you to align any single object to a precise location on the page or spread.)

Many of the options from the Align panel are also available in the Control panel; the Align options are also available in all the built-in workspaces. If you are using the Essentials workspace, the Distribute options are not available in the Control panel; you can turn them on by customizing the panel or by choosing the Advanced workspace option.

Align Right Edges, Align Horizontal Centers, Align Left Edges, Align Top Edges, Align Vertical Centers, Align Bottom Edges

Distribute Top Edges, Distribute Vertical Centers, Distribute Bottom Edges, Distribute Right Edges, Distribute Horizontal Centers, Distribute Left Edges

By default, the Distribute Object options equally space the selected objects within the outermost dimensions of the selection.

The Use Spacing option places a specific amount of space between the selected edge (or center) of selected objects.

The Distribute Spacing options place a specific amount of space between selected objects.

INDESIGN FOUNDATIONS

Project 1: Identity Package

Create and Edit Anchor Points and Curves

Vector objects are comprised of line segments and anchor points, even if you don't create each point manually with the Pen tool. You can create many objects by starting with basic shapes, and then editing the points and segments to produce the exact shape you want — in this case, the cross-piece of the T-square.

Note:

Unlike raster images, vector graphics can be resized without losing quality.

1. **With logo.indd open, use the Direct Selection tool to select only the horizontal rectangle.**

    Objects in InDesign are comprised of anchor points and line segments that connect those points. Using the Direct Selection tool, you can access and edit those anchor points and lines.

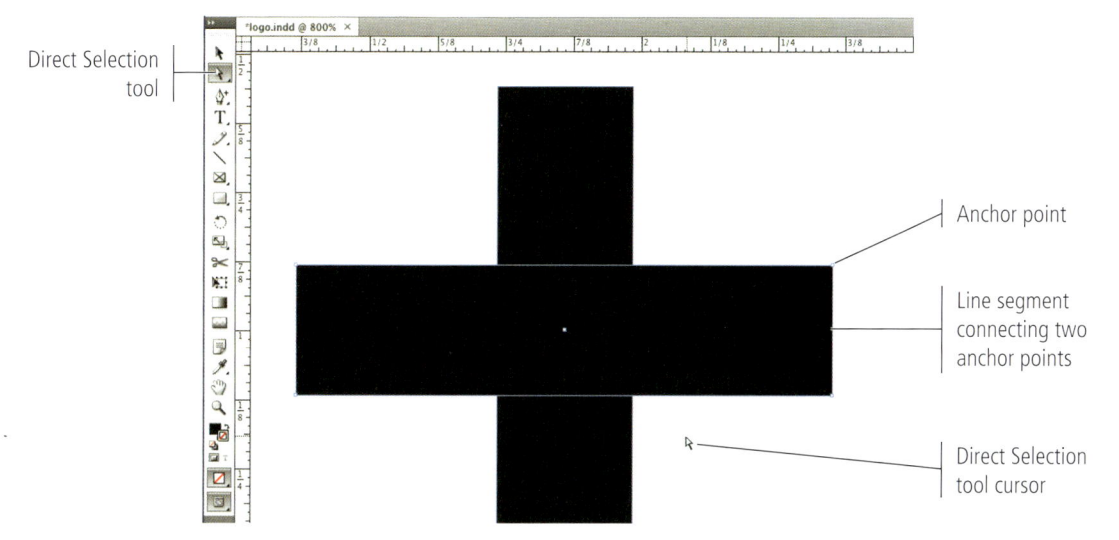

2. **In the Tools panel, click and hold the Pen tool and choose the Add Anchor Point tool from the menu of nested tools.**

3. **Place the cursor over the top edge of the horizontal rectangle and click to add an anchor point to the line segment.**

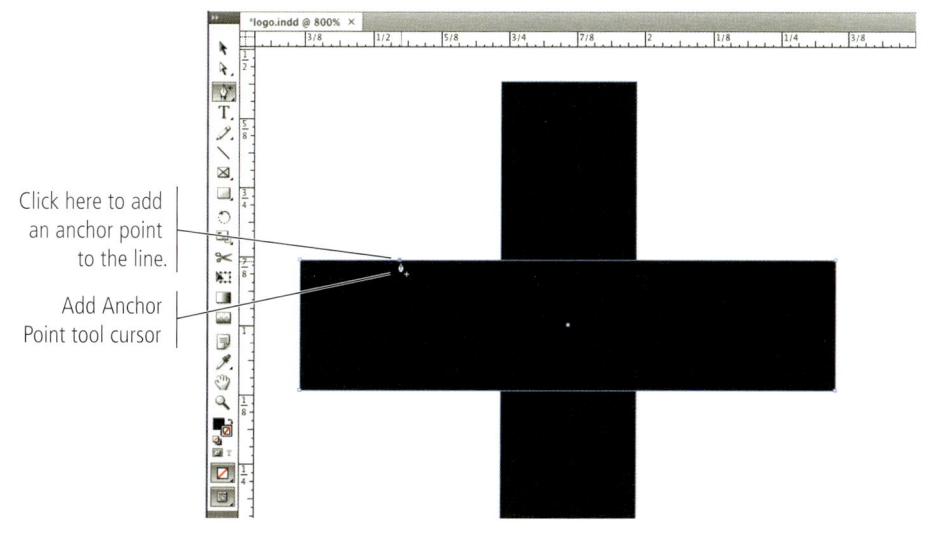

Project 1: Identity Package

4. **Repeat Step 3 to add two more anchor points, using the following image as a guide.**

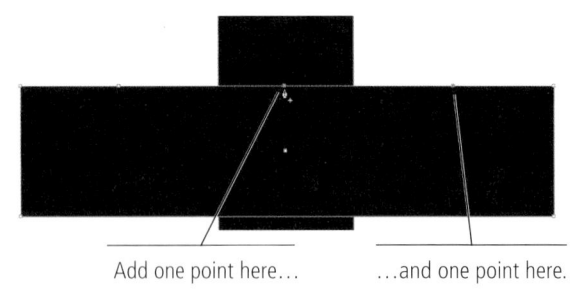

Add one point here… …and one point here.

5. **Choose the Direct Selection tool from the Tools panel and click the top-right anchor point of the rectangle.**

   As we mentioned earlier, the Direct Selection tool selects parts of objects — in other words, you can use the tool to select individual anchor points that make up a shape.

6. **Press the Shift key, click the top-right anchor point, and drag down to make the right edge approximately one-fourth its original height.**

   By pressing the Shift key, you constrain a point's movement to 45° angles — you can drag it straight up, down, across, or halfway between the two axes. (This technique works when moving any object or selection, using either selection tool.)

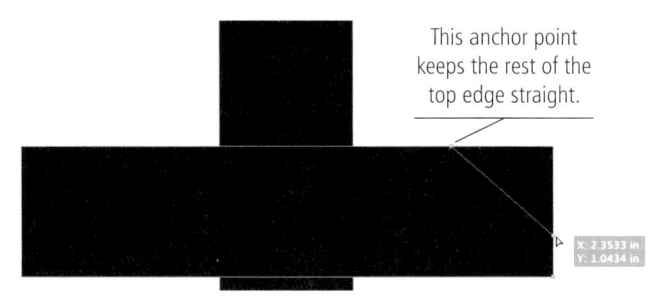

   This anchor point keeps the rest of the top edge straight.

7. **Drag the top-left point to match the Y position of the adjusted point on the right edge.**

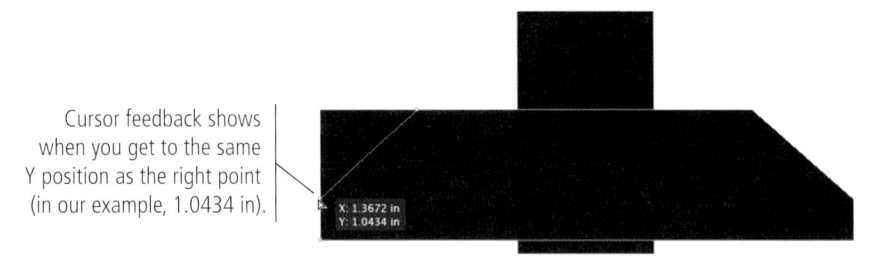

   Cursor feedback shows when you get to the same Y position as the right point (in our example, 1.0434 in).

8. **Using the Direct Selection tool, adjust the two points on the top edge of the shape to be halfway between their original position and the points you adjusted in Steps 6–7.**

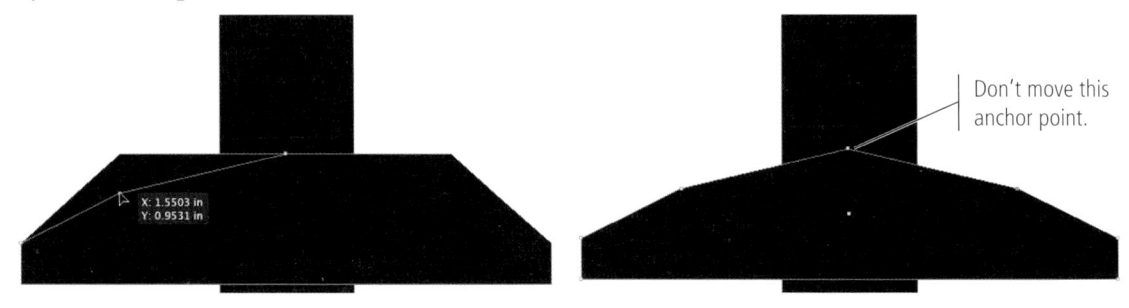

   Don't move this anchor point.

Project 1: Identity Package

9. **Choose the Convert Direction Point tool (nested under the Add Anchor Point tool).**

10. **Click the top-center anchor point of the shape and — without releasing the mouse button — drag to the left.**

    The Convert Direction Point tool changes a corner point to a smooth point. **Smooth points** have handles that control the size and shape of curves connected to the point. You can use the Direct Selection tool to drag handles for a selected anchor point.

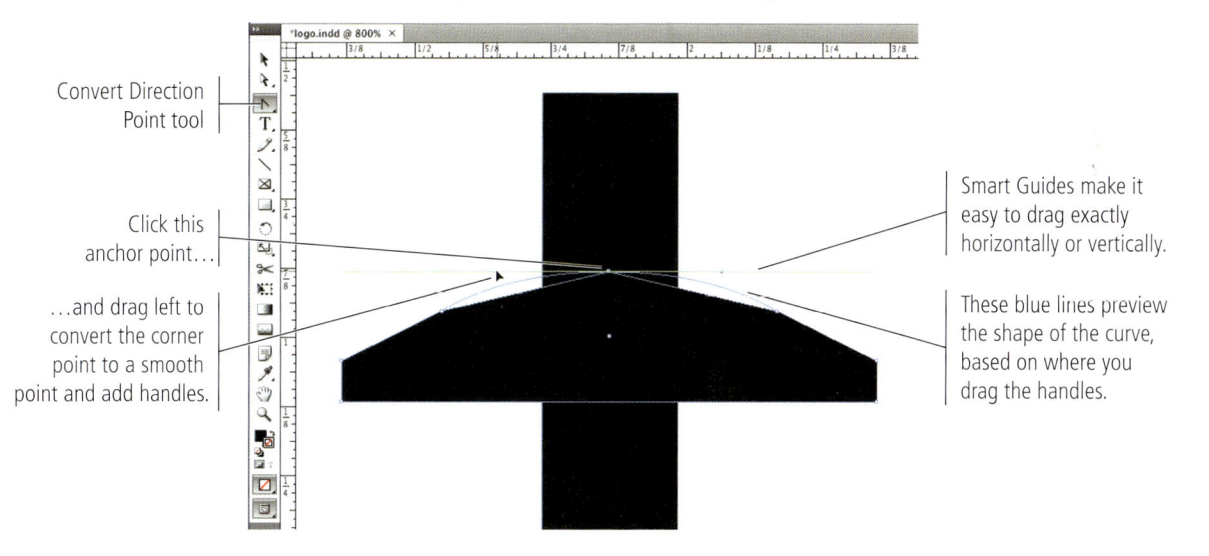

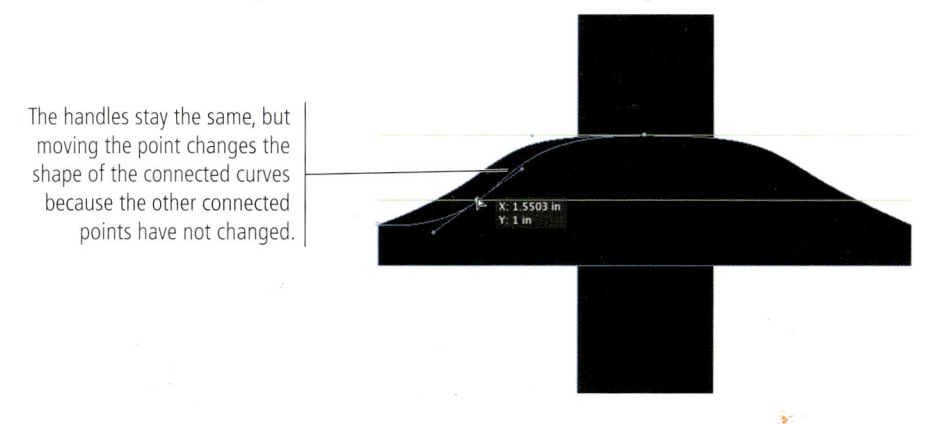

    Note:

    The lines that connect anchor points based on the angle and length of the control handles are called Bézier curves.

    Convert Direction Point tool

    Click this anchor point…

    …and drag left to convert the corner point to a smooth point and add handles.

    Smart Guides make it easy to drag exactly horizontally or vertically.

    These blue lines preview the shape of the curve, based on where you drag the handles.

11. **Repeat Step 10 to add handles to the other two points on the shape's top edge.**

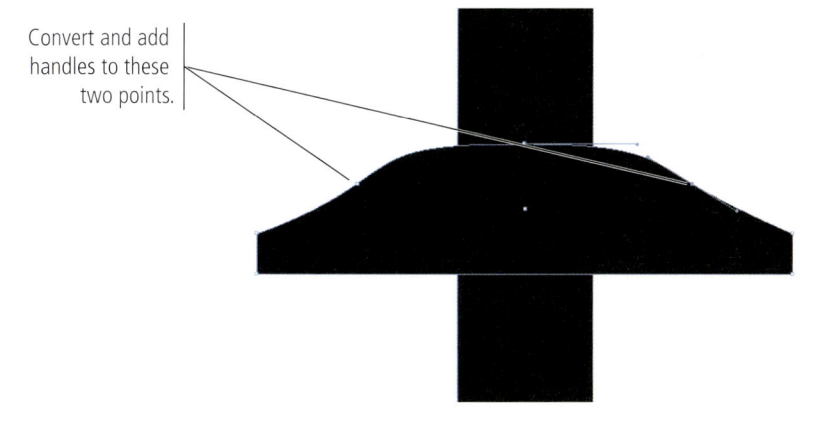

    Convert and add handles to these two points.

12. **Using the Direct Selection tool, drag the left-center point down until the Smart Guides identify the horizontal center of the shape.**

    The handles stay the same, but moving the point changes the shape of the connected curves because the other connected points have not changed.

    Project 1: Identity Package   47

Understanding Anchor Points and Handles

An anchor point marks the end of a line segment, and the point handles determine the shape of that segment. That's the basic definition of a vector, but there is a bit more to it than that. You can draw Bézier shapes from scratch using the Pen tool, or you can edit the curves that are created as part of another shape (such as a circle).

Each segment in a path has two anchor points and two associated handles. We first clicked to create Point A and dragged (without releasing the mouse button) to create Handle A1. We then clicked and dragged to create Point B and Handle B1; Handle B2 is automatically created as a reflection of B1 (Point B is a **symmetrical point**).

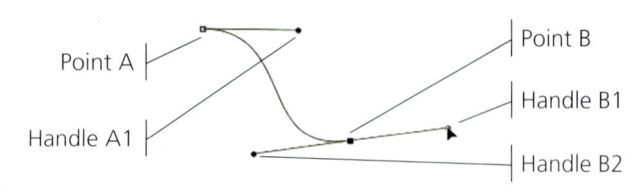

This image shows the result of dragging Handle B1 to the left instead of to the right. Notice the difference in the curve here, compared to the curve above. By dragging the handle, the segment arcs away from the direction of the handle.

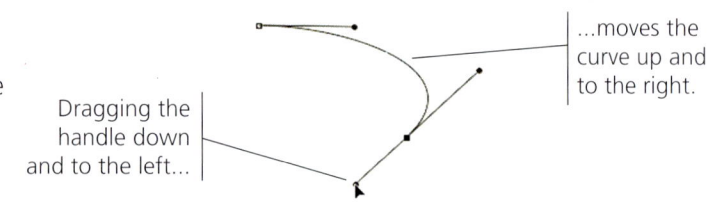

It's important to understand that a segment is connected to two handles. In this example, Handle A1 and Handle A2 determine the shape of Segment A. Dragging either handle to the right pulls out the arc of the connected segment.

Clicking and dragging a point creates a symmetrical point; both handles start out at equal length, directly opposite one another. Dragging one handle of a symmetrical point also changes the opposing handle of that point. (In the example here, dragging Handle B also moves Handle A, which affects the shape of Segment A.) You can, however, change the length of one handle without affecting the length of the other handle.

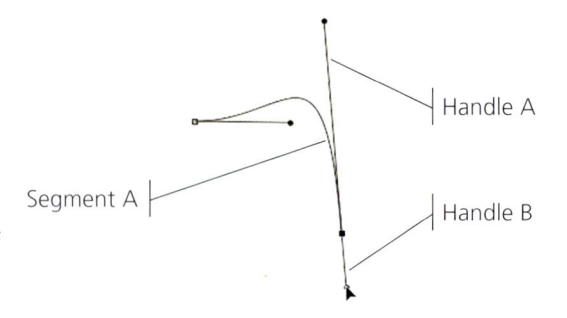

You can create corner points by simply clicking with the Pen tool instead of clicking and dragging. Corner points do not have their own handles; the connected segments are controlled by the handles of the other associated points.

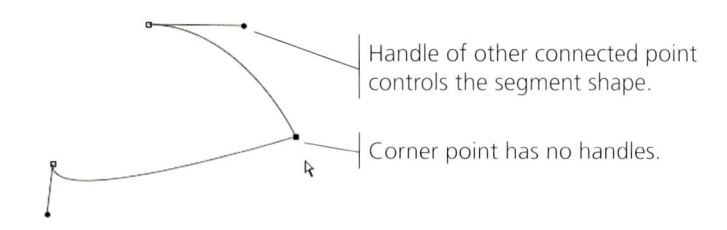

You can convert a symmetrical point into a corner point by clicking the point with the Convert Direction Point tool [▷] (nested under the Pen tool). You can also add a handle to only one side of an anchor point by Option/Alt-clicking a point with the Convert Direction Point tool and dragging.

INDESIGN FOUNDATIONS

48 Project 1: Identity Package

13. **Select the point on the center-right side and drag it down to match the point on the left.**

    Your shape doesn't have to be perfect. Remember that this logo should suggest the idea of a T-square — not be a photograph of a T-square.

    Note:

    Bézier curves can be difficult to master without a relatively deep understanding of geometry (at best) or trigonometry. The best training is to practice until you can recognize and predict how moving a point or handle will affect the connected segments.

14. **Save the file and continue to the next exercise.**

Apply Color to Page Elements

1. **With logo.indd open, use the Selection tool to click the vertical rectangle to select it.**

2. **Choose Object>Arrange>Bring to Front.**

    You can use this menu to change the **stacking order** (the top-to-bottom order) of objects relative to each other. You can move the selected object(s) to the front or back of the stack by choosing Bring to Front or Send to Back, or you can move objects one step up or back by choosing Bring Forward or Send Backward.

3. **Open the Color panel.**

    Remember, all panels can be accessed in the Window menu. Because workspace arrangement is a matter of personal preference, we won't tell you where to place or keep panels. If the Color panel is not in your panel dock, simply choose Window>Color to display that panel.

4. **In the Color panel, click the Fill swatch to bring it to the front (if it isn't already).**

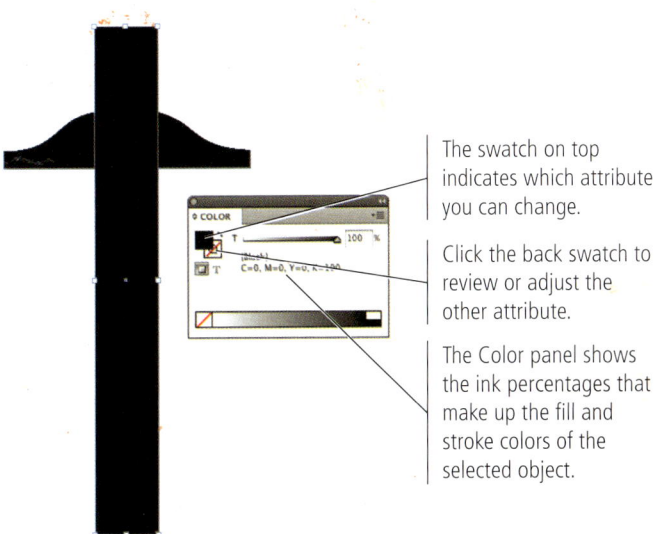

    The swatch on top indicates which attribute you can change.

    Click the back swatch to review or adjust the other attribute.

    The Color panel shows the ink percentages that make up the fill and stroke colors of the selected object.

Project 1: Identity Package

5. **Click the Percentage field to the right of the slider and type 15. Press Return/Enter to apply the change.**

    You can change the color by typing a specific value or by dragging the slider below the color gradient.

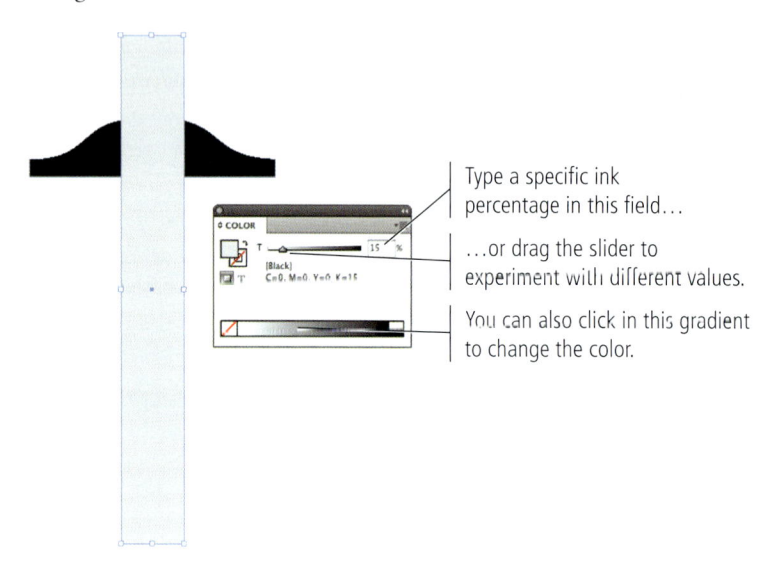

    Type a specific ink percentage in this field…

    …or drag the slider to experiment with different values.

    You can also click in this gradient to change the color.

    > *Note:*
    >
    > *When an object is selected, changing the fill and stroke values changes those attributes for the selected object. If you change the fill or stroke color value with no object selected, you can define the values for the next object you create.*

6. **Click the Stroke swatch to bring it to the front, and then change the stroke value to 100% black.**

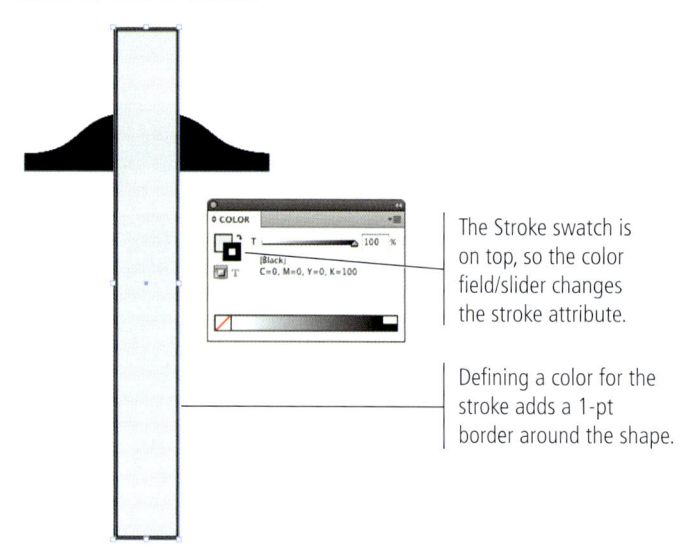

    The Stroke swatch is on top, so the color field/slider changes the stroke attribute.

    Defining a color for the stroke adds a 1-pt border around the shape.

7. **In the Control panel, open the Stroke Weight menu and choose 0.25 pt.**

    You can type any specific value in the Weight field or choose one of the predefined weights from the menu.

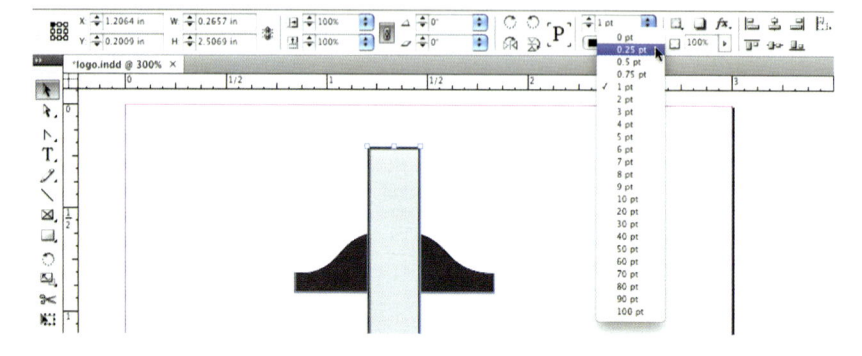

50   Project 1: Identity Package

8. **Using the same methods, select the horizontal shape and change the fill to 85% black, and change the stroke to 0.25 pt at 100% black.**

9. **Choose View>Hide Frame Edges.**

    This command turns off the blue border that outlines the two filled shapes so you can see the actual stroke values. Frame edges can be very valuable when you're working with some objects, but they can be distracting in other cases. Always remember that you can toggle the frame edges on and off in the View menu.

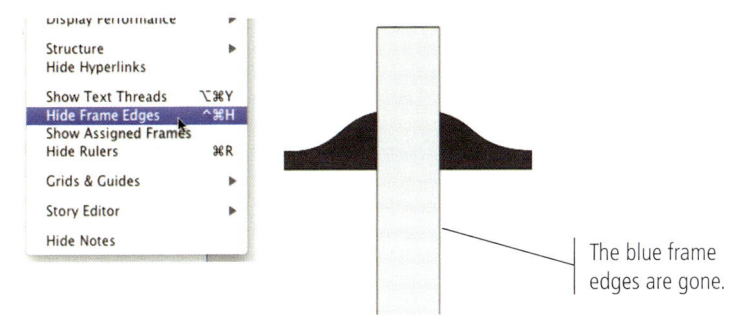

    The blue frame edges are gone.

10. **Save the file and continue to the next exercise.**

CREATE AND CONTROL LINES

InDesign includes two tools for creating lines: the Line tool for creating straight lines and the Pen tool for creating curved lines (although you can also create straight lines with the Pen tool). Working with straight lines is relatively straightforward, but don't dismiss them as inconsequential — straight lines are far more common than curved lines in a standard InDesign job.

1. **With logo.indd open, deselect both objects on the page.**

2. **Select the Line tool in the Tools panel.**

    The vertical bar in the T-square is basically a ruler, which means it should have marks indicating measurements. You're going to use lines to add those marks. (The logo you're creating will be representational, so you don't have to be precise with these lines.)

3. **In the Control panel (with nothing selected on the page), change the Weight field to 0.25 pt.**

    The default value for new lines is 1-pt black. For the marks on the ruler, 1 pt is too heavy, so you're going to create them at 0.25 pt.

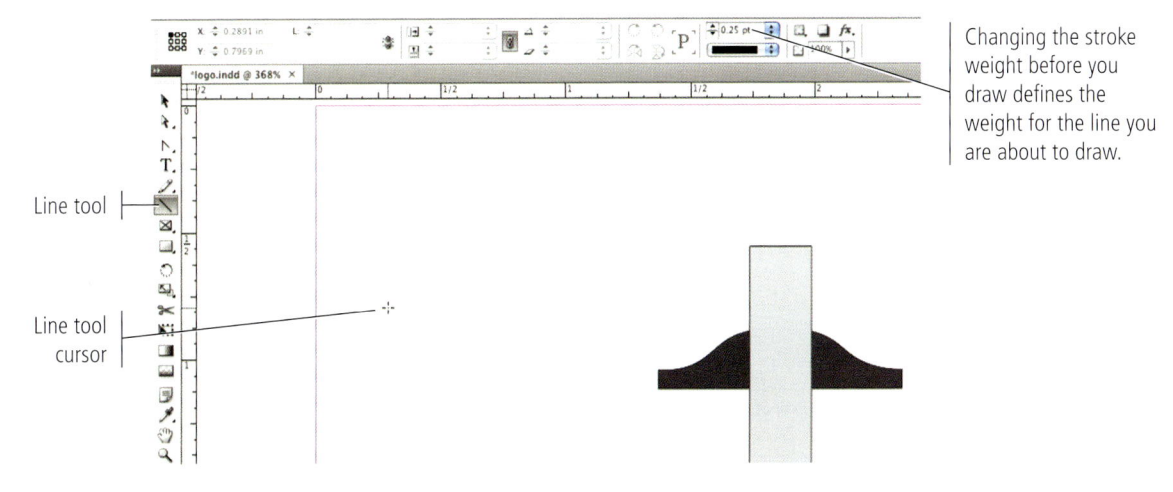

    Changing the stroke weight before you draw defines the weight for the line you are about to draw.

    Line tool

    Line tool cursor

    Project 1: Identity Package 51

4. **Near the top of the vertical "ruler," click about two-thirds of the way across, press the Shift key, and drag to the right edge of the rectangle.**

   Pressing Shift while drawing with the Line tool constrains the line to 45° increments.

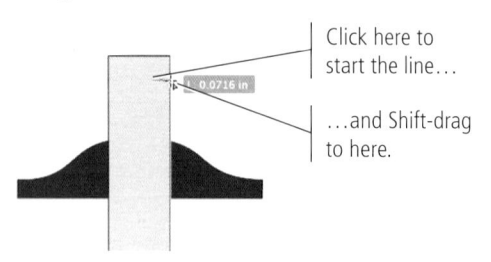

   Click here to start the line…
   …and Shift-drag to here.

   Note:

   You might want to zoom in to complete this part of the drawing.

5. **Click away from the line to deselect it.**

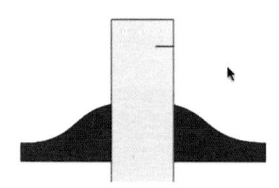

   Note:

   When drawing lines, cursor feedback shows the length of the segment you are drawing.

6. **Using the Selection tool, press Option/Alt, click the line you just drew, and drag down.**

   Pressing Option/Alt while you drag makes a copy of the original object (called **cloning**).

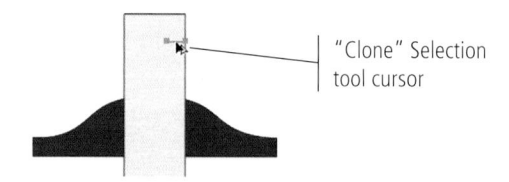

   "Clone" Selection tool cursor

   Note:

   You can press Shift to constrain the clone to 45° increments, but using Smart Guides make this unnecessary.

7. **Release the mouse button when the new line is approximately 1/8" below the original line. (Zoom in if necessary so you can see the small lines more clearly.)**

   When you release the mouse button, you have an exact copy of the line, placed directly under the original.

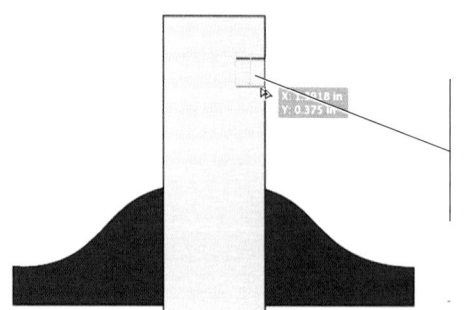

   The Smart Guides identify the left, right, and center points of the nearby (top) line. When you see all three Smart Guides, you know you are cloning the line exactly vertically.

Project 1: Identity Package

8. Choose the Direct Selection tool, and then click the left anchor point of the line.

9. Drag the left anchor point to the right, using the Smart Guides to keep the line horizontal and change the line to half its original length.

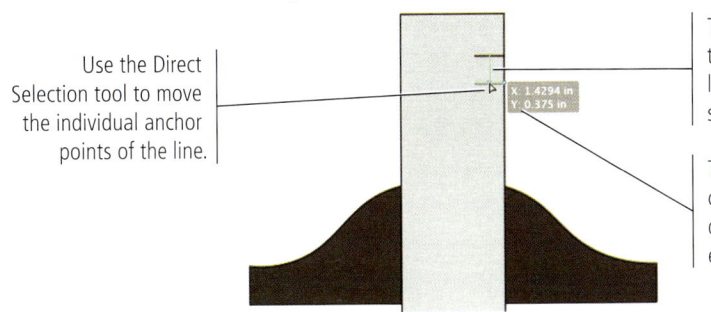

Use the Direct Selection tool to move the individual anchor points of the line.

The Smart Guide identifies the center point of the nearby line, allowing you to easily shorten the line by half.

The Y position should remain constant as you drag. (The original Y position in our example was 0.375 in.)

10. Choose the Selection tool, and then Shift-click to add the top line to the current selection.

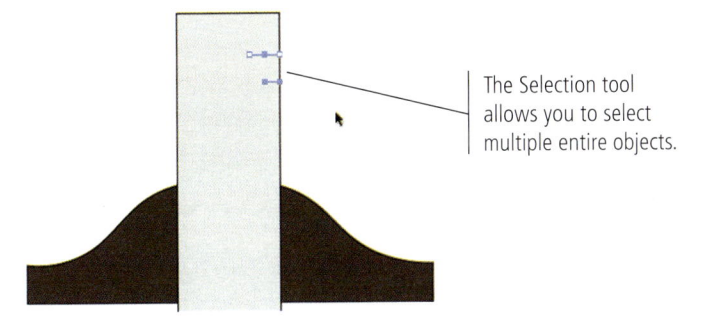

The Selection tool allows you to select multiple entire objects.

11. Press Option/Alt, then click and drag the selected objects down. When the Smart Guides to the right of the object show equality arrows between the original lines and the ones you're cloning, release the mouse button.

In addition to identifying the edges of objects, Smart Guides can also help to space and distribute objects relative to other objects on the page.

Note:

Pressing Option/Alt while dragging an object creates a copy of the object you drag. This method is called **cloning**.

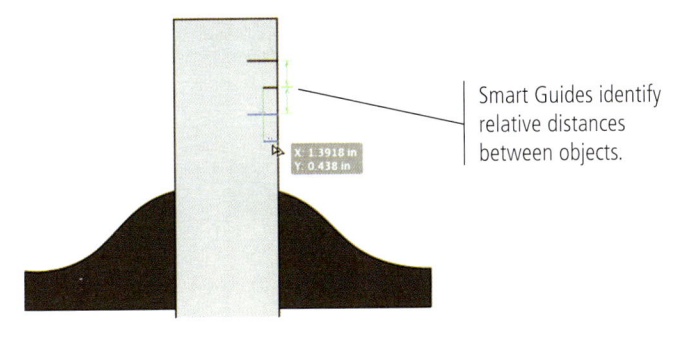

Smart Guides identify relative distances between objects.

Note:

If some menu commands are not visible, choose Show All Menu Items at the bottom of the Edit menu.

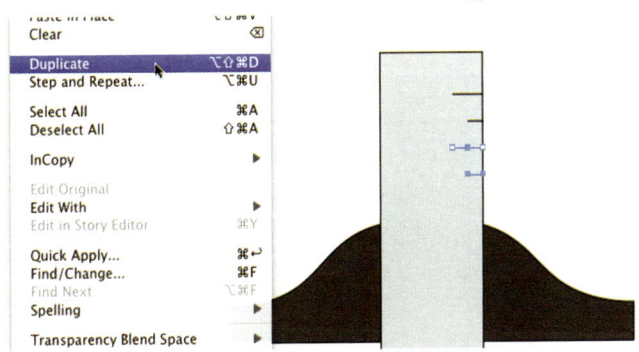

12. With the two cloned lines selected, choose Edit>Duplicate.

Project 1: Identity Package

13. **Using the Duplicate command, add equal-spaced marks to the entire length of the ruler.**

    When you clone an object, InDesign remembers the distance you moved the clone as the default step-and-repeat measurements (Edit>Step and Repeat). The Duplicate command creates one copy of the selected object using the default step-and-repeat values.

14. **Using the Selection tool, drag a marquee around the entire set of objects and choose Object>Group.**

    By grouping the selected objects, they are now treated as a single cohesive unit — which is appropriate whenever more than one object makes up an entire design.

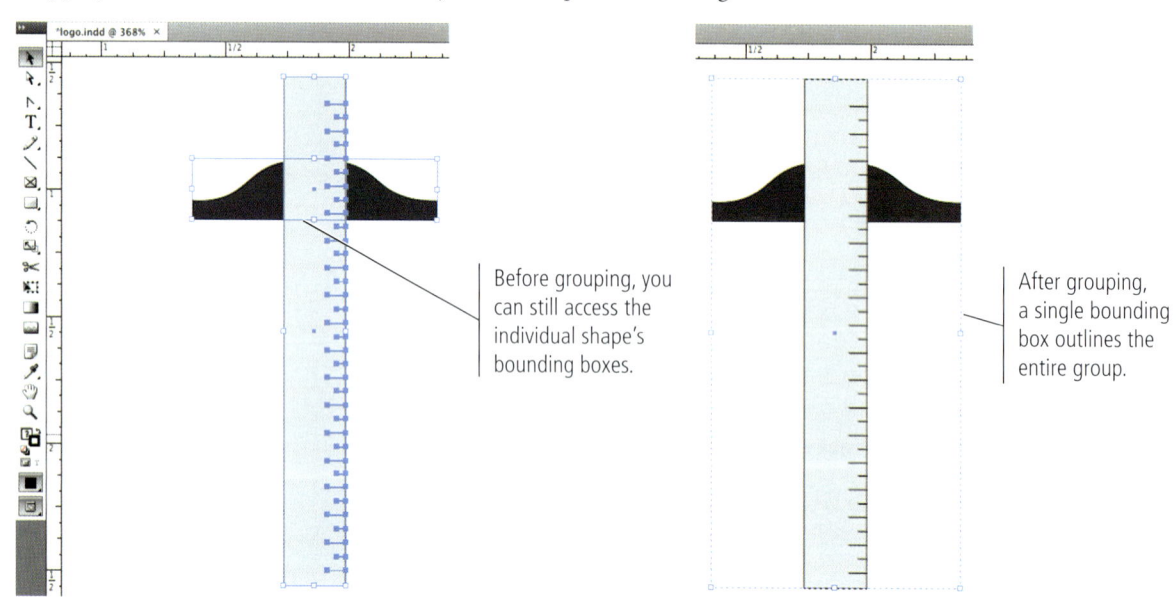

    Before grouping, you can still access the individual shape's bounding boxes.

    After grouping, a single bounding box outlines the entire group.

Project 1: Identity Package

15. **Choose the Direct Selection tool in the Tools panel.**

    Even when objects are grouped, you can still use the Direct Selection tool to access and modify each individual component of the grouped object.

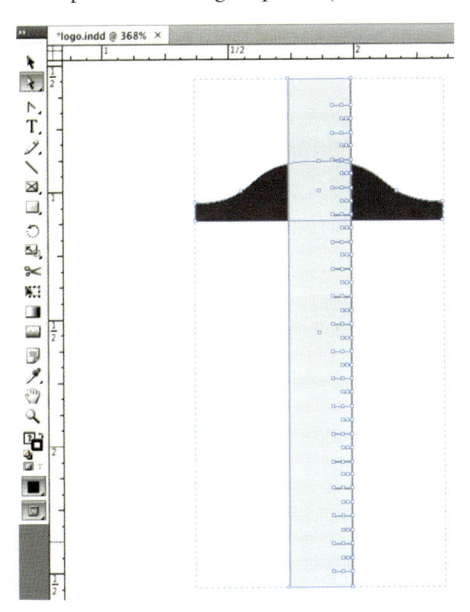

    Note:

    Group objects by pressing Command/Control-G.

    Ungroup objects by pressing Command/Control-Shift-G.

16. **Switch back to the Selection tool and (with the group still selected) use the Control panel to change the stroke weight to 0.5 pt.**

    Changing a fill or stroke attribute when a group is selected affects all objects in the selected group.

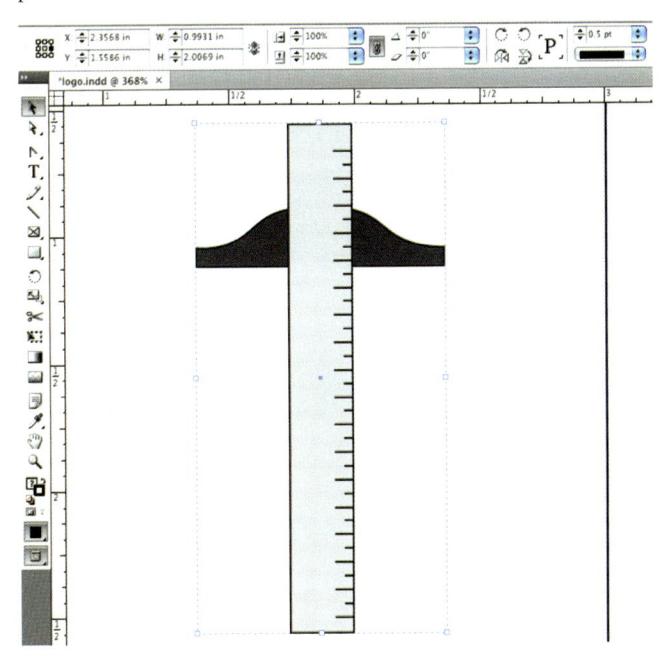

17. **Save the file and continue to the next exercise.**

Project 1: Identity Package   55

CREATE IRREGULAR SHAPES WITH THE POLYGON TOOL

Many designs require shapes other than rectangles and ovals. The Pen tool can create complex objects of any shape, based on Bézier curves. The middle ground is creating straight-sided shapes with anything other than four sides — which you can do with the Polygon tool.

1. **With logo.indd open, use the Selection tool to drag the existing group to the top-left corner of the page.**

2. **Choose the Polygon tool (nested under the Rectangle tool) in the Tools panel.**

The Stroke Panel in Depth

INDESIGN FOUNDATIONS

Although you can use the Control panel to change the stroke weight and style, other stroke options are only available in the Stroke panel. Most of these options are particularly relevant when working with thicker stroke weights; the thin blue line indicates the actual path, regardless of the specific stroke weight. The icons on the various buttons suggest what they do.

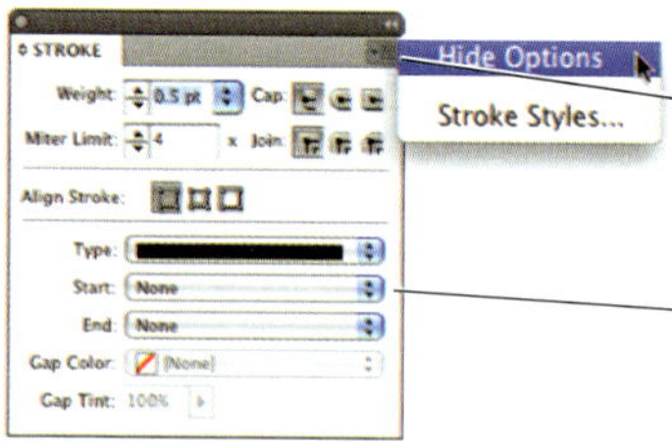

Toggle the Stroke panel options on and off in the panel submenu.

When the panel options are hidden, only the Stroke Weight field is visible.

The **Cap options** define the end treatment for a line segment; the end of a line can end exactly where the path ends, or it can extend beyond the end of the path with a rounded or flat cap. The Butt Cap option (left button) is the default setting.

Butt cap   Rounded cap   Projecting cap

The **Join options** determine the appearance of corner points. The default setting creates a mitered join, or you can choose rounded or beveled joints. The Miter Limit field specifies how long a corner point can be before it automatically converts to a beveled joint; the miter limit is a factor of the stroke weight, so a setting of 2 means the corner point can be no more than 2 times the stroke weight.

Mitered join   Rounded join   Beveled join

The **Align Stroke options** determine where the stroke is placed in relation to the actual path. The default option aligns the center of the stroke to the path; you can also move the stroke entirely inside or entirely outside the path.

The lower half of the Stroke panel includes options for changing the stroke style and applying special end treatments such as arrowheads. If you choose a style that has a gap (a space between pieces of the style), you can also define a different color for the stroke gaps.

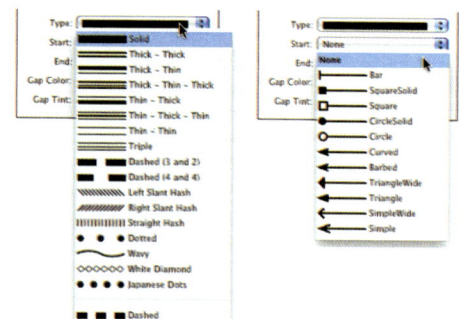

Align stroke to inside   Align stroke to outside   Align stroke to center

Project 1: Identity Package

3. **Click once on the right side of the page.**

   Clicking once opens the Polygon dialog box, where you can define the size of the new object, as well as the number of points and the inset percentage for every other point on the new shape.

4. **Change the Height and Width fields to 1.5 in. Change the Number of Sides field to 3, and make sure the Star Inset field is set to 0%.**

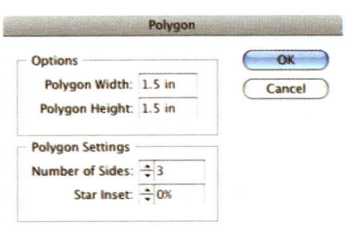

Note:

If you simply click and drag with the Polygon tool, you create a new shape with the tool's default settings.

Note:

*To create a starburst, every other anchor point in the shape needs to be closer to the object's center. The **Star Inset** field determines how much closer those inside points will be to the center; an inset of 0% creates all points at the same distance from the object's center.*

5. **Click OK to create the new shape.**

6. **If necessary, use the Selection tool to drag the new shape to be entirely within the page boundaries.**

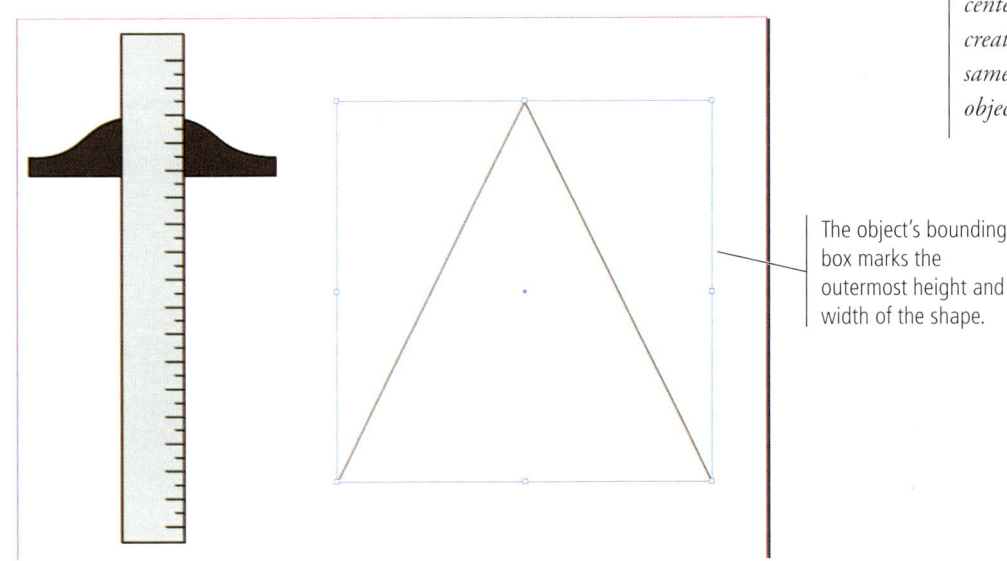

The object's bounding box marks the outermost height and width of the shape.

7. **Using the Direct Selection tool, drag the top anchor point until the left side of the triangle is approximately vertical.**

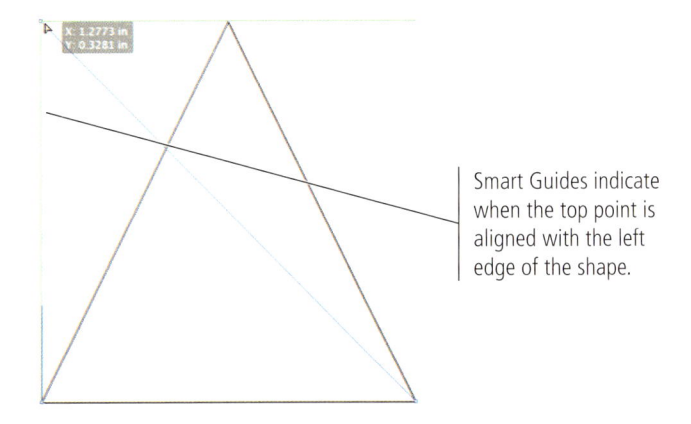

Smart Guides indicate when the top point is aligned with the left edge of the shape.

Project 1: Identity Package   57

8. **Switch to the Selection tool and choose Edit>Copy.**

9. **Choose Edit>Paste in Place to make an exact copy, placed exactly on top of the original.**

   Note:

   Remember: If you don't see certain menu commands, choose Edit>Show All Menu Items.

10. **Choose the Scale tool in the Tools panel, and then click once near the center of the triangle (do not click the bounding box).**

    By default, the Scale tool treats the object's bounding box center as the reference point (origin) for the transformation; you can change the origin to any location by clicking once with the Scale tool.

    Scale tool

    Clicking once with the Scale tool places the scale origin or reference point, which acts as the center of the transformation.

11. **Click the triangle's bottom-left bounding box handle, press Shift, and drag toward the center of the shape.**

    Pressing Shift constrains the object's proportions while you scale it.

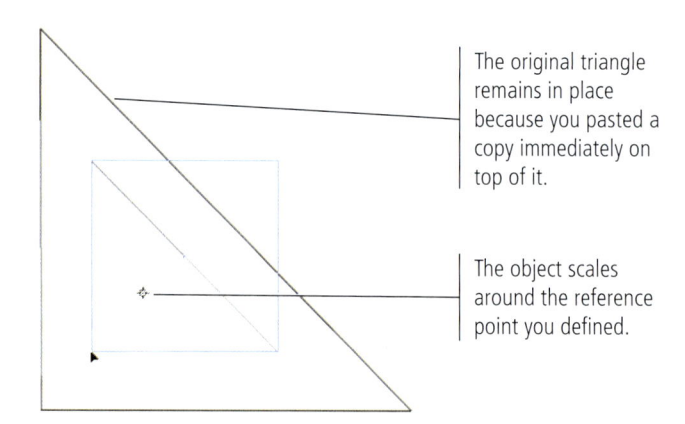

    The original triangle remains in place because you pasted a copy immediately on top of it.

    The object scales around the reference point you defined.

12. **Save the file and continue.**

Project 1: Identity Package

Use the Pathfinder Panel to Create Complex Objects

So far, you've created basic shapes and lines and edited anchor points to create a non-standard shape. Some shapes require multiple paths (called **compound paths**) to create empty or void areas, such as the open space in the middle of the letter "O" or the middle of an architect's triangle. In this exercise, you use the Pathfinder panel to create this type of shape.

1. **With logo.indd open, use the Rectangle tool to create a rectangle that completely covers both triangles. Fill the rectangle with 50% black and send it to the back of the stacking order (Object>Arrange>Send to Back).**

   The two triangles have no fill color, so you can see the entire gray rectangle. You want the space between the two rectangles to be solid.

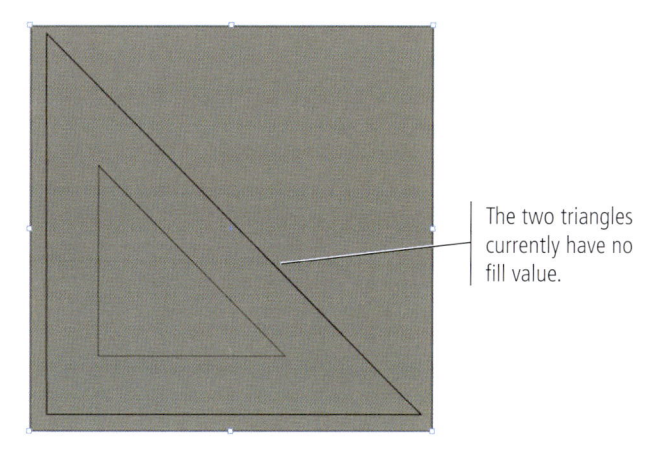

   The two triangles currently have no fill value.

2. **Change the fill of the larger triangle to 0% black.**

   There is a difference between no fill and 0% of a color. Using 0% of a color effectively creates a solid "white" fill. (In printing, solid white areas **knock out** or hide underlying shapes. A fill of None allows the underlying shape to show through.)

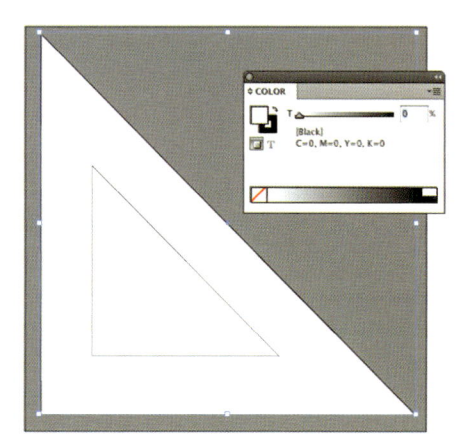

   You now need to remove the inner triangle from the outer triangle so the gray background is visible in the center of the shape.

3. **Shift-click with the Selection tool to select both triangle shapes, and then open the Pathfinder panel (Window>Object & Layout>Pathfinder).**

Project 1: Identity Package

4. **Click the Subtract button in the middle section of the Pathfinder panel.**

   The options in the Pathfinder panel can be used to combine multiple shapes or convert objects from one shape to another. The Subtract option removes the area of the front shape from the area of the back shape.

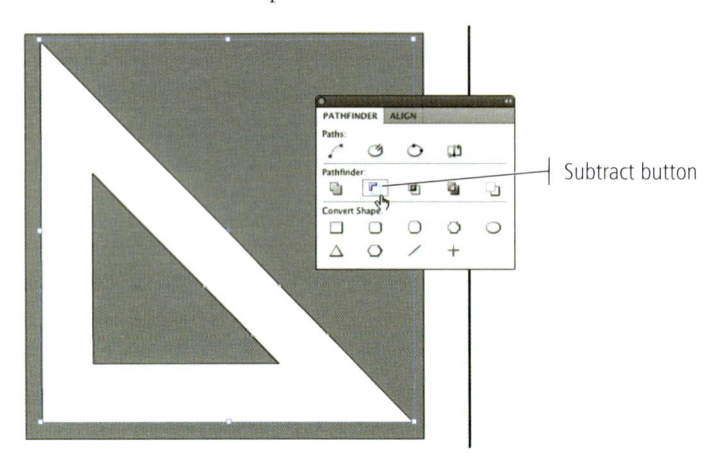

   Subtract button

   Note:

   You can accomplish the same result by choosing Object>Path>Make Compound Path.

5. **Select and delete the gray background rectangle, and then use the Line tool to add ruler marks around the outside edge of the triangle.**

6. **Select all the objects that make up the triangle, group the objects, and then change the stroke weight to 0.5 pt.**

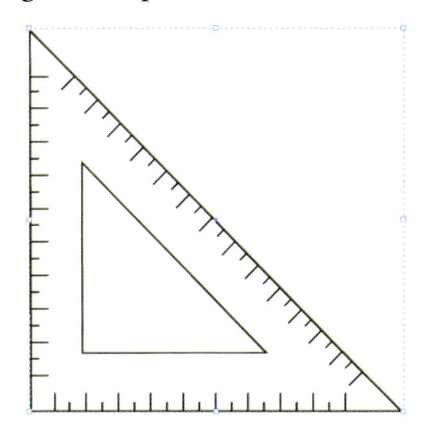

   Note:

   You can return the two triangles to regular, individual objects by choosing Objects>Paths>Release Compound Paths.

7. **Select the T-square group with the Selection tool.**

8. **Open the Control panel Options menu and uncheck the Adjust Stroke Weight when Scaling option.**

   By default, scaling an object proportionally scales the stroke weight. For example, scaling a circle with a 2-pt stroke by 50% results in a 1-pt stroke. In this case, you want to maintain the 0.5-pt stroke, so you are turning off this option.

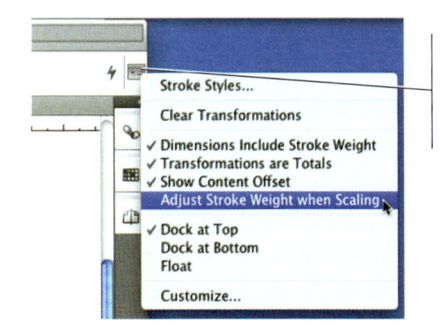

   Click this button (on the right end of the Control panel) to open the panel Options menu.

   Note:

   This option remembers the last-used setting. In many cases, you actually want the stroke weight to scale proportionally, so make sure you check this option if something looks wrong.

   60   Project 1: Identity Package

9. **Using the Control panel, change the group width to 1", the height to 2.5", and then rotate it by 15°. If necessary, drag the T-square group to be entirely within the page area.**

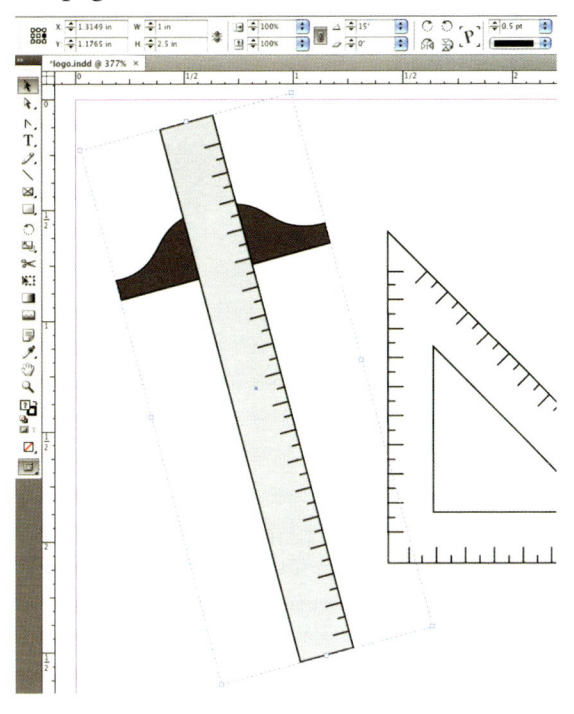

The Pathfinder Panel in Depth

You can apply a significant number of transformations to objects using the Pathfinder panel. (The options in the Pathfinder panel are the same as those in the Objects>Paths, Objects>Pathfinder, and Objects>Convert Shape submenus.)

- Join Path
- Open Path
- Close Path
- Reverse Path

- Add
- Subtract
- Intersect
- Exclude Overlap
- Minus Back

- Rectangle
- Rounded Rectangle
- Beveled Rectangle
- Inverse Rounded Rectangle
- Ellipse
- Triangle
- Polygon
- Line
- Horizontal/Vertical Line

Path options break (open) a closed path, connect (close) the endpoints of an open path, or reverse a path's direction (start becomes end and vice versa, which is relevant if you use stylized end treatments).

Convert Shape options change the overall appearance of an object using one of the six defined basic shapes, or using the default polygon settings; you can also convert any existing shape to a basic line or an orthogonal (horizontal or vertical) line.

Pathfinder options create complex objects by combining multiple existing objects. When you use the Pathfinder options, all but the Subtract function applies the attributes of the front object to the resulting shape; the Subtract function maintains the attributes of the back object.

- **Add** results in the combined shapes of all selected objects.
- **Subtract** returns the shape of the back object minus any overlapping area of the front object.
- **Intersect** results in the shape of only the overlapping areas of selected objects.
- **Exclude Overlap** results in the shape of all selected objects minus any overlapping areas.
- **Minus Back** results in the shape of the front object minus any area where it overlaps other selected objects.

Project 1: Identity Package

10. **Drag the triangle group to slightly overlap the ruler on the T-square group, using the following image as a guide.**

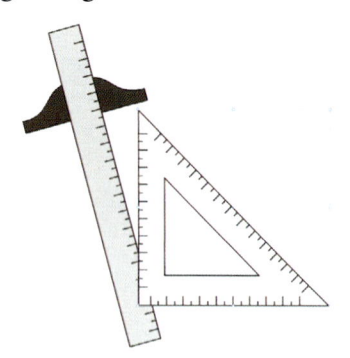

11. **Select both groups of objects and group them into a single group.**

12. **Save the file and continue to the next stage of the project.**

Stage 3 Create and Format Basic Text

Virtually every project you build in InDesign will involve text in one way or another. This logo project is no exception, even though you place and format only a single word. InDesign is ultimately a page-layout application, not an illustration program. **Page layout** means combining text and graphic elements in a meaningful way to convey a message. Text can be a single word (as in this logo) or thousands of pages of consecutive copy (as in a dictionary).

CREATE A SIMPLE TEXT FRAME

Page-layout software — especially InDesign — provides extremely precise control over virtually every aspect of every letter and word on the page. By completing the projects in this book, you learn how to control virtually every nuance of the text in your designs. For now, however, it's enough to learn how to place text on the page.

1. **With logo.indd open, select the Type tool in the Tools panel.**

2. **Click below the triangle and to the right of the T-square in the logo, and then drag down and right to create a text frame.**

   All text in InDesign (with the exception of type paths) must exist in a frame. To place text in a layout, you must first create the frame with the Type tool.

Note:

In an earlier exercise, you hid frame edges to see the thin strokes around shapes. If frame edges were visible here, you would see a thin blue line marking the shape of the frame you drew with the Type tool.

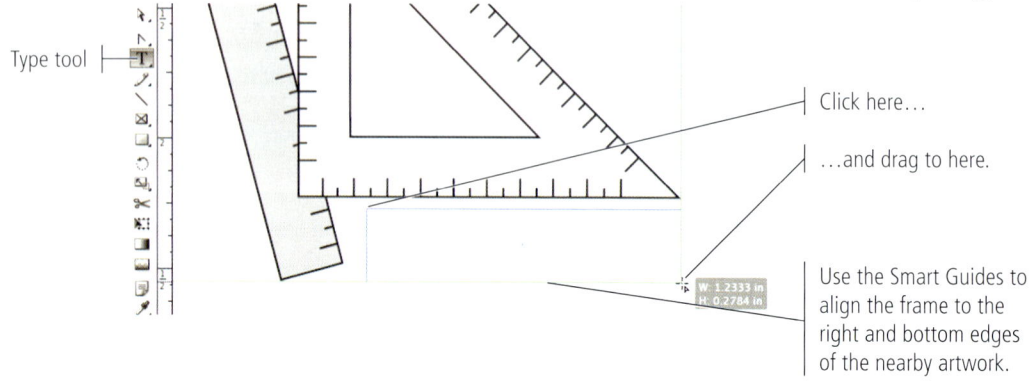

Type tool

Click here…

…and drag to here.

Use the Smart Guides to align the frame to the right and bottom edges of the nearby artwork.

When you release the mouse button, you see a flashing bar (called the **insertion point**) where you first clicked to create the text frame.

Project 1: Identity Package

3. **Type ASSOCIATES.**

   New text appears, beginning at the flashing insertion point.

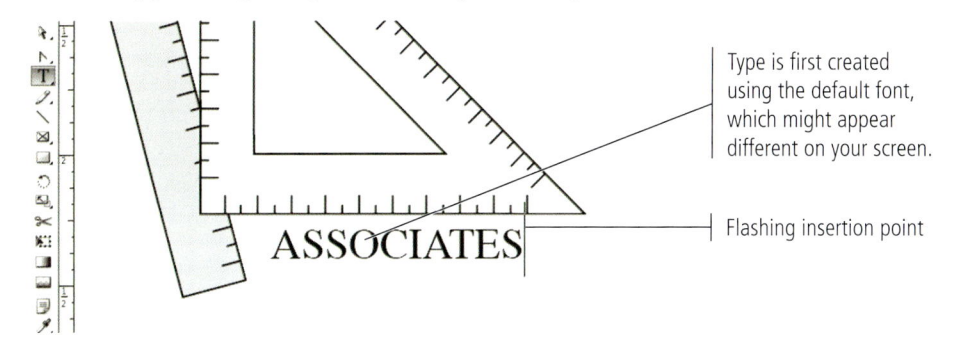

   Type is first created using the default font, which might appear different on your screen.

   Flashing insertion point

4. **Double-click the word you just typed to select it, and then review the options in the Control panel.**

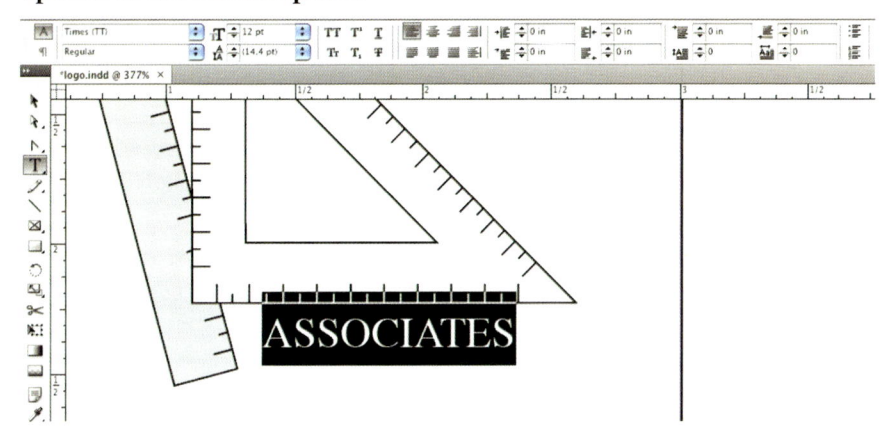

   Note:

   You explore all the available character formatting options in Project 2.

Selecting Text

INDESIGN FOUNDATIONS

You have a number of options for selecting type characters in a frame:

- Select specific characters by clicking with the Type tool and dragging.
- Double-click a word to select the entire word.
- Triple-click a word to select the entire line that contains the word.
- Quadruple-click a word to select the entire paragraph that contains the word.
- Place the insertion point and press Shift-Right Arrow or Shift-Left Arrow to select the character to the immediate right or left of the insertion point, respectively.
- Place the insertion point and press Shift-Up Arrow or Shift-Down Arrow to select all characters up to the same position as the insertion point in the previous or next line, respectively.
- Place the insertion point and press Command/Control-Shift-Right Arrow or Command/Control-Shift-Left Arrow to select the entire word immediately to the right or left of the insertion point, respectively.
- Place the insertion point and press Command/Control-Shift-Up Arrow or Command/Control-Shift-Down Arrow to select the rest of paragraph immediately before or after the insertion point, respectively.

5. **In the Control panel, highlight the Font field and type ATC M.**

   When you type in the Font field, InDesign scrolls to the first font that matches the characters you type. In this case, the ATC Maple font is automatically selected as soon as you type the letter M.

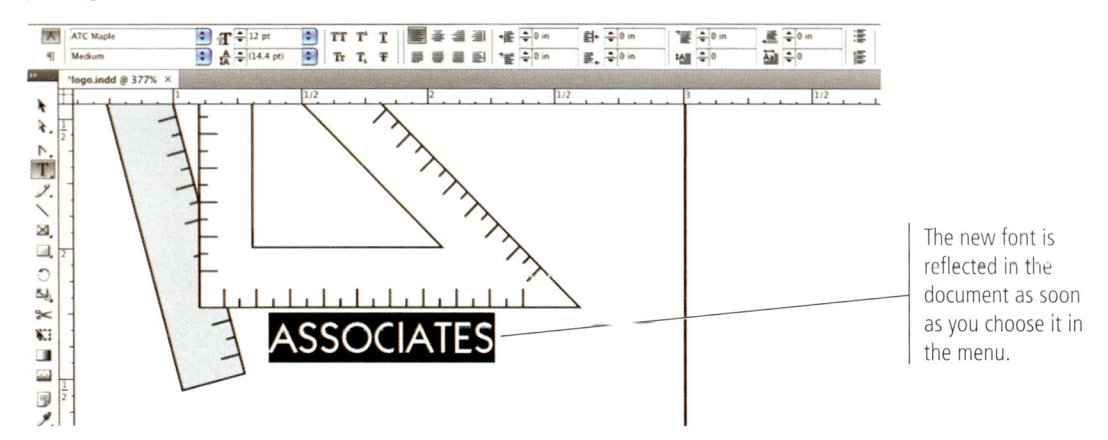

   The new font is reflected in the document as soon as you choose it in the menu.

6. **Open the Font Variation menu and choose Ultra from the list of options.**

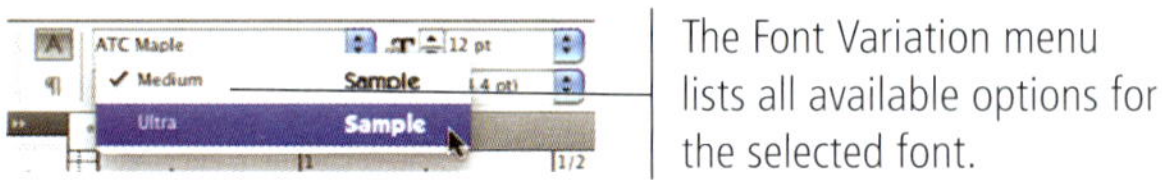

   The Font Variation menu lists all available options for the selected font.

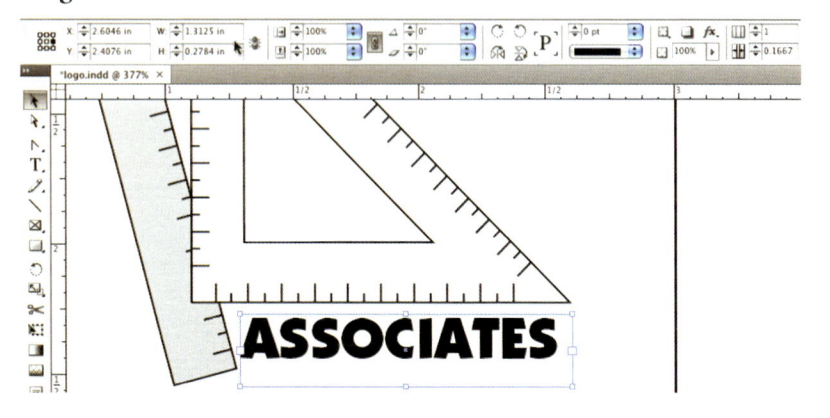

   Note:

   Remember from the Getting Started section at the beginning of this book: To complete the projects in this book, you should install and activate the ATC fonts that are provided on your Resource CD.

7. **Highlight the Type Size field and type 16, and then press Return/Enter to apply the change.**

   You don't need to type the unit "pt" for the type size; InDesign automatically applies the measurement for you.

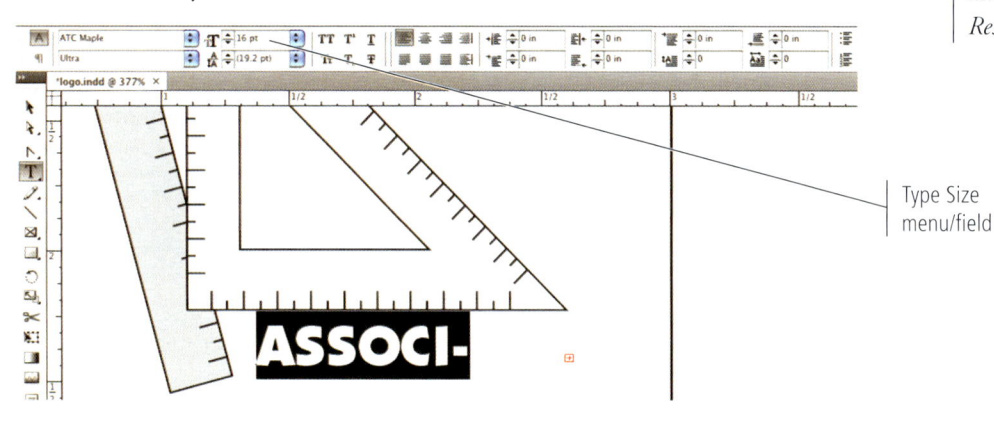

   Type Size menu/field

8. **If you see a red "X" on your frame border, select the right-center reference point in the Control panel and increase the frame width until all the text is visible again.**

64 Project 1: Identity Package

9. **With the text frame selected, open the Color panel.**

   Type defaults to a 100% black fill with no stroke. (You can apply a stroke to type, but you should be very careful when you do to avoid destroying the letter shapes.)

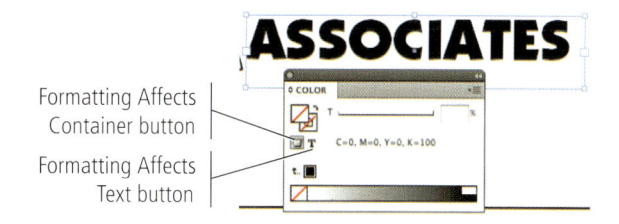

   Formatting Affects Container button
   Formatting Affects Text button

10. **In the Color panel, click the Formatting Affects Text button.**

    When this option is active, the Color panel shows color attributes of the selected text frame.

    When this option is active, the Color panel shows color attributes of the text within the frame.

11. **Open the Color panel Options menu and choose the CMYK color model.**

12. **In the Color panel, change the C (cyan) value to 100%, the M (magenta) value to 60%, and the K (black) value to 0%.**

13. **With the text frame selected, choose Type>Create Outlines.**

    When a job is printed, any font used in the job must be available on the computer that sends the file to the output device. Logos needs to be freely distributed to many people on many types of systems, so it's best if you don't use fonts in a logo file. By converting the text to outlines, you eliminate the potential problem of a missing font file.

    After converting the text to outlines, the text frame is gone; it is replaced by a bounding box for the group of letter shapes.

    Note:
    You can convert individual characters to inline objects by selecting specific characters before you choose Type>Create Outlines.

    Project 1: Identity Package   65

14. **Choose the Direct Selection tool in the Tools panel.**

   As with any other drawing object, you can access the individual anchor points using the Direct Selection tool.

15. **Switch back to the Selection tool, and then resize the group of letter shapes to completely fill the area below the triangle and to the right of the T-square.**

   Drag the bottom-center or right-center bounding box handles to resize the entire object (all grouped letter shapes).

16. **Select all the objects on the page and group them.**

17. **Using the Selection tool, drag the group until the Smart Guides indicate that the group is centered on the page both horizontally and vertically.**

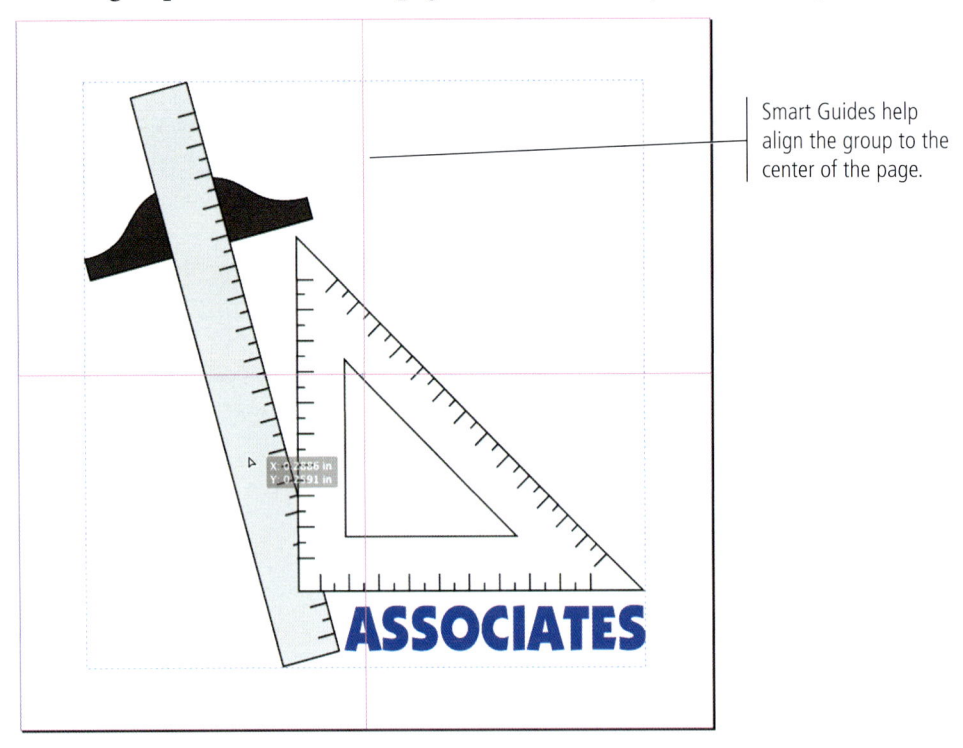

   Smart Guides help align the group to the center of the page.

18. **Save the file and continue to the next exercise.**

Why CMYK?

INDESIGN FOUNDATIONS

The CMYK color model, also called **process color**, uses subtractive color theory to reproduce the range of printable colors. The process color model recreates the range of printable colors by overlapping layers of cyan, magenta, yellow, and black inks in varying percentages from 0–100.

Using theoretically pure pigments, a mixture of equal parts of cyan, magenta, and yellow would produce black. Real pigments, however, are not pure; the actual result of mixing these three colors usually appears as a muddy brown. The fourth color, black (K), is added to the three subtractive primaries to extend the range of printable colors and to allow much purer blacks to be printed than is possible with only the three primaries. Black is abbreviated as "K" because it is the "key" color to which others are aligned on the printing press. Using K for black also avoids confusion with blue in the RGB color model.

In the following image, the left block is printed with 100% black ink. The right block is a combination of 100% cyan, 100% magenta, and 100% yellow inks.

In process color printing, the four process colors — cyan, magenta, yellow, and black (CMYK) — are imaged (or separated) onto individual printing plates. Each color separation is printed on a separate unit of a printing press. When printed on top of each other in varying percentages, the semi-transparent inks produce the range of colors in the CMYK **gamut** (range). Special (spot) colors are printed using specifically formulated inks as additional color separations.

Export EPS Files

Now that the logo is complete, you need to save it in the appropriate formats for the documents you will create (the letterhead, business card, and envelope).

1. **With logo.indd open, choose File>Export and navigate to your WIP>Identity folder.**

2. **In the Format/Save As Type menu, choose EPS.**

   The EPS (Encapsulated PostScript) format is ideal for logo files since the format maintains vector data and supports transparency (the "holes" in a graphic where the paper color should show).

   The file name defaults to the same name as the layout document you are exporting. InDesign automatically adds the correct extension.

Project 1: Identity Package   67

3. **In the Save As/File Name field, add _cmyk at the end of the file name, before the extension.**

4. **Click Save to review the Export EPS options, and then click Export.**

5. **In the layout, click the fill of any letter in the Associates group with the Direct Selection tool.**

   Because you grouped all the objects in the logo artwork, you can't use the Selection tool to select only the Associates letter shapes. However, if you click the fill of any one letter shape you select the entire group of letter shapes.

6. **Open the Swatches panel.**

   InDesign has a number of default options in the Swatches panel. There is one swatch for each primary color in the CMYK and RGB color models. There is also a special Registration color, which is used for trim and printer marks that need to appear on every separation of a job. Paper is basically white (a knock out), but more accurately named because the paper for a job might not be white.

   Note:

   Clicking any of these swatches applies that color to the selected object in the document.

7. **Open the Swatches panel Options menu and choose New Color Swatch.**

   Click here to open the Swatches panel Options menu.

Export EPS Options

In the General tab of the Export EPS dialog box, you can decide which page(s) you want to export, and whether to export single pages or spreads.

- **PostScript** defines compatibility with the various types of PostScript output devices (Level 2 or Level 3).

- **Color** specifies how color is represented in the exported file. The Leave Unchanged option leaves objects in their original color spaces. CMYK, Gray, and RGB convert all colors in the file to the respective color models.

- **Preview** controls the format of the embedded image preview for applications that can't display EPS files. TIFF can be viewed on Macintosh and Windows computers; PICT is a Macintosh-only file format.

- **Embed Fonts** specifies how to include fonts used in the pages you export. The None option does not embed the fonts; Complete embeds the entire font; Subset embeds only the necessary characters of fonts.

- **Data Format** determines how InDesign sends image data to a printer (ASCII or Binary).

- The **Bleed** fields determine how much of a bleed area will be included in the EPS file.

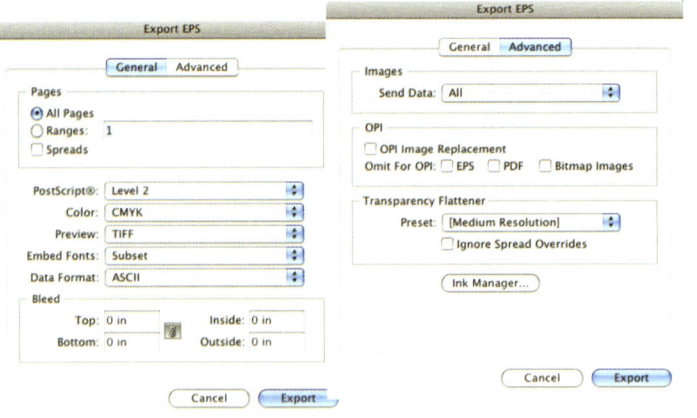

In the Advanced tab:

- The **Images** option determines how data in bitmap images is included in the exported file. The All option embeds all high-resolution data in the exported file; Proxy includes only low-resolution (72 dpi) versions.

- **OPI Image Replacement** is used if you are working in an Open Prepress Interface (OPI) server-based environment to replace low-resolution placement images with high-resolution graphics at output time. The Omit For OPI option selectively omits specific types of graphics.

- **Transparency Flattener** defines how transparent areas and effects (see Project 2) are output.

Project 1: Identity Package

8. **In the New Color Swatch dialog box, choose Spot in the Color Type menu.**

   Choose Spot in this menu.

9. **Choose Pantone Solid Coated in the Color Mode menu.**

   Spot colors are created with special premixed inks to produce a certain color with one ink layer; they are not built from the standard process inks used in CMYK printing. When you output a job with spot colors, each spot color appears on its own separation.

   Spot color inks are commonly used when a special color, such as a corporate color, is required. InDesign includes a number of built-in color libraries, including spot-color systems such as Pantone, Toyo, and DIC. In the United States, the most popular collections of spot colors are the Pantone Matching System (PMS) libraries. TruMatch and Focoltone are also used in the United States. Toyo and DICColor (Dainippon Ink & Chemicals) are used primarily in Japan.

   Even though you can choose a color directly from the library on your screen, you should look at a swatch book to verify that you're using the color you intend. Special inks exist because many of the colors cannot be reproduced with process inks, nor can they be accurately represented on a computer monitor. If you specify special colors and then convert them to process colors later, your job probably won't look exactly as you expect.

   Note:

   When choosing special colors, ask your printer which ink system they support. If you designate TruMatch, but they use Pantone inks, you won't get the colors you expect.

   Note:

   Spot colors are generally chosen from a swatch book — a book of colors printed with different inks, similar to the paint chip cards used in home decorating.

10. **Place the insertion point in the Pantone field and type 2718.**

    You can also scroll through the list and simply click a color to select it.

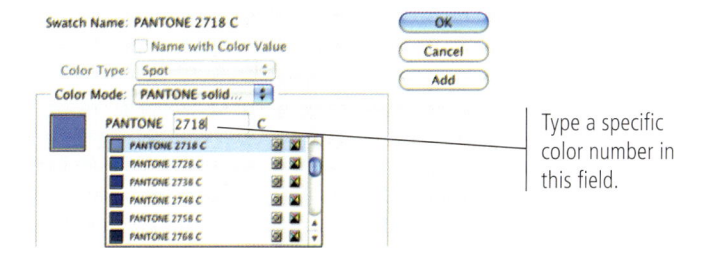

    Type a specific color number in this field.

Project 1: Identity Package

11. **Click OK to return to the document window.**

   The selected object is automatically changed to the new spot color.

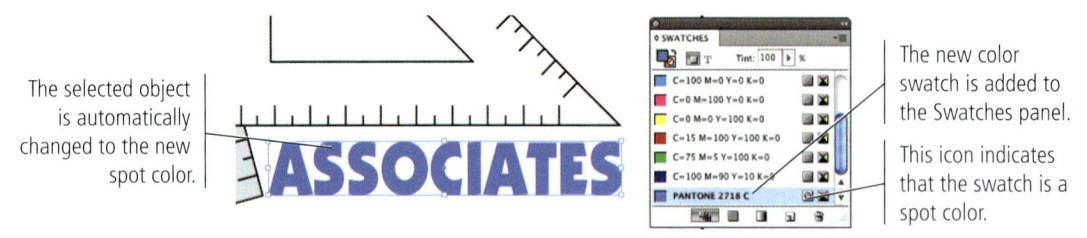

   The new color swatch is added to the Swatches panel.

   This icon indicates that the swatch is a spot color.

12. **Choose File>Export, navigate to the WIP>Identity folder, name the file logo_2c.eps, and click Save.**

   Remember, the printer for this complete identity package wants to print the envelope as a two-color job. That's why you need both the 4-color and 2-color versions of the logo.

13. **In the Export EPS dialog box, choose Leave Unchanged in the Color menu, and then click Export.**

   You must use this option to maintain the spot color information in the EPS file; if not, the color will be converted to CMYK.

14. **Close logo.indd (saving changes if asked), and then continue to the next stage of the project.**

Project 1: Identity Package

Stage 4 Creating a Cohesive Layout

Now that the logo is complete, it's time to put it together with the client's contact information — in other words, it's time to lay out the business card, letterhead, and envelope.

PLACE EXTERNAL GRAPHICS FILES

1. **Open td letterhead.indd from your WIP>Identity folder.**

2. **Click in the horizontal ruler and drag down to place a ruler guide at Y: 1.5″.**

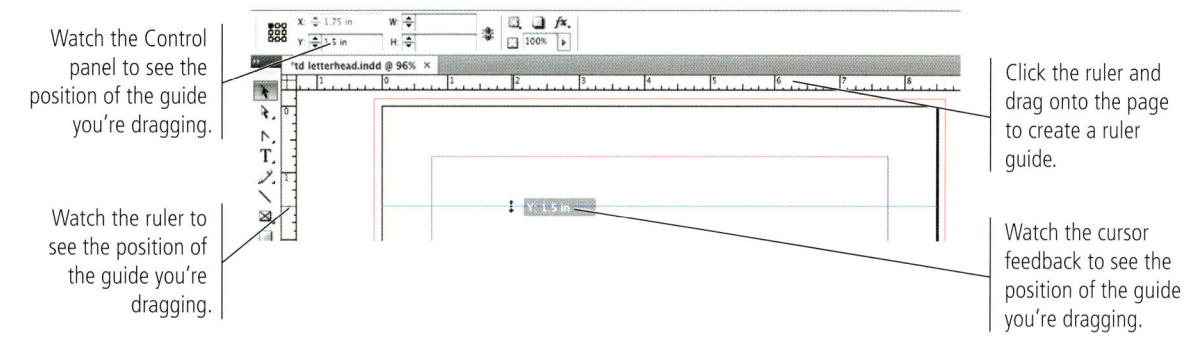

   Watch the Control panel to see the position of the guide you're dragging.

   Click the ruler and drag onto the page to create a ruler guide.

   Watch the ruler to see the position of the guide you're dragging.

   Watch the cursor feedback to see the position of the guide you're dragging.

3. **Choose File>Place, navigate to the RF_InDesign>Identity folder and select blueprint_cmyk.tif.**

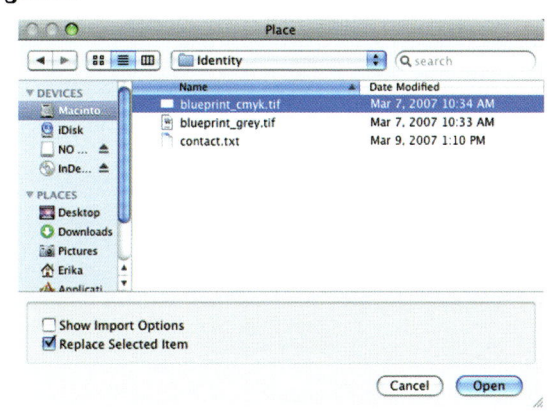

4. **Click Open to load the cursor with the placed file.**

   You still have to place the loaded image in the document.

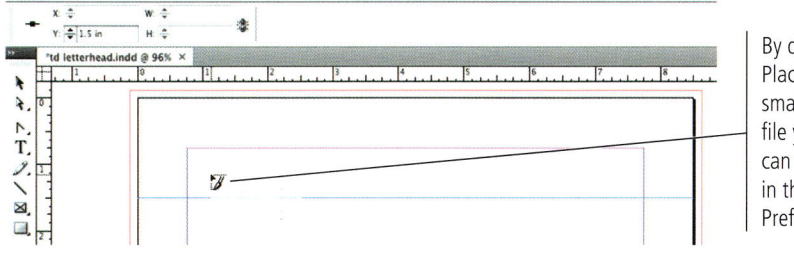

   By default, the loaded Place cursor shows a small thumbnail of the file you're placing. You can turn off this feature in the Interface Preferences dialog box.

Project 1: Identity Package   71

5. **Click near the top-left corner of the page to place the image, and then use the Selection tool to drag the image to the top-left bleed guides.**

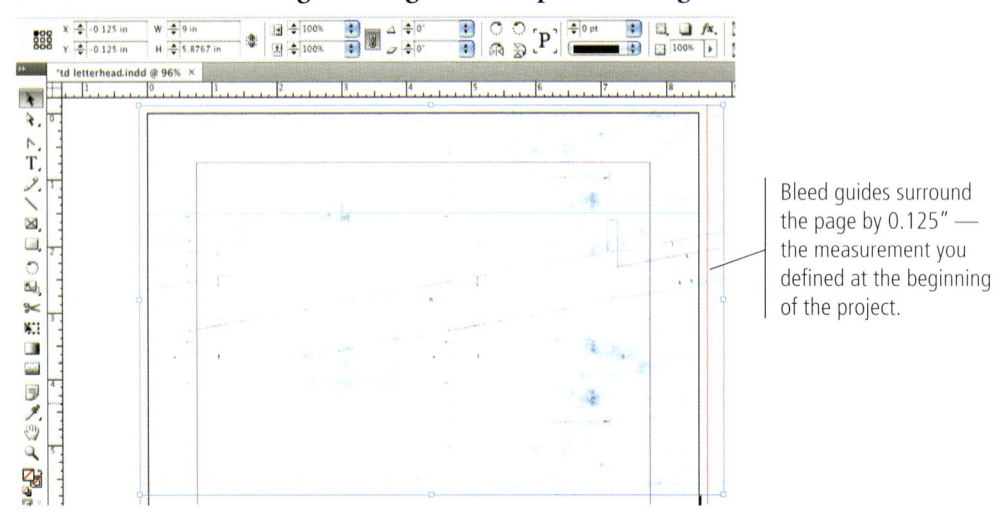

Bleed guides surround the page by 0.125″ — the measurement you defined at the beginning of the project.

6. **Click the bottom-center handle of the bounding box and drag up to the guide at 1.5″.**

   Similar to text, every image in an InDesign layout exists in a frame. When you place an image, the containing frame is automatically created for you. When you edit the dimensions of a graphics frame, the image contained within the frame remains unaffected.

7. **In the Control panel, select the top-left reference point and change the object width to 1.625″.**

Note:

Even though you can't see the entire image, InDesign still has to process the hidden data when you output the file. Whenever possible, it's a good idea to crop the actual image in Photoshop, and then place the cropped version into your InDesign layout.

8. **Choose the Direct Selection tool and click the placed image to select it.**

   The Direct Selection tool selects the image placed within the object. Options in the Control panel relate to the placed object, not the object containing the placed object.

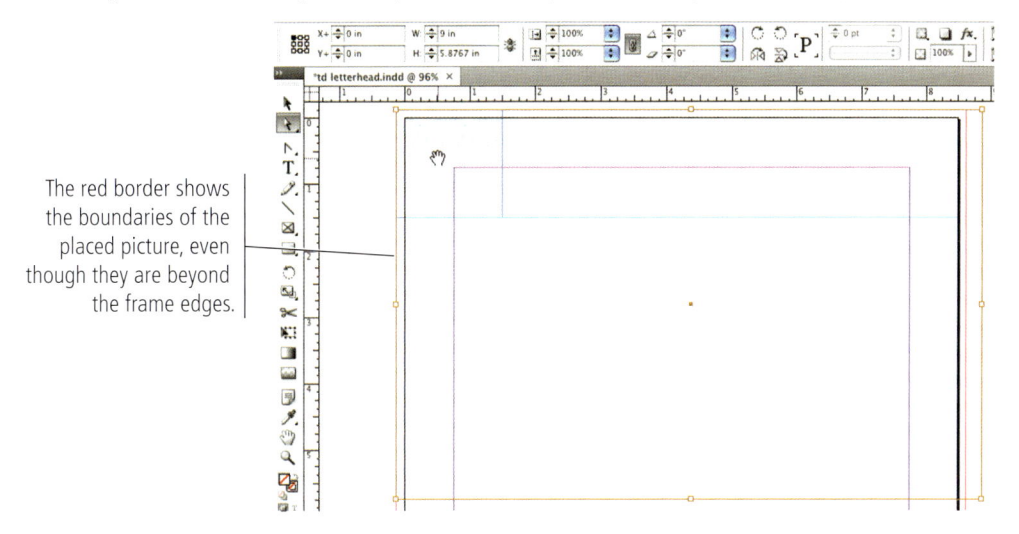

   The red border shows the boundaries of the placed picture, even though they are beyond the frame edges.

9. **Click and hold down the mouse button until you see a ghosted version of the entire image.**

10. **Drag to reposition the image within the frame. When you are satisfied with the visible portions of the image, release the mouse button.**

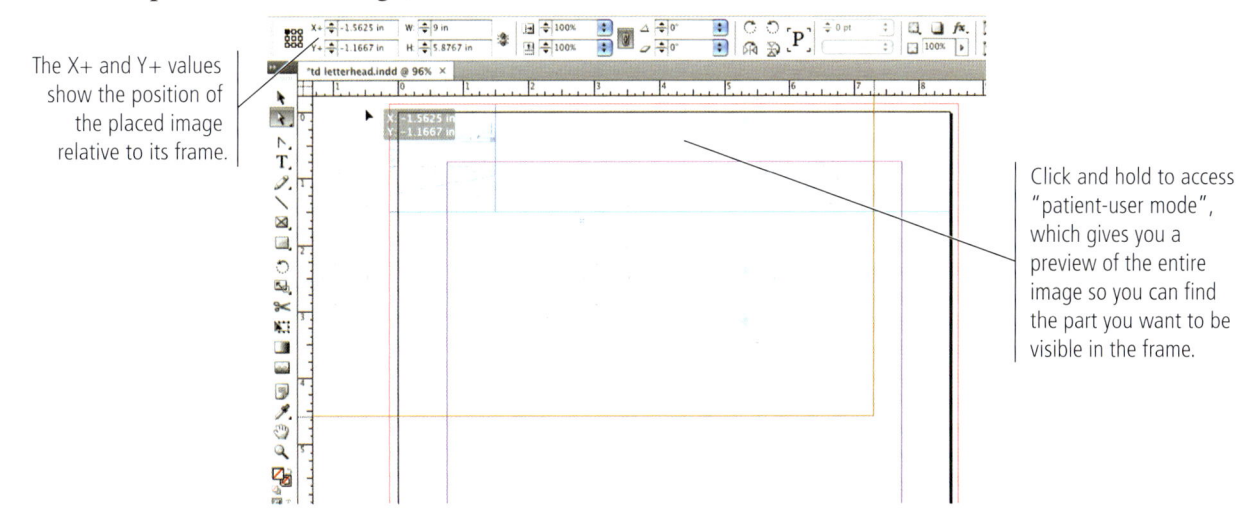

    The X+ and Y+ values show the position of the placed image relative to its frame.

    Click and hold to access "patient-user mode", which gives you a preview of the entire image so you can find the part you want to be visible in the frame.

Project 1: Identity Package 73

11. **Choose File>Place and navigate to your WIP>Identity folder. Select `logo_cmyk.eps` and uncheck the Replace Selected Item option.**

    If a frame is selected in the document and the Replace Selected Item option is checked, the file is automatically placed into the frame instead of loaded into the cursor. In this case, you want to add a new image, so the Replace Selected Item option should be unchecked (turned off).

    Make sure this option is not checked.

12. **Click Open, and then click to place the image on the page.**

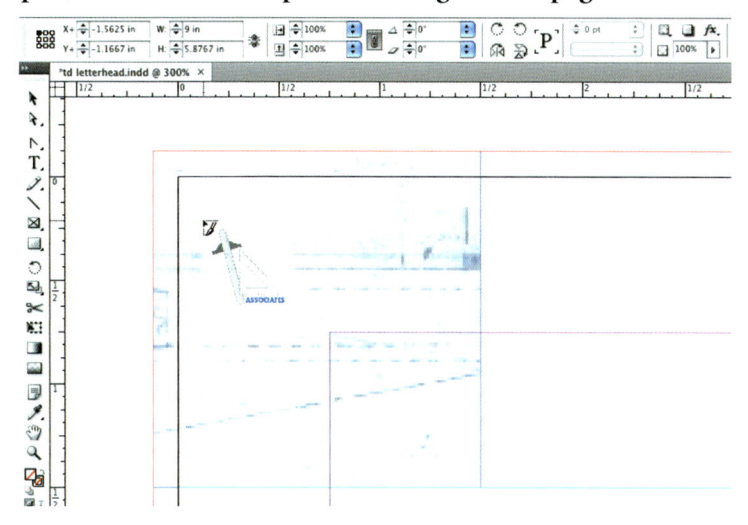

13. **Position the top-left edge of the placed logo frame at X: 0″, Y: 0″, and change the height and width to 1.5″.**

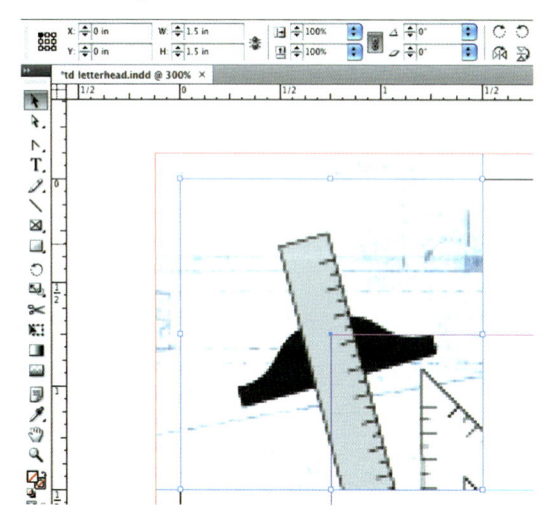

Project 1: Identity Package

14. **Choose the Direct Selection tool, Control/right-click the placed logo, and choose Fitting>Fit Content Proportionally from the contextual menu.**

    You can use these menu options to resize the frame and its content relative to each other. Choosing Frame Fitting Options opens a dialog box where you can define how much to clip each edge of the image, the alignment reference point, and how content will be scaled when placed into an empty frame.

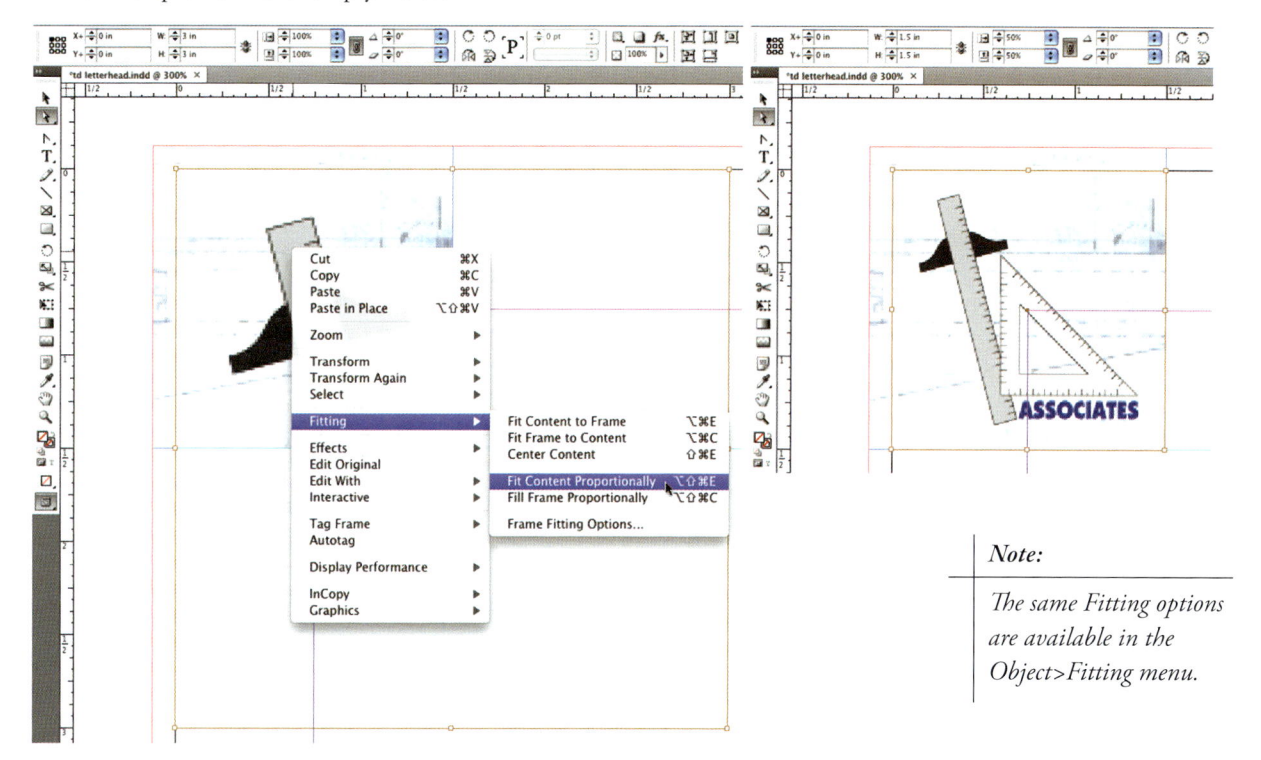

    Note:

    The same Fitting options are available in the Object>Fitting menu.

15. **Save the file and continue to the next exercise.**

PLACE AN EXTERNAL TEXT FILE

You already know how to create a text frame and enter text elements. You can also import text that was created in an external text editor or word-processing application, which is a common situation when creating page layout jobs.

1. **With td letterhead.indd open, make sure nothing is selected in the layout, and then choose File>Place.**

    If you leave the graphics frame selected from the previous exercise, the text might be placed into the graphics frame — which isn't what you want.

2. **Navigate to contact.txt in the RF_InDesign>Identity folder and click Open.**

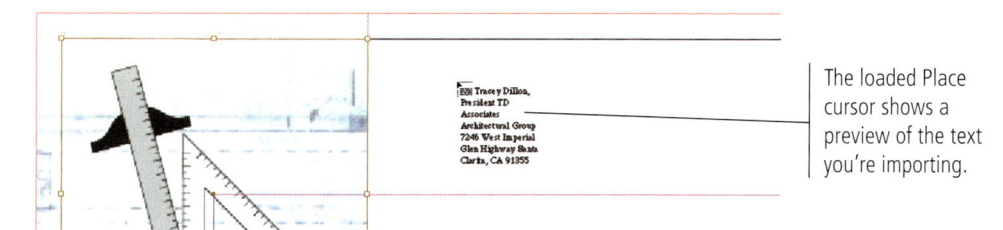

    The loaded Place cursor shows a preview of the text you're importing.

Project 1: Identity Package 75

3. **Click the loaded Place cursor near the top edge of the page, directly to the right of the placed graphics.**

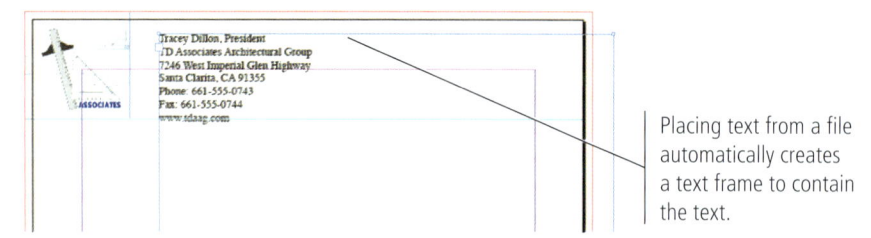

   Placing text from a file automatically creates a text frame to contain the text.

4. **Using the Selection tool, adjust the edges of the text frame to fit within the guides at the top of the page. Use the following image as a guide.**

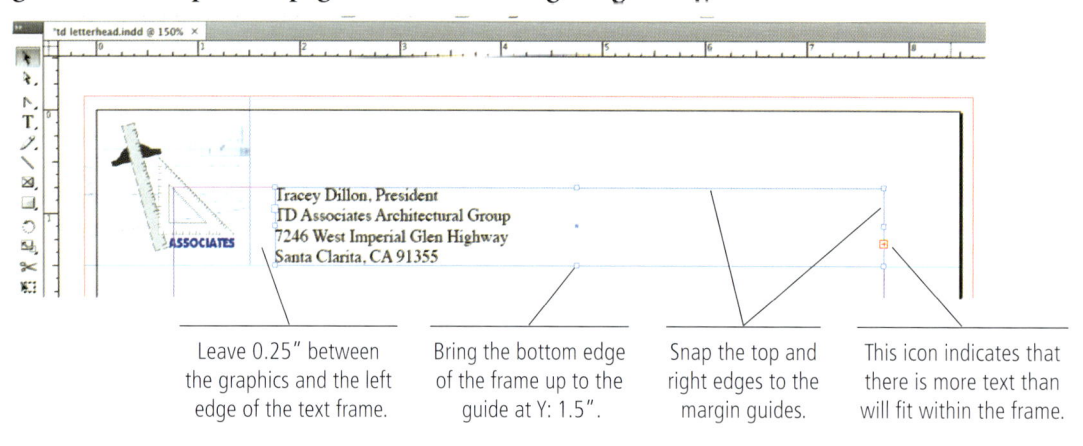

   Leave 0.25" between the graphics and the left edge of the text frame.

   Bring the bottom edge of the frame up to the guide at Y: 1.5".

   Snap the top and right edges to the margin guides.

   This icon indicates that there is more text than will fit within the frame.

5. **Choose Type>Show Hidden Characters.**

   Each line in this text is separated by a paragraph return character. When you reduce the height of the text frame, the seven paragraphs no longer fit within the available space.

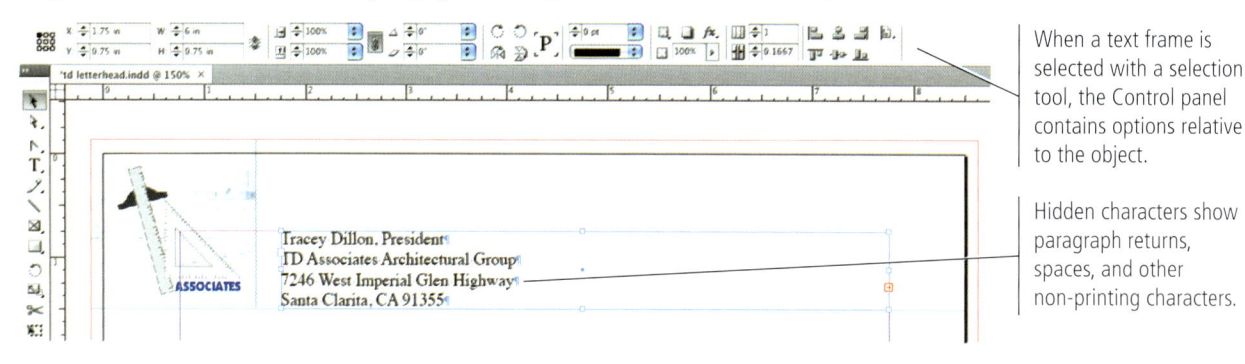

   When a text frame is selected with a selection tool, the Control panel contains options relative to the object.

   Hidden characters show paragraph returns, spaces, and other non-printing characters.

6. **Choose the Type tool and click in the text frame to place the insertion point.**

7. **Choose Edit>Select All to highlight all the text in the frame (including the text you can't see).**

8. **Using the Control panel, change the selected text to 8-pt ATC Pine Italic.**

   When text in a frame is selected with the Type tool, the Control panel contains options relative to the text.

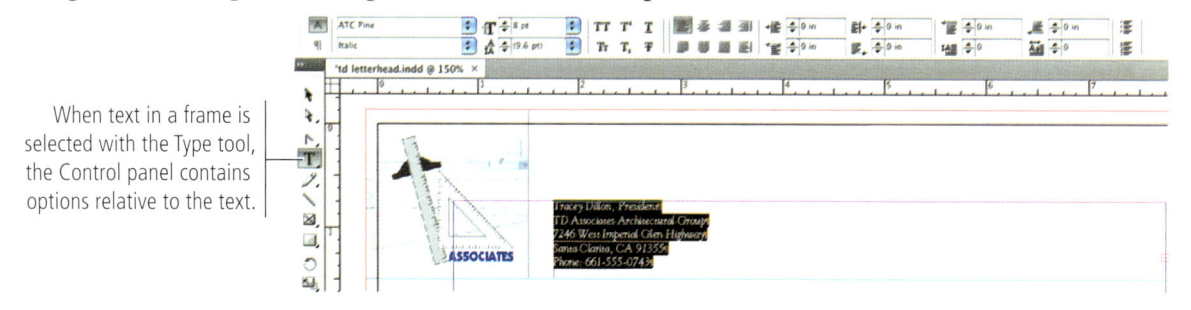

Project 1: Identity Package

9. Select the first line only, and then change the text to 18-pt ATC Maple Ultra.

10. Select the second line only, and change the text to 13-pt ATC Maple Medium.

11. Click at the end of the first address line to place the insertion point, and then press Shift-Right Arrow key to select the paragraph return character.

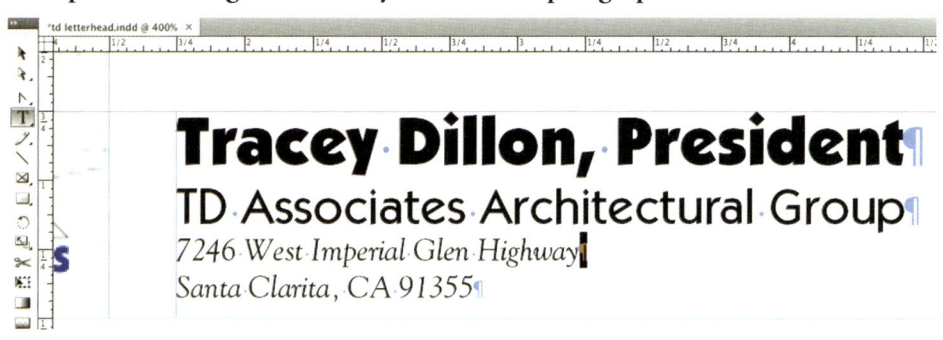

12. Type a comma, and then press the Spacebar.

    When you type with text highlighted — including hidden characters — whatever you type replaces the highlighted text.

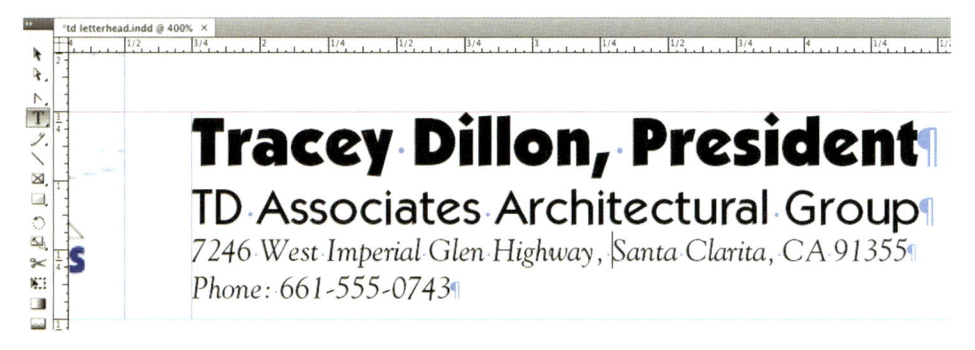

13. Highlight the paragraph return after the zip code. Press the Spacebar, type |, and then press the Spacebar again.

Project 1: Identity Package   77

14. **Repeat Step 13 to move all the remaining contact information onto the same line as the address.**

    Extra paragraph returns exist after the Web address, so InDesign thinks there is still more text than will fit. Remove the extra paragraph returns to get rid of the overset text icon on the edge of the text frame. You will often see this type of problem when working with imported text.

    The extra paragraph returns cause the overset text icon to show.

15. **Place the insertion point at the end of the line and press the Forward Delete key to remove the extra paragraph returns.**

    You can't delete the end-of-story character.   *The overset text icon is gone.*

16. **Highlight the first line of text only.**

17. **In the Color panel Options menu, make sure the Fill swatch is active and choose CMYK.**

    The Fill swatch should be on top of the stack.

    Because specific text is selected, the Formatting Affects Text option is automatically active.

18. **Change the color of the selected text to C=100 M=60 Y=0 K=0.**

19. **Save the file and continue to the next exercise.**

Project 1: Identity Package

Control Paragraph Formatting

Character formatting includes any option that affects the appearance of selected characters, such as font, size, horizontal scale, and a host of others. Paragraph formatting options, on the other hand, affect an entire paragraph (everything between two paragraph return characters). Paragraph formatting can control everything from indents to the space between paragraphs to lines above and below paragraphs.

Note:

You explore all the available paragraph formatting options in Project 2.

1. **With `td letterhead.indd` open, drag a horizontal guide that aligns with the bottom of the word "Associates" in the placed logo.**

Note:

If you want to apply the same formatting to more than one consecutive paragraph, you can drag to select any part of the target paragraphs. Any paragraph that's even partially selected will be affected.

2. **Click with the Type tool to place the text insertion point in the contact information paragraph.**

3. **In the Control panel, click the up arrow button of the Space Before Paragraph field to increase the spacing above the selected paragraph.**

   Changes to paragraph formatting apply to the entire paragraph; simply place the insertion point within the paragraph, rather than manually selecting the paragraph.

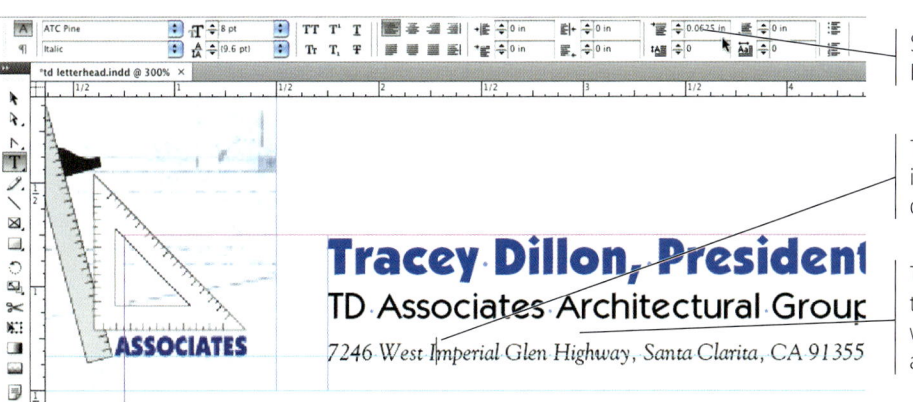

   Space Before Paragraph field

   The insertion point indicates the selected or active paragraph.

   The stepped increment for the Space Before Paragraph value adds too much space above the paragraph.

4. **Highlight the value in the Space Before Paragraph field and type `0.04 in`. Press Return/Enter to apply the change.**

   You can use the arrow buttons to increase or decrease the value in a Control panel field in specific increments, or you can type a specific value.

Note:

The arrow buttons for paragraph formatting options step through values in increments of 0.0625".

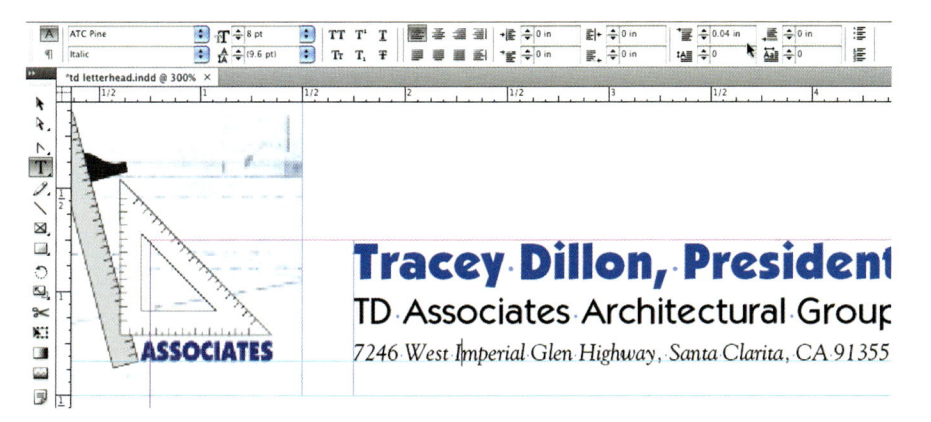

Project 1: Identity Package

5. **Using the Line tool, draw a horizontal line at Y: 1.5″ that bleeds past both page edges. Use the Color panel to change the stroke color to C=100 M=60 Y=0 K=0.**

6. **Use the Control panel to change the stroke weight to 4 pt, and use the Color panel to change the stroke color to C=100 M=60 Y=0 K=0.**

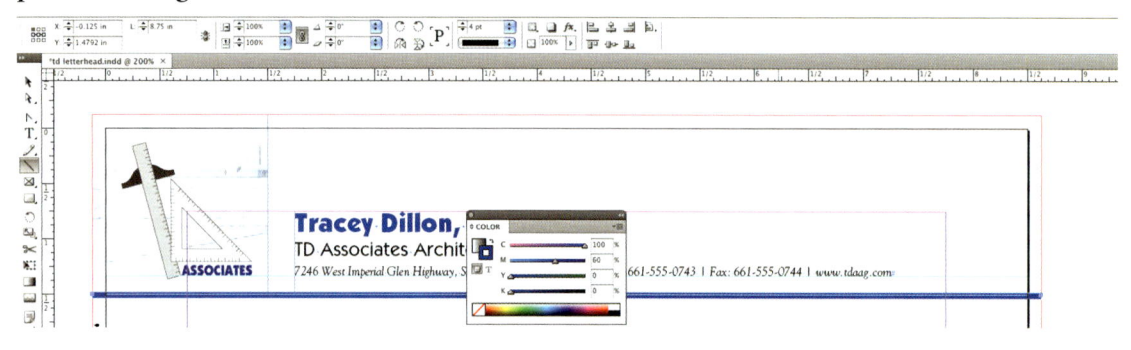

7. **Click the Screen Mode button in the Application/Menu bar and choose Preview.**

    Preview mode shows you the page without guides or frame edges. The pasteboard is gone, replaced by a gray background that runs up to the page edge.

8. **Choose Bleed in the Screen Mode menu.**

   Bleed mode extends Preview mode, showing the bleed area you defined in the New Document dialog box. You can use this mode to make sure all bleed objects extend far enough to meet the defined printer requirements. If any bleed object doesn't extend to the bleed edge, you should fix the problem before you output the file.

9. **Return to Normal screen mode, save the file, and continue to the next exercise.**

COPY OBJECTS AND IMPORT SPOT COLORS

At this point in the project, you've learned how to create various types of objects, how to import external graphics and text files, and how to control various objects and frames on the page. In this exercise, you create the 2-color envelope, which uses many of the same skills you already know, and introduces you to designing with spot colors.

1. **Open the td envelope.indd file from your WIP>Identity folder.**

2. **Activate the letterhead layout. Using the Selection tool, drag a marquee that selects all the objects at the top of the page except the horizontal line.**

   The letterhead layout is active.

   Select everything except this line.

3. **Choose Edit>Copy, and then close the letterhead layout.**

Project 1: Identity Package

4. **With the envelope layout window active, choose Edit>Paste.**

5. **Drag the pasted elements so the blueprint image extends 1/8″ past the top and left edges of the page.**

   You can copy elements from one layout to another by simply copying and pasting. This is a useful technique, but there are several problems in this case.

   First, the printer said the envelope layout can't bleed. You need to adjust the graphic elements to stay within the 1/4″ margin guides.

   Second, the envelope is going to be printed 2-color. The logo and blueprint image are both CMYK (4-color), as is the color used for your client's name. You need to replace these images with the 2-color versions.

   Third, the contact information is far too long for a business envelope. You need to reformat the text to be appropriate for an envelope.

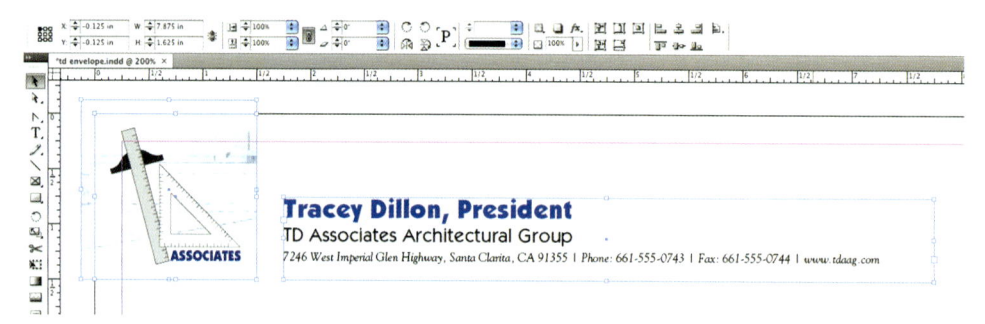

6. **Use the Selection tool to select the blueprint image, and then choose File>Place. Navigate to the `blueprint_gray.tif` file, click the Replace Selected Item check box, and then click Open.**

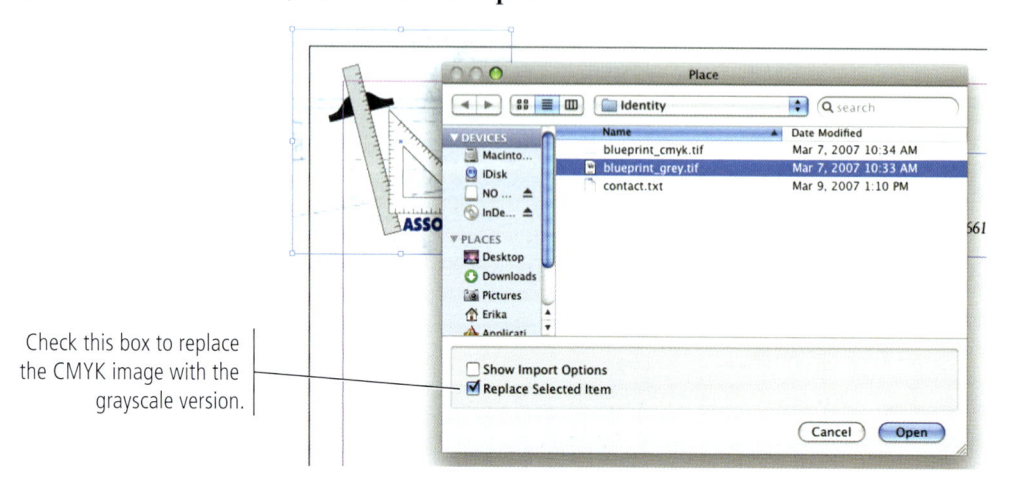

   Check this box to replace the CMYK image with the grayscale version.

Project 1: Identity Package

7. **Drag the top-left corner of the graphics frame to snap to the top-left margin guide.**

   The grayscale version of the image replaces the image in the selected frame.

8. **Using the same technique, replace the CMYK version of the logo file with the 2-color version you created earlier.**

9. **Drag the top-left corner of the graphics frame to the top-left margin guide, and then fit the content to its frame (choose Fitting>Fit Content Proportionally in the frame's contextual menu).**

   Drag the top-left frame handle to the margin guides… …then fit the content to its frame.

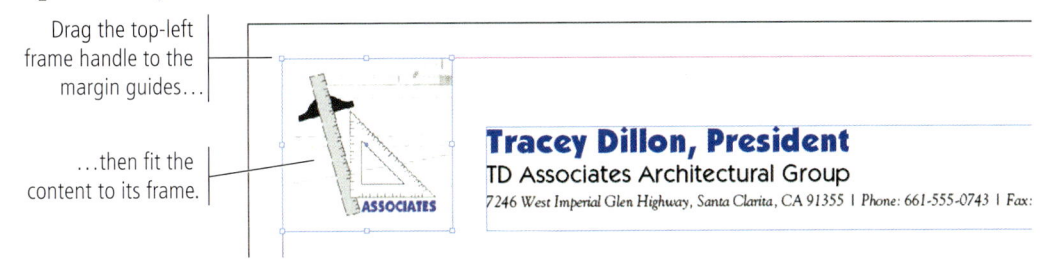

10. **With the logo frame selected, choose Object>Select>Next Object Below to select the blueprint image.**

    It can be difficult to select underlying objects, especially if they are completely covered by another object. The options in this menu allow you to easily navigate through the stacking order.

Project 1: Identity Package

11. **With the blueprint image selected, click the Pantone 2718 C swatch in the Swatches panel, and then change the Tint field to 10%.**

    This step was added to illustrate two points: First, when you place an EPS file that contains a spot color, the spot color swatch automatically imports into the InDesign Color panel. Second, the technique of applying a color to a grayscale image is a fairly common method for adding visual interest to a 2-color print job.

12. **Drag a marquee to select both graphics frames, and then group them.**

13. **Click the bottom-right handle of the group bounding box, press Command-Option-Shift/Control-Alt-Shift, and then drag up and to the left to resize the frames to a 1″ square.**

    Using all three modifier keys, you can dynamically resize both frames and their contained graphics.

14. **Adjust the text frame so the top edge snaps to the top margin guide, and the left edge is 1/8″ from the right edge of the graphics frames.**

15. **Make the following changes to the text:**
    - Change the first line of text to 12 pt and change the text color to Pantone 2718 C.
    - Change the second line of text to 10 pt.
    - Change the space before the address line to 0.02″.
    - In the address line, delete all the text after the zip code.
    - Add a paragraph return to move the city, state, and zip code to their own paragraph, and then delete the comma from the end of the street address.

    Note:

    When you add a paragraph return, the 0.02″ Space Before Paragraph value is also applied to the new paragraph.

16. **Save the file and continue to the next exercise.**

84 Project 1: Identity Package

Design the Business Card

Using all the skills you've learned so far, complete the business card layout. (Our solution is shown here; yours will probably be different in one or more ways.) Keep the following points in mind as you complete the layout:

- The most important point of a business card is to clearly present the contact information.

- The business card can bleed on all four sides.

- The business card will be printed in 4-color. Use the CMYK versions of the blueprint and logo.

- You are building a complete identity package, so all the pieces should have a consistent look. Use whatever fonts you prefer, but if you use different fonts on the business card, you should also change the fonts on the letterhead and envelope.

Stage 5   Printing InDesign Files

For a printer to output high-quality pages from Adobe InDesign, some method of defining the page and its elements is required. These definitions are provided by Page Description Languages (PDLs), the most widely used of which is Adobe PostScript 3.

When a file is output to a PostScript-enabled device, the raster image processor (RIP) creates a file that includes mathematical descriptions detailing the construction and placement of the various page elements; the print file precisely maps the location of each pixel on the page. In the printer, the RIP then interprets the description of each element into a matrix of ones (black) and zeros (white). The output device uses this matrix to reconstruct the element as a series of individual dots or spots that form a high-resolution bitmap image on film or paper.

Not every printer on the market is capable of interpreting PostScript information. Low-cost, consumer-level inkjet printers, common in the modern graphic design market, are generally not PostScript compatible. (Some desktop printers can handle PostScript, at least with an additional purchase; consult the technical documentation that came with your printer to make certain it can print PostScript information.) If your printer is non-PostScript compatible, some features in the InDesign Print dialog box will be unavailable and some page elements (particularly EPS files) might not output as expected.

Note:

If you do not have a PostScript output device, you can work around the problem by first exporting your InDesign files to PDF (see Project 2) and then open the PDFs in Acrobat to print a proof. This is a common workflow solution in the current graphic design industry.

Print Desktop Proofs

Not too long ago, every job sent to a commercial printer required a hardcopy proof to accompany the disk as an example of the layout content. As digital file submission continues to gain ground, however, physical printer proofs are becoming less common.

In general, every job you create will be printed at some point in the workflow — whether for your own review, as a client comp, or as a final proof that accompanies a file to the commercial printer. So, whether you need a basic proof or a final job proof, you should still understand what is possible in the InDesign Print dialog box.

Composite proofs print all colors on the same sheet, which allows you to judge page geometry and the overall positioning of elements. Final composite proofs that are provided to the printer should include **registration marks** (special printer's marks used to check the alignment of individual inks when the job is printed), and they should always be output at 100% size.

Note:

It is also important to realize that desktop inkjet and laser printers typically do not accurately represent color.

Project 1: Identity Package   85

1. **Open td letterhead.indd from your WIP>Identity folder.**

2. **Chose File>Print.**

   The Print dialog box includes dozens of options in eight different categories.

   The most important options you'll select are the Printer and PPD (PostScript printer description) at the top of the dialog box. InDesign reads the information in the PPD to determine which of the specific print options are available for the current output.

3. **Choose the printer you want to use in the Printer menu, and choose the PPD for that printer in the PPD menu (if possible).**

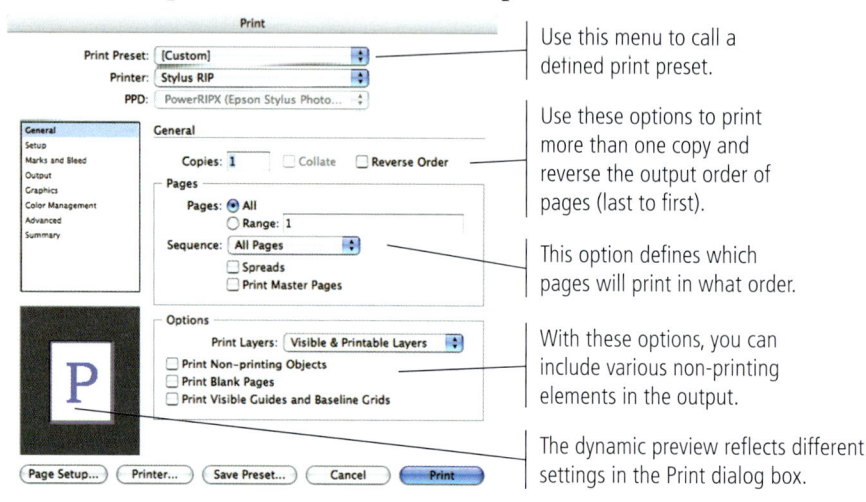

   Use this menu to call a defined print preset.

   Use these options to print more than one copy and reverse the output order of pages (last to first).

   This option defines which pages will print in what order.

   With these options, you can include various non-printing elements in the output.

   The dynamic preview reflects different settings in the Print dialog box.

   Note:

   *You might want to also print a set of **color-separated proofs** (each ink prints on a separate piece of paper) so you can make certain everything will print in the exact colors you specified. If you mistakenly left a spot color as process (or vice versa), nothing will alert you faster than separated proofs.*

   Note:

   A print preset is a way to store many different settings in a single menu choice. You can save print presets just as you save document presets for creating new documents.

4. **Click the Setup option in the list of categories in the left pane.**

   These options determine the paper size that will be used for the output (not to be confused with the page size), the paper orientation, and page scaling and positioning options relative to the paper size.

5a. **If your printer can print to tabloid-size paper, choose Tabloid in the Paper Size menu, and then choose Centered from the Page Position menu.**

   b. **If you can only print to letter-size paper, choose the landscape paper orientation option, and then activate the Tile check box.**

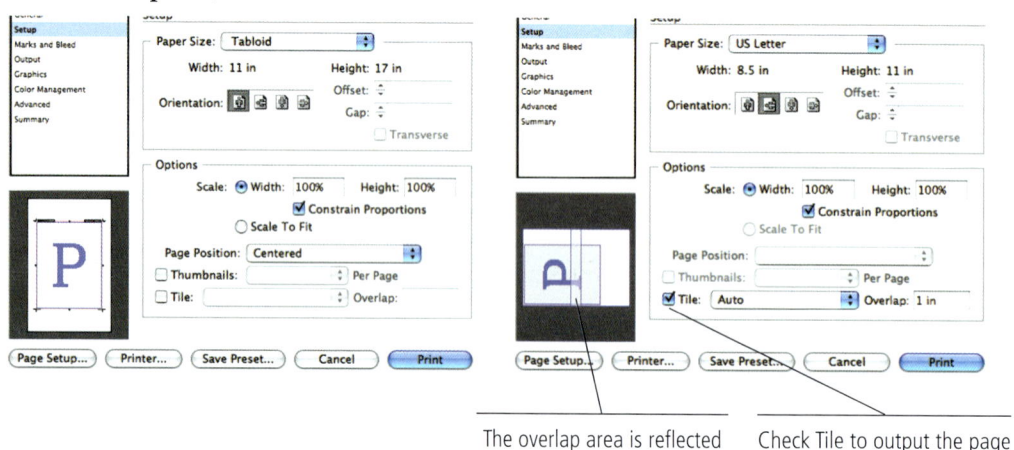

   Note:

   Offset and Gap fields should only be used when a job is output to an imagesetter or high-end proofing device. They define page placement on a piece of oversized film or on a printing plate.

   The overlap area is reflected in the preview; this area will print on both pieces of paper.

   Check Tile to output the page to multiple sheets of paper.

Project 1: Identity Package

6. **Click the Marks and Bleed option in the list of categories in the left pane. Activate the All Printer's Marks option and change the Offset field to 0.125″ (1/8″). Make sure the Use Document Bleed Settings option is checked.**

   You can specify individual printer's marks, or simply print them all. For proofing purposes, the crop and bleed marks are the most important options to include.

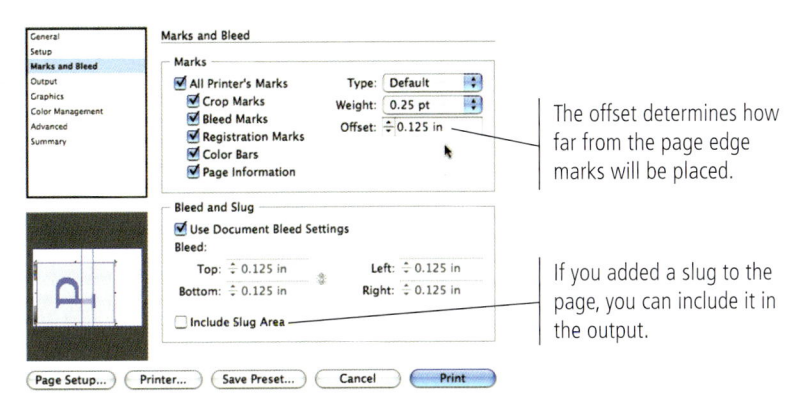

   The offset determines how far from the page edge marks will be placed.

   If you added a slug to the page, you can include it in the output.

   Note:

   To output a letter-size page at 100% on letter-size paper, you have to tile to multiple sheets of paper; using the landscape paper orientation allows you to tile to 2 sheets instead of 4 (as shown in the preview area).

7. **Click the Output option in the list of categories in the left pane. If you can print color, choose Composite CMYK or Composite RGB in the Color menu; otherwise, choose Composite Gray.**

   In the Color menu, you can choose the color model you want to use. (If you only have a black-and-white printer, this menu will default to Composite Gray.) If you chose either Separations option in the menu, the Inks list shows which inks (separations) will be included in the output.

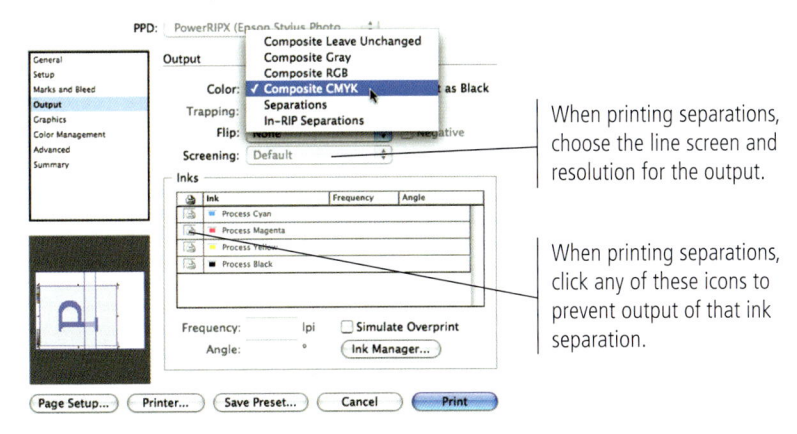

   When printing separations, choose the line screen and resolution for the output.

   When printing separations, click any of these icons to prevent output of that ink separation.

   Note:

   Some printers require printer's marks to stay outside the bleed area, which means the offset should be at least the same as or greater than the defined bleed area.

8. **Click Print to output the page.**

9. **When the document comes back into focus, save and close it.**

10. **Using what you just learned about the Print dialog box options, print full-size proofs (with printer's marks) of the envelope and business card layouts.**

11. **Close the layout files when you're finished.**

    Note:

    We're intentionally skipping the rest of the panes in the Print dialog box. We explain them in later projects when they are relevant to the project content.

Project 1: Identity Package 87

Project Review

fill in the blank

1. _____ is the area of an object that extends past the edge of a page to compensate for variations in the output process.

2. _____ is a special kind of raster image that has only two possible color values, black or white.

3. The _____ defines the outermost dimensions of an object; it is always a rectangle, regardless of the object's specific shape.

4. _____ are based on the concept of anchor points and their defining control handles.

5. _____ are the four primary colors used in process-color printing.

6. The _____ tool is used to select entire frames or other objects.

7. The _____ tool is used to select the image contained within a specific frame.

8. The _____ panel can be used to create complex shapes by combining multiple objects.

9. The _____ tool can create odd shapes with defined numbers of straight edges.

10. The _____ is context sensitive, reflecting different options depending on what is selected in the document.

short answer

1. Briefly explain the difference between a vector graphic and a raster image.

2. Briefly explain how resolution affects a page you lay out in InDesign.

3. Briefly explain the difference between process color and spot color.

Portfolio Builder Project

Use what you learned in this project to complete the following freeform exercise.
Carefully read the art director and client comments, then create your own design to meet the needs of the project.
Use the space below to sketch ideas; when finished, write a brief explanation of your reasoning behind your final design.

art director comments

The owner of your agency is pleased with your work on behalf of Dillon's new company. She has decided to create more formal branding for the design agency, and wants you to create a new logo and the accompanying collateral pieces with the new logo.

To complete this project, you should:

- ❏ Develop a compelling logo that suggests the agency's purpose (graphic design).
- ❏ Incorporate the agency's name (Creative Concepts) in the logo.
- ❏ Build the letterhead, envelope, and business cards with the same technical specs that you used to design the TD Associates pieces.

client comments

We've been so busy since opening that we never really took the time to brand our own business. But if we want to continue growing and winning new clients, I think it's time we corrected that oversight.

We've always focused on packaging design until now, but I want to diversify and offer a full range of graphic design solutions (corporate identity, direct mail, product marketing, etc.).

For the logo, I want something that really says 'graphic design' — how can we convince clients that we can design their logos if we don't have a good design for our own? Find some kind of imagery that people will immediately recognize as graphics or art related.

Use your own contact information as placeholder text for the collateral pieces. The business card needs to have space for a name, title, and email address. The letterhead should have the physical address, phone number, and Web site. The envelope should include only the physical address and Web site.

project justification

_____
_____
_____
_____
_____
_____
_____
_____
_____
_____
_____
_____
_____
_____
_____

Project Summary

Although logos are more commonly created in Adobe Illustrator, InDesign has many of the tools you need to create sophisticated vector graphics like the logo you created in this project. You used the basic shape tools and the Pen tool, as well as the Pathfinder panel, to create the final logo to your client's specifications.

Once you completed the logo, you used one of the most basic — and most important — features available in InDesign: creating new documents to meet specific project needs. You learned how to define page sizes and margins, and how to define bleed settings to meet the printer's stated requirements. You also learned about document presets, which can save common page settings so you can later apply the same choices in a single click. To create the three different pieces, you learned about the difference between "four-color" and "two-color" and generated different versions of the logo for each type of job.

You also learned the very basics of working with text and graphics frames — creating the frames and adding content, then applying basic formatting to the text you created. You will build on these basic skills as you complete the rest of the projects in this book.

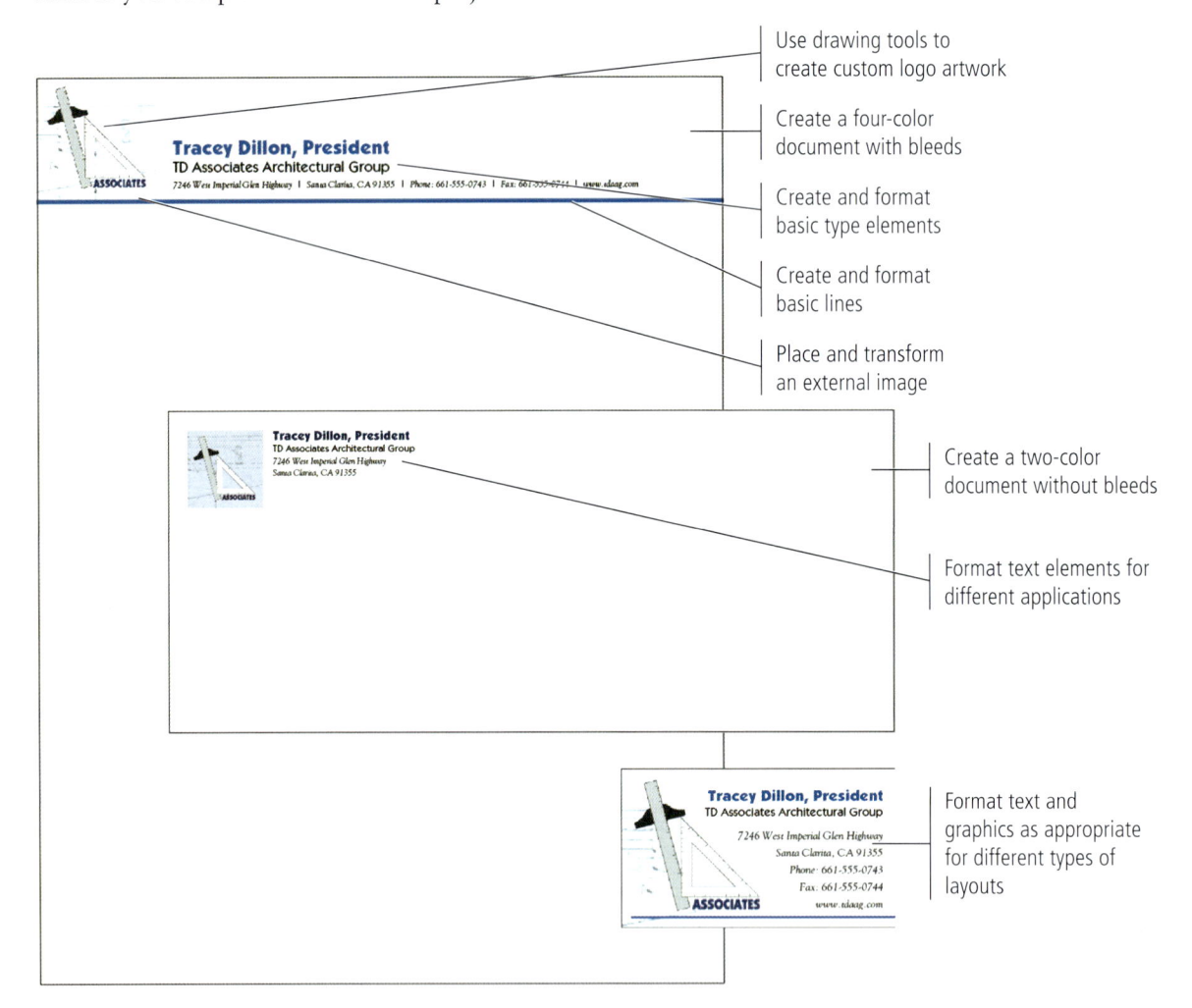

Use drawing tools to create custom logo artwork

Create a four-color document with bleeds

Create and format basic type elements

Create and format basic lines

Place and transform an external image

Create a two-color document without bleeds

Format text elements for different applications

Format text and graphics as appropriate for different types of layouts

Festival Poster

project 2

Your client is the promoter for the Miami Beach Jazz Festival, which is held annually at several locations throughout the South Beach area. The client wants to create posters that will be plastered all over the city, from local restaurants and clubs to bus stops and construction sites that don't say "Post No Bills." This type of poster should use very little text set in a large, easy-to-read font, and it needs to be eye-catching from a distance, with large, vivid graphics.

This project incorporates the following skills:

❏ Creating a file with the appropriate settings for a four-color, commercially printed poster

❏ Using gradients, graphics, and image effects to attract the viewer's attention

❏ Adding text elements and applying formatting as appropriate for a poster

❏ Threading a single text story across multiple text frames

❏ Understanding the various options for formatting characters and paragraphs

❏ Using inline graphics to highlight important text elements

❏ Creating a PDF file that meets the printer's requirements

Project Meeting

client comments

The poster to promote this festival is basically the "play bill," and we will plaster it all over the city. We want the poster to be very attractive, colorful, and vivid, so the main focus — and most of the poster real estate — should be on the graphics. But the text also has to be readable; I emailed the text I want you to place at the bottom of the poster this morning. Our posters for past years' festivals have always been 11 × 17", and we want to stick with that size.

This year's festival tag line is "Move Your Feet to the Beat." I found an excellent illustration of a saxophone player that we'd like to use as the main image, and we hope you can make the tag line look like it's coming out the end of the sax. I also found some nice beach images that might make good backgrounds, so we emailed those to you as well.

art director comments

We have all the pieces you need, based on what the client provided, so you can get started composing the layout. Most of this job is going to be compositing multiple images and formatting text, but I want you to go beyond basic image placement. InDesign includes many tools for manipulating images; use some of those to make sure this poster consists of more than just plain pictures.

You already know the page size, and according to the printer the poster needs a 1/4" bleed allowance just to be safe. The final poster should be saved as a PDF using the printer's specs, which I'll email to you.

project objectives

To complete this project, you will:

❏ Create a print layout using a master text frame

❏ Convert the content type of frames

❏ Create a custom gradient to add visual impact

❏ Create a custom frame using an image clipping path

❏ Apply visual effects to unify various graphic elements

❏ Thread the flow of text through multiple text frames

❏ Format text characters and paragraphs to effectively convey a message

❏ Place inline graphics to highlight important textual elements

❏ Create a PDF file for commercial output

Stage 1 Building Graphic Interest

In Project 1, you learned the basics of placing graphics into a layout and drawing shapes using the built-in InDesign tools. You know that graphics and text are contained in frames, and that objects (including graphics frames) can have stroke and fill attributes. You can use those foundational skills to build virtually any InDesign layout.

InDesign also includes a number of options for extending your artistic options beyond simply compositing text and graphics that were finalized in other applications. The first stage of this project incorporates a number of these creative tools to accomplish your client's stated goal of grabbing the viewer's attention with vivid, attractive graphics.

Define Color Swatches

The Swatches panel is used to apply predefined colors to any element in a layout. Six CMYK color swatches are included in the default set, as well as three special colors (Paper, Black, and Registration) and a None swatch that removes color from the selected attribute.

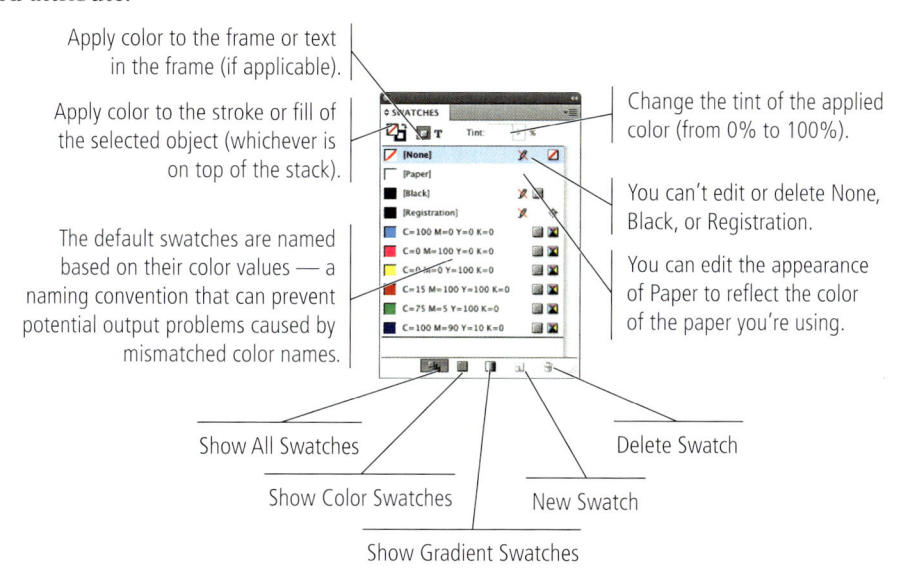

- Apply color to the frame or text in the frame (if applicable).
- Apply color to the stroke or fill of the selected object (whichever is on top of the stack).
- The default swatches are named based on their color values — a naming convention that can prevent potential output problems caused by mismatched color names.
- Change the tint of the applied color (from 0% to 100%).
- You can't edit or delete None, Black, or Registration.
- You can edit the appearance of Paper to reflect the color of the paper you're using.
- Show All Swatches
- Show Color Swatches
- Show Gradient Swatches
- Delete Swatch
- New Swatch

Note:

Anything colored with the Registration swatch will appear on every separation in a job. This color should typically be used for special marks or other information placed outside the trim area.

You can define colors based on one of three color models (CMYK, RGB, or LAB), as well as call spot colors from built-in libraries of special inks. Each different mode and type of color has an identifying icon in the Swatches panel.

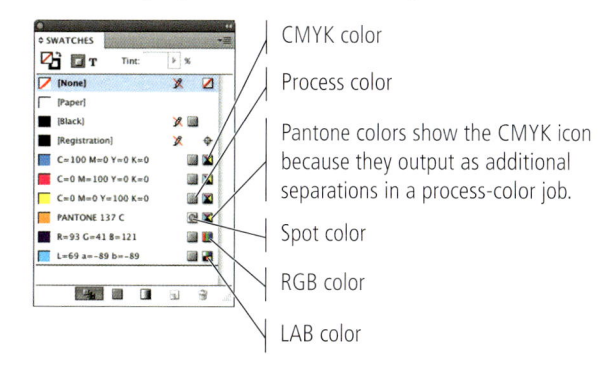

- CMYK color
- Process color
- Pantone colors show the CMYK icon because they output as additional separations in a process-color job.
- Spot color
- RGB color
- LAB color

Note:

When you work in files with large numbers of color and gradient swatches, it can be very helpful to view only swatches of a specific type.

Project 2: Festival Poster 93

1. **On your desktop, copy the Jazz folder from the WIP folder on your Resource CD to the WIP folder where you are saving you work.**

   Save all files for this project in your WIP>Jazz folder.

2. **Create a new file that is 11″ wide by 17″ high (Tabloid-size) with 1″ margins on all four sides and 0.25″ bleeds. Create the file with no master text frame and without facing pages.**

3. **Display the Swatches panel, and then open the panel Options menu.**

   This menu has options for creating four types of color swatches: Color, Tint, Gradient, and Mixed Ink.

   - **Color** swatches and **Gradient** swatches are self-explanatory.
   - A **Tint** swatch is a specific stored percentage of another swatch, which is useful if you frequently use (for example) a 30% tint of C=100 M=42 Y=0 K=73. You can apply that tint with a single click instead of applying the color, and then changing the tint of the applied color. Every click you save is a boost in productivity, especially if you're building layouts with multiple elements.
   - **Mixed Ink** swatches allow you to combine percentages of spot colors and process colors, or of multiple one-spot colors. This option is only available when at least one spot color exists in the file. (The **Mixed Ink Group** option allows you to build multiple swatches at once, based on specific incremental percentages of specific inks.)

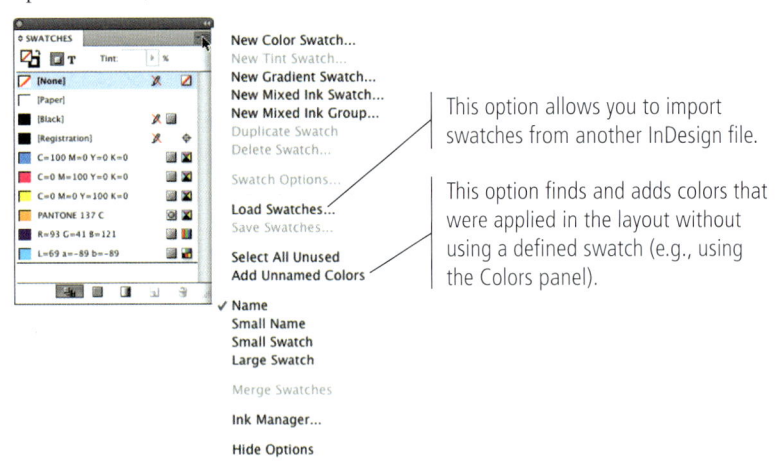

   Note:

   Industry standards typically call for a 0.125″ bleed, but in this case the printer specifically requested 0.25″ bleed allowance.

   This option allows you to import swatches from another InDesign file.

   This option finds and adds colors that were applied in the layout without using a defined swatch (e.g., using the Colors panel).

4. **Choose New Color Swatch in the panel Options menu.**

5. **Leave the Name with Color Value option checked. Make sure the Color Type is set to Process and the Color Mode is set to CMYK.**

   There is no industry standard for naming colors, but InDesign comes close with the Name with Color Value option. This type of naming convention — basing names on the color components — serves several purposes:

   - You know exactly what components the color contains, so you can easily see if you are duplicating colors.
   - You can immediately tell that the color should be a process build rather than a special ink or spot color.
   - You avoid mismatched color names and duplicate spot colors, which are potential disasters in the commercial printing production process.

Project 2: Festival Poster

Mismatched color names occur when a defined color name has two different values — one defined in the page layout and one defined in an image file you place into your layout. When the files are output, the output device might be confused by different definitions for the same color name; the imported value might replace the project's value for that particular color name (or vice versa). The change could be subtle, or it could be drastic.

A similar problem occurs when the same spot color is assigned different names in different applications. For example, you might define a spot color in InDesign as "Border Color"; another designer might define the same spot color in Illustrator as "Spec Blue." When the illustration is placed in the InDesign layout, two different spot-color separations exist, even though the different color names have the same values.

6. **Define the color with 0% Cyan, 70% Magenta, 95% Yellow, and 0% Black, and then click Add.**

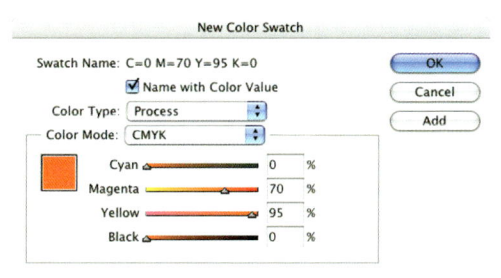

Color by Numbers

INDESIGN FOUNDATIONS

If you base your color choices solely on what you see on your monitor, it would be safe to assume that your perfect blue sky might not look quite right when it's printed with process-color inks. Even if you have calibrated your monitor, no monitor is 100% effective at simulating printed color. As long as monitors display color in RGB, there will always be some discrepancies.

Every designer should have some sort of process color chart, available from commercial publishers (some printers might provide the charts produced by the exact press on which your job will be printed). These charts contain small squares of process ink builds so that you can see, for example, what a process build of C=10 M=70 Y=30 K=20 will look like when printed. These guides usually show samples in steps of 5% or 10%, printed on both coated and uncoated paper (because the type of paper or substrate can dramatically affect the final result).

When you define process colors in an InDesign project, you should enter specific numbers in the CMYK fields to designate your color choices, rather than relying on your screen preview. As you gain experience defining colors, you will become better able to predict the outcome for a given process-ink build. Rely on what you know to be true rather than what you hope will be true.

The same concept also applies when using special ink libraries. You should have — and use — swatch books that show printed samples of the special inks. You cannot rely on the monitor preview to choose a special ink color. Rather, you should find the color in a printed swatch book, and then enter the appropriate number in the Pantone field (for example) below the color swatches.

Total Area Coverage

When defining the ink values of a process-color build, you must usually limit your **total area coverage** (TAC, also called **total ink coverage** or **total ink density**), or the amount of ink used in a given color.

This might sound complex, but it can be easily calculated by adding the percentages of each ink used to create the color. If a color is defined as C=45 M=60 Y=90 K=0, the total area coverage is 195% (45 + 60 + 90 + 0).

Maximum TAC limits are between 240% and 320% for offset lithography, depending on the paper being used. If you exceed the TAC limits for a given paper-ink-press combination, your printed job might end up with excess ink bleed, smearing, smudging, show-through, or a number of other printing errors because the paper cannot absorb all the ink.

7. **Create two more process-color swatches using the following ink values. Click OK/Done after adding the third color to close the dialog box.**

   Color 1: C=0 M=10 Y=75 K=0

   Color 2: C=0 M=40 Y=0 K=100

   The third color, 100% Black with 40% Magenta, is called a rich black or super black. By itself, plain black ink often lacks density. Rich blacks are commonly used to add density or "temperature" to flat black; adding magenta results in "warmer" blacks, and adding cyan results in "cooler" blacks.

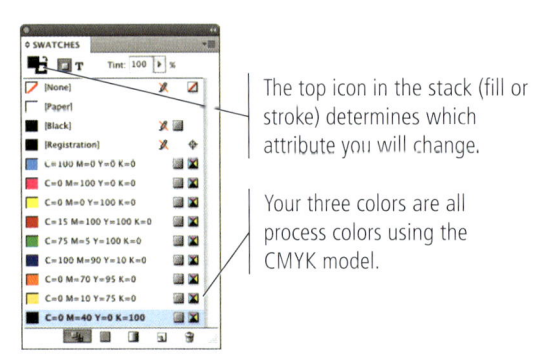

   The top icon in the stack (fill or stroke) determines which attribute you will change.

   Your three colors are all process colors using the CMYK model.

8. **Using the Rectangle tool, create a rectangle that covers the entire page and extends to the defined bleed guides.**

9. **In the Swatches panel, click the Stroke icon to make it active (bring it to the top of the stack). With the rectangle from Step 8 selected, click the None swatch to turn off the object's stroke color.**

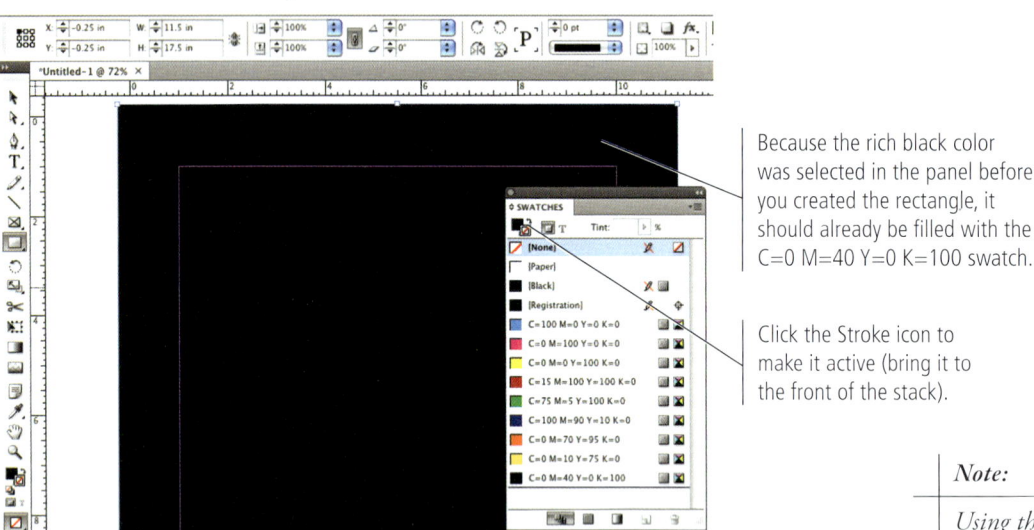

   Because the rich black color was selected in the panel before you created the rectangle, it should already be filled with the C=0 M=40 Y=0 K=100 swatch.

   Click the Stroke icon to make it active (bring it to the front of the stack).

   Note:

   Using the Fill and Stroke swatches at the top of the Swatches panel, you can apply different colors to the fill and stroke of selected text.

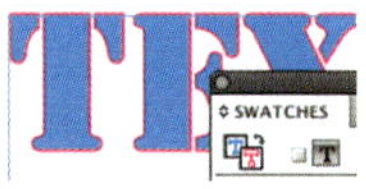

10. **Use the Selection tool to drag the rectangle's bounding box corners until they snap to the bleed guides.**

    By default, InDesign includes the defined stroke weight in an objects' dimensions. When you apply the None color to the stroke, the stroke is effectively removed, so the object's dimensions become smaller.

11. **Save the file as poster.indd in your WIP>Jazz folder and continue to the next exercise.**

96   Project 2: Festival Poster

Define and Apply a Gradient

A gradient, also called a blend, can be used to create a smooth transition from one color to another. You can apply a gradient to any object using the Gradient panel, or you can save a gradient swatch if you plan to use it more than once.

The Gradient panel controls the type and position of applied gradients. You can apply either linear or radial gradients, change the angle of linear gradients, and change the color and location for individual stops along the gradient ramp.

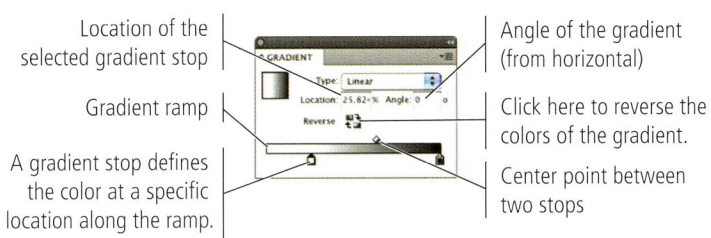

- Location of the selected gradient stop
- Gradient ramp
- A gradient stop defines the color at a specific location along the ramp.
- Angle of the gradient (from horizontal)
- Click here to reverse the colors of the gradient.
- Center point between two stops

1. **With `poster.indd` open, make sure nothing is selected in the layout, and then choose New Gradient Swatch from the Swatches panel Options menu.**

2. **Click the gradient stop on the left end of the gradient ramp to select it.**

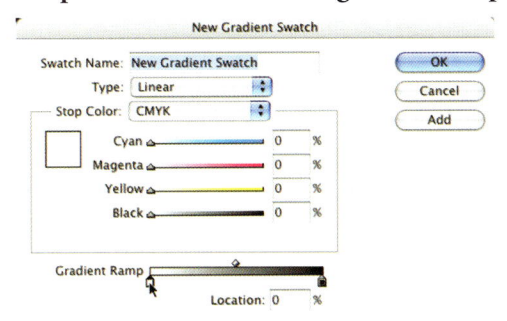

3. **Make sure Linear is selected in the Type menu, and then choose Swatches in the Stop Color menu.**

   You can define gradients using LAB values, CMYK percentages, RGB values, or existing color swatches.

4. **With the first stop selected, click the gold swatch you defined in the previous exercise.**

Project 2: Festival Poster   97

5. **Select the second gradient stop (on the right end of the ramp), and then click the orange swatch you created earlier.**

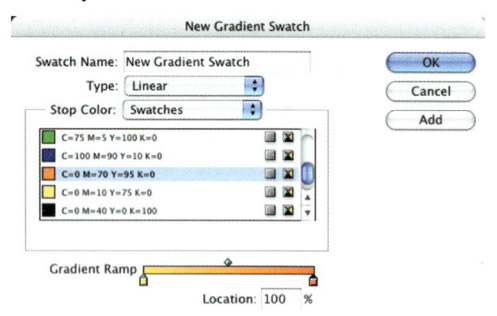

6. **Name the gradient Gold to Orange and click OK.**

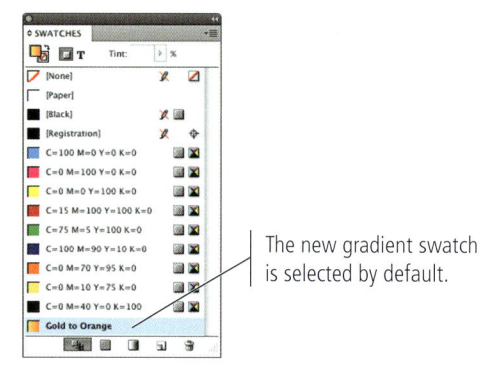

   The new gradient swatch is selected by default.

7. **Using the basic Rectangle tool, create a rectangle that fills the area within the margin guides.**

   If you continued directly from the previous exercise, the rectangle should be filled with the new gradient by default, since that swatch was selected in the Swatches panel and the Fill icon was active when you created the object.

8. **In the Swatches panel, make sure the Fill icon is active and click the Gold to Orange gradient swatch.**

   As you will soon see, gradients can also be applied to an object's stroke. Make sure the correct attribute (fill or stroke) is active when you change color attributes.

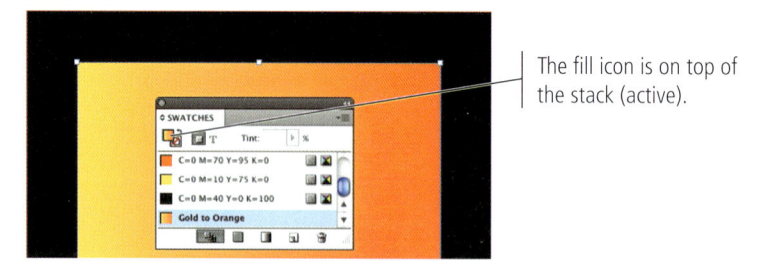

   The fill icon is on top of the stack (active).

   Note:

   Remember, all panels (whether docked or not) can be accessed from the Window menu. If you don't see a specific menu command, choose Edit>Show All Menu Items.

9. **Using either the Control panel or the Transform panel, activate the top-left reference point and change the rectangle height to 10″.**

Project 2: Festival Poster

10. **In the Gradient panel, change the Angle field to 90° to rotate the gradient.**

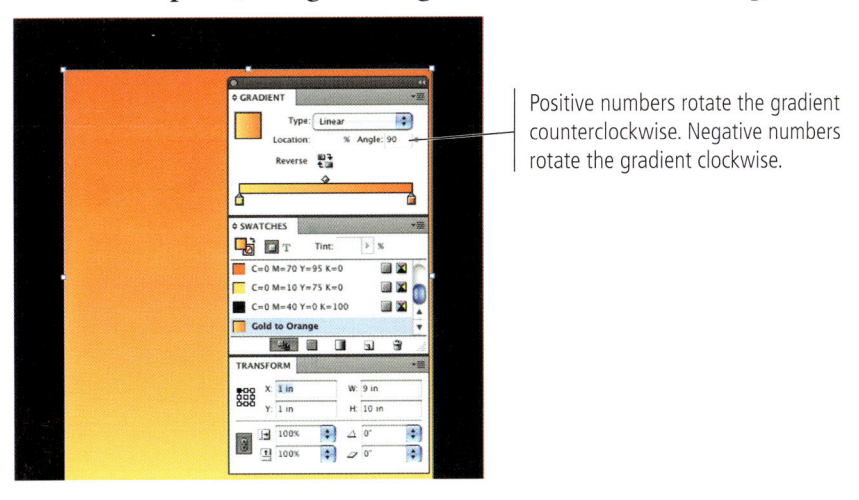

   Positive numbers rotate the gradient counterclockwise. Negative numbers rotate the gradient clockwise.

11. **Apply a 6-pt stroke to the gradient-filled rectangle.**

   You can use either the Stroke panel or the Control panel to change the object's stroke weight.

12. **Click the Stroke icon at the top of the Swatches panel to bring that attribute to the front, and then click the Gold to Orange gradient swatch to apply it to the stroke.**

   Remember that the attribute on top of the stack is the one you are currently changing. If the wrong attribute is on top of the stack, you will change the fill instead of the stroke (or vice versa).

13. **In the Gradient panel, change the gradient angle to −90° so the stroke goes from gold at the top to orange at the bottom (the reverse of the fill).**

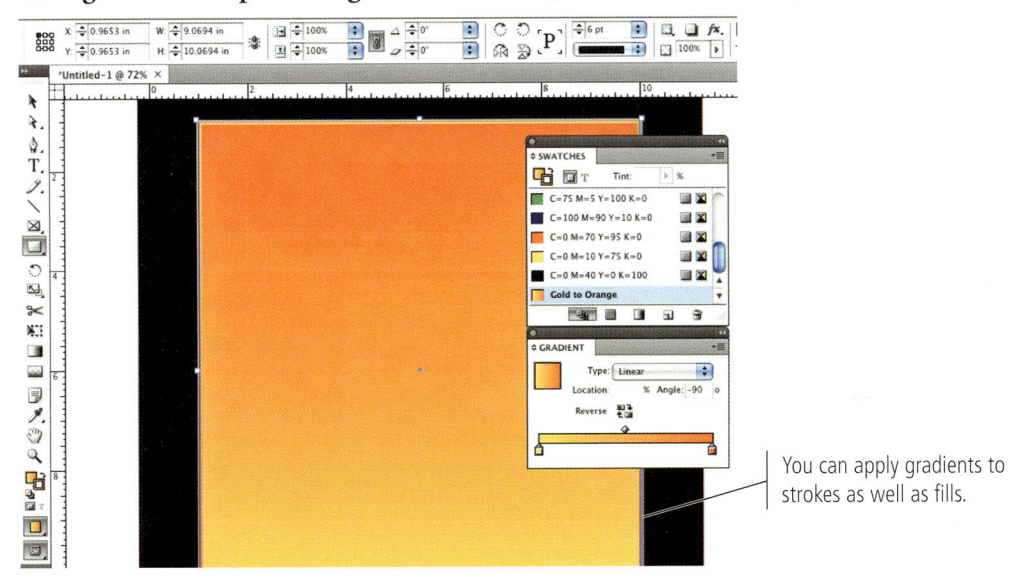

   You can apply gradients to strokes as well as fills.

14. **Save the file and continue to the next exercise.**

Project 2: Festival Poster

The Gradient Tools

Clicking a gradient swatch adds a gradient to the selected object, beginning at the left edge and ending at the right edge (for linear gradients), or beginning at the object's center and ending at the object's outermost edge (for radial gradients). When you drag with the Gradient tool, you define the length of the gradient without regard to the object you're filling.

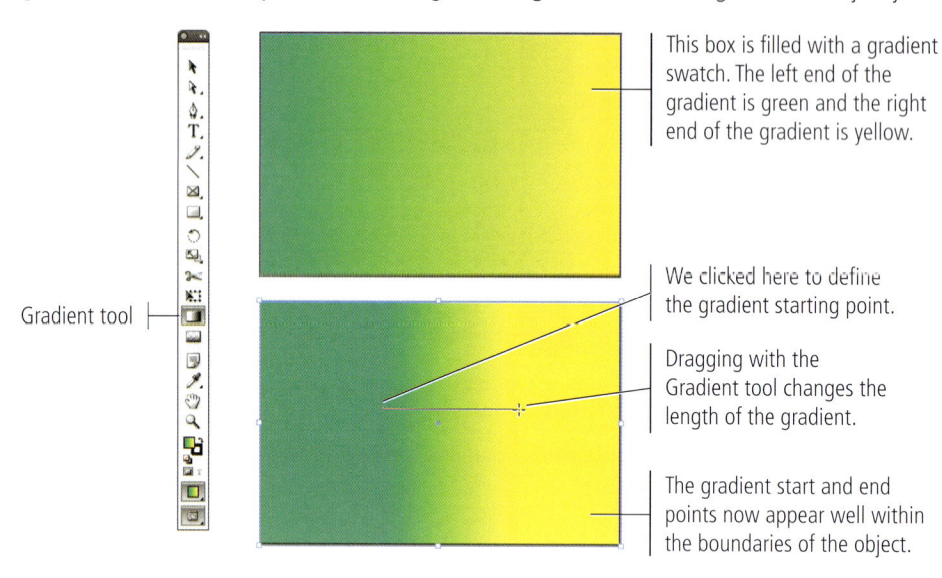

Gradient tool

This box is filled with a gradient swatch. The left end of the gradient is green and the right end of the gradient is yellow.

We clicked here to define the gradient starting point.

Dragging with the Gradient tool changes the length of the gradient.

The gradient start and end points now appear well within the boundaries of the object.

The Gradient Feather tool has a similar function but produces different results. Rather than creating a specific-colored gradient, the Gradient Feather tool creates a gradient mask that blends an object from solid to transparent.

Gradient Feather tool

Clicking here defines the starting point of the gradient mask (the area that will be entirely solid).

Dragging to here defines the end point of the gradient mask (the area that will be entirely transparent).

The gradient mask blends the object from solid to transparent, allowing background objects to show through.

Create Visual Impact with Transparency

The image effects and transparency controls in InDesign provide options for adding dimension and depth, allowing unprecedented creative control directly in the page layout. You can change the transparency of any object (or individual object attributes), apply different blending modes so objects blend smoothly into underlying objects, and apply creative effects such as drop shadows and beveling.

Transparency and effects are controlled in the Effects panel. You can change these options for an entire object (fill and stroke), only the stroke, only the fill, the text (if you're working with a text frame), the graphic (if you're working with a graphics frame), or all objects in a group.

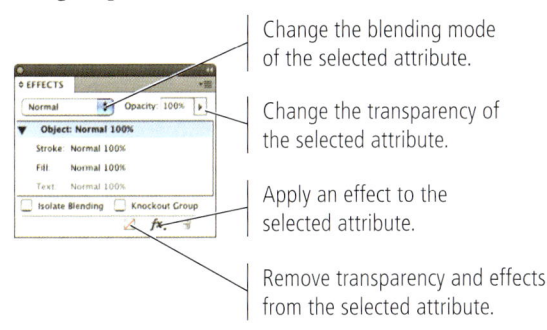

- Change the blending mode of the selected attribute.
- Change the transparency of the selected attribute.
- Apply an effect to the selected attribute.
- Remove transparency and effects from the selected attribute.

Note:

The Graphic option is only available when a placed graphic is selected with the Direct Selection tool. Group replaces Object in the list only when a group is selected with the Selection tool.

Note:

Effects applied to text apply to all text in the frame; you can't apply effects to individual characters.

Technical Issues of Transparency

Because all these features and options are related in some way to transparency, you should understand what transparency is and how it affects your output. **Transparency** is the degree to which light passes through an object so objects in the background are visible. In terms of page layout, transparency means being able to "see through" objects in front of the stacking order to objects in back of the stacking order.

Because of the way printing works, applying transparency in print graphic design is a bit of a contradiction. Commercial printing is, by definition, accomplished by overlapping a mixture of (usually) four semi-transparent inks in different percentages to reproduce a range of colors (the printable gamut). In that sense, all print graphic design requires transparency.

But *design* transparency refers to the objects on the page. The trouble is, when a halftone dot is printed, it's either there or it's not. There is no "50% opaque" setting on a printing press. This means that a transformation needs to take place behind the scenes, translating what we create onscreen into what a printing press produces.

When transparent objects are output, overlapping areas of transparent elements are actually broken into individual elements (where necessary) to produce the best possible results. Ink values in the overlap areas are calculated by the application, based on the capabilities of the mechanical printing process; the software converts what we create onscreen into the elements that are necessary to print.

When you get to the final stage of this project, you'll learn how to preview and control the output process for transparent objects.

Note:

Transparency is essentially the inverse of opacity. If an object is 20% transparent, it is also 80% opaque.

1. **In the open `poster.indd` file, use the Selection tool to select the gradient-filled rectangle.**

2. **Choose Object>Content>Graphic.**

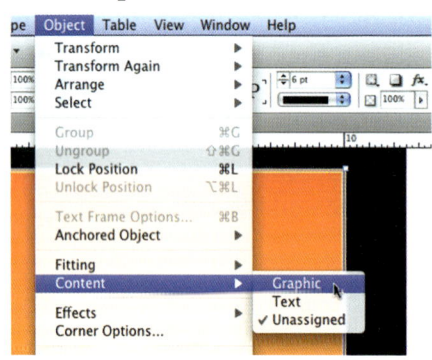

   Note:
   You can also Control/right-click an object and change its content type in the contextual menu.

   When you create a frame with one of the basic shape tools, it is considered "unassigned" because it is neither a text frame nor a graphics frame. You can convert any type of frame (graphics, text, or unassigned) to another type using this menu.

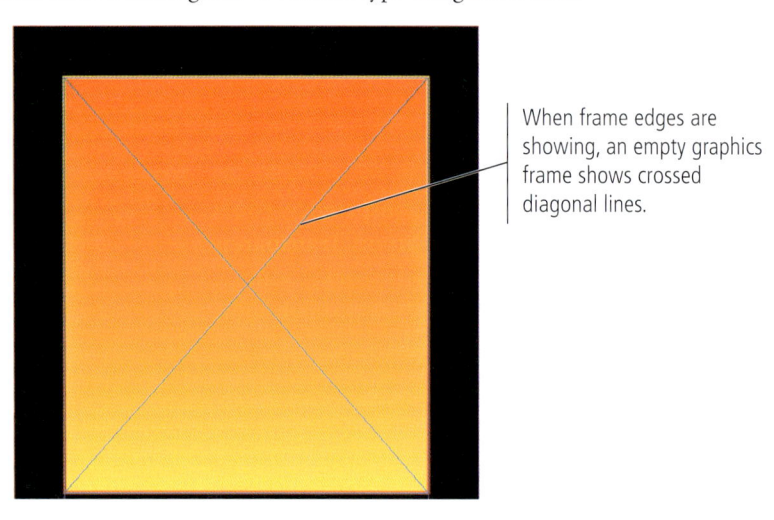

   When frame edges are showing, an empty graphics frame shows crossed diagonal lines.

3. **Open the Interface Preferences dialog box, and make sure the Show Thumbnails on Place option is checked.**

   Remember: Preferences can be accessed in the InDesign menu on Macintosh or in the Edit menu on Windows.

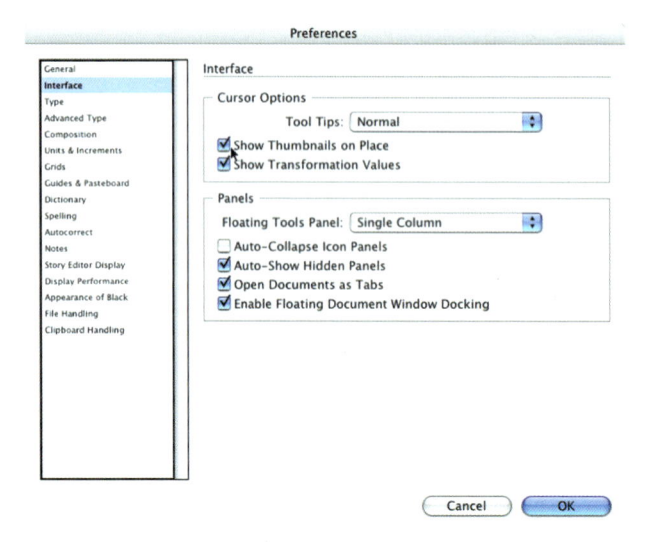

102   Project 2: Festival Poster

4. **Click OK to close the Preferences dialog box.**

5. **Choose File>Place. Navigate to the `RF_InDesign>Jazz` folder, choose `sunset.jpg`, and click Open.**

   When the Place dialog box closes, the image loads into the cursor. A small preview shows in the cursor icon.

6. **Click the loaded cursor anywhere inside the gradient-filled graphics frame.**

   By clicking the loaded cursor inside an existing frame, the image is placed inside the frame.

   Note:

   If Replace Selected Item was checked in the Place dialog box, the image will automatically be placed within the selected frame.

7. **Open the Effects panel (Window>Effects).**

   When you select an object with the Selection tool, you can apply various effects to the entire object, the object fill, the object stroke, or text within the object.

8. **Using the Direct Selection tool, click the sunset image to select only the image (not the frame).**

   When you select only the placed image, you can apply effects to the image itself, independent of the frame.

   Note:

   If you click in an empty area when the cursor is loaded, the image will be placed where you click; a new graphics frame will be created using the image's dimensions.

Project 2: Festival Poster — 103

9. **With the Graphic option selected in the Effects panel, choose the Screen option in the Blending Mode menu.**

   The image now blends into the gradient background, but there is still a hard line marking the bottom edge of the placed image.

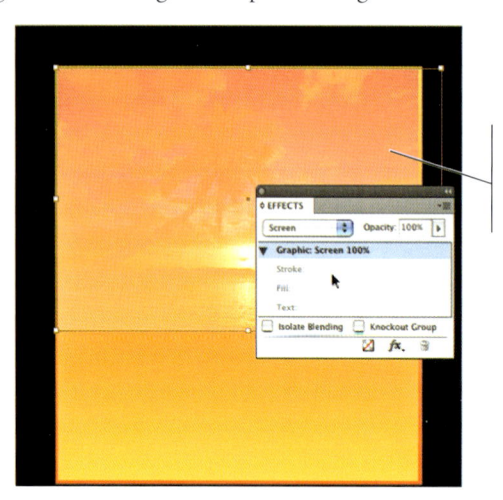

   The Screen blending mode merges the image colors into the object's gradient fill.

   Note:
   Remember, all panels can be accessed in the Window menu.

Blending Modes

Blending modes control how colors in an object interact with colors in underlying objects. Objects are set to Normal by default, which simply overlays the top object's color onto underlying objects. (If the top object is entirely opaque, there is no effect on underlying objects.)

- **Multiply** multiplies (hence the name) the base color by the blend color, resulting in a darker color. Multiplying any color with black produces black; multiplying any color with white leaves the color unchanged (think of math — any number times 0 equals 0).
- **Screen** is basically the inverse of Multiply, always returning a lighter color. Screening with black has no effect; screening with white produces white.
- **Overlay** multiplies or screens the blend color to preserve the original lightness or darkness of the base.
- **Soft Light** darkens or lightens base colors depending on the blend color. Blend colors lighter than 50% lighten the base color (as if dodged); blend colors darker than 50% darken the base color (as if burned).
- **Hard Light** combines the Multiply and Screen modes. Blend colors darker than 50% are multiplied, and blend colors lighter than 50% are screened.
- **Color Dodge** brightens the base color. Blend colors lighter than 50% significantly increase brightness; blending with black has no effect.
- **Color Burn** darkens the base color by increasing the contrast. Blend colors darker than 50% significantly darken the base color by increasing saturation and reducing brightness; blending with white has no effect.

- **Darken** returns the darker of the blend or base color. Base pixels that are lighter than the blend color are replaced; base pixels that are darker than the blend color do not change.
- **Lighten** returns whichever is the lighter color (base or blend). Base pixels that are darker than the blend color are replaced; base pixels that are lighter than the blend color do not change.
- **Difference** inverts base color values according to the brightness value in the blend layer. Lower brightness values in the blend layer have less of an effect on the result; blending with black has no effect.
- **Exclusion** is very similar to Difference, except that mid-tone values in the base color are completely desaturated.
- **Hue** results in a color with the luminance and saturation of the base color and the hue of the blend color.
- **Saturation** results in a color with the luminance and hue of the base and the saturation of the blend color.
- **Color** results in a color with the luminance of the base color and the hue and saturation of the blend color.
- **Luminosity** results in a color with the hue and saturation of the base color and the luminance of the blend color (basically the opposite of the Color mode).

Avoid applying the Difference, Exclusion, Hue, Saturation, Color, and Luminosity modes to objects with spot colors.

10. **Click the *fx* button at the bottom of the Effects panel, and choose Gradient Feather.**

   The Effects dialog box opens to the Gradient Effects options.

11. **In the Effects dialog box, click the Preview check box so you can preview your results before accepting/applying them.**

    The Gradient Feather effect creates a gradient mask so an object blends into underlying objects instead of leaving a hard edge. The mask is created using a black-to-white gradient. Anything under the black area of the gradient remains entirely visible, and anything under the transparent area of the gradient is hidden; areas in the middle of the gradient are partially visible.

    Note:

    If you create a mask with the Gradient Feather tool, the Gradient Feather effect is automatically applied.

12. **Click in the Angle circle and drag until the field shows −90° (the line should point straight down).**

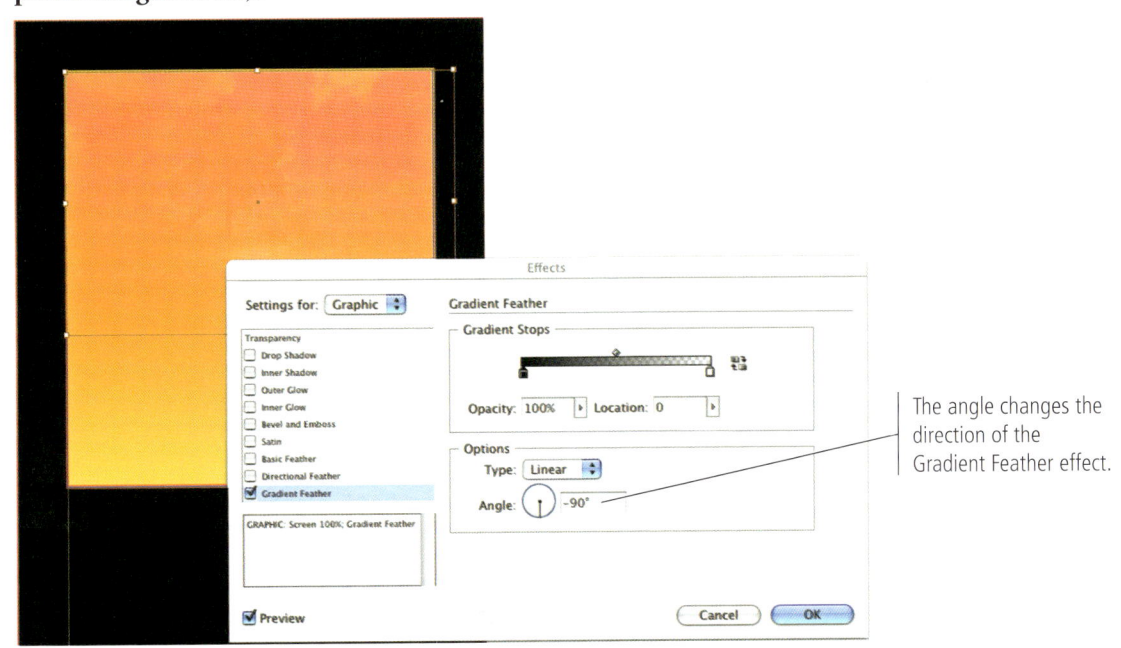

    The angle changes the direction of the Gradient Feather effect.

Project 2: Festival Poster

13. **Drag the left gradient stop until the Location field shows 75%.**

    By extending the solid black part of the gradient to the 75% location, the top three-quarters of the masked image remain entirely visible; only the bottom quarter of the image blends into the background.

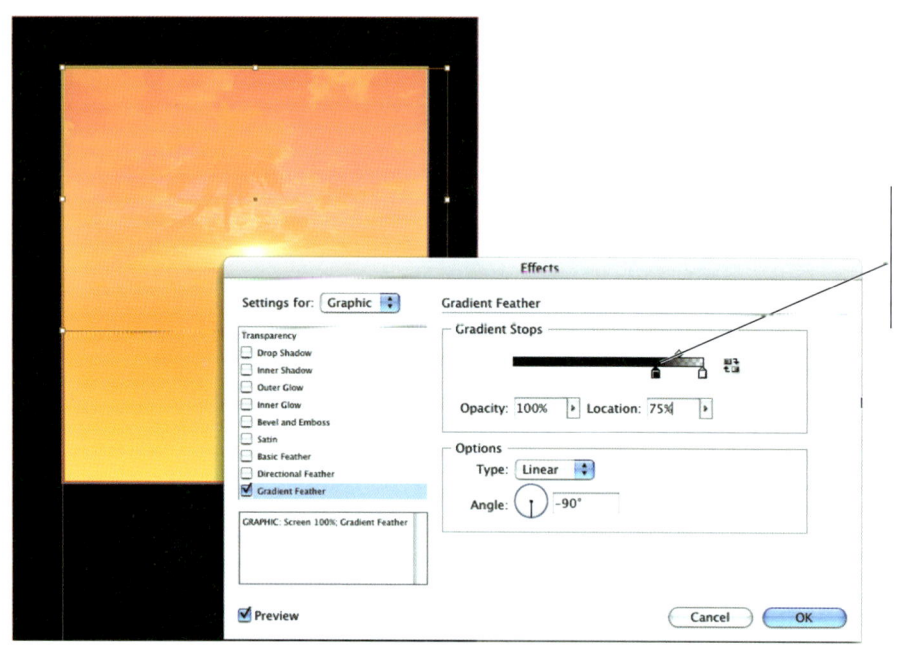

    Moving the first stop extends the black area of the gradient, which extends the part of the image that is entirely opaque.

14. **Click OK to close the Effects dialog box and apply your choices.**

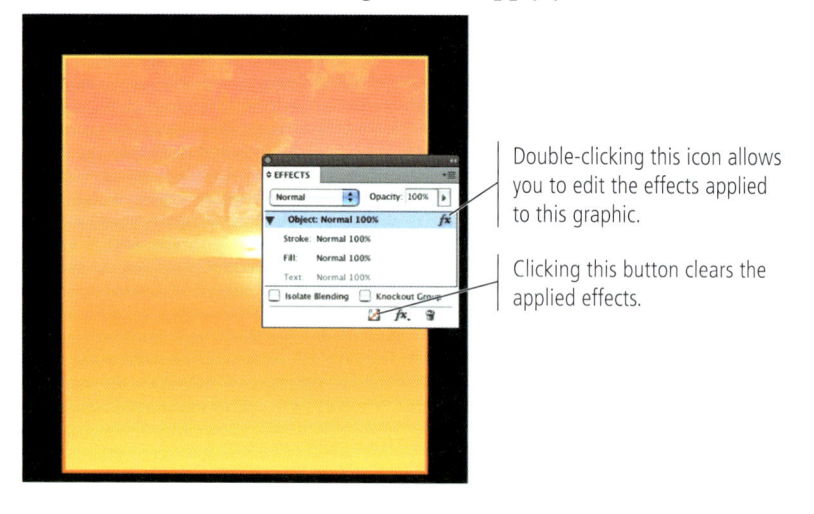

    Double-clicking this icon allows you to edit the effects applied to this graphic.

    Clicking this button clears the applied effects.

    Note:

    Effects in InDesign are non-destructive, which means they have no effect on the physical file data.

15. **Save the file and continue to the next exercise.**

Applying Effects

INDESIGN FOUNDATIONS

InDesign offers nine different effects options, which you can apply individually or in combinations to create unique flat and dimensional effects for any object. The effects can be applied by clicking the *fx* button at the bottom of the Effects panel, by clicking the *fx* button in the Control panel, or by choosing from the Object>Effects menu.

Drop Shadow and Inner Shadow

Drop Shadow adds a shadow behind the object. **Inner Shadow** adds a shadow inside the edges of the object. For both types, you can define the blending mode, color, opacity, angle, distance, offset, and size of the shadow.

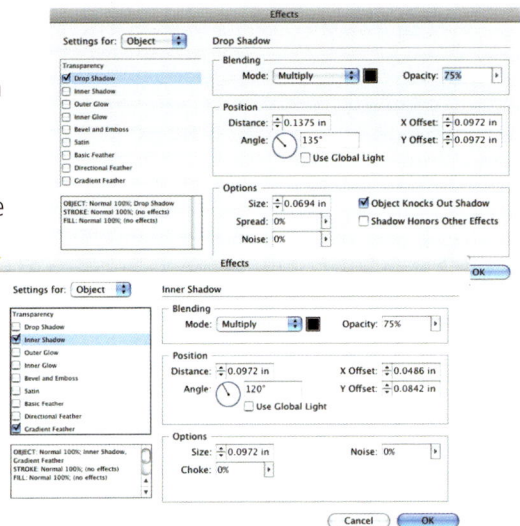

- **Distance** is the overall offset of the shadow, or how far away the shadow will be from the original object. The Offset fields allow you to define different horizontal and vertical distances.
- **Size** is the blur amount applied to the shadow.
- **Spread** (for Drop Shadows) is the percentage that the shadow expands beyond the original object.
- **Choke** (for Inner Shadows) is the percentage that the shadow shrinks into the original object.
- **Noise** controls the amount of random pixels that are added to the effect.

The **Object Knocks Out Shadow** option for drop shadows allows you to knock out (remove) or maintain the shadow underneath the object area. This option is particularly important if the original object is semi-transparent above its shadow.

The **Use Global Light** check box is available for the Drop Shadow, Inner Shadow, and Bevel and Emboss effects. When this option is checked, the style is linked to the "master" light source angle for the entire file. Changing the global light setting affects any linked shadow or bevel effect applied to any object in the entire file. (If Use Global Light is checked for an effect, changing the angle for that effect also changes the Global Light angle. You can also change the Global Light settings by choosing Object>Effects>Global Light.)

Outer Glow and Inner Glow

Outer Glow and **Inner Glow** add glow effects to the outside and inside edges (respectively) of the original object. For either kind of glow, you can define the blending mode, opacity, noise, and size values.

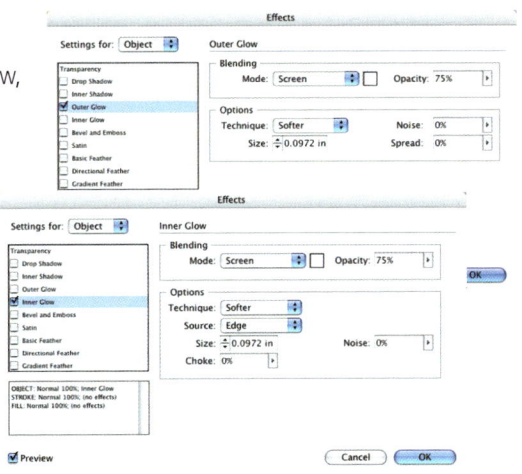

- For either kind of glow, you can define the **Technique** as Precise or Softer. **Precise** creates a glow at a specific distance; **Softer** creates a blurred glow and does not preserve detail as well as Precise.
- For Inner Glows, you can also define the **Source** of the glow (Center or Edge). **Center** applies a glow starting from the center of the object; **Edge** applies the glow starting from the inside edges of the object.
- The **Spread** and **Choke** sliders affect the percentages of the glow effects.

Project 2: Festival Poster

Applying Effects (continued)

Bevel and Emboss

This effect has five variations or styles:

- **Inner Bevel** creates a bevel on the inside edges of the object.
- **Outer Bevel** creates a bevel on the outside edges of the object.
- **Emboss** creates the effect of embossing the object against the underlying layers.
- **Pillow Emboss** creates the effect of stamping the edges of the object into the underlying layers.

Any of these styles can be applied as **Smooth** (blurs the edges of the effect), **Chisel Hard** (creates a distinct edge to the effect), or **Chisel Soft** (creates a distinct, but slightly blurred edge to the effect).

You can change the **Direction** of the bevel effect. **Up** creates the appearance of the layer coming out of the image; **Down** creates the appearance of something stamped into the image. The **Size** field makes the effect smaller or larger, and the **Soften** option blurs the edges of the effect. **Depth** increases or decreases the three-dimensional effect of the bevel.

In the Shading area, you can control the light source's **Angle** and **Altitude** (think of how shadows differ as the sun moves across the sky). Finally, you can change the blending mode, opacity, and color of both highlight and shadows created with the Bevel or Emboss effect.

Satin

Satin applies interior shading to create a satiny appearance. You can change the blending mode, color, and opacity of the effect, as well as the angle, distance, and size.

Basic Feather, Directional Feather, and Gradient Feather

These three effects soften the edges of an object:

- **Basic Feather** equally fades all edges of the selected object (or attribute) by a specific width. The **Choke** option determines how much of the softened edge is opaque (high settings increase opacity and low settings decrease opacity). **Corners** can be Sharp (following the outer edge of the shape), Rounded (corners are rounded according to the Feather Width), or Diffused (fades from opaque to transparent). Noise adds random pixels to the softened area.
- **Directional Feather** allows you to apply different feather widths to individual edges of an object. The **Shape** option defines the object's original shape (First Edge Only, Leading Edges, or All Edges). The **Angle** field allows you to rotate the feathering effect; if you use any angle other than a 90° increment (i.e., 90, 180, 270, 360), the feathering will be skewed.
- **Gradient Feather** creates a gradient mask that blends from solid (black) to transparent. This effect underlies the Gradient Feather tool. You can move the start and end stops to different locations along the ramp, or add stops to define specific transparencies at specific locations. You can also choose from a Linear or Radial Gradient Feather effect, and change the angle of a Linear Gradient Feather effect.

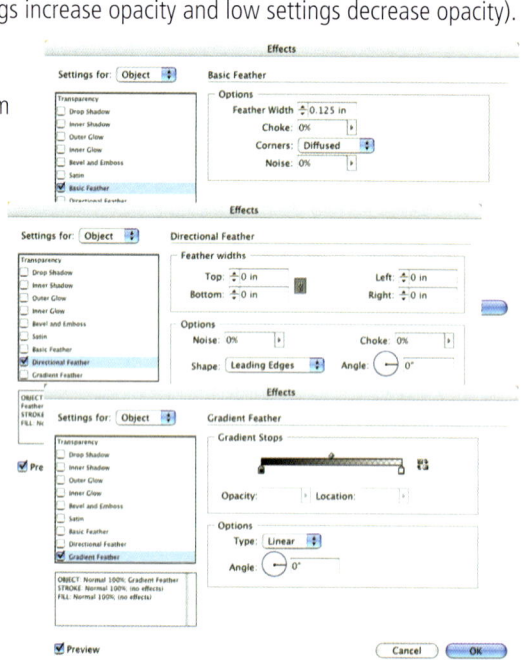

CREATE AN IRREGULAR GRAPHICS FRAME

You can create basic graphics frames using the Rectangle, Ellipse, and Polygon Frame tools. You can also create a Bézier shape with the Pen tool, and then convert the shape to a graphics frame — which means you can create a frame in virtually any shape. However, it requires a lot of work to trace complex graphics with the Pen tool; fortunately, you can use other options to create complex frames from objects in placed graphics.

1. **In the open `poster.indd` file, choose File>Place and navigate to the `JazzManOutline.ai` file in the `RF_InDesign>Jazz` folder.**

2. **Make sure the Replace Selected Item option is not selected, then click Open.**

   If the gradient rectangle had been selected, and the Replace Selected Item option turned on, the palms image would be placed in the gradient-filled frame instead of being loaded into the cursor.

3. **Click anywhere on the page edge to place the graphic.**

4. **Using the Control panel or the Transform panel, position the top-left corner of the graphic at X: 1″, Y: 3.3″.**

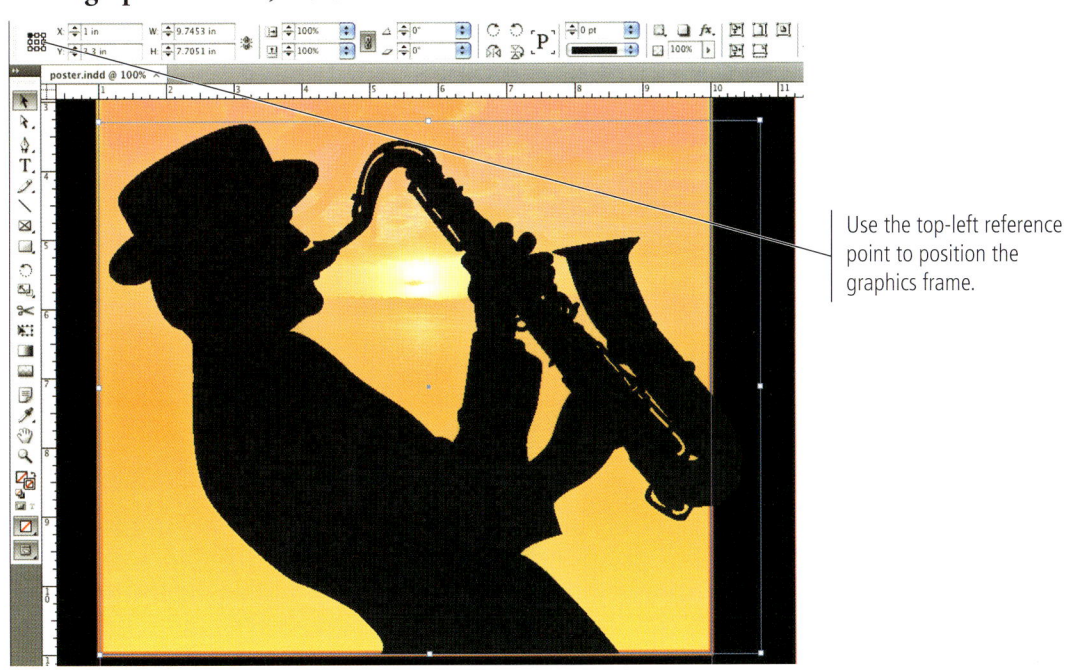

   Use the top-left reference point to position the graphics frame.

5. **Click the placed graphic with the Direct Selection tool, and then choose Object>Clipping Path>Options.**

   A **clipping path** is a hard-edged outline that masks an image. Areas inside the path are visible; areas outside the path are hidden.

Project 2: Festival Poster

6. **Make sure the Preview option is checked, and then choose Detect Edges in the Type menu.**

   InDesign can access Alpha channels and clipping paths that are saved in an image, or you can create a clipping path based on the image content.

   Because this graphic is a vector graphic filled with a solid color with well-defined edges, InDesign can create a very precise clipping path based on the information in the file.

   Note:

   The User-Modified Path option is selected by default if you use the Direct Selection tool to edit a path in the layout.

7. **Check the Include Inside Edges option.**

   When this option is not checked, InDesign generates a clipping path based only on the outside edges of the image. As you can see, the Include Inside Edges option generates a compound clipping path that removes holes in the middle of the outside path. (This is the same principle you used in Project 1 to remove the interior of the architect's triangle.)

   Including the inside edges removes internal areas from the path.

Project 2: Festival Poster

8. Click OK to close the dialog box and create the clipping path.

9. Choose Object>Clipping Path>Convert Clipping Path to Frame.

10. Using the Direct Selection tool, click inside the clipping path to select the placed JazzManOutline.ai file.

11. Press Delete/Backspace to delete the placed file but leave the frame you created.

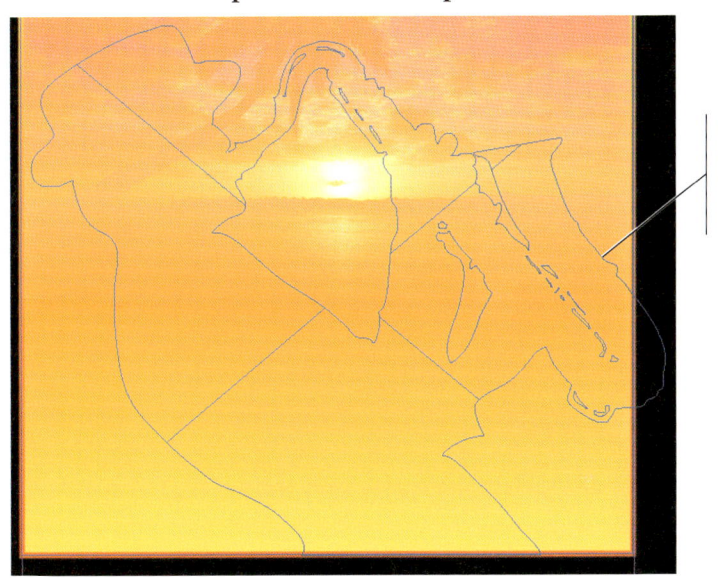

Deleting the original image leaves the frame you created, based on the InDesign-generated clipping path.

12. Choose File>Place, navigate to palms.jpg in the RF_InDesign>Jazz folder, and click Open.

13. Click inside the empty frame with the loaded cursor to place the image inside the frame.

14. Using the Direct Selection tool, click the palms image to select it.

Project 2: Festival Poster

15. **Using the Control panel, change the image's position within the frame to X: –0.25″, Y: –0.25″.**

    When you select an image with the Direct Selection tool, the Control panel fields define the position of the graphic *relative to* its containing frame. Negative numbers move the graphic up and to the left from the frame edge; positive numbers move the graphic down and to the right.

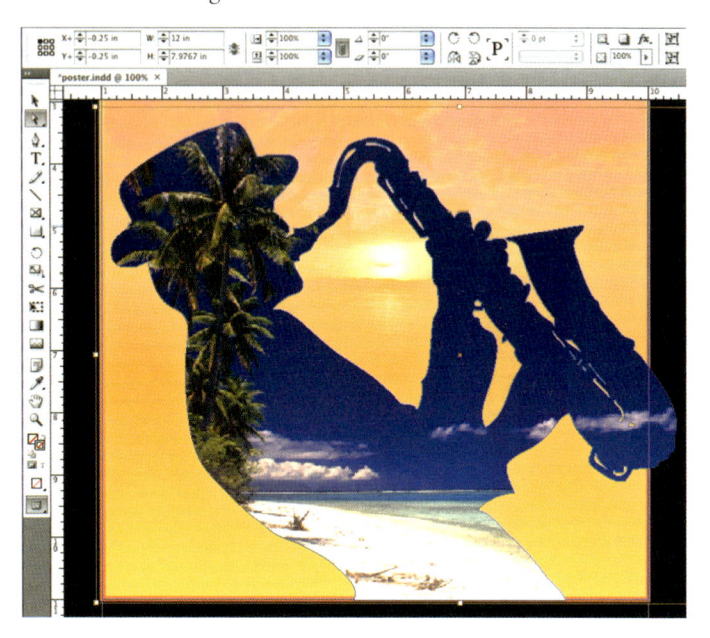

16. **Click the irregular frame with the Selection tool to select the frame (not the placed graphic).**

17. **In the Control panel, click the Drop Shadow button.**

    This button applies a drop shadow using the default settings; the Effects dialog box does not open.

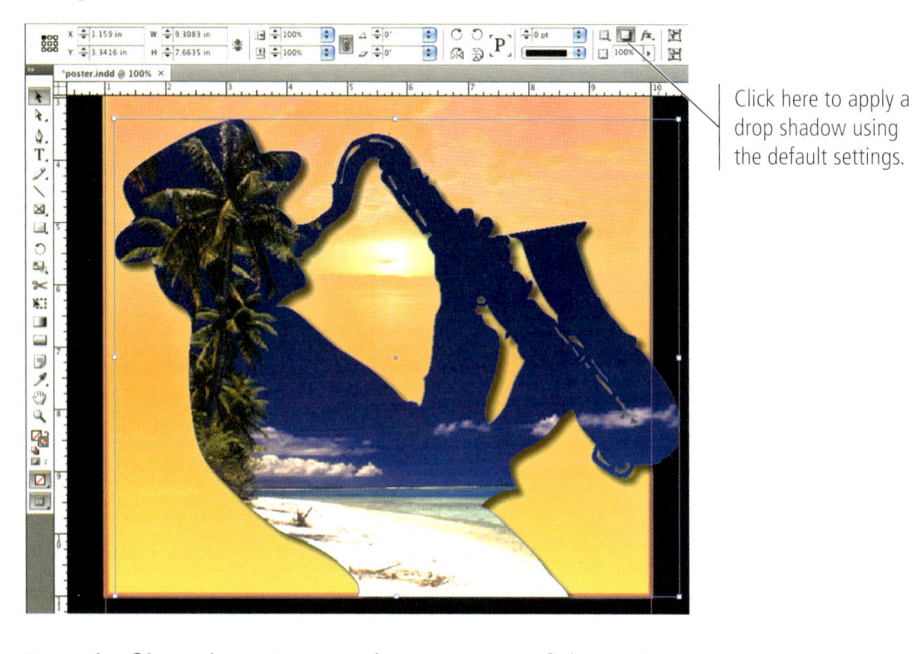

    Click here to apply a drop shadow using the default settings.

18. **Save the file and continue to the next stage of the project.**

Clipping Path Options

When you generate a clipping path in InDesign, you can refine the path using several different options.

Threshold specifies the darkest pixel value that will define the resulting clipping path. In this exercise, the placed image is filled with solid black, so you can set a very high Tolerance value to refine the clipping path. In images with greater tone variation (such as a photograph), increasing the Tolerance value removes lighter areas from the clipped area.

Tolerance specifies how similar a pixel must be to the Threshold value before it is hidden by the clipping path. Increasing the Tolerance value results in fewer points along the clipping path, generating a smoother path. Lowering the Tolerance value results in more anchor points and a potentially rougher path.

Inset Frame shrinks the clipping path by a specific number of pixels. You can also enter a negative value to enlarge the clipping path.

Invert reverses the clipping path, making hidden areas visible and vice versa.

Include Inside Edges creates a compound clipping path, removing inner areas of the object if they are within the Threshold and Tolerance ranges.

Restrict to Frame creates a clipping path that stops at the visible edge of the graphic. You can include the entire object — including areas beyond the frame edges — by unchecking this option.

Use High Resolution Image generates the clipping path based on the actual file data instead of the preview image.

Stage 2 Importing and Formatting Text

Placing text is one of the most important aspects of page-layout software, whether you create the text directly within InDesign or import it from an external file. InDesign provides all the tools you need to format text, from choosing a font to automatically creating hanging punctuation.

CONTROL TEXT THREADING

Some layouts require only a few bits of text, while others include numerous pages. Depending on how much text you have to work with, you might place all the layout text in a single frame, or you might cut and paste different pieces of a single story into individual text frames. In other cases, you might thread text across multiple frames — maintaining the text as a single story but allowing flexibility in frame size and position.

1. In the open `poster.indd` file, use the Type tool to create a text frame that is 1″ high and 9″ wide (it fills the width between the margin guides).

2. Select the frame with the Selection tool and then use the Control panel to make sure the top edge of the text frame is positioned at Y: 11.25″.

When the Selection tool is active, you can use the Control panel to change the position and dimensions of a text frame.

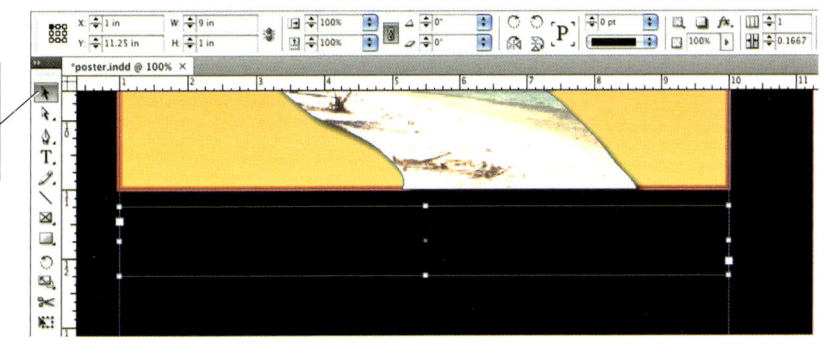

3. **Create three more text frames using the following parameters:**

Frame 2	X: 1″	W: 3.2″	Frame 4	X: 1″	W: 9″
	Y: 12.45″	H: 3.55″		Y: 16″	H: 0.5″
Frame 3	X: 5″	W: 5″			
	Y: 12.45″	H: 3.55″			

   Text Frame 1
   Text Frame 2
   Text Frame 3
   Text Frame 4

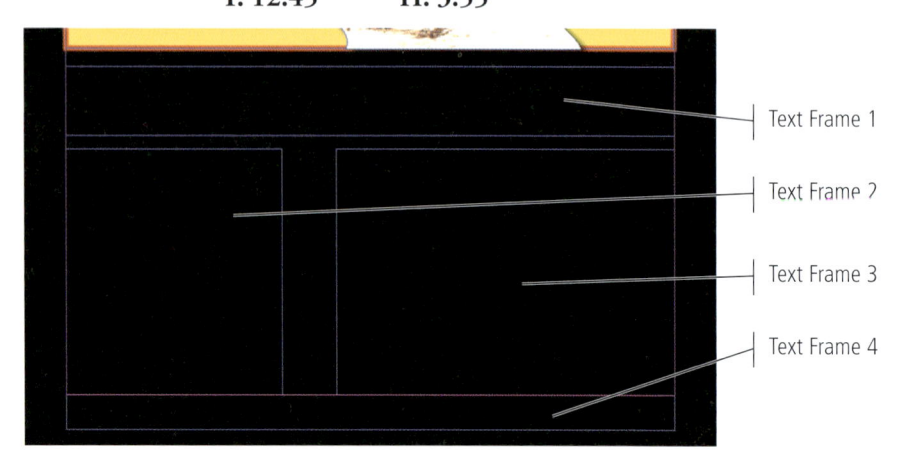

4. **Using the Selection tool, click in the white pasteboard area to deselect all the frames.**

5. **Choose File>Place. Navigate to the file named `jazzfest.doc` in the RF_InDesign>Jazz folder and click Open.**

   The cursor is loaded with the text file you selected.

   Note:

   If a frame were selected and the Replace Selected Item option checked, the text file would be placed directly into the selected frame.

6. **Click the loaded cursor in the first text frame.**

   Whenever a text frame is selected, you can see the In and Out ports that allow you to link one text frame to another. In this case, the Out port shows the **Overset Text icon**, indicating that the placed file has more text than can fit within the frame. The first linked text frame will not have an In port, but all other frames will have both In and Out ports.

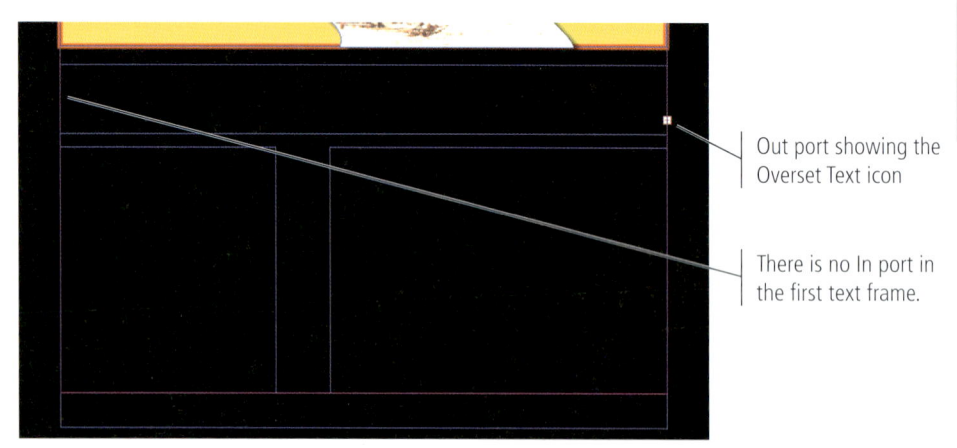

   Note:

   At this point, you can't see the text because text defaults to black, and your poster has a black background.

   Out port showing the Overset Text icon

   There is no In port in the first text frame.

7. **Using the Type tool, click anywhere in the first text frame.**

   When you click in a text frame with the Type tool, you see a flashing insertion point where you click (or in the top-left corner if there is no text in the frame). This insertion point marks the location where text will appear when you type or paste it into the document.

Project 2: Festival Poster

8. **Choose Edit>Select All to select all text in the frame (including the text that doesn't fit in the frame).**

   The Select All command selects all text in the story, whether that story exists in a single frame or threads across multiple frames. This command also selects overset text that doesn't fit into the current frame (or thread of frames).

   Note:

   If you see the Overset Text icon (the red plus sign), the story does not fit in the current frame (or series of frames). You should always correct overset text.

9. **In the Swatches panel, make sure the Text icon is selected at the top of the panel, and then click the Paper swatch.**

   In four-color (process) printing, there is no white ink. To achieve white, you have to remove the colors underneath the white areas, which is called a knockout. By removing or knocking out underlying colors, the paper shows through — whether white or some other color (e.g., if you print on yellow paper, knockout areas will show the yellow color). This is why InDesign refers to this swatch as "Paper" instead of "White."

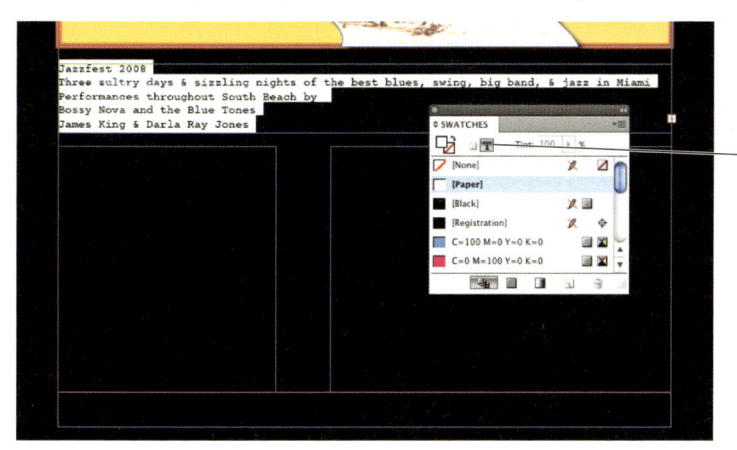

   This "T" icon means you are changing the text color instead of the object color.

10. **Using either Selection tool, click the Out port of the first text frame.**

    Clicking the Out port loads the cursor with the rest of the text in the story.

11. **Immediately click the second frame to link it to the first frame.**

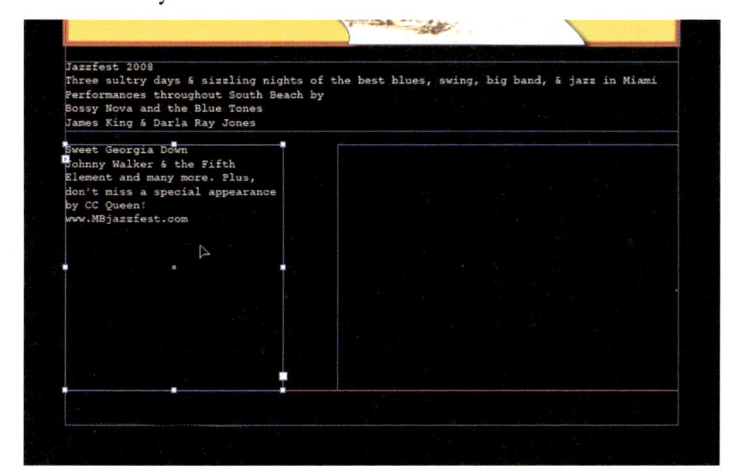

    Note:

    *Text that appears as a series of gray bars is called **greeked text**. By default, text smaller than 7 pt. (at 100%) is greeked to improve screen redraw time. You can change the greeking threshold in the Display Performance pane of the Preferences dialog box.*

    View percentage is part of the determination for greeking text; in other words, if your view percentage is 50%, 12-pt text appears as 6-pt text on screen, so it would be greeked using the default preferences.

12. **Repeat this process to link from the second frame to the third, and then from the third frame to the fourth.**

    You can define the thread of text frames even when there is no text to fill those frames. Simply use the Direct Selection tool to click the Out port of one frame, and then click the frame you want to add to the thread.

Project 2: Festival Poster   115

13. **Choose View>Show Text Threads.**

    As long as this option is toggled on, you see the thread arrows whenever one of the text frames in the thread is selected.

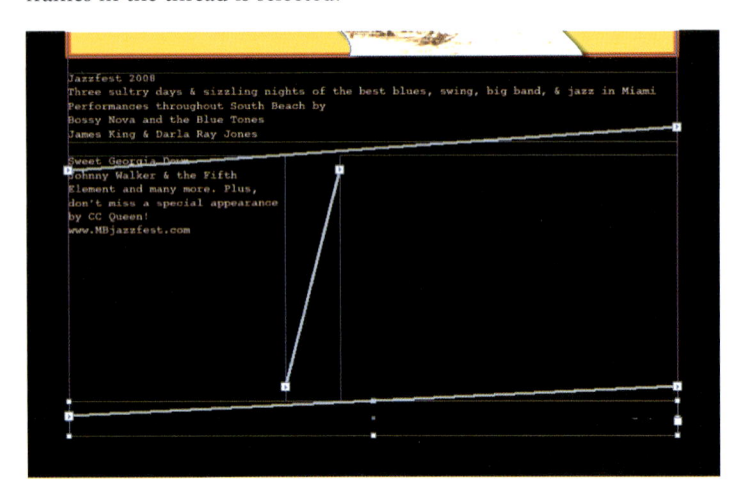

    Note:

    You can also press Command/Control while the Type tool is active to click a text-frame Out port and thread the frames.

14. **Save the file and continue to the next exercise.**

DEFINE MANUAL FRAME BREAKS

When you thread text from one frame to another (or to multiple columns in the same frame), you often need to control exactly where a story breaks from frame to frame. InDesign includes a number of commands for breaking text in precise locations.

1. **In the open `poster.indd` file, use the Type tool to click at the end of the first line (after "Jazzfest 2008") to place the insertion point.**

    As you complete the following exercises, feel free to zoom in as you think necessary to work with specific areas of a layout.

2. **Choose Type>Insert Break Character>Frame Break.**

    InDesign provides several special break characters that allow you to control the flow of text from line to line, from column to column, and from frame to frame. The Frame Break character forces all following text into the next frame in the thread.

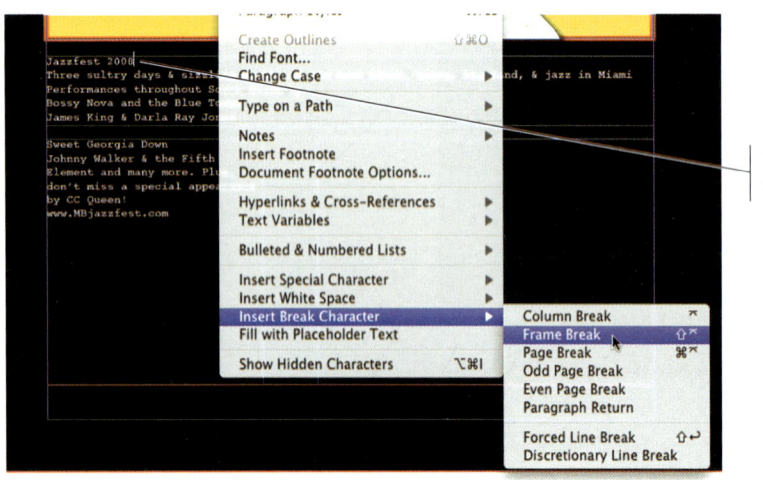

    The insertion point is at the end of the first paragraph.

116 Project 2: Festival Poster

3. **Choose Type>Show Hidden Characters.**

   When you placed the Frame Break character at the end of the first line, everything following was pushed to the next frame — including the paragraph return character that had been at the end of the first line.

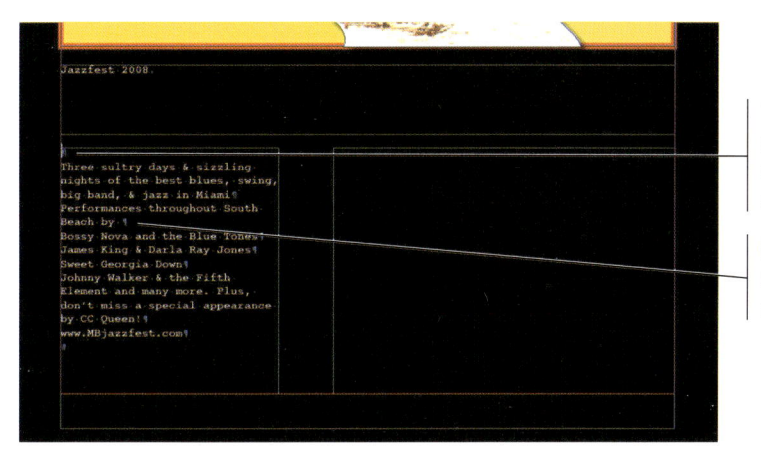

   The paragraph return that was at the end of the first paragraph is now the first paragraph in the second frame.

   Hidden characters include the paragraph return character, spaces, and the Frame Break character.

4. **With the insertion point flashing at the beginning of the second frame, press Forward Delete to remove the extra paragraph return.**

5. **With hidden characters visible, highlight the paragraph return character at the end of the first sentence in this frame (the second one).**

6. **Add another Frame Break character.**

   When text is highlighted — including hidden formatting characters — anything you type, paste, or enter using a menu command replaces the highlighted text.

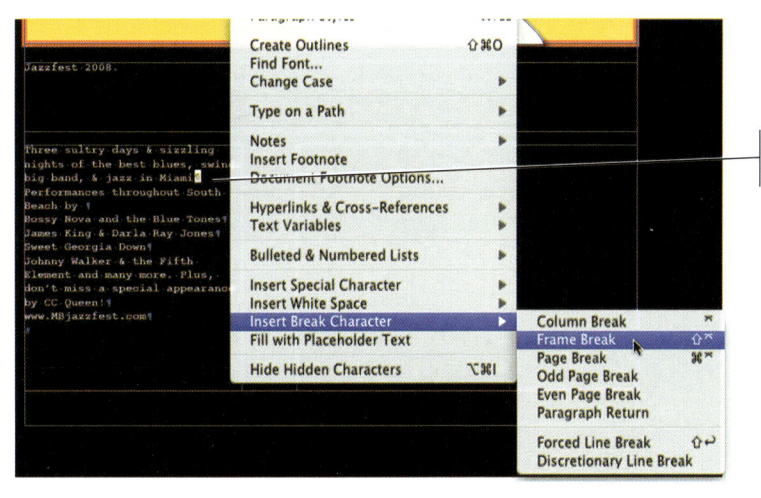

   Highlight this paragraph return character.

   Because the paragraph return was highlighted, the inserted Frame Break character replaces the paragraph return.

Note:

The Forward Delete key is the one directly below the Help key on most standard keyboards. If you are using a laptop, place the insertion point at the beginning of the first sentence in the second frame ("Three sultry days…") and press Delete/Backspace.

Project 2: Festival Poster

7. Use the same technique to move only the last paragraph (the Web address) into the fourth text frame.

Note:

Press Enter (numeric keypad) to add a Column Break.

Press Shift-Enter (numeric keypad) to add a Frame Break.

Press Command/Control-Enter (numeric keypad) to add a Page Break, which pushes all text to the first threaded frame on the next page.

Press Shift-Return/Enter to add a Line Break, which starts a new line without starting a new paragraph.

8. Save the file and continue to the next exercise.

Apply Character Formatting

Once text is in a frame, you can use character formatting attributes to determine the appearance of individual letters, such as the font and type size. These attributes can be controlled in the Character panel (Window>Type & Tables>Character) or the Control panel (depending on which options are visible in the Control panel; refer to Project 1 for information on changing the options that are available in the Control panel).

Note:

You can use the Up and Down Arrow keys to nudge paragraph and character style values when the insertion point is in a panel field.

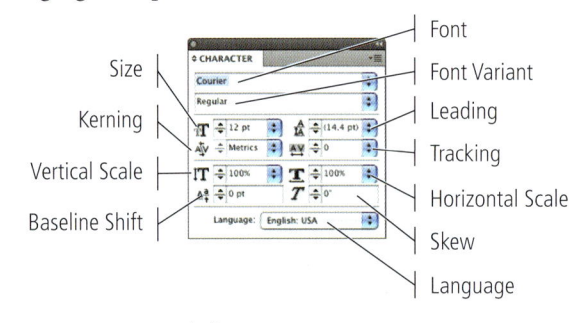

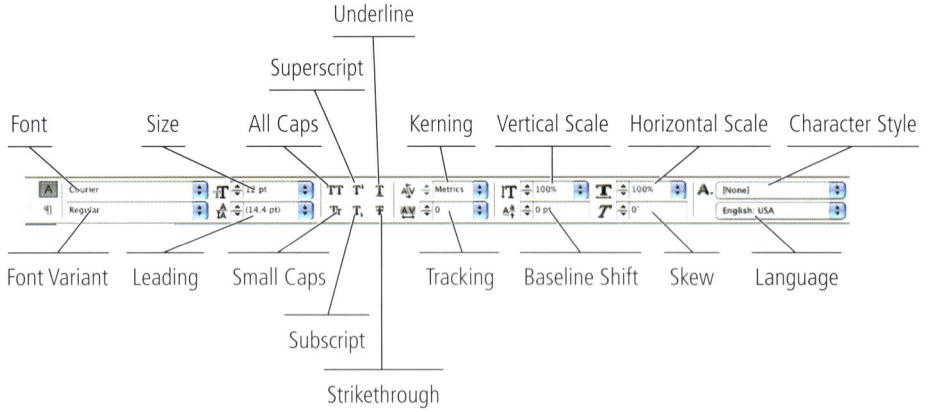

- A **font** contains all the characters (**glyphs**) that make up a typeface, including upper- and lowercase letters, numbers, special characters, etc. (Fonts must be installed and activated on your computer to be accessible in InDesign.)
- **Size** is the height of a typeface measured in points.

118   Project 2: Festival Poster

- **Leading** is the distance from one baseline to the next. InDesign treats leading as a character attribute, even though leading controls the space between lines of an individual paragraph. (Space between paragraphs is controlled using the Space Before/After options in the Paragraph panel.) To change leading for an entire paragraph, you must first select the entire paragraph. This approach means that you can change the leading for a single line of a paragraph by selecting any character(s) in that line; however, changing the leading for any character in a line applies the same change to the entire line that contains those characters.

- **Vertical Scale** and **Horizontal Scale** artificially stretch or contract the selected characters. This type of scaling is a quick way of achieving condensed or expanded type if those variations of a font don't exist.

- **Kerning** increases or decreases the space between pairs of letters. Kerning is used in cases where particular letters in specific fonts need to be manually adjusted to eliminate a too-tight or too-spread-out appearance. Manual kerning is usually necessary in headlines or other large type.

- **Tracking**, also known as "range kerning," refers to the overall tightness or looseness across a range of characters.

- **Baseline Shift** moves the selected type above or below the baseline by a specific number of points. Positive numbers move the characters up; negative values move the text down.

- **Skew** artificially slants the selected text, creating a false italic appearance. This option distorts the look of the type and should be used sparingly (if ever).

In addition to the options in the basic Character panel, several styling options are also available in the panel Options menu.

- **All Caps** changes all the characters to capital letters. This option only changes the appearance of the characters; they are not permanently converted to capital letters. To change the case of selected characters to all capital letters — the same as typing with Caps Lock turned on — use the Type>Change Case menu options.

- **Small Caps** artificially reduces the point size of a regular capital letter to a set percentage of that point size. If the font is an Open Type font that contains true small caps, InDesign uses the true small caps.

- **Superscript** and **Subscript** artificially reduce the selected character to a specific percentage of the point size; these options raise (for superscript) or lower (for subscript) the character from the baseline to a position that's a certain percentage of the leading. (The size and position of Superscript, Subscript, and Small Caps are controlled in the Advanced Type Preferences dialog box.)

- **Underline** places a line below the selected characters.

- **Strikethrough** places a line through the middle of selected characters.

- **Ligatures** are substitutes for certain pairs of letters, most commonly fi, fl, ff, ffi, and ffl. (Other pairs such as ct and st are common for historical typesetting, and ae and oe are used in some non-English-language typesetting.)

Note:

You can change this behavior by checking the Apply Leading to Entire Paragraph option in the Type Preferences dialog box.

Note:

Type that has been artificially condensed or expanded in this fashion looks bad — the scaling destroys the type's metrics. You should always use a condensed or expanded version of a typeface before resorting to horizontal or vertical scaling.

Note:

*Many commercial fonts have built-in kerning pairs, so you won't need to apply too much hands-on intervention with kerning. InDesign defaults to use the kerning values stored in the **font metrics**.*

Note:

*Tracking and kerning are applied in thousandths of an **em** (an em is technically defined as width that equals the type size).*

Note:

Choosing Underline Options or Strikethrough Options in the Character panel Options menu allows you to change the weight, offset, style, and color of the line for those styles.

1. With `poster.indd` open, triple-click the first line of text in the story to select it.

2. In the Control panel, click the Font menu and scroll to ATC Maple. Choose Ultra from the pop-up menu of font variations.

   There are three primary types of fonts: PostScript (Type 1), TrueType, and OpenType. InDesign identifies the font types with different icons in the Font menu.

   - **PostScript fonts** have two file components (outline and printer) that must both be available for successful output.
   - **TrueType fonts** have a single file, but (until recently) were primarily used on the Windows platform.
   - **OpenType fonts** are contained in a single file that can include more than 60,000 glyphs (characters) in a single font. OpenType fonts are cross-platform, which means the same font file can be used on both Macintosh and Windows systems.

   Note:

   There are other types of fonts, including PostScript Type 3 and Multiple Master, but these should generally be avoided.

3. Change the type size to 72 pt, and then click the All Caps button.

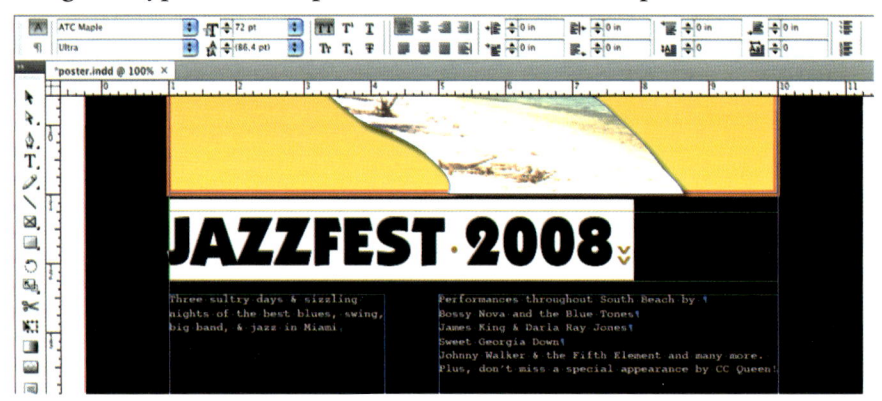

4. In the Character panel (Window>Type & Tables>Character), change the Tracking field to 200.

   Note:

   If you started with the Advanced workspace, or you modified the options in the Customize Control Panel dialog box, the Tracking control might be available in your Control panel. In any case, this option is always available in the Character panel.

Project 2: Festival Poster

5. **Click four times on the paragraph in the second frame to select the entire paragraph.**

    Clicking twice selects an entire *word*, clicking three times selects an entire *line*, and clicking four times selects the entire *paragraph*.

6. **Change the selected text to 34-pt ATC Pine Bold Italic.**

    Using these settings, the paragraph doesn't entirely fit within the available space (or at least, not yet). Because the frame is threaded, the paragraph flows into the third frame, and the rest of the text reflows accordingly.

    Note:

    Leave the Leading value at the automatic setting. By default, InDesign automatically applies leading as 120% of the type size.

7. **With the same text selected, change the Horizontal Scale field to 90%.**

    Horizontal and vertical scaling are useful for artificially stretching or contracting fonts that do not have a condensed or extended version. Be careful using these options, though, because the artificial scaling alters the character shapes and can make some fonts very difficult to read (especially at smaller sizes).

8. **Click three times to select the first line in the third frame, hold down the mouse button, and then drag down to select the other lines in the same frame.**

    When you triple-click to select an entire line, dragging up or down selects the entire lines above or below the one you first clicked.

9. **With all the text in the third frame selected, apply 22-pt ATC Pine Bold Italic with 90% horizontal scaling.**

Project 2: Festival Poster

10. Change the Web address in the fourth text frame to 26-pt ATC Maple Medium.

11. Save the file and continue to the next exercise.

APPLY PARAGRAPH FORMATTING

Paragraph formatting affects how your page looks and reads. Attributes that affect the entire paragraph — such as alignment, indents, and space before and after paragraphs — can be controlled in the Paragraph panel or the Control panel.

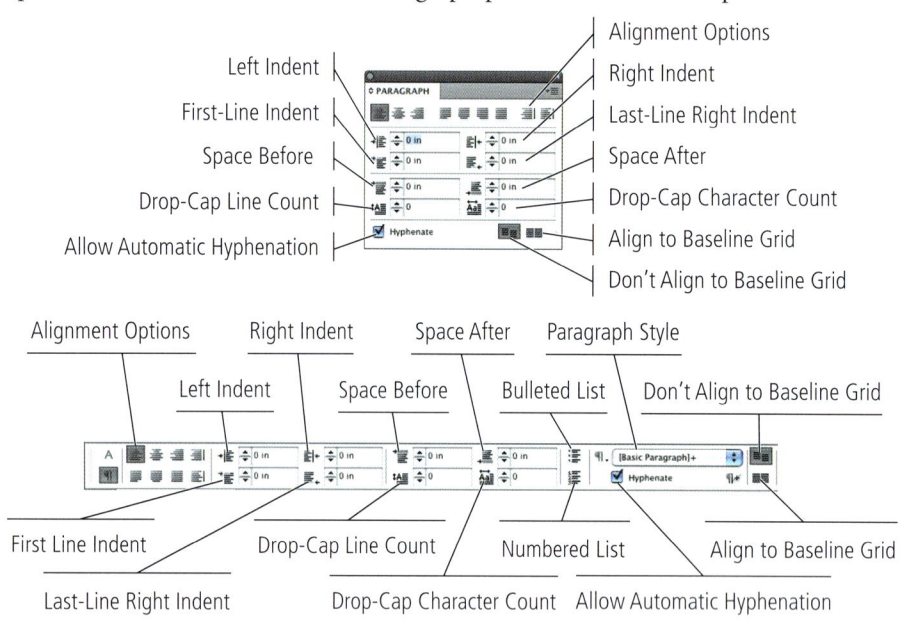

To apply paragraph formatting, you simply place the insertion point anywhere in a paragraph. Since paragraph formatting affects the entire paragraph, you don't have to select all the text manually.

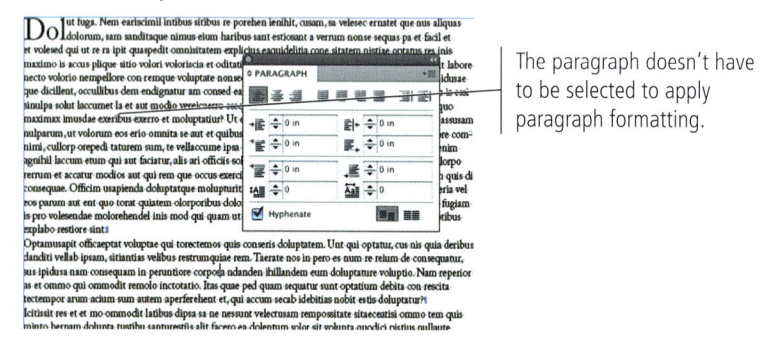

The paragraph doesn't have to be selected to apply paragraph formatting.

Project 2: Festival Poster

Understanding the Baseline Grid

The **baseline grid** is a type of non-printing guide, used for controlling and aligning type. You can show the baseline grid by choosing View>Grids & Guides>Show Baseline Grid. You'll see a series of light blue lines that extend down the entire page, placed at specific intervals.

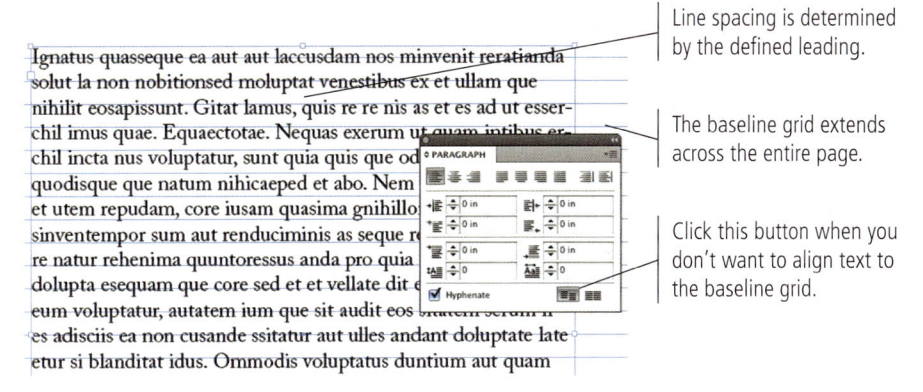

Line spacing is determined by the defined leading.

The baseline grid extends across the entire page.

Click this button when you don't want to align text to the baseline grid.

You can force paragraphs to align to the baseline grid, which overrides the defined leading.

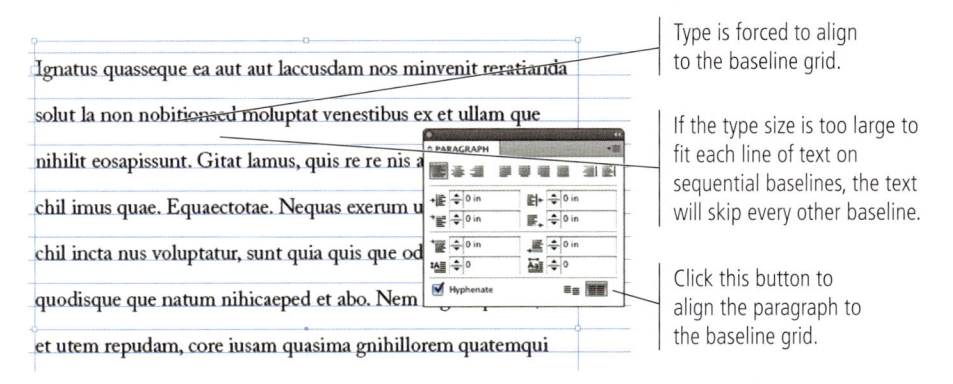

Type is forced to align to the baseline grid.

If the type size is too large to fit each line of text on sequential baselines, the text will skip every other baseline.

Click this button to align the paragraph to the baseline grid.

You can change the baseline grid in the Grids pane of the Preferences dialog box. The Start position can be relative to the top of the page (default) or to the top margin. You can also change the increment between lines (the default is approximately 1 pica). The View Threshold value determines the smallest view percentage at which the baseline grid will be visible.

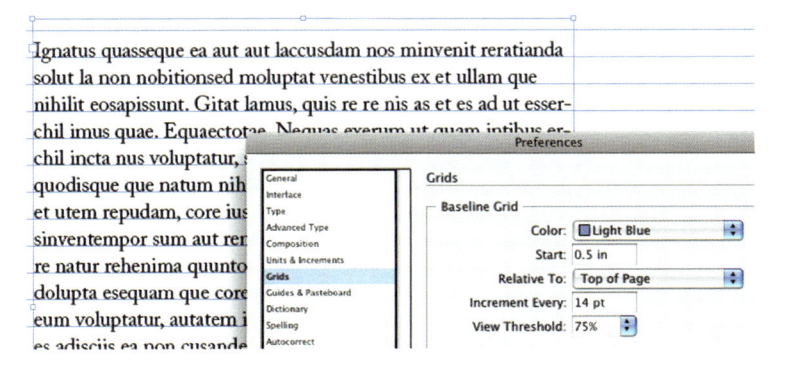

1. In the open `poster.indd` file, place the cursor anywhere in the paragraph in the second frame.

2. **In the Control panel, click the Right Paragraph Alignment button.**

   Paragraph formatting applies to the entire paragraph where the insertion point is placed, or to any paragraph that is entirely or partially selected. (A paragraph does not have to be entirely selected to change its paragraph formatting attributes.)

   Note:
   In InDesign, a paragraph is defined as all text between two paragraph return characters (¶), even if the paragraph exists on a single line.

   The insertion point is placed in this paragraph.

3. **Place the insertion point anywhere in the fourth frame (with the Web address) and apply centered paragraph alignment.**

4. **Place the insertion point in the last paragraph of the third frame and apply right paragraph alignment.**

5. **Select any part of the first through fifth lines in the third frame.**

6. **In the Control panel, change the Space Before Paragraph field to 0.09".**

   Space Before Paragraph

   These settings apply to any paragraph that is entirely or partially selected.

7. **Select any part of the second through fifth lines in the same frame and change the Left Indent field to 0.5".**

Left Indent

8. **Place the insertion point at the beginning of the sixth line (before the word "and") and press Return/Enter.**

   When you break an existing paragraph into a new paragraph, the attributes of the original paragraph are applied to the new paragraph.

   This is now a separate paragraph.

9. **Place the insertion point at the beginning of the fifth paragraph (before "Johnny") and press Delete/Backspace.**

Project 2: Festival Poster 125

10. **Press Return/Enter to separate the two paragraphs again.**

    This is an easy way to copy paragraph formatting from one paragraph to the next. When you re-separate the two paragraphs, the "Johnny" paragraph adopts the paragraph formatting attributes of the "Sweet Georgia Down" paragraph.

11. **Save the file and continue to the next exercise.**

USE OPTICAL MARGIN ALIGNMENT

At times, specific arrangements of text can cause a paragraph to appear out of alignment, even though it's technically aligned properly. Punctuation at the beginning or end of a line — such as quotation marks at the beginning of a line or the commas in lines four and five of the second text frame — often cause this kind of optical problem. InDesign includes a feature called Optical Margin Alignment to fix this type of problem.

1. **With `poster.indd` open, hide the text threads and hidden characters.**

    Although the paragraph is correctly right-aligned, the text in the second frame might appear misaligned because of the commas at the ends of lines three and four.

2. **Place the insertion point anywhere in the second text frame.**

3. **Open the Story panel (Window>Type & Tables>Story) and check the Optical Margin Alignment option.**

    When Optical Margin Alignment is turned on, punctuation marks move outside the text margins (either to the left for left-aligned text or right for right-aligned text). Moving punctuation outside the margins is often referred to as **hanging punctuation**.

    Note:

    You might want to turn on frame edges (View>Show Frame Edges) as you work on this exercise.

    The insertion point is in the text that was previously in the second frame.

4. **Place the insertion point in the first paragraph (the one that now infringes on the second frame).**

126   Project 2: Festival Poster

5. **Choose Ignore Optical Margin in the Paragraph panel Options menu.**

   The Optical Margin Alignment option applies to an entire story (including all text frames in the same thread), not just the selected paragraph. If necessary, you can manually turn this option off for individual paragraphs.

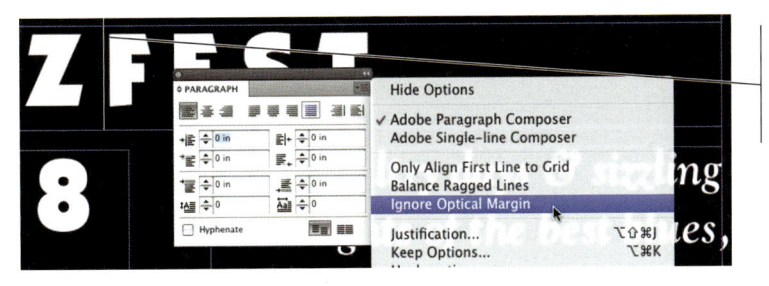

   The insertion point is in the first paragraph, which was thrown off by turning on the Optical Margin Alignment option.

6. **In the Story panel, change the Size field to 34 pt.**

   The field in the Story panel tells InDesign what size type needs to be adjusted. The best effect is usually created by defining the size of the type that needs adjustment.

   The commas now overhang the right margin.

7. **Save the file and continue to the next stage of the project.**

Copying Type Attributes with the Eyedropper Tool

INDESIGN FOUNDATIONS

You can use the Eyedropper tool to copy character and paragraph attributes (including text color), and then apply those attributes to other type.

To copy formatting from one piece of text to another, click with the Eyedropper tool on the formatting you want to copy. If any text is selected when you click the Eyedropper tool, the selected text is automatically re-formatted. If nothing is selected, the Eyedropper tool "loads" with the formatting attributes — the tool icon reverses directions and shows a small i-beam icon in the cursor.

The Eyedropper tool cursor when it is "loaded" with text formatting attributes

You can click the loaded Eyedropper tool on any text to change its formatting, or you can click and drag to format multiple paragraphs at once. As long as the Eyedropper tool remains selected, you can continue to select text to apply the same formatting. You can also change the formatting in the Eyedropper tool by pressing Option/Alt and clicking text with the new formatting attributes you want to copy.

By default, the Eyedropper tool copies all formatting attributes. You can change that behavior by double-clicking the tool in the Tools panel to access the Eyedropper Options dialog box. Simply uncheck the options you don't want to copy (including individual options in each category), and then click OK.

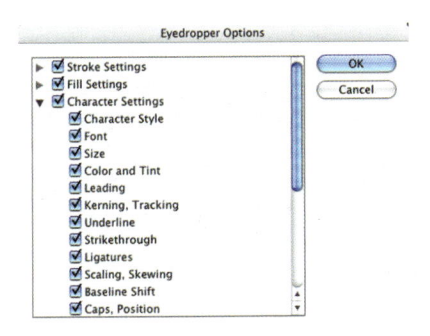

Project 2: Festival Poster 127

Stage 3 Graphics as Text and Text as Graphics

Now that you're familiar with the basic options for formatting characters and paragraphs, you can begin to add style to a layout using two techniques — flowing text along a path, and placing graphics inline with text. (There is, of course, much more to say about working with text than what you're doing in this project. You'll learn much more as you complete the rest of the projects in this book.)

PLACE INLINE GRAPHICS

The graphics frames you create on a page float over the other elements in the layout. You can position graphics frames over other objects to hide underlying elements, or you can apply a runaround so text will wrap around a picture box.

You can also place images as inline graphics, which means they are anchored to the text in the position you place them. If the text reflows within the text box, inline objects reflow with the text and maintain the correct position. This feature can be very useful for placing custom bullets (which you do in this exercise), or for a variety of other purposes where sidebar text needs to remain in proximity to the main body copy.

There are two methods for creating inline objects. For simple applications, such as a graphic bullet, you can simply place the graphic and format it as a text character. (An inline graphic is treated as a single text character in the story; it is affected by many of the paragraph-formatting commands, such as space before and after, tab settings, leading, and baseline position.) For more complex applications, you can use the options in the Object>Anchored Object menu.

1. **With poster.indd open, place the insertion point at the beginning of the second line in the third frame (before the word "Bossy").**

2. **Choose File>Place and navigate to note.ai in the RF_InDesign>Jazz folder.**

3. **Make sure the Replace Selected Item option is checked, and then click Open.**

   If the insertion point is flashing in a story when you place a graphic using the Replace Selected Item option, the graphic is automatically placed as an inline object.

The actual Space Before Paragraph value is unchanged.

The line spacing automatically adjusts to accommodate the placed image.

Note:

You can also select an existing object, cut or copy it, place the insertion point, and then paste the object inline where the insertion point flashes.

4. **Select the inline graphic with the Selection tool, and then scale the graphic and frame to 50% horizontally and vertically.**

   Although inline graphics are anchored to the text, they are still graphics contained in graphics frames. You can apply the same transformations to inline graphics that you would to any other placed graphic.

Note:

When you select the frame with the Selection tool, resizing the frame also resizes the frame content.

Use these fields to scale the placed graphic and the containing frame.

After you finalize the scaling, the fields show 100% when the frame is selected with the Selection tool.

Working with Anchored Objects

INDESIGN FOUNDATIONS

The Anchored Object Options dialog box controls the position of an anchored object relative to the frame in which it's placed. Anchored objects can be aligned inline (such as the bullets you created in the previous exercise) or above the line.

When an object is anchored using the Above Line option, the object can be anchored to the left, right, or center of the frame. If you're using facing pages, you can also choose Toward Spine or Away from Spine so that an anchored object will be placed in the appropriate position relative to the spread center (for example, all sidebars have to be on the inside edge, close to the spine). Finally, you can choose Text Alignment, which is the alignment applied to the paragraph (including indent values).

The Inline option aligns the object with the text baseline, adjusted by the Y Offset value.

The Above Line option moves the object above the line where the object is anchored.

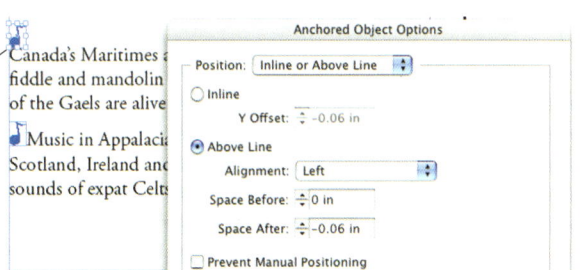

When you use the Above Line option, you can also define the space before and after the anchored object. The Space Before option defines the position of the object relative to the bottom of the previous line of text. A positive value moves the object (and the following text) down; a negative value moves the following text up toward the object. The Space After option defines the position of the object relative to the first character in the line below the object. A positive value moves the following text down, and a negative value moves the following text up.

When you work with anchored objects, you can use the Selection tool to drag the object up or down (in other words, change its position relative to the text to which it's anchored). If the Prevent Manual Positioning option is checked, you can't drag the anchored object in the layout.

Project 2: Festival Poster 129

5. **Choose Object>Anchored Object>Options.**

6. **Make sure the Inline option is checked, and then change the Y Offset field to −0.07".**

   A negative number moves the anchored object down; a positive number moves the anchored object up.

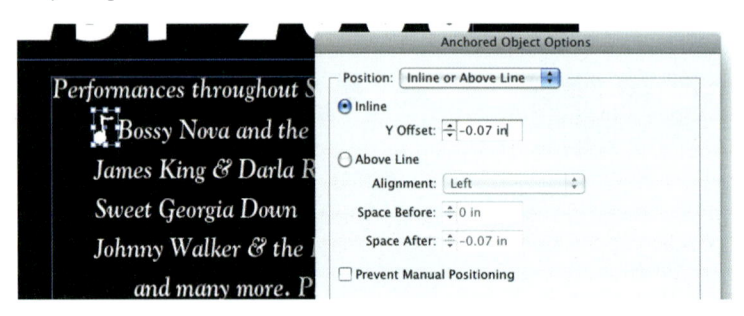

7. **Click OK, and then place the insertion point between the anchored object and the letter "B."**

Anchored Object Size and Text Position

INDESIGN FOUNDATIONS

When an anchored object is larger than the defined leading for the text in which it is placed, it might appear that changing the Y Offset values moves the text instead of the anchored object. In a way, this is true, because the text will move until it reaches the defined leading value; after that, greater changes will move the object and not the text.

Default text position without the anchored object

Text position after placing the anchored object.

Adjusting the anchored object position allows the text to move back into its original place based on the defined leading and paragraph spacing.

Adjusting the anchored object farther moves the actual object.

130 Project 2: Festival Poster

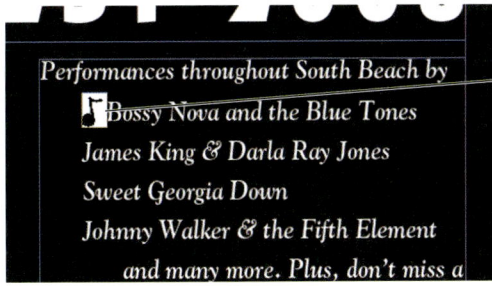

8. **Press Shift-Left Arrow key to select the anchored object, and then copy the highlighted object/character.**

An anchored graphic can be selected just as you would select any other text character.

Custom Anchor Options

For complex applications — such as moving an anchored object outside a text frame — you can choose Custom in the Anchored Object Options Position menu.

The **Relative to Spine** option, which aligns objects based on the center spread line, is only available if your layout has facing pages. When selected, objects on one side of a spread (such as a sidebar in the outside margin) remain on the outside margin even if the text reflows to a facing page.

The **Anchored Object Reference Point** defines the location on the object that you want to align to the location on the page.

The **Anchored Position Reference Point** defines the page location where you want to anchor an object.

The **X Relative To** field defines what you want to use as the basis for horizontal alignment — Anchor Marker, Column Edge, Text Frame, Page Margin, or Page Edge. The **X Offset** setting moves the object left or right.

The **Y Relative To** field specifies how the object aligns vertically — Line (Baseline), Line (Cap Height), Line (Top of Leading), Column Edge, Text Frame, Page Margin, Page Edge. The **Y Offset** setting moves the object up or down.

When the **Keep Within Top/Bottom Column Boundaries** is checked, the anchored object stays inside the text column if reflowing the text would otherwise cause the object to move outside the boundaries (for example, outside the top edge of the frame if the anchoring text is the first line in a column). This option is only available when you select a line option such as Line (Baseline) for Y Relative To.

You can manually reposition a custom-anchored object by simply dragging the anchored object with the Selection tool. You can also review the anchored position by choosing View>Show Text Threads.

The anchored object is outside the text frame; it is positioned with custom values.

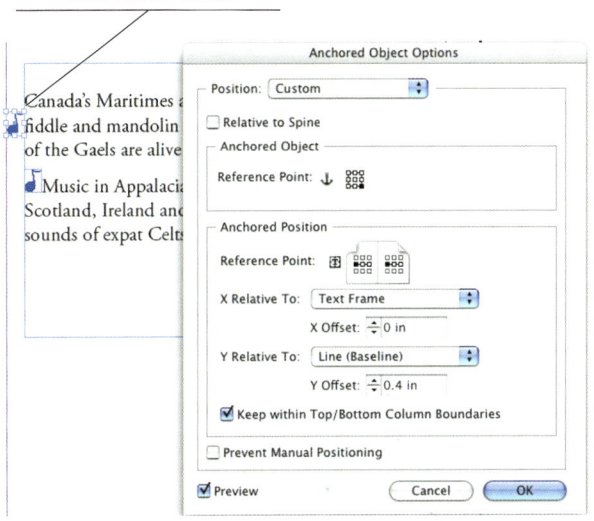

When text threads are showing, a dashed blue line indicates the position of anchored objects.

Creating Anchored Placeholders

If you want to create an anchored object but don't yet have the content, you can use the Object>Anchored Object>Insert option to define the placeholder object.

This dialog box allows you to create a frame (unassigned, graphics, or text) of a specific size, and even apply object and paragraph styles (if those exist). The Position options are the same as those in the Anchored Object Options dialog box. (You can always resize and reposition the anchored object later.)

Project 2: Festival Poster

9. **Place the insertion point at the beginning of the next paragraph and paste the copied object.**

10. **Paste the anchored graphic again at the beginning of the next two paragraphs.**

11. **Save the file and continue to the next exercise.**

CREATE TYPE ON A PATH

Instead of simply flowing text into a frame, you can also create unique typographic effects by flowing text onto a path. A text path can be any shape that you can create in InDesign, whether created with one of the basic shape tools, a complex graphic you drew with the Pen tool, or a path created by converting a clipping path to a frame.

1. **With poster.indd open, place the file text_path.tif from the RF_InDesign>Jazz folder in the layout and position it at X: 0″, Y: 0″.**

   When this image is loaded into the cursor, click outside the defined bleed area to place the image and not replace the content in one of the existing frames. Then use the Control panel to position the image correctly. (This image is simply a guide that you will use to create the shape of the text path for this exercise.)

2. **Choose the Pen tool. Change the stroke value to 1-pt Magenta (C=0 M=100 Y=0 K=0) and change the fill value to None.**

   Because the line in the placed image is black, you're using magenta so you can differentiate your line from the one in the image.

3. **Using the Pen tool, click once on the left end of the line in the placed image.**

   This first click anchors the first point of the path you're drawing.

4. **Click about half way between the point you just set and the topmost arc of the curve, and then drag right to create handles for the second anchor point.**

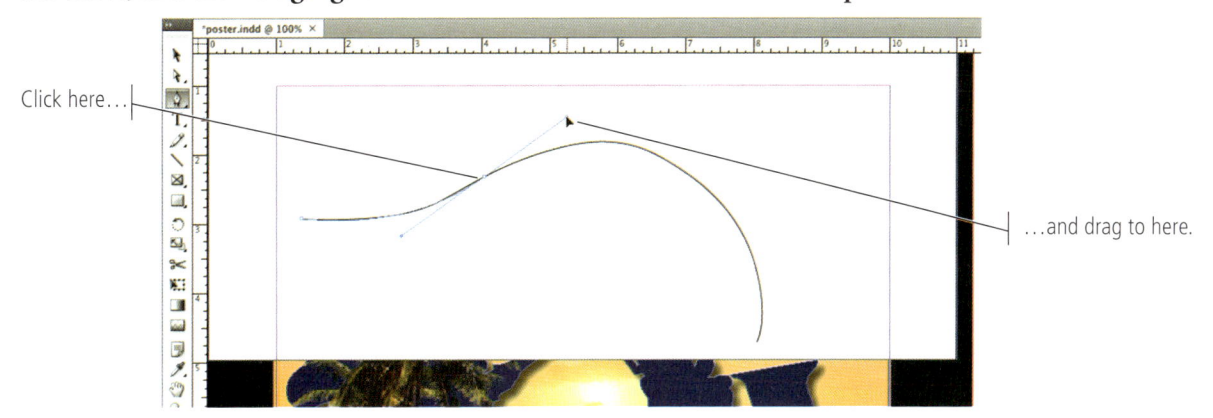

Click here…

…and drag to here.

5. **Click again near the middle of the arc on the right, and then drag to create handles for the point.**

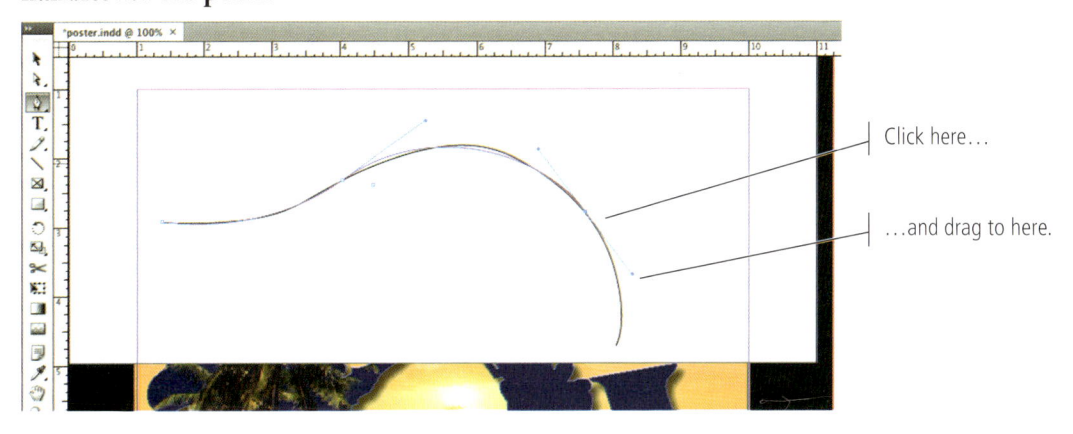

Click here…

…and drag to here.

6. **Click a final time on the right end of the line.**

   Don't worry if your path isn't perfect the first time; you can always edit the anchor points and handles with the Direct Selection tool.

7. **Using the Direct Selection tool, drag the handles of the two middle anchor points until your line closely resembles the one in the placed image.**

8. **Choose the Type on a Path tool. Move the cursor near the path until the cursor shows a small plus sign in the icon, and then click the path.**

   This action converts the line from a regular path to a type path.

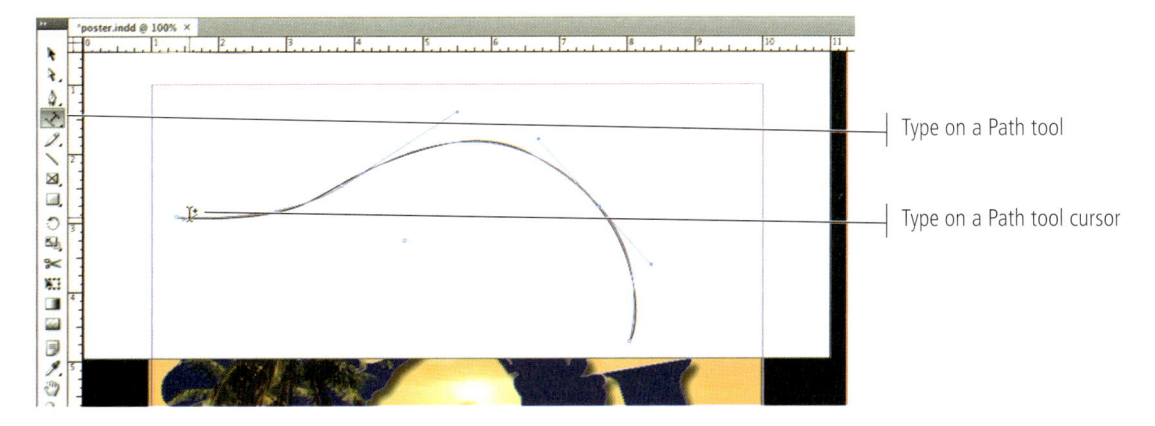

Type on a Path tool

Type on a Path tool cursor

Project 2: Festival Poster   133

9. Type **Move your feet to the beat!**.

10. **Format the path type as 49-pt ATC Maple Ultra.**

11. **Delete the text_path.tif image you used as a guide.**

12. **Click the text path line with the Selection tool to select it.**

When the path is selected, the Swatches panel defaults to show attributes of the path (not the type).

Note:

When a text path has no stroke color, you can still view the path by choosing View>Show Frame Edges.

Type on a Path Options

You can control the appearance of type on a path by choosing Type>Type on a Path>Options. You can apply one of five effects, change the alignment of the text to the path, flip the text to the other side of the path, and adjust the character spacing around curves (higher Spacing values remove more space around sharp curves).

- The **Rainbow** (default) effect keeps each character's baseline parallel to the path.
- The **Skew** effect maintains the vertical edges of type while skewing horizontal edges around the path.
- The **3D Ribbon** effect maintains the horizontal edges of type while rotating the vertical edges to be perpendicular to the path.
- The **Stair Step** effect aligns the left edge of each character's baseline to the path.
- The **Gravity** effect aligns the center of each character's baseline to the path, keeping vertical edges in line with the path's center.

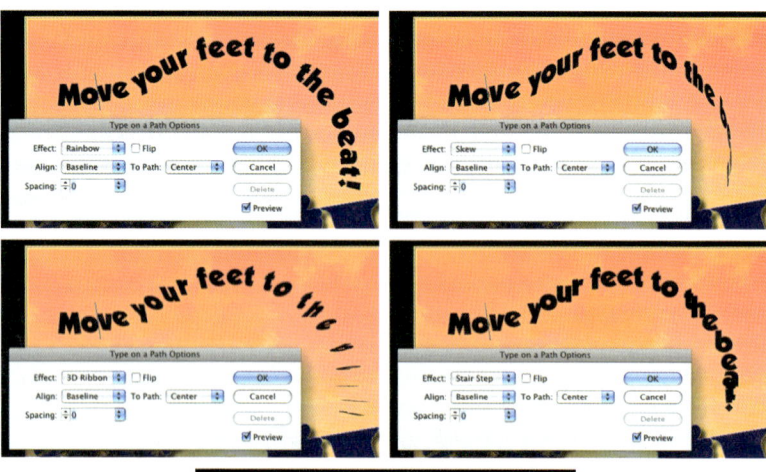

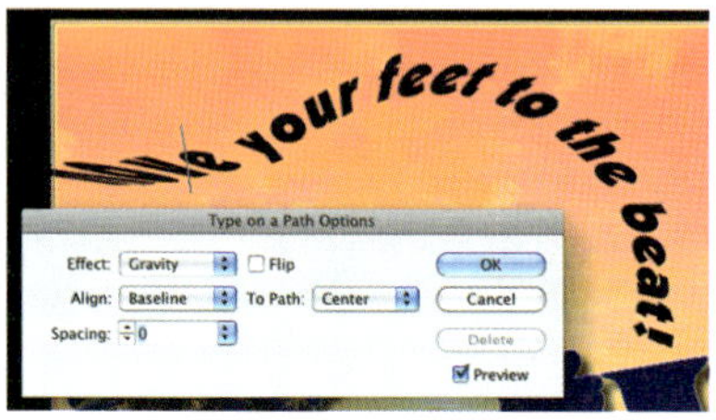

The **Align options** determine which part of the text (Baseline, Ascender, Descender, or Center) aligns to which part of the path (Top, Bottom, or Center).

INDESIGN FOUNDATIONS

Project 2: Festival Poster

13. **In the Swatches panel, change the object's fill and stroke values to None.**

    A text path can have a fill and stroke value just like any other path.

14. **Click the Text Color button at the top of the Swatches panel, and then click the rich black swatch (C=0 M=40 Y=0 K=100) to change the text color.**

    You don't have to select the actual text on a path to change its color. You can use the buttons at the top of the Swatches panel to change the color attributes of either the path or the text.

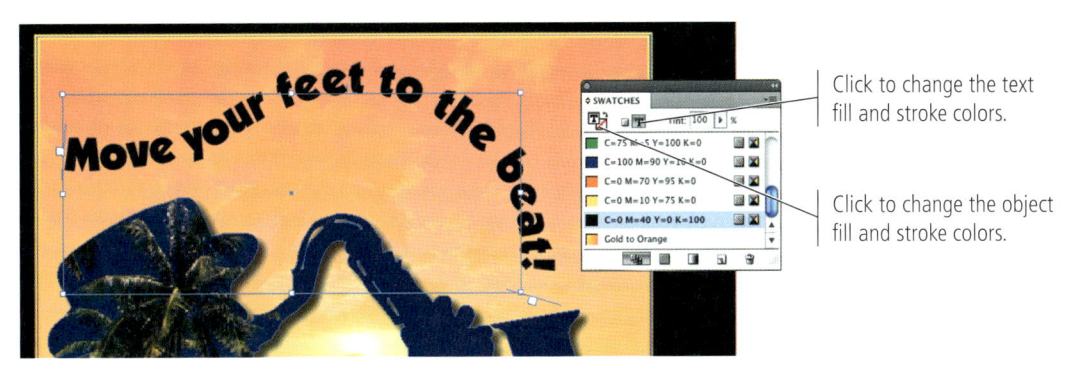

    Click to change the text fill and stroke colors.

    Click to change the object fill and stroke colors.

15. **Click the bar at the left edge of the text path and drag right about 1/4".**

    When you release the mouse button, the left edge of the text moves to the point where you dragged the line. This marks the orientation point of the text on the path.

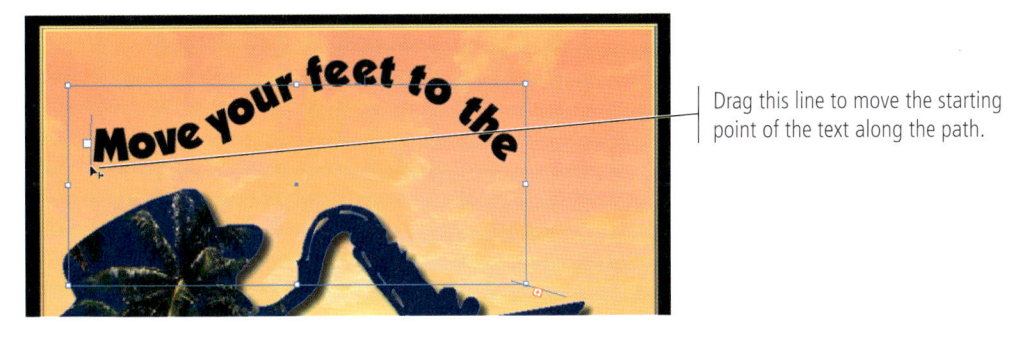

    Drag this line to move the starting point of the text along the path.

16. **Press Command/Control-Z to return the orientation point to the left end of the line.**

17. **Place the insertion point in the text path and apply right paragraph alignment.**

    You can control paragraph formatting on a path just as you can format paragraphs in a frame.

18. **Save the file and continue to the final stage of the project.**

Stage 4 Outputting the File

If your layout contains transparency or effects, those transparent areas will typically need to be flattened for output. **Flattening** divides transparent artwork into the necessary vector and raster objects. Transparent objects are flattened according to the settings in the selected flattener preset, which you choose in the Advanced options of the Print dialog box (or in the dialog box that appears when you export as PDF, EPS, or another format).

When you work with transparency, InDesign converts affected objects to a common color space (either CMYK or RGB) so transparent objects of different color spaces can blend properly. To avoid color mismatches between different areas of the objects on screen and in print, the blending space is applied for screen and in the flattener. You can define which space to use in the Edit>Transparency Blend Space menu; for print jobs, make sure the CMYK option is selected.

Flattener Presets

InDesign includes three default flattener presets:

- **Low Resolution** works for desktop proofs that will be printed on low-end black-and-white printers and for documents that will be published on the Web.
- **Medium Resolution** works for desktop proofs and print-on-demand documents that will be printed on PostScript-compatible color printers.
- **High Resolution** works for commercial output on a printing press and for high-quality color proofs.

You can create your own flattener presets by choosing Edit>Transparency Flattener Presets and clicking New in the dialog box. You can also use the Transparency Flattener Presets dialog box to load flattener presets created on another machine — such as one your service provider created for their specific output device and/or workflow.

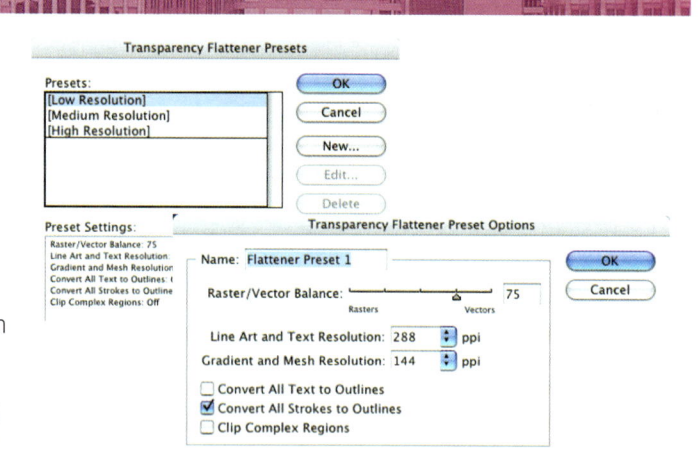

- The preset **Name** will be listed in the related output menus. You should use names that suggest the preset's use, such as "PDF for XL Printing Company." (Using meaningful names is a good idea for any asset that can have a name — from color swatches to output presets. "My Preset 12" is meaningless, possibly even to you after a few days, while "Preset for HP Indigo" tells you exactly when to use those settings.)
- **Raster/Vector Balance** determines how much vector information will be preserved when artwork is flattened. This slider ranges from 0 (all information is flattened as rasters) to 100 (maintains all vector information).
- **Line Art and Text Resolution** defines the resulting resolution of vector elements that will be rasterized, up to 9600 ppi. For good results in commercial printing applications, this option should be at least 600–1200 ppi (ask your output provider what settings they prefer you to use).
- **Gradient and Mesh Resolution** defines the resolution for gradients that will be rasterized, up to 1200 ppi. This option should typically be set to 300 ppi for most commercial printing applications.
- **Convert All Text to Outlines** converts all type to outline shapes; the text will not be editable in a PDF file.
- **Convert All Strokes to Outlines** converts all strokes to filled paths.
- **Clip Complex Regions** forces boundaries between vector objects and rasterized artwork to fall along object paths, reducing potential problems that can result when only part of an object is rasterized.

Export a PDF File for Print

1. **In the open `poster.indd` file, choose File>Export.**

2. **In the Export dialog box, navigate to your WIP>Jazz folder as the destination and choose Adobe PDF in the Format/Save As Type menu.**

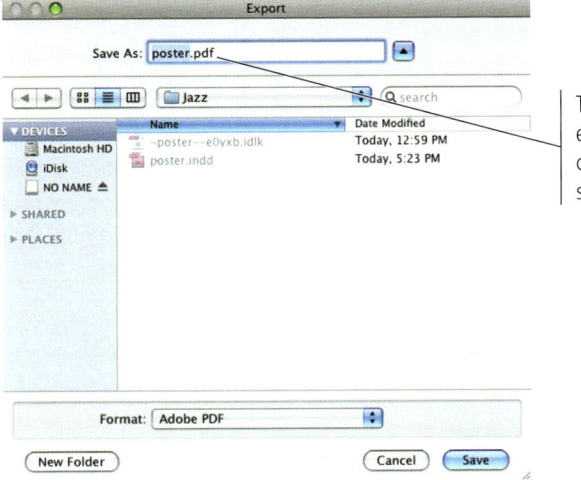

   The file name defaults to the existing name, but with the correct extension for the selected format.

3. **Click Save.**

   Before the PDF is saved, you have to define the settings that will be used to generate the PDF file.

Using the Flattener Preview Panel

INDESIGN FOUNDATIONS

Because of the potential problems that can arise when transparent elements are flattened, you can use the Flattener Preview panel (Window>Output>Flattener Preview) to highlight areas that will be affected by flattening. If you are working on a layout with multiple pages or spreads, you can apply different flattener settings to individual spreads by displaying a specific spread, and then choosing Spread Flattening in the Pages panel Options menu.

You can highlight different kinds of areas and determine which flattener preset to use. Clicking Refresh displays a new preview based on your settings. You can also choose Auto Refresh Highlight.

- **None** displays the normal layout.
- **Rasterized Complex Regions** highlights areas that will be rasterized based on the Raster/Vector Balance defined in the applied preset.
- **Transparent Objects** highlights objects with opacity of less than 100%, objects with blending modes, objects with transparent effects (such as drop shadows), and objects with feathering.
- **All Affected Objects** highlights all objects affected by transparency, including the transparent objects and the objects overlapped by transparent objects. All of these objects will be affected by flattening.
- **Affected Graphics** highlights all placed image files affected by transparency.
- **Outlined Strokes** highlights all strokes that will be converted to filled objects when flattened.
- **Outlined Text** highlights all text that will be converted to outlines when flattened.
- **Raster-Fill Text and Strokes** highlights text and strokes that will have rasterized fills as a result of flattening.
- **All Rasterized Regions** highlights objects (and parts of objects) that will be rasterized when flattened.

Project 2: Festival Poster

4. **Choose High Quality Print in the Adobe PDF Preset menu.**

   The Adobe PDF Preset menu includes six PDF presets that meet common industry output requirements.

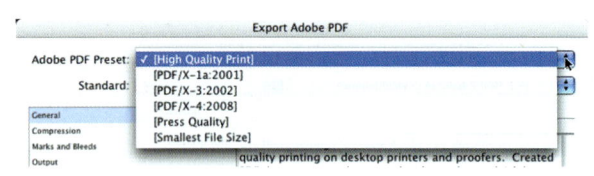

   Because there are so many ways to create a PDF — and not all of those ways are optimized for the needs of commercial printing — the potential benefits of the file format are often undermined. The PDF/X specification was created to help solve some of the problems associated with bad PDF files entering the prepress workflow. PDF/X is a subset of PDF that is specifically designed to ensure files have the information necessary for the digital prepress output process. Ask your output provider whether you should apply a PDF/X standard to your files, and if so, which version to use.

   Note:

   You can manage PDF Presets by choosing File>Adobe PDF Presets>Define. The dialog box that appears lists the built-in presets, as well as any presets you have created. You can also import presets from other users or export presets to send to other users.

   The Compatibility menu determines which version of the PDF format you will create. This is particularly important if your layout uses transparency. PDF 1.3 does not support transparency, so the file will require flattening. If you save the file to be compatible with PDF 1.4 or later, transparency information will be maintained in the PDF file.

5. **Review the options in the General pane.**

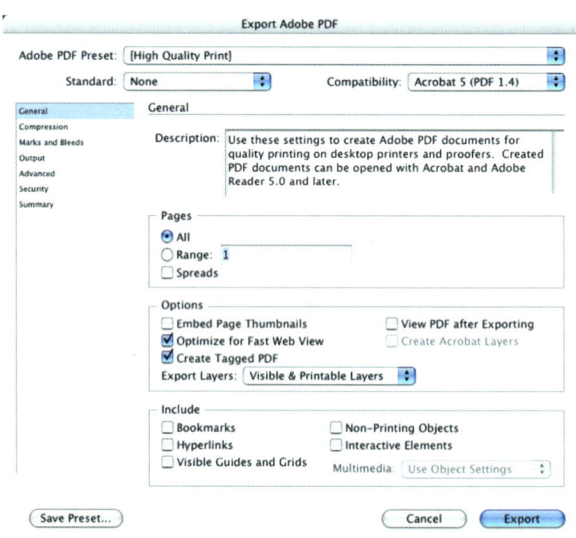

   - **Pages** options determine which pages to output, and whether to output facing pages on a single page.
   - **Embed Page Thumbnails** creates a thumbnail for each page being exported, or one thumbnail for each spread if the Spreads option is selected.
   - **Optimize for Fast Web View** optimizes the PDF file for faster viewing in a Web browser by allowing the file to download one page at a time.
   - **Create Tagged PDF** automatically tags elements based on a subset of Acrobat tags (including basic formatting, lists, and more).
   - **View PDF after Exporting** opens the PDF file after it has been created.
   - **Create Acrobat Layers** saves each InDesign layer as an Acrobat layer within the PDF. Printer's marks are exported to a separate marks and bleeds layer. (Create Acrobat Layers is only available only when Compatibility is set to Acrobat 6 (PDF 1.5) or later.)
   - **Export Layers** determines whether you are outputting All Layers (including hidden and non-printing layers), Visible Layers (including non-printing layers), or Visible & Printable Layers.
   - **Include** options can be used to include specific non-printing elements.

Project 2: Festival Poster

6. **Review the Compression options.**

   The compression options determine what and how much data will be included in the PDF file. This set of options is one of the most important when creating PDFs, since too-low resolution results in bad-quality printing, and too-high resolution results in extremely long download times.

   Before you choose compression settings, you need to consider your final goal. If you're creating a file for commercial printing, resolution is more important than file size. If your goal is a PDF that will be posted on the Web, file size is equally (if not more) important than pristine image quality.

   You can define a specific compression scheme for color, grayscale, and monochrome images. Different options are available depending on the image type:

   - **JPEG compression** options are lossy, which means data is thrown away to create a smaller file. When you use one of the JPEG options, you can also define an Image Quality option (from Low to Maximum).
   - **ZIP compression** is lossless, which means all file data is maintained in the compressed file.
   - **CCITT compression** was initially developed for fax transmission. Group 3 supports two specific resolution settings (203 × 98 dpi and 203 × 196 dpi). Group 4 supports resolution up to 400 dpi.
   - **Run Length Encoding** (RLE) is a lossless compression scheme that abbreviates sequences of adjacent pixels. If four pixels in a row are black, RLE saves that segment as "four black" instead of "black-black-black-black."

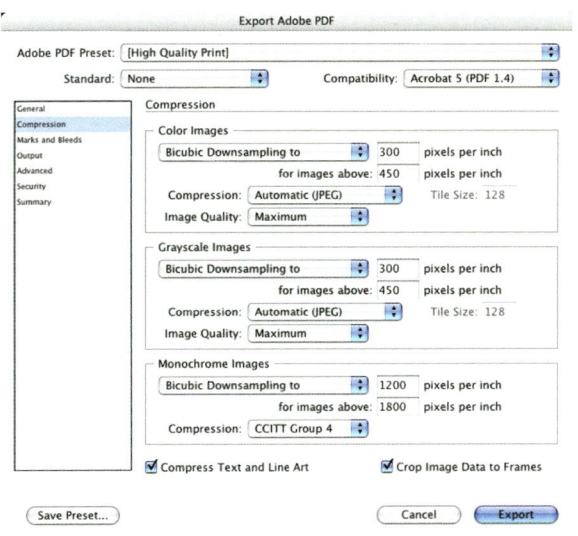

   Note:

   Since you chose the High Quality Print preset, these options default to settings that will produce the best results for most commercial printing applications.

Resolution Options for PDF

When you resize an image in the layout, you are changing its effective resolution. The **effective resolution** of an image is the resolution calculated after any scaling has been taken into account. This number is equally — and sometimes more — important than the original image resolution. The effective resolution can be calculated with a fairly simple equation:

   Original resolution / (% magnification / 100) = Effective resolution

If a 300-ppi image is magnified 150%, the effective resolution is:

   300 ppi / 1.5 = 200 ppi

If you reduce the same 300-ppi image to 50%, the effective resolution is:

   300 ppi / 0.5 = 600 ppi

In other words, the more you enlarge a raster image, the lower its effective resolution becomes. Reducing an image results in higher effective resolution, which can result in unnecessarily large PDF files.

When you create a PDF file, you also specify the resolution that will be maintained (for each of the three image types) in the resulting PDF file. The Resolution option is useful if you want to throw away excess resolution for print files, or if you want to create low-resolution files for proofing or Web distribution.

- **Do Not Downsample** maintains all the image data from the linked files in the PDF file.
- **Average Downsampling To** reduces the number of pixels in an area by averaging areas of adjacent pixels. Apply this method to achieve user-defined resolution (typically 72 or 96 dpi for Web-based files or 300 dpi for print files).
- **Subsampling To** applies the center pixel value to surrounding pixels. If you think of a 3 × 3-block grid, subsampling enlarges the center block (pixel) — and thus, its value — in place of the surrounding eight blocks.
- **Bicubic Downsampling To** creates the most accurate pixel information for continuous-tone images. This option also takes the longest to process, and it produces a softer image. To understand how this option works, think of a 2 × 2-block grid — bicubic downsampling averages the value of all four of those blocks (pixels) to interpolate the new information.

7. In the Marks and Bleed options, check the Crop Marks option and change the Offset field to **0.125″** (1/8″). Check the Use Document Bleed Settings option.

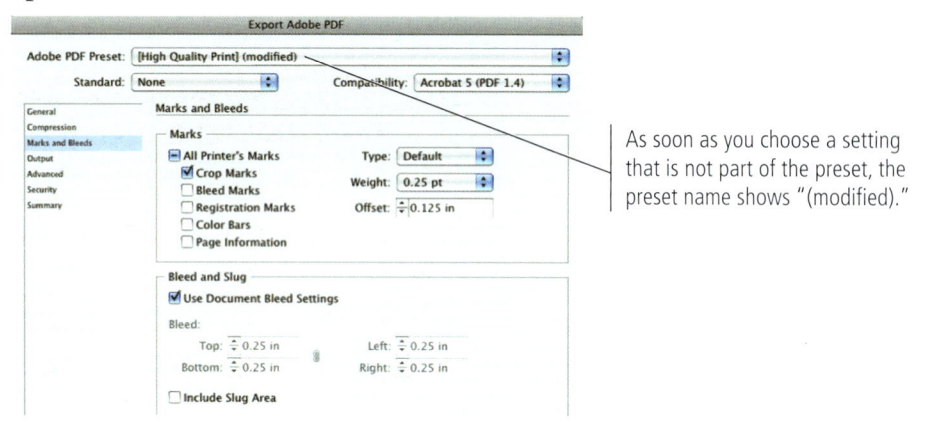

As soon as you choose a setting that is not part of the preset, the preset name shows "(modified)."

8. In the Compatibility menu, choose Acrobat 4 (PDF 1.3).

9. In the Advanced options, choose High Resolution in the Transparency Flattener Preset menu.

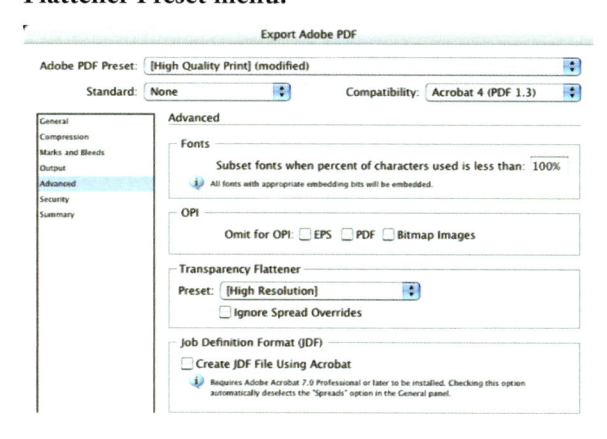

Note:

The Output options relate to color management, which you will use in Project 6. The Security options allow you to add password protection to a PDF file.

10. Click the Save Preset button in the bottom-left corner of the dialog box. Name the new preset **High Quality Print - Flattened**.

11. Click OK to close the Save Preset dialog box, and then click Export to create your PDF file. If you see a warning message, click OK.

    Your PDF file will be flattened, so some features (hyperlinks, bookmarks, etc.) will be unavailable. You didn't use those features in this project, however, so you don't have to worry about this warning.

12. When the spooling window (Generating PDF) closes, your file is complete. Close the InDesign file.

Project Review

fill in the blank

1. The _____ tool can be used to draw the direction and position of a gradient within a frame.

2. The _____ menu command reveals characters such as paragraph returns and tabs.

3. _____ is the space between specific pairs of letters. To change this value, you have to place the insertion point between two characters.

4. The _____ is the theoretical line on which the bottoms of letters rest.

5. The _____ indicates that more text exists in the story than will fit into the available frame (or series of linked frames).

6. The _____ can be used to copy type formatting from one type element to another.

7. The _____ panel is used to apply optical margin alignment.

8. _____ are objects that are attached to specific areas of text.

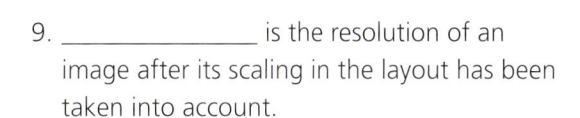

9. _____ is the resolution of an image after its scaling in the layout has been taken into account.

10. _____ compression for color and grayscale raster images is lossy, which means data is thrown away to reduce the file size.

short answer

1. Briefly explain how transparency is applied to objects in an InDesign page layout.

2. Briefly define a clipping path; provide at least two examples of how they might be useful.

3. Briefly explain the differece between character formatting and paragraph formatting.

Project 2: Festival Poster   141

Portfolio Builder Project

Use what you learned in this project to complete the following freeform exercise.
Carefully read the art director and client comments, then create your own design to meet the needs of the project.
Use the space below to sketch ideas; when finished, write a brief explanation of your reasoning behind your final design.

art director comments

The former marketing director for the Miami Jazz Festival recently moved to California to be the director of the Laguna Beach Sawdust Festival. She was pleased with your work on the jazz festival project, and would like to hire you to create the advertising for next year's art festival event.

To complete this project, you should:

❏ Develop some compelling visual element that will be the central focus of the ads.

❏ Create an ad that fits on a tabloid-size newspaper page (9 1/2 × 11 1/2″ with no bleeds).

❏ Create a second version of the same ad to fit a standard magazine trim size (8 1/4 × 10 7/8″ with 1/8″ bleeds).

client comments

The Sawdust Festival is one of the longest running and well-known art shows in California, maybe even the entire United States. We're planning our advertising campaign for the 2010 summer.

You might want to poke around our Web site to get some ideas. There's information about the festival's history, as well as images from previous shows.

We need an ad that will be placed in the pull-out sections of regional newspapers, and another version of the same ad that can go into magazines for travel/tourism audiences (like the WestWays magazine from AAA). Both ads should be four-color, although you should keep in mind the basic color scheme that we use on our Web site.

The ads need to have all the relevant information (we sent you the text, in the RF_Builders>Sawdust folder). But just as important, we want the ad to be art in its own right; the visual element you create will actually be repurposed for festival souvenirs like shirts, posters, and so on.

project justification

Project Summary

This project combined form and function — presenting the client's information in a clear, easy-to-read manner, while using large graphic elements to grab the viewer's attention and reinforce the message of the piece. As the client requested, the main focus is on the graphics in the top two-thirds of the piece while the relevant text is large enough to be visible but isn't the primary visual element.

Completing this poster required a number of different text formatting options, including more sophisticated paragraph controls and controlling the flow of text across multiple frames. You should now understand the difference between character and paragraph formatting, and know where to find the different options when you need them.

The graphics options in InDesign give you significant creative control over virtually every element of your layouts. Custom colors and gradients add visual interest to any piece, while more sophisticated tools like non-destructive transparency and other effects allow you to experiment entirely within your page layout until you find exactly the look you want to communicate your intended message.

- Create and format text on a path
- Create custom swatches and gradients for frame fills and strokes
- Use blending modes to blend an image into the frame background fill
- Use a gradient feather to add soft edges to a placed image
- Create a custom graphics frame from an image's clipping path
- Place graphics as anchored inline objects
- Use optical margin alignment to align punctuation outside the text frame
- Control text flow across multiple text frames

Project 2: Festival Poster

project 3

HeartSmart Newsletter

Your client is a non-profit foundation that focuses on health education and public awareness. It publishes a monthly newsletter for people on various mailing lists, which are purchased from a list-management vendor. The editor wants to change the existing newsletter template, and wants you to take over the layout once the template has been revised.

This project incorporates the following skills:

❑ Opening and modifying an existing layout template
❑ Managing missing font and link requests
❑ Replacing graphics files to meet specific color output needs
❑ Formatting text with template styles
❑ Controlling text-frame inset, alignment, and wrap attributes
❑ Creating a table with data from a Microsoft Excel worksheet
❑ Preflighting the final layout and creating a job package

Project Meeting

client comments

In the past our newsletter was printed black-only, since we ran it off a digital copier. We recently received a grant that will allow us to broaden our reach. The printer said that because we're going to print so many copies, we can go to four-color printing and still pay less per piece than we used to pay for the black-only copies. The printer also recommended using a self-mailer format, which will save us money on envelopes and postage.

We need some other changes too. We want to go from four columns to three on the front, and from three columns to two on the back. The checkerboard area on the front usually has four random pictures, and the bar at the top of the back has a single image. Those all used to be gray, but now you can add color.

We'd like you to make modifications to the template, and then use the template to create the current issue. We sent you the pictures we want to use for this issue, as well as the three text pieces (the main article, a sidebar for the front, and the story for the back). There's also a table in Microsoft Excel format that we want to include on the back.

art director comments

Whenever you work with a file that someone else created, there is always the potential for problems. When you first open the template, you'll have to check the fonts and images and make whatever adjustments are necessary. Make sure you save the file as a template again before you build the new issue.

Moving from grayscale to color isn't too big a deal — it's actually easier than going from color to grayscale since color adds possibilities instead of limiting them. You have the opportunity to add color to common design elements (including styles), and you should also use the color version of the nameplate instead of the grayscale one.

The printer said they prefer to work with native application files instead of PDF, so when you're finished implementing the layout, you'll need to check the various elements, and then create a final job package.

project objectives

To complete this project, you will:

❏ Handle requests for missing fonts and images

❏ Edit master page elements to meet new requirements

❏ Save a layout file as a template

❏ Access master page elements on the layout pages

❏ Format imported text using template styles

❏ Build and format a table using data from a Microsoft Excel spreadsheet

❏ Create a final job package for the output provider

Stage 1   Working with Templates

Templates are commonly used whenever you have a basic layout that will be implemented more than once — for example, the structure of a newsletter remains the same, but the content for each issue changes. InDesign templates are special types of files that store the basic structure of a project. Well-planned templates can store layout elements such as nonprinting guides that mark various areas of the job; placeholder frames that will contain different stories or images in each revision; elements that remain the same in every revision, such as the nameplate; and even formatting information that will be applied to different elements so the elements can be consistent from one issue to the next.

When you work with a template file (with the extension ".indt"), you open and build onto a copy of the original template. Instead of simply saving your changes to the existing layout file, working from a template file means the first time you save you must use the Save As command and save the file under a new name. Opening a template is similar to creating a new untitled file from scratch, except the new file from the template has all the bits and pieces that are part of the template layout.

Manage Missing Fonts and Images

Templates can store a wealth of information, including a number of options for formatting text. Placeholder text frames and styles include font information. When you work with digital layout files, it's important to understand that fonts are external files of data that describe the font for on-screen display and for the output device. The fonts you use in a layout need to be available on any computer that will be used to open and work with the file. InDesign stores a reference to the fonts you use, but it does not store the actual font data.

1. **Copy the HeartSmart folder from the WIP folder on the Resource CD to the WIP folder where you're saving your work.**

    Use your WIP>HeartSmart folder to save all files for this project.

2. **Open the file heartsmart.indt from the RF_InDesign>HeartSmart folder.**

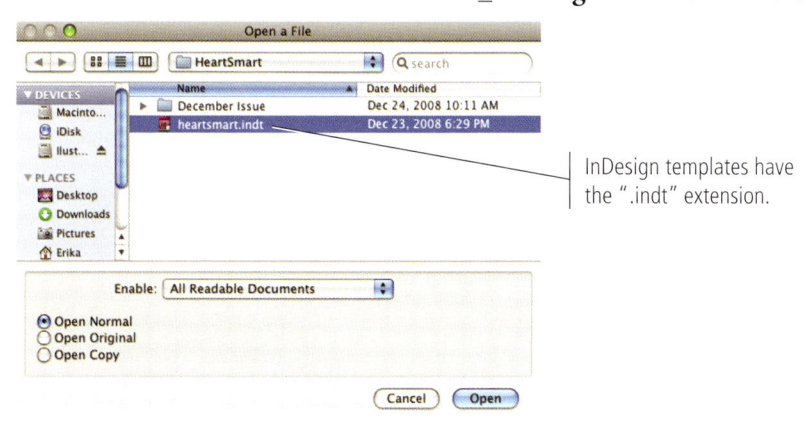

    InDesign templates have the ".indt" extension.

    Note:

    Missing fonts are one of the most common problems in the digital graphics output process. This is one of the primary advantages of using PDF files for output — PDF can store actual font data so you don't need to include the separate font files in your job package. However, PDF can't solve the problem of fonts used in a layout template.

3. **Review the warning message, then click OK.**

    InDesign stores links to images placed in a layout; the actual placed-file data is not stored in the InDesign file. If placed files are not available in the same location as when they were originally placed, you'll see a warning message when you open the file. You'll use the InDesign Links panel to correct this problem in the next exercise.

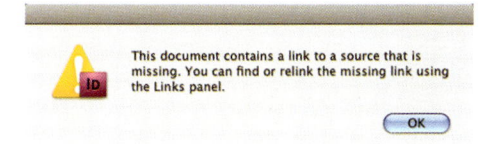

4. **Review the information in the Missing Fonts dialog box, and then click OK.**

   Any time you open a file that calls for fonts you don't have, you see this warning. You could blindly fix the problem now (without knowing what will be affected), but we prefer to review problem areas before making changes.

5. **Open the Pages panel.**

   The Pages panel is the easiest way to navigate through the pages in a layout, including the master page(s). You can navigate to any page in the layout by simply double-clicking the page's icon.

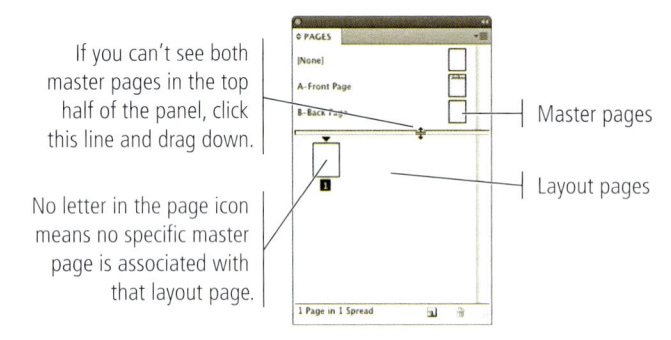

   If you can't see both master pages in the top half of the panel, click this line and drag down.

   No letter in the page icon means no specific master page is associated with that layout page.

   Master pages

   Layout pages

   Think of master pages as templates for different pages within the layout. This file, for example, has two master pages: Front Page and Back Page. The letters preceding each master page name are automatically added and used to identify which layout pages are associated with which master page. (This will make more sense shortly.)

6. **Double-click the A-Front Page icon to display that layout in the document window.**

   The top area of the newsletter (the **nameplate** area) includes the newsletter logotype, as well as the "Published by…" line and the issue date. A pink highlight around the type shows that the font used in this area is not available.

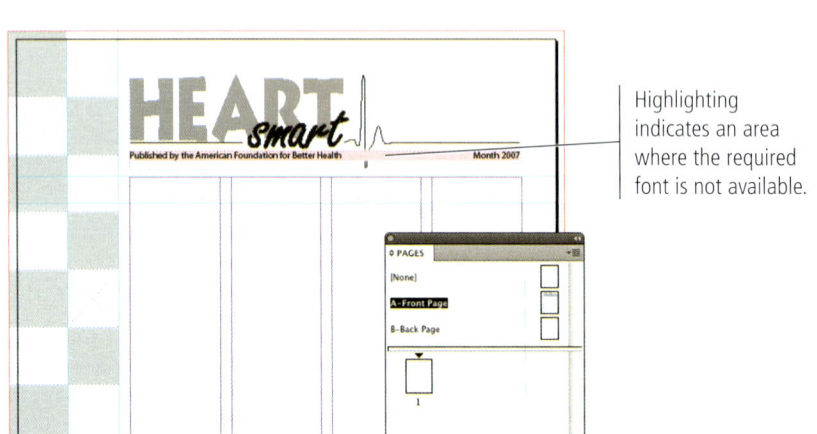

   Highlighting indicates an area where the required font is not available.

   Note:

   If the nameplate information is not highlighted, open the Composition pane of the Preferences dialog box and make sure the Highlight Substituted Fonts option is checked.

7. **Using the Type tool, click the frame with the missing font to place the insertion point.**

   The Control panel shows the missing font name in brackets. Any time you see a font name in brackets, you know you have a potential problem.

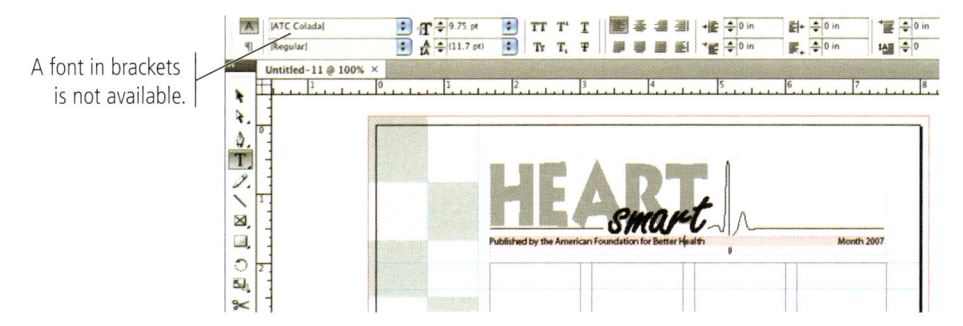

   A font in brackets is not available.

8. **Choose Type>Find Font.**

   The Find Font dialog box lists every font used in the layout — including missing ones (with a warning icon). You can use this dialog box to replace any font — including missing ones — with another font that is available on your system.

9. **Highlight ATC Colada in the Fonts in Document list and click the More Info button.**

   The bottom section of the dialog box shows information about the selected font, including the places where it's used (in this case, 66 characters on the A-Front Page).

10. **In the Replace With area, choose ATC Oak Normal in the Font Family menu.**

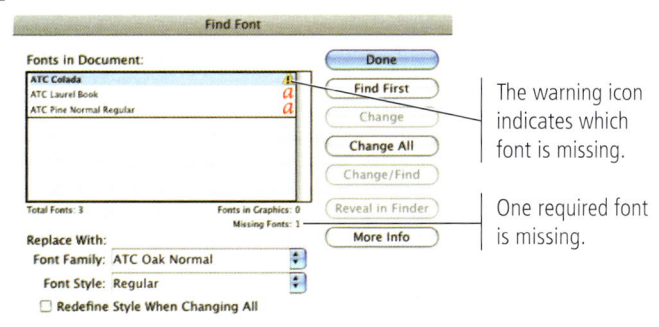

    The warning icon indicates which font is missing.

    One required font is missing.

    Note:

    If a font is used in styles, you can apply your font replacement choices to style definitions by checking the Redefine Style When Changing All option.

11. **Click Change All to replace all instances of ATC Colada with ATC Oak Normal.**

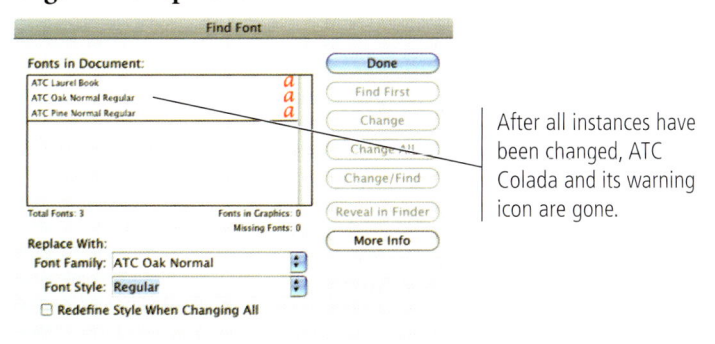

    After all instances have been changed, ATC Colada and its warning icon are gone.

    Note:

    You can click the Find Next button to review individual instances of a missing font, or you can click the Change or Change/Find button to replace and review individual instances of the selected font.

Project 3: HeartSmart Newsletter   149

12. **Click Done to close the Find Font dialog box.**

    Once you've replaced the missing font, the pink highlighting disappears.

13. **Save the file as** template_working.indd **in your WIP>HeartSmart folder and continue to the next exercise.**

REPLACE MISSING GRAPHICS

Placed graphics can cause problems if those files aren't where they're supposed to be (or at least where InDesign thinks they should be). Placed graphics files can be either **missing** (they were moved from the location from which they were originally placed in the layout, or the name of the file was changed) or **modified** (they were resaved after being placed into the layout, changing the linked file's "time stamp" but not its location or file name). In either case, you need to correct these problems before the file can be successfully output.

1. **With** template_working.indd **open, display the Links panel (Window>Links).**

    The Links panel lists every file that is placed in your layout. Missing images show a red stop-sign icon; modified images show a yellow yield sign.

2. **Click** nameplate_gray.ai **in the list, and click the Go to Link button.**

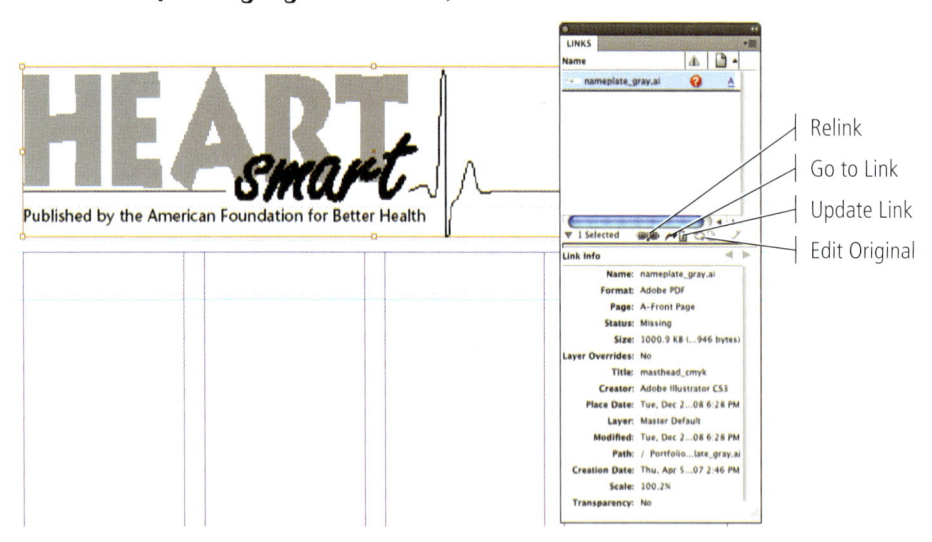

    Relink
    Go to Link
    Update Link
    Edit Original

3. **With the file still selected in the panel, click the Relink button.**

150 Project 3: HeartSmart Newsletter

4. **Navigate to `nameplate_color.ai` in the RF_InDesign>HeartSmart> December Issue folder and click Open.**

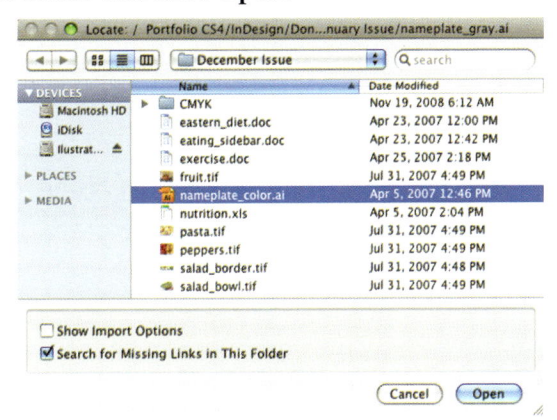

Note:

If the Search for Missing Links option is checked, InDesign will scan the selected folder to find other missing image files.

5. **Save the file and continue to the next exercise.**

The Warning icon is gone.

The Links Panel in Depth

INDESIGN FOUNDATIONS

The Links panel lists all files that have been placed into a layout. By default, the panel shows the item name, the status (missing or modified), and the location of that item in the layout. The lower half of the panel shows important information for the selected link, such as color space and resolution. If you open the Panel Options dialog box (from the Links panel Options menu), you can change which information appears in each section of the panel.

Click the column headings to sort based on specific criteria (e.g., filename, status, or page).

Multiple instances of the same image are grouped together.

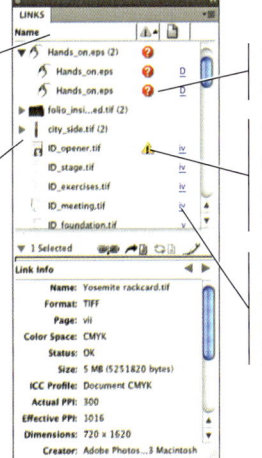

The red icon indicates a file is missing.

The yellow icon indicates a file has been modified since being placed into the layout.

Click the hot-text page number to navigate to a specific item in the layout.

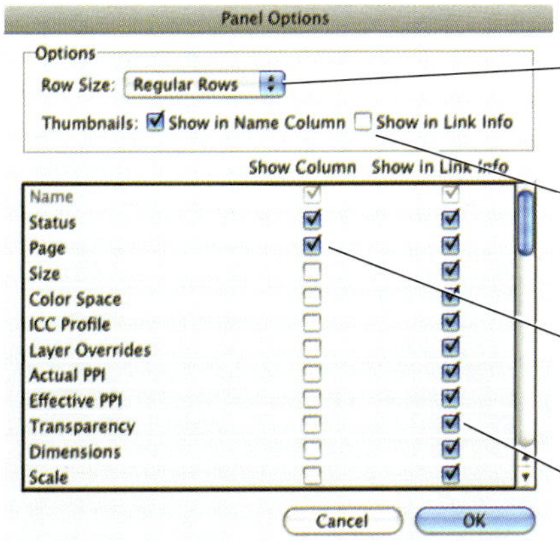

Use this menu to change the size of item thumbnails in the panel.

Check to include item thumbnails in the lower half of the panel.

Use these options to change what appears in the top half of the panel.

Use these boxes to change what appears in the lower half of the panel.

Project 3: HeartSmart Newsletter   151

EDIT MARGIN AND COLUMN GUIDES

Your client wants to make several changes to the layout, including fewer columns and incorporating color into various elements. These changes will recur from one issue to the next, so you should change the template instead of simply changing the elements in each individual issue.

1. **With template_working.indd open, and with the A-Front Page master layout visible in the document window, choose Layout>Margins and Columns.**

   Every layout has a default setup, which you define when you create the file. Master pages have their own margin and column settings that might or might not be different than the default document settings.

   Note:

   You can change the default margins and columns for a layout by choosing File>Document Setup.

2. **In the resulting Margins and Columns dialog box, change the Columns field to 3 and the Gutter field to 0.2 in, and then click OK.**

   Changing the column guides has no effect on the text frame; you have to change the text frame independently.

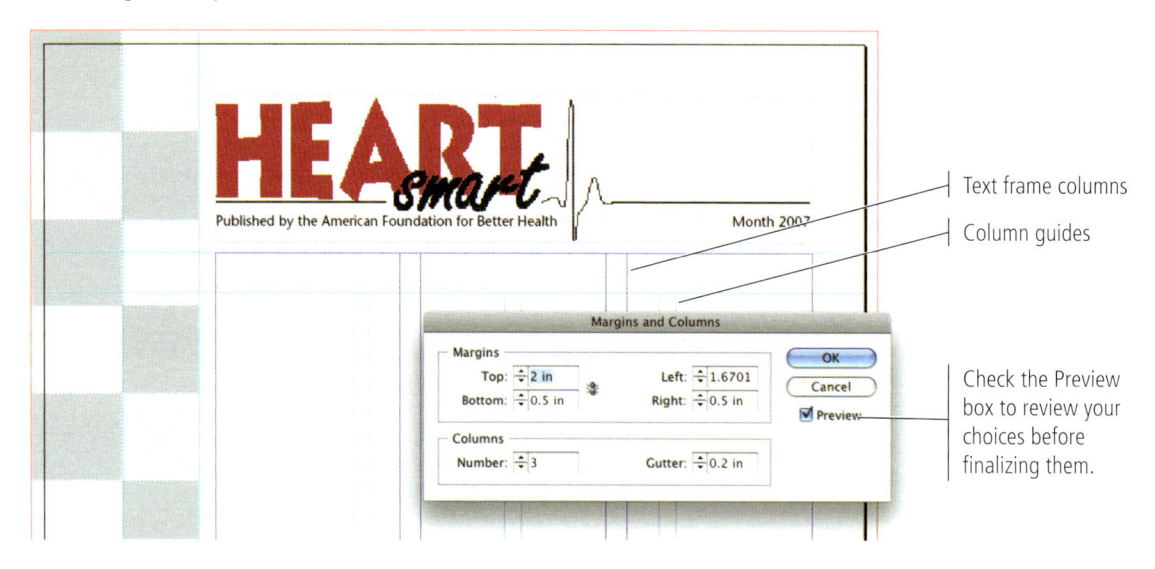

   Text frame columns
   Column guides

   Check the Preview box to review your choices before finalizing them.

3. **Using the Selection tool, click to select the 4-column text frame, and then Control/right-click the frame and choose Text Frame Options from the contextual menu.**

   Note:

   You can also access the Text Frame Options dialog box from the Object menu.

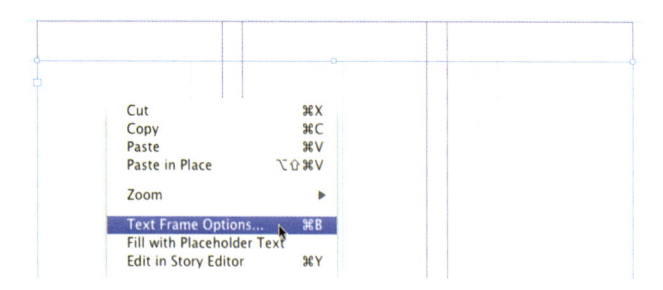

Project 3: HeartSmart Newsletter

4. Change the Number of Columns field to **3** and the Gutter field to **0.2 in** to match the changes you made to the column guides. Click OK to close the dialog box.

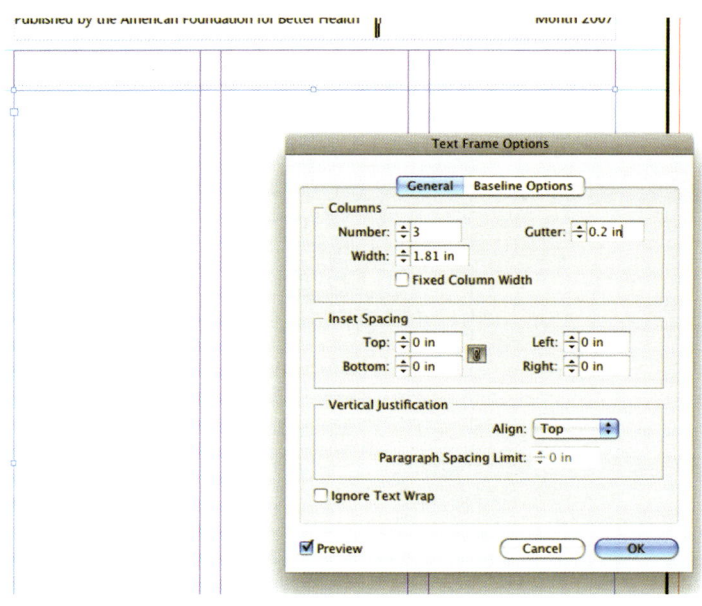

5. In the Pages panel, double-click the B-Back Page icon to display that layout in the document window.

6. Click the horizontal page ruler at the top of the window and drag a page guide to the vertical center of the page (5″).

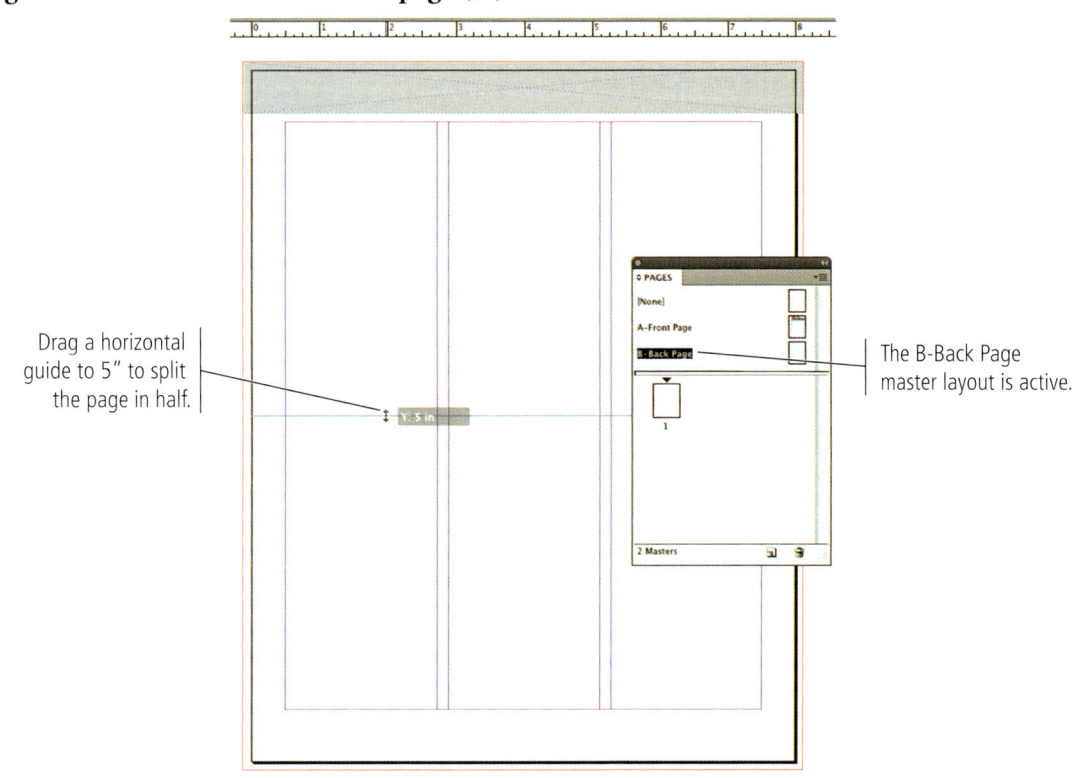

Drag a horizontal guide to 5″ to split the page in half.

The B-Back Page master layout is active.

7. Choose Layout>Margins and Columns.

Project 3: HeartSmart Newsletter 153

8. **Change the Bottom Margin setting to 5.25 in, change the Columns field to 2, change the Gutter to 0.2 in, and then click OK.**

   This brochure is a **self mailer**, which means it won't be put into an envelope for delivery. The bottom half of the back page will include return address and postage information, which is why you are defining such a large bottom margin.

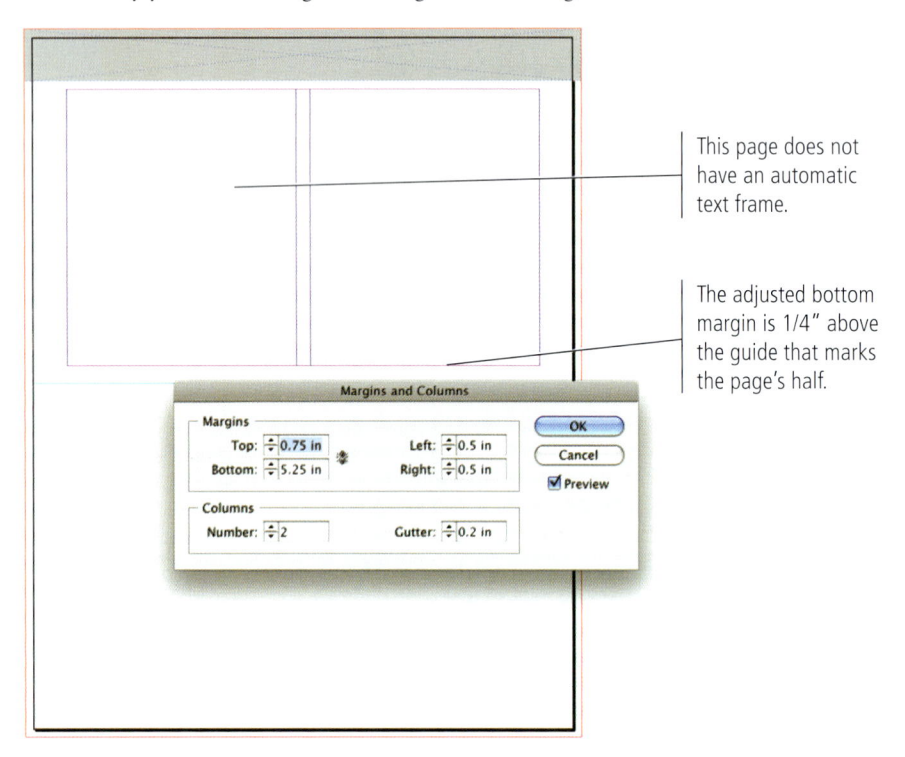

   This page does not have an automatic text frame.

   The adjusted bottom margin is 1/4" above the guide that marks the page's half.

9. **Save the file and continue to the next exercise.**

CHANGE REPEATING TEMPLATE AND MASTER PAGE ELEMENTS

One of the advantages to using a template is eliminating repetitive tasks. So you don't have to redo the same work for future issues of the newsletter, you're going to add the mailing information and color on the master page of the template file.

1. **With template_working.indd open, and with the B-Back Page master visible in the document window, place the file nameplate_color.ai into the layout.**

   Click in the lower half of the page (away from the existing frames) to place the image without replacing existing content.

2. **Select the placed image with the Selection tool. Using the Control panel, scale the placed file to 55% proportionally and position it (using the top-left reference point) at X: 0.5″, Y: 5.25″.**

   You can scale a placed picture (and its frame) by selecting it with the Selection tool. You can scale the placed picture within its frame (without affecting the frame) by selecting it with the Direct Selection tool.

Project 3: HeartSmart Newsletter

Understanding Master Pages

INDESIGN FOUNDATIONS

There are two kinds of pages in InDesign:

- **Layout pages** are the pages on which you place text and images.
- **Master pages** are the pages on which you place recurring information, such as running heads (information at the top of the page) and running footers (information at the bottom of the page).

Master pages are one of the most powerful features in professional layout software. Think of a master page as a template for individual pages; anything on the master appears on the related layout page(s). Changing something on a master layout applies the same changes to the object on related layout pages (unless you already changed the object on the layout page, or detached the object from the master).

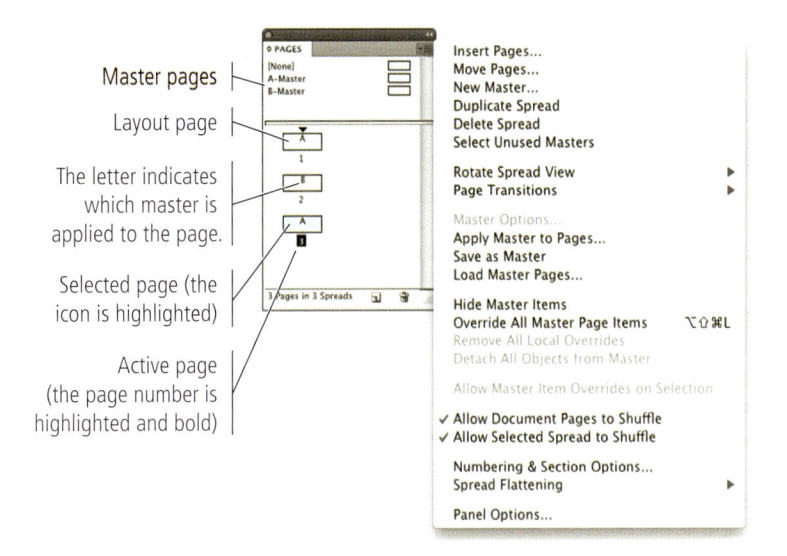

Master pages are accessed and controlled in the top half of the Pages panel. Layout pages, in the lower half of the panel, show the letter that corresponds to the master applied to that page. The Pages panel Options menu has a number of indispensable options for working with master pages:

- **New Master** opens a dialog box where you can assign a custom prefix, a meaningful name, whether the master will be based on another master page, and the number of pages (from 1 to 10) to include in the master layout.

- **Select Unused Masters** highlights all master pages not associated with at least one layout page (and not used as the basis of another master page). This option can be useful if you want to clean up your layout and remove extraneous elements.

- **Master Options** opens a dialog box with the same options you defined when you created a new master.

- **Apply Master to Pages** allows you to apply a specific master to selected pages. You can also apply a specific master to a layout by dragging the master icon onto the layout page icon in the lower half of the panel.

- **Save as Master** is useful if you've built a layout on a layout page and want to convert that layout to a master. Instead of copying and pasting the page contents, you can simply activate the page and choose Save as Master.

- **Load Master Pages** allows you to import entire master page elements from one InDesign file to another. Assets such as colors and styles used on the imported masters will also be imported into the current InDesign file.

- **Hide/Show Master Items** toggles the visibility of master items on layout pages.

- **Override All Master Page Items** allows you to access and change master items on a specific layout page. (It's important to realize that this command functions on a page-by-page basis.) You can also override individual objects by pressing Command/Control-Shift and clicking the object you want to override.

- **Remove All Local Overrides** reapplies the settings from the master items to related items on the layout page. (This option toggles to **Remove Selected Local Overrides** if you have a specific object selected on the layout page.)

- **Detach All Objects from Master** breaks the link between objects on a layout page and objects on the related master; in this case, changing items on the master has no effect on related layout page items. (This selection toggles to **Detach Selection from Master** if you have a specific object selected on the layout page.)

- **Allow Master Overrides on Selection**, active by default, allows objects to be overridden on layout pages. You can protect specific objects by selecting them on the master layout and toggling this option off.

Project 3: HeartSmart Newsletter

3. Create a new text frame with the following dimensions:

   X: 0.5″   W: 2.25″
   Y: 5.9″   H: 0.5″

4. In the new text frame, type:

   American Foundation for Better Health
   P.O. Box 76936
   Houston, TX 77020

   The text won't all fit into the frame; you need to change the formatting.

5. Select all the text (Edit>Select All) and format it as 8-pt ATC Oak Normal.

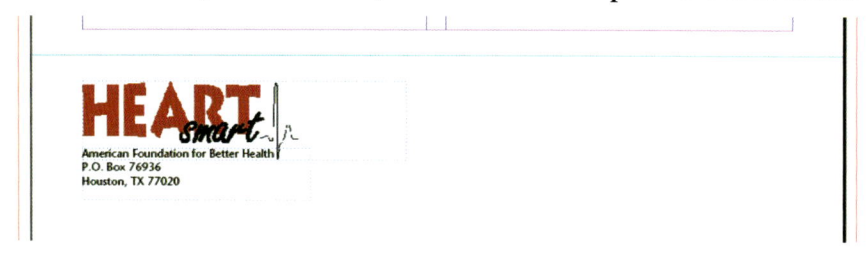

6. Using the Type tool, create a text frame that fills the margins on the Back Page layout.

7. Control/right-click the text frame and choose Text Frame Options from the contextual menu. Change the frame to 2 columns with a 0.2″ gutter, and then click OK.

   Since every issue of the newsletter has a story in this area of the back, it makes sense to create the text frame as part of the master page (and template).

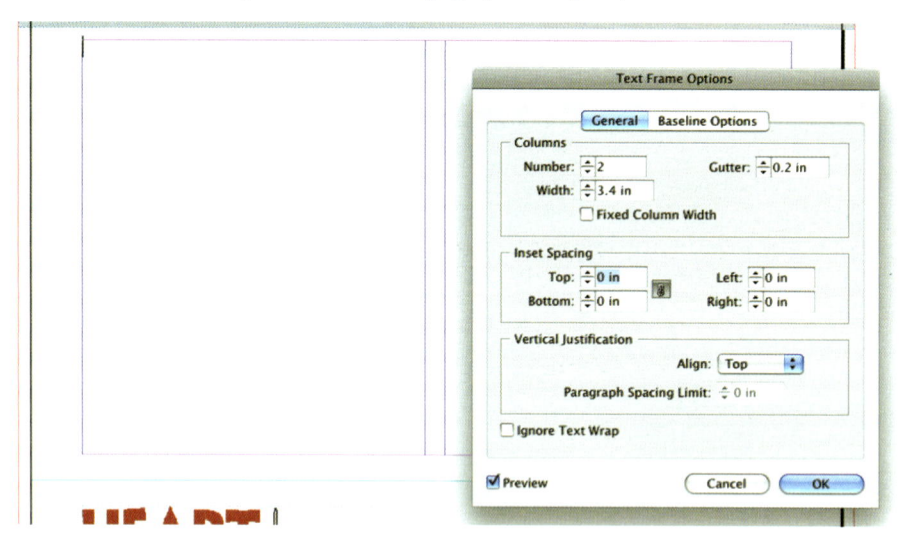

8. Using the Selection tool, select the gray box at the top of the page.

Project 3: HeartSmart Newsletter

9. **In the Swatches panel, make sure the Fill icon is active, and then click Pantone 1945 C to change the color of the frame.**

   The gray rectangle was actually filled with 20% black; changing the color does not affect the tint, so the rectangle is now filled with 20% of the Pantone color.

   Note:

   The Pantone color is used in the logo file, so you are using it to add consistent color in other areas of the layout. Before you package this file for final output you will convert the spot-color swatch to a process-color build.

10. **Double-click the A-Front Page icon in the Pages panel.**

11. **Click the gray square in the top-left corner of the page, and then change the fill to Pantone 1945 C.**

    Because all the gray squares were created by overlaying white ("Paper") frames on top of a single gray rectangle, you have to change the color only once.

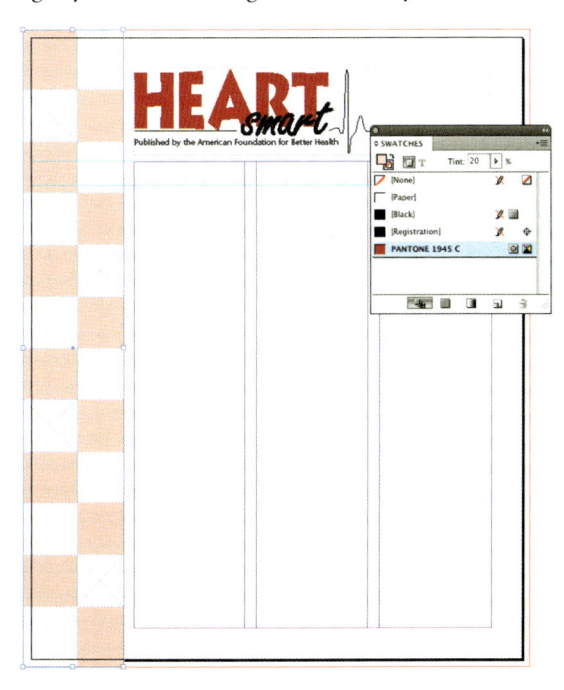

12. **Save the file and continue to the next exercise.**

SAVE A NEW TEMPLATE

Every issue has the same page structure — one front page and one back page. These layouts are already prepared as master pages, but you have to apply those master pages to the layout pages for individual issues. Since this occurs for every issue, it will remove two more clicks from the process if you set up the layout pages as part of the template.

1. **With template_working.indd open, double-click the Page 1 icon in the Pages panel.**

2. **Drag the A-Front Page master icon onto the Page 1 icon in the lower half of the Pages panel.**

   When a master page is applied to a layout page, everything on the master page is placed on the layout page.

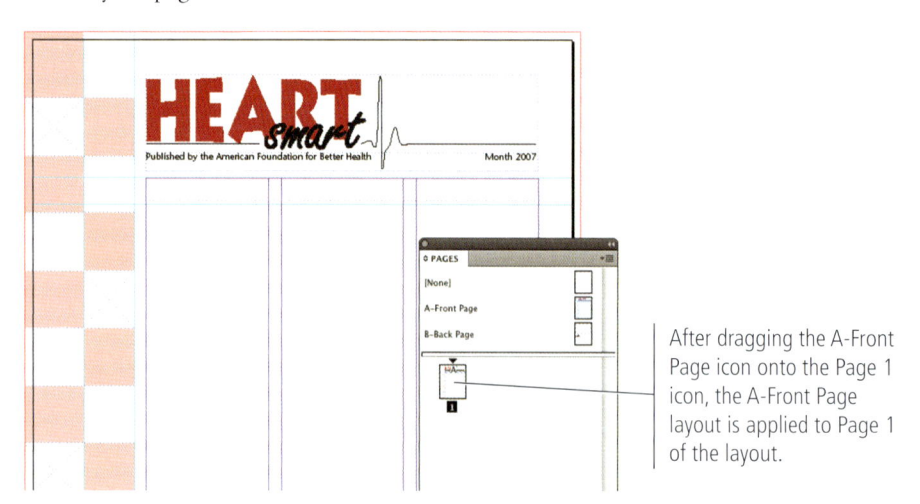

   After dragging the A-Front Page icon onto the Page 1 icon, the A-Front Page layout is applied to Page 1 of the layout.

3. **Click the B-Back Page icon and drag it into the bottom half of the Pages panel (below the Page 1 icon).**

   You can add new pages to your layout by dragging any of the master page icons into the lower half of the panel.

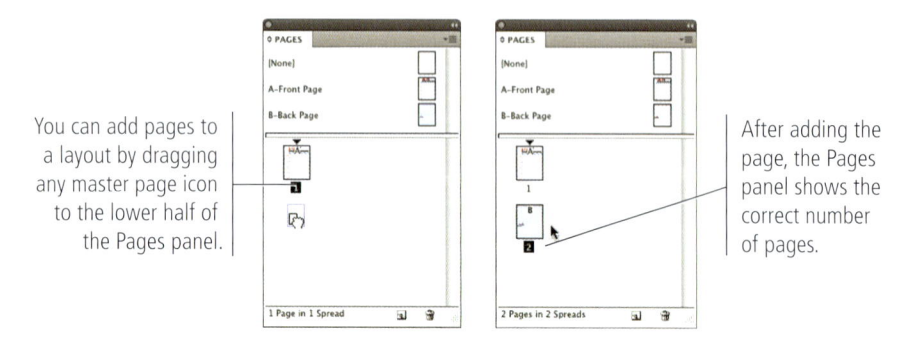

   You can add pages to a layout by dragging any master page icon to the lower half of the Pages panel.

   After adding the page, the Pages panel shows the correct number of pages.

4. **Choose File>Save As.**

5. **Navigate to your WIP>HeartSmart folder as the location for saving the template.**

6. Change the file name to **heartsmart_new.indd**.

7. In the Format/Save As Type menu, choose **InDesign CS4 Template**.

The extension automatically changes to ".indt," the correct extension for InDesign template files.

8. Click Save to save the template file.

9. When the save is complete, close the InDesign file.

CREATE A NEW FILE BASED ON THE TEMPLATE

Now that you've made the client's requested changes and saved a new template, you can easily begin each new issue by simply opening the template. Only a few things need to be addressed before you're ready to work on the current issue of the newsletter.

1. Choose File>Open and navigate to your WIP>HeartSmart folder.

2. Click the **heartsmart_new.indt** file and click Open.

   When creating a new file from a template, you have to open the template file. Opening a template file actually opens a new untitled document with all the same elements that are saved in the template.

3. Double-click the Page 1 icon in the Pages panel to show Page 1 in the document window.

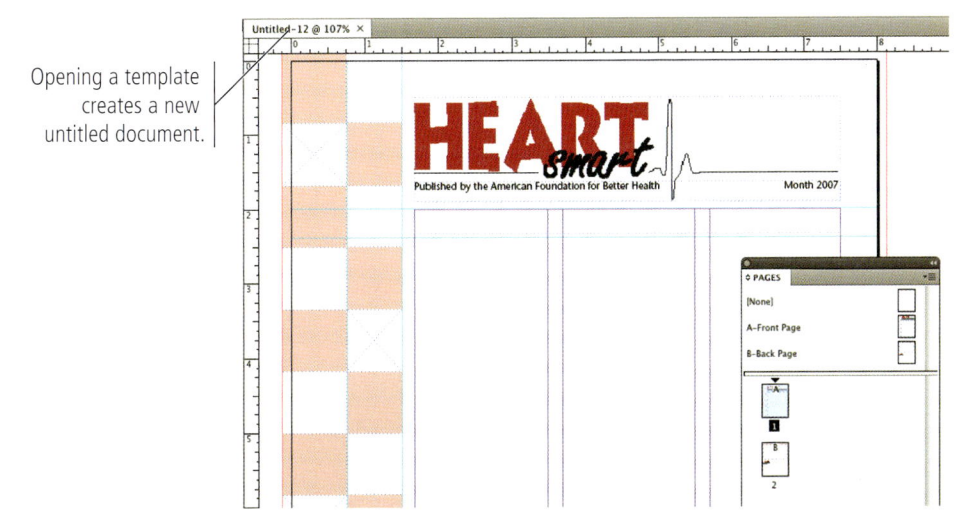

Opening a template creates a new untitled document.

Project 3: HeartSmart Newsletter 159

4. **Try to select the empty text frame near the top margin guide by clicking with the Selection tool.**

   This step will have no effect, and nothing will be selected. By default, you can't select master page items on a layout page; changes have to be made on the master page.

   When you change an object on a master page, the same changes reflect on associated layout pages. For example, if you change the red box to blue on A-Front Page, the red box will turn blue on Page 1 as well.

   In many cases, however, you might need to change a master page item for only a single page in the layout — a common occurrence when you use placeholder text or graphics frames on a master page. In this case, you have to override the master page layout for the specific layout page (or for a specific item by Command/Control-Shift-clicking that item), so you can select and change the overridden master page items.

5. **Control/right-click the Page 1 icon and choose Override All Master Page Items from the contextual menu.**

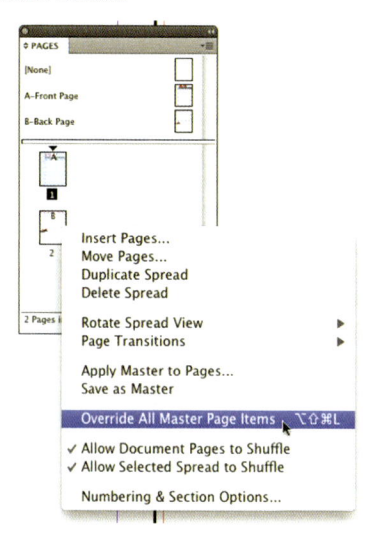

6. **Now click near the top margin guide to select the empty text frame.**

   By overriding the master page layout for this page, you can now select and change master page items — including the text frame — on the layout page.

7. **Double-click the Page 2 icon to show that page in the document window.**

Project 3: HeartSmart Newsletter

8. **Control/right-click the Page 2 icon and choose Override All Master Page Items from the contextual menu.**

   You can now select and change the text frame on Page 2, as well as the other objects from the B-Back Page master.

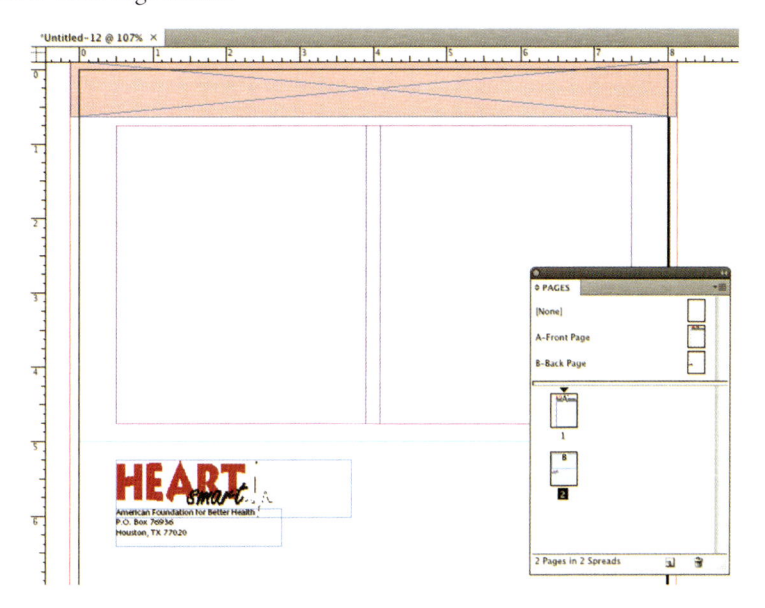

9. **Choose File>Save As and navigate to the WIP>HeartSmart folder.**

10. **Change the file name to heartsmart_new.indd, and then choose InDesign CS4 Template in the Format/Save As Type menu.**

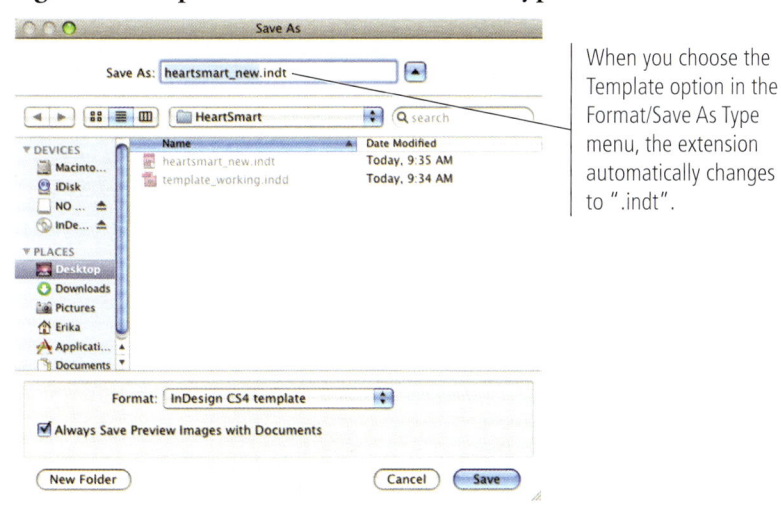

    When you choose the Template option in the Format/Save As Type menu, the extension automatically changes to ".indt".

    Note:

    The previous eight steps would need to be completed for every issue of the newsletter, so you can save yourself time by resaving the template with these new changes.

11. **Click Save. When you see a warning message asking if you want to overwrite the existing template, click Replace/Yes.**

    Templates sometimes require changes, as is the case in this project. You can overwrite the original template by choosing File>Save As, navigating to the original template location, and saving the revised template with the exact same file name.

12. **Close the template file.**

Project 3: HeartSmart Newsletter

Implement the Newsletter Template

By saving your work as a template, you've eliminated a significant amount of repetitive work that would otherwise need to be redone for every issue. There are still some tasks that will need to be done for each issue, such as changing the issue date and adding images to the front and back pages. These elements will change in each issue, so they can't be entirely "templated." But if you review the layout as it is now, you'll see that the template includes placeholders for these elements — so adding these elements is greatly simplified.

1. **Open the file heartsmart_new.indt from your WIP>HeartSmart folder.**

2. **Immediately save the file as an InDesign CS4 document named heartsmart_dec.indd in your WIP>HeartSmart folder.**

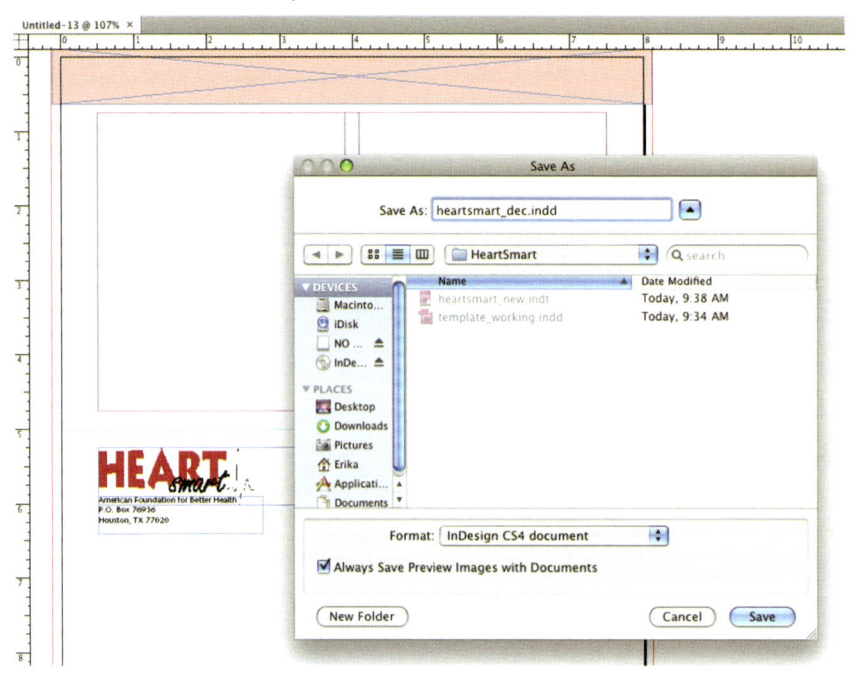

3. **Navigate to Page 1 of the file. Using the Type tool, highlight "Month 2007" in the nameplate area of Page 1 and type December 2009.**

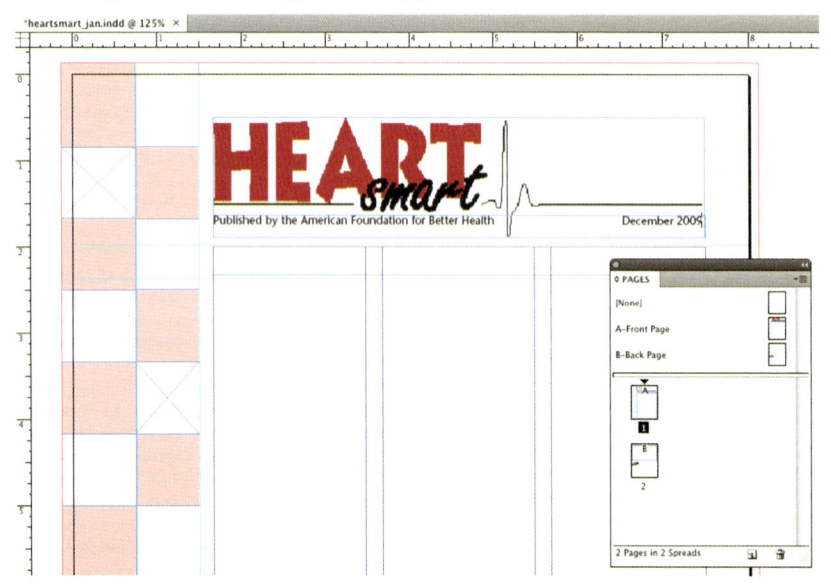

162 Project 3: HeartSmart Newsletter

4. Select the first empty graphics frame in the checkerboard pattern on the left side of the page.

5. Choose File>Place. Navigate to the file `fruit.tif` in the RF_InDesign>HeartSmart>December Issue folder. Make sure the Replace Selected Item is checked, and then click Open.

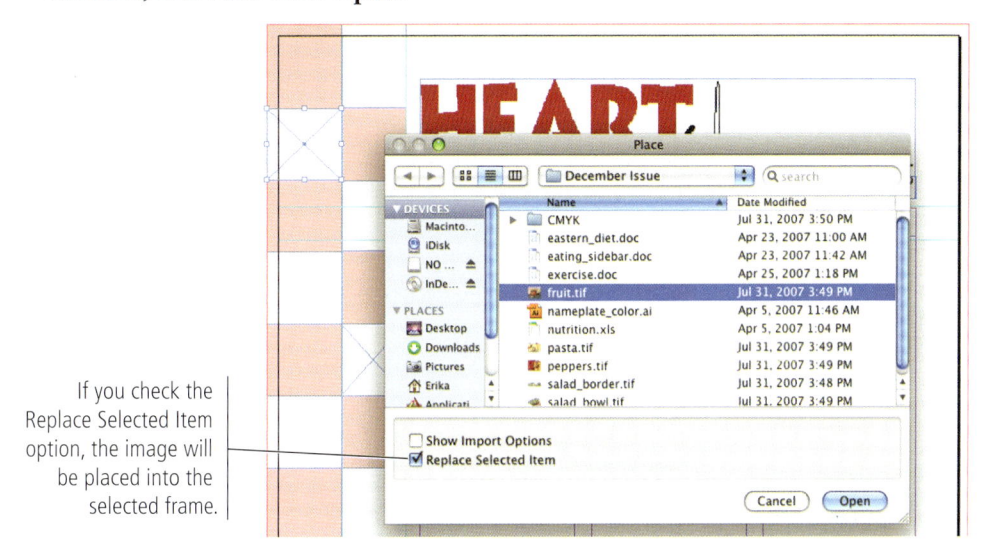

If you check the Replace Selected Item option, the image will be placed into the selected frame.

6. Click the placed graphic with the Direct Selection tool to select only the graphic (not the containing frame).

7. Scale the placed graphic (not the frame) to 60% proportionally, and drag the picture inside the frame so the peach is roughly centered in the space.

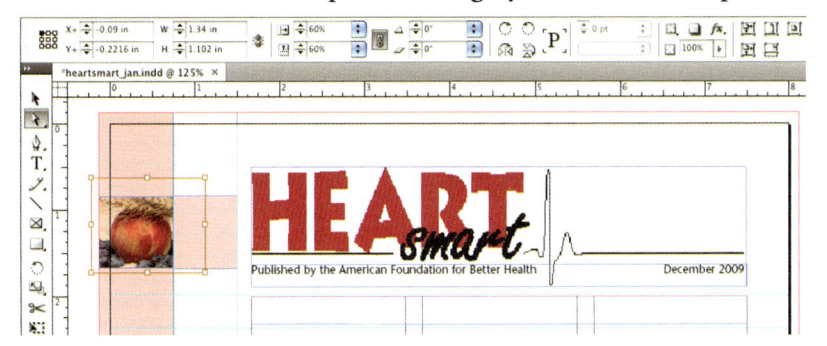

Note:

To scale the picture and not the frame, select the picture with the Direct Selection tool and use either the Transform panel or Control panel.

8. Using the same technique, place the following images in the remaining three graphics frames in the checkerboard pattern:

    Second frame: `pasta.tif`, scaled to 50%

    Third frame: `peppers.tif`, scaled to 50%

    Fourth frame: `salad_bowl.tif`, scaled to 75%

9. **Drag each image within its frame until you are satisfied with the visible area of the pictures.**

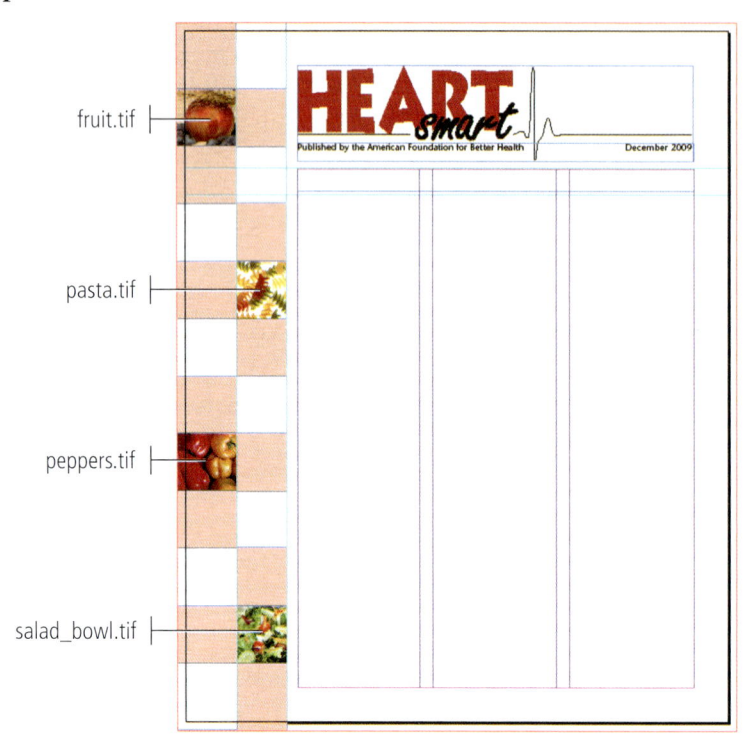

10. **On Page 2, place the file `salad_border.tif` into the graphics frame at the top of the page.**

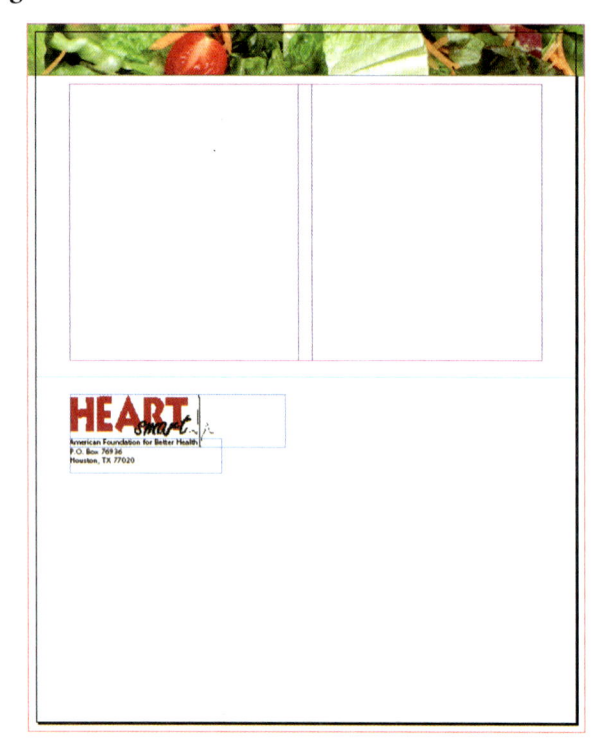

11. **Save the file and continue to the next stage of the project.**

Project 3: HeartSmart Newsletter

Stage 2 Working with Styles

The principles of good design state that headings, subheadings, body copy, and other editorial elements should generally look the same throughout a single job — in other words, editorial elements should be consistent from one page to another, whether the job is two pages or two hundred.

In Project 2 you learned about the various text formatting options that can be applied in an InDesign layout. For any bit of text, there are dozens of character- and paragraph-formatting options, from the font and type size to the space above and below paragraphs. Whenever you work with longer blocks of copy, you'll apply the same group of formatting options to multiple pieces of text.

If you were to change each editorial element manually, you would have to make hundreds of clicks to create a two-page newsletter. Fortunately, InDesign includes the ability to easily store groups of text-formatting options as **styles**, which can be applied to any text with a single click.

The major advantages of using styles are ease of use and enhanced efficiency. Changes can be made instantly to all text defined as a particular style. For example, you might easily modify leading in the Body Copy style or change the font in the Subhead style from Helvetica to ATC Oak Bold. When a style definition changes, any text that uses that style automatically changes, too.

Note:

Styles ensure consistency in text and paragraph formatting throughout a publication. Rather than trying to remember how you formatted a sidebar 45 pages ago, you can simply apply a predefined Sidebar style.

InDesign supports both character styles and paragraph styles. **Character styles** apply only to selected words; this type of style is useful for setting off a few words in a paragraph without affecting the entire paragraph. **Paragraph styles** apply to the entire body of text between two ¶ symbols; this type of style defines the appearance of the paragraph, combining the character style used in the paragraph with line spacing, indents, tabs, and other paragraph attributes.

Styles are most advantageous when working with text-intensive documents that have recurring editorial elements, such as headlines, subheads, and captions; when working with several people concurrently on the same project; and when creating projects with specific style requirements, such as catalogs or magazines.

Note:

Paragraph styles define character attributes and paragraph attributes; character styles define only the character attributes. In other words, a paragraph style can be used to format text entirely — including font information, line spacing, tabs, and so on.

In this project, the client's original template included a number of styles for formatting the text in each issue. Because the text frames already exist in the template layout, you only need to import the client's text and apply the existing styles. (In Project 4, you import styles from a Microsoft Word file and another InDesign file. In Project 5, you define your own styles from scratch.)

Apply Template Styles

Most InDesign jobs incorporate some amount of client-supplied text, which might be sent to you in the body of an email or saved in any number of text file formats. Many text files will be supplied from Microsoft Word, the most popular word-processing application in the United States market.

Microsoft Word includes fairly extensive options for formatting text (although not quite as robust or sophisticated as what you can do with InDesign). Many Microsoft Word users apply '**local formatting** (selecting specific text and applying character and/or paragraph attributes); more sophisticated Microsoft Word users build text formatting styles similar to those used in InDesign.

Note:

All text files for this project are in the RF_InDesign> HeartSmart>December Issue folder.

1. With Page 1 of `heartsmart_dec.indd` open, make sure nothing is selected in the file. Choose File>Place and navigate to the file `exercise.doc`.

2. **Make sure the Show Import Options box is checked and Replace Selected Item is not checked, and then click Open.**

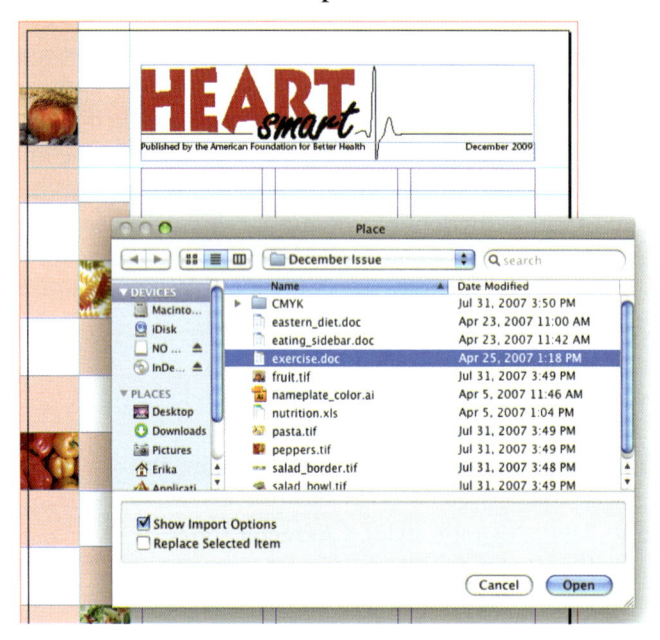

3. **In the resulting dialog box, review the options in the Formatting section.**

   When you import a Microsoft Word file into InDesign, you can either preserve or remove formatting saved in the Microsoft Word file (including styles defined in Microsoft Word).

4. **Make sure the Preserve Styles and Formatting option is selected and the Import Styles Automatically radio button is selected. Choose Auto Rename in both conflict menus, and then click OK.**

5. **If you see a Missing Fonts warning, click OK.**

   You're going to replace the Microsoft Word formatting with InDesign styles, which should correct this problem.

6. **Click the loaded cursor in the empty text frame at the top (the one that touches the top margin guide).**

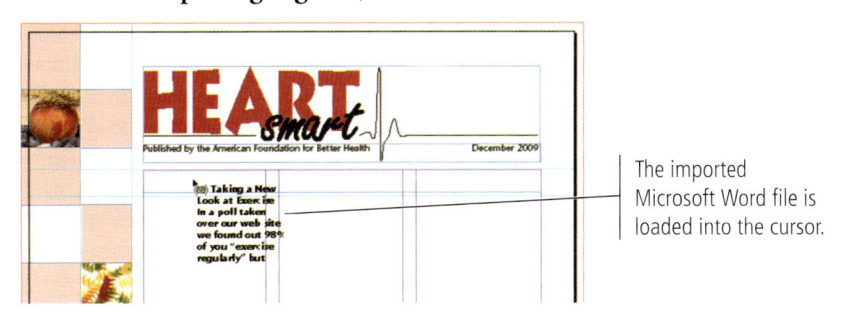

   The imported Microsoft Word file is loaded into the cursor.

   Clicking with the loaded cursor places the loaded text into the text frame.

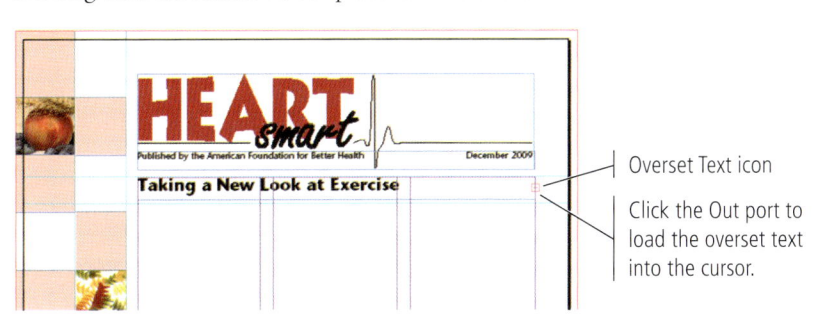

   Overset Text icon

   Click the Out port to load the overset text into the cursor.

   Note:

   When you load the cursor with overset text, the loaded cursor shows the text from the beginning of the story — even though the beginning is already placed. This is a quirk of the software; when you click with the loaded cursor, the text will flow into the new frame at the proper place in the story.

7. **Click the Out port on the text frame to load the rest of the story into the cursor, and then click the loaded cursor in the empty 3-column frame below the heading.**

   Overset text from the first frame is loaded into the cursor.

   After clicking, the overset text flows into the three-column frame.

8. **Open the Paragraph Styles panel (Window>Type & Tables>Paragraph Styles).**

9. **Place the insertion point in the first paragraph of the imported story (the main heading) and look at the Paragraph Styles panel.**

   When you imported the Microsoft Word file, you preserved the formatting in the file; this is usually a good idea so you can see what the writer intended. However, now that the text is imported into your layout, you want to apply the template styles to make the text in this issue consistent with other issues.

   When you import text into InDesign, any number of new styles may appear in the Styles panels; the most common imported style is Normal. Text in a Microsoft Word file is typically formatted with the Normal style — even if you don't realize it; user-applied formatting is commonly local (meaning it is applied to selected text instead of using a defined style).

   The imported text appears to be preformatted, but the Paragraph Styles panel tells a different story. This paragraph is formatted as "Normal+." Whenever you see a plus sign next to a style name, the selected text includes some formatting other than what is defined in the style.

   Note:

   You should be able to guess the purpose of these styles from their names. It's always a good idea to use indicative names whenever you create styles or other user-defined assets.

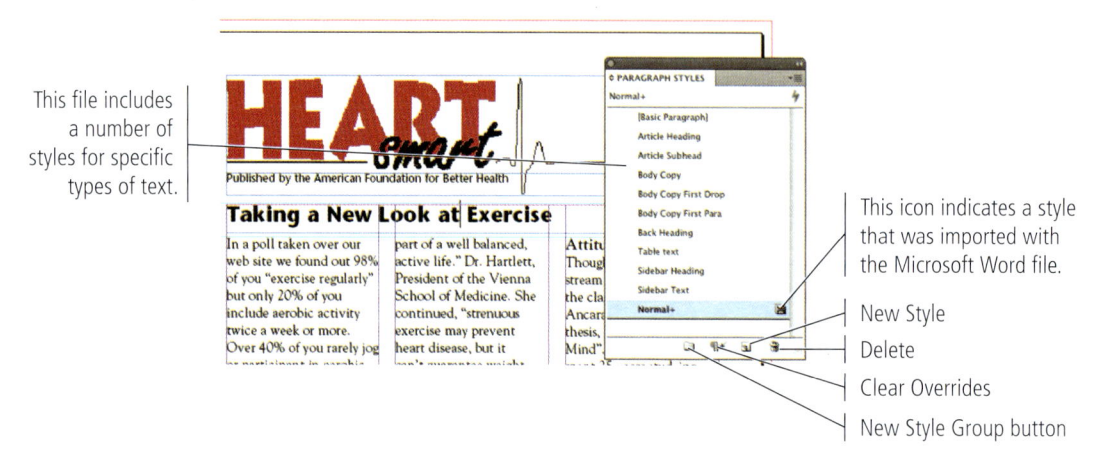

10. **With the insertion point still in place, click the Article Heading style in the Paragraph Styles panel.**

    Using styles, you can change all formatting attributes of selected text with a single click.

    Note:

    You can reapply the basic style definition to selected text by clicking the Clear Overrides button at the bottom of the Paragraph Styles panel, or by Option/Alt clicking the applied style name.

    Note:

    Paragraph styles can include character attributes as well as paragraph attributes; character styles can only define character-formatting attributes.

11. **Place the insertion point anywhere in the first paragraph of body copy, and then drag to select the rest of the visible text in the 3-column frame.**

Project 3: HeartSmart Newsletter

12. **Click the Body Copy style in the Paragraph Styles panel.**

    Paragraph styles apply to any paragraph that is partially or entirely selected. You don't have to select an entire paragraph before applying a paragraph style.

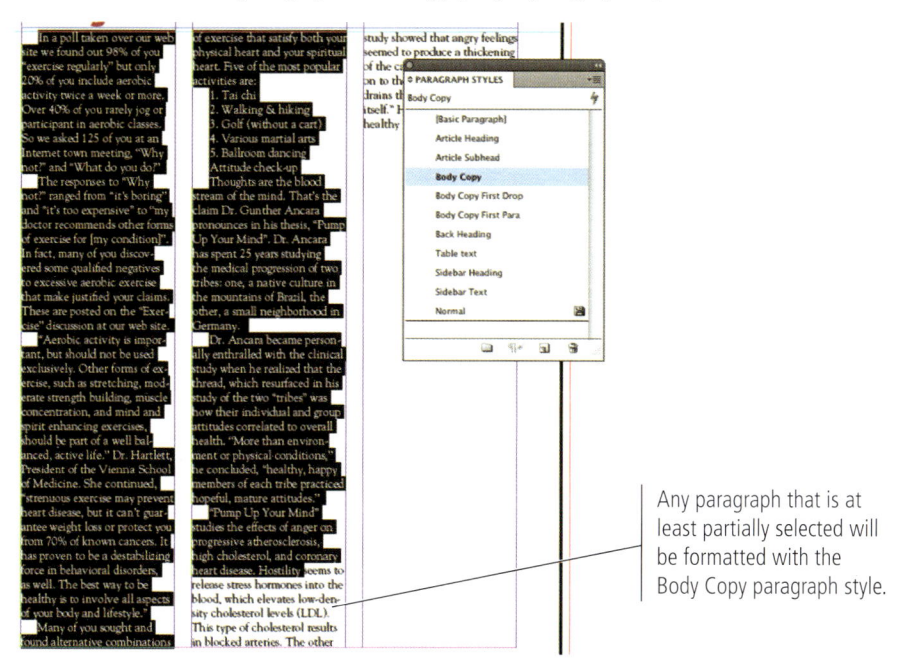

    Any paragraph that is at least partially selected will be formatted with the Body Copy paragraph style.

13. **Format the first paragraph using the Body Copy First Drop style.**

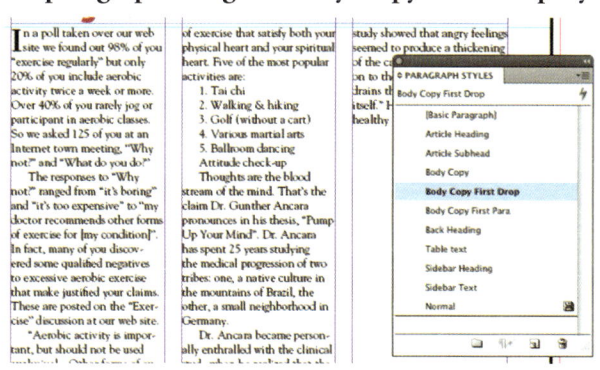

14. **In the second column, format the subheading ("Attitude Checkup", after the numbered list) with the Article Subhead style.**

15. **Format the next paragraph (after the subhead) with the Body Copy First Para style.**

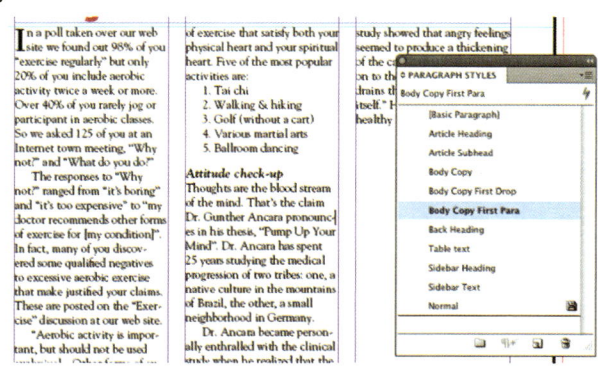

Project 3: HeartSmart Newsletter 169

16. Navigate to Page 2 of the layout and click with the Type tool to place the insertion point inside the 2-column text frame.

17. Choose File>Place. Navigate to the file `eastern_diet.doc` and make sure both Show Import Options and Replace Selected Item are checked.

The insertion point should be flashing in the 2-column text frame.

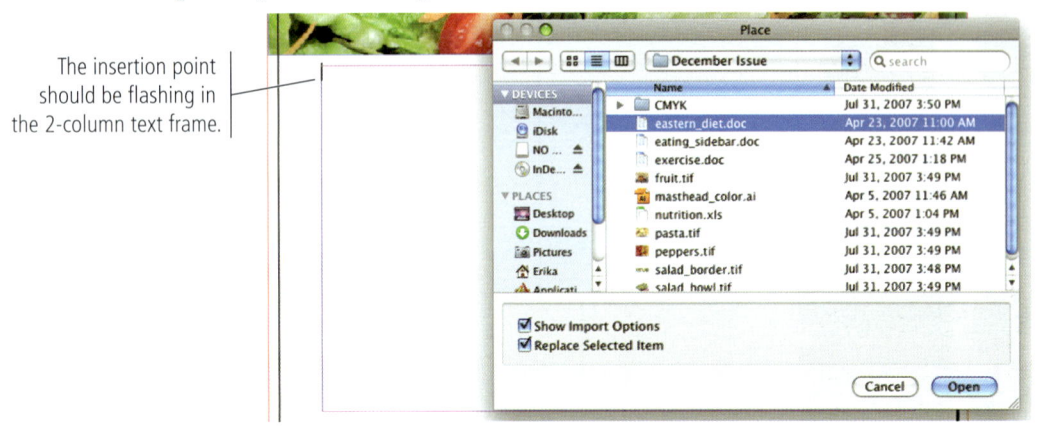

18. Click Open, then click OK to accept the default import options.

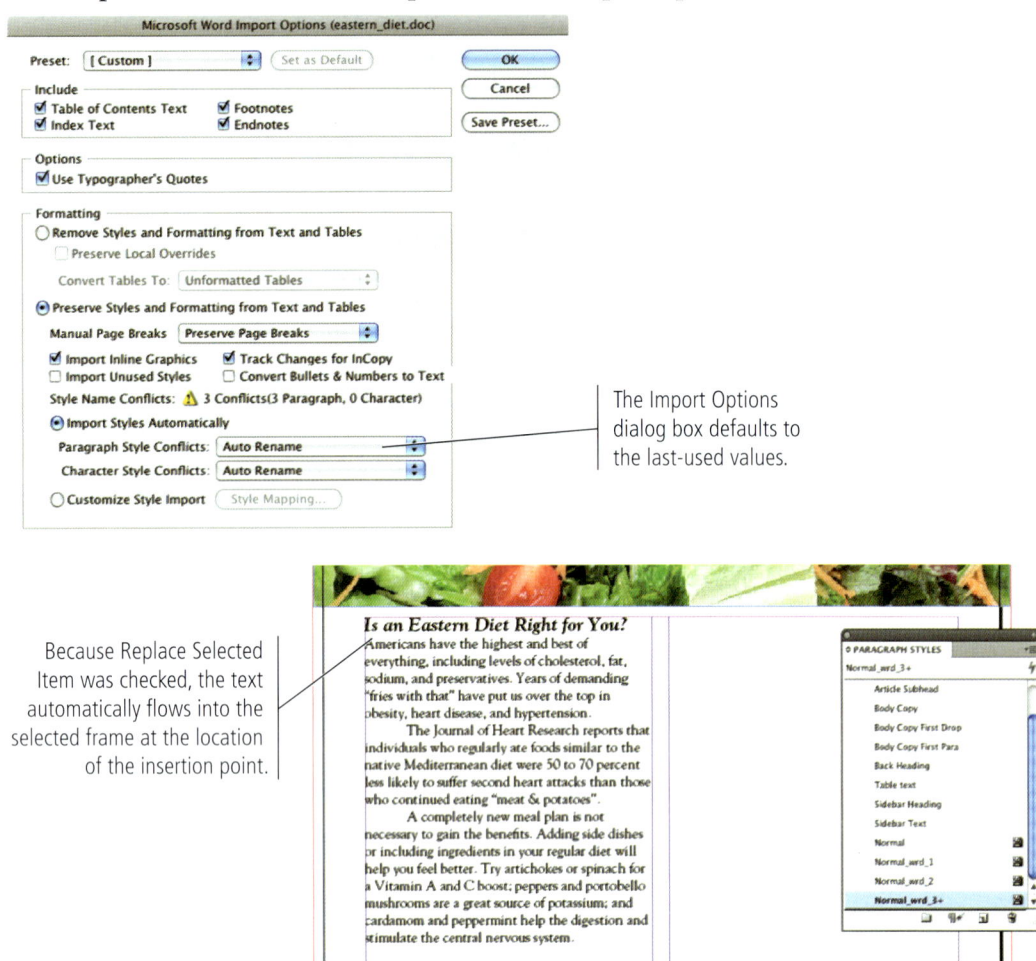

The Import Options dialog box defaults to the last-used values.

Because Replace Selected Item was checked, the text automatically flows into the selected frame at the location of the insertion point.

170   Project 3: HeartSmart Newsletter

Working with Microsoft Word Files

INDESIGN FOUNDATIONS

Microsoft Word files can include a fairly sophisticated level of formatting attributes, from basic text formatting to defined paragraph and character styles to automatically generated tables of contents. When you import a Word file into InDesign, you can determine whether to include these elements in the imported text, as well as how to handle conflicts between imported elements and elements that already exist in your InDesign layout.

If these elements exist in the Microsoft Word file, checking the associated boxes imports those elements into your InDesign file.

Choose this option to convert straight quote marks to typographer's or "curly" quotes.

Choose this option to strip out all formatting applied in the file and import the file as plain text.

Choose this option to import the Microsoft Word file, including formatting.

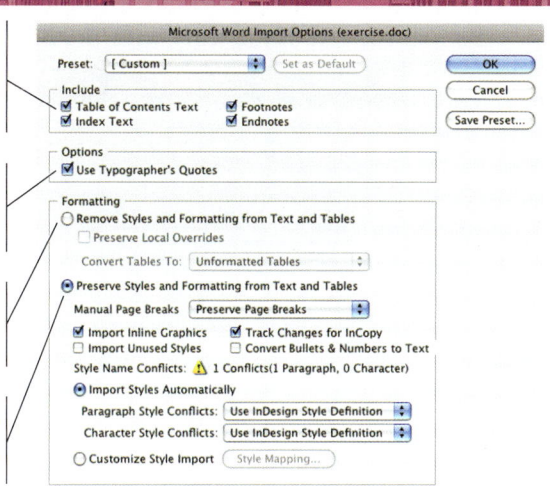

The **Manual Page Breaks** menu determines how page breaks in Word translate to InDesign. You can preserve manual breaks, convert them to column breaks, or ignore them. This option is important because Word users tend to force breaks where appropriate in the file — which rarely translates to a properly formatted InDesign layout. More often than not, you'll end up removing these page breaks, but it might be a good idea to include them in the import and remove them after you've reviewed the imported text.

If graphics have been placed into a Word file, the **Import Inline Graphics** option allows you to include those graphics as anchored objects in the InDesign story. If you choose to include graphics, it is extremely important to understand that the graphics might be embedded into the story instead of linked to the original data file (depending on how the graphic was placed into the Word file).

If you choose **Import Unused Styles**, all styles in the Word file will be imported into the InDesign layout. The most significant issue here is that styles might require fonts you don't have.

Word includes a powerful collaboration tool call Track Changes, which allows one person to review another person's changes to a file. (As publishers, we use this feature every day so editors and authors can review each other's changes before permanently changing the text). If you check the **Track Changes** option, any tracked changes from the Word file will be included in your InDesign layout. This might cause a lot of items to show up in your text that aren't supposed to be there (typos, errors, or, for example, something the general counsel office removed from the original text for a specific legal reason).

Convert Bullets & Numbering to Text allows you to convert automatically generated numbering and bullet characters into actual text characters. This option is extremely useful if the text includes lists; if you don't check this option, you'll have to manually re-enter the bullets or line numbers into the imported text.

The **Style Name Conflicts** area warns you if styles in the Word file conflict with styles in the InDesign file (in other words, they have the same style names but different definitions in the two locations). If you are importing styles from the Word file, you have to determine how to resolve these conflicts.

Import Styles Automatically allows you to choose how to handle conflicts in paragraph and character styles. **Use InDesign Style Definition** preserves the style as you defined it; text in the Word file that uses that style will be reformatted with the InDesign definition of the style. **Redefine InDesign Style** replaces the layout definition with the definition from the Word file. **Auto Rename** adds the Word file to the InDesign file with "_wrd_1" at the end of the style name.

If you choose **Customize Style Import**, the Style Mapping button opens a dialog box where you can review and control specific style conflicts. Click an option in the InDesign Style column to access a menu, where you can choose which InDesign style to use in place of a specific Word style.

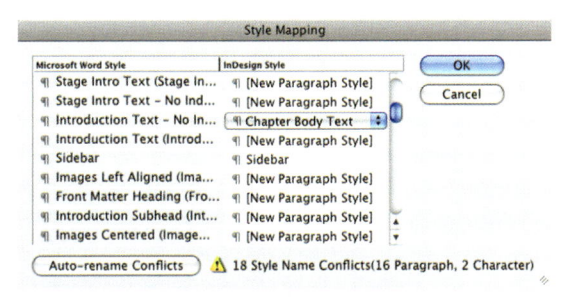

Project 3: HeartSmart Newsletter   171

19. **Format the first paragraph with the Back Heading style.
Format the second paragraph with the Body Copy First Para style.
Format the rest of the story with the Body Copy style.**

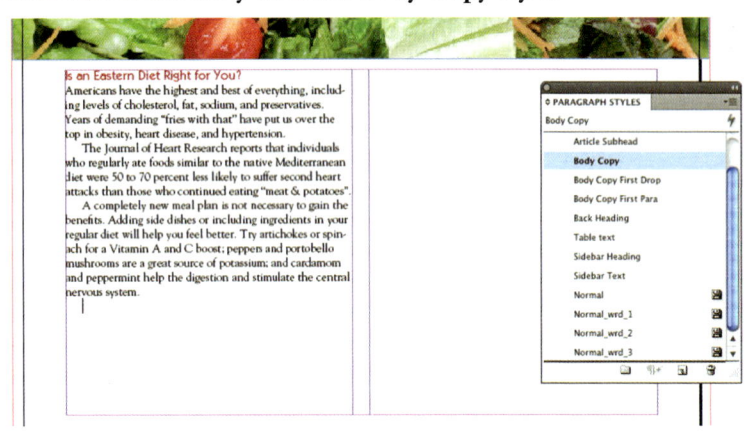

20. **Save the file and continue to the next exercise.**

Text Frame Options

INDESIGN FOUNDATIONS

You can change any number of text frame attributes using the Text Frame Options dialog box (Object>Text Frame Options, or choose Text Frame Options in the object's contextual menu).

Any text frame can have up to 40 columns, with a gutter (the space between columns) between 0 and 120". If **Fixed Column Width** is selected, changing the number of columns changes the width of the frame to accommodate the defined number of columns. (For example, 3 columns at 2" each with a 0.25" gutter would require the frame to be 6.5" wide.) If Fixed Column Width is not checked, the number of columns is evenly divided in the existing frame width.

Inset Spacing is the distance at which text is moved in from frame edges. You can define different values for each edge, or you can link all four edges to a consistent value.

If you check the **Ignore Text Wrap** option, the frame is not affected by wrap attributes of overlapping objects.

Clicking any of the arrow buttons changes the field value by 0.0625".

When this button is active (dark gray), all four inset values are the same.

Text can be aligned to the top, center, or bottom of a frame, or justified (stretched) to fill the frame height.

Click this check box to immediately see the results of your choices.

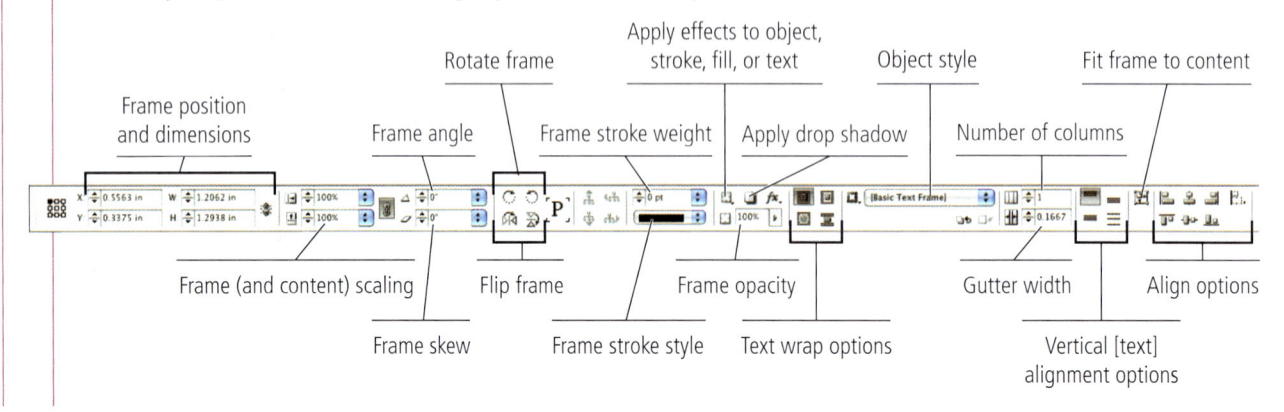

Some of these options are also available in the right side of the Advanced Workspace Control panel (or if you manually edit the panel options) when a frame is selected with one of the selection tools. It is important to note that some changes to text frames also affect the text inside the frame; scaling, flipping, rotating, or skewing a frame also scales, flips, rotates, or skews the text inside that frame.

Control panel callouts (top row): Frame position and dimensions · Rotate frame · Apply effects to object, stroke, fill, or text · Object style · Fit frame to content · Frame angle · Frame stroke weight · Apply drop shadow · Number of columns

Control panel callouts (bottom row): Frame (and content) scaling · Flip frame · Frame opacity · Gutter width · Align options · Frame skew · Frame stroke style · Text wrap options · Vertical [text] alignment options

Project 3: HeartSmart Newsletter

CREATE A SIDEBAR BOX

Many page layouts have a primary story (which might flow across multiple pages), as well as related-but-not-connected stories called **sidebars**. These elements are usually not linked to the main story, and they are often placed in their own boxes with some unique formatting to draw attention to the box. Amateur designers often create three separate elements to achieve this effect — an unnecessary degree of complexity when you can change multiple text frame options to create the effect with a single object.

1. **On Page 1 of `heartsmart_dec.indd`, create a text frame with the following dimensions (based on the top-left reference point):**

   X: 3.67″   W: 3.95″
   Y: 6.6″   H: 3″

2. **Fill the text frame with a 20% tint of Pantone 1945 C.**

3. **Place the file `eating_sidebar.doc` into the new frame, preserving the formatting in the imported file.**

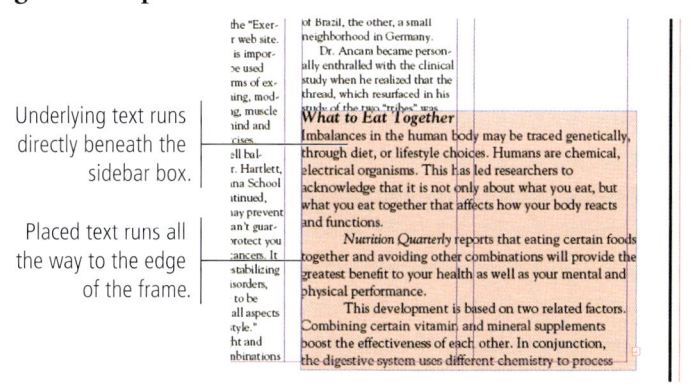

   Underlying text runs directly beneath the sidebar box.

   Placed text runs all the way to the edge of the frame.

4. **Format the first line of the sidebar with the Sidebar Heading style.**

5. **Format the rest of the text in this frame using the Sidebar Text style.**

   If a paragraph includes local formatting, simply clicking a new style name might not work perfectly. As you can see in this example, the first two words are italicized; in the Paragraph Styles panel, the Sidebar Text style shows a plus sign — indicating that some formatting other than the style definition has been applied.

6. **Place the insertion point in the second paragraph of body copy in the sidebar box.**

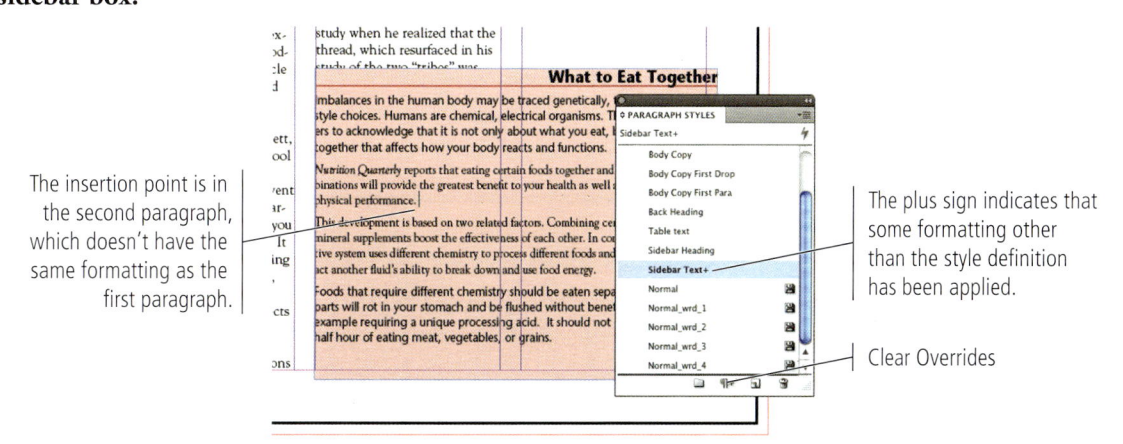

   The insertion point is in the second paragraph, which doesn't have the same formatting as the first paragraph.

   The plus sign indicates that some formatting other than the style definition has been applied.

   Clear Overrides

7. **Click the Clear Overrides button at the bottom of the Paragraph Styles panel.**

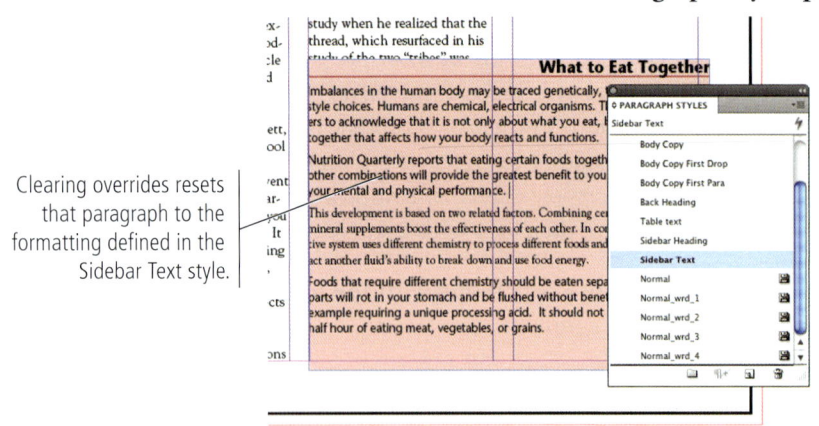

   Clearing overrides resets that paragraph to the formatting defined in the Sidebar Text style.

8. **Click in the third sidebar paragraph, and then click the Clear Overrides button again.**

9. **Select the first two words of the second sidebar paragraph. Change the font to ATC Oak and choose Italic in the Font Style menu.**

10. **Control/right-click the sidebar box and choose Text Frame Options from the contextual menu.**

11. **Make sure the Preview option is checked, and then change the Top Inset field to `0.1 in`.**

    Text inset is the distance text is moved from the inside edge of its containing frame.

12. **Make sure the chain icon is active so all four inset values are the same, and then press Tab to move the highlight and apply the new Inset Spacing value.**

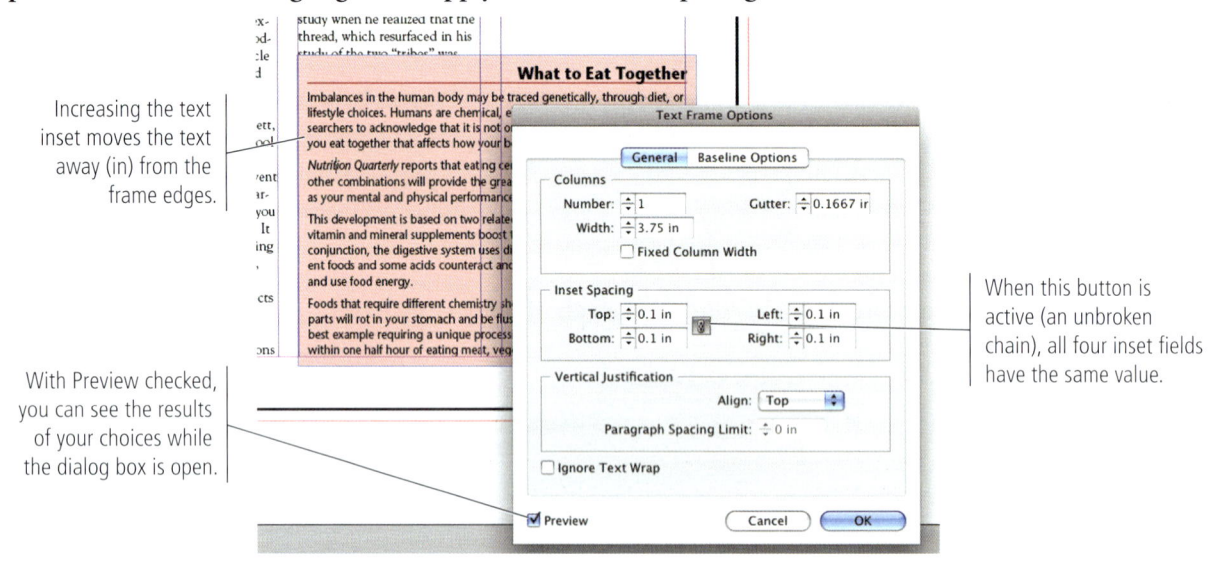

    Increasing the text inset moves the text away (in) from the frame edges.

    With Preview checked, you can see the results of your choices while the dialog box is open.

    When this button is active (an unbroken chain), all four inset fields have the same value.

Project 3: HeartSmart Newsletter

13. **In the Vertical Justification Align menu, choose Justify.**

    Text can be vertically aligned to the top, bottom, or center of its containing frame, or it can be justified — stretched to extend the entire height of the containing frame.

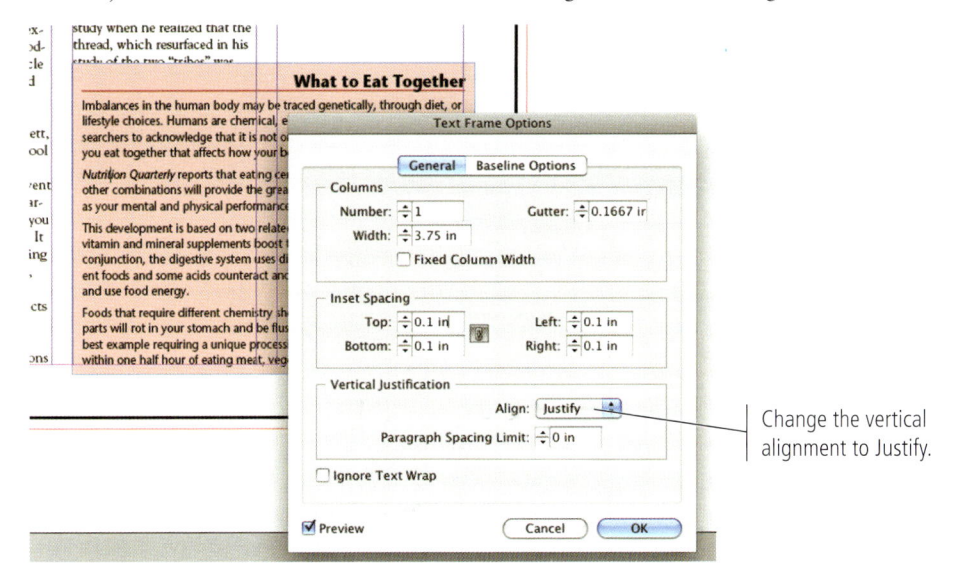

    Change the vertical alignment to Justify.

14. **Click OK to close the dialog box and apply your choices.**

15. **Open the Text Wrap panel (Window>Text Wrap).**

    Text wrap is the distance underlying text flows around the edge of a frame or other object.

16. **Click the sidebar frame with the Selection tool, and then click the second button from the left in the Text Wrap panel.**

17. **Change the Top Wrap field to `0.1 in` and make sure the Link option is active so all four wrap values are the same.**

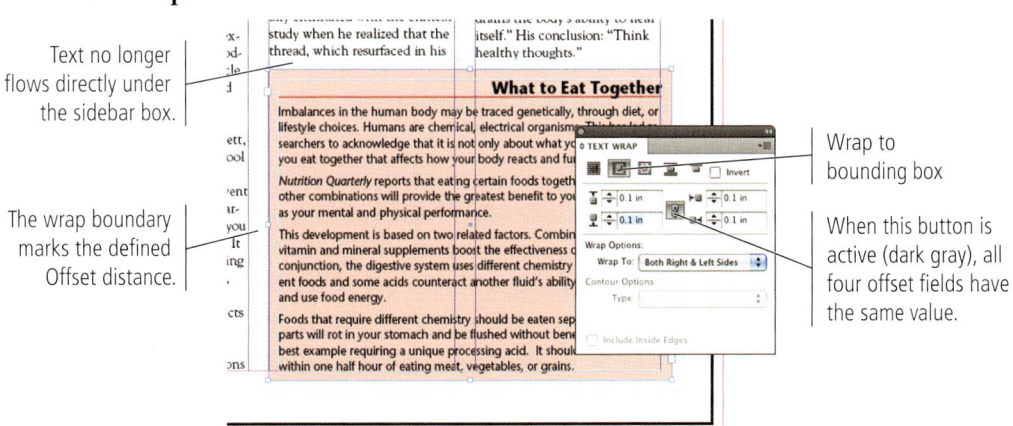

    Note:

    When you vertically justify type, the Paragraph Spacing Limit field defines the maximum space that can be added between paragraphs to fill the frame.

    Text no longer flows directly under the sidebar box.

    The wrap boundary marks the defined Offset distance.

    Wrap to bounding box

    When this button is active (dark gray), all four offset fields have the same value.

    Project 3: HeartSmart Newsletter 175

18. **Select the 3-column text box and open the Text Frame Options dialog box. Choose Justify in the Vertical Justification Align menu and click OK.**

    This command aligns the bottom lines in the two right columns.

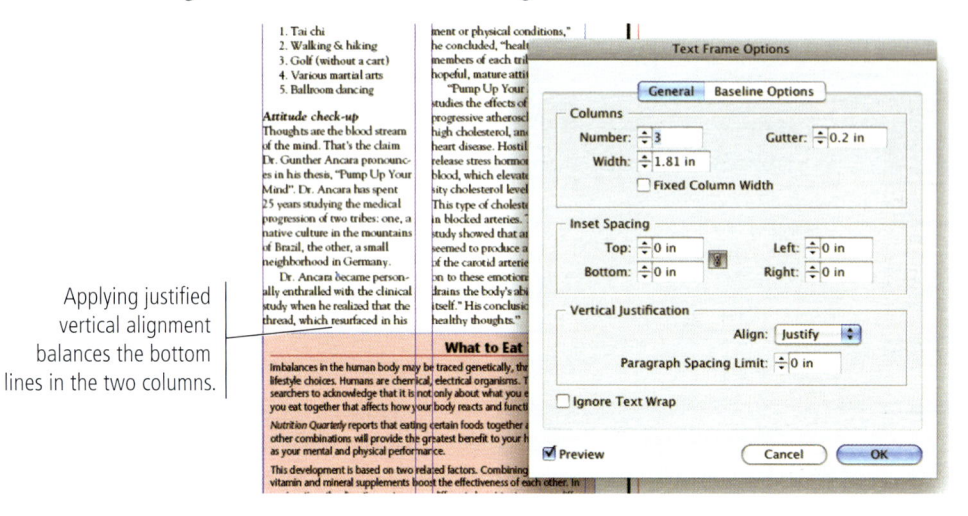

    Applying justified vertical alignment balances the bottom lines in the two columns.

19. **Save the file and continue to the next stage of the project.**

Text Wrap Options

INDESIGN FOUNDATIONS

Text wraps are largely controlled in the Text Wrap panel (Window>Text Wrap), although you can change the basic wrap attributes in the Control panel. InDesign provides five options for wrapping text around an object:

- **No Text Wrap** allows text to run directly under the object.
- **Wrap Around Bounding Box** creates a straight-edged wrap around all four sides of the object's bounding box.
- **Wrap Around Object Shape** creates a wrap in the shape of the object. In this case, you can also define which contour to use:
  - **Bounding Box** creates the boundary based on the object's bounding box.
  - **Detect Edges** creates the boundary using the same detection options you use to create a clipping path.
  - **Alpha Channel** creates the boundary from an Alpha channel saved in the placed image.
  - **Photoshop Path** creates the boundary from a path saved in the placed image.
  - **Graphic Frame** creates the boundary from the containing frame.
  - **Same as Clipping** creates the boundary from a clipping path saved in the placed image.
  - **User-Modified Path** appears by default if you drag the anchor points of the text wrap boundary.
- **Jump Object** keeps text from appearing to the right or left of the frame.
- **Jump to Next Column** forces surrounding text to the top of the next column or frame.

No Text Wrap / Wrap Around Bounding Box / Wrap Around Object Shape / Jump Object

Jump to Next Column — When this button is active (dark gray), all four offset fields have the same value.

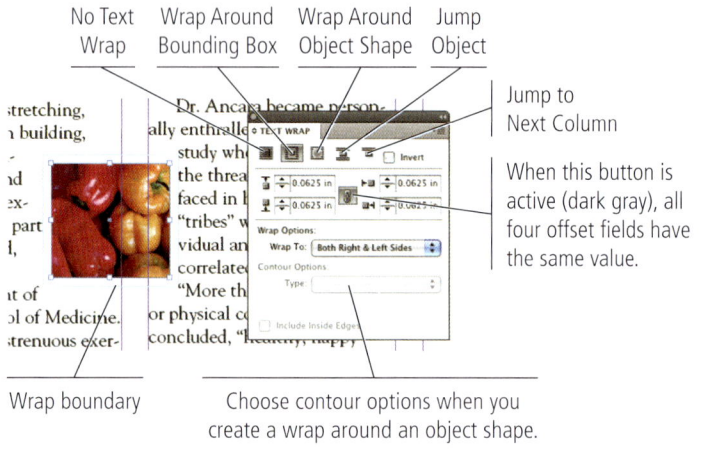

Wrap boundary

Choose contour options when you create a wrap around an object shape.

Regardless of which wrap you apply, you can define the Offset value, or the distance surrounding text will remain from the object. (If you use the Object Shape wrap option, you can define only a single Offset value; for the other three types, you can define a different offset value for each edge.

If you use the Bounding Box or Object Shape wrap option, you can also define the Wrap To options — whether the wrap is applied to a specific side (right, left, right and left, or the largest side), or toward or away from the spine.

176   Project 3: HeartSmart Newsletter

Stage 3 Working with Tables

Many page layouts incorporate tables of information, from basic tables with a few rows and columns to multi-page catalog spreadsheets with thousands of product numbers and prices. InDesign includes a number of options for building tables, each having advantages and disadvantages depending on what you need to accomplish. Regardless of which method you use to create a table, the same options are available for formatting the table, the cells in the table, and the content in the cells.

When you place an insertion point in an existing text frame, you can create a new table from scratch by choosing Table>Insert Table. This method allows you to define your own table parameters, including the number of rows and columns, the number of header and footer rows (top and bottom rows that appear in every instance of the table if the table breaks across multiple columns or frames), and even a defined style for the new table (table styles store formatting options such as gridline weight and color, cell inset, and other attributes that you learn about in this stage of the project).

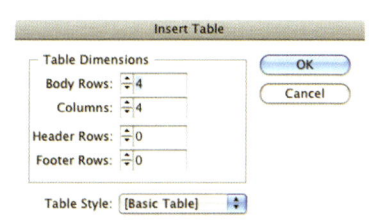

You can also create a table by selecting a series of tab-delimited text in the layout and choosing Table>Convert Text to Table. (Tab-delimited means that the content of each column is separated by a tab character.) Using this method, the new table becomes an inline object in the text frame that contained the original tabbed text.

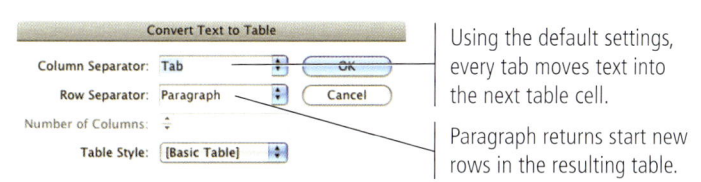

Using the default settings, every tab moves text into the next table cell.

Paragraph returns start new rows in the resulting table.

Note:

Pressing Tab moves the insertion point from one table cell to the next (from left to right, top to bottom). This means you can't press Tab to insert a tab character into text in an InDesign table; you have to choose Type>Insert Special Character>Other>Tab.

Finally, you can create a new table in InDesign by placing a Microsoft Excel file (Microsoft Excel is probably the most common application for creating spreadsheets). You'll use this method to complete this stage of the HeartSmart newsletter project.

Place a Microsoft Excel Table

Microsoft Excel spreadsheets can be short tables of text or complex, multi-page spreadsheets of data. In either case, Microsoft Excel users tend to spend hours formatting their spreadsheets for business applications. Those formatting options are typically not appropriate for commercial printing applications, but they give you a better starting point in your InDesign file than working from plain tabbed text.

1. Display Page 2 of the file **heartsmart_dec.indd**.

2. Choose File>Place and navigate to the file **nutrition.xls** in the RF_InDesign>HeartSmart>December Issue folder.

3. **Uncheck the Replace Selected Item option, make sure Show Import Options is checked, and click Open.**

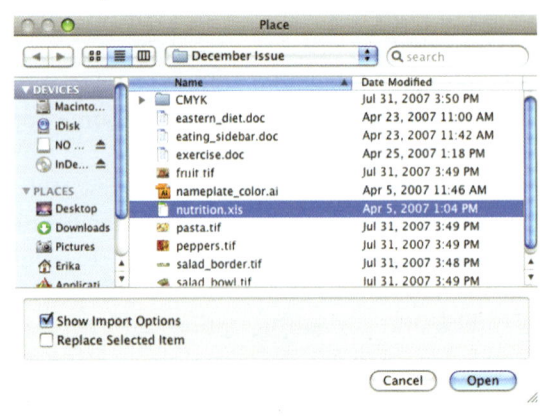

4. **Review the options in the resulting dialog box. Make sure your options match what is shown in the following image, and then click OK.**

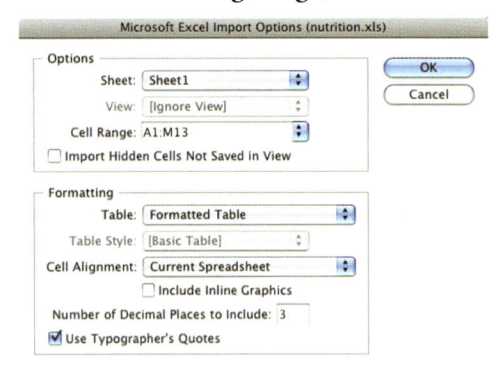

   If you see a warning about missing fonts, click OK; you're going to reformat the table text in the next exercise, so missing fonts won't be a problem.

5. **With the table loaded into the cursor, click in the empty area in the lower half of the page.**

   The new table is placed into the layout; a text frame is automatically created to contain the table. (The table currently extends beyond the right edge of the text frame, and the Overset Text icon in the frame's Out port indicates that the frame is not high enough to fit all the rows of the table).

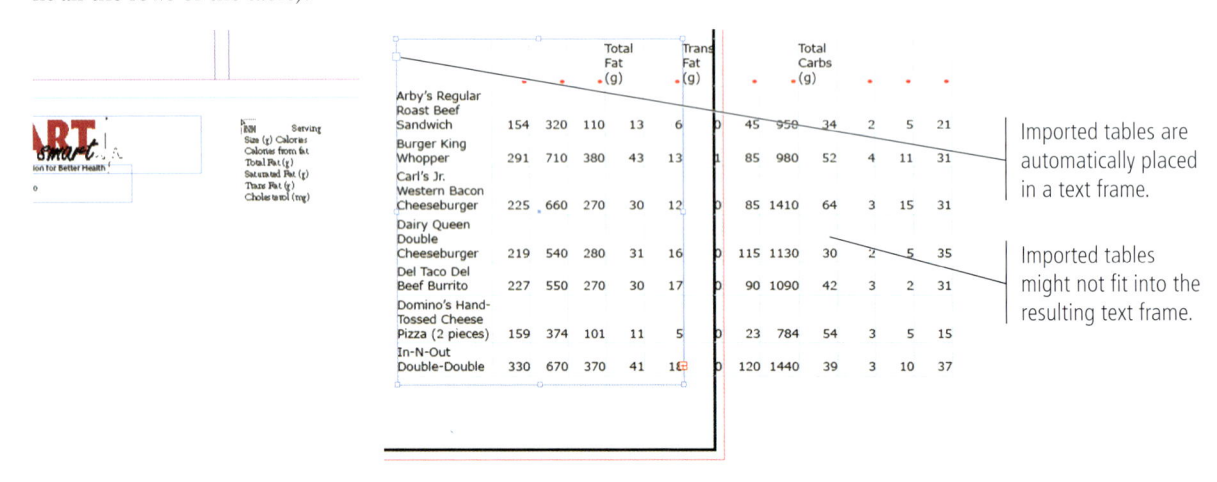

   Imported tables are automatically placed in a text frame.

   Imported tables might not fit into the resulting text frame.

   Obviously this table still needs some significant modification to make it a cohesive part of the newsletter layout. Some placed tables require more work than others, but be prepared to do at least some clean-up work whenever you place a spreadsheet/table.

6. **Drag the text frame with the table into the right column of the top half of the page.**

7. **Control/right-click the table and choose Fitting>Fit Frame to Content.**

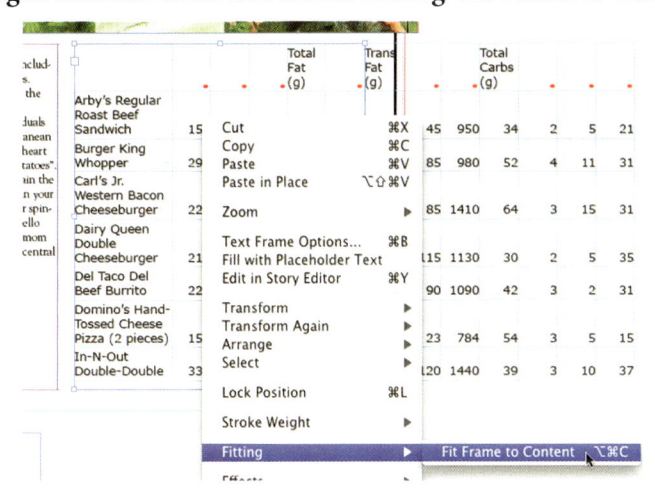

This is the same command you can use to resize a graphics frame; in this case, you're making the text frame big enough to show the entire table width. You should now be able to see the bottom row of the table.

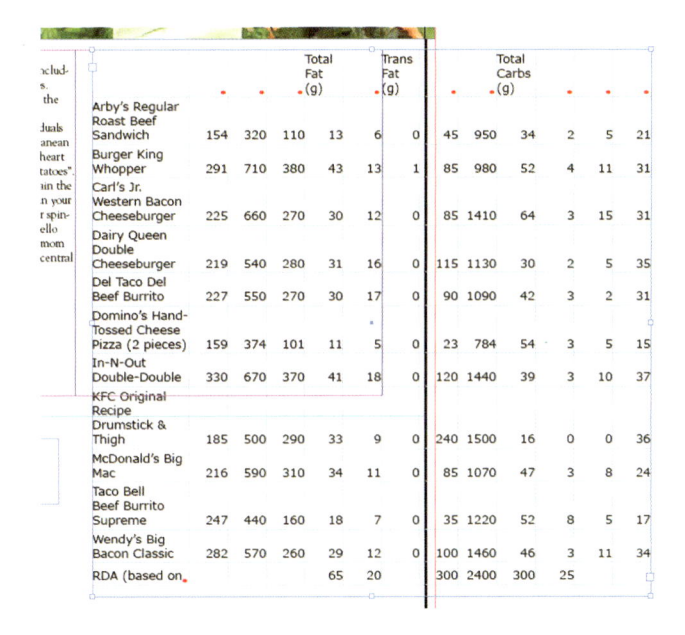

8. **Save the file and continue to the next exercise.**

FORMAT CELL CONTENTS

When you work with tables in InDesign, think of the cells as a series of text frames. Text in a table cell is no different than text in any other text frame; it can be formatted using the same options you've already learned, including paragraph and character styles.

1. **With `heartsmart_dec.indd` open, select the Type tool and click in the top-left cell of the table.**

2. **Drag to the bottom-right table cell to highlight all cells in the table.**

3. **Click Table Text in the Paragraph Styles panel to format all the text in the selected table cells.**

Project 3: HeartSmart Newsletter 179

4. **Click the Clear Overrides button at the bottom of the Paragraph Styles panel to apply only the base style definition to the text.**

   As with files from Microsoft Word, some options in Microsoft Excel spreadsheets might require this two-step process to apply your style definitions to the selected text.

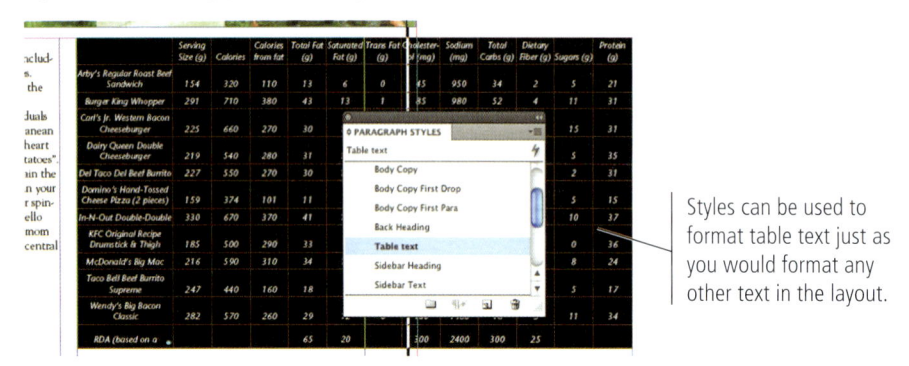

   Styles can be used to format table text just as you would format any other text in the layout.

5. **Click in any cell to deselect all table cells.**

6. **Place the cursor over the top edge of the first column of the table. When you see a down-pointing arrow, click to select the entire column.**

   You can also select rows by placing the cursor immediately left of a row and clicking when the cursor changes to a right-facing arrow.

   The down-pointing arrow means you can click to select the entire column.

   Note:

   You have to use the Type tool to select table cells, either individually in a specific area, or as entire rows/columns.

7. **Using the Control panel, change the selected column to left paragraph alignment.**

   Note:

   Text is still text, even though it's placed inside a table cell. You can apply all the same text-formatting options to table text that you can apply to text in a regular text frame.

8. **Save the file and continue to the next exercise.**

Project 3: HeartSmart Newsletter

FORMAT CELL ATTRIBUTES

As we mentioned in the previous exercise, table cells are very similar to regular text frames. Individual cells can have different attributes such as height and width, text inset, vertical positioning, and text orientation. These options can be controlled in the Table panel, the Control panel, and the Cell Options dialog box.

1. With `heartsmart_dec.indd` open, click in the second cell of the first row, and then drag to select all cells in the row except the first cell.

2. In the Table panel (Window>Type & Tables>Table), choose Exactly in the Row Height menu, and then change the field to **0.875 in**.

3. Change the Column Width field to **0.2785 in**.

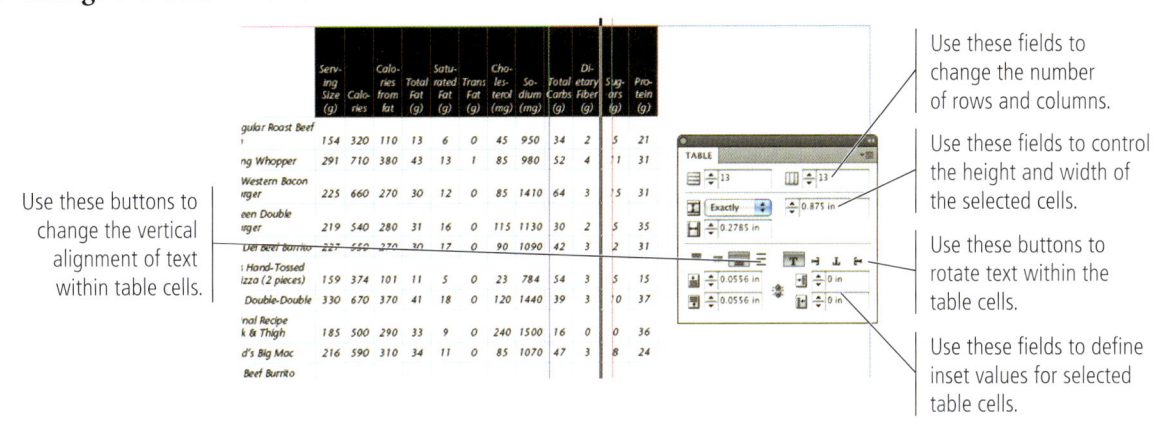

   Use these buttons to change the vertical alignment of text within table cells.

   Use these fields to change the number of rows and columns.

   Use these fields to control the height and width of the selected cells.

   Use these buttons to rotate text within the table cells.

   Use these fields to define inset values for selected table cells.

4. Click the Rotate Text 270° button so the left edge of the text aligns to the bottom edge of the cell.

5. Click the Align Center button so the text in each cell is centered top to bottom.

   Because the text is rotated, this button actually aligns the text between the left and right cell edges. It's important to remember that the vertical align options are based on the orientation of the text.

6. Using the Control panel, apply left paragraph alignment to the selected text.

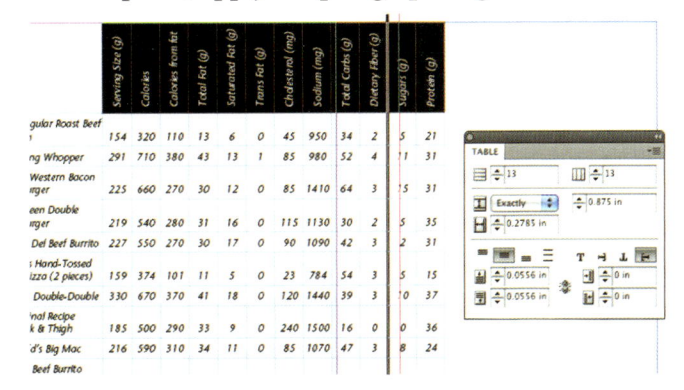

7. Click the second cell in the second row and drag to select all the cells that contain numeric data.

8. **Apply centered vertical alignment to the selected cells.**

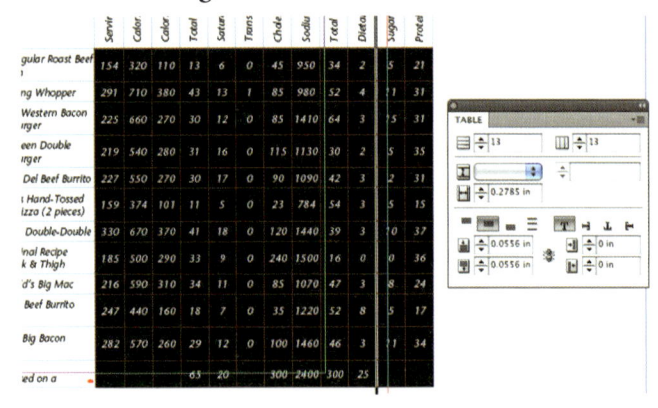

9. **Select the first four cells in the last row and choose Table>Merge Cells.**

    This function extends the contents of a single cell across multiple cells.

10. **Select the entire first column of the table and change the Left Inset value to 0.0625 in.**

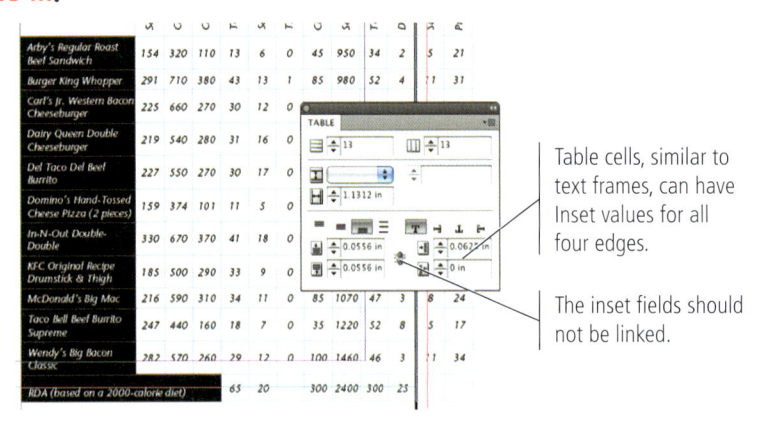

    Table cells, similar to text frames, can have Inset values for all four edges.

    The inset fields should not be linked.

11. **Place the cursor over the right edge of the first column until the cursor becomes a two-headed arrow.**

    When you see this cursor, you can drag the gridline to resize a column or row.

12. **Drag right until the column is wide enough to allow the Wendy's Big Bacon Classic to fit on one line.**

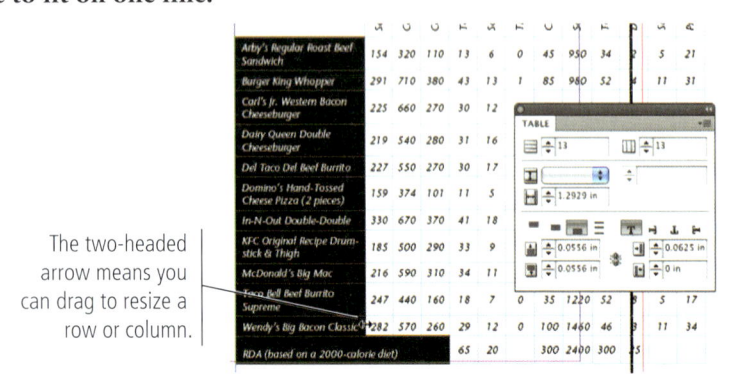

    The two-headed arrow means you can drag to resize a row or column.

Note:

Resizing the width of a cell resizes the entire column; resizing the height of a cell resizes the entire row.

13. **Place the insertion point in the cell with the Wendy's product name.**

    When you make the column wide enough to fit the text, the row automatically shrinks to one row. In the Table panel, you can see that the Row Height menu is set to At Least; this option allows cells to shrink to fit the height of cell contents, down to the defined minimum height.

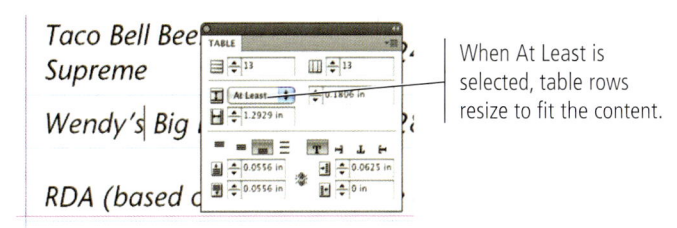

    When At Least is selected, table rows resize to fit the content.

14. **Save the file and continue to the next exercise.**

Controlling Cell Attributes

INDESIGN FOUNDATIONS

Basic attributes of individual table cells can be defined in the Text tab of the Cell Options dialog box (Table>Cell Options). Most table cell options are exactly the same as for regular text frames; the only choice unique to tables is **Clip Contents to Cell**. If you set a fixed row height that's too small for the cell content, an Overset icon appears in the lower-right corner of the cell. (You can't flow text from one table cell to another.) If you check the Clip Contents to Cell option, any content that doesn't fit in the cell will be clipped.

As with any text frame, a table cell can have its own fill and stroke attributes. These attributes can be defined in the Strokes and Fills tab (or using the Swatches and Stroke panels). You can turn individual cell edges (strokes) on or off by clicking specific lines in the preview.

The Rows and Columns tab controls row height and column width. If **At Least** is selected in the Row Height menu, you can define the minimum and maximum possible row height; rows change height if you add or remove text, or if you change the text formatting in a way that requires more or less space. If **Exactly** is selected, you can define the exact height of the cell.

If you're working with an extremely long table, you can break the table across multiple frames by threading (as you would for any long block of text). The **Keep Options** can be used to keep specific (selected) rows together after a break, and they determine where those rows will go, based on your choice in the Start Row menu.

You can add diagonal lines to specific cells using the Diagonal Lines tab. You can apply lines in either direction (or both) and choose a specific stroke weight, color, style, and tint. The Draw menu determines whether the line is created in front of or behind the cell's contents.

Many of these options are also available in the Table panel (and in the Control panel).

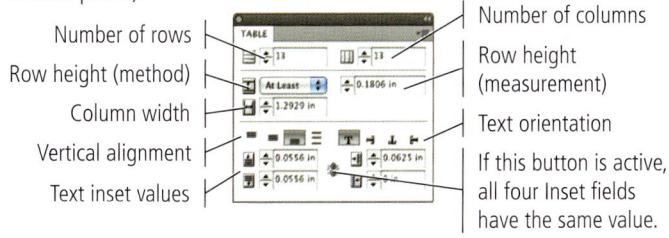

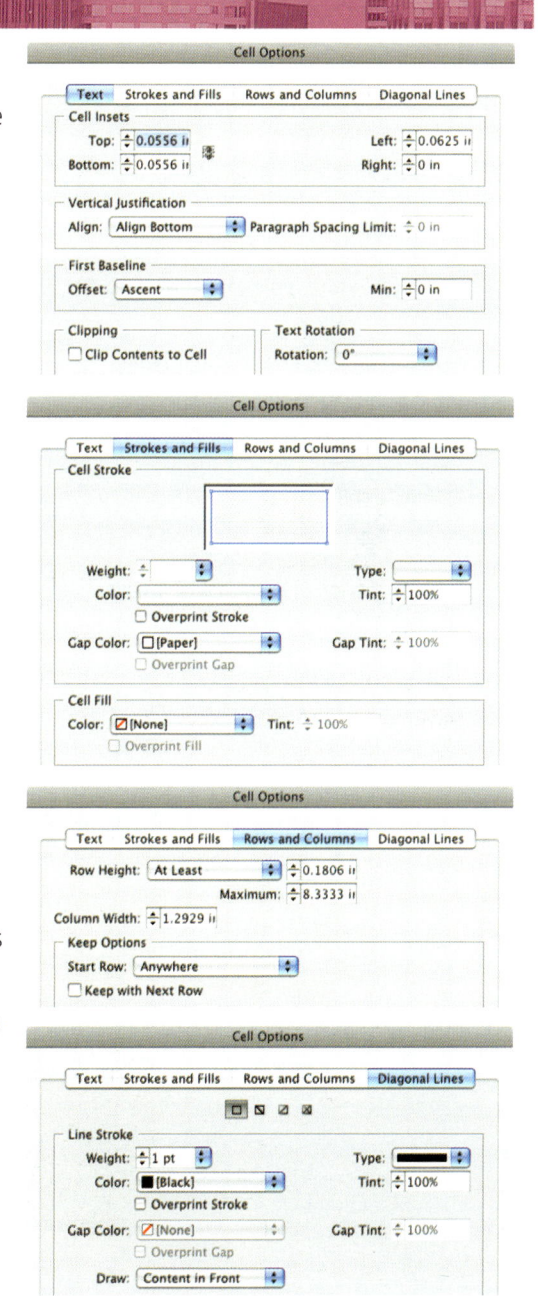

- Number of rows
- Row height (method)
- Column width
- Vertical alignment
- Text inset values
- Number of columns
- Row height (measurement)
- Text orientation
- If this button is active, all four Inset fields have the same value.

Project 3: HeartSmart Newsletter   183

Define Table Fills and Strokes

Like text frames, table cells can also have fill and stroke attributes. InDesign includes a number of options for adding color to tables, from changing the stroke and fill of an individual cell to defining patterns that repeat every certain number of rows and/or columns.

1. **With `heartsmart_dec.indd` open, open the Table panel Options menu. Choose Table Options>Table Setup.**

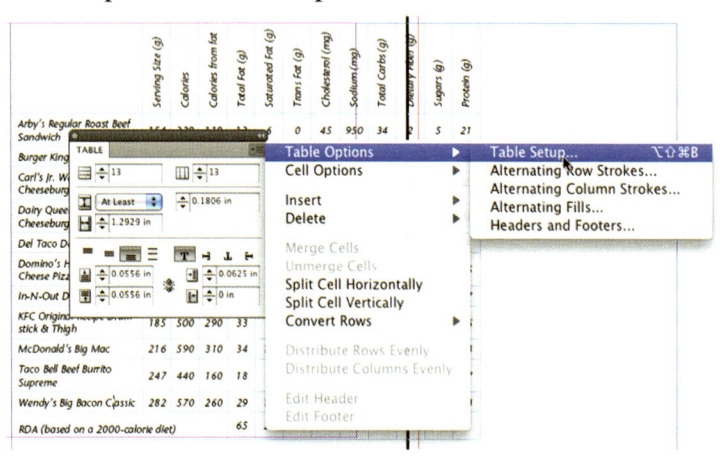

Note:

You can also choose Table>Table Options> Table Setup to access the dialog box.

Strokes and Fills in Tables

INDESIGN FOUNDATIONS

In the Table Options dialog box, you can use the Row Strokes and Column Strokes tabs to define stroke patterns based on the sequence you choose in the Alternating Pattern menus. Alternating rows can have different styles, weights, colors, and tints; you can also skip a specific number of rows at the top and bottom of a table.

You can also define patterns for filling different rows in the table, again based on your choice in the Alternating Pattern menu.

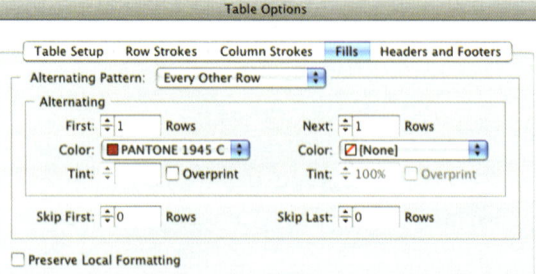

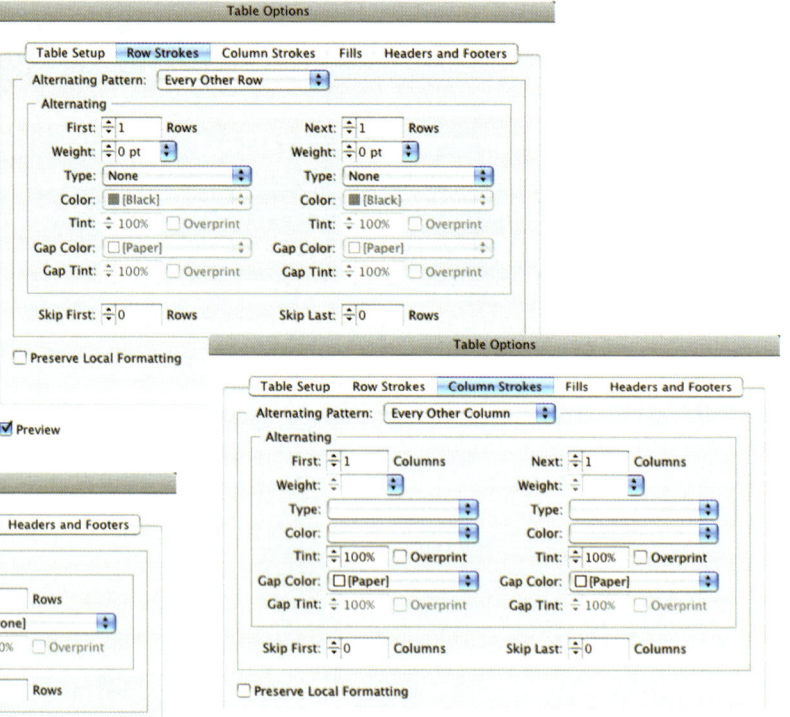

184 Project 3: HeartSmart Newsletter

2. **In the Table Setup tab, apply a 0.5-pt solid border of 100% Pantone 1945 C.**

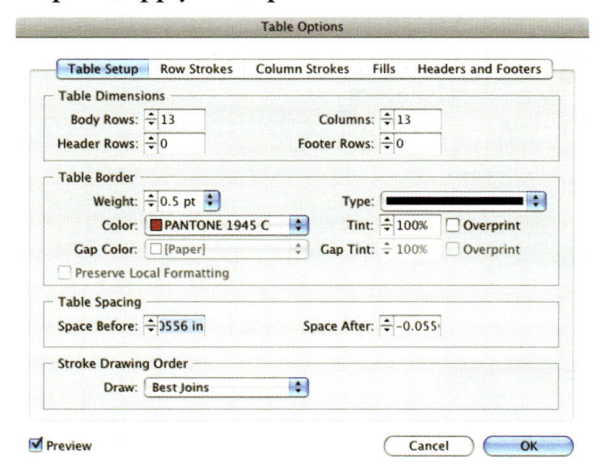

   Note:

   If you can't see the borders and strokes, try hiding frame edges (View>Hide Frame Edges) while you experiment with these options.

3. **In the Fills tab, choose Every Other Row in the Alternating Pattern menu.**

4. **Set the First field to 1 row and apply 20% Pantone 1945 C.**

5. **Set the Next field to 1 row and apply None as the color.**

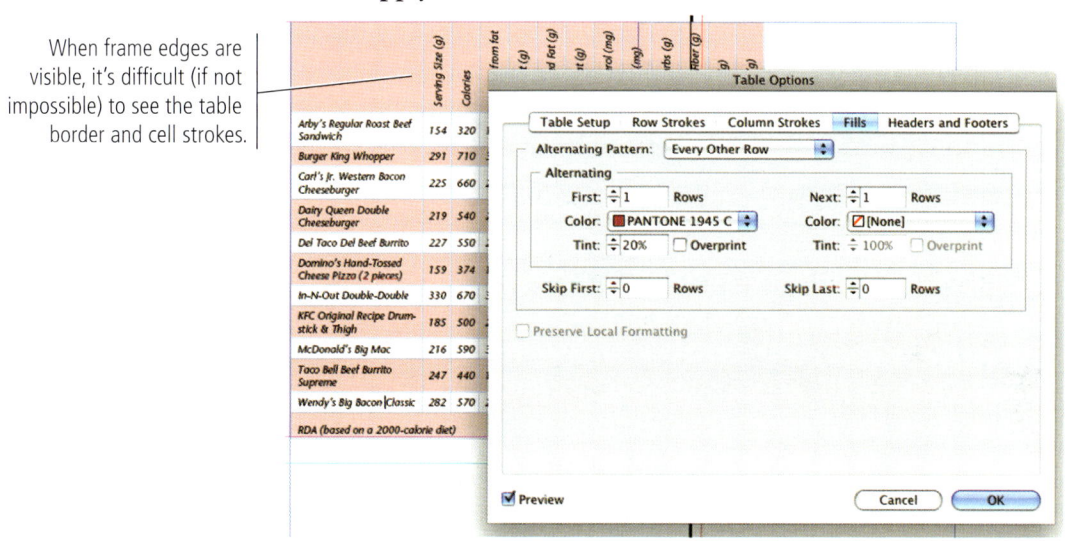

   When frame edges are visible, it's difficult (if not impossible) to see the table border and cell strokes.

6. **Click OK to apply your choices.**

7. **Select the last row in the table. Using the Swatches panel, change the cell fill tint to 50%.**

   Remember, table cells are very similar to individual text frames. You can change the color of cell fills and strokes using the Swatches panel, and you can change the cell stroke attributes using the Stroke panel.

   Cell fills can be changed in the Swatches panel, just as you would change the fill of a text frame.

Project 3: HeartSmart Newsletter

8. **Select all cells in the table. Open the Table panel Options menu and choose Cell Options>Strokes and Fills.**

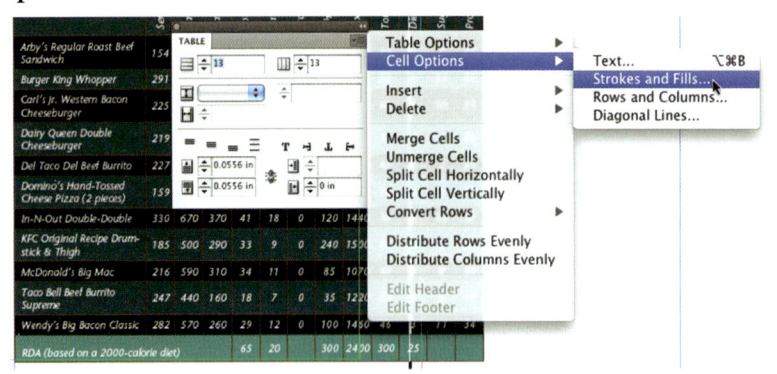

   Note:

   If you place the cursor at the top-left corner of the table, it changes to a diagonal arrow icon. Clicking with this cursor selects all cells in the table.

9. **In the preview area of the dialog box, click all three horizontal lines to remove the strokes from the tops and bottoms of the cells.**

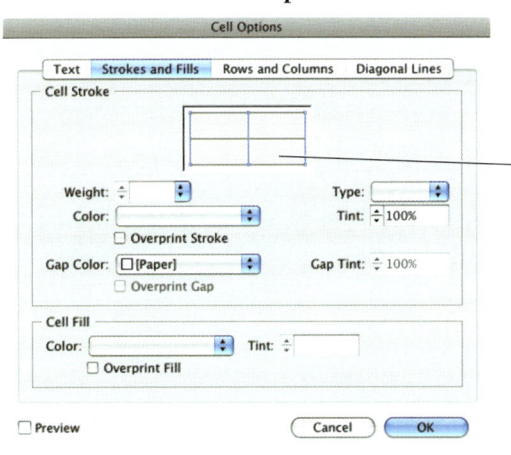

   By deselecting the horizontal lines before defining the stroke, you can add a stroke to the vertical gridlines only.

Managing Table Setup

INDESIGN FOUNDATIONS

The Table Setup tab of the Table Options dialog box (Table>Table Options>Table Setup) defines the table dimensions, table border, spacing above and below the table, and how strokes are applied to the table.

The **Stroke Drawing Order** allows you to control the appearance where gridlines of different styles or colors meet. If Best Joins is selected, styled strokes such as double lines result in joined strokes and gaps.

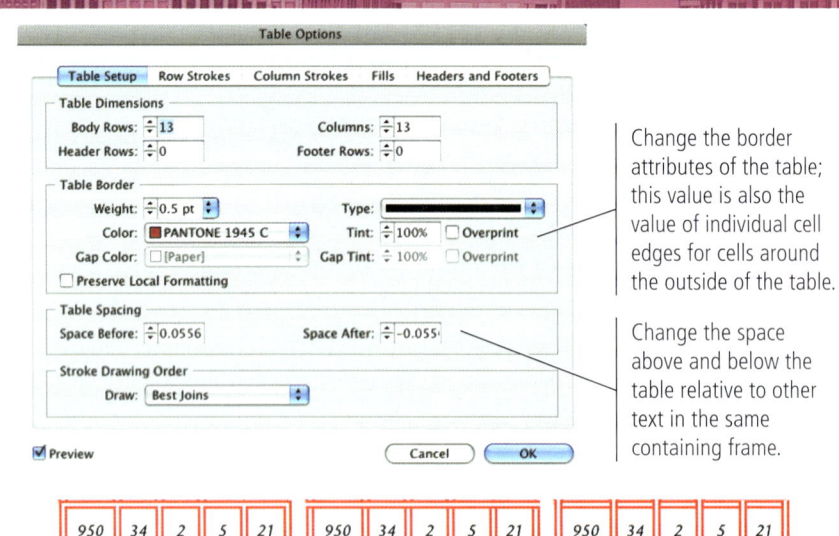

Change the border attributes of the table; this value is also the value of individual cell edges for cells around the outside of the table.

Change the space above and below the table relative to other text in the same containing frame.

Best Joins   Row Strokes in Front   Column Strokes in Front

186   Project 3: HeartSmart Newsletter

10. **Apply a 0.5-pt, 100% Pantone 1945 C stroke value, using the Solid stroke type.**

    These settings change the attributes for the vertical gridlines for all selected cells.

    Note:

    You can apply different stroke values to every cell in a table (although you probably wouldn't want to).

11. **Click OK to apply the stroke values to your table.**

12. **Click away from the table to deselect it, and then choose View>Hide Frame Edges to review the table formatting.**

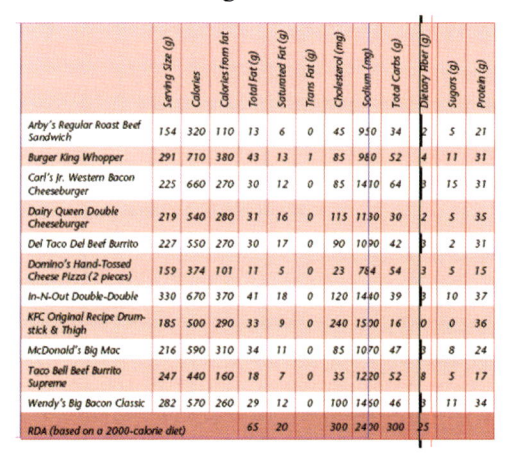

13. **Choose View>Show Frame Edges and then continue working.**

14. **Using the Selection tool, Control/right-click the table and choose Fitting>Fit Frame to Content from the contextual menu.**

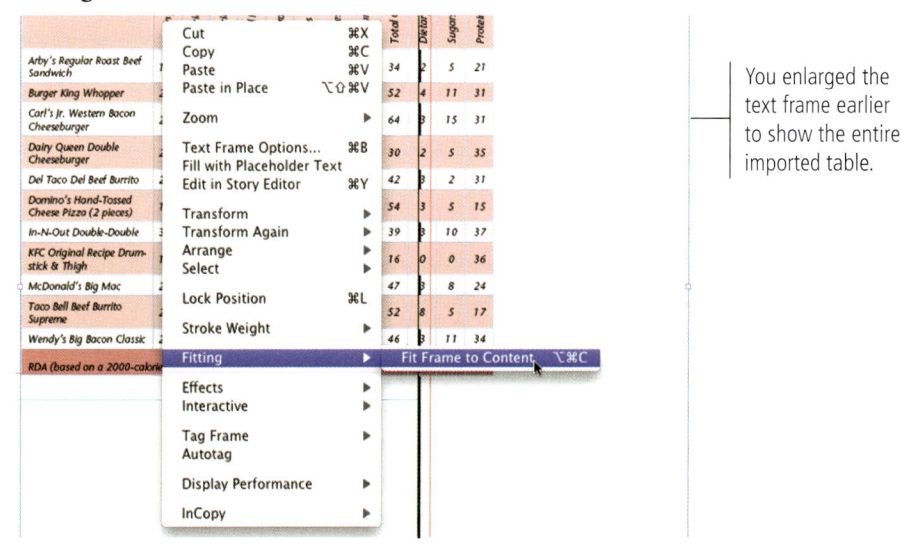

    You enlarged the text frame earlier to show the entire imported table.

Project 3: HeartSmart Newsletter

15. **Drag the table until the top-right corner of the frame snaps to the top-right margin guide on Page 2.**

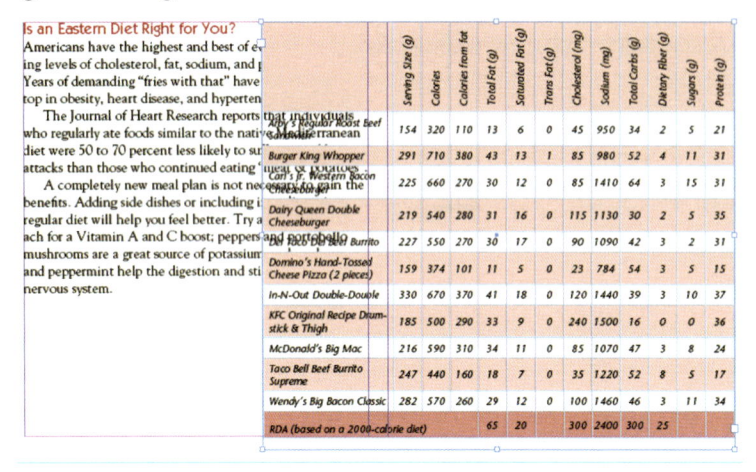

16. **With the frame still selected, click the second button in the Text Wrap panel so the Eastern Diet story wraps around the frame that contains the table. Change the Left Wrap field to 0.125 in.**

    A table is always contained inside a text frame. To control the wrap around a table, you have to actually apply the wrap attributes to the frame that contains the table.

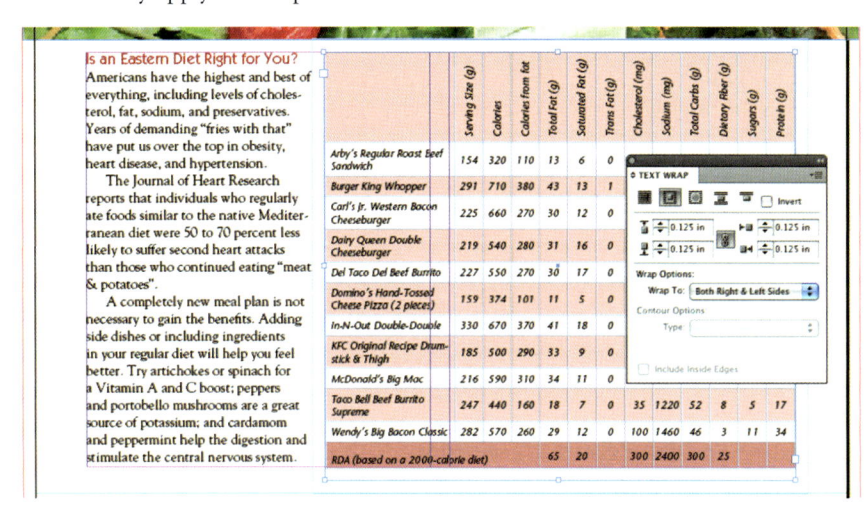

    Note:

    Remember, you can turn off the Link button in the Text Wrap panel to apply different wrap values to each side of the frame.

17. **Save the file and continue to the final stage of the project.**

Creating Table Headers and Footers

INDESIGN FOUNDATIONS

Long tables of data often require more than one text frame (or column, depending on the table). In this case, you can break a table across multiple frames and use repeating headers and footers for information that needs to be part of each instance of the table (for example, column headings). Repeating headers and footers eliminate the need to manually insert the repeating information in each instance of the table.

- Header row
- Body rows
- Footer row
- One table broken into two columns

Repeating header and footer rows are dynamically linked; this means that changing one instance of a header or footer changes all instances of the same header or footer.

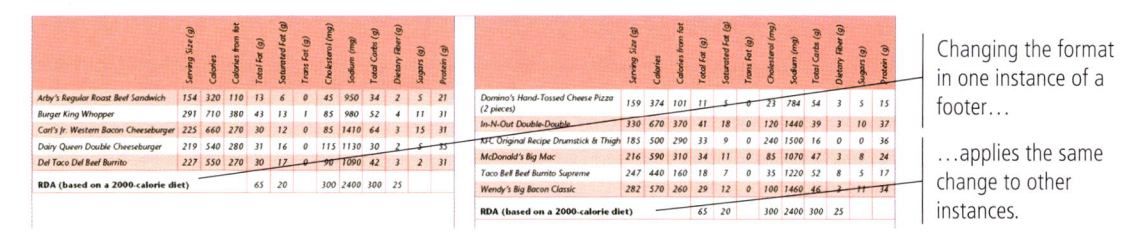

- Changing the format in one instance of a footer…
- …applies the same change to other instances.

Finally, this capability also means the headers and footers remain at the top and bottom of each instance, even if other body rows move to a different instance.

- The header row remains in place at the top of the second instance.
- Resizing the containing frame allows an extra body row to fit into the first instance.

You can add new header and footer rows to a table when you create the table, or by changing the options in the Headers and Footers tab of the Table Options dialog box. You can also convert existing rows to headers or footers by selecting one or more rows and choosing Table>Convert Rows>To Header or To Footer. You can also control these elements in the Headers and Footers dialog box.

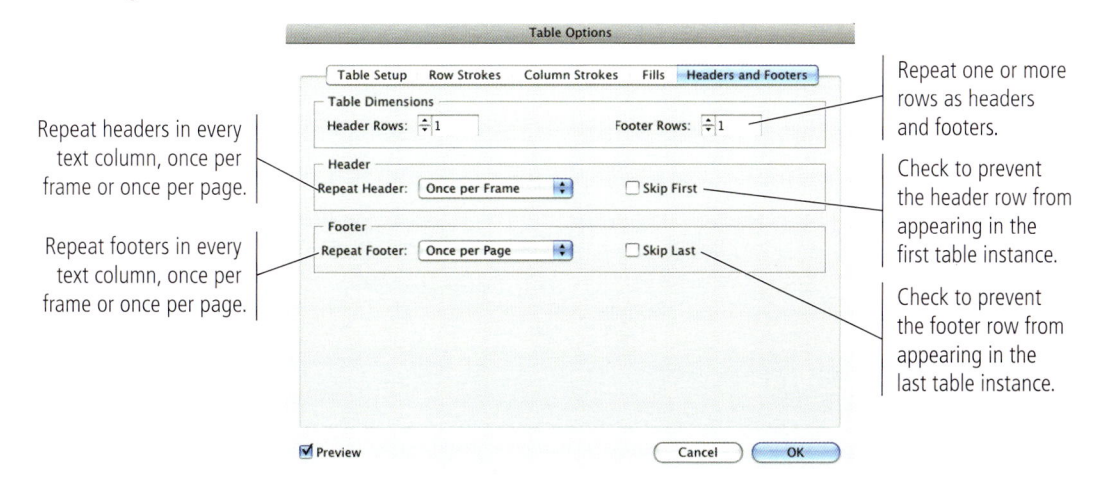

- Repeat headers in every text column, once per frame or once per page.
- Repeat footers in every text column, once per frame or once per page.
- Repeat one or more rows as headers and footers.
- Check to prevent the header row from appearing in the first table instance.
- Check to prevent the footer row from appearing in the last table instance.

Project 3: HeartSmart Newsletter   189

Table Styles

If you've spent any amount of time refining the appearance of a table, and you think you might want to use the same format again, you can save your formatting choices as a style. InDesign supports both table styles and cell styles, which are controlled in the Table Styles panel and Cell Styles panel.

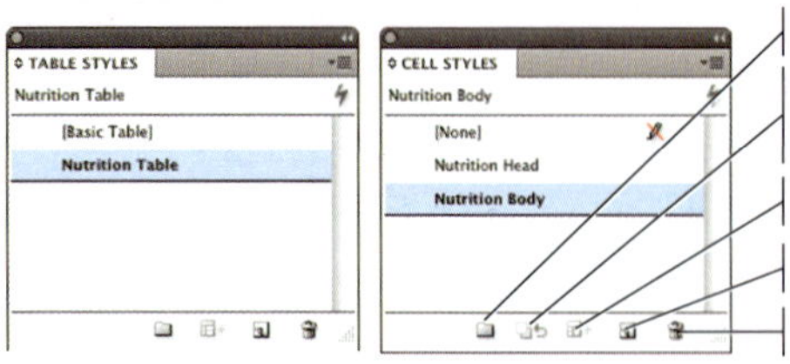

Table and cell styles use the same concept as text-formatting styles. You can apply a cell style by selecting the cells and clicking the style name in the Cell Styles panel. Clicking a style in the Table Styles panel applies the style to the entire selected table.

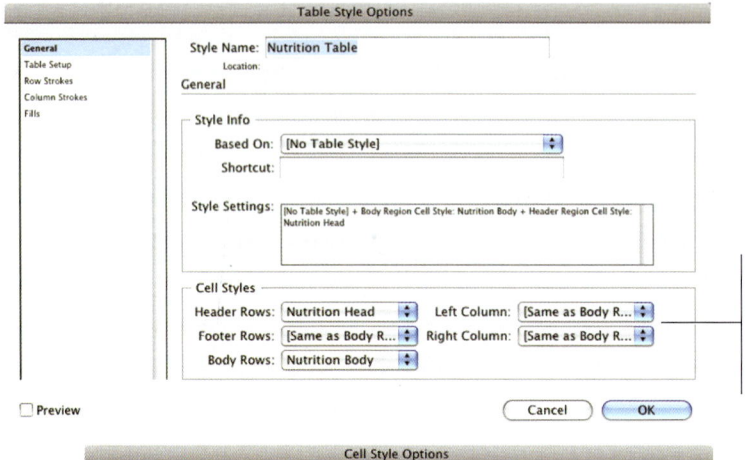

The Clear Overrides button clears text-formatting options; the Clear Attributes button clears cell attributes.

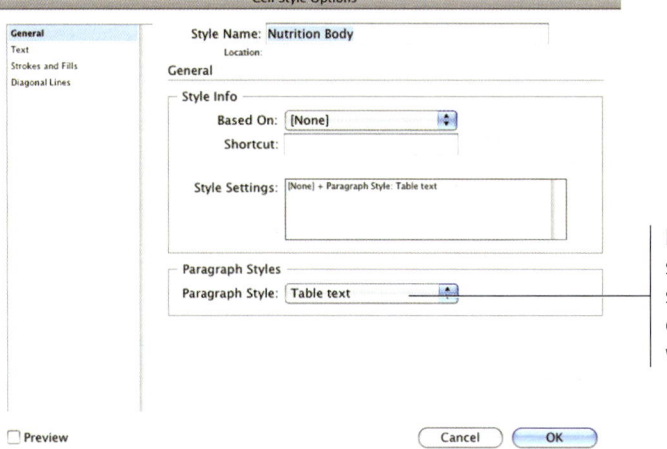

Table styles store all options that can be defined in the Table Setup dialog box (except the options for header and footer rows). You can also define cell styles (called **nesting styles**) for specific types of rows, as well as the left and right columns in the table.

Cell styles store all options that can be defined in the Cell Options dialog box. You can also define the paragraph style applied to cells using that style.

INDESIGN FOUNDATIONS

- New style group
- Clear attributes not defined by style
- Clear Overrides
- New style
- Delete

Nest cell styles for specific types of table rows, as well as for the left and right columns.

Nest a paragraph style into a cell style to format the cell contents, as well as the cell.

190 Project 3: HeartSmart Newsletter

Stage 4   Preflighting and Packaging the Job

When you submit an InDesign layout to a commercial output provider, you need to send all the necessary pieces of the job — the layout file, any placed (linked) graphics or other files, and the fonts used in the layout. Before you copy everything to a disk and send it out, however, you should check your work to make sure the file is ready for commercial printing.

When you opened the original template at the beginning of this project, you replaced missing fonts and graphics — two of the most common problems with digital layout files. However, successful output on a commercial press has a number of other technical requirements that — if you ignore them — can cause a file to output incorrectly or not at all. InDesign includes a preflighting utility that makes it easy to check for potential errors, as well as a packaging utility that gathers all the necessary bits for the printer.

Define a Preflight Profile

InDesign includes a dynamic, built-in preflighting utility that can check for common errors as you build a file. If you introduce a problem while building a file, the bottom-left corner of the document window shows a red light and the number of potential errors. In the following exercise, you define a profile to check for errors based on the information you have. This is certainly not an exhaustive check for all possible output problems. You should always work closely with your output provider to build responsible files that will cause no problems in the output workflow.

Note:

Ask your output provider if they have defined an InDesign preflight profile that you can load into your application to check for the problems that will interrupt their specific workflows.

1. **With heartsmart_dec.indd open, look at the bottom-left corner of the document window.**

   This area shows the number of errors in the file (if any).

2. **Click the arrow to the right of the No Errors message and choose Preflight Panel from the menu.**

   The message currently shows no errors, but at this point you don't know exactly what is being checked. The Preflight panel provides an interface for defining preflight profiles, as well as reviewing the specific issues identified as errors.

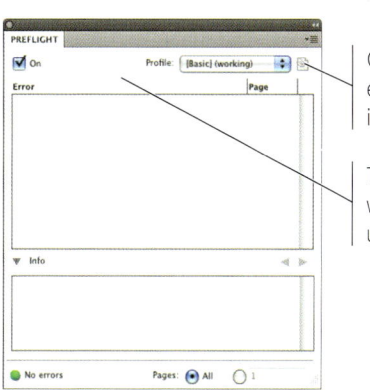

   Click this button to embed the current profile into the active document.

   The Preflight panel shows which profile is being used to check for errors.

Project 3: HeartSmart Newsletter

3. **Open the Preflight panel Options menu and choose Define Profiles.**

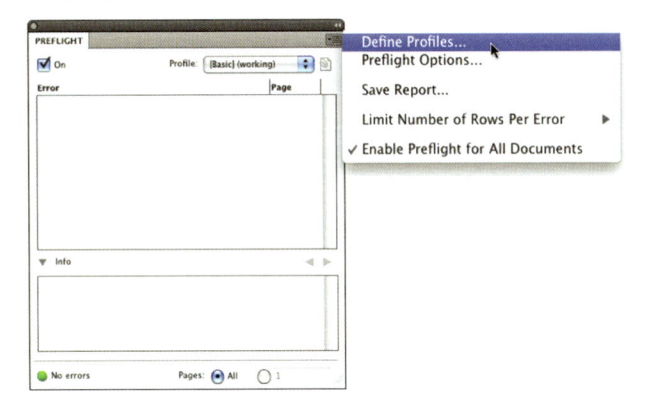

4. **In the Preflight Profiles dialog box, click the "+" button in the left side of the dialog box to create a new profile.**

    Rather than relying on generic built-in profiles, you should be aware of and able to control exactly what is (and is not) an error.

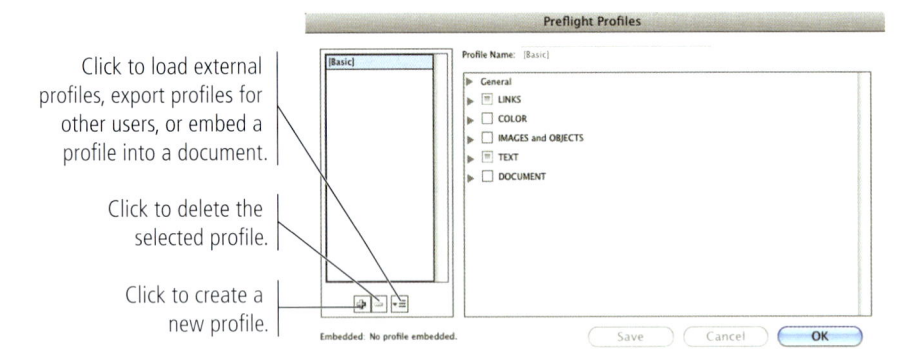

    Click to load external profiles, export profiles for other users, or embed a profile into a document.

    Click to delete the selected profile.

    Click to create a new profile.

    Note:

    Preflight profiles become part of the application, but are not linked to or saved in a specific document unless you intentionally embed the profile.

5. **Type `HeartSmart Check` in the Profile Name field, then click the empty area below the list of profiles to finalize the new name.**

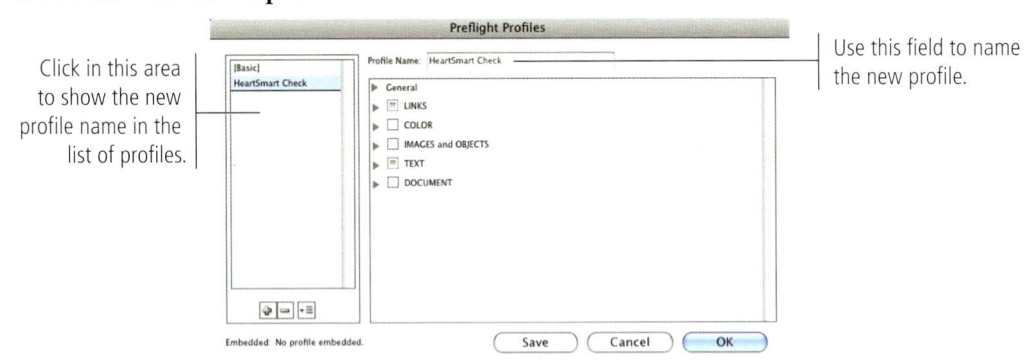

    Click in this area to show the new profile name in the list of profiles.

    Use this field to name the new profile.

Project 3: HeartSmart Newsletter

6. **With the HeartSmart Check profile selected on the left side of the dialog box, expand the General category on the right. In the Description field, type Verify newsletter for 4c press.**

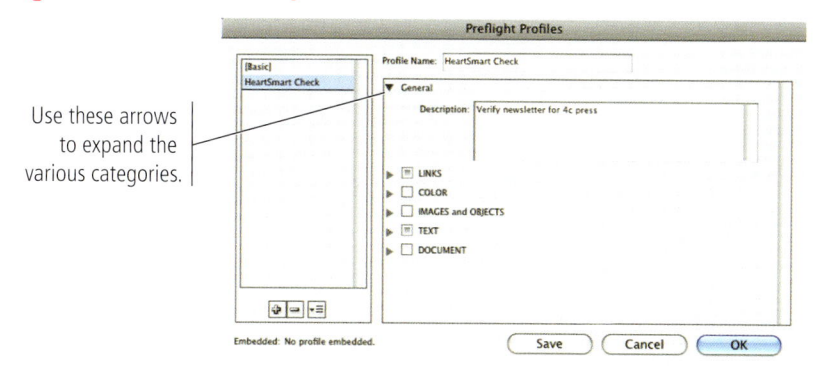

Use these arrows to expand the various categories.

Note:

This description is simply a reminder of the profile's intent.

7. **Collapse the General category and expand the Links category. Check the Links Missing or Modified option.**

   Image files placed in a layout need to be available when the job is output. By checking this option, you are warned if any placed image has been moved or modified since it was placed into the layout.

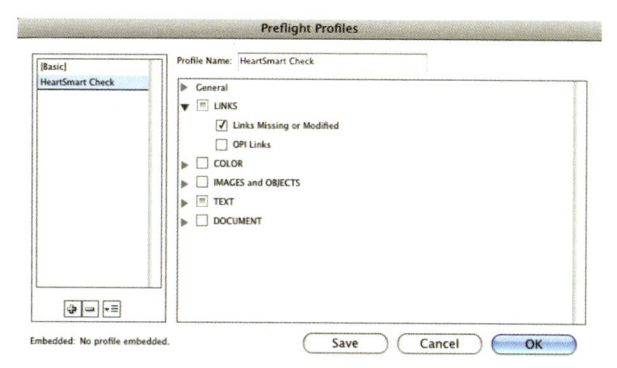

8. **Collapse the Links category and expand the Color category. Check and expand the Color Spaces and Modes Not Allowed option, and then check the RGB and Spot Color options.**

   You know this newsletter is going to be output as a 4-color job. Spot colors will create an extra separation, which can be a very costly error. By setting these options, you will receive a warning if you create a spot color in a job that should be output as 4-color.

   Some output processes use a method called in-RIP separation to convert RGB images to CMYK during the output process. However, the conversion process can cause significant color shift if it is not controlled. To achieve the best-quality, predictable output, it's a good idea to check for RGB images and control the conversion process in an image-editing application (i.e., Photoshop).

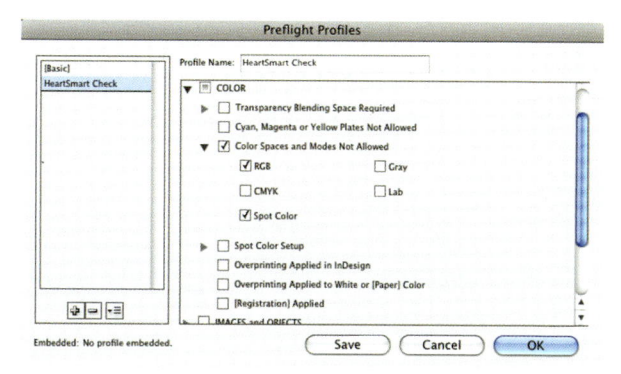

Project 3: HeartSmart Newsletter 193

9. **Collapse the Color category and expand the Images and Objects category. Check and expand the Image Resolution option. Check the three Minimum Resolution options. Change the Color and Grayscale minimums to 300 and change the 1-bit option to 1200.**

    As you learned in Project 1, commercial output devices typically require at least 300 ppi to output raster images at good quality. By setting these minimum restrictions, you will receive a warning if your (or your client's) images do not have enough resolution to output at good quality using most commercial printing processes.

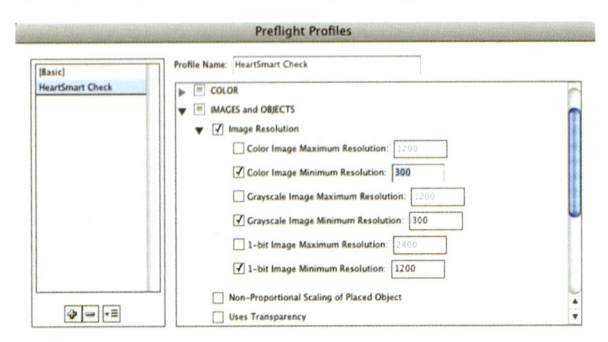

    Note:

    Remember: Required resolution is actually two times the line screen (lpi) used for a specific job. If you don't know the lpi, 300 ppi resolution is a safe choice for most printing.

10. **Collapse the Images and Objects category and expand the Text category. Check the Overset Text and Font Missing options.**

    Overset text could simply be the result of extra paragraph returns at the end of a story. However, you should always check these issues to be sure that some of the client's text has not been accidentally overset.

11. **Collapse the Text category and expand the Document category. Check the Number of Pages Required option. Expand that option, choose Exactly in the menu, and type 2 in the field.**

    You know that every issue of the newsletter should be exactly 2 pages. If your file has more or less than 2 pages, you will receive an error message.

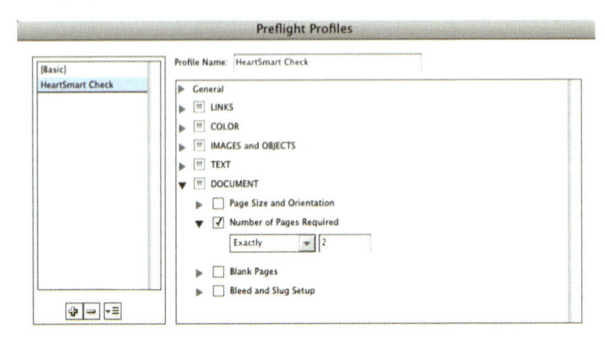

12. **Click OK to save the profile and close the dialog box.**

13. **Continue to the next exercise.**

194   Project 3: HeartSmart Newsletter

What's in a Preflight Profile?

The Preflight Profiles dialog box includes a number of options for identifying potential errors. If you are going to build responsible files, you should have a basic understanding of what these options mean.

This is by no means an exhaustive list of all the potential problems in digital page layout files; it's a list of the problems Adobe included in the Preflight Profile dialog box. Other problems are beyond the scope of most graphic designers and are better left to prepress professionals to correct, given the specific equipment conditions in their workflows.

It should also be noted that some of these issues are not necessarily errors, but nonetheless should be reviewed before a job is output. For example, blank pages might be intentionally placed into a document to force a chapter opener onto a right-facing page; in this case, the blank page is not an error. In other cases, a blank page might be left over after text is edited; in this case, the blank page would be an error. You can use the Preflight panel to find definite errors, but also use it to verify that what you have is exactly what you want.

Links

- **Links Missing or Modified.** Use this option to receive a warning if a placed file has been moved (missing) or changed (modified) since it was placed into a layout. If a placed file is missing, the output will use only the low-resolution preview that appears in the file. If a placed file has been modified, the output will reflect the most up-to-date version of the placed file — which could be drastically different than the original, which can in turn destroy your overall layout.
- **OPI Links.** OPI is a workflow tool that allows designers to use low-resolution FPO (for placement only) files during the design stage of a job. When the job is processed for output, the high-resolution versions are swapped out in place of the FPO images. Although not terribly common anymore (thanks to larger storage and higher processing speeds on desktop computers), some larger agencies still use OPI workflows.

Document

- **Page Size and Orientation.** Use this option to cause an error if the document size is not a specific size; you can also cause an error if the current document is oriented other than the defined page size (i.e., portrait instead of landscape or vice versa).
- **Number of Pages Required.** Use this option to define a specific number of pages, the smallest number of pages that can be in the document, or whether the document must have pages in multiples of a specific number (for example, multiples of 16 for 16-page signature output).
- **Blank Pages.** Use this option to find blank pages in the document.
- **Bleed and Slug Setup.** Use this option to verify the document's bleed and slug sizes against values required by a specific output process.

Color

- **Transparency Blending Space Required.** Use this option to define whether CMYK or RGB should be used to flatten transparent objects for output. (Refer to Project 2 for more on transparency flattening.)
- **Cyan, Magenta, or Yellow Plates Not Allowed.** Use this option to verify layouts that will be output with only spot colors, or with black and spot colors.
- **Color Spaces and Modes Not Allowed.** Use this option to create errors if the layout uses RGB, CMYK, Spot Color, Gray, or LAB color models. (Different jobs have different defined color spaces. The CMYK option can be useful, for example, if you are building a layout that will be output in black only.)
- **Spot Color Setup.** Use this option to define the number of spot colors a job should include, as well as the specific color model that should be used (LAB or CMYK) when converting unwanted spot colors for process printing.
- **Overprinting Applied in InDesign.** Use this option to create an error if an element is set to overprint instead of trap. (These issues are explained in Project 6.)
- **Overprinting Applied to White or [Paper] Color.** By definition, White or [Paper] is technically the absence of other inks. Unless you are printing white toner or opaque spot ink, white cannot, by definition, overprint. Use this option to produce an error if White or [Paper] elements are set to overprint.
- **[Registration] Applied.** The [Registration] color swatch is a special swatch used for elements such as crop and registration marks. Any element that uses the [Registration] color will output on all separations in the job. Use this option to find elements that are incorrectly colored with the [Registration] color instead of (probably) black.

What's in a Preflight Profile? (continued)

Images and Objects

- **Image Resolution.** Use this option to identify placed files with too little or too much resolution. As you know, commercial output devices typically require 300 ppi to output properly. The maximum resolution options can be used to find objects that, typically through scaling, result in unnecessarily high resolutions that might take considerable time for the output device to process.
- **Non-Proportional Scaling of Placed Object.** Use this option to find placed files that have been scaled with different X and Y percentages.
- **Uses Transparency.** Use this option to find any element affected by transparency. As you learned in Project 2, you should carefully preview transparency flattening before outputting the job.
- **Image ICC Profile.** Use this option to find placed images that have embedded ICC profiles. Typically used in color-managed workflows, placed images often store information — in the form of profiles — about the way a particular device captured or created the color in that image. You can cause errors if the image profile results in CMYK conversion, or if the embedded image profile has been overridden in the layout.
- **Layer Visibility Overrides.** Use this option to find layered Photoshop files in which the visibility of specific layers has been changed within InDesign.
- **Minimum Stroke Weight.** There is a limit to the smallest visible line that can be produced by any given output device. Use this option to find objects with a stroke weight smaller than a specific point size.
- **Interactive Elements.** Use this option to find elements with interactive properties (more on this in Project 7).
- **Bleed/Trim Hazard.** Use this option to find elements that fall within a defined distance of the page edge, or spine for facing-page layouts (i.e., outside the live area).

Text

- **Overset Text.** Use this option to find any frames with overset text.
- **Paragraph Style and Character Style Overrides.** Use this option to find instances where an applied style has been overridden with local formatting.
- **Font Missing.** Use this option to create an error if any required font is not available on the computer.
- **Glyph Missing.** Use this option to identify glyphs that aren't available (more on glyphs in Project 5).
- **Dynamic Spelling Detects Errors.** Use this option to cause an error if InDesign's dynamic spelling utility identifies any errors in the document.
- **Font Types Not Allowed.** Use this option to prohibit specific font types that can cause problems in modern output workflows.
- **Non-Proportional Type Scaling.** Use this option to identify type that has been artificially stretched or compressed in one direction (i.e., where horizontal or vertical scaling has been applied).
- **Minimum Type Size.** Use this option to identify any type set smaller than a defined point size. You can also identify small type that requires more than one ink to reproduce (a potential registration problem on commercial output devices).
- **Cross-References.** Use this option to identify dynamic links from one location in a file to another. You can cause errors if a cross reference is out of date or unresolved.
- **Conditional Text Indicators Will Print.** Use this option to create an error if certain visual indicators will appear in the final output. (You explore conditional text in Project 5.)

EVALUATE THE LAYOUT

Now that you have defined the issues you know are errors, you can check your file for those issues and make the necessary corrections.

1. **With heartsmart_dec.indd open, click the Profile menu in the Preflight panel and choose HeartSmart Check as the profile to use.**

2. **In the bottom of the panel, make sure the All radio button is checked.**

   When the All option is active, the entire document is checked. You can use the other radio button to define a specific page or range of pages to preflight.

   As soon as you call the HeartSmart Check profile, the panel reports 10 errors.

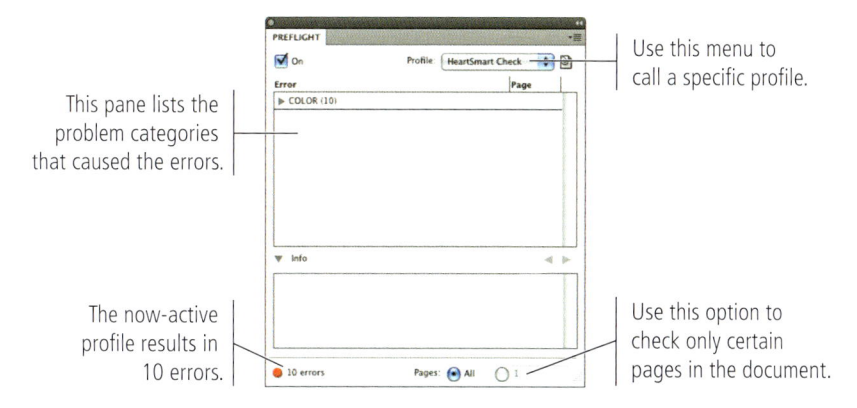

   This pane lists the problem categories that caused the errors.

   Use this menu to call a specific profile.

   The now-active profile results in 10 errors.

   Use this option to check only certain pages in the document.

3. **Click the arrow to expand the Color list, and then click the arrow to expand the Color Space Not Allowed list.**

4. **Click the Page Item listing to select it, and then click the hot text page number for that item.**

   The hot text link on the right side of the Preflight panel changes the document window to show the specific item that caused the error. The Info area offers information about the error, and offers suggestions for fixing the problem.

   Click the hot text to navigate to a specific instance of the problem.

Project 3: HeartSmart Newsletter 197

5. **In the Swatches panel, Control/right-click the Pantone 1945 C swatch and choose Swatch Options from the contextual menu.**

Note:

Spot colors are not always errors. Check the project's specifications carefully before you convert spot colors to process. Also, be aware that spot colors are often outside the CMYK gamut; converting a spot color to process can result in drastic color shift.

6. **In the Swatch Options dialog box, change the Color Type menu to Process.**

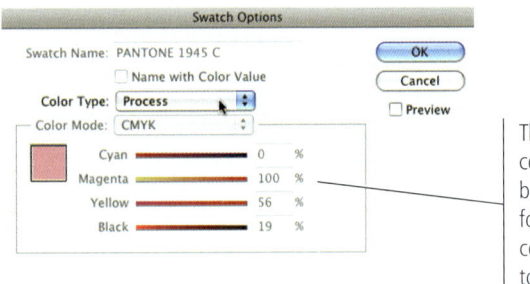

The color was already converted to a CMYK build, but someone forgot to change the color type from spot to process.

Note:

The type of error described in Step 6 is a common error. If not fixed, it would result in an extra, unwanted separation when the file is output for press — a costly mistake.

7. **Click OK to apply the new swatch options.**

The former spot color now shows the process color icon.

Nine of the errors have been corrected by fixing this single issue.

8. **Select the remaining problem instance in the Preflight panel and click the hot text link to show that element in the layout.**

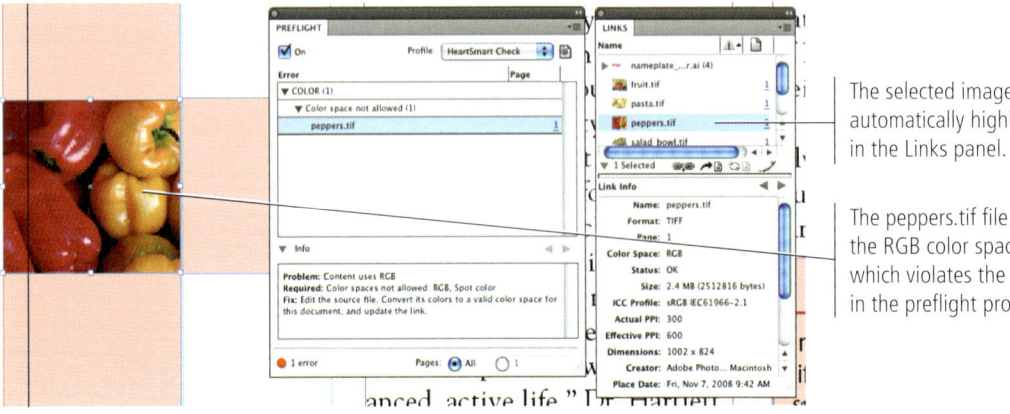

The selected image is automatically highlighted in the Links panel.

The peppers.tif file uses the RGB color space, which violates the rule in the preflight profile.

Project 3: HeartSmart Newsletter

9. **In the Links panel, click the Relink button. Navigate to the file `peppers_cmyk.tif` in the RF_InDesign>HeartSmart>December Issue>CMYK folder and click Open. If you see the Image Import Options dialog box, click OK to accept the default options.**

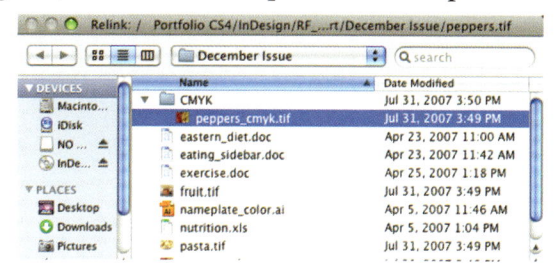

10. **Save the file and continue to the next exercise.**

After linking to the CMYK version of the image, the file shows no errors (based on the profile you defined).

CREATE THE JOB PACKAGE

Now that your file is error-free, you can package it for the output provider. As we have already stated, the images and fonts used in a layout must be available on the computer used to output the job. When you send the layout file to the printer, you must also send the necessary components. InDesign includes a Package utility that makes this process very easy.

1. **With `heartsmart_dec.indd` open, choose File>Package.**

2. **Review the information in the Package dialog box, and then click Package.**

    If you had not preflighted the file before opening the Package dialog box, you would see warning icons identifying problems with image color space or missing fonts. Because you completed the previous exercise, however, potential errors have been fixed, so this dialog box simply shows a summary list of information about the file you are packaging.

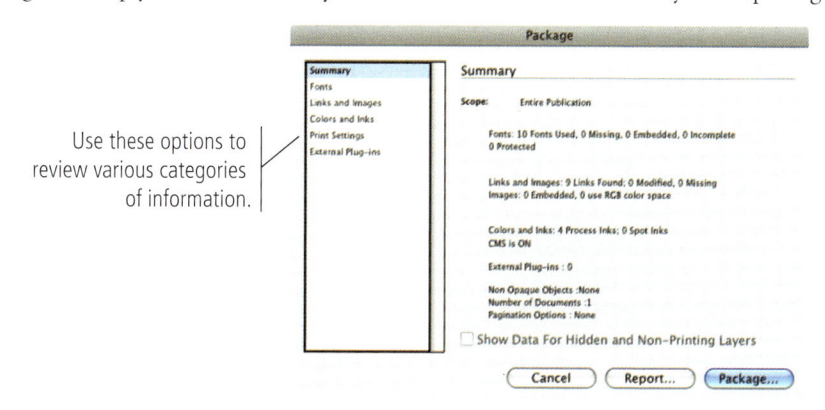

    Use these options to review various categories of information.

Project 3: HeartSmart Newsletter 199

3. **If you see a message asking you to save, click Save.**

4. **In the Printing Instructions dialog box, add your contact information, and then click Continue.**

5. **Navigate to your WIP>HeartSmart folder as the target location. Make sure the Copy Fonts, Copy Linked Graphics, and Update Graphic Links options are checked, and then click Save/Package.**

   When you create a job package, InDesign automatically creates a new folder for the job.

   This setting defines the name of the folder that will be created. All files for the job will be placed in this folder.

6. **Read the resulting warning and click OK.**

   As with any software, you purchase a license to use a font — you do not own the actual font. It is illegal to distribute fonts freely, as it is illegal to distribute copies of your software. Most (but not all) font licenses allow you to send your copy of a font to a service provider, as long as the service provider also owns a copy of the font. Always verify that you are not violating font copyright before submitting a job.

   When the process is complete, the necessary job elements appear in the job folder (in your WIP>HeartSmart folder).

7. **Close the InDesign file.**

Project 3: HeartSmart Newsletter

Project Review

fill in the blank

1. An image file that has been renamed since it was placed into an InDesign layout shows the status of _____.

2. The _____ is used to monitor the status of images that are placed into a layout.

3. _____ is the distance between the edge of a frame and the text contained within that frame.

4. _____ is the distance between the edge of an object and text in other overlapping frames.

5. _____ apply only to selected text characters; this is useful for setting off a few words in a paragraph without affecting the entire paragraph.

6. _____ apply to the entire body of text between two ¶ symbols.

7. While working in a table, the _____ key has a special function; pressing it does not insert the associated character.

8. When the _____ row height method is selected, table rows change height if you add or remove text from the table cells, or if you change the text formatting in a way that requires more or less space.

9. A(n) _____ is a special kind of table row that repeats at the top of every instance of the same table.

10. _____ is the process of checking a layout for errors before it goes to print.

short answer

1. Briefly explain the significance of a Missing Font warning.

2. List three advantages of using templates.

3. Briefly define "styles" in relation to text formatting.

Portfolio Builder Project

Use what you learned in this project to complete the following freeform exercise.
Carefully read the art director and client comments, then create your own design to meet the needs of the project.
Use the space below to sketch ideas; when finished, write a brief explanation of your reasoning behind your final design.

art director comments

The Humane Society wants to create a wall calendar to give away as a part of its annual fundraising drive. Each month will be on one sheet, which can be flipped when the month is over.

To complete this project, you should:

❏ Design a layout that incorporates the month grid, as well as space for an image and four coupons.

❏ Use whatever page size you think is most appropriate for the job.

❏ Use the master page to build the basic structure of each page (month) in the calendar.

❏ Find images or illustrations for each month that don't require a licensing fee.

client comments

As a not-for-profit organization, we try to dedicate most of our finances to caring for our furry (and feathery, and leathery) friends. The printer has donated the resources to print the job, and your agency has donated your time as well — for which we're extremely grateful.

We want each month to have a different picture of cute, cuddly, happy pets and people to encourage adoption. Make sure you include different kinds of animals; the Humane Society isn't just for dogs and cats. Can you find images that won't cost anything to use?

Each month will also include a set of three coupons for local pet-related businesses. When you build the layout, plan space for those; when the layout's done, we'll let our donor companies know how much space they have for the coupons.

One final thing: we thought it might be fun to include a monthly 'fun fact' about animals. Can you find some little text snippets to include each month?

project justification

Project Summary

This project introduced a number of concepts and tools that will be very important as you work on more complex page layout jobs. Importing text content from other applications — specifically, Microsoft Word and Microsoft Excel — is a foundational skill that you will use in most projects; this newsletter showed you how to control that content on import, and then re-format it as appropriate in the InDesign layout.

Templates, master pages, and styles are all designed to let you do the majority of work once and then apply it as many times as necessary; virtually any InDesign project can benefit from these tools, and you will use them extensively in your career as a graphic designer. This project provided a basic introduction to these productivity tools; you will build on these foundations as you complete the remaining five projects of this book.

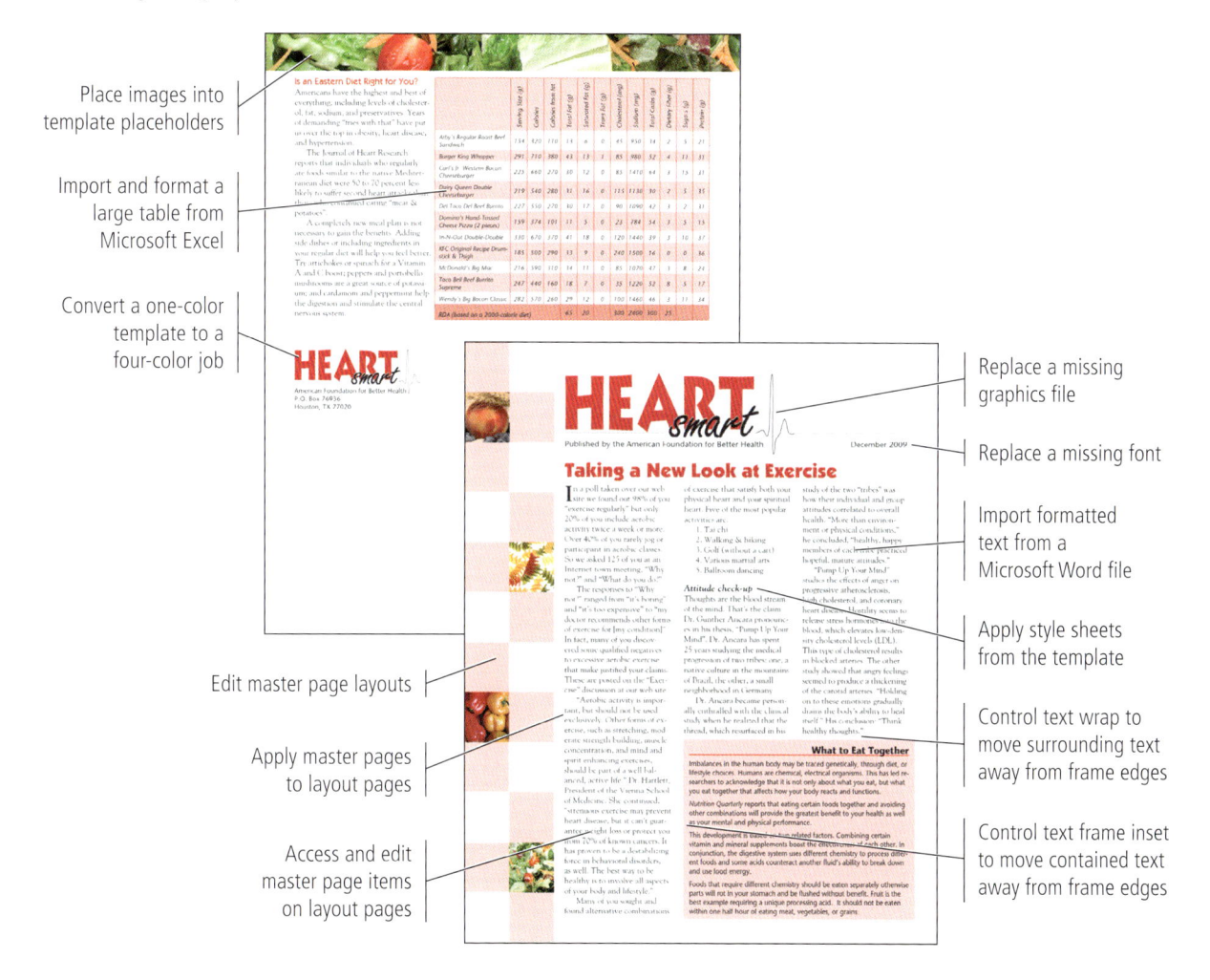

- Place images into template placeholders
- Import and format a large table from Microsoft Excel
- Convert a one-color template to a four-color job
- Edit master page layouts
- Apply master pages to layout pages
- Access and edit master page items on layout pages
- Replace a missing graphics file
- Replace a missing font
- Import formatted text from a Microsoft Word file
- Apply style sheets from the template
- Control text wrap to move surrounding text away from frame edges
- Control text frame inset to move contained text away from frame edges

Project 3: HeartSmart Newsletter 203

Letterfold Catering Menu

Your client is a local patisserie that offers corporate catering services in addition to its in-store breakfast, brunch, and bakery products. To promote their business, the client wants to create a letterfold brochure that highlights the breakfast catering menu. They also want to include a basic form that people can fill out and enter to win a free office breakfast — a common technique for gathering potential clients' contact information.

This project incorporates the following skills:

❏ Building a template for specific folding requirements
❏ Importing text from a Microsoft Word file
❏ Editing imported style sheets
❏ Controlling tabs to format columns of text
❏ Using object styles to reduce repetitive tasks
❏ Working with embedded clipping paths and Alpha channels
❏ Controlling irregular text wraps
❏ Using a library to access frequently used objects

Project Meeting

client comments

Our business has been doing well, but we're hoping to expand our catering services. We want you to create a simple brochure featuring our breakfast catering menu, with lots of pictures to go with the text. We also want to include a little form that we can use to gather prospective clients' contact information, as well as a quote from one of our happy customers. (We put one at the end of the text. If you can use it, great; if not, just delete it.)

art director comments

A lot of people design folding documents incorrectly. Some use a six-page layout with each page the size of the final folded job; others use two pages, each divided into three equal "columns." In both cases, all panels on the job are the exact same width — which is wrong.

Paper has inherent thickness; any panel that folds "in" to the other panels needs to be smaller than the other panels. In the case of a letterfold brochure such as the one you're designing here, the inside panel needs to be 1/16″ smaller than the other panels.

Different types of folding documents also have different facing- or non-facing page requirements. For a letterfold, the job needs to be set up as facing pages because the front and back need to mirror each other. The right-facing page has the front panel, back panel, and the outside of the folding flap; the left-facing page has the three inside panels.

The last item to remember is that the brochure will be a self-mailer; the back panel needs to be left blank, with only the return address in the upper-left corner.

project objectives

To complete this project, you will:

❏ Create a template that accommodates specific folding requirements

❏ Create a folding grid on a master page

❏ Use the slug area to mark folding panels

❏ Import and edit style sheets from a Microsoft Word file

❏ Create new styles based on existing formatting in the layout

❏ Create a basic form using tabs, fill characters, and box inset values

❏ Use object styles to apply consistent formatting to multiple frames

❏ Call a TIFF file clipping path

❏ Apply a feathered Alpha channel that's embedded in a Photoshop file

❏ Control text wraps around basic frames and irregular shapes

❏ Create an InDesign library file to store frequently used objects and groups

Stage 1 Building a Folding Template

When working with folding (multi-panel) documents, many people mistakenly assume that the trim size of the job is the size it appears after folding. In fact, the trim size of a folded document is actually the size of the sheet before it's folded. In this stage of the project, you learn how to properly set up multi-panel documents that fold in a variety of ways.

There are two basic principles to remember when dealing with documents that fold:

- Paper has thickness. The thicker the paper, the more allowance you need to plan for the fold.

- Folding machines are mechanical devices. They process large amounts of material and are accurate to about 0.0125″. Paper sometimes shifts as it flows through the machine's paper path, just as it can in a laser printer or photocopier.

Facing vs. Non-Facing Pages

As a general rule, you should use facing pages any time the design will be read like a book — left to right, Page 2 printed on the back of Page 1 and facing Page 3, and so on. For facing-page layouts, the left page mirrors the right page of each spread. The side margins are referred to as "Inside" (near the spine or binding) and "Outside" (away from the binding) instead of "Left" and "Right."

When you plan a nonstandard folding document, it is also important to decide whether it should be created with or without facing pages. The fold marks on the front and back of a sheet should line up. This means that if one panel of a document is a different size than the others, the back side of the sheet must mirror the front.

In the following illustration, a document has one fold — a smaller panel that folds over to cover half of the inside of the brochure. Fold marks on the outside layout must mirror the inside of the brochure so that, when folded, the two sides line up properly.

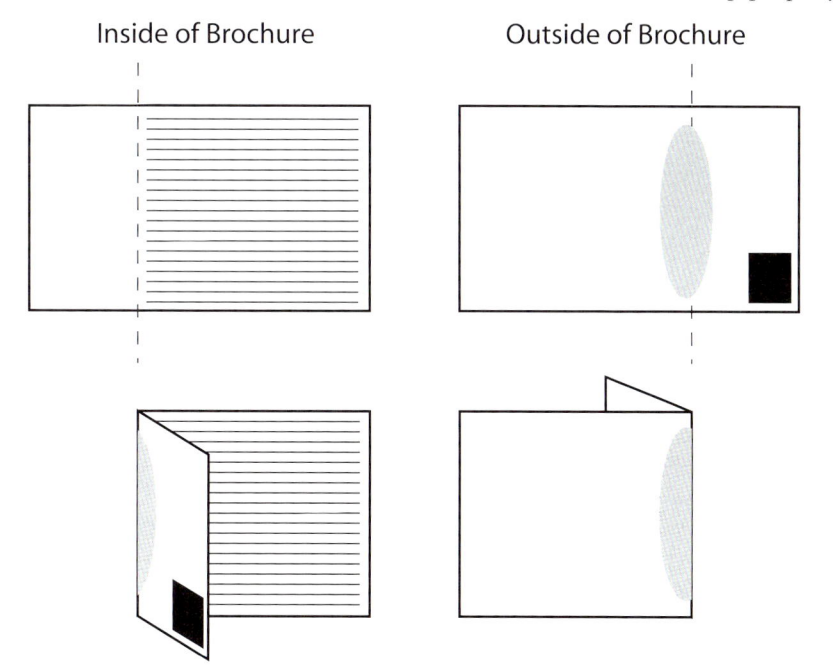

Inside of Brochure   Outside of Brochure

Note:

Layout pages can be viewed as individual pages, or they can be viewed as two or more pages at a time, which is called a **spread**.

Note:

Depending on the job you're designing — including some jobs that are printed on two sides of the same page — you might need to create facing pages or non-facing pages.

Note:

Some service providers give their clients folding templates to use for building a layout. You should ask your service provider if these templates are available before you waste time and effort reinventing the wheel.

Project 4: Letterfold Catering Menu

Basic Types of Folds

There are several standard types of folded documents, each with specific formulas for setting up the layout.

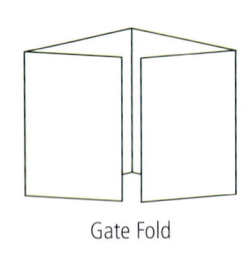

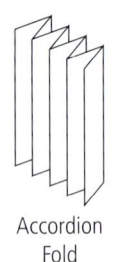

Letterfold   Gate Fold   Accordion Fold   Double Parallel Fold   Barrel Fold

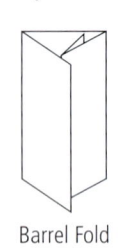

Letterfold (often incorrectly called "trifold" because it results in three panels) brochures can be printed at any size. There are three panels to a side and two folds; letterfold brochures should be created with facing pages because the two sides of the sheet need to mirror each other.

The formula for creating a letterfold brochure typically requires the panel that folds in to be 1/16" narrower than the two outside panels. (Ask your service provider if 1/16" allowance is enough based on the type of paper you're using.) Half of the area removed from the inside panel (1/32") is added to each of the outside two panels.

    Trim size ÷ 3 = Starting panel size

    Fold-in panel = Starting panel size − 1/16"

    Outside panels = Starting panel size + 1/32"

Gate folds result in a four-panel document. The paper is folded in half, and then each half is folded in half toward the center so the two ends of the paper meet at the center fold. The formula for creating a gate fold is similar to the formula for the letterfold brochure; the panels that fold in are 1/16" narrower than the two outside panels. Gate-fold brochures can be created with non-facing pages.

    Trim size ÷ 4 = Starting panel size

    Fold-in panels = Starting panel size − 1/32"

    Outside panels = Starting panel size + 1/32"

Accordion folds — a comparatively unusual format — can have as many panels as you prefer. When it has six panels (three on each side), it's often referred to as a "Z-fold" because it looks like the letter Z. Because the panels don't fold into one another, an accordion-fold document has panels of consistent width. Accordion-fold brochures can be created with non-facing pages.

    Paper size ÷ Number of panels = Panel size

Double-parallel folds are commonly used for eight-panel rack brochures (such as those you often find in a hotel or travel agency). Again, the panels on the inside are 1/16" narrower than the outside panels. This type of fold uses facing pages because the margins need to line up on the front and back sides of the sheet. Double parallel-fold brochures should be created with facing pages.

    Trim size ÷ 4 = Starting panel size

    Outside panels = Starting panel size + 1/32"

    Fold-in panels = Starting panel size − 1/32"

Barrel folds (also called **roll folds**) are perhaps the most common fold for 14 × 8.5" brochures. The two outside panels are full size, and each successive panel is 1/16" narrower than the previous one. Barrel-fold brochures should be created with facing pages.

    Trim size ÷ 4 = Starting panel size

    Outside panels = Starting panel size + 1/32"

    Fold-in panel 1 = Starting panel size − 1/32"

    Fold-in panel 2 = Starting panel size − 3/32"

Set Up Folding Guides

It's important to consider the output process when planning a job with documents that are not just a single sheet of standard-size paper — documents with multiple pages folded one or more times, or other non-standard page sizes. The mechanics of commercial printing require specific allowances for cutting, folding, and other finishing processes.

You should note that the issues presented here have little to do with the subjective elements of design. Layout and page geometry are governed by specific variables, including mechanical limitations in the production process. These principles are rules, not suggestions. If you don't leave adequate margins, for example, design elements will be cut off or won't align properly from one page to the next.

1. **On your desktop, drag the Menu folder from the WIP folder on your Resource CD to the WIP folder where you're saving your work.**

2. **Create a new document with a page size of 11 × 8.5″ (landscape orientation), with 0.25″ margins on all four sides and one column.**

3. **Select the Facing Pages option and deselect the Master Text Frame option.**

4. **Define a 0.125″ bleed and 0.5″ slug on all four sides of the layout.**

5. **Click OK to create your new file.**

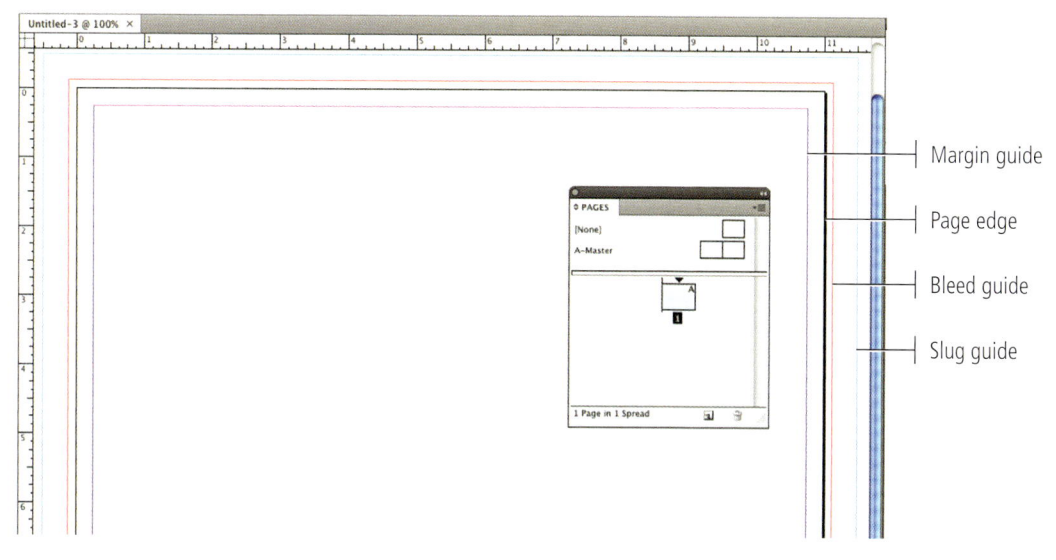

Project 4: Letterfold Catering Menu — 209

6. **In the Pages panel, double-click the A-Master page icon to access the master-page layout.**

   It doesn't matter if you double-click the master-page name or icon; both display the master page in the document window.

   It's a good idea to create folding grids on a master-page layout so you can easily apply the same set of guides to any page in the layout. Doing so is far quicker than manually placing the guides on individual pages.

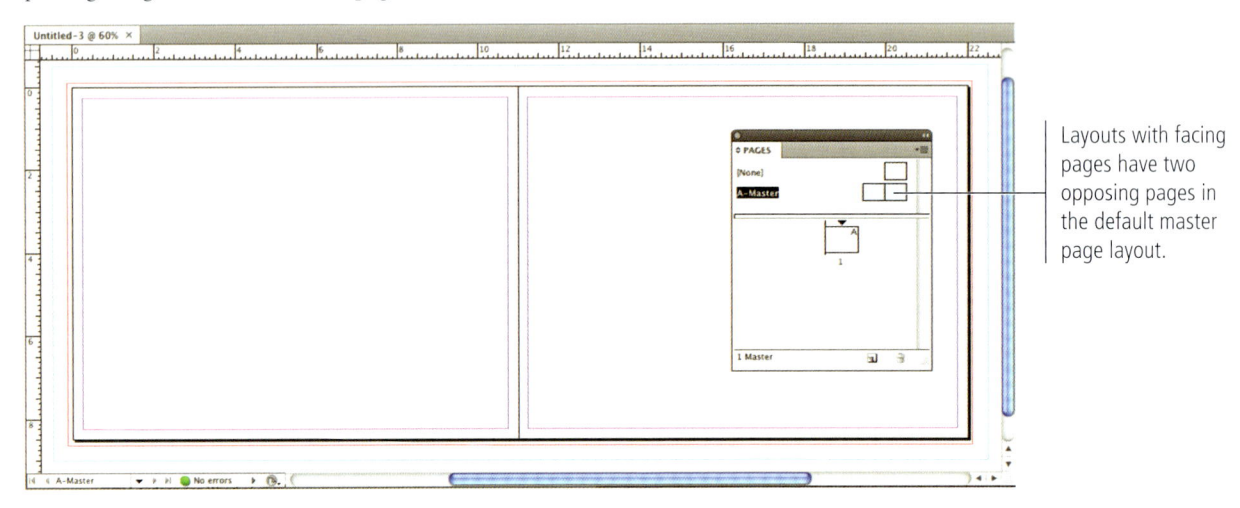

   Layouts with facing pages have two opposing pages in the default master page layout.

7. **On the left page of the master-page layout, drag vertical guides for the folds to the following X positions: 3.6875″ and 7.375″.**

   Smart Guides can be very useful for placing precise guides on a page or spread. You can also place exact guides by dragging a guide onto the page, and then changing the guide position in the Control panel. (The Control panel also shows the dynamic location of guides as you drag them.)

   Note:

   The left-facing page will be the inside panels of the brochure. The right-facing page will be the outside panels.

   Use the Control panel to precisely position each guide.

   Smart Guides give X and Y coordinates when guides and objects are dragged in the document.

8. **Show the right page of the spread in the layout and look at the ruler above the spread line.**

   By default, InDesign rulers are based on the top-left corner of the entire spread. The ruler above the spread line (the black line between the two pages of the spread) continues at 11″ instead of starting again at 0 for the right page.

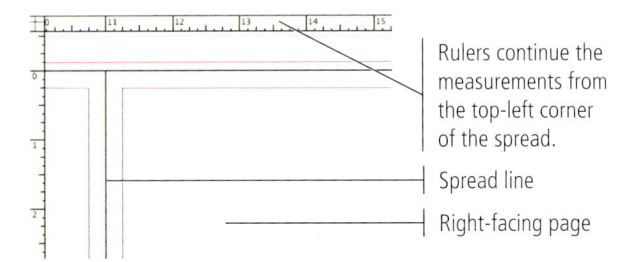

   Rulers continue the measurements from the top-left corner of the spread.

   Spread line

   Right-facing page

Project 4: Letterfold Catering Menu

9. **In the Units & Increments pane of the Preferences dialog box, choose Page in the Ruler Units Origin menu, and then click OK.**

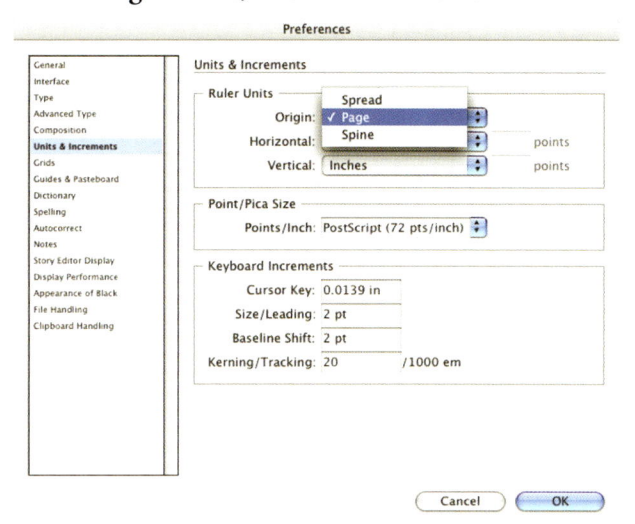

Above the spread line, the ruler now starts over at 0 for the right-facing page.

Note:

If the Spine option is selected as the Ruler Units Origin menu, the right-hand page is measured from left to right and the left-hand page is measured from right to left. This can be useful when preparing pages in which objects are mirrored.

10. **On the right-facing page, place vertical guides at X: 3.625″ and 7.3125″.**

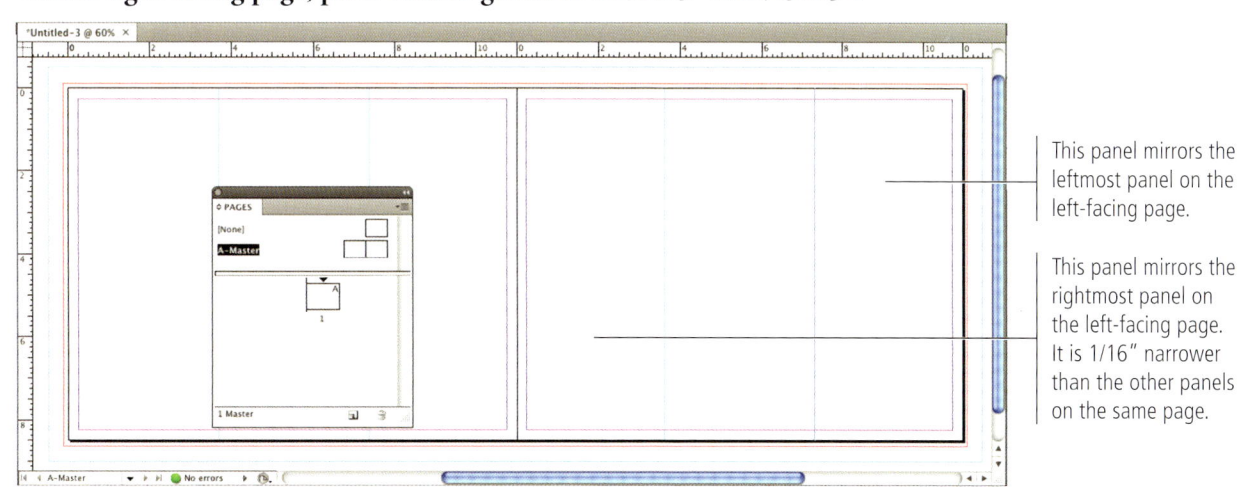

This panel mirrors the leftmost panel on the left-facing page.

This panel mirrors the rightmost panel on the left-facing page. It is 1/16″ narrower than the other panels on the same page.

11. **Drag the zero point crosshairs (in the top-left corner of the project window) to the first vertical guide on the left master page.**

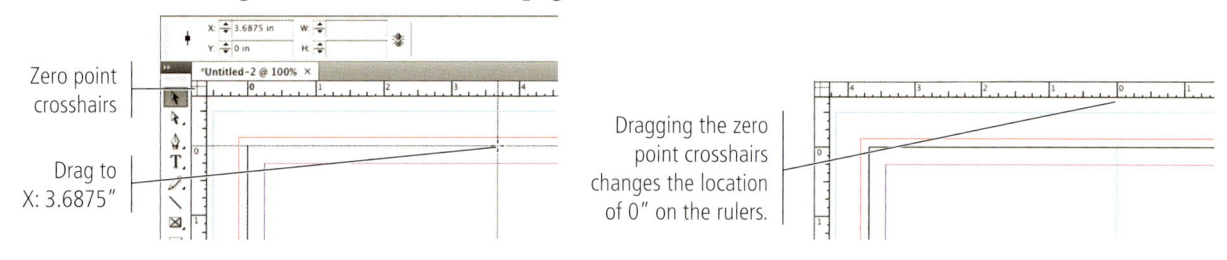

Zero point crosshairs

Drag to X: 3.6875″

Dragging the zero point crosshairs changes the location of 0″ on the rulers.

Project 4: Letterfold Catering Menu   211

12. **Drag vertical guides 0.25″ on both sides of the fold guide to create margin areas around the fold.**

    Once the zero point is placed over the folding guide, margins can easily be set at 0.25″ on either side of the folding guide.

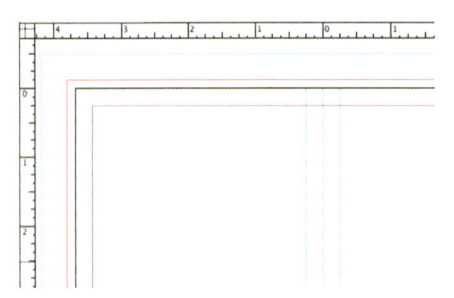

13. **Repeat this process to place guides at 0.25″ on both sides of each fold guide on the master layout (left- and right-facing pages).**

14. **Double-click the zero point crosshairs (in the top-left corner of the project window) to reset the zero point to the top-left corner of the layout page.**

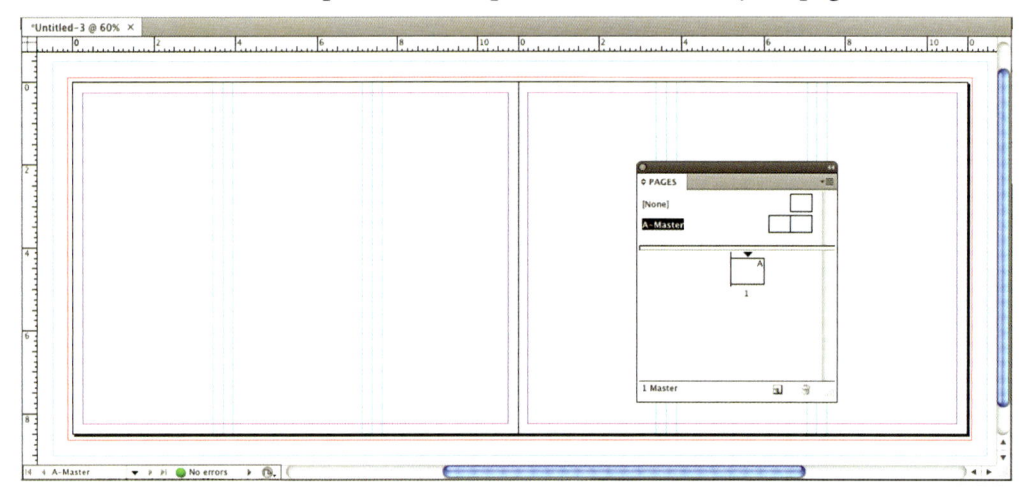

15. **Choose View>Grids & Guides>Lock Guides to prevent the guides from being accidentally moved.**

16. **Save the file in your WIP>Menu folder as `letterfold.indd`.**

Add Slug Information and Placeholders

When you work with folding grids, it's easy to forget which panel goes where. You can use the layout slug area to add nonprinting elements as self-reminders, as well as place folding marks that the output provider can use as references. These elements, like the guides, should be placed on the master page layout.

1. **With `letterfold.indd` open, make sure the A-Master layout is showing in the document window.**

2. **Select the Type tool and create a text frame above the left panel of the left-facing page, between the bleed and slug guides.**

Project 4: Letterfold Catering Menu

3. Type **INSIDE LEFT PANEL** in the frame, and then apply centered paragraph alignment and centered vertical frame alignment.

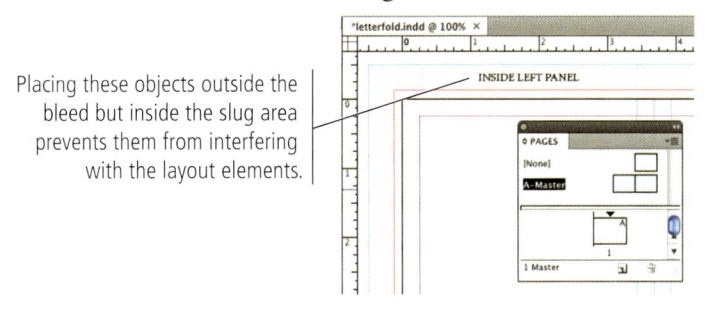

Placing these objects outside the bleed but inside the slug area prevents them from interfering with the layout elements.

4. Choose Window>Attributes to open the Attributes panel.

5. Make sure the text frame is selected with the Selection tool and check the Nonprinting box in the Attributes panel.

    These objects are for your information only; they should not be included in the output.

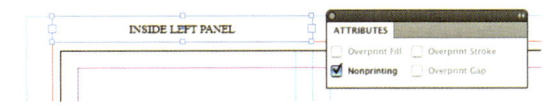

    Note:

    If you want to print these frames, you can override this setting using the Print Nonprinting Objects option in the General print settings.

6. Control/right-click the text frame and choose Allow Master Item Overrides to deactivate the option and protect this object on associated layout pages.

    This item should be unchecked.

7. Using the Selection tool, press Option/Alt-Shift and drag the text frame to the right.

    By pressing Option/Alt while dragging, you are creating an exact copy or **clone** of the original object.

    Note:

    Pressing Shift while cloning constrains the clone movement to 45° angles from the original object.

8. Change the text in the clone to **INSIDE CENTER PANEL**.

9. **Repeat this process to place a text frame over each panel on both sides of the spread, using the following text:**

Right column, left page	**INSIDE RIGHT PANEL**
Left column, right page	**FOLD-IN FLAP**
Center column, right page	**BACK PANEL (MAILING AREA)**
Right column, right page	**FRONT PANEL**

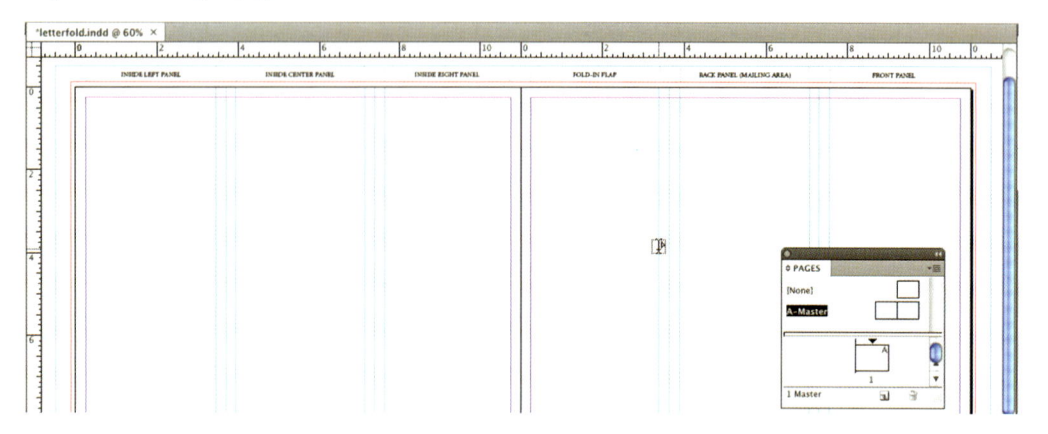

10. **Using the Line tool, click in the slug area above the first fold guide on the left page.**

11. **Press Shift and drag down to the bleed guide.**

    Pressing Shift constrains the line to a 45° angle.

    Remember, the area outside the bleed is the slug area.

12. **Using the Control panel, change the line's X position to 3.6875″ (the same as the first folding guide).**

13. **In the Stroke panel, change the line Weight to 0.5-pt and choose Dashed in the Type menu. After applying the Dashed line type, type 3 pt in the first Dash and Gap fields at the bottom of the panel.**

    If you don't see the Type menu in the Stroke panel, open the panel Options menu and choose Show Options.

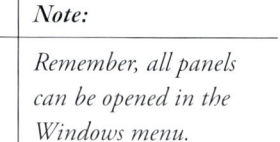

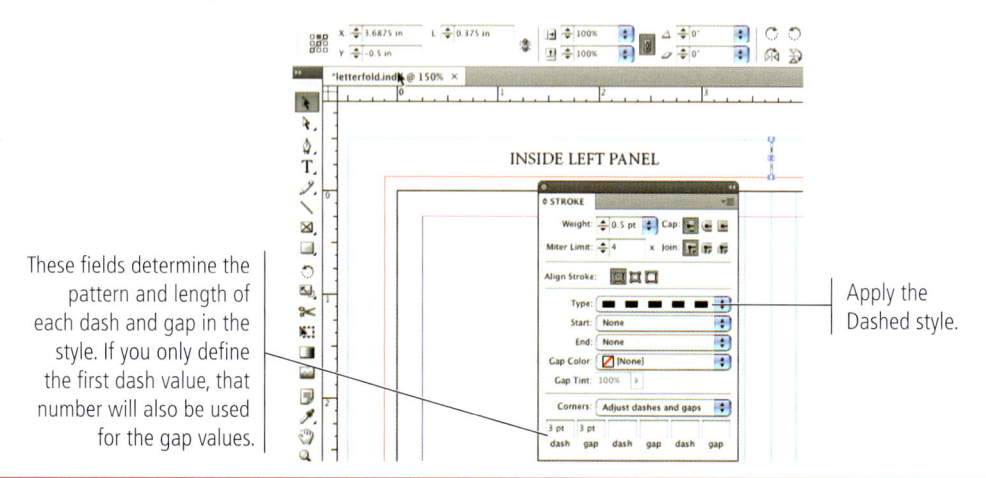

    Note:

    Remember, all panels can be opened in the Windows menu.

    These fields determine the pattern and length of each dash and gap in the style. If you only define the first dash value, that number will also be used for the gap values.

    Apply the Dashed style.

Project 4: Letterfold Catering Menu

14. **Control/right-click the dashed line and toggle off the Allow Master Item Overrides option.**

15. **Clone the line and place copies above and below each folding guide on both pages of the spread.**

    | Line 2 | X: 7.375" (left-facing page) |
    | Line 3 | X: 3.625" (right-facing page) |
    | Line 4 | X: 7.3125" (right-facing page) |

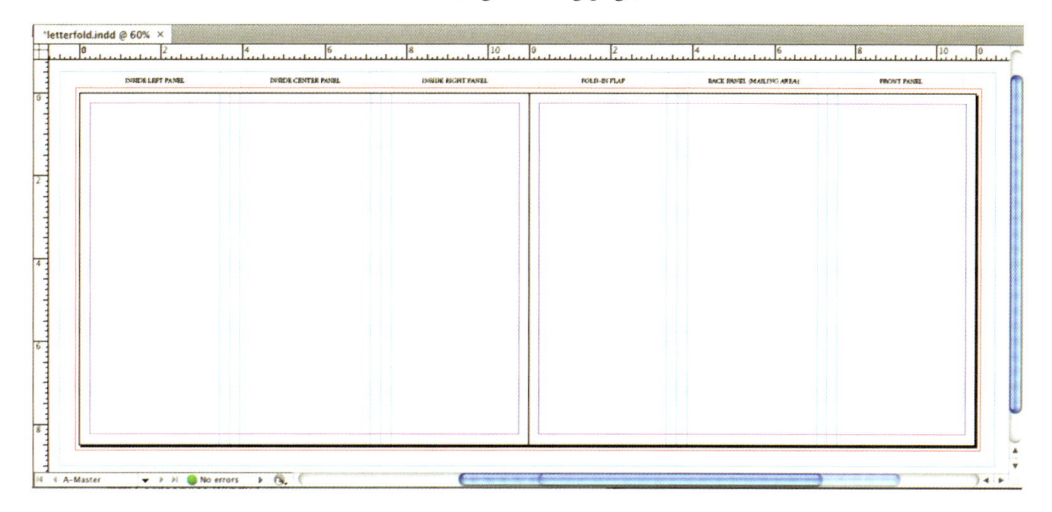

16. **Save the file and continue to the next exercise.**

Save a Template

As the previous exercises demonstrated, setting up a brochure properly can be time-consuming. Once you create a folding grid, it's a good idea to save the layout as a template so the same guides can be applied to any similar type of layout. Every time you want to create a letterfold brochure, you can open the template and begin with an empty file that contains the correct guides and marks.

1. **With A-Master of `letterfold.indd` visible, create a text frame in each panel of the layout (snapping to the margin guides for each panel).**

    These placeholders will be available whenever you implement the layout. Remember, every click you can save by adding template elements will save that much time later — every time you re-use the same template.

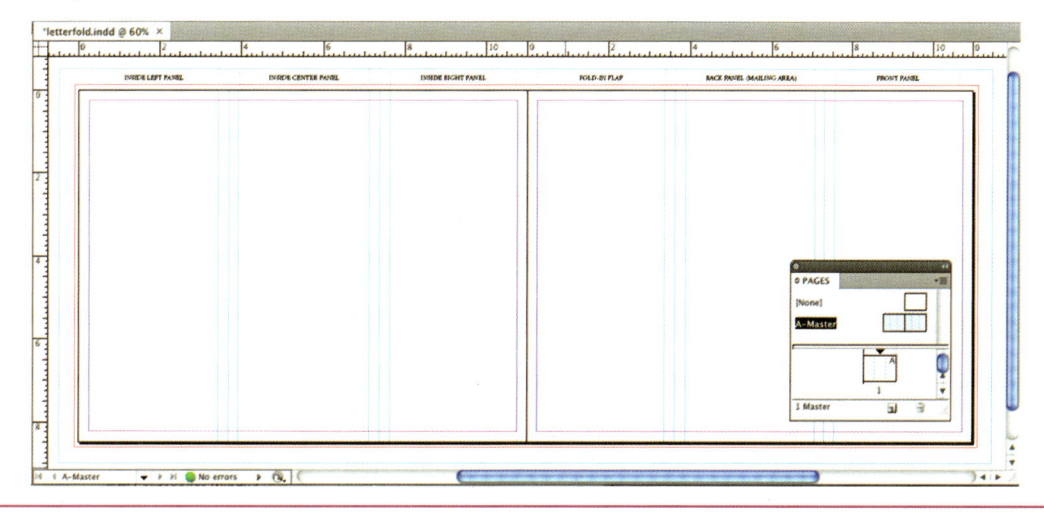

Project 4: Letterfold Catering Menu   215

2. **Choose File>Save As and navigate to your WIP>Menu folder.**

3. **Choose InDesign CS4 Template in the Format/Save As Type menu and click Save.**

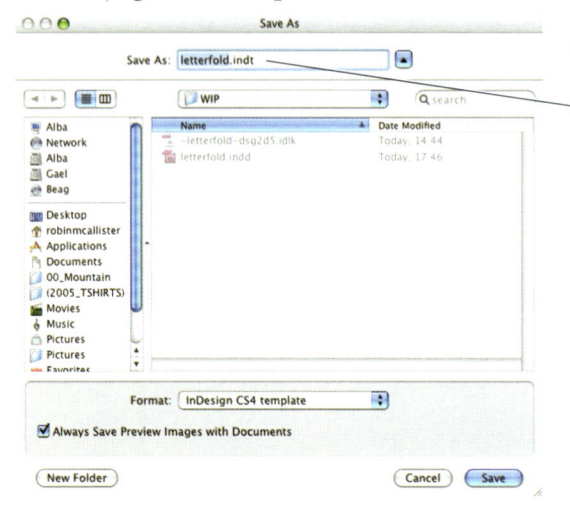

   Choosing the template option in the Format/Save As Type menu automatically changes the extension to "indt."

4. **Close the file and continue to the next stage of the project.**

Pages Panel Options

In Project 3, you learned about the options for working with master pages. In addition to those, the Pages panel Options menu has a number of other choices for working with document pages.

- **Insert Pages** allows you to insert from 1 to 9999 pages before or after a specific page, or at the start or end of the document. You can also determine which master page to base the new pages on.

- **Move Pages** allows you to reposition specific pages anywhere in the current document or in another open document.

- **Duplicate Page/Spread** allows you to replicate the selected page (or spread), including all elements on that page or spread.

- **Delete Page/Spread** removes the page (or spread) from the document.

- **Rotate Spread View** changes the appearance of the page within the document window. This option does not affect the physical dimensions of the page, but is useful for working with a page that's oriented differently than the overall document.

- **Page Transitions** are visual effects that apply when a document is exported as a PDF or SWF file that will be distributed digitally.

- **Allow Document Pages to Shuffle** is checked by default. You can toggle off this option if you want to create spreads of more than two pages (called an **island spread**).

- **Allow Selected Spreads to Shuffle** is checked by default. If you toggle this option off, adding pages before an island spread maintains the island spread pages as you created them.

- **Numbering & Section Options** give you control over the manner in which pages and chapters are numbered, where page or chapter numbers begin, and what format is used for page numbers.

- **Spread Flattening** allows you to apply flattener settings to individual spreads in a document, overriding the document flattener settings. Default uses the document settings. None (Ignore Transparency) eliminates any function that requires transparency. Custom opens the Custom Spread Flattener settings.

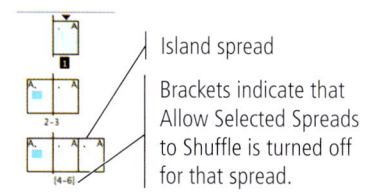

   Island spread

   Brackets indicate that Allow Selected Spreads to Shuffle is turned off for that spread.

Project 4: Letterfold Catering Menu

Stage 2 Working with Imported Text

In Project 3, you used styles in an InDesign template to format the text imported from a Microsoft Word file. You learned that by applying styles, you can apply multiple formatting attributes — both character and paragraph — with a single click. InDesign is not the only software that supports text-formatting styles; Microsoft Word also incorporates this functionality.

Many of your clients will submit text with local formatting — they highlight some text and change the font, size, spacing, etc. — that you will strip out and replace with the proper InDesign translations. More sophisticated users, however, will send files that are extensively formatted with Microsoft Word styles. In this case, you can import the styles from Microsoft Word directly into your InDesign layout to use as the basis for your work.

IMPORT AND THREAD TEXT ACROSS FRAMES

1. **Create a new file from the letterfold.indt template (WIP>Menu).**

   Remember, to create a new file from a template, you have to open the template file.

2. **Double-click the Page 1 icon to make it active in the document window.**

   Page 1 of a new document — whether created from scratch or based on an existing template — is automatically associated with the default master page (A-Master).

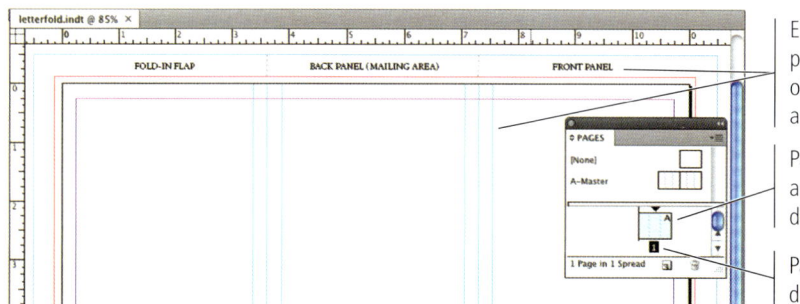

   Elements from the master page — including guides and objects in the slug area — are visible on the layout page.

   Page 1 is automatically associated with the default master page.

   Page 1 is active in the document window.

3. **Open the Pages panel Options menu and choose Insert Pages.**

   Note:

   You can disassociate Page 1 from the default master by dragging the [None] master-page icon onto the Page 1 icon.

4. **In the Insert Pages dialog box, make sure you are adding 1 page, after Page 1, using the A-Master page layout.**

   This dialog box allows you to add a specific number of pages, in a specific location, using any existing master page layout as the master.

   Note:

   You can also add new pages into the layout by dragging a master-page icon into the lower half of the Pages panel.

5. **Click OK to add the second page to the layout.**

    In a layout with facing pages, new pages are added sequentially as left- or right-facing pages. Following convention, right-facing pages have odd numbers and left-facing pages have even numbers. (You can override this option using section numbering, which you do in the next project.)

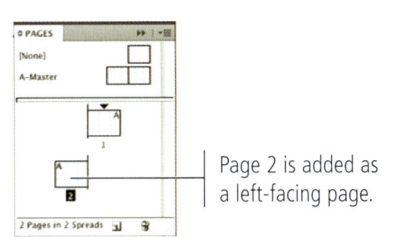

    Page 2 is added as a left-facing page.

    Note:

    You can Shift-click to select multiple pages in the Pages panel and override master page items for all selected pages at one time.

6. **Control/right-click the Page 1 icon in the Pages panel and choose Override All Master Page Items.**

    This command allows you to access the text frames you created on the master layout. You won't be able to access the guides, which are locked, or the nonprinting slug items, which you protected by toggling off the Allow Master Item Overrides option.

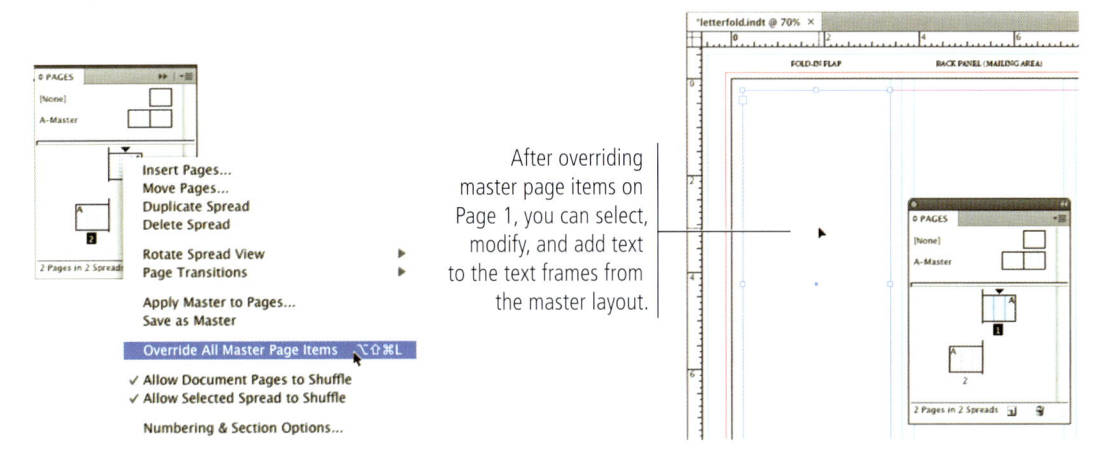

    After overriding master page items on Page 1, you can select, modify, and add text to the text frames from the master layout.

7. **Repeat Step 6 for Page 2.**

8. **Save the file as cafe.indd in your WIP>Menu folder and continue to the next exercise.**

Import Styles from Microsoft Word

In the previous project you learned the basics of importing the Normal style from a Microsoft Word file. When your clients use more sophisticated styles in their layouts, you need to understand what to do with those styles when you import the files into your InDesign layout.

1. **With `cafe.indd` open, display Page 2 in the document window and choose File>Place.**

2. **Navigate to the RF_InDesign>Menu folder and choose `menu.doc`.**

3. **Make sure the Show Import Options box is checked and click Open.**

   The Formatting section of the resulting Import options dialog box shows that one conflict exists between the styles in the Microsoft Word file and the styles in the InDesign file.

4. **Under Preserve Styles and Formatting from Text and Tables, make sure the Import Styles Automatically option is selected, and then choose Auto Rename in the Paragraph Style Conflicts menu. Click OK.**

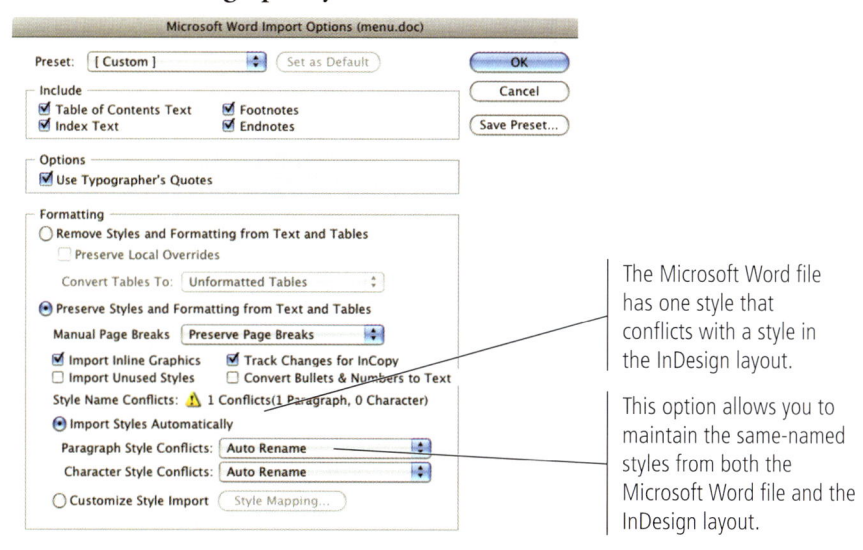

Note:

Since you haven't created any styles in the InDesign file yet, you could simply use the imported style. But we generally prefer to import everything the client created so we can see important issues, and then make whatever changes are necessary in the InDesign file.

The Microsoft Word file has one style that conflicts with a style in the InDesign layout.

This option allows you to maintain the same-named styles from both the Microsoft Word file and the InDesign layout.

5. **If you see a Missing Font warning, review the information and then click OK.**

   When you import Microsoft Word files with their formatting, you see this warning more often than not.

   Many actions in Microsoft Word — such as using the B or I buttons to apply **faux bold** or **faux italic** type styles — can cause problems in InDesign because InDesign tries to translate those faux formatting options to the best-possible "real" font variants required for commercial printing applications.

   The good news is that in many cases, you can replace the fonts used in the Microsoft Word file with something more appropriate for your overall design. It would be a waste of time to correct these font problems until you know you need to do so. In this case, you're eventually going to replace the style that calls for the missing fonts, so there's no point in spending time resolving the missing-font problem.

6. **In the document window, press Option/Alt and move the cursor over the text frame on the left side of Page 2 (the inside of the brochure).**

   Normally, clicking with the loaded text cursor fills the current frame and leaves overset text as overset text. By pressing Option/Alt before clicking, however, you can keep overset text loaded in the cursor so you can choose the next frame where the story will thread (called **semi-automatic text flow**).

   Pressing Option/Alt converts the loaded text cursor to the semi-auto flow cursor so you can direct the flow of the story into more than one text frame.

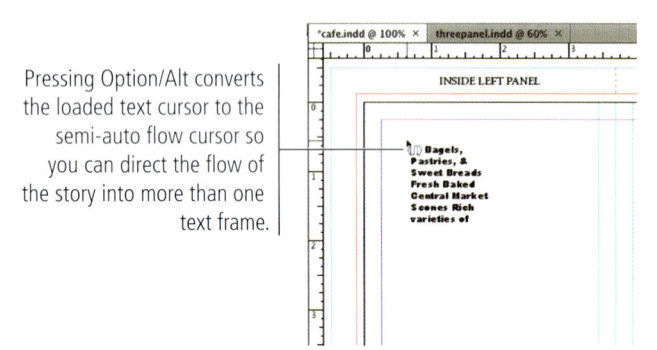

   Note:

   Semi-automatic text flow works on one frame at a time, so you have to Option/Alt-click each frame to keep overset text loaded in the cursor. You can automatically flow an entire story by Shift-clicking with the loaded cursor. In this case, pages are added as necessary to accommodate the entire story.

7. **While holding down the Option/Alt key, click in the text frame on the left side of the page.**

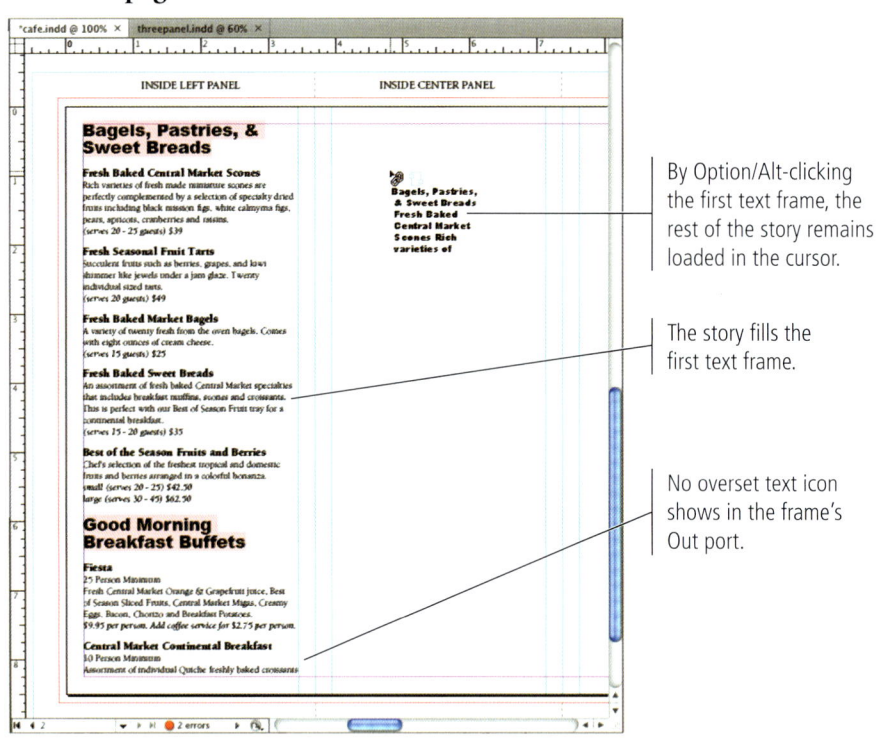

   By Option/Alt-clicking the first text frame, the rest of the story remains loaded in the cursor.

   The story fills the first text frame.

   No overset text icon shows in the frame's Out port.

Project 4: Letterfold Catering Menu

8. **Option/Alt-click the second text frame on the page to place more of the story.**

9. **Click the third frame to place the rest of the story.**

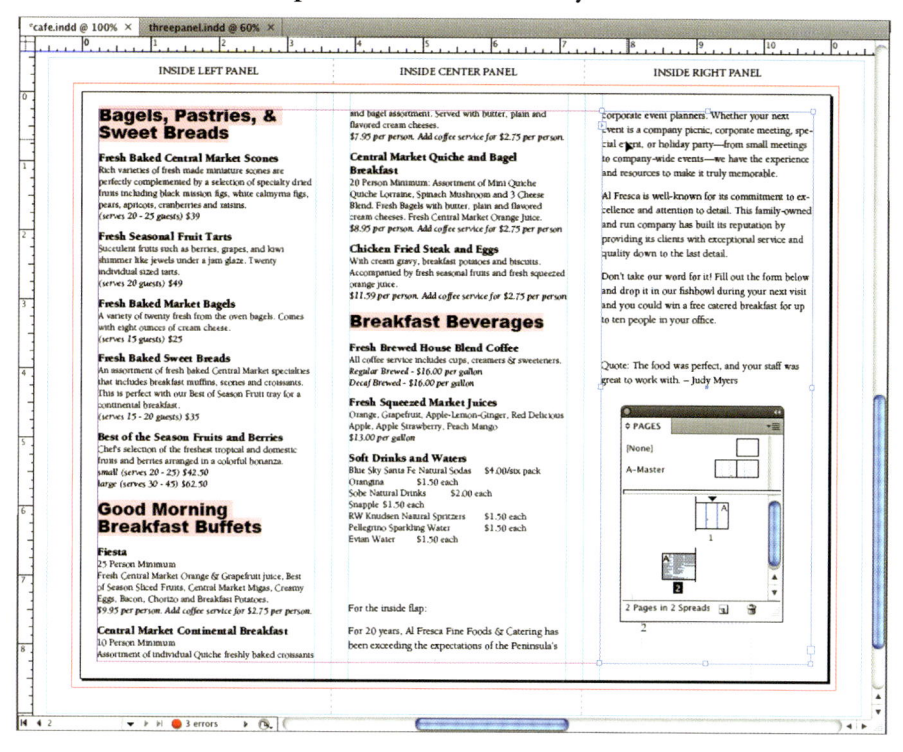

10. **Place the insertion point in the first paragraph of the story and look at the Paragraph Styles panel.**

    The Paragraph Styles panel shows what style is applied to the current paragraph — in this case, Heading 1. (The pink highlight also shows the location of missing fonts.)

11. **Click in different areas with different formatting throughout the story and review which styles are applied to which paragraphs.**

12. **Save the file and continue to the next exercise.**

Import and Replace InDesign Styles

In many instances, the styles you need for a particular job have already been created for another job. For example, a particular client likes to use 12-pt Garamond with 14-pt leading for the main body copy in every job. If you've already spent the time to create styles once, you can simply import them into your current file instead of repeatedly recreating the same styles.

1. **With `cafe.indd` open, choose Load All Text Styles from the Paragraph Styles panel Options menu.**

    You could also choose Load Paragraph Styles, but the Load All Text Styles allows you to access both character and paragraph styles in a single pass, instead of requiring two steps to import the two different types of styles.

2. **Navigate to the file `cafe_styles.indd` in the RF_InDesign>Menu folder and click Open.**

    This file contains several styles that were used when the café created its in-store menus. For consistency, the client would like to use some of the same styles in the mailing brochure, too.

3. **The Load Styles dialog box shows all styles available in the cafe_styles.indd file.**

    Anything with an option in this column conflicts with a style already in the InDesign file.

4. **Click the box to the left of [Basic Paragraph] to uncheck that style.**

    Anything checked will import; anything unchecked will not import.

5. **Click Description Text, and then choose Auto-Rename in the Conflict with Existing Style menu.**

    Note:

    As with style conflicts in Microsoft Word files, it's a good idea to maintain the imported information until you determine exactly what you need.

222 Project 4: Letterfold Catering Menu

6. **Click OK to import the selected styles (three paragraph and three character).**

   The imported InDesign styles do not show the disk icon.

7. **Using the Selection tool, click anywhere in the pasteboard to deselect the text frames in the layout.**

8. **In the Paragraph Styles panel, drag Heading 1 to the trash icon at the bottom of the panel.**

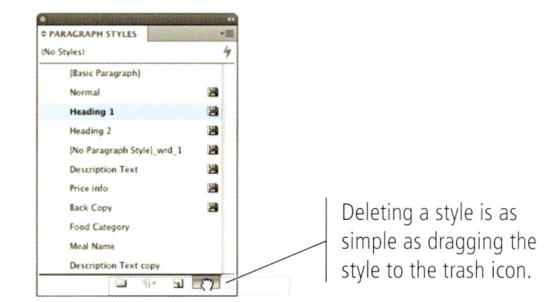

   Deleting a style is as simple as dragging the style to the trash icon.

   Note:

   You can also simply select a style in the panel and click the panel Delete button (the trash can).

9. **In the resulting dialog box, choose Food Category in the Replace With menu and click OK.**

   If you delete a style sheet that's being used, you have to determine what to do with text that uses the style you want to delete. If you want to maintain the formatting of that text without applying a different style, you can choose [No Paragraph Style].

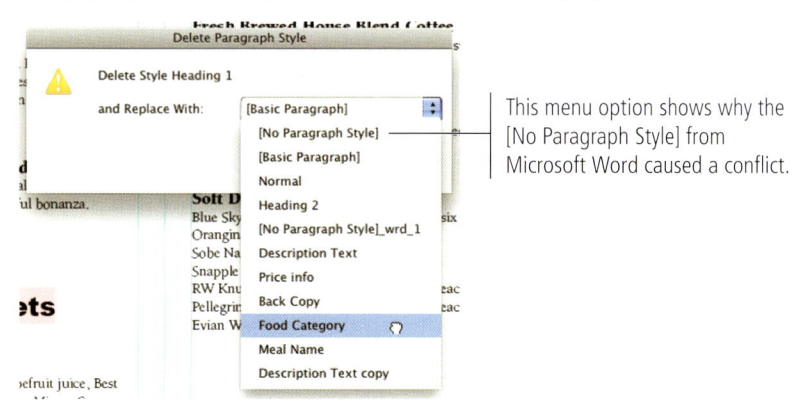

   This menu option shows why the [No Paragraph Style] from Microsoft Word caused a conflict.

Project 4: Letterfold Catering Menu 223

After the Heading 1 style has been replaced with the Food Category style, the associated headings in the layout change in appearance to match the new style definition.

Food Category does not call for Arial Black Italic, so the pink highlighting disappears.

10. **Delete Heading 2 and replace it with Meal Name.**

11. **Delete Description Text and replace it with Description Text Copy.**

12. **Delete [No Paragraph Style]_wrd_1 and replace it with [No Paragraph Style]. In this case, make sure the Preserve Formatting option is selected.**

    InDesign's default [No Paragraph Style] is not a style — in fact, it is the express lack of a defined style. The imported [No Paragraph Style] is considered a style, so you have to decide what to do with the formatting that was applied.

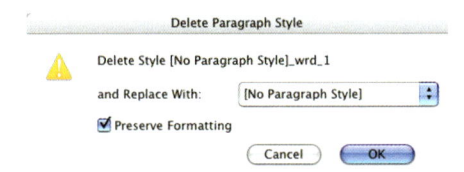

Note:

Any time you choose [No Paragraph Style] in the Replace With menu, the Preserve Formatting option becomes available in the Delete Paragraph Style dialog box.

Note:

You can edit the default type settings for a layout by editing the [Basic Paragraph] style. You can edit the default type settings for all new InDesign layouts by editing the [Basic Paragraph] style when no file is open.

13. **Delete Normal and replace it with [Basic Paragraph].**

    In InDesign, [Basic Paragraph] is essentially the same as Microsoft Word's Normal style. If you define or apply no other styles, all new text in an InDesign document will be automatically set in the [Basic Paragraph] style.

    Your computer might or might not have the Italic variant of the Times font available; if not, you will see the missing font indicated by a pink highlight. You change the Price Info definition in the next exercise, so don't worry if you see pink highlighting now.

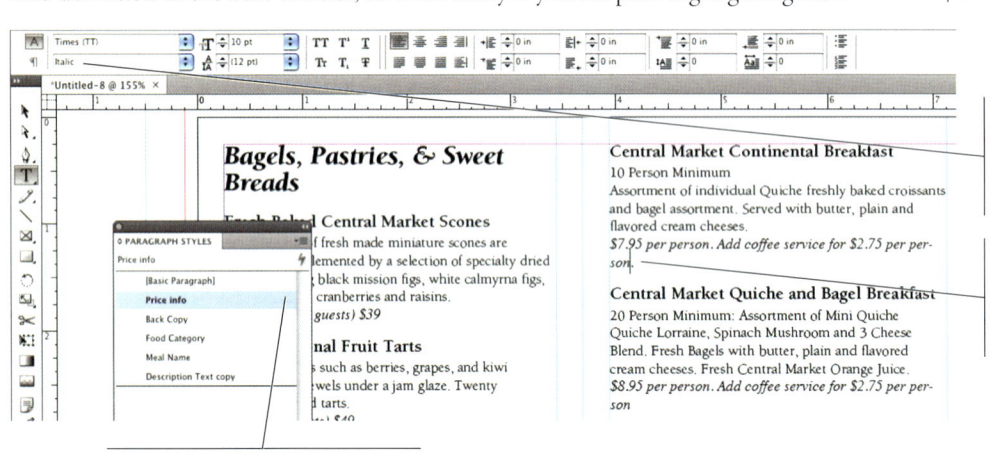

The style calls for the Italic variant of Times, which might not exist on your computer.

The Price Info style, which was based on the Normal style, is now based on the [Basic Paragraph] style.

Changing the definition of Price Info (by deleting Normal) removes the disk icon from the imported style.

14. **Save the file and continue to the next exercise.**

Project 4: Letterfold Catering Menu

What's in a Paragraph Style?

By completing the first three projects, you've already learned about a considerable number of options for formatting text — both character and paragraph attributes — but there's still more to learn. The important point here is that styles can store a very large number of settings, which you'll see when you complete the next exercise.

Use the following chart as a reminder of exactly what can be stored in a paragraph style definition, as well as where to find the equivalent in the application interface for selected text. (Character styles include a subset of these same options: General, Basic Character Formats, Advanced Character Formats, Character Color, OpenType Features, Underline Options, and Strikethrough Options.)

Category	Options			Application Equivalent
General	Based On Style Settings	Next Style Reset to Base	Shortcut Apply Style to Selection	N/A
Basic Character Formats	Font Family Leading	Style Kerning	Size Tracking	Character panel
	Case	Position	Styles	Character panel options menu
Advanced Character Formats	Horizontal Scale Skew	Vertical Scale Language	Baseline Shift	Character panel
Indents and Spacing	Alignment Left & Right Indent Space Before	Balance Ragged Lines First Line Indent Space After	Ignore Optical Margin Last Line Indent Align to Grid	Paragraph panel
Tabs	X position	Leader	Align On	Tabs panel (Type menu)
Paragraph Rules	Rule Above On Width Rule attributes (Weight, Type, Color, etc.)	Rule Below On Offset	Left & Right Indents Gap attributes	Paragraph panel Options menu
Keep Options	Keep with Next [N] Lines Start Paragraph		Keep Lines Together	Paragraph panel Options menu
Hyphenation	Hyphenate On/Off (and all related options)			Paragraph panel Options menu
Justification	Word Spacing Auto Leading	Letter Spacing Single Word Justification	Glyph Scaling Composer	Paragraph panel Options menu
Drop Caps and Nested Styles	Number of Lines	Number of Characters		Paragraph panel
	Character Style for Drop Characters Scale for Descenders	Nested Styles	Align Left Edge Nested Line Styles	Paragraph panel Options menu
Bullets and Numbering	List Type Text After Bullet	List Style Character Style	Bullet Character Bullet/Number Position	Paragraph panel Options menu
Character Color	Fill Color, Tint, Overprint attributes Stroke Color, Tint, Weight, Overprint attributes			Swatches panel
OpenType Features	Titling, Contextual, & Swash Alternates Ordinals, Fractions, Discretionary Ligatures, Slashed Zero, Figure Style, Positional Form Stylistic Sets			Character panel Options menu
Underline Options	Underline On	Stroke attributes	Gap attributes	Character panel Options menu
Strikethrough Options	Strikethrough On	Stroke attributes	Gap attributes	Character panel Options menu

✋ EDIT STYLE DEFINITIONS

In most cases, styles you import with a text file will need at least some modification — if for no other reason than InDesign has more sophisticated options that are relevant to commercial printing. In addition, your clients are not designers, so their formatting choices are most likely not up to par with professional-quality graphic design.

1. **With `cafe.indd` open, place the insertion point in the small italic text at the end of one of the item descriptions.**

   The Paragraph Styles panel shows that this text is formatted with the Price Info style. The Control panel shows that the style calls for the Italic variant of Times (which might not be available).

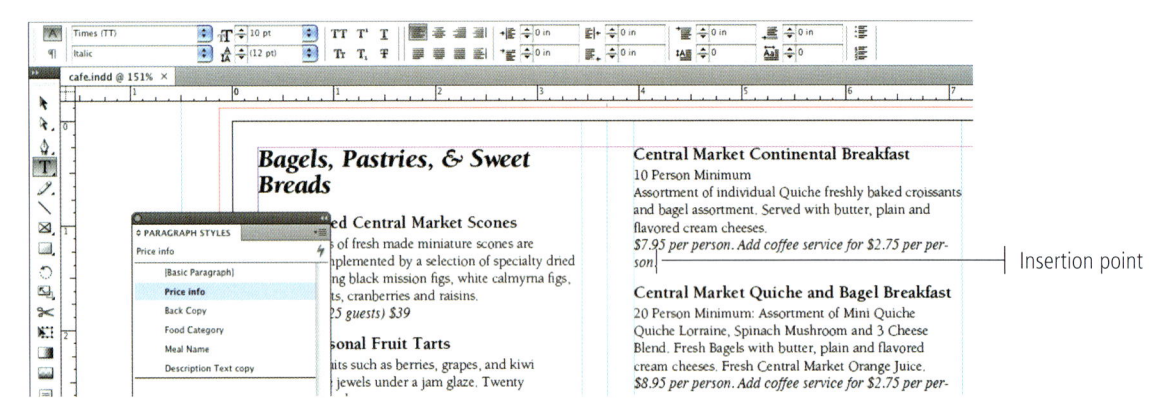

2. **Control/right-click Price Info in the Paragraph Styles panel and choose Edit "Price Info" in the contextual menu.**

   Editing styles is both easy and efficient. When you change the options in a style definition, any text formatted with that style reformats with the changed definition.

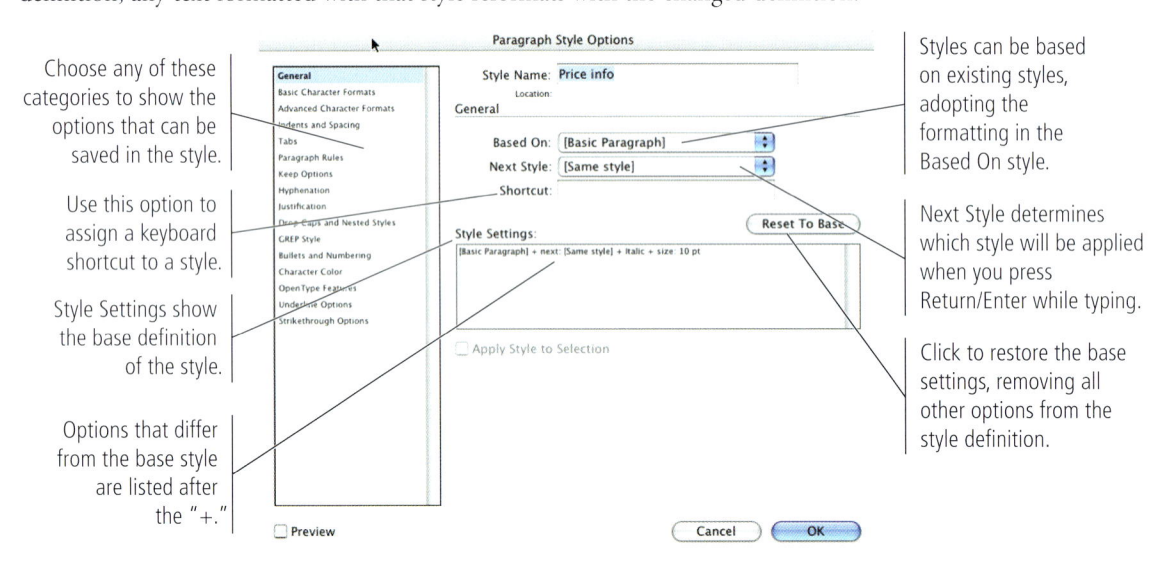

226 Project 4: Letterfold Catering Menu

3. **Click Basic Character Formats in the list of categories and choose ATC Laurel in the Font Family menu.**

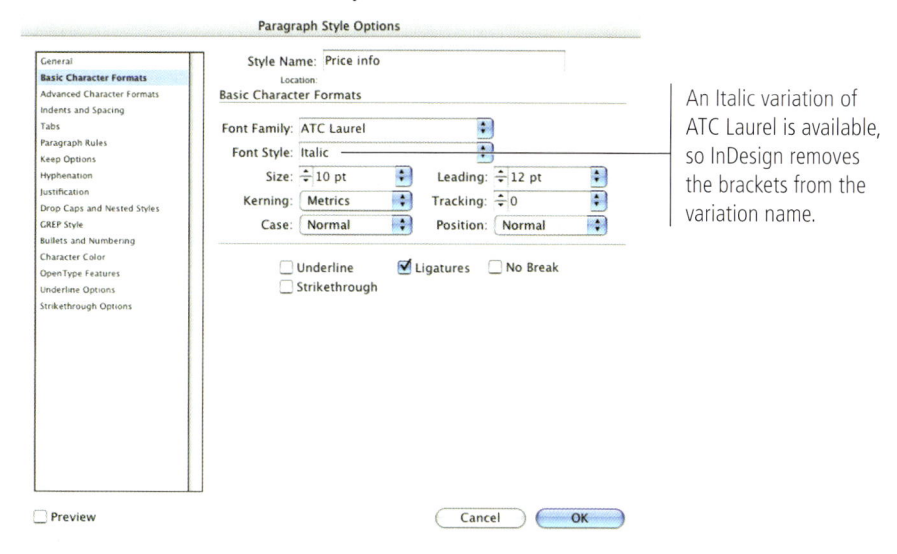

An Italic variation of ATC Laurel is available, so InDesign removes the brackets from the variation name.

Note:

*When one style refers to or calls another in some way (called **nesting styles**), the style on which another style is based is called the **parent** in the parent-child relationship. If a paragraph style calls a character style as part of its formatting definition, the paragraph style is considered the parent in the nesting relationship. See the discussion on Understanding Nested Styles (page 232).*

4. **Click OK to return to the document.**

The new font is applied to text formatted with the Price Info style.

5. **Control/right-click the Food Category style in the Paragraph Styles panel and choose Edit "Food Category".**

6. **Click Paragraph Rules in the list of formatting categories and make sure the Preview option is checked.**

Paragraph rules are simply lines that are attached to a specific paragraph. Rules can be placed above or below any paragraph (or above *and* below a paragraph) to add visual interest and importance to specific text elements.

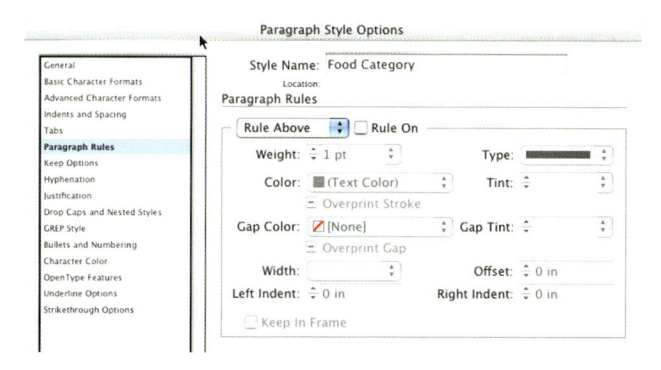

Note:

Paragraph rules do not need to be applied as part of a style. You can apply paragraph rules to paragraphs in the layout by placing the insertion point, and then choosing Paragraph Rules in the Paragraph panel Options menu.

Project 4: Letterfold Catering Menu   227

7. **With Rule Below selected in the first menu, check the Rule On box.**

   If Rule Above appears in the menu, click to open the menu and choose Rule Below.

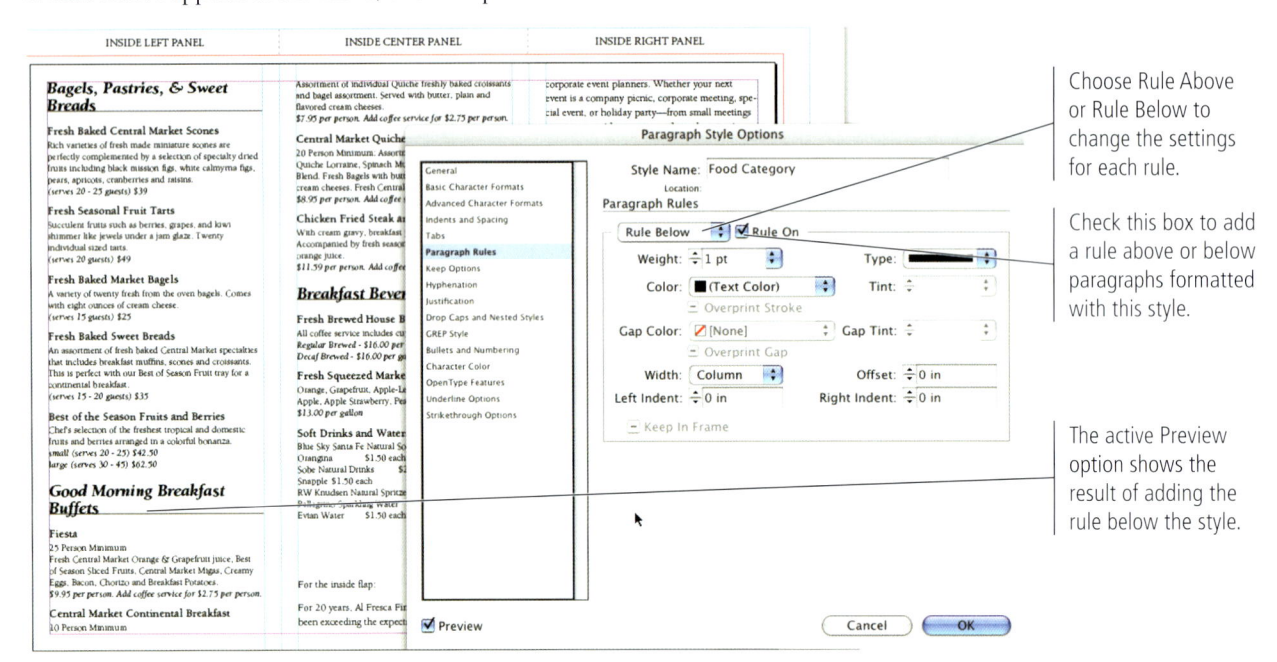

   Choose Rule Above or Rule Below to change the settings for each rule.

   Check this box to add a rule above or below paragraphs formatted with this style.

   The active Preview option shows the result of adding the rule below the style.

8. **Change the rule weight to 6 pt. Change the rule color to C=100 M=25 Y=50 K=25 with a 20% tint.**

   This swatch is used by one of the styles you imported from another InDesign file in the previous exercise. When you import a style from one InDesign file to another, any other required assets — such as color swatches — are also imported into the current file.

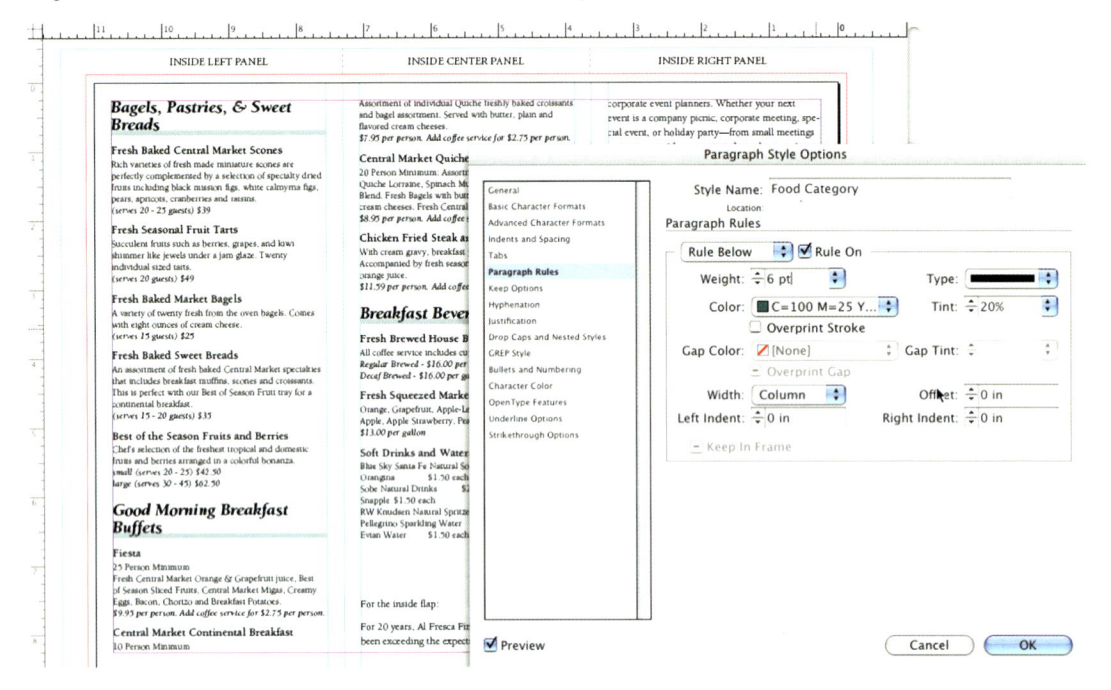

228   Project 4: Letterfold Catering Menu

9. **Change the Offset field to −0.03 in.**

   By default, paragraph rules align to the baseline of the text (the top edge of the rule touches the text baseline). The Offset value moves the position of the rule relative to the baseline; negative numbers move the rule up, and positive numbers move the rule down.

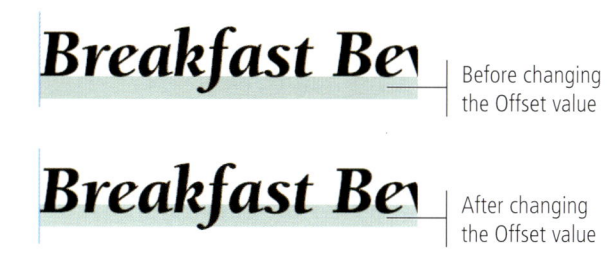

   Before changing the Offset value

   After changing the Offset value

   The Width option defines whether the rule extends the length of the text in the paragraph or across the entire width of the column (or frame, if it's a one-column frame). You can also use the Left Indent and Right Indent fields to move the rule in from the column (or frame) edge by a specific distance.

10. **Click OK to close the dialog box and return to the layout.**

    By editing the style definition, you simultaneously changed the appearance of all three paragraphs formatted with the Food Category style.

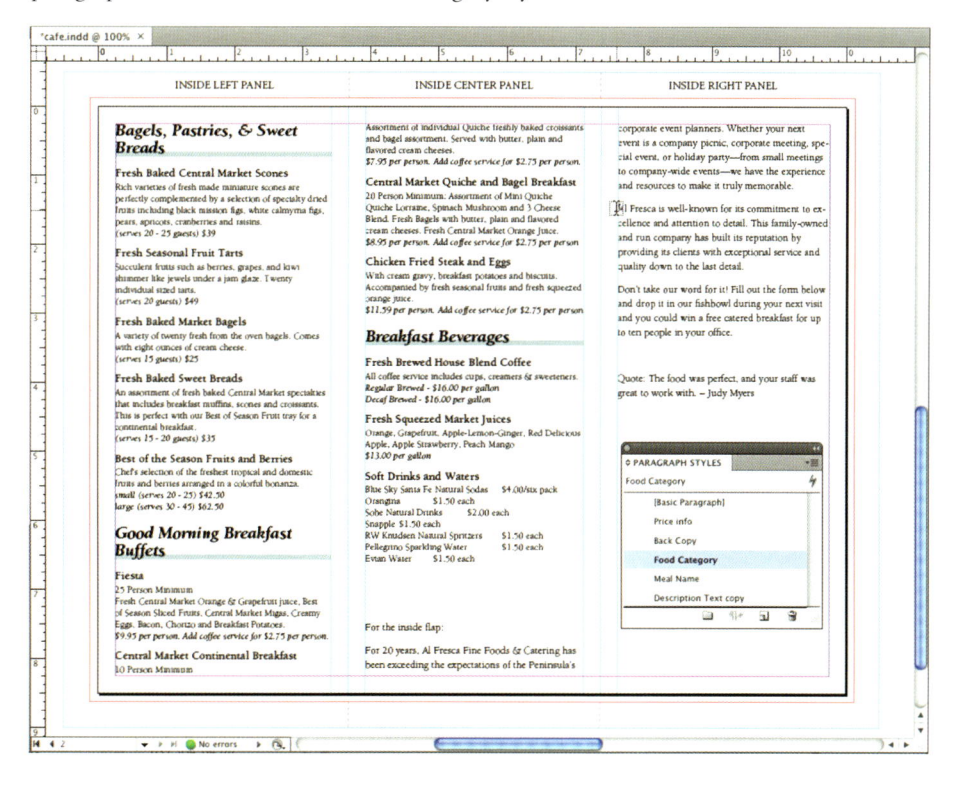

11. **Save the file and continue to the next exercise.**

Project 4: Letterfold Catering Menu   229

Cut and Delete Text

In some cases, you may want to thread text across multiple frames (as you did for the three text frames on the inside of this brochure). In other cases, you may want to break a single story into multiple stories to prevent text from accidentally flowing into the wrong place.

In this brochure, you need to move the inside flap copy to the text frame on the inside flap (on Page 1). Rather than creating a thread from Page 2 to Page 1, you are going to cut the text from Page 2 and move it to Page 1.

1. **With `cafe.indd` open, highlight all text including and after the paragraph "For the inside flap:".**

    This kind of notation is common in imported client text.

2. **Cut the text from the frame (Edit>Cut or Command/Control-X).**

    When you cut text from a story, the text is stored in the Clipboard so you can paste it somewhere else.

3. **Using the Type tool, click the empty text frame on the left side of Page 1 and paste the text you cut from Page 2 (Edit>Paste or Command/Control-V).**

4. **Highlight the entire first paragraph in the frame ("For the inside flap:", including the paragraph-return character) and press Delete/Backspace.**

    Pressing Delete/Backspace removes the selected text from the story; the deleted text is not stored in the Clipboard.

5. **Highlight the last paragraph in the frame (the one that begins with the word "Quote") and cut it.**

Project 4: Letterfold Catering Menu

6. **Create a new text frame with the following parameters (based on the top-left reference point):**

   X: 1.875"   W: 1.5"
   Y: 2.9"   H: 1.5"

   You need to create the text frame on the pasteboard, or somewhere on the page where no frame currently exists, then select the frame and use the Control panel to define the frame position and dimensions.

7. **Apply a text wrap (Window>Text Wrap) to the frame based on the frame's bounding box.**

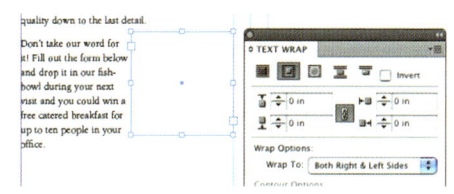

8. **Place the insertion point in the empty text frame and paste the text you cut in Step 5.**

9. **Delete the word "Quote" (and the space character that follows) from the pasted text.**

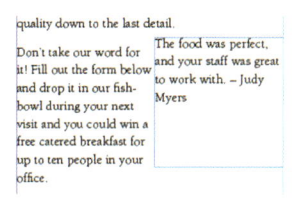

10. **Save the file and continue to the next exercise.**

CREATE A STYLE FOR PULL QUOTES

Your client asked you to include a **pull quote**, which is a special visual treatment for text that is either pulled from the story (hence the name) or somehow supports the surrounding text. For the pull quote in this layout, use the following structure:

- Format the first character in the pull quote as a quotation mark using the Quote Character character style.

- Format the text of the quote with the Quote Copy character style. All quotes have one or more paragraphs.

- Format the author's name (preceded by an en dash) with the Quote Author character style.

You could simply format these elements in the layout, but nested styles allow you to create the structure once and apply it anywhere.

1. **On Page 1 of the open `cafe.indd` file, change the pull-quote frame's vertical alignment to bottom,**

2. **In the layout, copy the en dash before the author's name.**

3. **Place the insertion point anywhere in the pull quote text frame, and then apply right paragraph alignment to the paragraph.**

Project 4: Letterfold Catering Menu   231

Understanding Nested Styles

InDesign supports two kinds of nested styles. The first is the basic parent/child relationship, in which one style is based on another. When you base one style on another, you change all related styles by changing the parent style.

Body Copy uses 10-pt Jansen Text with a 0.3" first-line indent.

Body Copy No Indent is based on Body Copy, with the first-line indent changed to 0".

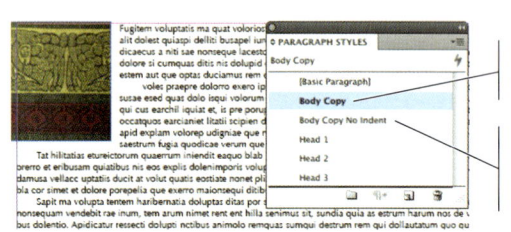

Changing Body Copy to use Optima…

…applies the same change to Body Copy No Indent.

The second type of nested style incorporates different character styles for specific parts of a paragraph. You can use nested character styles for drop caps, bulleted lists, and numbered lists.

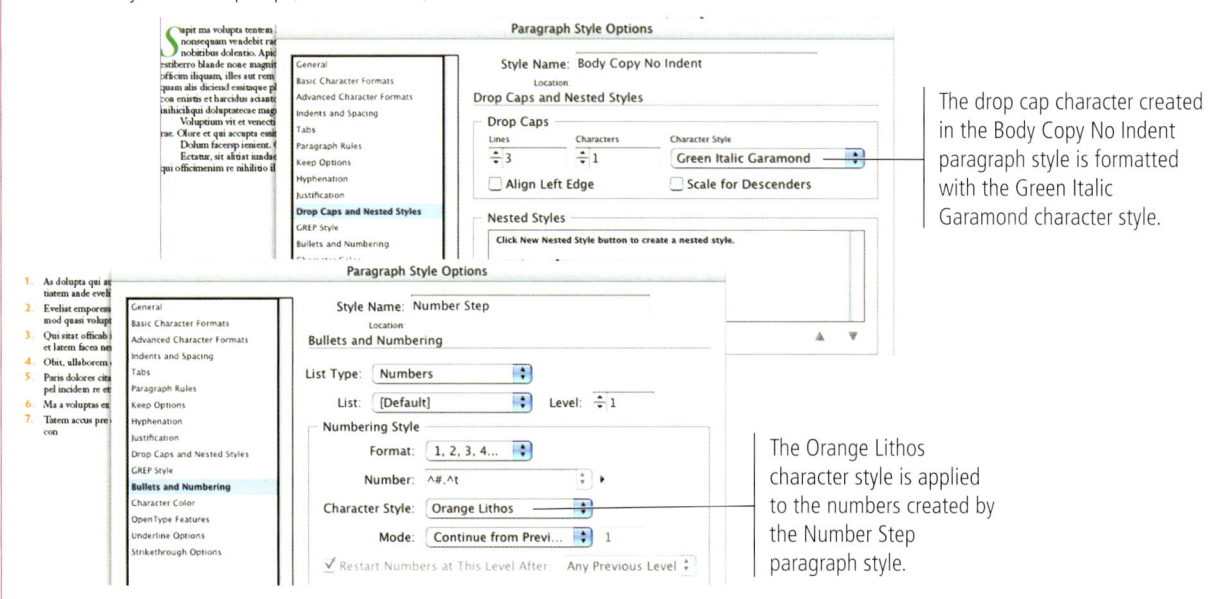

The drop cap character created in the Body Copy No Indent paragraph style is formatted with the Green Italic Garamond character style.

The Orange Lithos character style is applied to the numbers created by the Number Step paragraph style.

Nested Line Styles (at the bottom of the dialog box) affect the appearance of entire lines of text. You can define specific character styles to apply to a specific number of lines; the Repeat option allows you to continue a sequence of defined styles for the remainder of the paragraph. In this example, a paragraph style ("Chart") has been applied to the chart paragraph.

The first two items in the Nested Line Styles area tell InDesign to apply the Cyan Band character style to the first line of the paragraph, and then apply the Yellow Band character style to the second line of the paragraph. The third item in the list — [Repeat] — determines what to do with the remaining lines of the paragraph; in this example, InDesign will repeat the last 2 lines of the Nested Line Styles list.

The Chart paragraph style defines a sequence of two character styles that will be applied to every other line in the paragraph.

This entire chart is a single paragraph; each line is forced by a soft-return character.

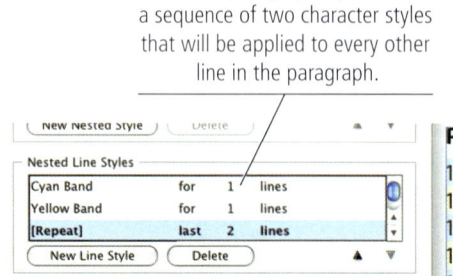

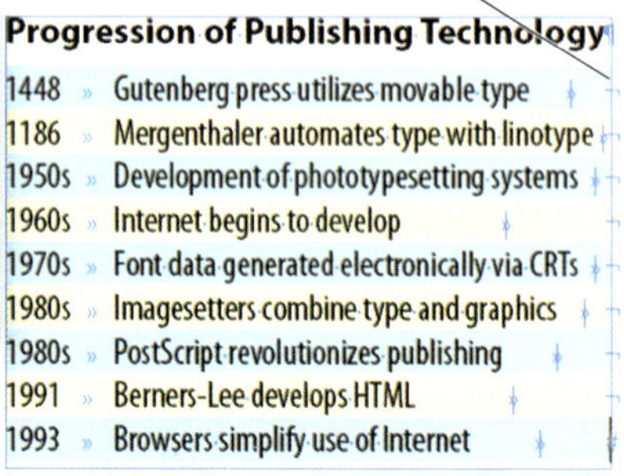

4. **With the insertion point anywhere in the quote paragraph, click the Create New Style button in the Paragraph Styles panel.**

The plus sign indicates that formatting other than the style definition has been applied to the current selection (insertion point location).

The new style is automatically named.

Insertion point

En dash

Create New Style button

5. **Without moving the insertion point, click Paragraph Style 1 in the panel.**

When you create a new style, the style has the same formatting as the currently selected text (or location of the insertion point). When you click the new style to apply it, nothing changes in the layout because the style already has the same formatting as the selected paragraph.

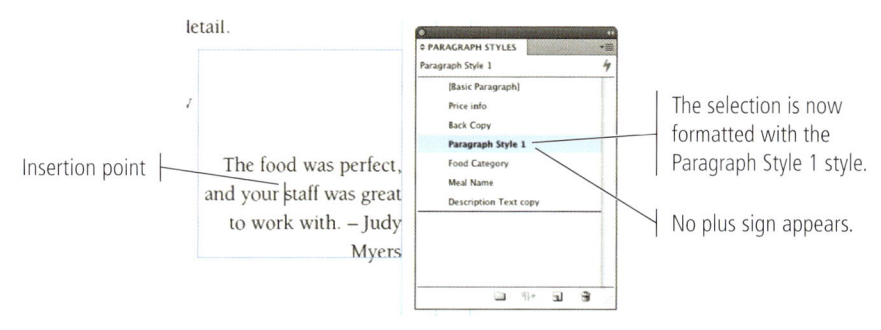

Insertion point

The selection is now formatted with the Paragraph Style 1 style.

No plus sign appears.

Building Complex Nested Styles

You can also set up complex arrangements of nested styles to apply specific character formatting to certain ranges of text within a paragraph. To automatically format a bold run-in paragraph, for example, you can define one character style for the first sentence of a paragraph, and then switch to another character style for the rest of the paragraph. For a sequence of paragraphs with the same formatting structure (such as a glossary), you can even loop back to the first style in the sequence.

In the following example, the TOC 2 paragraph style includes a sequence of nested character styles to format the different parts of each listing:

- The first two words of each paragraph ("Stage N") are formatted with the Stage Number character style.
- The paragraph switches to the Stage Name character style up to the first tab character it finds.
- The paragraph switches to the Page Number character style through the next four characters (to accommodate the tab character and up to three-digit page numbers).

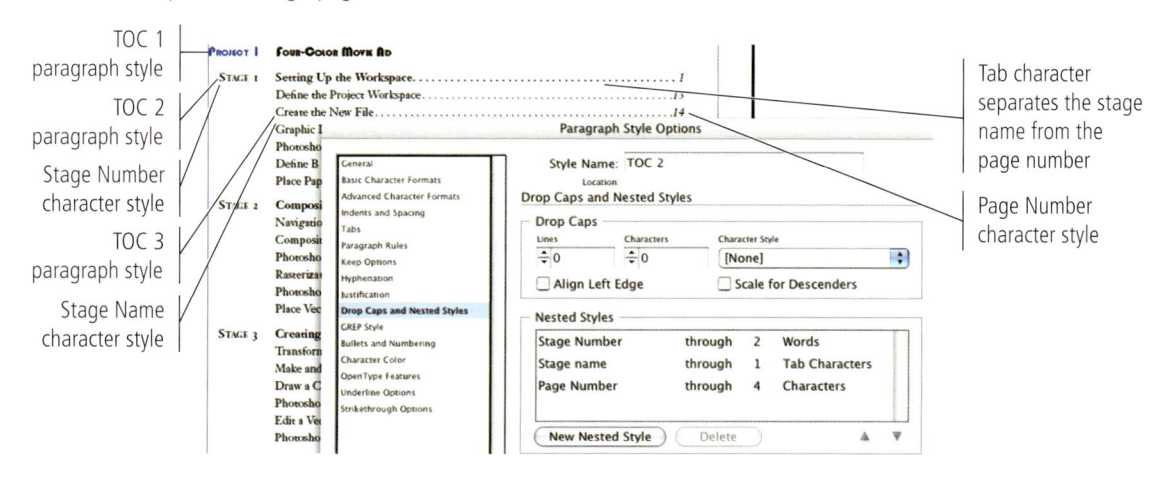

TOC 1 paragraph style

TOC 2 paragraph style

Stage Number character style

TOC 3 paragraph style

Stage Name character style

Tab character separates the stage name from the page number

Page Number character style

6. **Control/right-click Paragraph Style 1 in the panel and choose Edit "Paragraph Style 1".**

7. **Change the style name to Pull Quote and make sure the Preview check box is active.**

8. **Click Drop Caps and Nested Styles in the list of categories to display those options.**

9. **Click the New Nested Style button.**

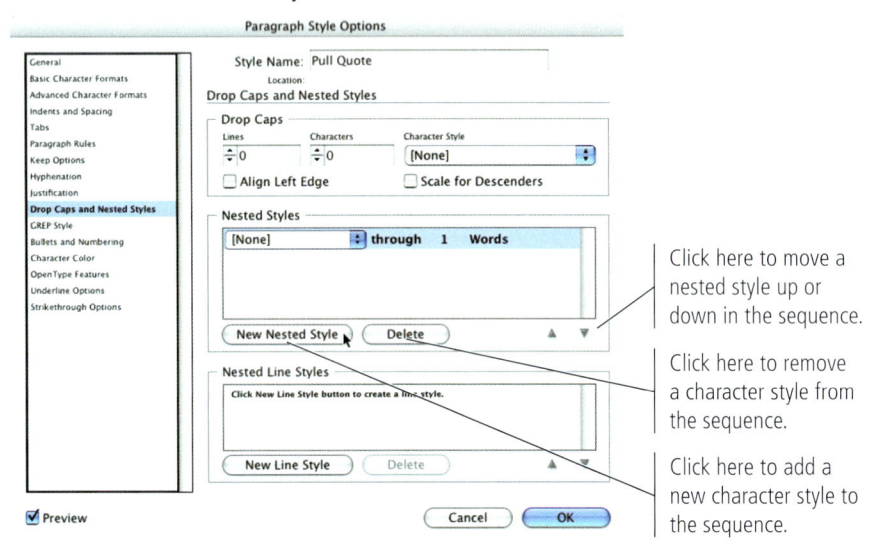

Note:

Double-click a paragraph style name in the panel to open the Paragraph Style Options dialog box.

10. **Click the first menu (the one that says "[None]") and choose Quote Character in the list of available character styles.**

11. **Click the Words menu and choose Characters from the list.**

   Nested styles can be applied up to or through a specific character sequence; if you choose the Through option, the character(s) you define will be formatted with the character style you define.

   The first character in any pull quote will be formatted with the Quote Character style; in this case, you can leave the default Through option.

234 Project 4: Letterfold Catering Menu

Because the Preview option is checked, the layout shows a dynamic preview of your choices.

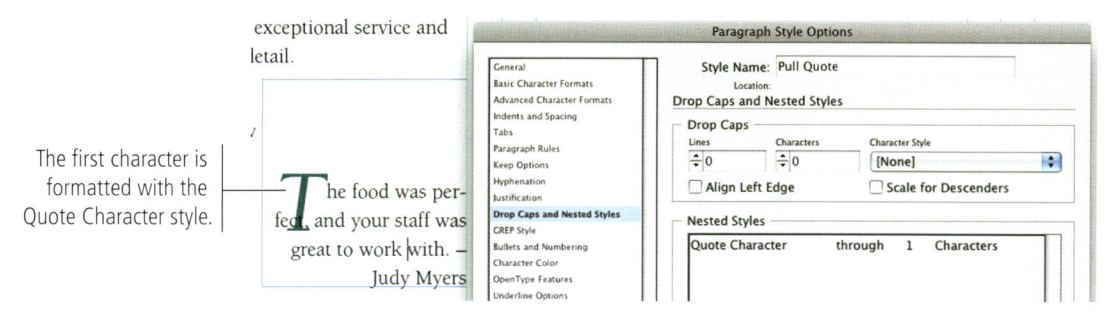

The first character is formatted with the Quote Character style.

12. **Add another nested style to the list, applying the Quote Copy character style and using the Up To option instead of the Through option. Choose Characters in the fourth menu.**

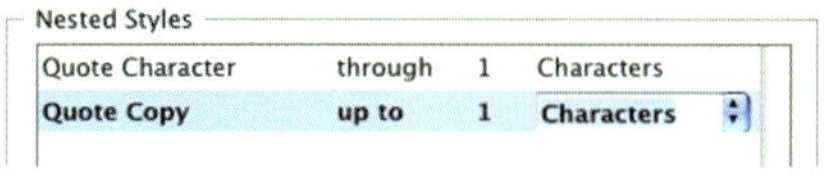

13. **Select the word "Characters" in the menu and press Command/Control-V to paste the en dash you copied in Step 2.**

    You can define a specific character by selecting the menu and typing the character. In this case, you're formatting all text up to the en dash preceding the author's name.

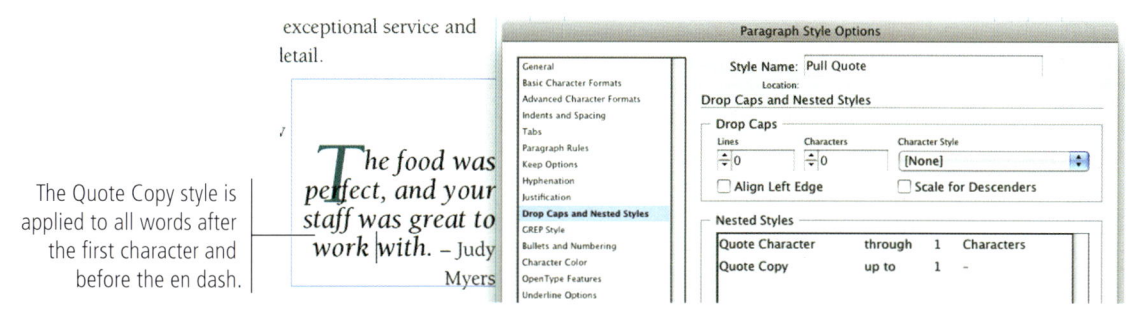

    The Quote Copy style is applied to all words after the first character and before the en dash.

    Option/Alt-Hyphen is the key command for inserting an **en dash**, which is a special character typically used to separate ranges (as in 2–5 hours or January 13–15) in place of the word "through." Macintosh users can actually type the en dash in the dialog box field; this doesn't work for Windows users, who have to copy the character from the layout and paste it into the dialog box field.

14. **Add a third nested style to the list, applying the Quote Author character style through six words.**

    In this case, you want the style to go through the end of the paragraph. The Words option looks at space characters to determine where a "word" starts and ends. Using six words should cover most names (including titles, initials, etc.). If you found a name with more than six words, you could edit the style to include more words.

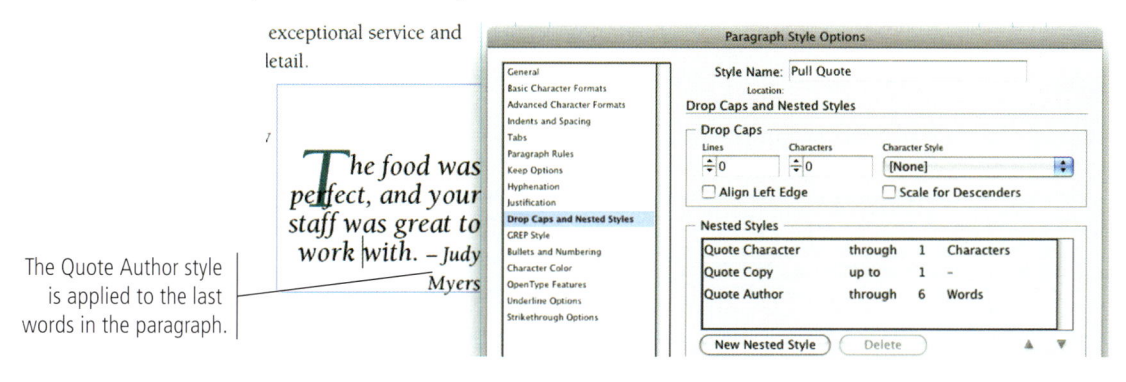

    The Quote Author style is applied to the last words in the paragraph.

Project 4: Letterfold Catering Menu

15. **Display the Basic Character Formats category of options and change the Leading value to 18 pt.**

   Increasing the paragraph style leading adds more space to accommodate the formatting applied through nested styles.

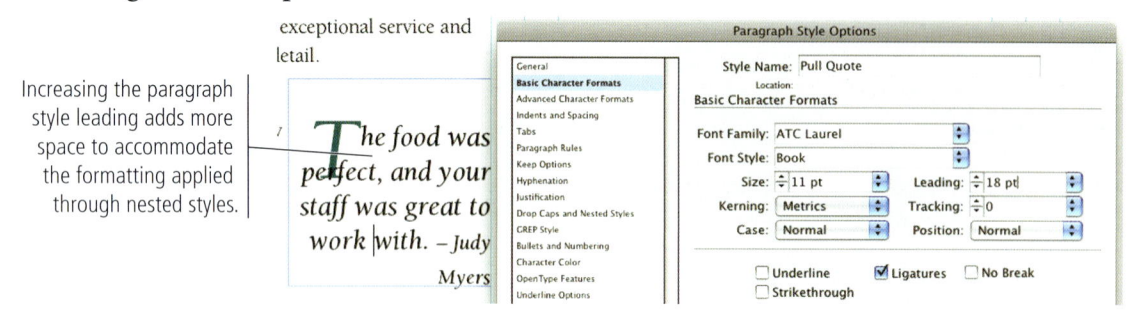

16. **Click OK to return to the document.**

17. **Place the insertion point at the beginning of the pull quote and add a quotation mark.**

   The nested styles apply the Quote Character style to the first character in the paragraph. When you type a new first character (the quotation mark), the style is applied to the new character instead of the letter "T".

18. **Place the insertion point before the en dash and press Shift-Return/Enter.**

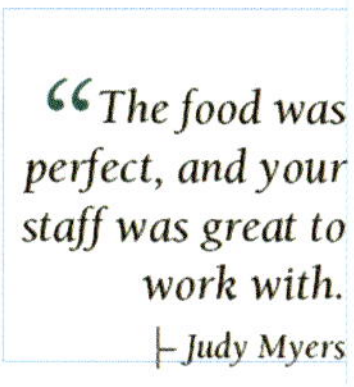

   Note:
   Remember, Shift-Return/Enter is the key command for a forced line break or "soft return," which starts a new line without starting a new paragraph.

19. **Save your work and continue to the next exercise.**

Nested Style Character Options

- **Sentences** applies the style up to or through the defined number of sentences. InDesign recognizes the end of a sentence as the location of a period, question mark, or exclamation point. (Quotation marks following punctuation are included as part of the sentence.)
- **Words** applies the style up to or through the defined number of words. InDesign recognizes the division of individual words by space characters.
- **Characters** applies the style up to or through the defined number of characters. Nonprinting characters (tabs, spaces, etc.) are included in the character count.
- **Letters** applies the style up to or through the defined number of letters.
- **Digits** applies the style up to or through the defined number of Arabic numerals (0–9).
- **End Nested Style Character** applies the style up to or through a manually added End Nested Style Here character (Type>Insert Special Character>Other>End Nested Style Here).
- **Tab Characters** applies the style up to or through a nonprinting tab character. (Choose Type>Show Hidden Characters to see tab characters in the text.) 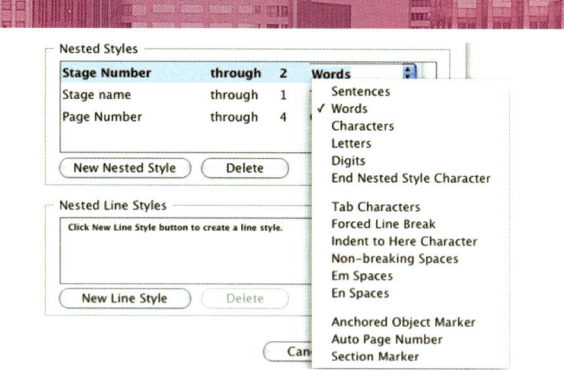
- **Forced Line Break** applies the style up to or through a nonprinting forced line break character.
- **Indent to Here Character** applies the style up to or through a nonprinting Indent to Here character.
- **Non-Breaking Spaces**, **Em Spaces**, and **En Spaces** apply the style up to or through these space characters.
- **Anchored Object Marker** applies the style up to or through an inline graphic (which exists by default wherever you have an inline object in the text).
- **Auto Page Number** and **Section Marker** apply the style up to or through page or section markers.

INDESIGN FOUNDATIONS

Project 4: Letterfold Catering Menu

CONTROL TAB FORMATTING

Some people incorrectly rely on the spacebar for aligning columns of text, or they rely on the default tab stops (usually every half-inch in InDesign and Microsoft Word) and add as many tab characters as they need to align text. Both methods can be time consuming, and both are unnecessary to properly format tabbed text.

1. **With Page 2 of the open cafe.indd file visible, make sure hidden characters are showing (Type>Show Hidden Characters).**

2. **Select the seven paragraphs after the Soft Drinks heading and choose Type>Tabs.**

    This is the only InDesign panel not accessed in the Window menu. Depending on your document window, the Tabs panel might appear randomly on your screen. If the top edge of the active text frame is visible, the Tabs panel will automatically appear at the top of the frame.

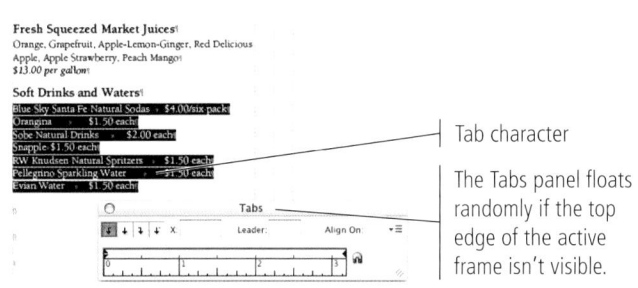

    Tab character

    The Tabs panel floats randomly if the top edge of the active frame isn't visible.

    Note:

    Many client files will have multiple tab characters separating one bit of text from another. You should almost always remove extra tab characters and use tab-formatting options to create the appropriate columns.

3. **Make sure the top of the selected text frame is visible and click the Snap Above Frame button to position the Tabs panel above the text frame.**

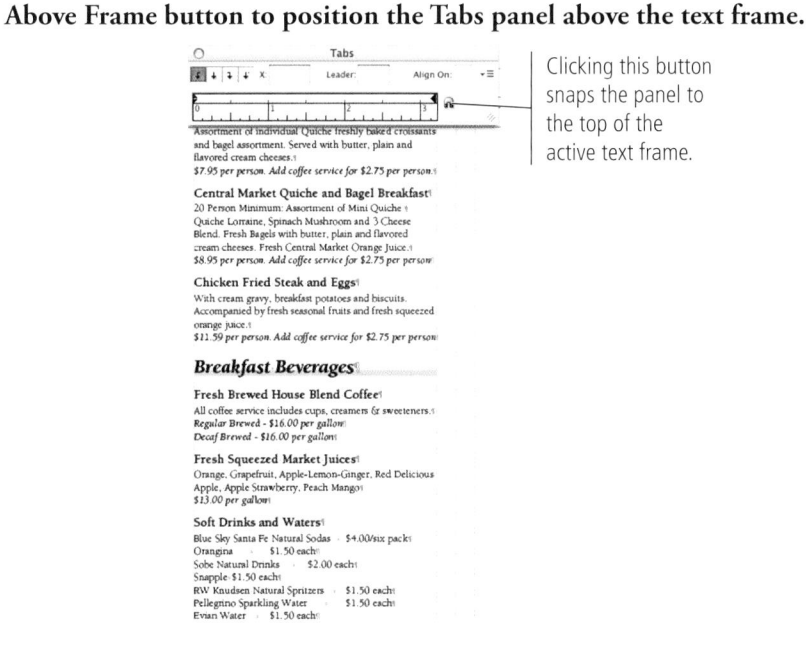

    Clicking this button snaps the panel to the top of the active text frame.

Project 4: Letterfold Catering Menu   237

4. **Click the right-justified tab marker in the Tabs panel, and then click the ruler to add a tab stop.**

   Left-justified tab
   Center-justified tab
   Right-justified tab
   Align-on-Decimal tab

   Drag these arrows on the ruler to dynamically change the paragraph indents.

   This line shows the position of the tab you're placing.

   Note:

   If you use the Align-on-Decimal tab, you can define a different alignment character in the Align On field.

5. **With the stop you added in Step 4 selected on the ruler, change the X field to 3.1″ and the Leader field to period-space.**

   You can either drag markers on the ruler to place tab stops, or you can define a precise location.

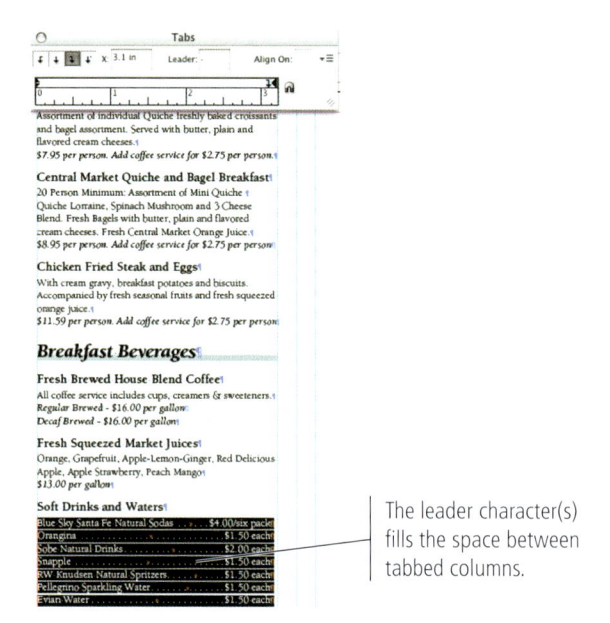

   The leader character(s) fills the space between tabbed columns.

6. **With the same lines selected, create a new paragraph style, change its name to** Price Line**, and then apply that style to the selected text.**

7. **Save the file and continue to the final stage of the project.**

Stage 3 Editing Advanced Frame Options

You've already learned how to place graphics and control them within their frames. There are, of course, many more options for working with graphics. Some of these (such as object styles and InDesign libraries) improve your productivity by automating repetitive tasks. Other options (such as accessing elements stored in image files) enhance your creative capabilities when designing a page layout.

Define an Object Style

Like paragraph and character styles, an object style stores multiple formatting options in a single unit so you can apply all settings with one click. Also similar to text-formatting styles, object styles are dynamic — which means that changing an object style automatically changes the appearance of any object that uses that style. Object styles can include virtually any attribute you can apply to a frame in the layout.

Object styles are accessed and managed in the Object Styles panel (Window>Object Styles). Every layout includes a default [Basic Graphics Frame] and a default [Basic Text Frame], which are applied to all frames you create in the layout.

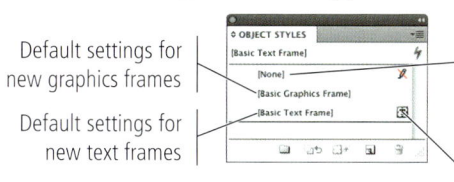

Default settings for new graphics frames
Default settings for new text frames

Click [None] to separate a specific (selected) frame from the [Basic] default.

Drag one of these icons to another style to change the default graphics and text frame settings to a different existing style.

Note:

If you want to change the default attributes of new frames, you should edit the [Basic Graphics Frame] or [Basic Text Frame] object style.

1. **With cafe.indd open, create a rectangle graphics frame in the right panel of Page 1 using the following dimensions (based on the top-left reference point):**

   X: 9.1"   W: 2.1"
   Y: 1.85"   H: 1.5"

2. **Apply a 2-pt frame using the C=100 M=25 Y=50 K=25 swatch at 100%.**

3. **In the Object Styles panel, click the Create New Style button.**

   Object styles follow the same basic principles as text-formatting styles. When you create a new style, it is added with the default name "Object Style [N]" (where "N" is a sequential number) and has the same settings as the currently selected object.

   New object style
   Create New Style button

4. **Control/right-click Object Style 1 in the panel and choose Edit Object Style 1 in the contextual menu.**

5. **In the Object Style Options dialog box, change the style name to Green Stroke Frame.**

Note:

Double-click an object style in the panel to open the Object Style Options dialog box for that style.

Project 4: Letterfold Catering Menu 239

6. **In the Style Settings window, expand the Stroke options to review the settings.**

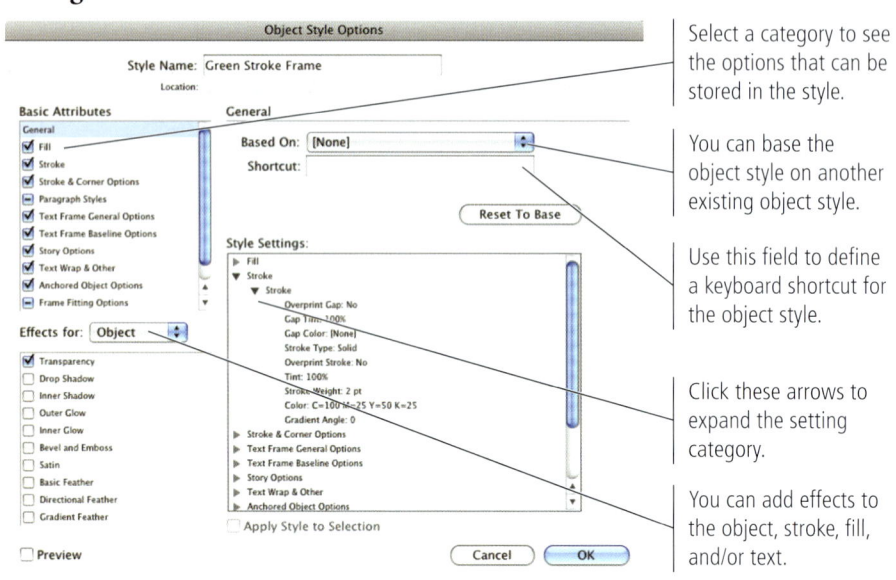

Select a category to see the options that can be stored in the style.

You can base the object style on another existing object style.

Use this field to define a keyboard shortcut for the object style.

Click these arrows to expand the setting category.

You can add effects to the object, stroke, fill, and/or text.

What's in an Object Style?

Use the following chart as a reminder of exactly what can be stored in an object style definition, as well as where to find the equivalent in the application interface for a selected object.

Category	Options		Application Equivalent
General	Based on Reset to base	Shortcut	N/A
Fill	Color	Tint	Swatches panel
Stroke	Color	Tint	Swatches panel
	Weight Gap attributes	Type	Stroke panel
Stroke & Corner Options	Stroke alignment End cap End treatment (arrowheads)	Join Miter limit Corner effects (bevel, etc.)	Stroke panel
Paragraph Styles	Default paragraph style for frame		Paragraph Styles panel
Text Frame General Options	Columns Vertical justification	Inset spacing Ignore text wrap	Text Frame Options dialog box (Object>Text Frame Options)
Text Frame Baseline Options	First baseline	Custom baseline grid options	Text Frame Options dialog box (Object>Text Frame Options)
Story Options	Optical margin alignment		Story panel
Text Wrap & Other	Text wrap type Wrap options	Offset Contour options	Text Wrap panel
	Nonprinting check box		Attributes panel
Anchored Object Options	Position (Inline, Above Line, Custom) Prevent manual positioning		Anchored Object Options dialog box (Object>Anchored Object>Options)
Frame Fitting Options	Crop amount Fitting on empty frame	Alignment reference point	Frame Fitting Options dialog box (Object>Fitting>Frame Fitting Options)
Effects	Effect (including Transparency) for object, fill, stroke, or text		Effects panel

INDESIGN FOUNDATIONS

240 Project 4: Letterfold Catering Menu

7. **Click OK to rename the style and return to the document.**

8. **With the original graphics frame still selected, click Green Stroke Frame in the Object Styles panel to apply the style to the frame.**

   Even though the object style is based on the selected object, you still have to manually apply the new style to the object. It's easy to forget this step.

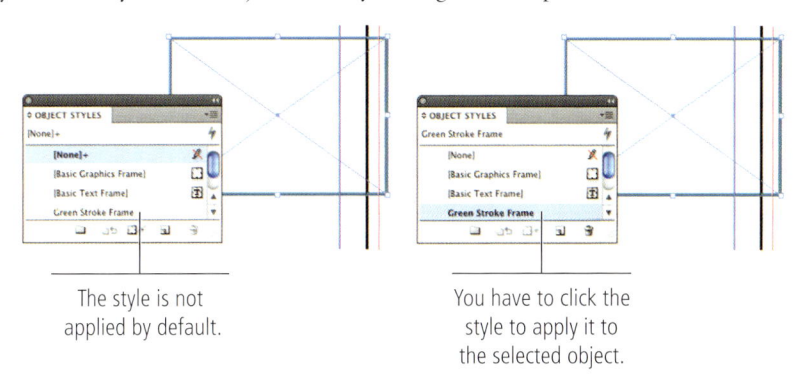

   The style is not applied by default.

   You have to click the style to apply it to the selected object.

   Note:

   If you double-clicked Object Style 1 to open the Object Style Options dialog box, you don't need to complete this step since the style will be applied to the selected object when you double-click.

9. **Option/Alt-Shift-click the graphics frame and drag down to create an exact clone of the object. Repeat this two more times to end up with four graphics frames, aligned vertically.**

10. **Position the bottom frame to align with the bottom margin guide, and then use the Align panel (Window>Object & Layout>Align) to distribute the vertical centers of the four frames.**

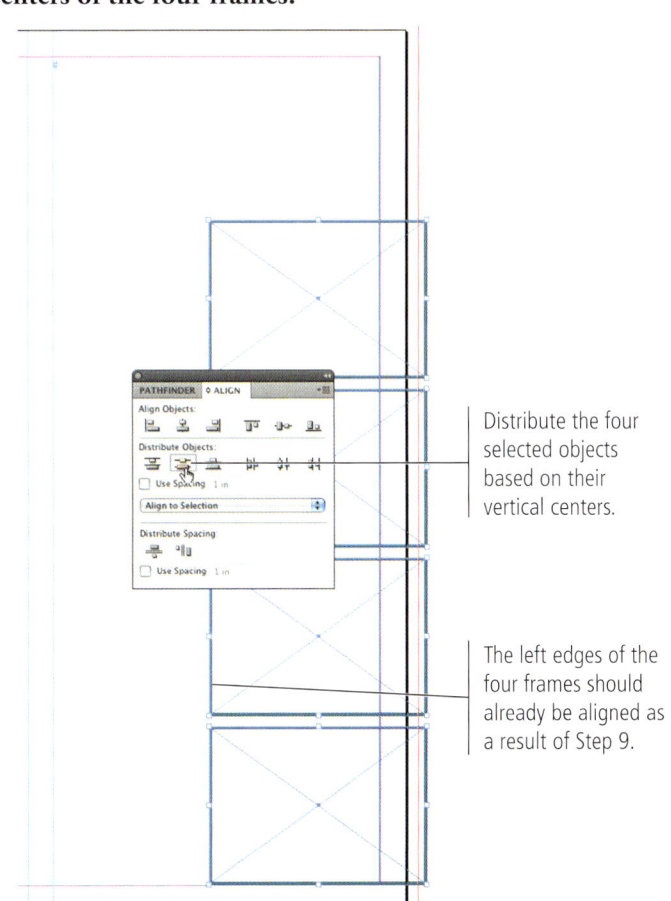

    Distribute the four selected objects based on their vertical centers.

    The left edges of the four frames should already be aligned as a result of Step 9.

    Note:

    Object styles do not store the dimensions or position of a frame.

    Note:

    Refer to Project 1 for a more in-depth explanation of the Align and Distribute options.

Project 4: Letterfold Catering Menu 241

11. Place (File>Place) images into the graphics frames, using the following image as a guide. (If Show Options is checked in the Place dialog box, either uncheck it or click OK in the resulting Image Options dialog box.) Drag each placed image within its frame so the main food item is roughly centered.

crepe.tif
scaled to 80%

crumpet.tif
scaled to 85%

sandwich.tif
scaled to 100%

omelet.tif
scaled to 100%

Note:

When you place the images within the frames, keep an eye on the panel's right page edge. Although the frames extend beyond these points, the frame area on the front panel is the "real" area you have to work with.

Note:

Because you used an object style to format all four of these frames, you can change the attributes of all four frames by changing the style definition.

12. Control/right-click Green Stroke Frame in the Object Styles panel and choose Edit "Green Stroke Frame".

13. Click Stroke in the list of Basic Attributes and change the stroke weight to 0 pt.

14. Click the Drop Shadow option in the Effects For list to add a drop shadow to the style. Change the drop shadow Distance value to 0.07″ and the Angle to 45°.

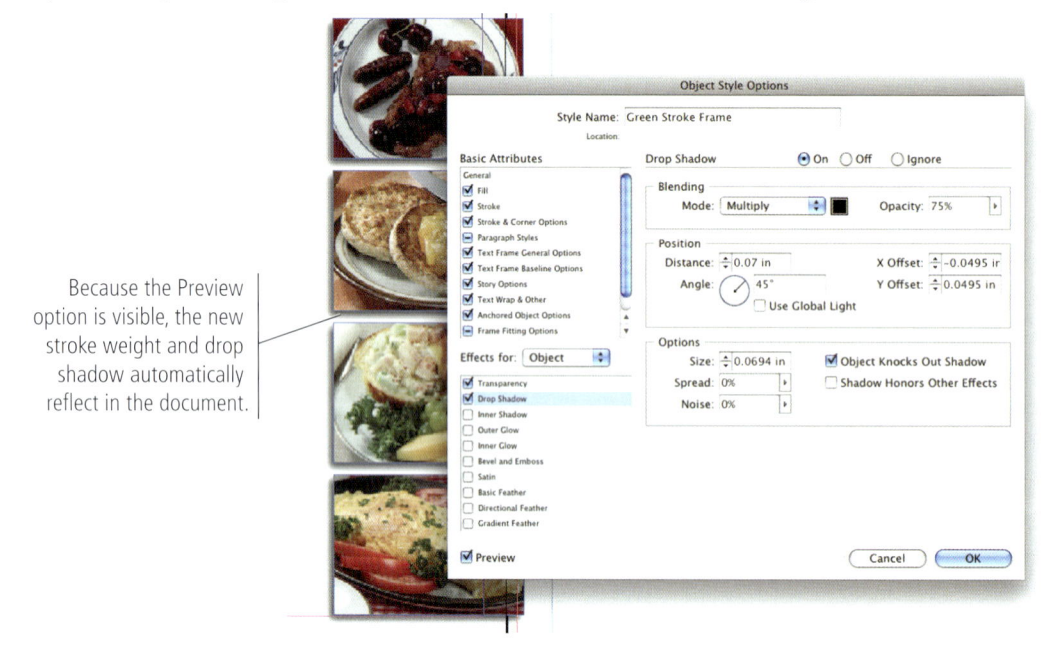

Because the Preview option is visible, the new stroke weight and drop shadow automatically reflect in the document.

15. Click OK to redefine the object style.

16. Save the file and continue to the next exercise.

EDIT THE BASIC GRAPHICS FRAME STYLE

You can edit object styles just as you edit a text-formatting style; changes to the style automatically apply to objects that use the style. In this exercise, you apply and change the Basic Graphics Frame style — which exists by default in every layout — so a number of frames can have the same basic settings with no stroke value and with a defined text wrap attribute.

1. With Page 2 of cafe.indd showing, create a new empty graphics frame using the following dimensions:

    X: –0.125"   W: 5.5"
    Y: 5.3"   H: 3.325"

2. With the new graphics frame selected, click [Basic Graphics Frame] in the Object Styles panel.

    Note:

    If you are using the Advanced workspace, or you edited the content of your Control panel, you might be able to access object style options directly in the Control panel.

3. Create a second graphics frame using the following dimensions, and then apply the [Basic Graphics Frame] object style to the new frame:

    X: 3.687"   W: 3.7"
    Y: –0.125" H: 2.5"

4. Create a third graphics frame using the following dimensions, and then apply the [Basic Graphics Frame] object style to the new frame:

    X: 7.375"   W: 3.75"
    Y: 3.825"   H: 4.8"

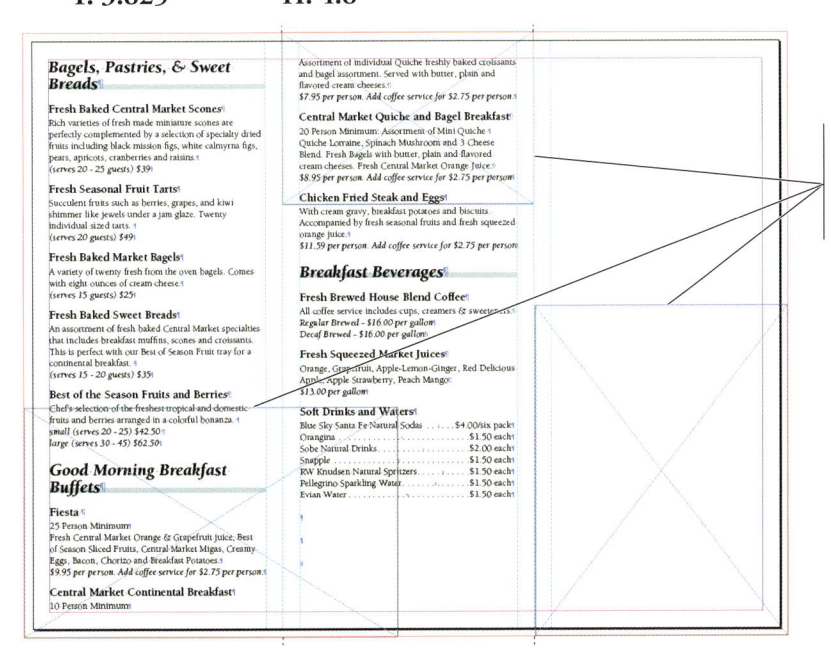

All three frames use the [Basic Graphics Frame] style (1-pt black stroke with no text wrap).

Note:

By default, the [Basic Graphics Frame] style has a 1-pt black stroke and no text wrap. You're going to change the default settings so you can apply the same settings to all three graphics on the page.

Project 4: Letterfold Catering Menu   243

5. **In the Object Styles panel, Control/right-click [Basic Graphics Frame] and choose Edit [Basic Graphics Frame].**

6. **Click Stroke in the Basic Attributes list and change the weight to 0 pt.**

7. **Click Text Wrap & Other in the Basic Attributes list and apply a text wrap based on the object bounding box with a 0.1″ offset on all four sides.**

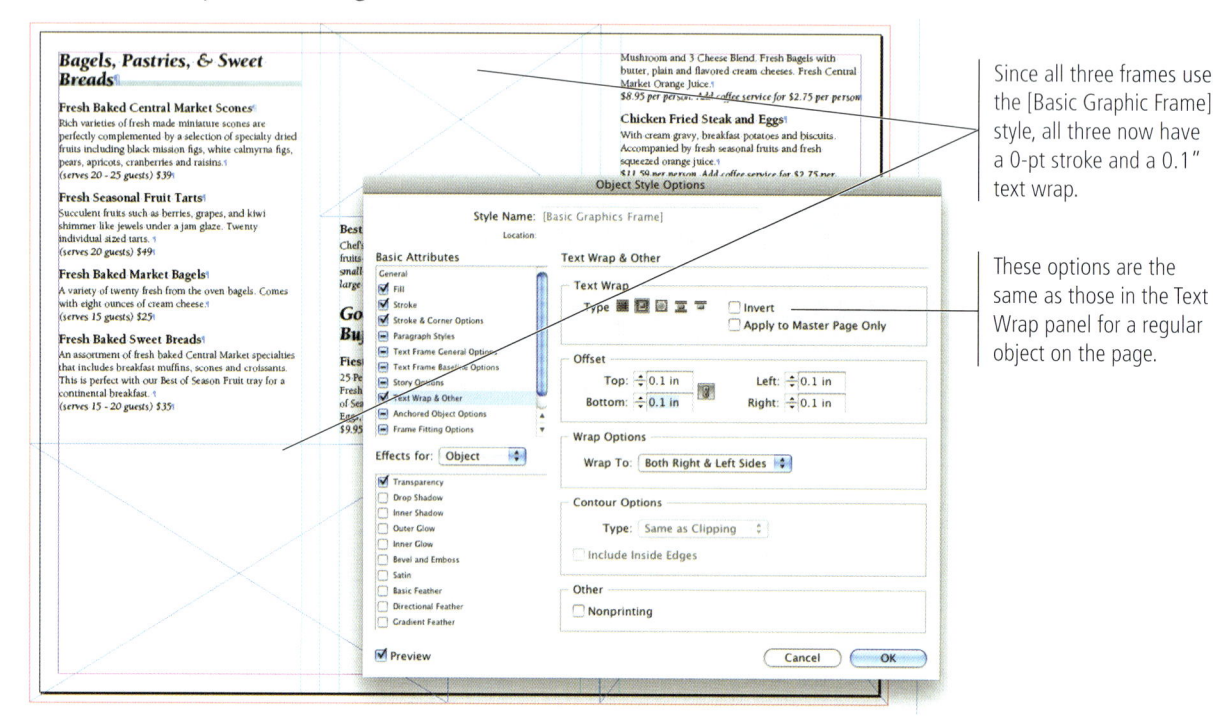

Since all three frames use the [Basic Graphic Frame] style, all three now have a 0-pt stroke and a 0.1″ text wrap.

These options are the same as those in the Text Wrap panel for a regular object on the page.

8. **Click OK to return to the layout.**

9. **Save the file and continue to the next exercise.**

Access Embedded Clipping Paths and Alpha Channels

At times, you might want to show a specific part of an image instead of the entire image. You can accomplish this task in a number of ways, but the two most common methods are using Alpha channels and clipping paths stored in the image.

A **clipping path** is a vector-based path used to mask (cover) specific parts of an image; areas inside the path are visible, and areas outside the path are hidden. Because the clipping path is a vector-based object, clipping paths always result in hard edges on the clipped image.

An **Alpha channel** is a special type of image channel that masks specific parts of an image by determining the degree of transparency in each pixel. (In other words, a 50% value in the Alpha channel means that particular spot of the image will be 50% transparent). Alpha channels allow you to design with degrees of transparency; the soft edge created by a blended Alpha channel means you can blend one image into another, blend one layer into another, or blend an entire image into a background in a page-layout application.

1. With Page 2 of cafe.indd showing, place the file muffins.tif into the frame at the top of the middle panel.

2. Select the empty frame in the right panel. Open the Place dialog box (File>Place) and navigate to the file coffee.tif. Make sure the Show Import Options box is checked and click Open.

3. In the Image tab of the Image Import Options dialog box, activate the Apply Photoshop Clipping Path option and click OK.

The clipping path hides the background area in the placed image.

4. With the placed file selected, choose Object>Clipping Path>Options.

5. In the Clipping Path dialog box, make sure the Preview option is checked and choose None in the Type menu.

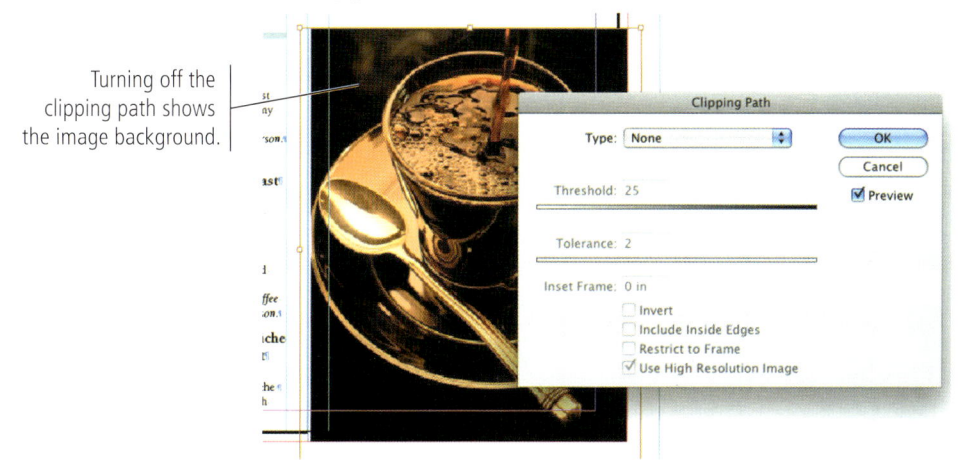

Turning off the clipping path shows the image background.

Project 4: Letterfold Catering Menu 245

6. **Click Cancel to leave the clipping path in place.**

7. **Select the empty frame in the left panel. Open the Place dialog box and navigate to the file `bread_bowl.psd`. Make sure the Show Import Options box is checked and click Open.**

8. **In the Image tab of the Image Import Options dialog box, choose Bowl in the Alpha Channel menu and click OK.**

   Although you can turn embedded clipping paths on and off in the application interface, this is the only way to access an embedded Alpha channel.

   Note:

   If this menu isn't available, the image doesn't include an Alpha channel.

9. **Scale the placed image (not the frame) to 85%.**

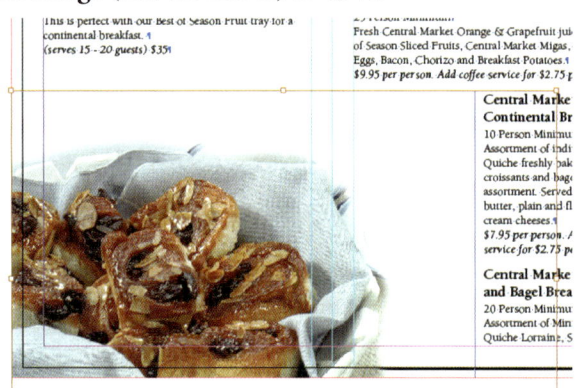

10. **In the Text Wrap panel, apply the Wrap Around Object Shape type of wrap and change the Offset value to 0.1″. In the Contour Options Type menu, choose Alpha Channel.**

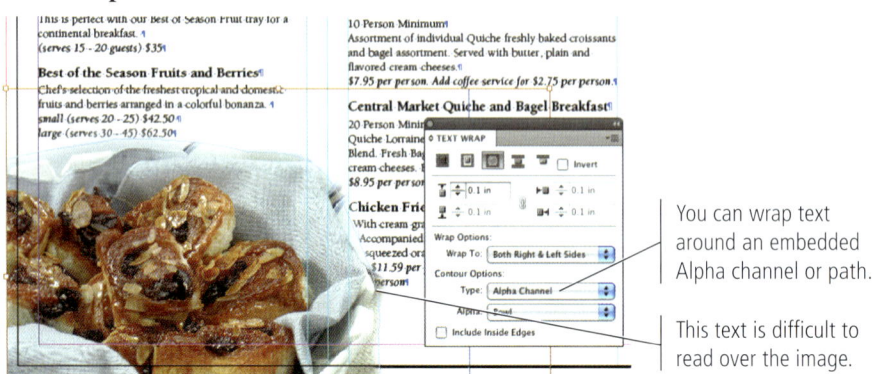

    Note:

    Remember, all panels can be opened in the Window menu.

    You can wrap text around an embedded Alpha channel or path.

    This text is difficult to read over the image.

    Project 4: Letterfold Catering Menu

11. **Click the placed image with the Direct Selection tool so you can see the anchor points of the text-wrap boundary line.**

12. **Drag the anchor points of the text-wrap boundary until you're satisfied with the position of the text at the bottom of the center panel.**

    Depending on your monitor size and current view percentage, it might help to zoom in for this step.

    When you change the boundary, this menu defaults to User-Modified Path.

    Edit the boundary anchor points to move the text away from the image.

13. **Add soft returns (Shift-Return/Enter) in the first two food category headings, and add one soft return in the last line of the center panel.**

    This final clean-up step fixes the **orphans** (single short words at the end of a paragraph that result in an unbalanced appearance in the paragraph). Page 2 is now finished.

Project 4: Letterfold Catering Menu   247

14. **Place the insertion point at the end of the last line on the right panel of Page 2. Use the Forward Delete key to remove extra paragraph returns at the end of the story.**

    If leading for the last line of the table changes after you have deleted all the extra paragraph returns, reapply the Price Line style.

    Place the insertion point here and delete any extra paragraph returns from the end of the story.

15. **Save the file and continue to the next exercise.**

IMPORT OBJECT STYLES

If you've already taken the time to build an element once, why not save yourself time and effort by reusing that same element? Object styles are not limited to the file in which you create them. You can import object styles, like text-formatting styles, from one InDesign file to another.

1. **With Page 1 of cafe.indd showing, choose Load Object Styles in the Object Styles panel Options menu.**

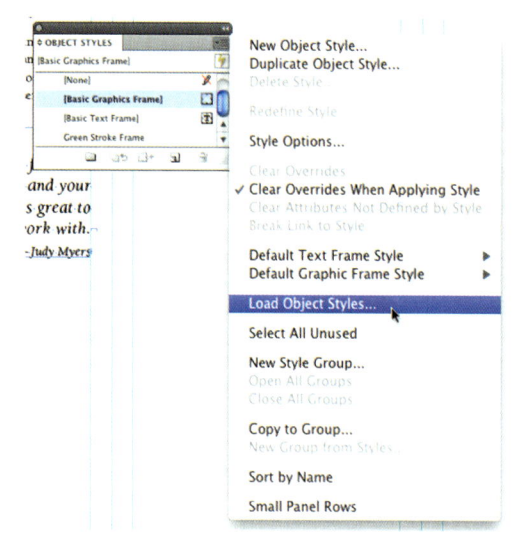

2. **Navigate to the file form_styles.indd in the RF_InDesign>Menu folder and click Open.**

3. **Uncheck the two basic frame styles, leaving only the Form Box option checked.**

    If you change the [Basic Graphics Frame] style for a file (as you did in an earlier exercise), be careful when importing object styles from one InDesign file to another. You could inadvertently overwrite the changes you already made, meaning you would have to redo your earlier work.

    The Form Box style was not created based on the Basic frame style, so there should be no conflict if you import only the Form Box style.

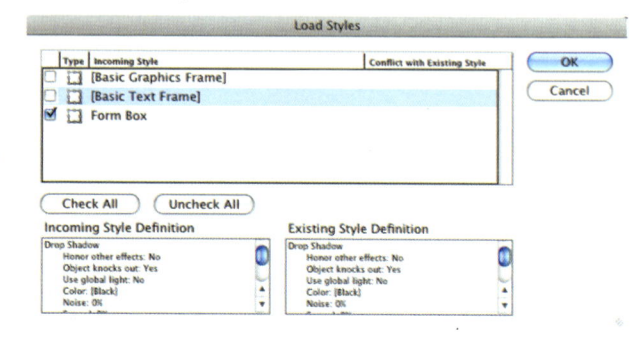

4. **Click OK to import the Form Box object style.**

   The Form Box style is imported.

   A new style, defined as part of the object style, is also imported into the InDesign file.

5. **Create a new text frame on Page 1 that fills the width of the left panel, with a height of 2.25″. Position the frame at X: 0.25″, Y: 4.75″ (based on the top-left reference point).**

6. **With the insertion point in the new frame, click [Basic Paragraph] in the Paragraph Styles panel (if it is not already selected). In the new frame, type:**

   Sign me up to win breakfast for my office!
   Name[Tab]
   Company[Tab]
   Address[Tab]
   City[Tab]
   State[Tab]
   Zip[Tab]
   Phone[Tab]

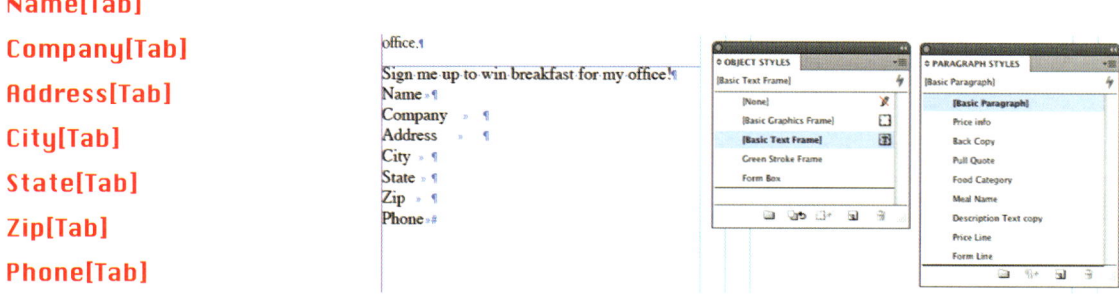

7. **Click the frame with the Selection tool, and then click Form Box in the Object Styles panel.**

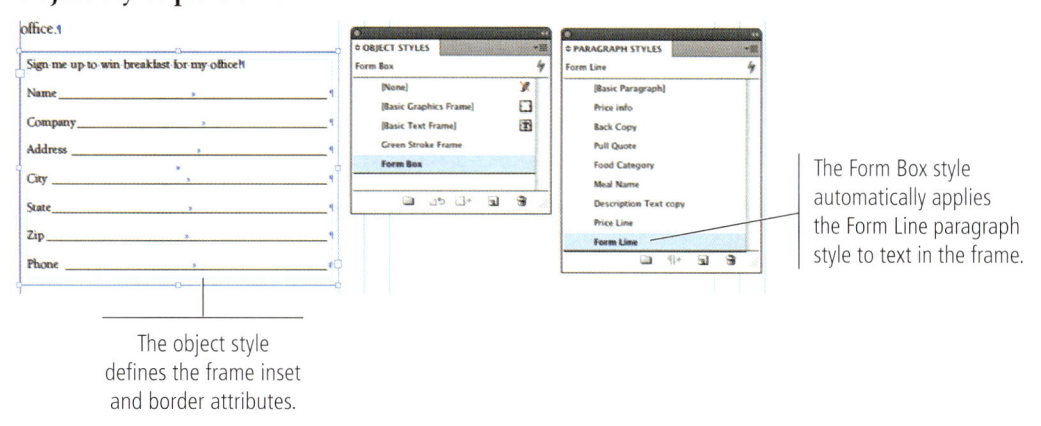

   The object style defines the frame inset and border attributes.

   The Form Box style automatically applies the Form Line paragraph style to text in the frame.

8. **Save the file and continue to the next exercise.**

Project 4: Letterfold Catering Menu 249

Add the Logo and Address Information

The final elements of this brochure are the logo and company address, which will appear on all three outside panels. Whenever you have multiple instances of the same object (or objects), you can create a library item to speed your workflow.

1. With `cafe.indd` open, choose File>Place. Make sure the Show Options box is not checked, select `al_fresca.eps` (in the RF_InDesign>Menu folder) and click OK.

2. Place the loaded image onto Page 1, and scale it (and the frame) to 65%. Position the graphics frame (based on the top-left corner) at X: 8″, Y: 0.5″.

3. If the frame shows an applied text wrap, click the Clear Overrides button in the Object Styles panel.

4. Create a new text frame with the following dimensions:

   X: 7.333″   W: 3.8″
   Y: 1.4″   H: 0.5″

5. Select the text frame with the Selection tool, and then click the Clear Overrides button in the Object Styles panel to remove the frame text wrap.

6. Inside the frame, type:

   2218 Pacific Crest Highway
   Monterey Heights, CA 95313

7. Format the text as 8-pt ATC Oak Normal with left paragraph alignment.

8. Using the Swatches panel, fill the text frame with a 15% tint of the C=100 M=25 Y=50 K=25 swatch.

9. Open the Text Frame Options dialog box. Define 0.9″ left inset spacing and apply centered vertical alignment. Click OK to apply the changes.

10. Choose Object>Arrange>Send to Back to move the text frame behind the placed graphics.

11. **Using the Rectangle tool, create a frame that is 0.25″ wide and extends from the top bleed guide to the bottom bleed guide. Position the left edge of the frame at X: 8″.**

12. **Apply the [None] object style to the frame, and then fill the frame with a 35% tint of the C=100 M=25 Y=50 K=25 swatch.**

13. **Send the rectangle from Steps 11–12 to the back (Object>Arrange>Send to Back).**

14. **Save the file and continue to the next exercise.**

CREATE AN INDESIGN LIBRARY

Object styles allow you to apply the same attributes to a frame, considerably lessening your workload if you need to repeatedly use the same settings. In other cases, you might need to use the same content (such as a logo) or the same group of objects with different content (such as a graphics frame with a grouped text frame for the caption) throughout a document. Object styles don't manage placed graphics or grouped objects. In these situations, you can use an InDesign library to quicken the process.

1. **With cafe.indd open, choose File>New>Library.**

2. **Navigate to your WIP>Menu folder as the target location. Change the file name to alfresco.indl.**

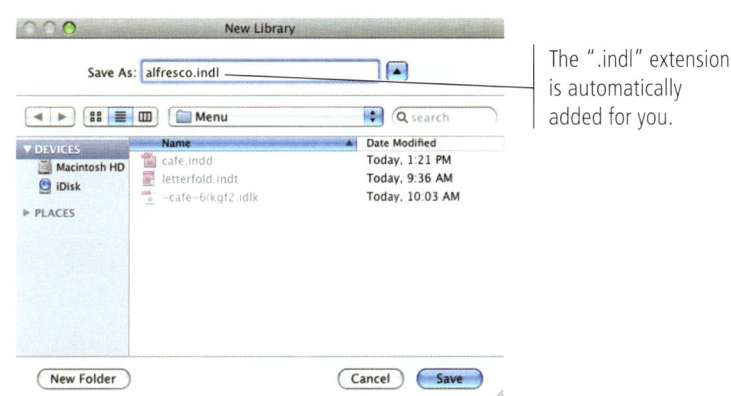

The ".indl" extension is automatically added for you.

Note:

Library items store the links to placed graphics files. Because the graphic is not embedded in the library item, you have to make sure the links are up to date before outputting the file.

Project 4: Letterfold Catering Menu 251

3. **Click Save to create the new library.**

   A library is a special type of file that stores objects (including the objects' content) for use in any InDesign file. Library files are not linked or specific to any individual layout (indd) file, so you can open and use items from an existing library in any layout you build.

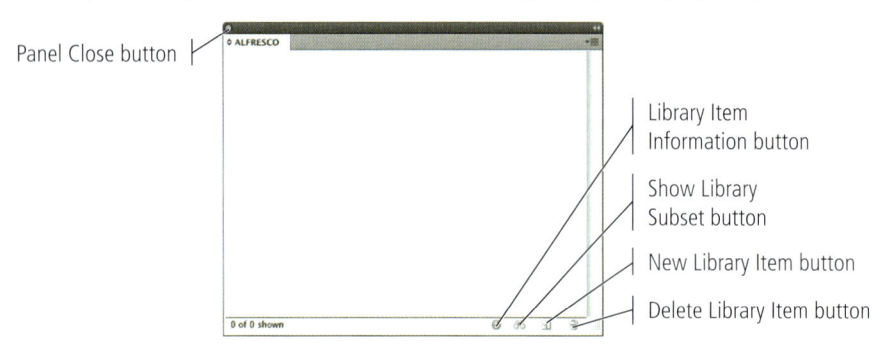

   Note:

   Library items do not store fonts. If a library item uses a specific font, that font must be active on whatever system uses the library.

4. **In the layout, select only the logo graphic frame and the frame with the address. Click the New Library Item button in the alfresca panel.**

5. **With the Untitled item selected, click the Library Item Information button at the bottom of the panel.**

6. **In the Item Information dialog box, change the Item Name field to Logo With Address and click OK.**

   You can also use this dialog box to change the object type and add a description for any library item.

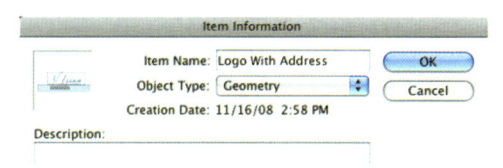

   Note:

   You can also simply drag an object from the layout into the Library panel. Doing so has no effect on the object already placed in the layout.

   Choose Add Items On Page [N] As Separate Objects in the Library panel Options menu to add all objects on the page as separate library items.

   Choose Add Items On Page [N] in the panel Options menu to add all objects on the page as a single library item.

7. **Drag the Logo With Address item from the Library panel into the layout.**

8. **Position the new objects at the bottom of the left panel on Page 1. Use the following image as a positioning guide.**

9. **Drag a third copy of the library item into the layout. With both objects from the library item selected, rotate the selection 90° counterclockwise.**

10. **Position the rotated objects on the center panel of Page 1.**

11. **Select only the address text frame. Change the right edge of the frame to end at the same point as the logo frame, and then drag the left edge to meet the bottom bleed guide.**

    There is no dynamic link between items in the library and instances placed in a layout. Changing one placed instance has no effect on the original library item or on other placed instances of the same item.

    This edge should align with the right edge of the logo frame.

    This edge should meet the bottom bleed guide.

    Note:

    Deleting an object from the library has no effect on placed instances in the layout. Deleting a placed instance has no effect on the item in the library.

    Note:

    Styles in library items are automatically added to any layout where you place an instance of that item. If a library item uses a style (text or object) that conflicts with a style in the document where you're placing an instance, the style definition from the document overrides the style definition from the library item.

12. **Click the Close button on the Library panel to close the library file.**

    This project is only a two-page brochure, and all instances of the library item appear on the same page. But think of a layout with more than a few pages — a newsletter, a booklet, or even a multi-file multi-chapter book. You can use library items to easily access common graphics such as logos; maintain consistency between sidebars on Page 1 and Page 42; and even use the same graphic-and-text-frame structure for graphics with captions on every page of a 240-page book.

    Now think about combining libraries with the other InDesign tools you've learned about. For example, let's say you create a library item with a graphics frame and a caption frame. The graphics frame is formatted with an object style, and the caption frame has placeholder text formatted with a paragraph style. You can use the library to place and change the content in individual instances, change the object and paragraph styles as necessary, and still maintain consistency throughout the document.

13. **Save the file, and then use the Package utility (File>Package) to create a final job folder. When the job folder is created, close the InDesign file.**

Managing Libraries

INDESIGAN FOUNDATIONS

If you have a large collection of objects in a library, you can show a subset of the library by clicking the Show Library Subset button (or choosing Show Subset from the Library panel Options menu). The Show Subset dialog box allows you to define what you want to find, based on the item name, creation date, object type, or description text. You can always restore the entire library by choosing Show All in the Library panel Options menu.

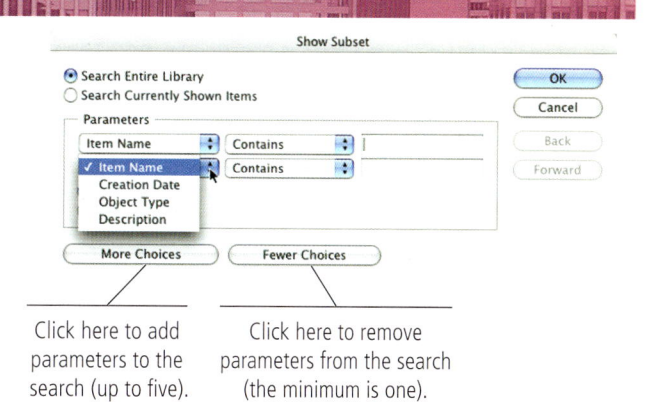

Click here to add parameters to the search (up to five).

Click here to remove parameters from the search (the minimum is one).

Project Review

fill in the blank

1. _____ have inside and outside margins instead of left and right margins.

2. A(n) _____ folds three times, resulting in four panels on each side of the sheet. The paper is folded in half, and then each half is folded in half toward the center so the two ends of the paper meet at the center fold

3. A(n) _____ is a spread with more than two pages.

4. You can use the _____ panel to determine whether certain objects are printed when the job is output.

5. The _____ dialog box is used to resolve conflicts in text formatting styles that you are importing from another InDesign layout.

6. A(n) _____ is a special visual treatment for text that is either pulled from the story or somehow supports surrounding text.

7. You can use the _____ option to create a parent/child relationship between two styles, in which changes made to the parent style reflect in the child style as well.

8. A(n) _____ can be used to define multiple styles that will be used for different portions of the same paragraph, based on specific sequences of characters or markers.

9. A(n) _____ is used to format entire lines of text within a single paragraph.

10. A(n) _____ can be used to apply the same attributes (such as text wrap and stroke weight) to multiple text frames.

short answer

1. Briefly explain the difference between facing pages and non-facing pages.

2. Briefly explain the rules regarding panels that fold into other panels in a folding document.

3. Explain three different ways that text formatting styles might appear in an InDesign file.

Project 4: Letterfold Catering Menu

Portfolio Builder Project

Use what you learned in this project to complete the following freeform exercise.
Carefully read the art director and client comments, then create your own design to meet the needs of the project.
Use the space below to sketch ideas; when finished, write a brief explanation of your reasoning behind your final design.

art director comments

The owner of Hollywood Sandwich Shoppe wants you to design new menus that can be printed every month at the local quick printer.

To complete this project, you should:

❏ Plan the overall layout of the piece using a letter-size sheet as the basic flat size, with no bleeds.

❏ If you decide to design the menu with folds, create a document grid that incorporates the necessary folding allowances.

❏ Import the client's text, then develop a text-formatting scheme (using styles) that will communicate the theme of the restaurant.

❏ Find supporting artwork or images that will support the restaurant's theme.

client comments

A menu is the single most important tool that a restaurant can develop to promote the business. Be creative, but also be sure that the menu is readable.

The cover needs to include the restaurant's logo, name, and address. We gave you the logo, and the address is in the menu text file (in the RF_Builders>Hollywood folder).

Somewhere on the menu, you need to include space for a "special feature" that will include a description of the monthly special and a picture of the star that it's named after — we'll send this to you as soon as we finalize the first two months' specials. For now, can you just use placeholders?

Since we have to print new menus every month, we just take them to the local quick printer. We want something we can print on letter-size paper — nothing fancy or overly expensive. We might be willing to print in color if it's important, but black-only is much cheaper so we'll probably stick with that.

project justification

Project Summary

This project built on the skills you learned in previous projects. To begin the letterfold layout, you built a technically accurate folding guide on a facing-page master layout, incorporating nonprinting fold guides and text frames into the slug area. To speed up the process for the next time you need to build one of these common letterfold jobs, you saved your initial work as a template.

Completing this project also required extensive work with imported text, specifically importing styles from a Microsoft Word file and then editing those styles. You also worked with several advanced text options, including nested styles and tab formatting, to fine-tune the text in this project.

You also learned about two more options for improving workflow. Object styles allow you to store and apply multiple frame-formatting options (including nested paragraph styles) in a single click. Libraries store entire objects or groups of objects (including their formatting and even contents) so you can place as many instances as necessary on any page of any file.

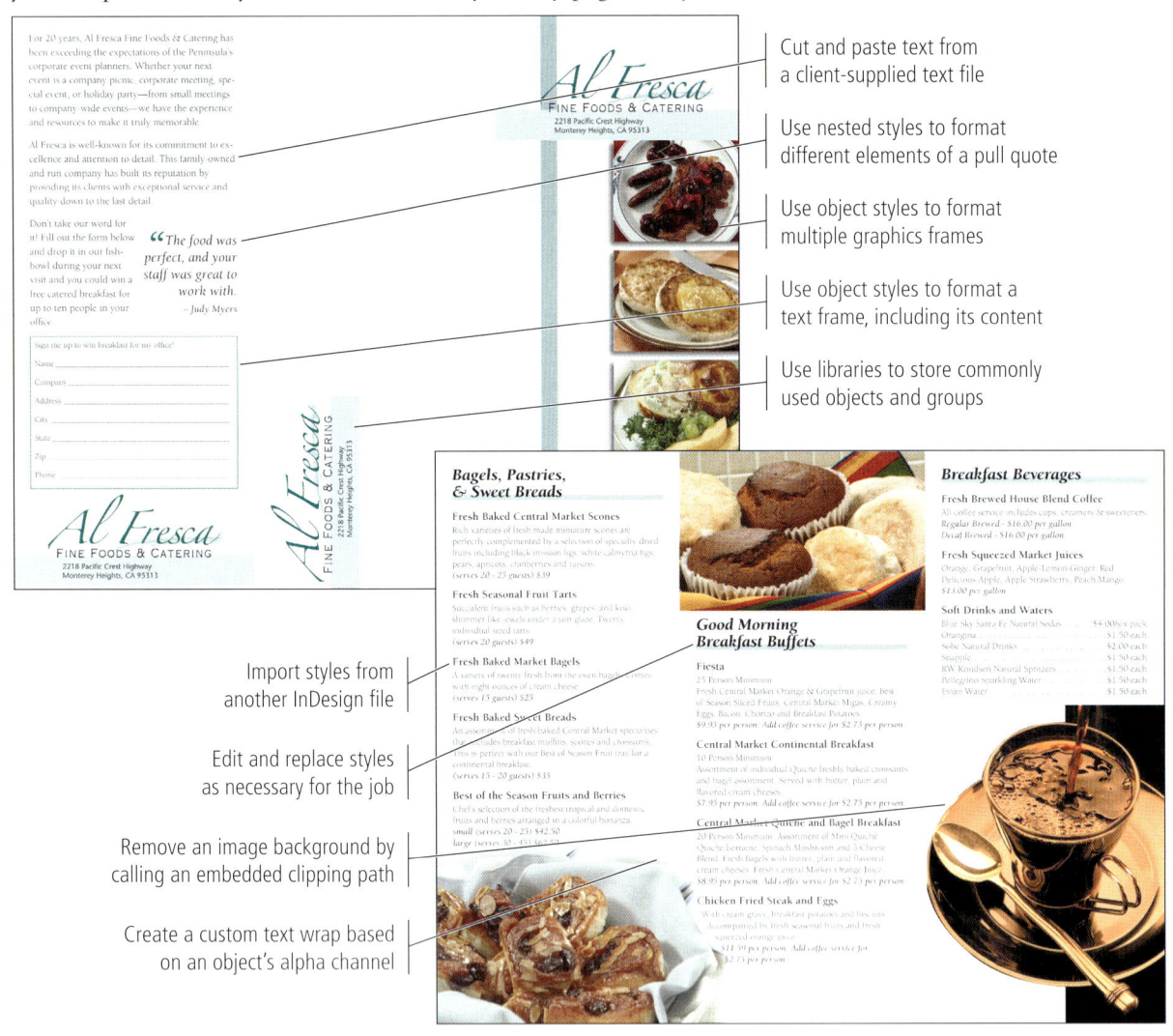

- Cut and paste text from a client-supplied text file
- Use nested styles to format different elements of a pull quote
- Use object styles to format multiple graphics frames
- Use object styles to format a text frame, including its content
- Use libraries to store commonly used objects and groups
- Import styles from another InDesign file
- Edit and replace styles as necessary for the job
- Remove an image background by calling an embedded clipping path
- Create a custom text wrap based on an object's alpha channel

project 5

Realtor Collateral Booklet

Your client is the Southern California Realtors Association, which provides support materials for member realtors. They hired you to create a booklet with tips for sellers who want to make their homes more attractive to buyers. The booklet will be printed in very large quantities and distributed to agents' offices, so the individual realtors can use it as a tool when they are contacted about listing a home for sale. The ultimate consumer for this piece is the home seller (not the agent), so it needs to be visually inviting and easy to read.

This project incorporates the following skills:

❏ Understanding and controlling facing-page layouts
❏ Using master pages to apply repetitive layout elements
❏ Converting regular layout pages to master pages
❏ Automatically flowing text across multiple pages
❏ Using special characters, markers, and text variables
❏ Basing style sheets on other style sheets to improve consistency
❏ Applying bulleted list formatting
❏ Controlling page breaks with paragraph Keep options
❏ Controlling automatic hyphenation
❏ Printing a booklet using built-in imposition options
❏ Exporting a PDF file with animated page transitions
❏ Using conditional text to output multiple file versions

Project Meeting

client comments

The idea behind this booklet is to give realtors something they can hand to potential sellers — kind of a tactful way to point out what a homeowner needs to do to prepare their house for sale. This way the agents don't have to blatantly say things like "scrub the mold off your bathtub before showing it." So really, the booklet is a tool for the agents to hand out, but ultimately it's for the sellers to use as a checklist of things to do before an open house.

The text was created in Microsoft Word, using a custom template with all the text formats we use in a number of similar collateral pieces. We're also sending you some images from our agents' files; we have permission to use them in marketing materials without paying a specific licensing fee. Our research shows that a 5.5 × 8.5″ booklet is well received by most consumers, so we want the finished booklet to be that size.

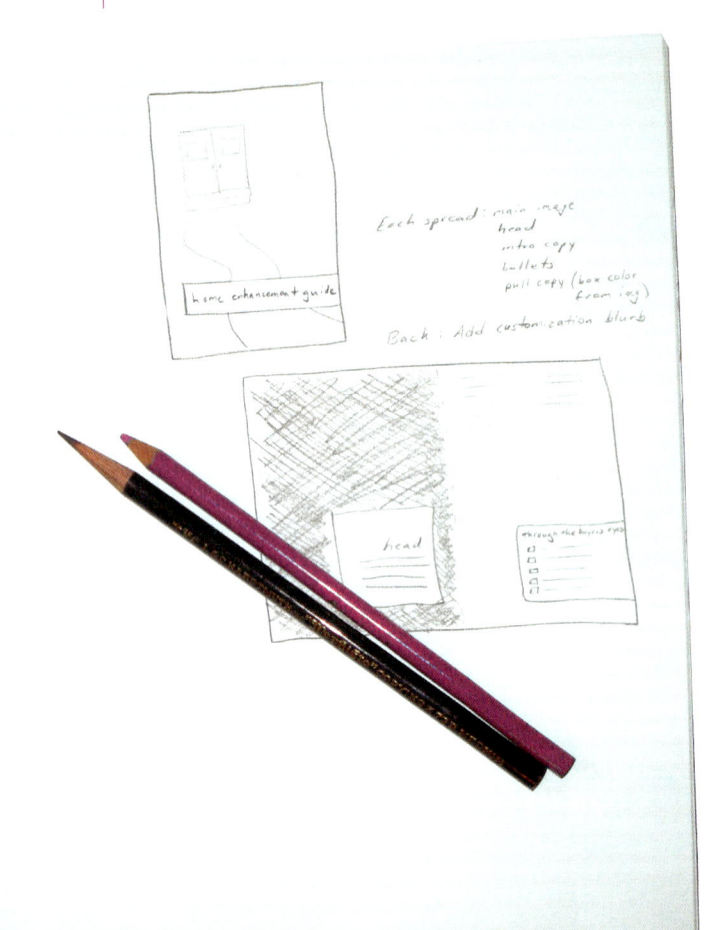

art director comments

This booklet was originally specified as 16 pages with a separate cover, but the client decided that a self-cover will work just as well. We had already designed the front and back covers for the initial pitch, so you can import the cover layouts into the main booklet file.

People don't like to read long blocks of body copy, and this project has a large amount of text. A lot of it will work well as lists, however, so you'll use bullets to break up most of the body text. Each spread will also have a large picture and a callout box to add visual interest.

This project — like most documents with a lot of text — will also require tighter control over the text flow than when you work with smaller bits of text. Long documents like this one require special attention to detail to prevent problems such as bad line and page breaks.

Consistency is important for any document with more than a few pages; the same basic grid should be used for most internal pages in the booklet. Completing this project will be much easier if you take the time to build the basic layout on master pages.

project objectives

To complete this project, you will:

❑ Use master pages with placeholders for the different elements of the layout

❑ Convert layout pages to master pages and import them into the main booklet file

❑ Create a custom slug with text variables to keep track of the file status

❑ Define styles based on other styles to improve consistency and facilitate changing multiple styles at once

❑ Format paragraphs as bulleted lists to improve readability

❑ Control paragraph positioning using widow and orphan controls

❑ Control automatic hyphenation to prevent bad line breaks

❑ Print a sample booklet for client approval

❑ Export a PDF version with page transitions

❑ Create personalized versions for different end users

Stage 1 Working with Master Pages

In Project 3, you worked with the existing master pages in a newsletter template. In Project 4, you used master pages to build a technically accurate folding grid on facing pages of a spread. To complete this booklet project, you dig much deeper into the capabilities and advantages of master pages.

Create the Booklet File

Multi-page documents (such as the booklet you build in this project) typically require special layout considerations so the pages will appear in the correct arrangement when the job is finished. Called **imposition**, you'll deal with output considerations in Stage 3. For now, however, you need to understand two issues related to setting up this type of file:

- Books and booklets usually have facing pages, which means opposing left and right pages of a spread mirror each other.

- Files with facing pages can have different margin values on the inside (near the spread center) and outside (away from the spread center) edges.

1. **On your desktop, copy the Realtors folder from the WIP folder on your Resource CD to the WIP where you are saving your work.**

2. **Choose File>New.**

3. **In the New Document dialog box, choose Letter – Half in the Page Size menu, using portrait orientation.**

    The 5.5 × 8.5″ document size is common enough to be included in the default InDesign settings.

4. **Make sure the Facing Pages and Master Text Frame options are checked.**

    The Master Text Frame option creates an automatic text frame that snaps to the defined margins, using the number of columns and gutter width defined in the Columns area of the dialog box. This frame is placed on the default master page layout, so it will also appear on every layout page associated with the default master page layout.

5. **In the Columns area, define 2 columns with a 0.2″ gutter.**

6. **In the Margins area, apply a 0.5″ margin to all four sides of the page.**

7. **Define a 0.125″ bleed and a 0.5″ slug on all four sides.**

    If you can't see the Bleed and Slug options, click the More Options button below the Save Preset button.

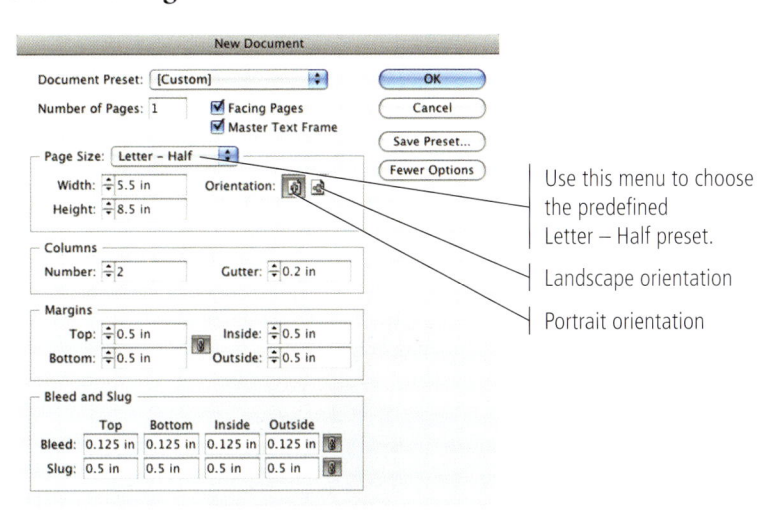

Project 5: Realtor Collateral Booklet

8. **Click OK to create the new document.**

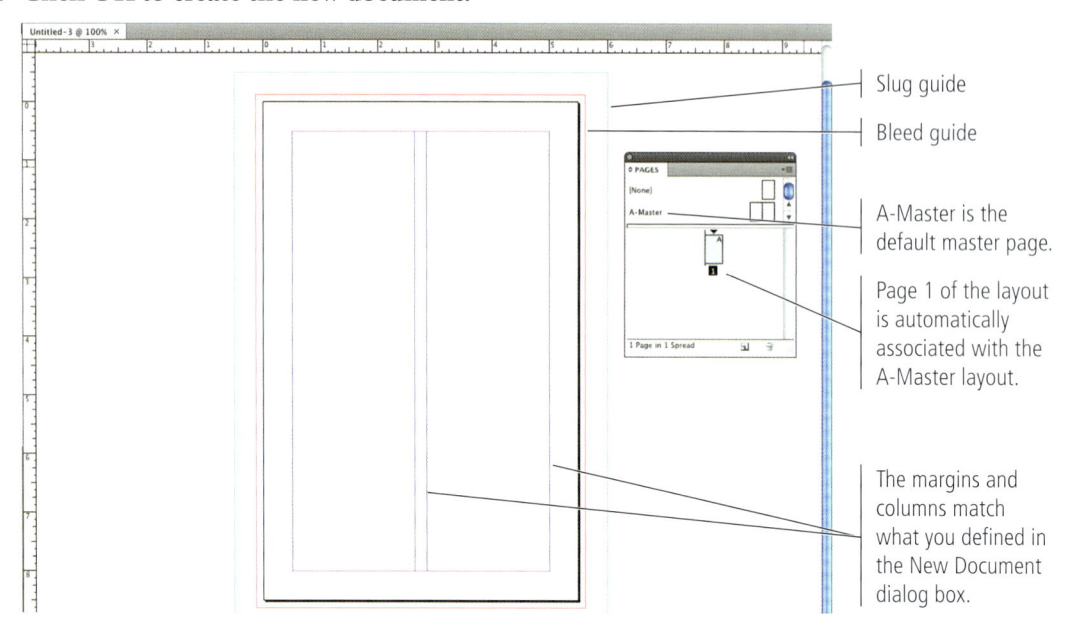

Slug guide

Bleed guide

A-Master is the default master page.

Page 1 of the layout is automatically associated with the A-Master layout.

The margins and columns match what you defined in the New Document dialog box.

9. **Save the file as `booklet_working.indd` in your WIP>Realtors folder and continue to the next exercise.**

CREATE MASTER PAGES FROM LAYOUT PAGES

This project was originally defined as a 16-page booklet "plus cover." In other words, the main booklet file would have 16 pages, but the cover would be created and printed as a separate file. Once printed, the two pieces would be combined and bound together into a single finished piece.

Based on the amount of text they created, your clients have decided to create the booklet as 16 pages "including self cover," which means the first and last pages of the main booklet file will be the front and back covers (respectively). The first step in completing this project is to bring the cover pages into the main layout.

1. **Open the file `cover.indd` from the RF_InDesign>Realtors folder.**

    This layout includes two pages — the front cover and the back cover. Like many projects, however, these pages were not created using master pages.

    Although you could simply copy the page contents from this file into your main file, it is a better idea to work with master pages whenever possible. Doing so gives you the most flexibility and control over the various layouts. As master pages, you can easily import the layouts into other files and apply the layouts to specific layout pages as necessary.

    Fortunately, it is very easy to create a master page layout from a regular page layout.

Note:

If you receive a message about missing images, use the Links panel to relink the missing images. The necessary files are in the RF_InDesign>Realtors folder.

The front cover was designed on Page 1.

The back cover was designed on Page 2.

260 Project 5: Realtor Collateral Booklet

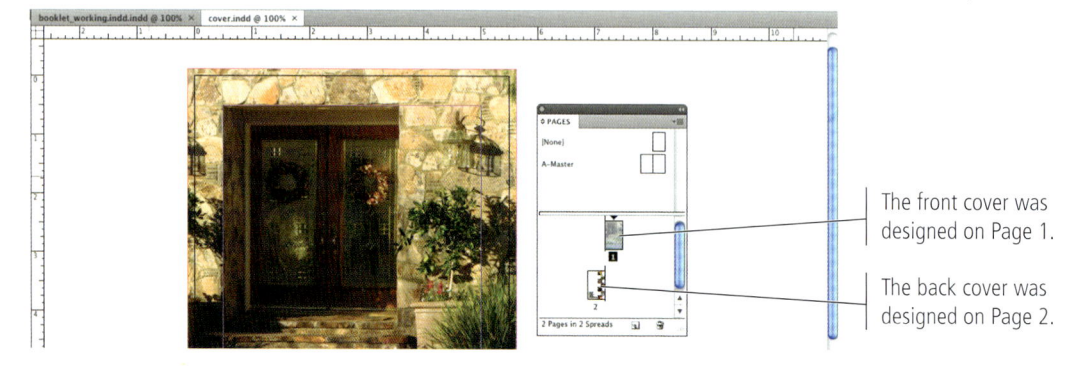

2. **In the Pages panel, Control/right-click the Page 1 icon and choose Save as Master from the contextual menu.**

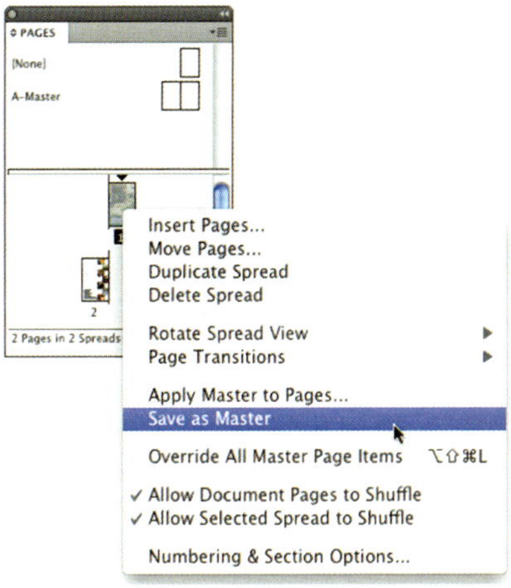

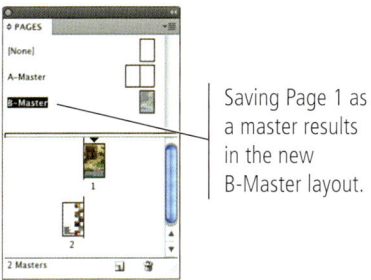

Saving Page 1 as a master results in the new B-Master layout.

Understanding Master Page Icons

INDESIGN FOUNDATIONS

When you work with facing pages, the default master page is actually a spread. In the Pages panel, the A-Master layout icon shows two pages, representing the two pages in the master page spread. Depending on your needs, you can also create master pages with a single page instead of a spread.

Change this field to "1" if you want a master layout with only a single page.

If you double-click the name of a master page in the Pages panel, you select the entire page or spread that makes up that master layout. You can select only one page of a master page spread by clicking the left or right page icon for that master.

In a facing-page document, the default A-Master has two pages — a spread.

You can add a single-page master layout to a facing-page document.

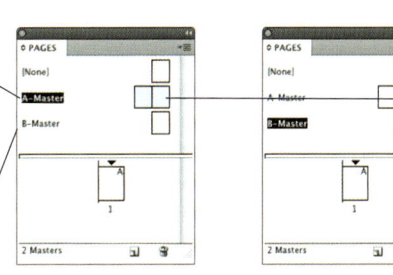

Double-clicking the master page name selects all pages in the master layout.

If an entire master page spread is already selected (both page icons are highlighted), you have to first deselect the spread to select only one page of the spread. You can do this by simply clicking any other page icon — master page or regular page— in the panel.

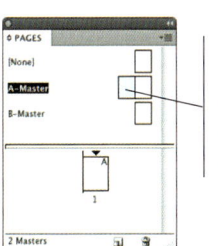

Single-click either page icon in a master page spread to select only that page, rather than the entire spread.

When you add pages to the layout by dragging a master page, the selected page icons determine what will be added. If both pages of a master spread are highlighted, dragging the selected icons into the lower half of the panel will add the entire master page spread. If only one page of the master spread is selected, you can add a single page to the layout.

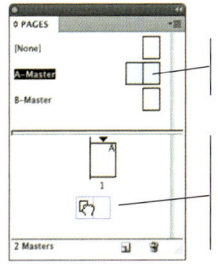

Both pages of the spread are selected.

By dragging the selected master into the layout, two pages will be added.

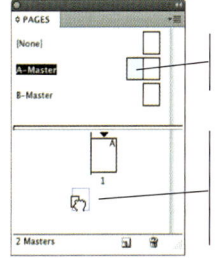

One page of the spread is selected.

By dragging the selected master into the layout, one page will be added.

Project 5: Realtor Collateral Booklet   261

3. **Control/right-click the new B-Master icon (in the top section of the Pages panel) and choose Master Options for "B-Master" from the contextual menu.**

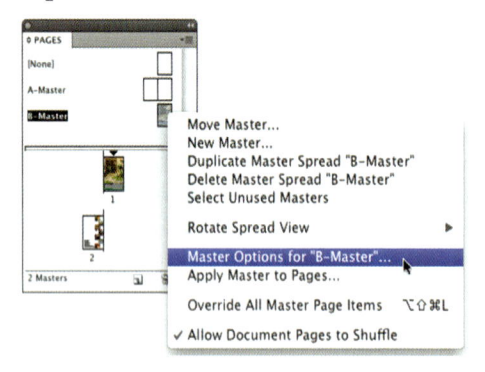

4. **In the resulting Master Options dialog box, change the name to Front Cover and click OK.**

5. **Repeat this process to convert the Page 2 layout to a master page layout named Back Cover.**

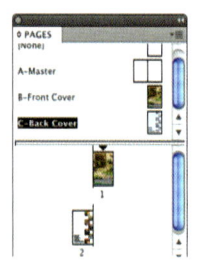

6. **In the top section of the Pages panel, Control/right-click the A-Master layout name and choose Delete Master Spread "A-Master" from the contextual menu.**

   The default master layout in this file was never used, so you can simply delete it.

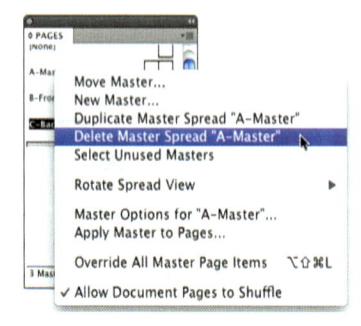

7. **Save the file as cover_masters.indd in your WIP>Realtors folder, and then close the file.**

8. **Continue to the next exercise.**

IMPORT MASTER PAGES

Now that the front and back covers are saved as master pages, you can easily import and apply them in the booklet file you created.

1. **With `booklet_working.indd` open, choose Load Master Pages from the Pages panel Options menu.**

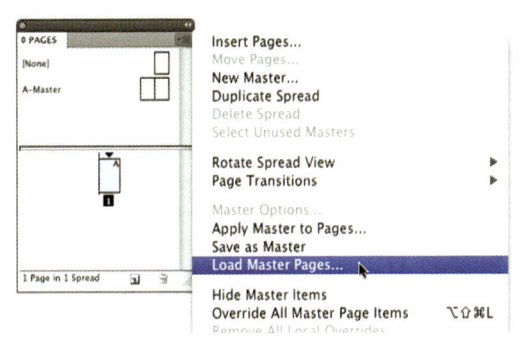

2. **In the resulting dialog box, navigate to the file `cover_masters.indd` in your WIP>Realtors folder and click Open.**

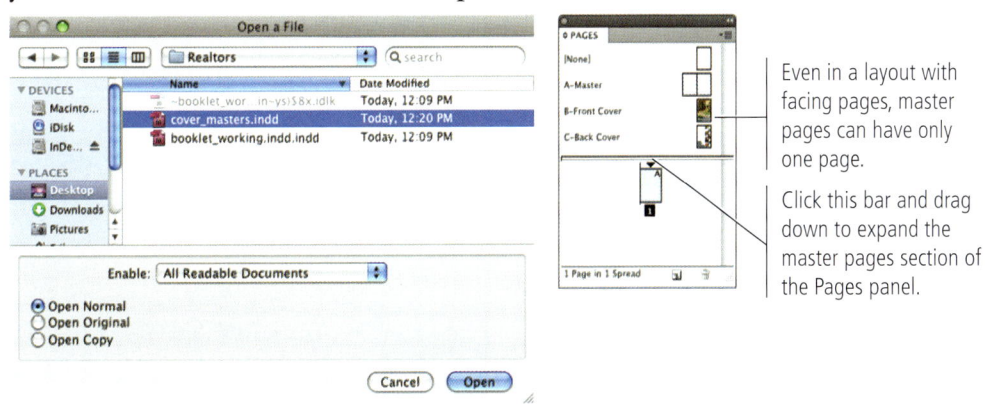

   Even in a layout with facing pages, master pages can have only one page.

   Click this bar and drag down to expand the master pages section of the Pages panel.

3. **Open the Swatches and Paragraph Styles panels.**

   Loading master pages from one file to another is an all-or-nothing process. Both master pages from the cover_masters.indd file are now part of the new file.

   When you load a master page from one file to another, all required assets (styles, swatches, etc.) are also imported. One color swatch has been added to the Swatches panel; two paragraph styles have been added to the Paragraph Styles panel.

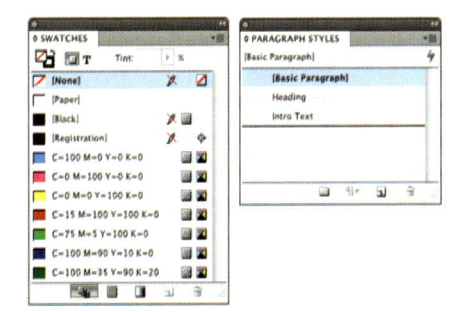

   Note:

   There is no dynamic link between the master pages now in the booklet file and the master pages in the original cover file. Changing one version of the front cover master (for example) will not affect the other version.

Project 5: Realtor Collateral Booklet | 263

4. **In the Pages panel, drag the B-Front Cover icon onto the Page 1 icon.**

   By default, Page 1 of any new file is associated with the A-Master layout. You can change this by simply dragging a different master onto the page icon.

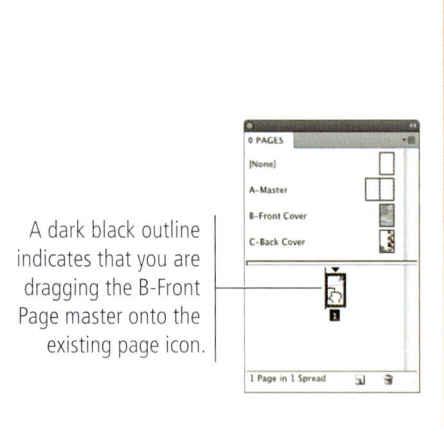

   A dark black outline indicates that you are dragging the B-Front Page master onto the existing page icon.

   After releasing the mouse button, Page 1 is now associated with the B-Front Page master.

5. **In the Pages panel, select only the left page of the A-Master spread and drag it below the Page 1 icon.**

   Using facing pages, new pages are added to the left and right of the spread center. When you release the mouse button, the new Page 2 is automatically added on the left side of the spread center.

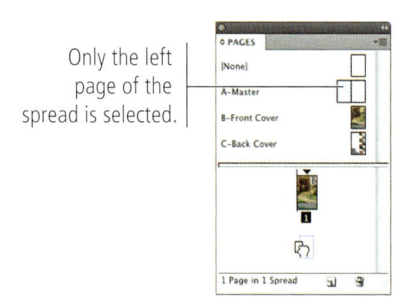

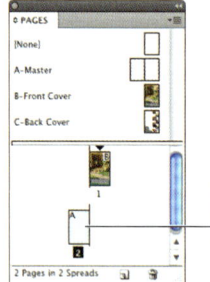

   Only the left page of the spread is selected.

   Page 2 is automatically added to the left side of the spread center.

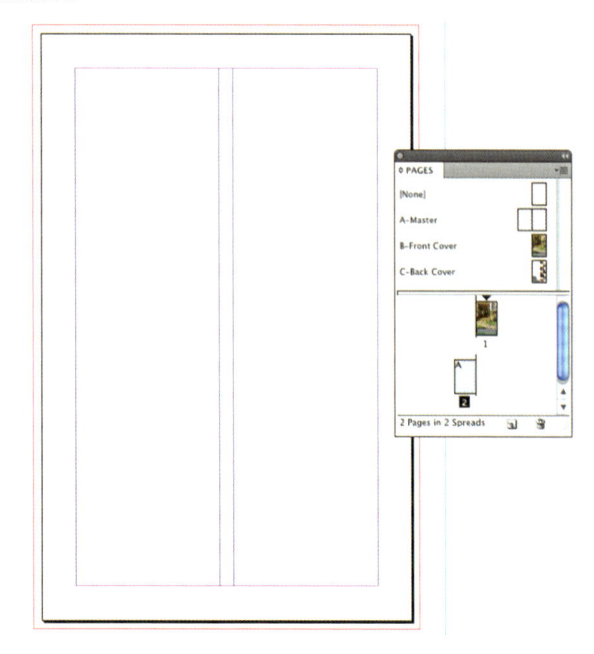

   Note:

   You can also Control/right-click a page icon in the lower section of the Pages panel and choose Apply Master to Page from the contextual menu.

   Note:

   *Pages on the left side of the spread center are called **left-facing** or **verso** pages.*

   *Pages on the right side of the spread center are called **right-facing** or **recto** pages.*

   Note:

   By convention, odd-numbered pages are right-facing and even-numbered pages are left-facing.

6. **Double-click the Page 2 icon in the Pages panel to show that page in the document window.**

264 Project 5: Realtor Collateral Booklet

7. **Drag the C-Back Cover icon onto the Page 2 icon to change the associated master.**

8. **Make sure guides (View>Grids & Guides>Show Guides) and frame edges (View>Show Frame Edges) are visible.**

   Two objects now appear on Page 2 — a text frame and a graphics frame. The frame edges appear as dotted lines instead of solid lines. This indicates that the objects are from the associated master page; you can't select them on the layout page unless you override the master page items for that layout page.

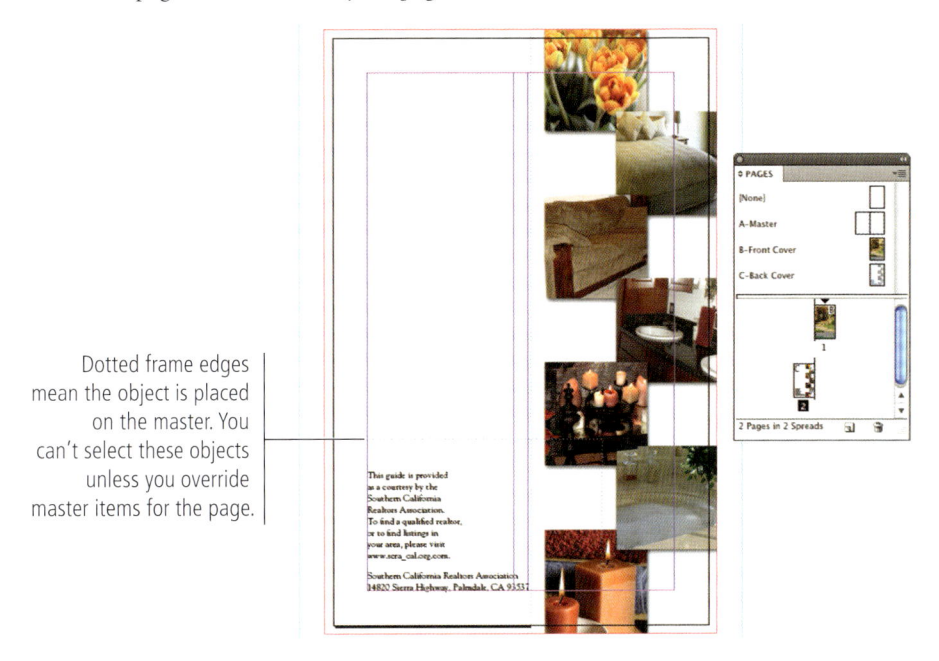

   Dotted frame edges mean the object is placed on the master. You can't select these objects unless you override master items for the page.

9. **In the Pages panel, drag the left page of the A-Master spread to the left of the Page 2 icon.**

   Before you release the mouse button, a vertical black bar indicates the potential position of the new page.

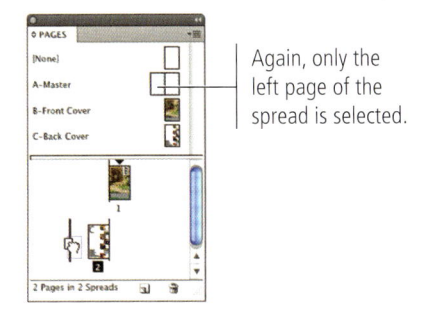

   Again, only the left page of the spread is selected.

Project 5: Realtor Collateral Booklet 265

After you release the mouse button, the new page is automatically added before Page 2. Because this is a facing-page layout, the new Page 2 becomes the left-facing page, and the old Page 2 — now Page 3 — moves to the right side of the spread.

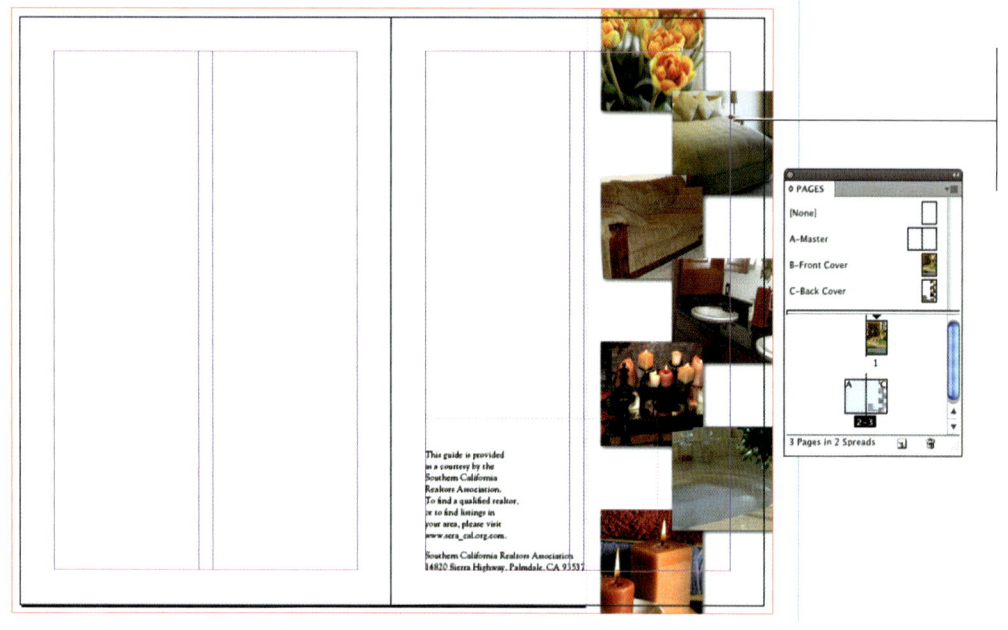

Objects from the C-Back Cover master still appear in the same position relative to the page.

10. **Save the file and continue to the next exercise.**

Edit the Default Master Page

The main body of the booklet will be 14 pages in 7 spreads; each spread will have the same basic layout:

- A large image, which fades to white, fills the background of each left-facing page.
- A heading and introductory paragraph sits at the bottom of each left-facing page.
- The right-facing page of each spread has two columns of body copy.
- Each right-facing page has a callout box of related checklist items.
- The right-facing page of each spread includes the page number and the words "Home Enhancement Guide."

Because these elements are common to most pages in the layout, it makes sense to create them on a master page layout. You could either create a new master page for the body spread or simply edit the existing default master page.

1. **With `booklet_working.indd` open, double-click the words "A-Master" in the top section of the Pages panel.**

   Double-clicking a master page navigates to that master layout in the document window.

   Each page of the A-Master spread has the margin and column settings you defined in the New Document dialog box.

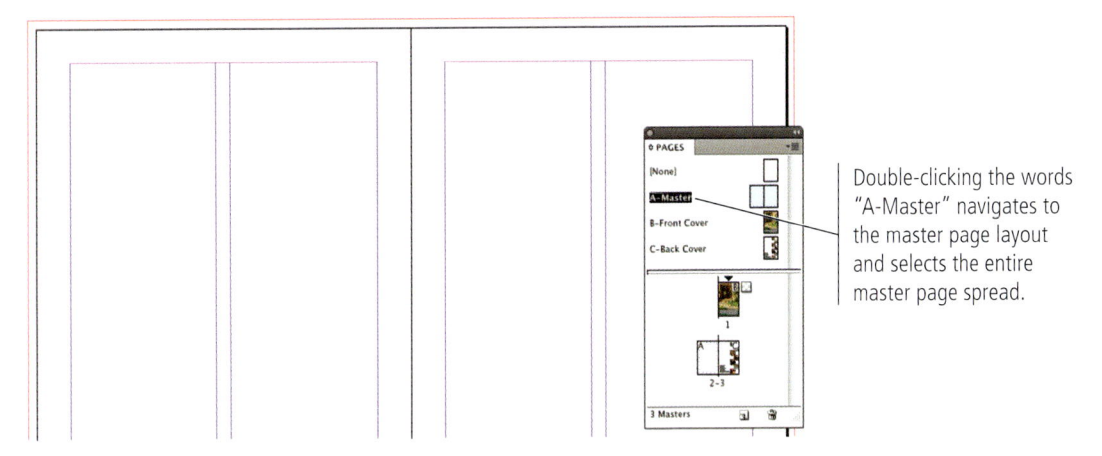

   Double-clicking the words "A-Master" navigates to the master page layout and selects the entire master page spread.

   Based on the specified elements of the interior pages, each page in this spread has different margin and column requirements. Fortunately, InDesign allows you to modify those settings for individual pages in the spread.

2. **Click once on any page other than the A-Master spread in the Pages panel.**

   When you double-click the master page name in the Pages panel, the entire spread is selected (highlighted) in the panel. To change the setting for only one page of the spread, you have to first deselect the spread (by selecting some other page), and then select the specific page you want to modify.

   You can click a regular page or a master page icon; the important point is to deselect the A-Master spread.

   Note:

   Clicking a page icon once selects that page without changing the visible page in the document window.

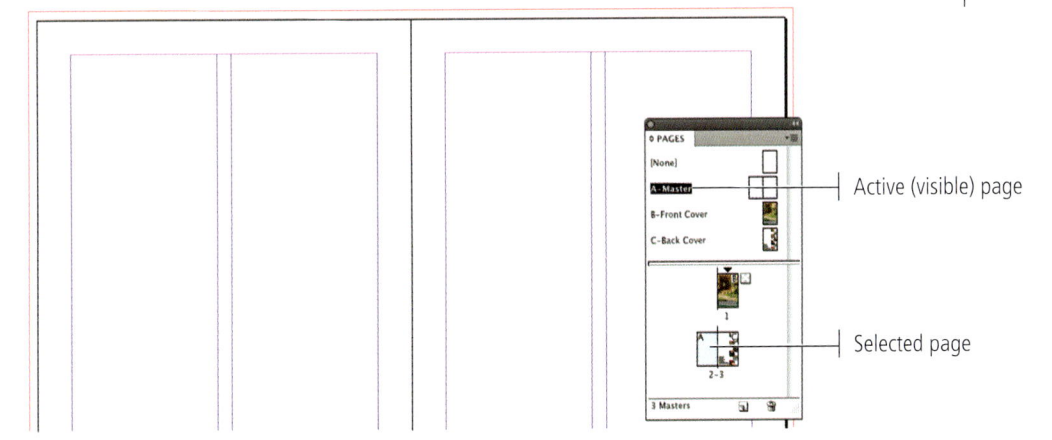

   Active (visible) page

   Selected page

3. **In the Pages panel, click once on the left page icon of the A-Master spread.**

4. **With the left page of the A-Master layout selected, choose Layout>Margins and Columns.**

Understanding Relative Object Positioning

You need to understand the difference between spread master pages and single-page master pages, especially when working with facing pages. In the booklet file you're building now, you have both kinds of master pages— the covers are single-page masters and the A-Master layout is a spread of two facing pages.

In the previous exercise, you added a page in front of the back cover page. The back cover page, which had been Page 2, moved to Page 3; the objects on the page stayed in the same position relative to the page (in other words, they also moved from Page 2 to Page 3). This happened because the back page master is a single page, so the objects on the master (and the associated layout pages) are positioned relative to the single page.

When you work with a spread master page, the objects on the master page layout are positioned relative to the entire spread. Objects on regular layout pages, however, are positioned relative to the page on which they are created.

Understanding this concept is particularly important if:

- You are working with objects that bleed off the left or right side of a page
- You override the master page items on a specific page

When you move a page from one side of a spread to the other (e.g., from left to right), any bleed object will continue to bleed past the same edge of its new page position — possibly interfering with the other page of the spread.

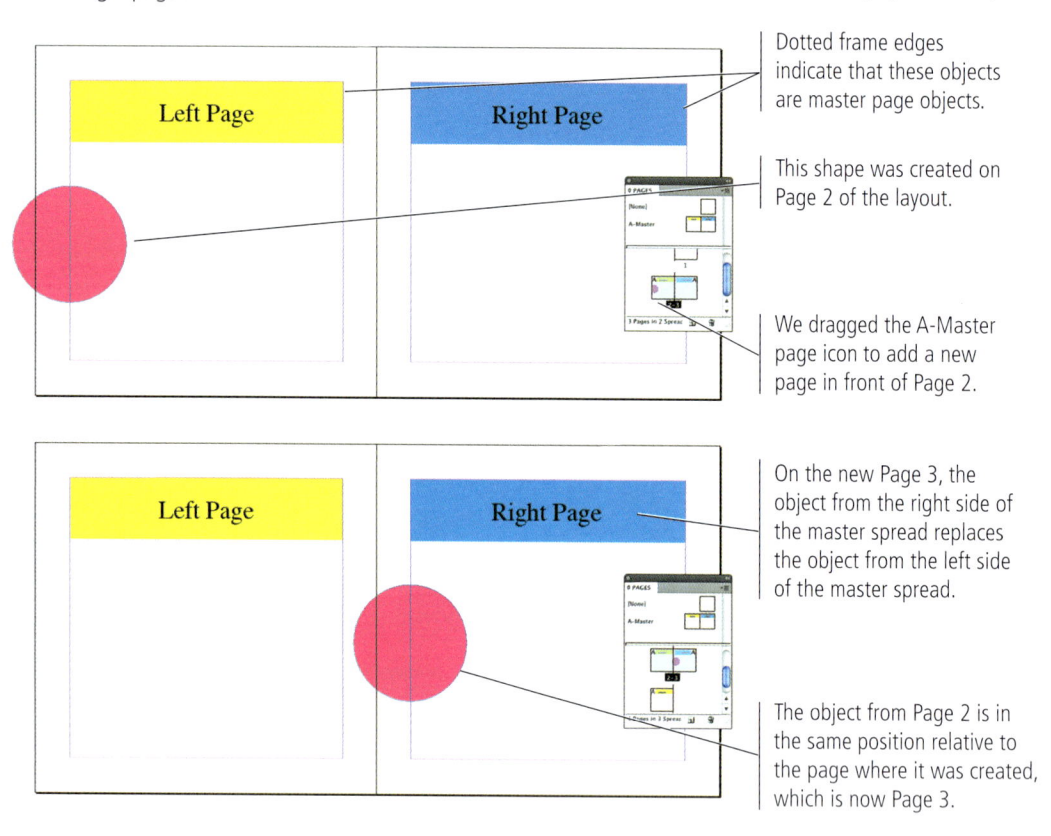

Dotted frame edges indicate that these objects are master page objects.

This shape was created on Page 2 of the layout.

We dragged the A-Master page icon to add a new page in front of Page 2.

On the new Page 3, the object from the right side of the master spread replaces the object from the left side of the master spread.

The object from Page 2 is in the same position relative to the page where it was created, which is now Page 3.

Understanding Relative Object Positioning (continued)

A related problem occurs when you override and change master page items on regular layout pages. When you override master page items, they become regular layout page items. Adding pages to the middle of a layout moves those items relative to their new page position; the original master page objects are added directly behind the overridden objects. (If necessary, you can eliminate the overridden objects by choosing Remove All Local Overrides from the Pages panel Options menu, or you can select specific objects and choose Remove Selected Local Overrides.)

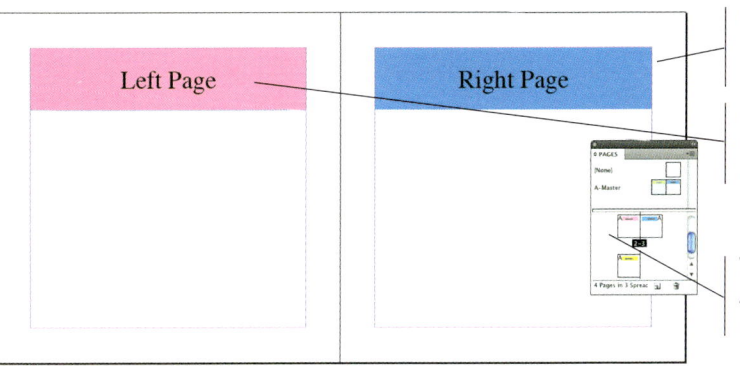

Dotted frame edges indicate that this object is a master page object.

We overrode master page items for Page 2, then changed the object fill color from yellow to magenta.

We then dragged the A-Master page icon to add a new page in front of Page 2.

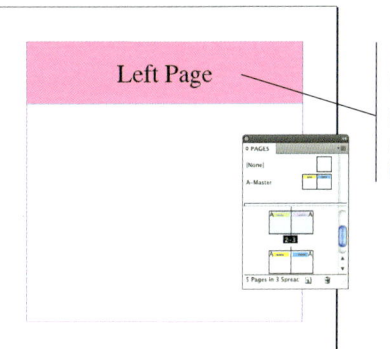

Because overriding master page items converts them into regular page items, the overridden object moves relative to the page on which it is placed (the moved Page 2).

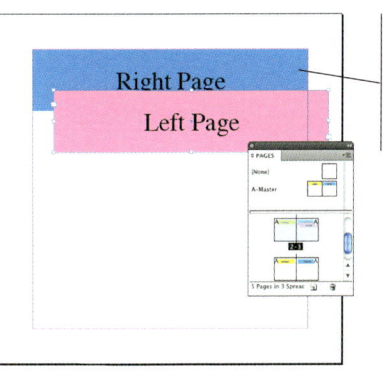

Moving the overridden object shows that the correct master page object has been added to the page, directly behind the overridden object.

5. **With the Preview option checked, change the top margin to 5", change the outside margin to 2", and change the number of columns to 1.**

   Make sure the Lock icon between the margin fields is a broken chain. If the icon shows an unbroken chain, changing one margin field changes the other three fields to match.

   Unfortunately, changing the margins and columns does not automatically change the settings of the master text frame. You have to change those separately.

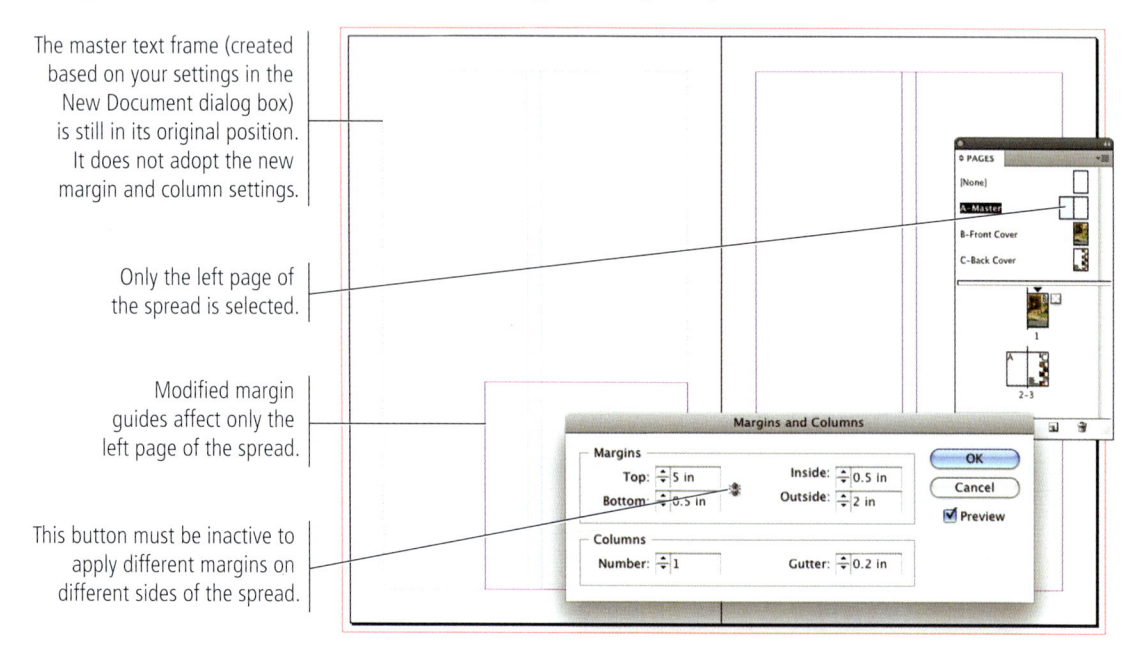

   The master text frame (created based on your settings in the New Document dialog box) is still in its original position. It does not adopt the new margin and column settings.

   Only the left page of the spread is selected.

   Modified margin guides affect only the left page of the spread.

   This button must be inactive to apply different margins on different sides of the spread.

6. **Click OK to apply the changes.**

7. **In the document window, use the Selection tool to resize the master text frame to match the new margin guides.**

8. **Control/right-click the frame, choose Text Frame Options from the contextual menu, and change the number of columns to 1. In the Inset Spacing area, change all four values to 0.125". In the Vertical Justification area, change the Align menu to Center. Click OK.**

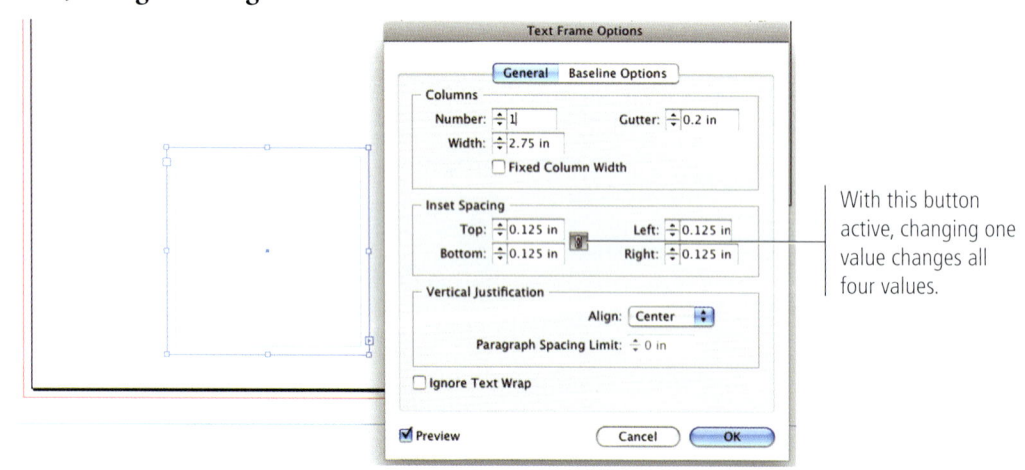

   With this button active, changing one value changes all four values.

Project 5: Realtor Collateral Booklet

9. In the Pages panel, select only the right page of the A-Master spread. Choose Layout>Margins and Columns and change the bottom margin to 3.25″. Click OK.

10. Using the Selection tool, drag the bottom edge of the text frame to match the new bottom margin guide on the right page of the spread.

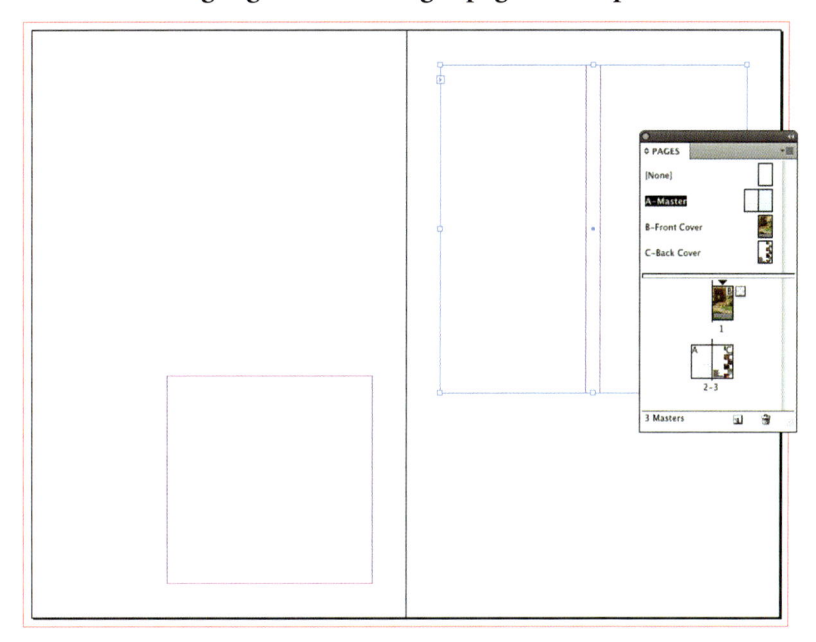

11. Save the file and continue to the next exercise.

Add Common Elements to a Master Page Layout

In addition to the master text frame, you need several other elements to appear on every body spread: the graphics frame on the left side of the spread, as well as the callout box and page footer on the right page of the spread. Again, it makes sense to create master page placeholders for these objects rather than to recreate the objects on individual layout pages. Doing so reduces the number of repetitive tasks as much as possible to maximize your productivity.

The client's content is supplied in a single file, and the callout text for each spread appears within the main body of the text. The text includes the heading "Through the Buyer's Eyes," so you can identify the appropriate text.

1. With the file booklet_working.indd open, make sure the A-Master layout is showing in the document window.

2. Create a new text frame with the following dimensions (based on the top-left reference point):

   X: 7.375″   W: 3.75″
   Y: 5.65″   H: 2.35″

Note:

By default, InDesign measurements reflect an object's position relative to the entire spread; the X: 7.375″ position is actually 1.875″ from the left edge of the right page. You can change this behavior by changing the Ruler Units origin in the Units & Increments pane of the Preferences dialog box.

Project 5: Realtor Collateral Booklet   271

3. **Using the Swatches panel, fill the new text frame with the C=100 M=35 Y=90 K=20 swatch.**

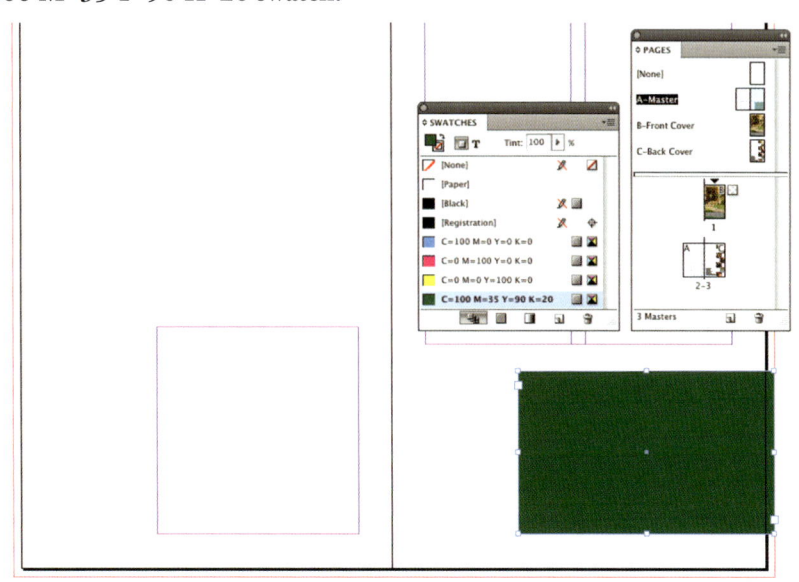

4. **Control/right-click the new frame and choose Text Frame Options from the contextual menu. Change the Top, Bottom, and Left Inset Spacing fields to 0.125″, and change the Right Inset field to 0.625″. Click OK to apply the change.**

   Because the frame bleeds off the page edge, you need to adjust the frame inset on only the bleed side to match the rest of the layout. Instead of overlaying two frames — one with the green fill and one with the text frame — you can use uneven inset spacing to achieve the same goal.

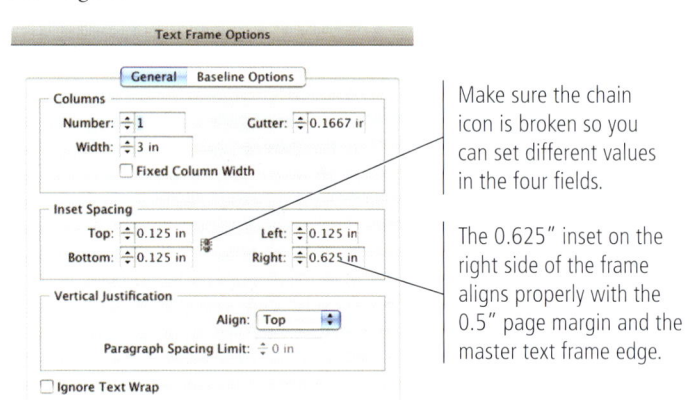

   Make sure the chain icon is broken so you can set different values in the four fields.

   The 0.625″ inset on the right side of the frame aligns properly with the 0.5″ page margin and the master text frame edge.

5. **Using the Selection tool, click the master text frame on the right page of the spread. Click the Out port of the master text frame, and then immediately click the green text frame to link the two frames.**

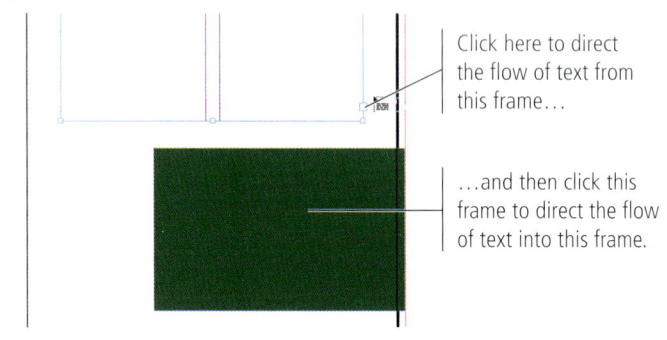

   Click here to direct the flow of text from this frame…

   …and then click this frame to direct the flow of text into this frame.

Project 5: Realtor Collateral Booklet

6. **Choose View>Show Text Threads.**

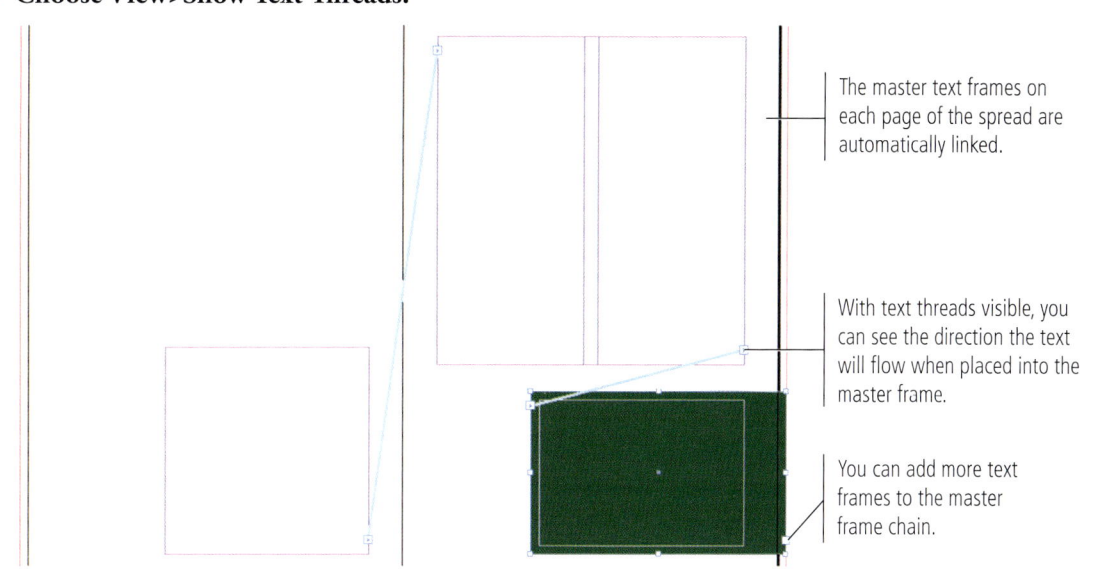

   The master text frames on each page of the spread are automatically linked.

   With text threads visible, you can see the direction the text will flow when placed into the master frame.

   You can add more text frames to the master frame chain.

7. **Turn off the text threads (View>Hide Text Threads).**

8. **Create an empty graphics frame that fills the entire left page of the spread (including the bleed area). Fill the frame with a 20% tint of the dark green swatch, and then choose Object>Arrange>Send to Back to move the graphics frame behind the text frame.**

   Each spread in the booklet will include a large image on the left side of the spread. Placing it on the master layout eliminates the need to manually draw the frame on each spread. You added the fill color simply as a visual reference for placing the image.

9. **Select the master text frame on the left page of the spread. Change the fill color to Paper and change its Opacity value to 85%.**

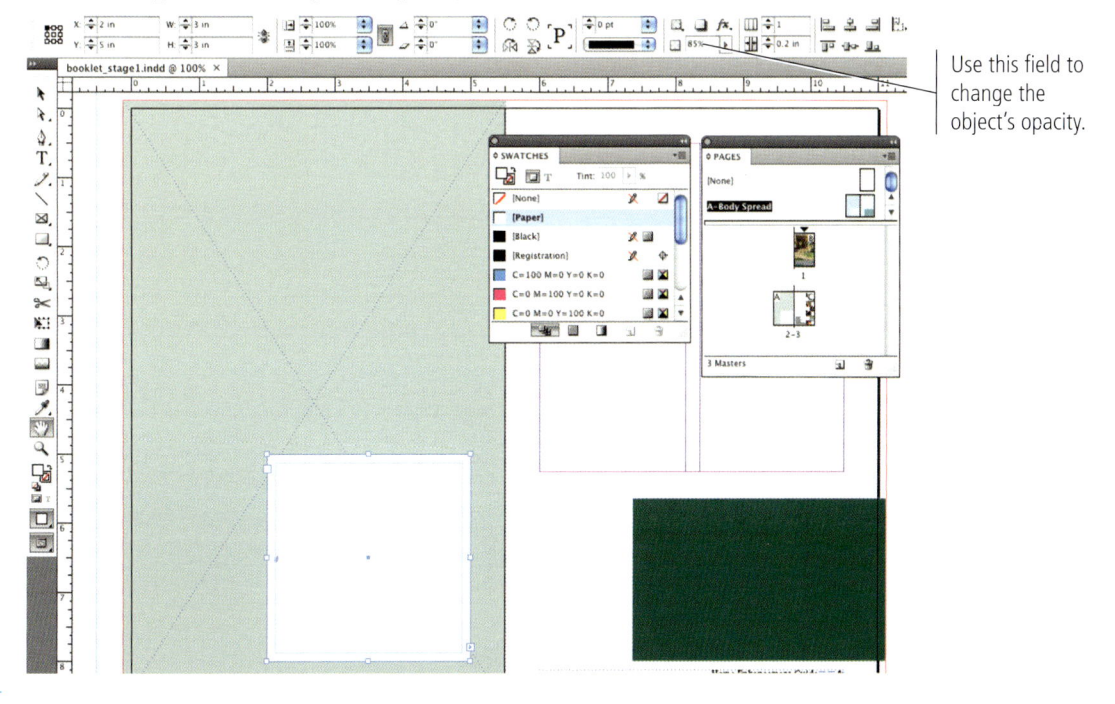

   Use this field to change the object's opacity.

10. **Make sure the frame edges are visible (View>Show Frame Edges).**

11. **Save the file and continue to the next exercise.**

Project 5: Realtor Collateral Booklet 273

PLACE AUTOMATIC PAGE NUMBER MARKERS

The next item to add to the master page layout is the page footer information — the page number and the name of the booklet. Rather than manually numbering each page in the booklet, which can be time consuming and invites human error, you can use special characters to automatically number the pages in any layout.

1. With booklet_working.indd open, make sure the A-Master layout is showing.

2. Create a new text frame with the following dimensions (based on the top-left reference point):

    X: 6"   W: 4.5"
    Y: 8.125"   H: 0.25"

Special Characters and White Space

A number of special characters can be accessed in the Type submenus. Use the following chart as a how-and-why guide for accessing these characters.

Menu			What it's used for
Insert Special Character	Markers	Current Page Number	Places the current page number
		Next Page Number	Places the page number of the next frame in the same story
		Previous Page Number	Places the page number of the previous frame in the same story
		Section Marker	Places a user-defined text variable that is specific to the current layout section. (You'll work with section numbering in Project 8.)
		Footnote Number	Inserts a number character based on the options defined in the Footnote Options dialog box
	Hyphens and Dashes	Em Dash	Places a dash that has the same width as the applied type size
		En Dash	Places a dash equivalent to one-half of an em dash
		Discretionary Hyphen	Allows you to hyphenate a word in a location other than what is defined by the currect dictionary, or hyphenate a word when automatic hyphenation is turned off; the discretionary hyphen only appears if the word is hyphenated at the end of a line
		Nonbreaking Hyphen	Places a hyphen character that will not break at the end of a line; used to keep both parts of a phrase on the same line of the paragraph
	Quotation Marks	Double Left Quotation Marks	"
		Double Right Quotation Marks	"
		Single Left Quotation Mark	'
		Single Right Quotation Mark	'
		Straight Double Quotation Marks	"
		Straight Single Quotation Mark	'
	Other	Tab	Forces following text to begin at the next defined or default tab stop
		Right Indent Tab	Forces following text to align at the right indent of the column or frame
		Indent to Here	Creates a hanging indent by forcing all following lines in the paragraph to indent to the location of the character
		End Nested Style Here	Interrupts nested style formatting before the defined character limit
		Non-joiner	Prevents adjacent characters from being joined in a ligature or other alternate character connection

3. **Type Home Enhancement Guide, and then change the formatting to 12-pt ATC Laurel Bold with right paragraph alignment.**

4. **Place the insertion point immediately after the word "Guide" and press the Spacebar once.**

   Because the text is right-aligned, the Space character is not visible; a space at the end of a line is not considered in the line length or type position when InDesign aligns paragraphs.

   The space character is not visible at the end of the line.

Special Characters and White Space (continued)

Menu		What it's used for
Insert White Space	Em Space	Space equivalent to applied type size
	En Space	One-half of an em space
	Nonbreaking Space	Places a space character the same width as pressing the Spacebar; this character prevents a line break from occurring, which allows you to keep related words together on the same line.
	Nonbreaking Space (Fixed Width)	Same as the regular nonbreaking space, but does not change size when a paragraph uses justified alignment.
	Hair Space	One-twenty-fourth of an em space
	Sixth Space	One-sixth of an em space
	Thin Space	One-eighth of an em space
	Quarter Space	One-fourth of an em space
	Third Space	One-third of an em space
	Punctuation Space	Same width as a period in the applied font
	Figure Space	Same width as a number in the applied font
	Flush Space	Variable space in a justified paragraph placed between the last character of the paragraph and a decorative character (called a "bug") used to indicate the end of a story
Insert Break Character	Column Break	Forces text into the next available column (or frame, if used in a one-column frame or the last column of a multi-column frame)
	Frame Break	Forces text into the next available frame
	Page Break	Forces text into the first available frame on the next page, skipping any available frames or columns on the same page
	Odd Page Break	Forces text into the first available frame on the next odd-numbered page
	Even Page Break	Forces text into the first available frame on the next even-numbered page
	Paragraph Return	Creates a new paragraph (same as pressing Return/Enter)
	Forced Line Break	Creates a new line without starting a new paragraph (called a "soft return")
	Discretionary Line Break	Creates a new line if the character falls at the end of the line; if the character falls in the middle of the column, the line is not broken

INDESIGN FOUNDATIONS

5. **With the insertion point flashing after the space character (which you can't see), choose Type>Insert Special Character>Markers>Current Page Number.**

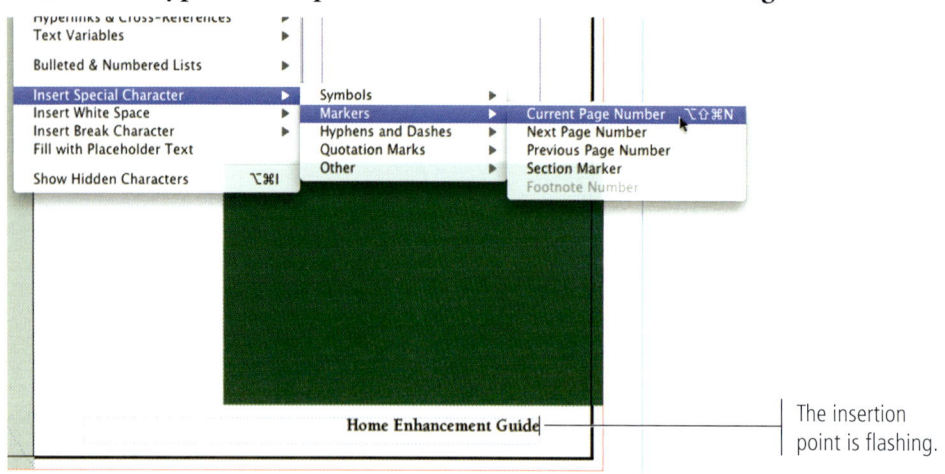

The insertion point is flashing.

Keyboard Shortcuts for Special Characters

Character	Keyboard Shortcut Macintosh	Keyboard Shortcut Windows
Current page number	Command-Option-Shift-N	Control-Alt-Shift-N
Em dash	Option-Shift-Hyphen (-)	Alt-Shift-Hyphen (-)
En dash	Option-Hyphen	Alt-Hyphen
Discretionary hyphen	Command-Shift-Hyphen	Control-Shift-Hyphen
Nonbreaking hyphen	Command-Option-Hyphen	Control-Alt-Hyphen
Double left quotation marks	Option-[	Alt-[
Double right quotation marks	Option-Shift-[	Alt-Shift-[
Single left quotation mark	Option-]	Alt-]
Single right quotation mark	Option-Shift-]	Alt-Shift-]
Straight double quotation marks	Control-Shift-'	Alt-Shift-'
Straight single quotation mark	Control-'	Alt-'
Tab	Tab	Tab
Right indent tab	Shift-Tab	Shift-Tab
Indent to here	Command-\	Control-\
Em space	Command-Shift-M	Control-Shift-M
En space	Command-Shift-N	Control-Shift-N
Nonbreaking space	Command-Option-X	Control-Alt-X
Thin space	Command-Option-Shift-M	Control-Alt-Shift-N
Column break	Enter (numeric keypad)	Enter (numeric keypad)
Frame break	Shift-Enter (numeric keypad)	Shift-Enter (numeric keypad)
Page break	Command-Enter (numeric keypad)	Control-Enter (numeric keypad)
Paragraph return	Return	Enter
Forced line break	Shift-Return	Shift-Enter

6. **If the hidden characters are not visible, choose Type>Show Hidden Characters.**

   The Current Page Number command inserts a special character that reflects the correct page number of any page where it appears. Because you placed this character on the A-Master page, the character shows as "A" in the text box.

   Now that the Space character is no longer the last character in the line, you can see it — as long as hidden characters are showing.

   Space character
   Current Page Number character
   End of Story character

   In this case, the single, regular Space character is not enough to separate the booklet name from the page number. InDesign provides a number of options for increasing (and decreasing) white space without simply pressing the Spacebar numerous times.

7. **Highlight the Space character before the Page Number character.**

8. **Choose Type>Insert White Space>Em Space.**

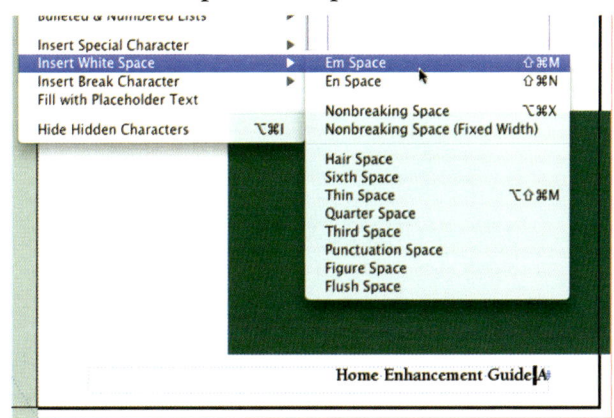

   An **em** is a typographic measure equivalent to the applied type size. An em space is white space equal to one em.

   Em Space character

9. **Add a second Em Space character immediately after the first.**

10. **Select all text in the footer and change the type size to 10 pt.**

    Special and hidden characters are still characters; changing the type formatting affects these characters in the same way as regular characters.

11. **Save the file and continue to the next exercise.**

Project 5: Realtor Collateral Booklet | 277

CREATE TEXT VARIABLES

The final item to add on the master page is a custom slug, which is file information that will be printed outside the trim and bleed areas. You already defined the slug area in the first exercise of this project; you can now use text variables to place the same information on each of the three master pages in the layout.

1. **With `booklet_working.indd` open, make sure the A-Master layout is showing.**

2. **Create a new text frame in the slug area above the left page of the spread.**

3. **With the insertion point flashing in the new text frame, choose Type> Text Variables>Insert Variable>Modification Date.**

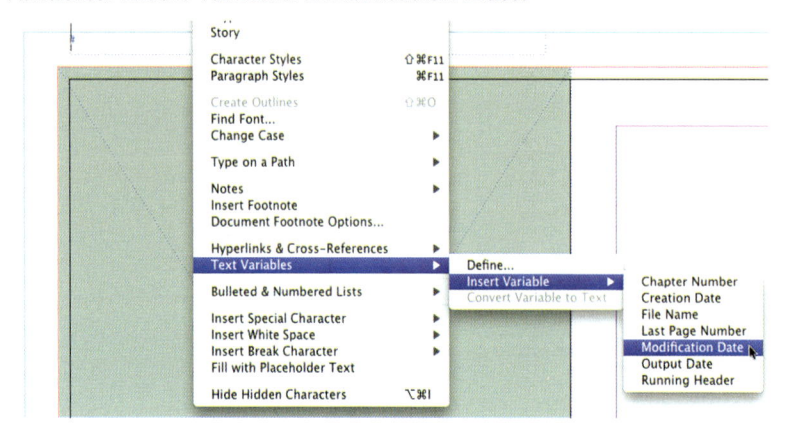

   InDesign includes several common default variables, including the Modification Date variable, which places the date and time when the file was last saved.

   The text variable is surrounded by a faint gray border; this string of text is treated as a single anchored object in the slug text frame.

4. **Choose Type>Text Variables>Define.**

   This dialog box allows you to change the built-in text variables, or you can define your own text variables to meet the specific needs of a project.

   In this case, you're going to create a "status" variable that reflects the current stage of the file. This information should appear over every spread, which means it needs to be placed on all three master page layouts. You could accomplish the same result by simply typing the stage in the slug of each master page; however, you would have to make the same change on each of those three master pages in each stage of the project.

   By defining a text variable that you will place on all three master pages, you can simply change the variable definition for each stage of the project, and then all instances of the placed variable will automatically reflect the same change.

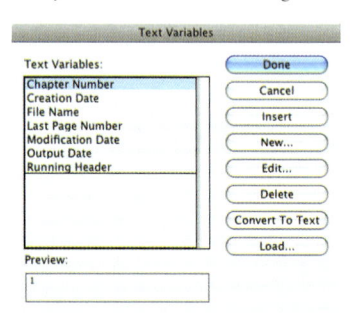

Note:

Even though you can't select the actual characters within the text variable instance, you can still change the formatting of variables by highlighting the instance in the layout and making whatever changes you want.

Note:

You can convert text variable instances to regular text by selecting an instance in the layout and choosing Type>Text Variables>Convert Variable to Text. You can convert all instances of a specific variable to regular text by opening the Text Variables dialog box, selecting a specific variable, and clicking the Convert to Text button.

278 Project 5: Realtor Collateral Booklet

5. **In the Text Variables dialog box, click the New button.**

6. **In the Name field of the New Text Variable dialog box, type File Status.**

7. **In the Type menu, choose Custom Text.**

   Eight of these options place specific text (using the formatting you define in this dialog box). These variable types are the same as the ones that already appear in the Text Variables>Insert Variables submenu. You can, however, define more than one variable for a single type. For example, you can define two different modification date variables — one that shows the day, month, year, and time; and one that shows only the day and month.

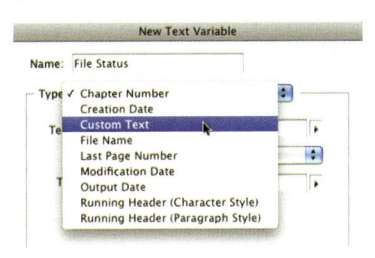

Note:

If you delete a variable that is used in the layout, you can choose to replace placed instances with a different variable, convert the instances to regular text, or simply remove the placed instances.

8. **Click the menu to the right of the Text field.**

   Using the Custom Text option, you can determine what text appears in the variable. The menu provides access to common special characters (these are the same characters you can access in the Type>Insert Special Character submenus).

9. **Choose Ellipsis from the menu.**

10. **With the insertion point after the code for the Ellipsis character, type Stage 1.**

Project 5: Realtor Collateral Booklet 279

11. **Click OK to close the New Text Variable dialog box.**

    The new File Status variable now appears in the list.

12. **Click Done to close the Text Variables dialog box.**

13. **With the insertion point flashing after the Modification Date text variable in the slug text frame, press Tab, and then choose Type>Text Variables>Insert Variable>File Status.**

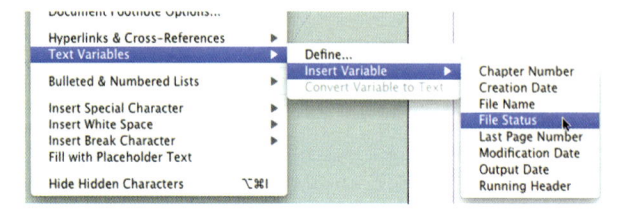

    The variable text you defined is placed immediately after the Tab character. Because it is a variable instance, it is surrounded by a gray border.

14. **Click the Selection tool in the Tools panel.**

    Because the slug text frame was already active, it is automatically selected.

15. **Press Command/Control-C to copy the frame.**

16. **In the Pages panel, double-click the B-Front Cover master page.**

17. **Press Command/Control-V to paste the copied frame, and then drag the frame into the slug area above the page.**

    The B-Front Cover layout is active.

Project 5: Realtor Collateral Booklet

18. **Navigate to the C-Back Cover layout and paste the copied text frame into the slug area above the page.**

   The C-Back Cover layout is active.

19. **In the top section of the Pages panel, Control/right-click the A-Master layout name and choose Master Options for "A-Master" from the contextual menu.**

20. **In the Master Options dialog box, change the Name field to `Body Spread` and click OK.**

   It's always a good idea to use a meaningful name for any element you define in InDesign, including a master page.

   After you click OK, the new name appears in the Pages panel.

21. **Save the file as `booklet_stage1.indd` in your WIP>Realtors folder, and then continue to the next stage of the project.**

Custom Text Variable Options

INDESIGN FOUNDATIONS

The built-in text variables (in the Type>Text Variables>Insert Variable menu) are based on the types of variables you can define. When you choose Type>Text Variables>Define, the dialog box lists those default variables. You can select any of these variables and click Edit to change the options for the selected variable, or you can create a new variable by clicking the New button.

Your choice in the Type menu of the New/Edit Text Variable dialog box, whether editing an existing variable or creating a new one, determines what options are available.

Click here to open the New Text Variable dialog box and define a new text variable.

Click here to open the Edit Text Variable dialog box and change the formatting options of the selected variable.

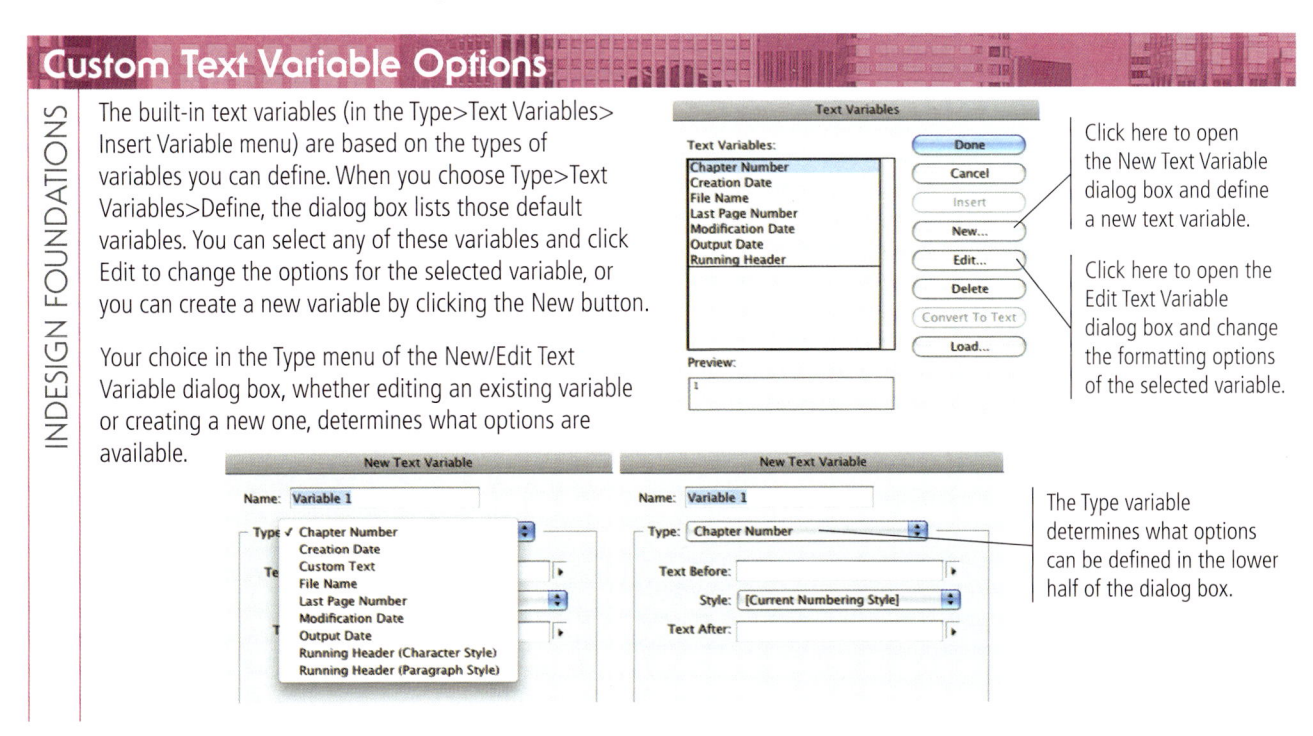

The Type variable determines what options can be defined in the lower half of the dialog box.

Project 5: Realtor Collateral Booklet   281

Custom Text Variable Options (continued)

For all but the Custom Text variable, you can define the characters that precede (Text Before field) or follow (Text After field) the variable information. You can type specific information in either of these fields, or you can use the associated menus to place symbols, em or en dashes, white-space characters, or typographer's quotation marks.

The **Chapter Number** variable inserts the chapter number based on the file's position in a book document (you will work with InDesign books in Project 8). You can use the Style menu to format the chapter number as lowercase or uppercase letters, lowercase or uppercase Roman numerals, or Arabic numbers.

The **Creation Date** variable inserts the time the document is first saved. The **Modification Date** variable inserts the time the document was last saved. The **Output Date** variable inserts the date the document was last printed, exported to PDF, or packaged. You can use the **Date Format** menu to modify the date format for all three of these variables. You can either type a format directly into the field, or you can use the associated menu to choose the options you want to include. If you want to simply type the format into the field, you have to use the correct abbreviations.

The **File Name** variable inserts the name of the open file. You can use the check box options to include the entire folder path and the file extension. (The path and extension will not appear until you save the file at least once.)

Abbreviation	Description	Example
M	Month number	1
MM	Month number (two digits)*	01
MMM	Month name (abbreviated)	Jan
MMMM	Month name (full)	January
d	Day number	3
dd	Day number (two digits)*	03
E	Weekday name (abbreviated)	Wed
EEEE	Weekday name (full)	Wednesday
yy	Year number (last two digits)	09
yyyy	Year number (four digits)	2009
G	Era (abbreviated)	AD
GGGG	Era (full)	Anno Domini
h	Hour	1
hh	Hour (two digits)*	01
H	Hour (24-hour format)	16
HH	Hour (two digits, 24-hour format)*	16
m	Minute	9
mm	Minute (two digits)*	09
s	Second	2
ss	Second (two digits)*	02
a	AM or PM	AM
z	Time zone (abbreviated)	PST
zzzz	Time zone (full)	Pacific Standard Time

*The two-digit formats force a leading zero in front of numbers lower than 10 (for example, 9/25/09 would appear as 09/25/09 if you use the two-digit Month format).

The **Last Page Number** variable can be used to create a "Page x of y" notation. This variable can indicate the last page number of the entire document or the current section (in the Scope menu). You can also determine the numbering style (with the same options as in the Chapter Number variable).

The **Running Header** variables can be used to find content on the page based on applied paragraph or character styles.

In the Style menu, you can choose the paragraph or character style to use as the variable content. The Use menu identifies which instance of the defined style (first or last on the page) to use as the variable content. For example, say you have a glossary page and all the terms are formatted with the Glossary Term character style. You could define two Running Header (Character Style) variables — one that identifies the first use of the Glossary Term style and one that identifies the last use of the Glossary Term style on the current page. You can then place the two variables in a text frame to create a running header that shows the first and last terms on the page — e.g., [First Term] – [Last Term].

The Delete End Punctuation option identifies the text without punctuation. For example, you can identify a Bold Run-In character style that is applied to text that always ends with a period. When the style is identified as the variable, the period will not be included in the variable text.

The Change Case options determine capitalization for the variable text:

- Upper Case capitalizes the entire variable.
- Lower Case removes all capitalization.
- Title Case capitalizes the first letter in every word.
- Sentence Case capitalizes only the first word.

The **Custom Text** variable inserts whatever text you define in the associated field.

Stage 2 Controlling Text Flow

Because you imported the covers as master pages and built a spread layout to hold the various body elements, all the necessary pieces are in place to import the client's provided text and graphics. The time you spent building effective master pages will enable you to quickly place the layout content and create a multi-page document; you significantly reduce overall development time because you don't have to manually create these elements on each page.

CHANGE THE CUSTOM TEXT VARIABLE

The File Status variable you defined in the previous exercise allows you to monitor the status of the project while you work. As you begin the second stage of the project, you should change the variable to reflect the new status.

1. **With booklet_stage1.indd open, immediately save the file as booklet_stage2.indd in your WIP>Realtors folder.**

2. **Double-click the Page 2 icon in the Pages panel to navigate to that page.**

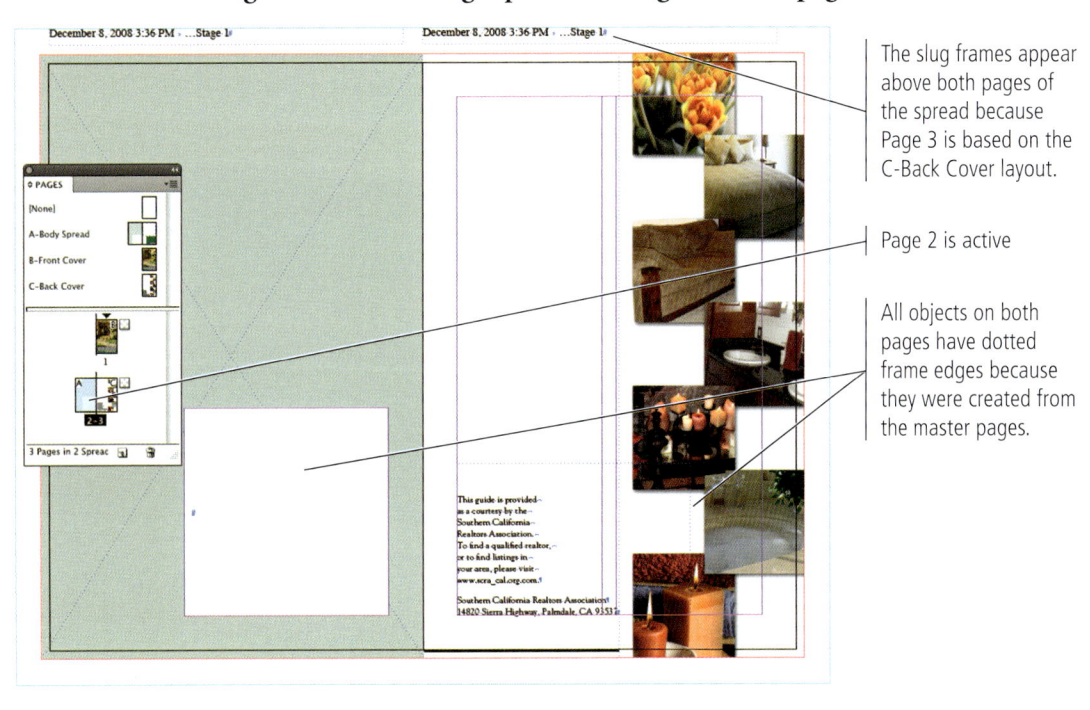

The slug frames appear above both pages of the spread because Page 3 is based on the C-Back Cover layout.

Page 2 is active

All objects on both pages have dotted frame edges because they were created from the master pages.

3. **Choose Type>Text Variables>Define.**

4. **Select File Status in the list and click Edit.**

5. **In the Text field, change Stage 1 to Stage 2.**

Project 5: Realtor Collateral Booklet   283

6. **Click OK, and then click Done to return to the layout.**

   Because you placed the File Status variable on each master page layout, changing the variable definition automatically changes all placed instances. And by placing the variable instances on the master page layouts, the same change automatically reflects on the associated layout pages.

7. **Save the file and continue to the next exercise.**

IMPORT AND AUTO-FLOW CLIENT TEXT

You are building a document with 16 facing pages. You could manually insert the necessary pages, and then manually link the text from one page to the next. But anytime you see the word "manually," you should look for ways to automate some or all of the process. The ability to automate work is one of the defining characteristics of professional page-layout software such as InDesign.

1. **With Page 2 of `booklet_stage2.indd` visible, open the Type pane of the Preferences dialog box.**

2. **Make sure the Smart Text Reflow option is checked, choose End of Story in the Add Pages To menu, and check the Delete Empty Pages option.**

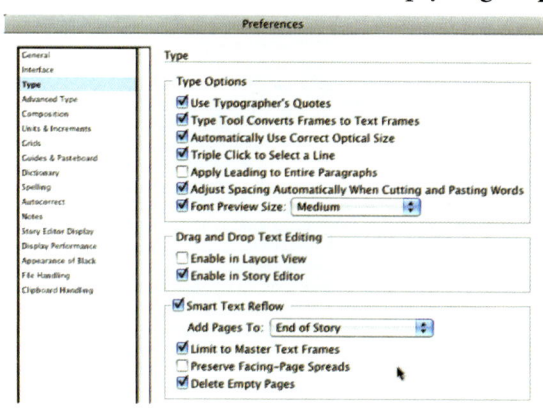

   When Smart Text Reflow is active, InDesign automatically adds pages to accommodate an entire story that is placed in a master text frame. This option applies to adding text within a story, and to changing formatting in a way that affects the number of required pages — which you will do in a later exercise.

   - You can use the **Add Pages To** menu to determine where pages are added to the file (at the end of the current story, the current section, or the current document).

   - If **Limit To Master Text Frames** is checked, you can add or remove pages when editing text in frames other than a master text frame. This option only applies if the existing frame is already part of a text thread with at least one other frame. (New pages added when the text frame is not a master text frame have a single-column text frame that matches the default page margins for the file.)

   - If **Preserve Facing-Page Spreads** is active, pages added to the middle of a document are added as document spreads based on the applied master layout. When unchecked, only the necessary pages will be added; subsequent existing pages are reshuffled (left-facing to right-facing) if necessary.

   - If **Delete Empty Pages** is active, unnecessary pages are removed from the layout if you delete text (or format text to require less space).

3. **Choose File>Place. Navigate to the file booklet.doc in the RF_InDesign> Realtors folder. Make sure the Show Import Options box is checked and click Open.**

4. **In the Import Options dialog box, make sure the Preserve Styles and Formatting option is selected.**

5. **In the Manual Page Breaks menu, choose No Breaks.**

   This command removes any page and section breaks that exist in the client's Microsoft Word file.

6. **Select the Import Styles Automatically option, and choose Auto Rename in both conflict menus.**

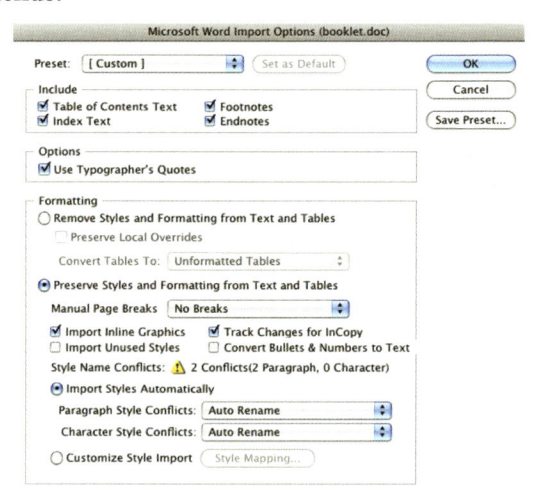

7. **Click OK to import the text.**

   When you see the Missing Fonts warning, click OK. You're going to change the style definitions for the text, so you don't have to worry about finding the missing fonts.

   This is a common workflow issue when you work with client-supplied files. Every situation is different, but we find it best to import client formatting so we can review the editorial priority, and then edit or define styles as necessary to complete the page layout.

Project 5: Realtor Collateral Booklet   285

8. **Click the loaded text cursor inside the margin guides on Page 2.**

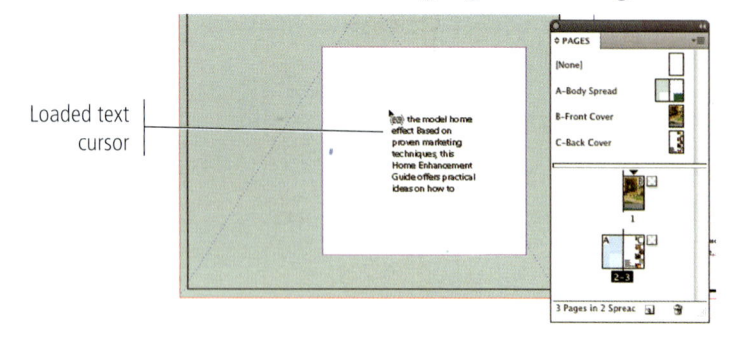

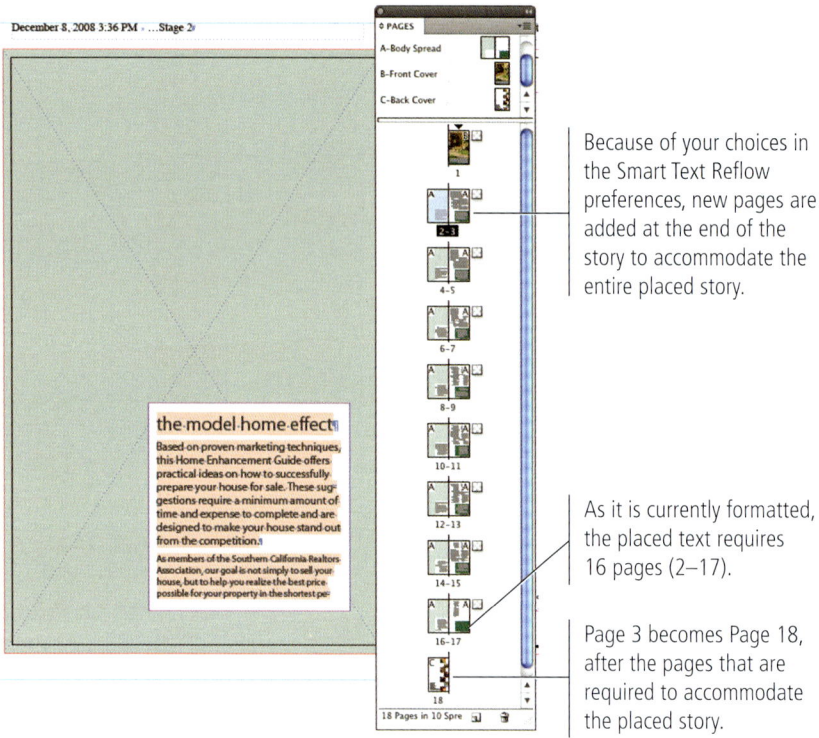

Loaded text cursor

Because of your choices in the Smart Text Reflow preferences, new pages are added at the end of the story to accommodate the entire placed story.

As it is currently formatted, the placed text requires 16 pages (2–17).

Page 3 becomes Page 18, after the pages that are required to accommodate the placed story.

Note:

If Smart Text Reflow is not active, you can press Shift and click the loaded text cursor to automatically flow the entire story; InDesign adds pages as necessary to accommodate the entire story. (In this case, new pages are always added at the end of the document, regardless of the position of the text box where you first click to place the text.)

9. **Save the file and continue to the next exercise.**

Review, Replace, and Edit Imported Styles

As you can see in the current booklet file, the text is just a long block with little to identify the editorial priority (e.g., headings, subheadings, and so on). Fonts used in the client's file aren't available, as indicated by the pink "missing font" highlight.

This type of situation occurs frequently. When it does, you should begin by reviewing the text to see if applied styles can provide any clues about which elements belong where and at what editorial priority.

1. **With Page 2 of `booklet_stage2.indd` showing, click the Type tool in the first paragraph (the model home effect).**

2. **Look at the Paragraph Styles panel.**

   The first paragraph is formatted with the Section Head style. You can assume that other text with the same basic appearance is also a section head.

   Insertion point

   The highlighted style is applied to the selected text (insertion point).

   These two styles — Heading and Intro Text — were imported when you loaded the cover master page layouts into the booklet file.

   The disk icon shows that the style was imported with the text file.

3. **In the Paragraph Styles panel, Control/right-click the Section Head style and choose Delete Style from the contextual menu.**

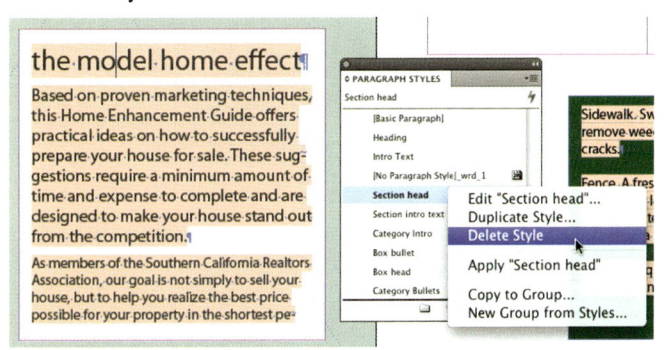

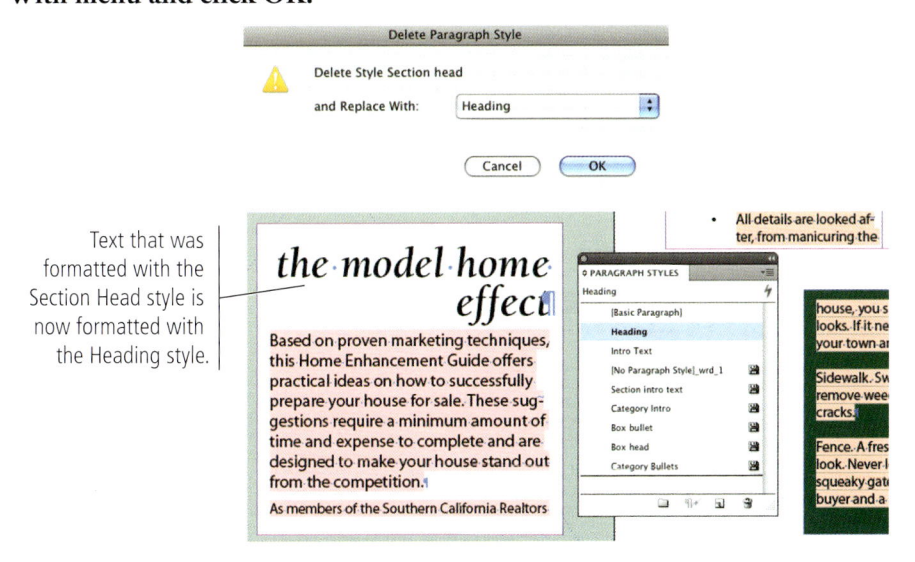

   Note:

   You can also edit a style by double-clicking the style in the panel. However, double-clicking a style in the panel applies the style to the current text, and then opens the Paragraph Style Options dialog box.

   By Control/right-clicking the style in the panel, you can edit the style without applying it to the currently selected text.

4. **In the Delete Paragraph Style dialog box, choose Heading in the Replace With menu and click OK.**

   Text that was formatted with the Section Head style is now formatted with the Heading style.

   Project 5: Realtor Collateral Booklet   287

5. **Move the insertion point to the next paragraph.**

    The second paragraph is formatted with the Section Intro Text style. Again, you can assume that other text with the same appearance is also introductory text for a section.

6. **Using the same process, replace the Section Intro Text style with the Intro Text style.**

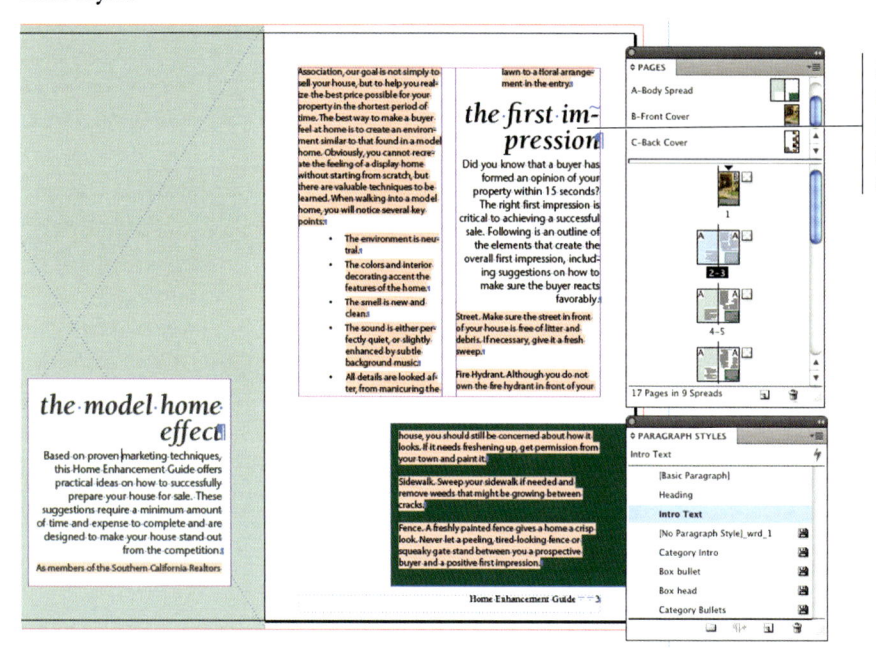

    Zooming out shows multiple instances of the Heading and Intro Text styles on the Page 2–3 spread.

7. **Place the insertion point in the third paragraph.**

    This paragraph is formatted with the Category Intro style.

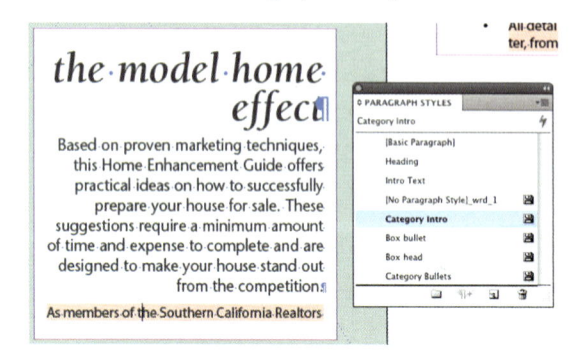

8. **Control/right-click the Category Intro style and choose Edit "Category Intro" from the contextual menu.**

9. **In the Basic Character Formats options, change the formatting to 9.5-pt ATC Pine Normal.**

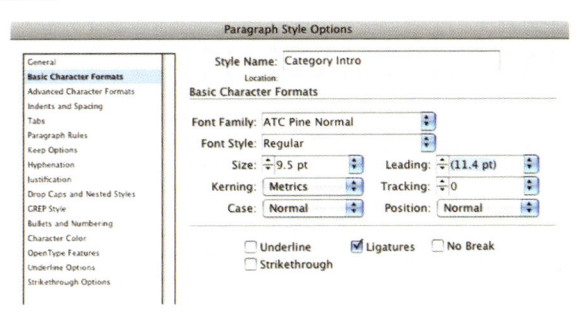

10. **In the Indents and Spacing options, change the Space Before field to 0.1″ and change the Space After field to 0″.**

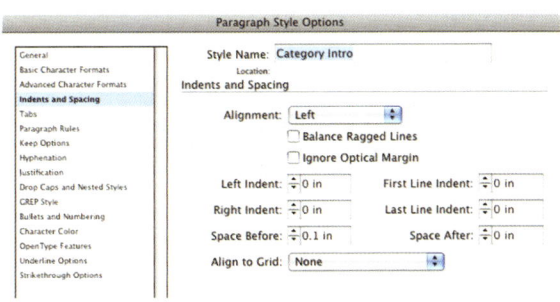

Note:

Remember, if you check the Preview box in the Paragraph Style Options dialog box, you can see the effect of your changes before you click OK.

11. **Click OK to change the style definition.**

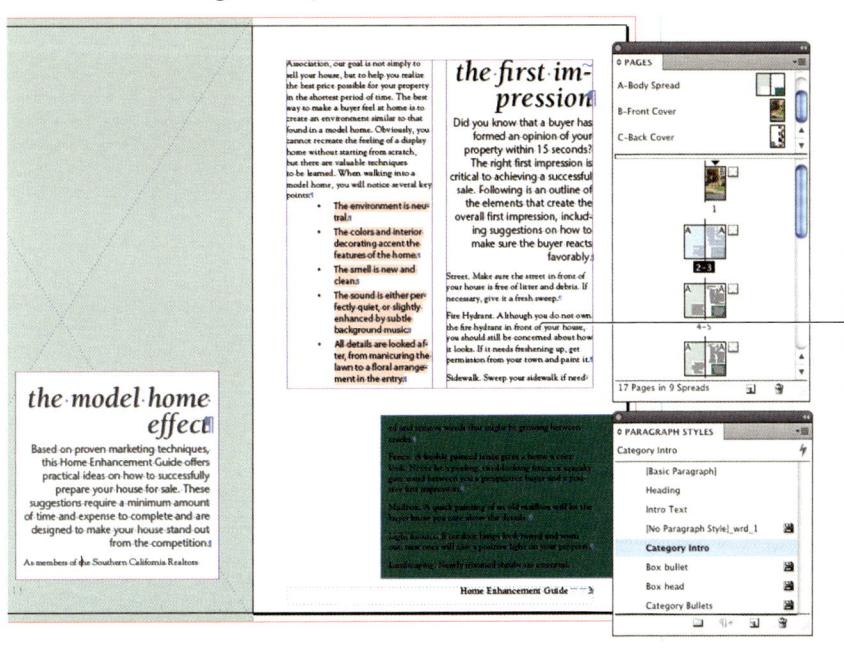

Much of the text in this layout is formatted with the Category Intro style. That text now reflects the updated definition.

12. **Save the file and continue to the next exercise.**

Project 5: Realtor Collateral Booklet   289

DEFINE PARENT-CHILD STYLE RELATIONSHIPS

There are two important points to remember about designing long documents. First, changing the definition of a style changes all text formatted with that style. Second, text should be consistently formatted from one page to the next; body copy (for example) should use the same basic font throughout the entire layout.

If you think of these two points together, consider what happens if you decide to change the font for the main body copy (for example, changing from Times New Roman to Adobe Garamond). Changing the main body font means you should also change any related styles that are variations of the main body text, such as bulleted or numbered lists.

The best way to manage this type of situation is to create secondary styles that are based on the main style. This way, changes to the main style also reflect in styles that are based on the main style.

1. **With Pages 2–3 of `booklet_stage2.indd` visible, place the insertion point in the first bulleted paragraph where the font is still missing.**

    This text is formatted with the Category Bullets style. The plus sign to the right of the style name indicates that some formatting other than the style definition has been applied to the selected paragraph — called a **local formatting override**.

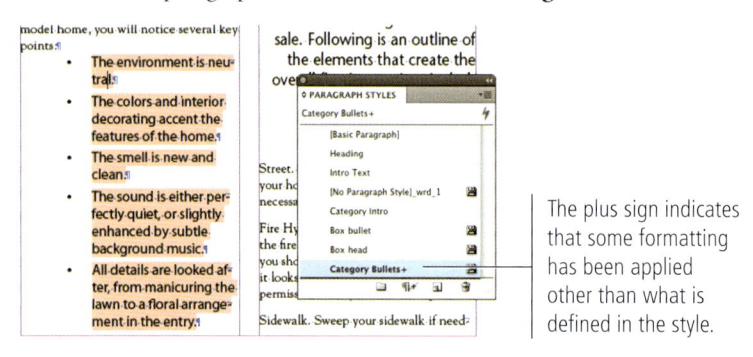

    The plus sign indicates that some formatting has been applied other than what is defined in the style.

    Note:

    Local formatting overrides are common when you import text from a client-supplied Microsoft Word file.

2. **Control/right-click the Category Bullets style in the Paragraph Styles panel and choose Edit "Category Bullets" from the contextual menu.**

3. **In the General options pane, choose Category Intro in the Based On menu.**

    When you redefine an existing style to be based on another style, InDesign tries to maintain the formatting of the original style instead of the one it is being based on. In the Style Settings area, you can see the style will be Category Intro +. Everything after the plus sign is different than the style defined in the Based On menu (called the **parent style**).

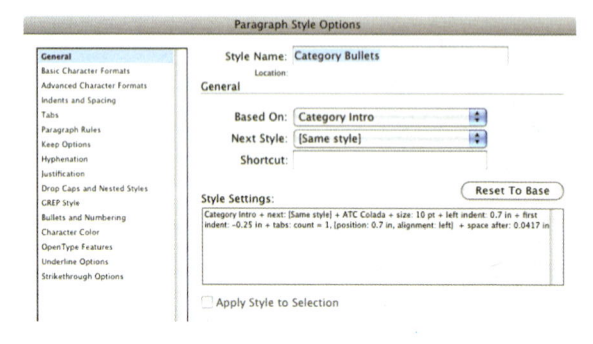

Project 5: Realtor Collateral Booklet

4. **Click the Reset To Base button above the Style Settings area.**

5. **In the Indents and Spacing options, change the Space Before field to 0.05″ and click OK.**

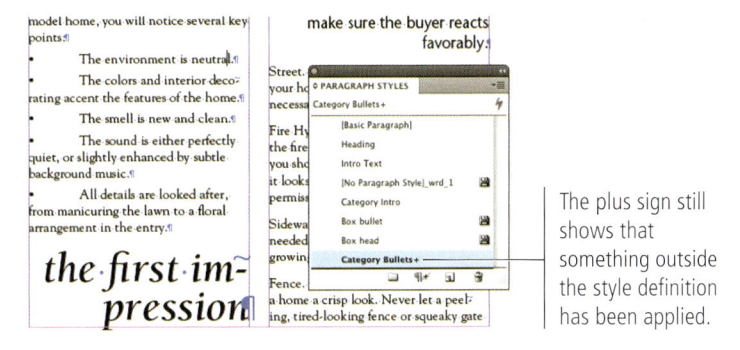

   The plus sign still shows that something outside the style definition has been applied.

6. **With the insertion point anywhere in the selected text, choose Edit>Select All to select the entire story.**

   You can clear overrides for any selected text, whether for a single character or an entire story. In this case, all overrides were created in the original Microsoft Word file; rather than manually clearing overrides in each paragraph, you can simply select the entire story and clear all overrides at once.

7. **At the bottom of the Paragraph Styles panel, click the Clear Overrides button.**

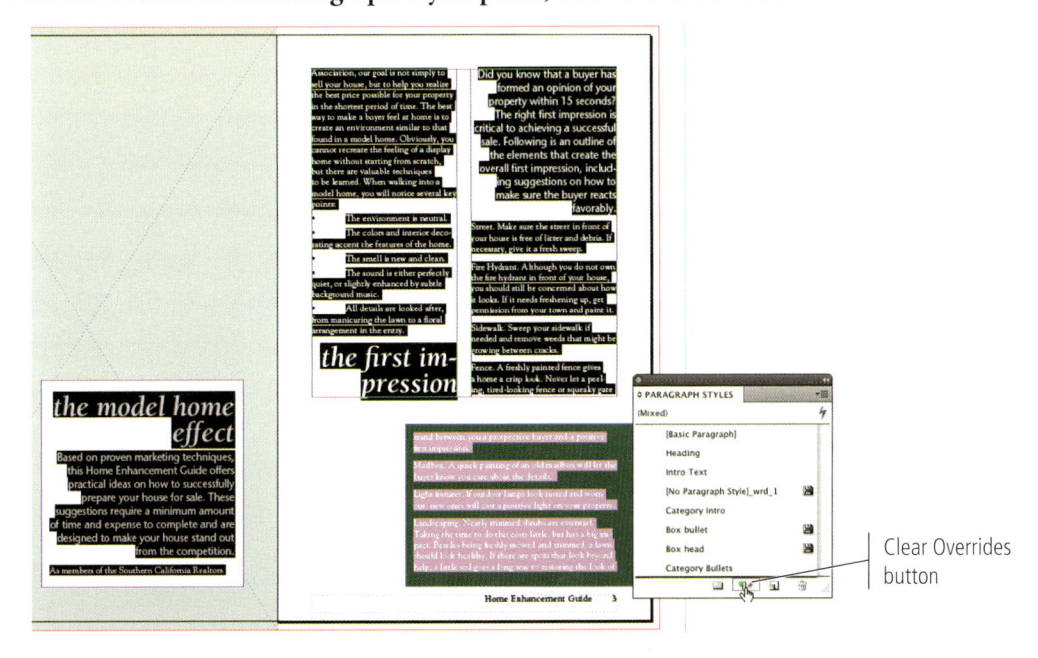

   Clear Overrides button

Project 5: Realtor Collateral Booklet 291

By clearing overrides, the bullet characters are removed from the Category Bullets style. You will add these back in later when you edit the style definition.

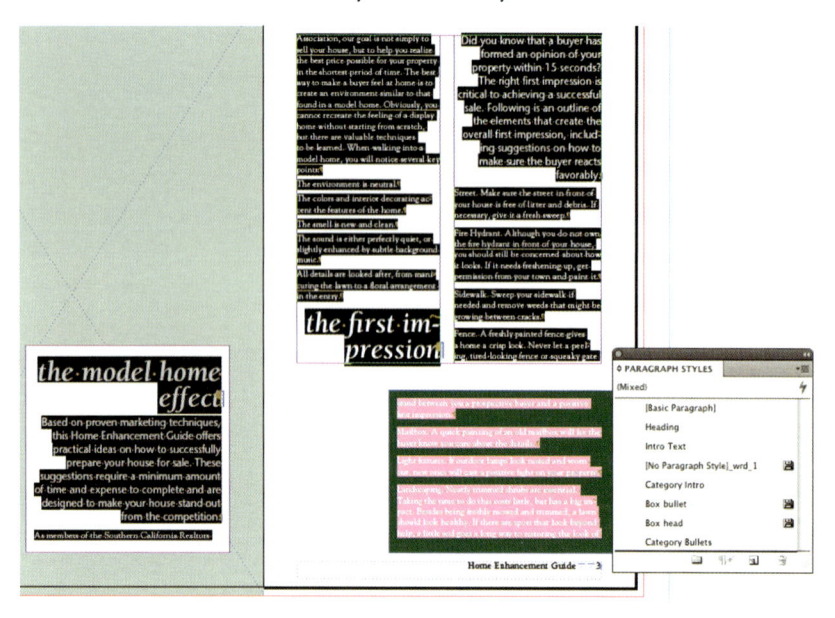

8. **Deselect all text, navigate to Page 5, and place the insertion point in the first paragraph with the missing font highlight.**

   This text is formatted with the Box Head style.

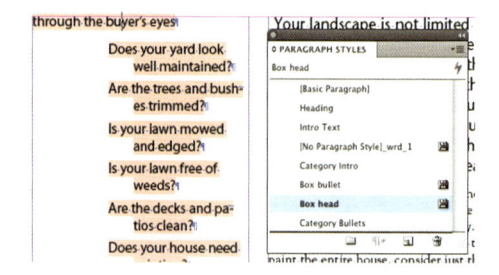

9. **Using the same method as in Steps 2–5, edit the Box Head style to be based on the Heading style with the following modifications:**

   Size: 15 pt

   Leading: Auto

   Paragraph Alignment: Left

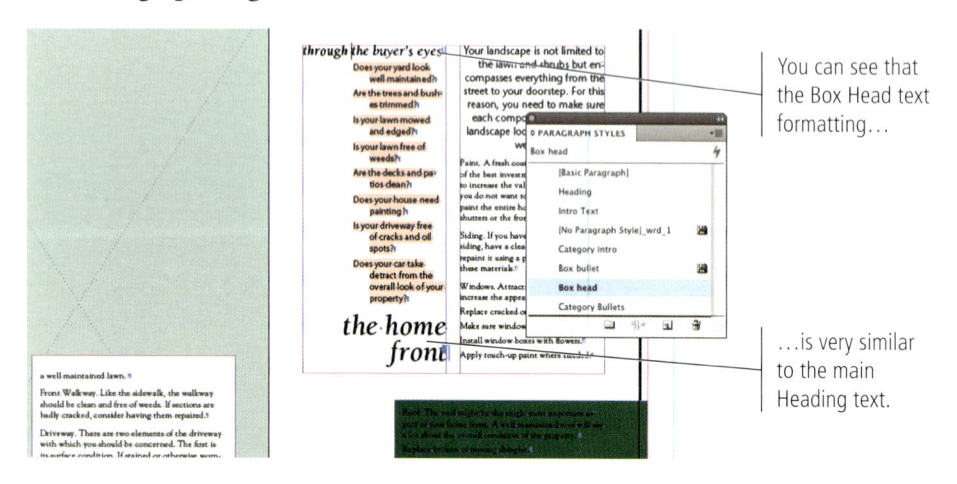

   You can see that the Box Head text formatting…

   …is very similar to the main Heading text.

   292 Project 5: Realtor Collateral Booklet

10. **Place the insertion point in the first bulleted paragraph with the missing font highlight.**

    This text is formatted with the Box Bullet style.

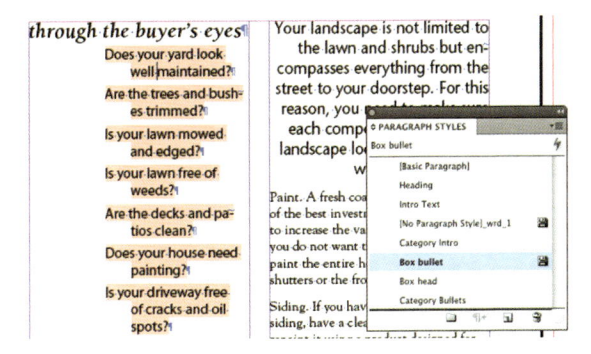

11. **Using the same method from Steps 2–5, change the Box Bullet style to be based on the Category Intro text style with a 0.05" Space Before value.**

    You could actually base this style on the Category Bullet style, but we try to avoid too many levels of nested styles. More levels of nesting means greater complexity when you need to make changes.

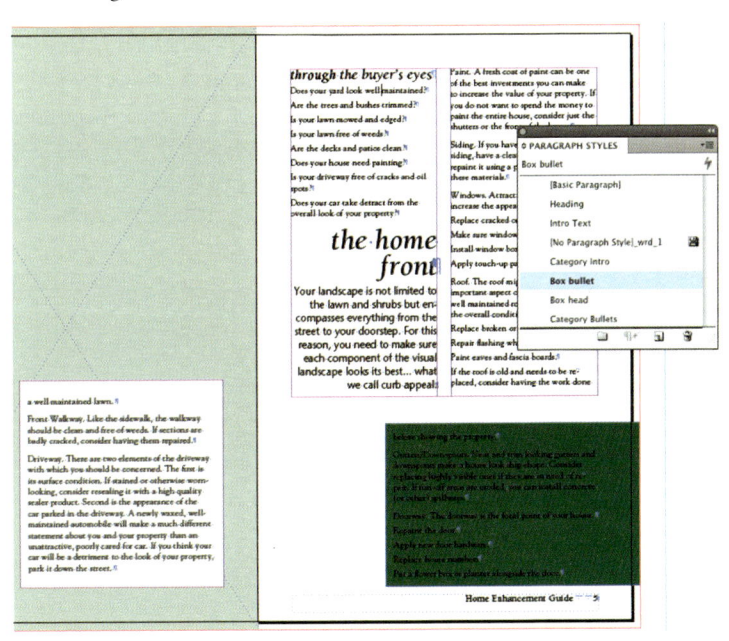

12. **Save the file and continue to the next exercise.**

Define Bullets and Numbering Options

By changing the style definitions in the previous exercise, you removed the bullets from two different types of lists (the category bulleted lists and the box bulleted lists); these bullets need to be replaced. You also need to convert the Category Intro text paragraphs to bullets to create improved visual separation.

You could manually type the bullet characters at the beginning of each line, but it's much easier and more efficient to use the Bullets and Numbering formatting options.

1. **With `booklet_stage2.indd` open, Control/right-click Category Intro in the Paragraph Styles panel and choose Edit "Category Intro" from the contextual menu.**

2. **In the Paragraph Style Options dialog box, display the Bullets and Numbering options.**

3. **In the List Type menu, choose Bullets.**

    By default, you can apply the Bullets or Numbers type of list.

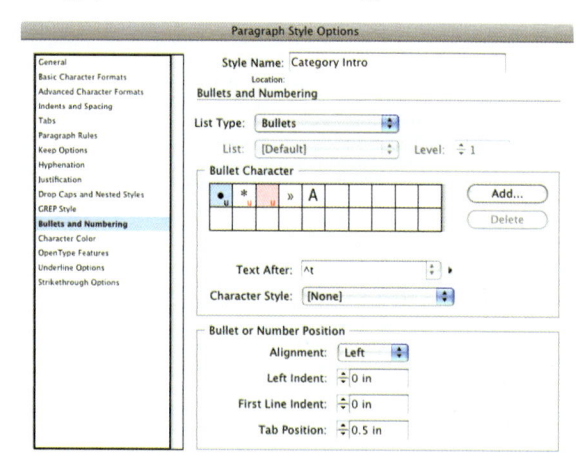

Note:

You can also define custom lists by choosing Type>Bulleted & Numbered Lists>Define Lists. If you've defined a custom list type, it will be available in the List Type menu of the Paragraph Style Options dialog box.

4. **Click the Add button to the right of the Bullet Character list.**

    The Add Bullets dialog box allows you to choose a character for the bullet. This character defaults to the same font used in the style, but you can choose any font and font style from the menus at the bottom of the dialog box.

5. **In the Add Bullets dialog box, find and select the Tilde character.**

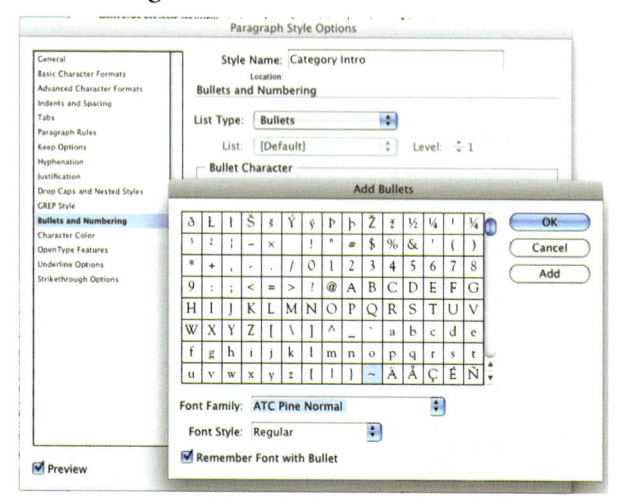

Project 5: Realtor Collateral Booklet

6. **Make sure the Remember Font with Bullet option is checked, and then click OK to return to the Paragraph Style Options dialog box.**

   The selected bullet character is added to the list of available bullet characters. If you don't check the Remember Font with Bullet option, the character will be applied in whatever font is used for the style.

7. **Click the Tilde character in the grid of available characters to select it.**

8. **Leave the Text After field to the default (^t, which is the code for a Tab character).**

9. **In the Bullet or Number Position area, change the Left Indent value to 0.125″, and change the First Line Indent value to –0.125″. Leave the Tab Position value at its default.**

   This negative first-line indent is called a **hanging indent**.

Note:

The Remember Font with Bullet option can be important if you use extended characters or decorative or dingbat fonts as bullet characters. If you select the solid square character in the Zapf Dingbats font (■), for example, changing to a different font would show the letter "n" as the bullet character.

Note:

Changing these fields also changes the same fields in the Indents and Spacing options.

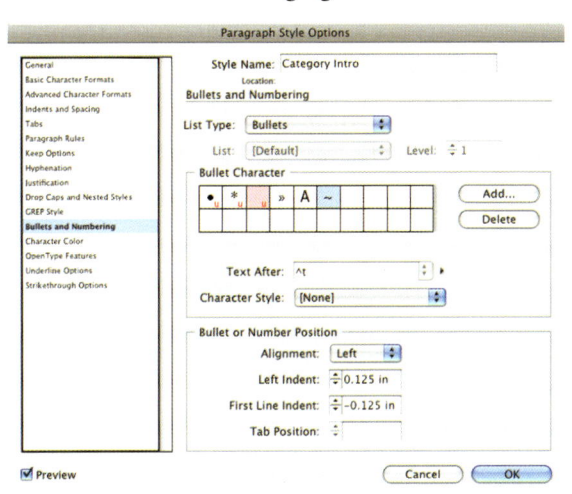

10. **Click OK to change the style definition and return to the layout.**

    Because the two bullet styles are based on the Category Intro style, virtually all text in the layout (except the heading and intro text) now has the initial Tilde character and the hanging indent you just defined.

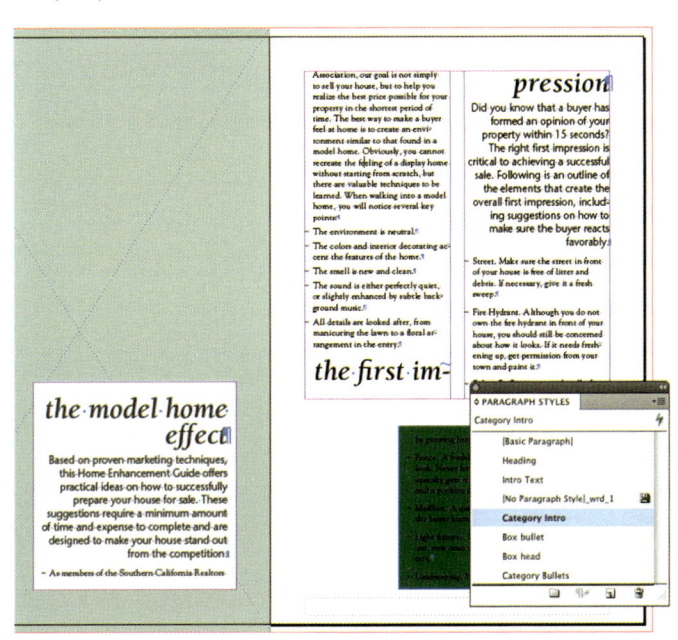

Project 5: Realtor Collateral Booklet   295

11. **Control/right-click the Category Bullets style and choose Edit "Category Bullets" in the contextual menu.**

12. **In the Bullets and Numbering options, click the Double-Chevron character from the default Bullet Character list.**

13. **Change the Left Indent field to 0.25" and click OK.**

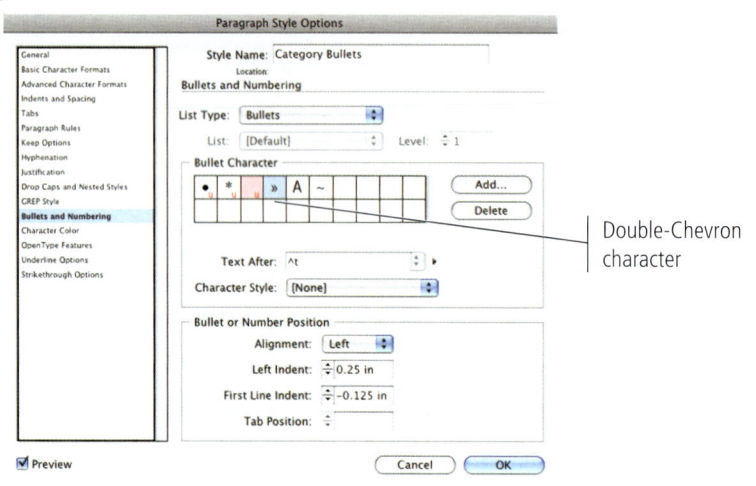

14. **Navigate through the layout to review the effect of changing the character and indent options for the secondary bulleted list.**

    The Category Bullet paragraphs are indented 0.125" from the column edge because the negative first-line indent was not equal to the first-line indent value. In other words:

    Left Indent + First-Line Indent = Indent location of the first line

    0.25 + (−0.125) = 0.125

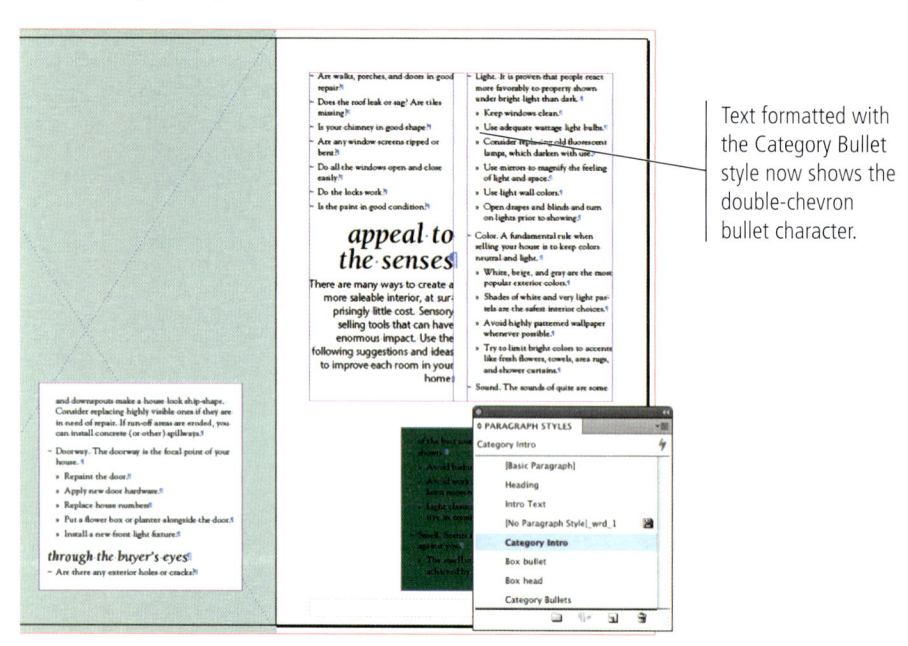

15. **Edit the Box Bullet style to use a check box-like character as the bullet character, with a 0.2″ left indent and −0.2″ first-line indent.**

    For the bullet character, try the "o" character from the Zapf Dingbats (Macintosh) or Wingdings (Windows) fonts. If you don't have one of these fonts, use any character from any font that you think works well as a bullet character.

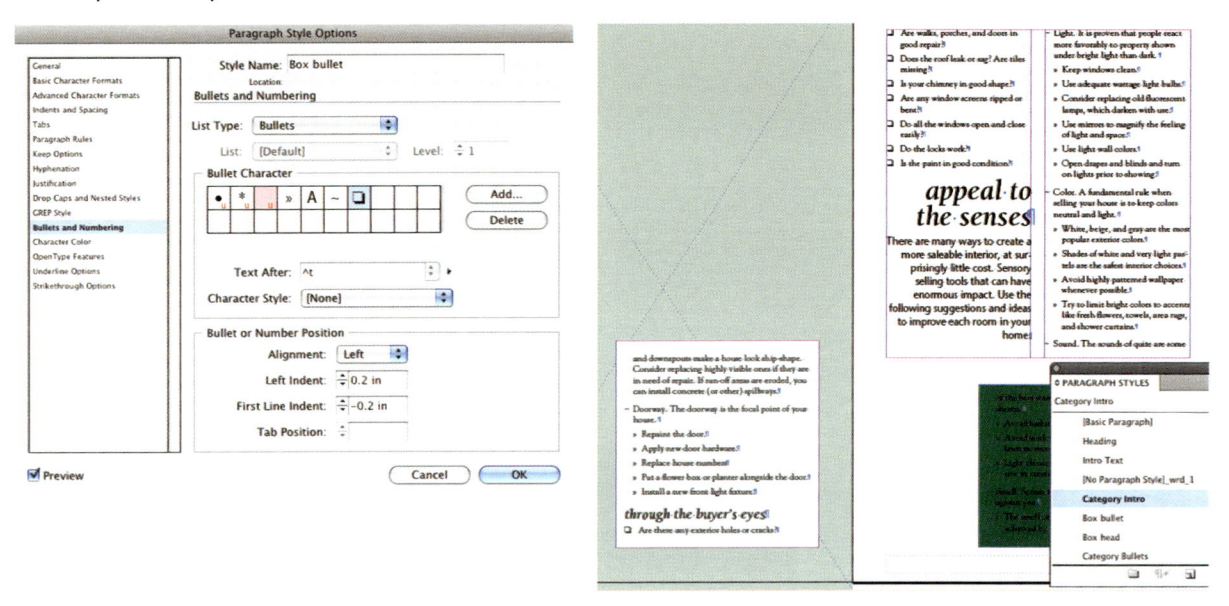

16. **Save the file and continue to the next exercise.**

The Glyphs Panel

ASCII is a text-based code that defines characters with a numeric value between 001 and 256. The standard alphabet and punctuation characters are mapped from 001 to 128. **Extended ASCII characters** are those with ASCII numbers higher than 128; these include symbols (bullets, copyright symbols, etc.) and some special characters (en dashes, accent marks, etc.). Some of the more common extended characters can be accessed in the Type>Insert submenus.

OpenType fonts can store more than 65,000 **glyphs** (characters) in a single font — far beyond what you could access with a keyboard (even including combinations of the different modifier keys). The large glyph storage capacity means that a single OpenType font can replace the multiple separate "Expert" fonts that contain variations of fonts (Minion Swash, for example, is no longer necessary when you can access the Swashes subset of the Minion Pro font).

Unicode fonts include two-bit characters that are common in some foreign language typesetting (e.g., Cyrillic, Japanese, and other non-Roman or pictographic fonts).

The Glyphs panel (Window>Type & Tables>Glyphs or Type>Glyphs) provides access to individual glyphs in a font, including basic characters in regular fonts, extended ASCII and OpenType character sets, and even pictographic characters in Unicode fonts.

Using the Glyphs panel is simple: make sure the insertion point is flashing where you want a character to appear, and then double-click the character you want to place. You can view the character set for any font by simply changing the menu at the bottom of the panel. By default, the panel shows the entire font, but you can show only specific character sets using the Show menu.

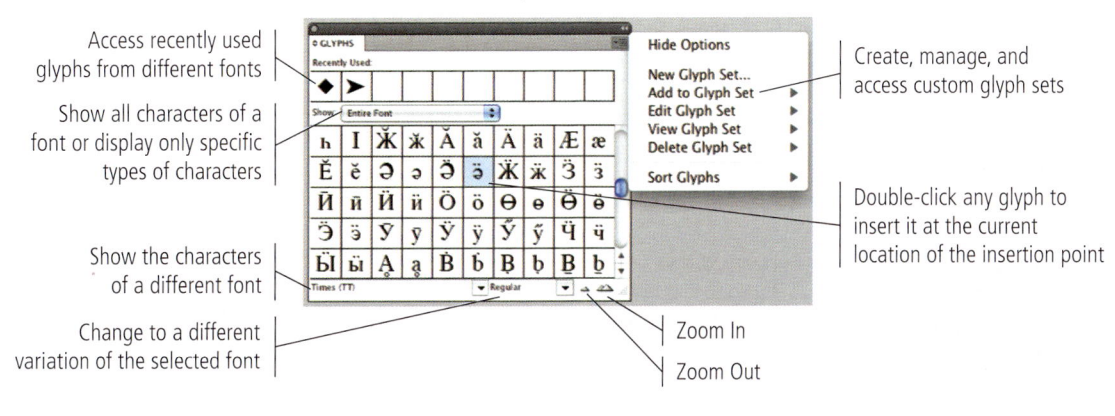

Access recently used glyphs from different fonts

Show all characters of a font or display only specific types of characters

Show the characters of a different font

Change to a different variation of the selected font

Create, manage, and access custom glyph sets

Double-click any glyph to insert it at the current location of the insertion point

Zoom In

Zoom Out

Project 5: Realtor Collateral Booklet 297

CONTROL PAGE AND FRAME BREAKS

In the completed booklet, each spread will have a single section heading followed by a section intro on the left page. The main and secondary bullet points will all appear on the right side, and the "through the buyer's eyes" bullets will appear in the colored frame. Rather than manually placing page and frame breaks, you can use styles and paragraph formatting options to automatically place text in the correct frame on the correct side of the spread.

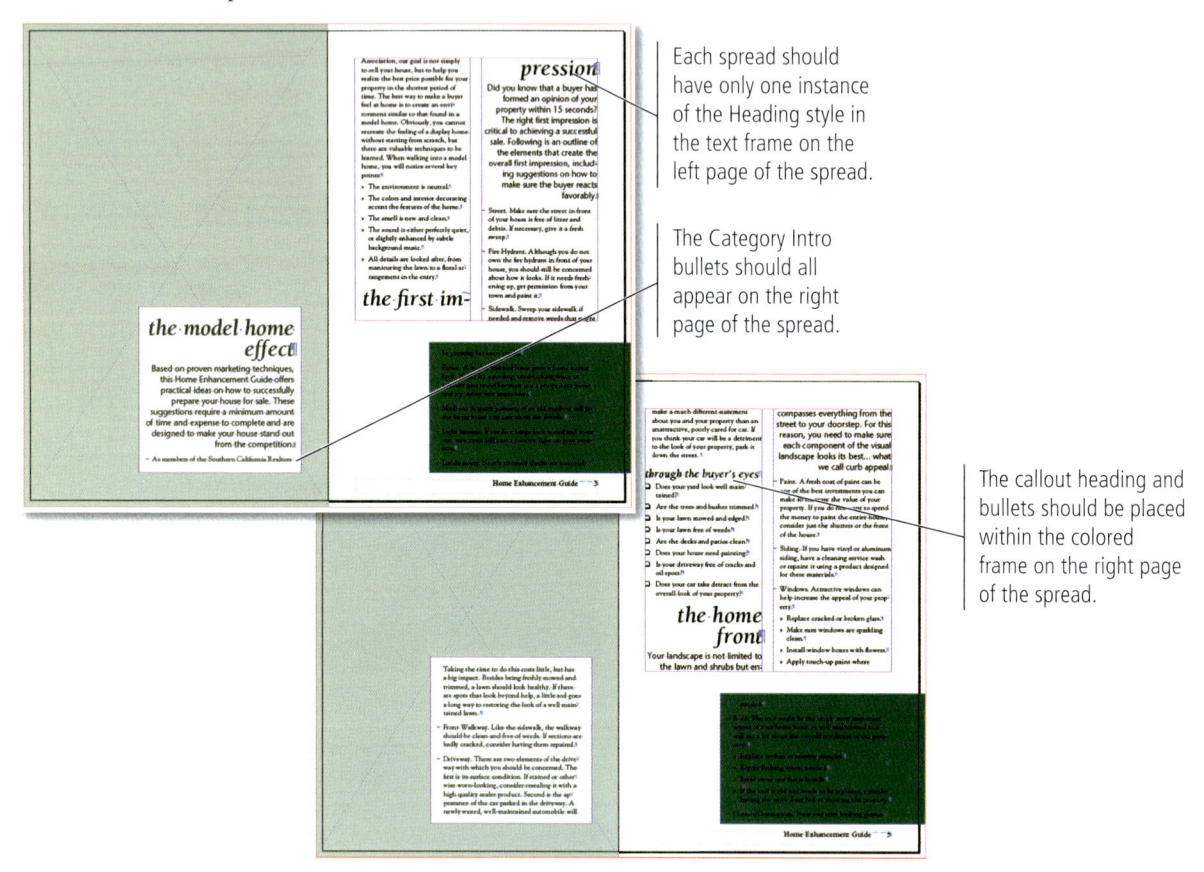

Each spread should have only one instance of the Heading style in the text frame on the left page of the spread.

The Category Intro bullets should all appear on the right page of the spread.

The callout heading and bullets should be placed within the colored frame on the right page of the spread.

1. **With the Page 2–3 spread of `booklet_stage2.indd` visible, Control/right-click Heading in the Paragraph Styles panel and choose Edit "Heading" from the contextual menu.**

2. **Display the Keep options. In the Start Paragraph menu, choose On Next Even Page. Click OK to change the style definition.**

   Each section heading should appear on the left page of a spread, and left-facing pages are even-numbered.

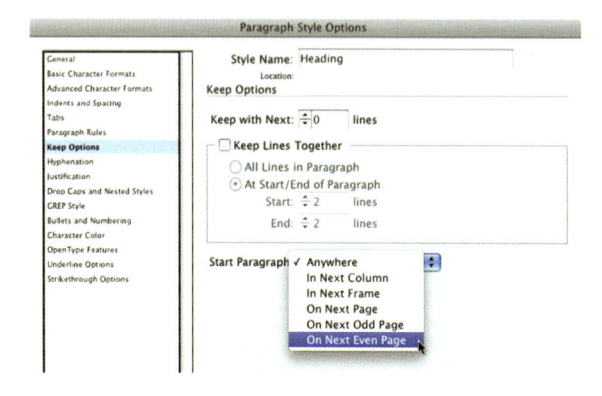

298 Project 5: Realtor Collateral Booklet

3. **Navigate through the layout and review the results.**

   When you get to Page 6, you might notice a problem — the "through the buyer's eyes" heading has moved to the wrong place. Because the Box Head style is based on the Heading style, it adopts the Start Paragraph option that requires this heading to appear on the next even-numbered page. It should move to the green frame on the right side of the spread, which requires a different Start Paragraph option.

   The extra heading from Page 3 correctly moves to Page 4.

   The box heading from Page 5 incorrectly moves to Page 6.

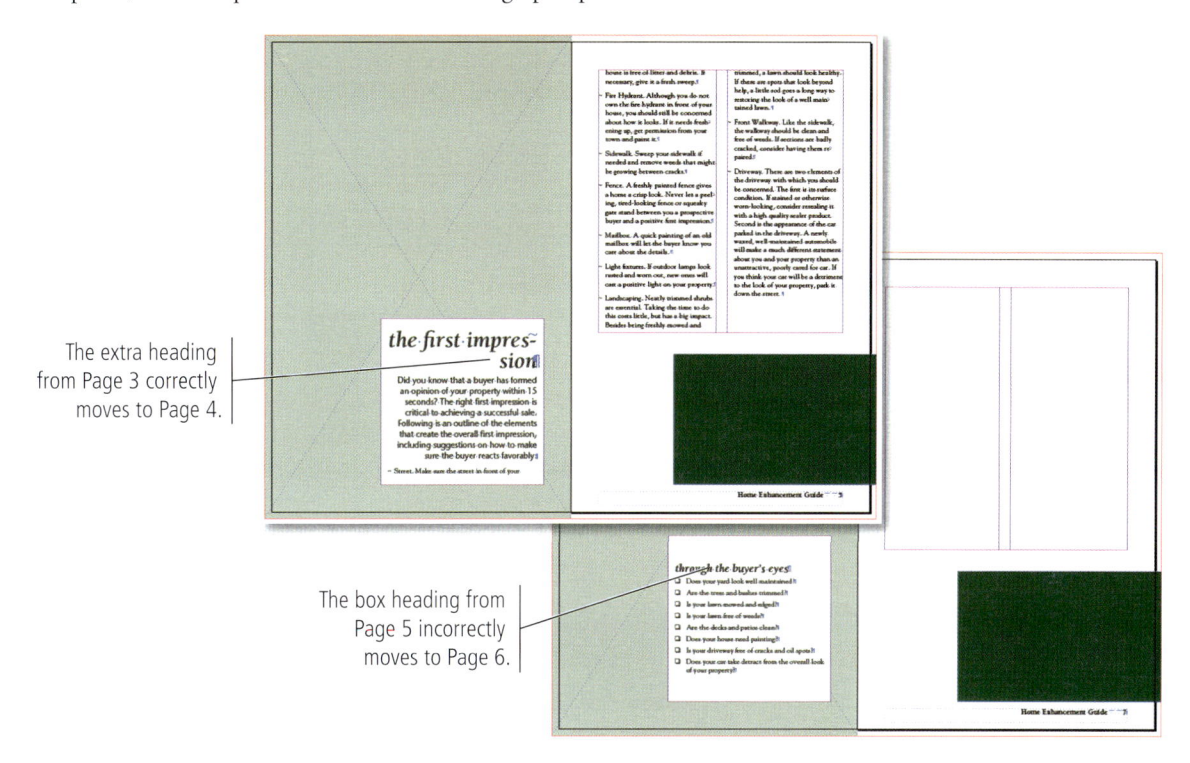

4. **Control/right-click the Box Head style and choose Edit "Box Head" from the contextual menu. In the Keep options, choose In Next Frame in the Start Paragraph menu and click OK to redefine the style.**

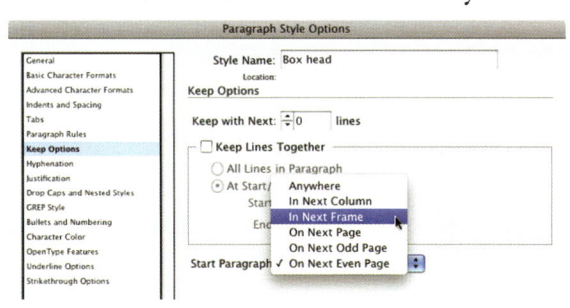

Project 5: Realtor Collateral Booklet

5. **Navigate through the layout and review the results.**

   The even-numbered pages show another problem in the current formatting. The left page of the spread should contain only the heading and the intro text; you need to force all remaining text onto the right side of the spread. You could do this manually, but a new style can handle the formatting for you.

   This paragraph should begin on the right page of the spread.

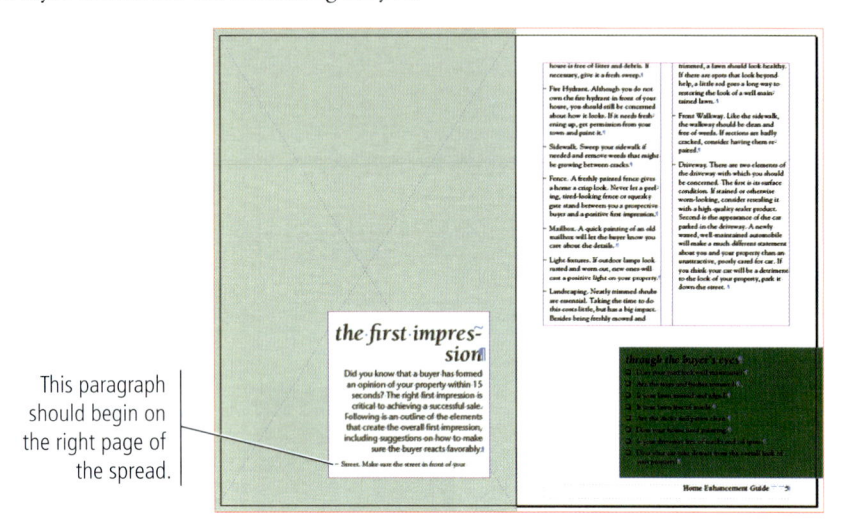

6. **Control/right-click the Category Intro style and choose Duplicate Style from the contextual menu.**

7. **Change the Style Name field to Category Intro - First and choose Category Intro in the Based On menu. In the Keep options, choose In Next Column from the Start Paragraph menu and click OK.**

   The In Next Column option moves a paragraph to the next column in the same frame or to the next frame if the text is already in the last (or only) column of a frame.

   Note:

   As with the bulleted lists, it's a good idea to base the new style on the existing style so later changes will reflect in the duplicate style.

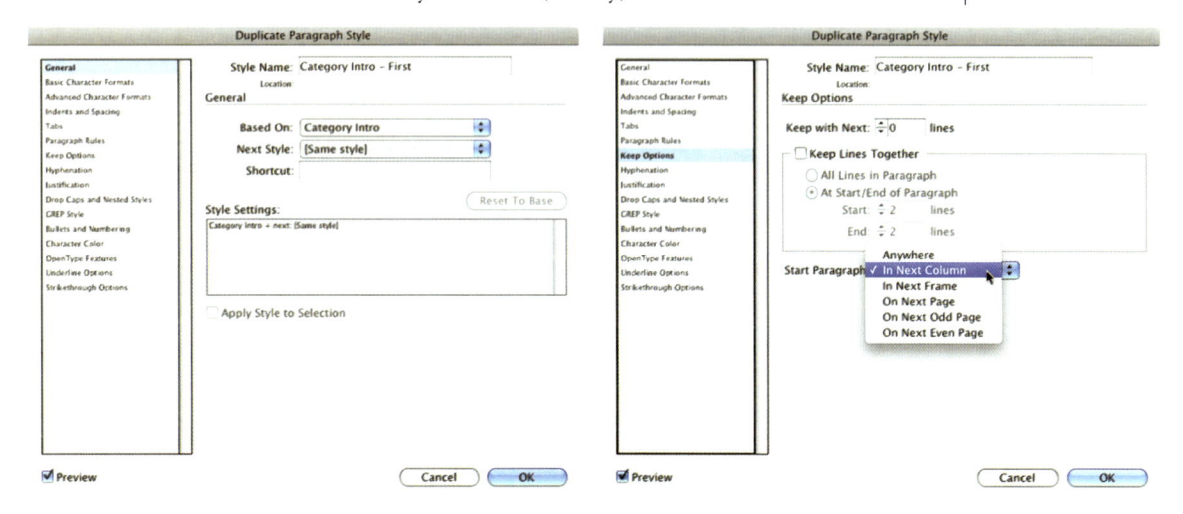

   300 Project 5: Realtor Collateral Booklet

8. **Place the insertion point in the first Category Intro paragraph on Page 4 (the first paragraph with a tilde character as the bullet character), and then click the Category Intro – First style in the Paragraph Styles panel.**

   As soon as you apply the style, the paragraph automatically moves to the next available frame in the text chain.

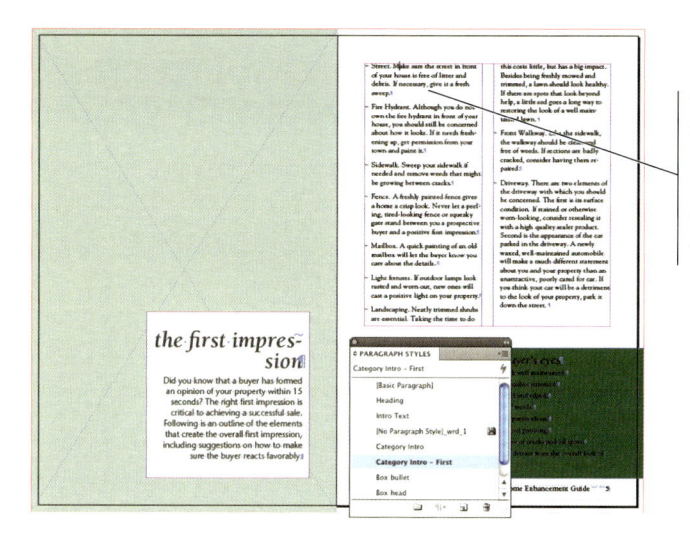

   The In Next Frame option forces the paragraph to begin in the correct location (the left column of the frame on the right page of the spread).

9. **Navigate through the layout and apply the Category Intro – First style to the third paragraph on each spread.**

10. **Navigate through the layout and review your work.**

    Page 7 highlights another potential issue with the position of text in the layout. Despite all the available automation and productivity options, some things simply must be resolved manually. There is no way to tell InDesign, for example, "If only one secondary bullet fits in the first column, move the preceding primary bullet to the next column." Resolutions to issues such as these, which add polish to a professional layout, must be determined and applied manually.

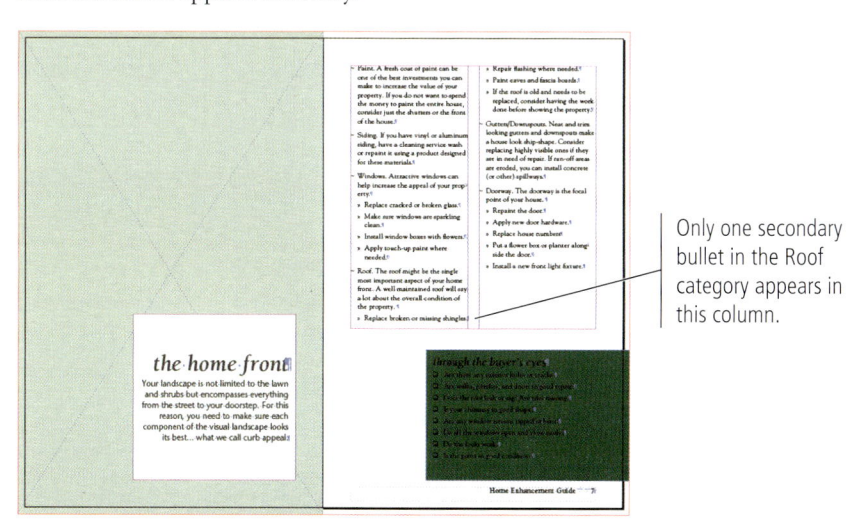

    Only one secondary bullet in the Roof category appears in this column.

Project 5: Realtor Collateral Booklet   301

11. On Page 7, place the insertion point in the intro paragraph of the Roof category, and then apply the Category Intro – First style.

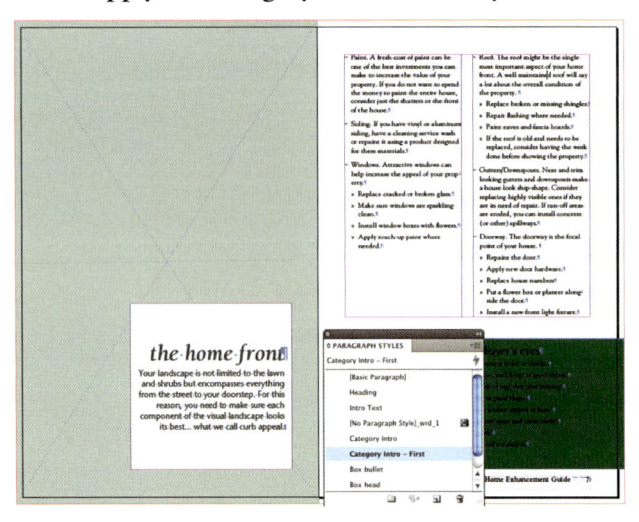

12. **Navigate through the layout and apply the same change as necessary.**

    We applied the formatting on Pages 11 and 15.

13. **Navigate through the layout and review your work.**

    Page 4 shows a problem with unbalanced columns, in this case resulting from a few lines of one paragraph remaining at the bottom of the left column.

    In addition to determining where a paragraph can start, the Keep options are also used to control **orphans** (single words at the end single lines of a paragraph at the end of a column) and **widows** (single lines of a paragraph at the top of a column). Typography conventions suggest that at least two lines of a paragraph should be kept together at the beginning and end of a column or frame. (Headings at the end of a frame or column are also sometimes considered orphans.)

    Two lines is not technically an orphan, but breaking this paragraph across the columns creates an unbalanced appearance on the page.

    Note:

    These same options can be applied to any specific paragraph by choosing Keep Options from the Paragraph panel Options menu.

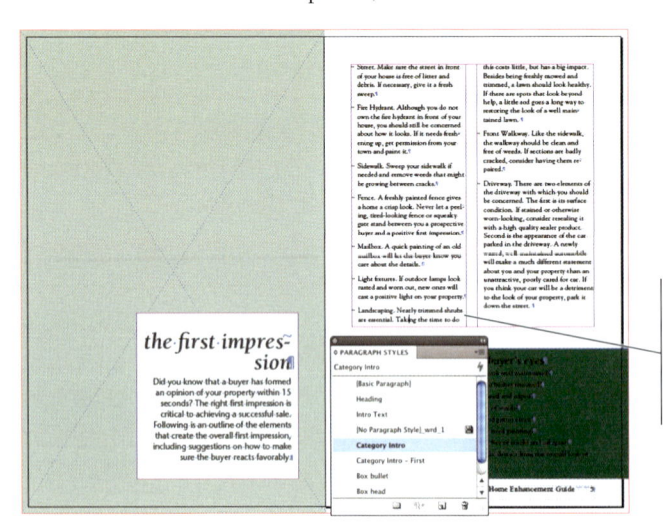

Project 5: Realtor Collateral Booklet

14. **Control/right click Category Intro in the Paragraph Styles panel and choose Edit "Category Intro" from the contextual menu. In the Keep options, activate the Keep Lines Together check box and choose the All Lines in Paragraph option. Click OK to change the style definition.**

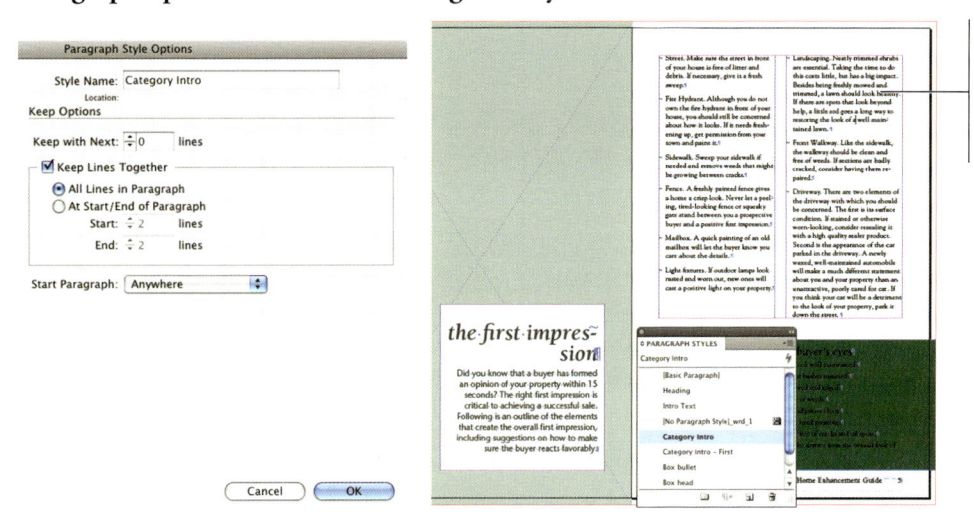

This entire paragraph moves to the next column because all lines in the paragraph must be kept together.

15. **Save the file and continue to the next exercise.**

Control Automatic Hyphenation

Automatic hyphenation is another key to professional page layout. Typographic conventions recommend no hyphenation in headings, no more than three hyphens in a row, and at least three characters before or after a hyphen. Some designers follow stricter rules, such as not hyphenating proper nouns; others prefer no hyphenation at all. Whatever your requirements, you can control the hyphenation of any paragraph either locally or in a style definition.

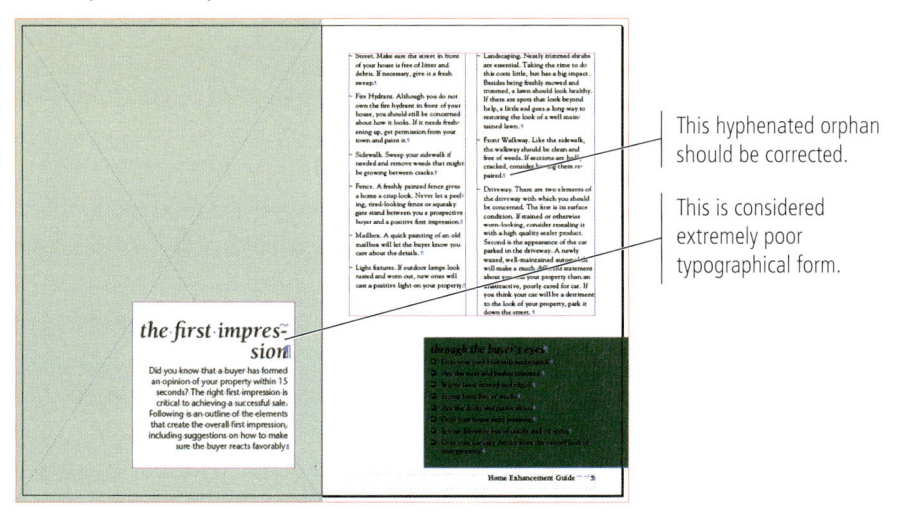

This hyphenated orphan should be corrected.

This is considered extremely poor typographical form.

1. **With the Page 4–5 spread of `booklet_stage2.indd` visible, Control/right-click the Heading style and choose Edit "Heading" from the contextual menu.**

2. **In the Paragraph Style Options dialog box, show the Hyphenation options.**

Project 5: Realtor Collateral Booklet   303

3. **Uncheck the Hyphenate option and click OK.**

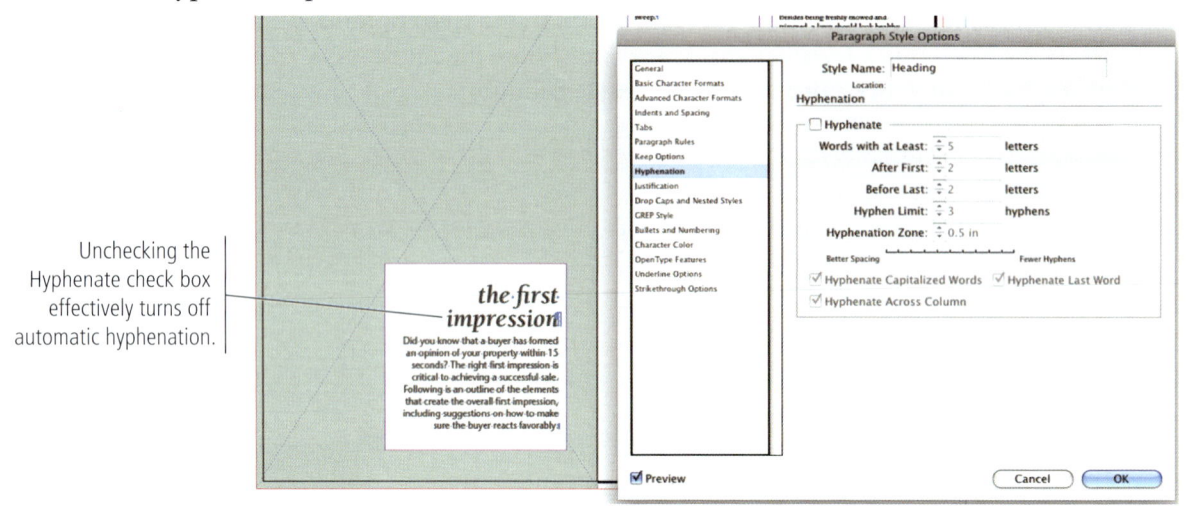

Unchecking the Hyphenate check box effectively turns off automatic hyphenation.

4. **Control/right-click the Category Intro style and choose Edit "Category Intro" from the contextual menu.**

   Remember, most of the other styles are based on the Category Intro style; by changing the hyphenation options for this style, you also change the options for all styles based on it.

5. **In the Hyphenation options, change the After First and Before Last fields to 3. Click OK to change the style definition.**

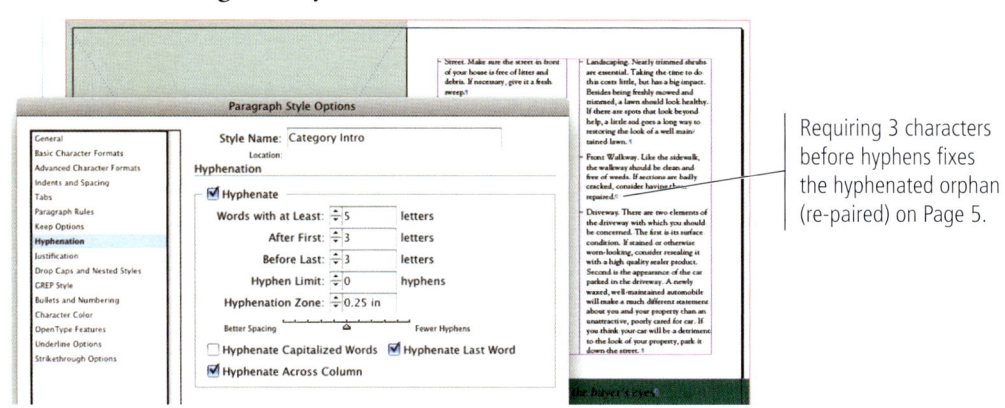

Requiring 3 characters before hyphens fixes the hyphenated orphan (re-paired) on Page 5.

The Hyphenation options allow you to control the way InDesign hyphenates text. (If the Hyphenate box is unchecked, InDesign will not hyphenate text in the paragraph.)

- **Words With At Least _ Letters** defines the minimum number of characters that must exist in a hyphenated word.
- **After First _ Letters** and **Before Last _ Letters** define the minimum number of characters that must appear before and after a hyphen.
- **Hyphen Limit** defines the maximum number of hyphens that can appear on consecutive lines. (Remember, you are defining the limit here, so zero means there is no limit — allowing unlimited hyphens.)
- **Hyphenation Zone** defines the amount of white space allowed at the end of a line of unjustified text before hyphenation begins.
- If **Hyphenate Capitalized Words** is checked, capitalized words (proper nouns) can be hyphenated.
- If **Hyphenate Last Word** is checked, the last word in a paragraph can be hyphenated.
- If **Hyphenate Across Column** is checked, the last word in a column or frame can be hyphenated.

Note:

These options can be applied to any specific paragraph by choosing Hyphenation from the Paragraph panel Options menu.

6. **Navigate to Page 2.**

   As with balancing columns, there is some subjective element to balancing lines of copy — especially headlines.

7. **Place the insertion point before the word "home" in the heading and press Shift-Return/Enter.**

   This character, called a **soft return**, forces a new line without starting a new paragraph.

   Line break character

8. **Navigate through the layout and add soft returns as necessary to balance the two-line headings.**

   We adjusted the headings on Pages 8, 10, and 14.

9. **Save the file and continue to the next exercise.**

Overriding Automatic Hyphenation

INDESIGN FOUNDATIONS

InDesign applies automatic hyphenation based on the defined language dictionary. You can override the hyphenation as defined in the dictionary by choosing Edit>Spelling>Dictionary.

If you highlight a word before opening the dictionary, it automatically appears in the Word field. Clicking the Hyphenate button shows the possible hyphenation locations as defined in the dictionary. You can override the automatic hyphenation by adding or deleting the consecutive Tilde characters in the Word field. When you change the hyphenation of a word, you have to click the Add button to add the new hyphenation scheme to the dictionary.

Default hyphenation locations

After adding the exception to the list, the word "photography" will now only hyphenate between the "o" and the "g".

Project 5: Realtor Collateral Booklet 305

REDEFINE STYLES BASED ON LOCAL FORMATTING OVERRIDES

You might have noticed one final formatting problem when you reviewed the current layout: The black text in the callout boxes (on the right-facing pages) is very difficult to read because the boxes have a dark fill color. Although you are going to change the box color on each spread, you are going to use other dark colors that still make the black text difficult to read.

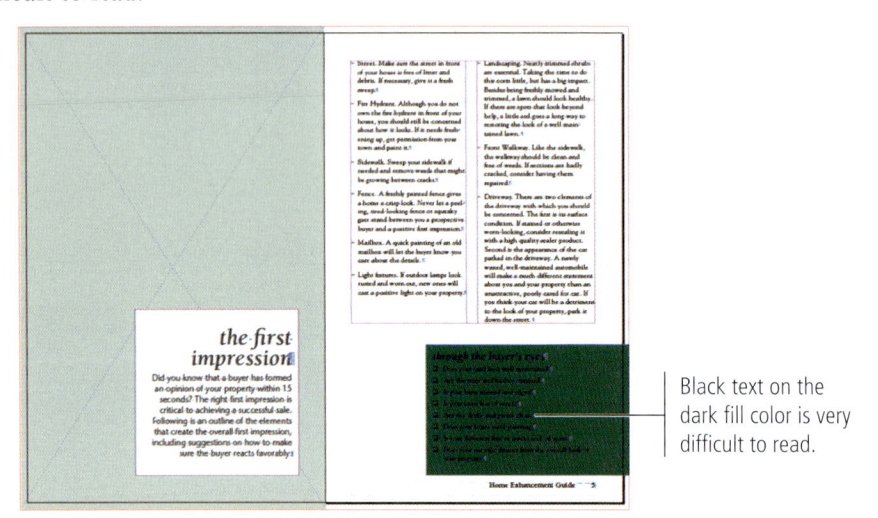

Black text on the dark fill color is very difficult to read.

Paragraph Composition Options

INDESIGN FOUNDATIONS

InDesign offers two options for controlling the overall flow of text (called **composition**) within a paragraph: **Adobe Paragraph Composer** (the default) and **Adobe Single-line Composer**. Both methods create breaks based on the applied hyphenation and justification options for a paragraph.

You can change the composition method for an individual paragraph in the Paragraph panel Options menu or the Justification dialog box; or you can change the composition method for a paragraph style in the Justification pane of the Paragraph Style Options dialog box.

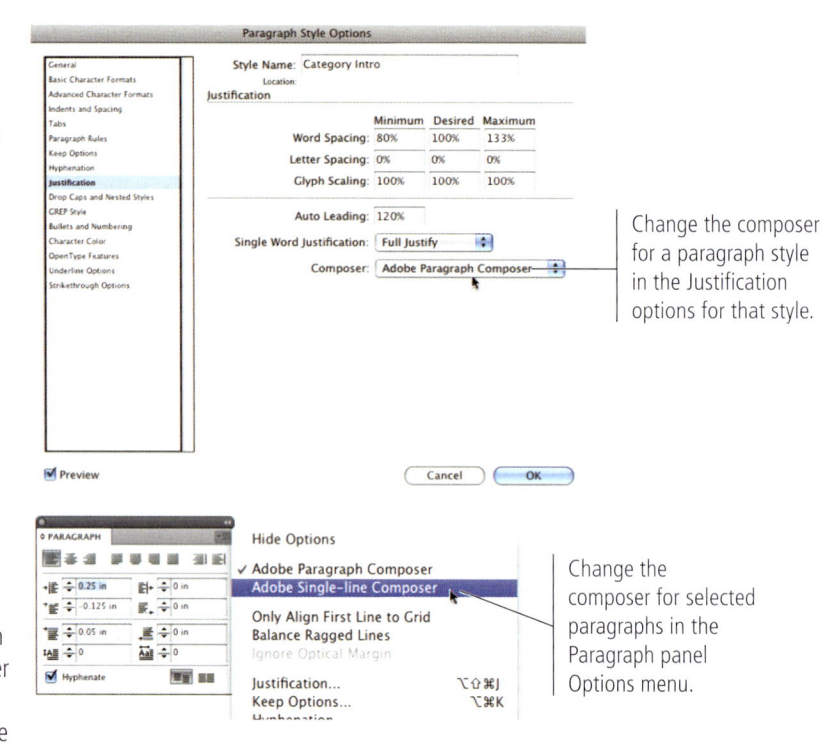

Change the composer for a paragraph style in the Justification options for that style.

The Adobe Paragraph Composer evaluates the entire paragraph as a unit; changing one line of a paragraph might alter other lines in the paragraph (including earlier lines) to create what the software defines as the "best" overall paragraph composition. For example, adding a manual line break on Line 6 to eliminate a hyphen might also cause Lines 2 through 5 to reflow if InDesign determines the shift will create a better overall paragraph. (Although primarily a matter of personal preference, Adobe Paragraph Composer can be annoying for anyone who wants tight or exact control over the text in a layout.)

Change the composer for selected paragraphs in the Paragraph panel Options menu.

The Adobe Single-line Composer is a better choice if you prefer to control your own text flow. Using Single-line Composer, adding a manual line break on Line 6 (for example) will not affect preceding lines in the paragraph.

Project 5: Realtor Collateral Booklet

Rather than simply changing the style definitions for text in the colored boxes, you are going to experiment with different options within the layout. When you're satisfied with the results, you're going to use local formatting to redefine the applied styles.

1. **With `booklet_stage2.indd` open, navigate to the green box on Page 5.**

2. **Select the entire first paragraph in the green box (through the buyer's eyes).**

3. **Using the Swatches panel, change the text color to 10% of the dark green swatch.**

4. **Move the insertion point to the end of the paragraph and review the results.**

   The light tint of the green swatch makes the text far more readable. However, in the next exercise you are going to change the box color to match the image on the left-facing page of the spread. Rather than use a light tint of the green swatch — which won't match the end result — you should use the Paper swatch to knock out the text from the background color.

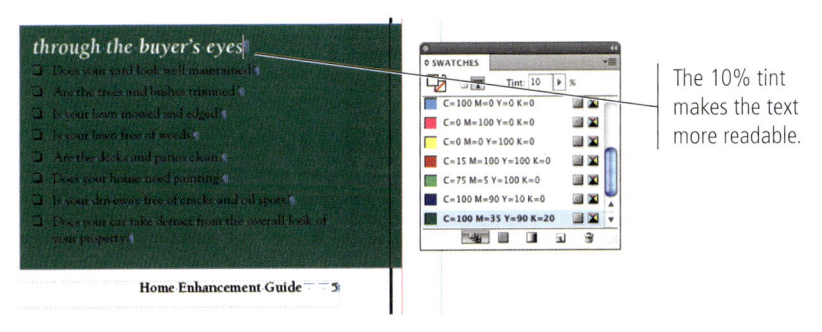

   The 10% tint makes the text more readable.

5. **Select the paragraph again and change the text color to Paper, then move the insertion point to any location within the reformatted heading.**

6. **Open the Paragraph Styles panel Options menu and choose Redefine Style.**

   This option makes it easy to experiment with formatting within the context of the layout, and then change a style definition to match what you created with local formatting.

   The insertion point should be anywhere within this paragraph.

   The Paper color is not part of the Box head style, so a plus sign indicates local formatting overrides.

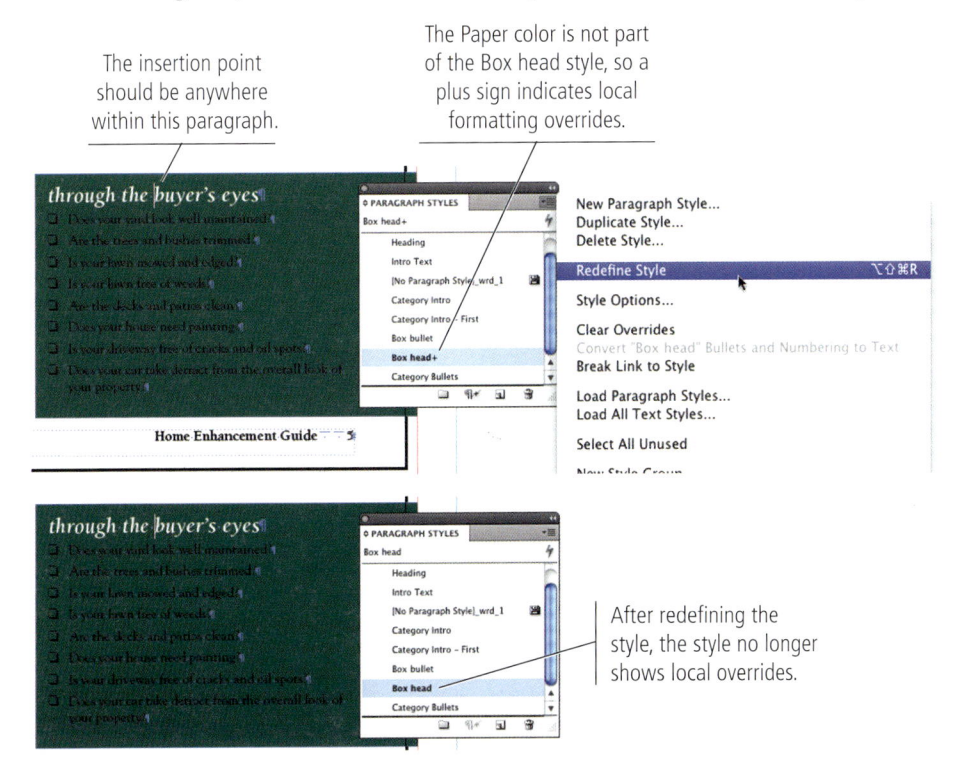

   After redefining the style, the style no longer shows local overrides.

Project 5: Realtor Collateral Booklet 307

7. **Select one of the bulleted paragraphs (below the heading) and change the text color to Paper.**

   By default, changing the color of text in the paragraph also changes the color of the applied bullet.

8. **With the same paragraph selected, open the Paragraph Styles panel Options menu and choose Redefine Style.**

   Because more than one Box Bullet paragraph appears on this page, you can see how redefining the style based on local formatting affects all text where that style is applied.

   Redefining the style changes all text formatted with that style.

9. **With the same paragraph selected, change the font to ATC Oak Normal, then redefine the Box bullet style to match the local formatting override.**

   White text on a colored background is called **knockout text**. As you learned in an earlier project, colors are reproduced with overlapping dots of four primary ink colors. Anything "white" is actually removed from the colored areas because you typically don't print white ink.

   Knocking out small text — especially text set in a serif font, such as this 9.5-pt ATC Pine Normal text — can cause problems in the output process. To help minimize potential output problems on press, you are changing the formatting for the small knockout text to a sans-serif font.

   The sans-serif font will help to minimize potential problems when the booklet is output on a commercial printing press.

   Changing the font of the selected paragraph does not affect the bullet character because that character is defined only in the Bullets and Numbering options of the style. It is technically not a character in the paragraph.

10. **Save the file and continue to the next exercise.**

308   Project 5: Realtor Collateral Booklet

Finalize the File

For all intents and purposes the booklet text is finished. The final task is to place the images. Because you placed the graphics frame on the master page layout, you can simply place most of these images into the existing frames without any additional intervention.

1. With `booklet_stage2.indd` open, navigate to Page 2 of the layout and choose File>Place.

2. Navigate to the file `front.tif` (in the RF_InDesign>Realtors folder) and turn off the Show Import Options and Replace Selected Item options.

3. Click Open to load the image into the cursor, and then click inside the graphics frame on Page 2 to place the image.

   Note:

   As with placing text into the master text frame, you don't have to override the master page to place the image into the graphics frame. InDesign assumes that clicking inside an existing frame — even one from the master page — means you want to place the image inside that frame.

4. Place the remaining images on the left page of each layout spread:

Page 4	doorway_outside.tif
Page 6	doorway_inside.tif
Page 8	candles.tif
Page 10	flowers.tif
Page 12	bathroom.tif
Page 14	storage.tif

5. Navigate to Page 3 of the layout. Using the Selection tool, select and delete the green-filled text frame.

6. **Place the file `squares.tif` onto Page 3 and position the file as shown in the following image.**

7. **Deselect the squares.tif image.**

   The page number is obscured by the white area of the placed image.

8. **Command/Control-Shift-click the text frame at the bottom of the page.**

   Command/Control-Shift-clicking a master page object allows you to detach a single master page item without detaching the entire page from the master page.

   Command/Control-Shift-clicking detaches the object from the master layout.

9. **With the text frame selected, choose Object>Arrange>Bring to Front. Delete the words "Home Enhancement Guide" from the text frame, leaving only the page number.**

10. **Navigate to the Page 4–5 spread. Use the Selection tool to select the green text frame on the right-facing page.**

11. **Make sure the Fill Color icon is active in the Tools panel. Use the Eyedropper tool to click a dark green area in the image on the left side of the spread.**

   In addition to copying text formatting, the Eyedropper tool can be used to pull or **sample** colors from a placed image. Using the same colors from one page to the next makes it easier to unify different elements of the design.

   Eyedropper tool

   The Fill Color icon is active.

   We sampled this color from the image.

   Clicking with the Eyedropper tool changes the active attribute of the selected object.

12. **Repeat the process from Steps 10–11 to change the box color on each spread of the layout.**

13. **Choose Type>Text Variables>Define. Select File Status in the list and click Edit. In the Text field, change Stage 2 to** Final**. Click OK, then click Done to return to the document.**

14. **Save the file as** `booklet_final.indd`**, and then continue to the next stage of the project.**

Project 5: Realtor Collateral Booklet   311

Stage 3 Outputting Variations of Files

The final stage of this project requires three versions of output:

- A desktop proof for your client, showing the spreads as they will appear in the final bound booklet
- A low-resolution PDF file that prospective clients can download from the organization's Web site
- High-resolution, print-quality PDF files, including personalization information for specific agents

InDesign includes a number of tools that make it easy to create all three versions without destroying the integrity of the original layout file.

Note:

*A **reader's spread** is a set of two pages that appear next to each other in a printed document — Page 2 faces Page 3, and so on.*

*A **printer's spread** refers to the way pages align on a press sheet so, after a document is folded and cut, the reader's spreads will be in the correct locations.*

Create a Folding Dummy

When a page is printed, it is typically output on a sheet larger than the job's trim size. Multiple pages are often **imposed** (arranged) on a single press sheet, and the printed pieces are later cut from the press sheet and trimmed to their final size. In some cases, entirely different jobs can be **ganged** (combined) together to make the best use of available space on the press sheet.

Multi-page documents that use facing pages have special output requirements; understanding these requirements means you will also be able to see how your design might be affected by output processes after the file leaves your desk. When multiple-page books and booklets are produced, they are not printed as individual pages. Instead, they are printed in signatures of eight, sixteen, or more pages at a time. A **signature** consists of multiple pages of a document, all printed on the same press sheet, which is later folded and cut to the final trim size. Each signature is composed of two flats. (The term **flat** is a relic of the days when film was manually stripped together on a light table; it is still sometimes used to describe one side of one signature.)

Layouts are designed in reader's spreads, but arranged into printer's spreads on the printing plate. (**Imposition** refers to the arrangement of a document's pages on a printing plate to produce the final product.)

Note:

In printer's spreads, the sum of pairs of page numbers always totals the number of pages in the signature, plus 1. For example, in a 16-page signature, Page 4 faces Page 13, Page 16 faces Page 1, and so on.

If a saddle-stitched (stapled) book is made up of multiple signatures, the page numbers on printer's spreads equal the total number of pages in the publication, plus 1. For example, a saddle-stitched booklet is 32 pages, made up of two 16-page signatures. The page numbers on each printer's spread total 33: Page 16 faces Page 17, Page 22 faces Page 11, and so on.

1. **Fold a piece of paper in half lengthwise, and then in half lengthwise again.**

2. **While the paper is still folded, write the sequential page numbers 1 through 8 on the folded sections.**

3. **Unfold it and you will see the printer's spreads for an eight-page document.**

   The dummy unfolds to show how an eight-page signature is laid out. Page 8 and Page 1 create a single printer's spread.

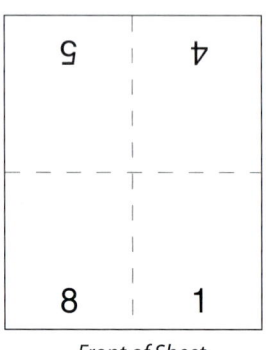

Front of Sheet   Back of Sheet

Project 5: Realtor Collateral Booklet

PRINT A BOOKLET PROOF

You probably don't want to (and really, you shouldn't have to) think about creating full impositions for a press. At times, however, you might want to print proofs in printer's spreads to show clients. You could work through a complicated manual process of rearranging pages, but the InDesign Print Booklet command is far easier — and it's non-destructive.

1. **With booklet_final.indd open, choose File>Print Booklet.**

   This dialog box shows only the output options related to printing printer's spreads. These options are set; you can't directly change the printer that will be used for output.

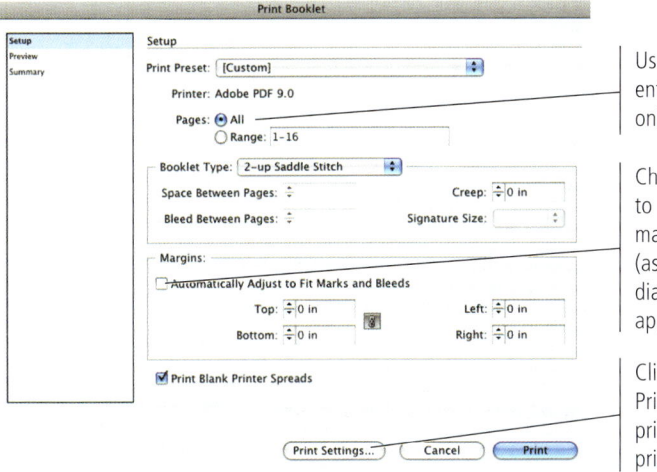

   Use these options to output the entire file as a booklet, or output only a specific range of pages.

   Check this box to allow InDesign to automatically calculate the margins to accommodate bleeds (as defined in the Document Setup dialog box) and printer's marks (as applied in the Print dialog box).

   Click this button to access the Print dialog box and change the printer-specific settings and define printer's marks.

2. **In the Setup pane of the dialog box, make sure 2-up Saddle Stitch is selected in the Booklet Type menu.**

   In the Booklet Type menu, you can choose what kind of imposition to create.

   - **2-up Saddle Stitch** creates two-page printer's spreads from the entire layout or selected page range. If the layout doesn't contain enough pages to create the necessary printer's spreads, InDesign automatically adds blank pages at the end of the layout.
   - **2-up Perfect Bound** creates two-page printer's spreads that fit within the specified signature size (4, 8, 12, 16, or 32 pages). If the number of layout pages to be imposed is not divisible by the selected signature size, InDesign adds blank pages as needed at the end of the finished document.
   - **Consecutive** creates a two-, three-, or four-page imposition appropriate for a foldout brochure.

   You can also define settings to adjust for imposition issues related to printer's spreads versus reader's spreads.

   - **Space Between Pages** defines the gap between pages in the printer's spread. This option is available for all but saddle-stitched booklet types.
   - **Bleed Between Pages** defines the amount that page elements can bleed into the space between pages in a printer's spread (from 0 to half the defined space between the pages) for perfect-bound impositions.
   - **Creep** defines the amount of space necessary to accommodate paper thickness and folding on each signature.
   - **Signature Size** defines the number of pages in each signature for perfect-bound impositions.
   - **Print Blank Printer Spreads** determines whether any blank pages added to a signature will be printed.

3. **Click the Print Settings button.**

4. **In the Print dialog box, choose the printer and PPD you will use to output the booklet.**

5. **In the Setup options, choose Letter in the Paper Size menu and choose landscape orientation.**

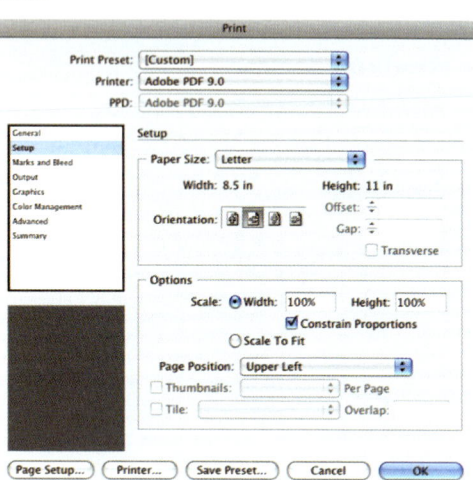

Note:

If you have a printer with tabloid-paper capability, you could output the file with marks and bleeds, and then trim the proof to size. Doing so would eliminate any issue with the margins required by some desktop printers, which would prevent the pages from printing the outer edges of the layout.

Understanding Imposition

If you fold a piece of paper in half twice, number the pages, and then unfold the paper, you will see the basic imposition for an eight-page signature.

If you look at your folded piece of paper, you can see that the tops of all the pages are folded together. If elements bleed to the top of a page, given the inaccuracy of folding machines (±0.03125″), that ink would appear on the edge of the page it abutted on the signature (for example, see Pages 12 and 13 in the following illustration).

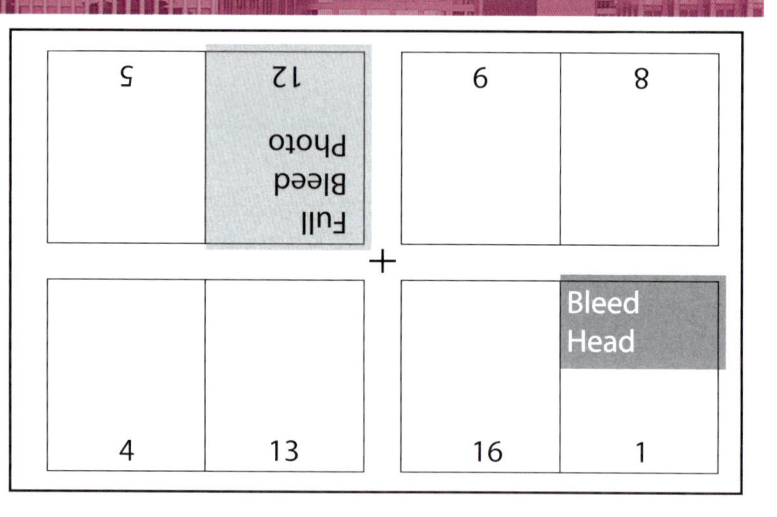

The pages of a signature must be cut apart at the top, which requires at least 1/8″ at the top of the page for the trim. The outside edge of half the pages also must be cut apart (this is called a **face trim**) so the pages of the finished piece can be turned. This face trim also requires 1/8″ around the page edge. That trim would shorten an 8.5 × 11″ book to 8.375 × 10.875″. This shorter size might be fine, but it could also ruin a design and layout. There's a better solution.

On the press-sheet layout, space is added between the tops of the printer's spreads to allow room for bleed and cutting apart the pages. This separation is probably all that's required for a 16-page saddle-stitched booklet printed on a 70# text-weight paper. If you use a heavier paper (for example, a 100# coated sheet for an annual report), or if you have more than one 16-page signature, you need to allow room for **creep**, which is the progressive extension of interior pages of the folded signature beyond the trim edge of the outside pages.

If you have questions about folds or imposition, you should always call your service provider. Somebody there will be able to advise you on the best course to take. In most cases, these issues will be handled entirely by the service provider, often using software specifically designed for the prepress workflow. If you try to do too much, you might cause them extra work (and yourself extra expense).

6. In the Marks and Bleed options, uncheck the All Printer's Marks and Use Document Bleed Settings options, and change all four Bleed values to 0".

7. Click OK to return to the Print Booklet dialog box.

8. In the Print Booklet dialog box, uncheck the Automatically Adjust to Fit Marks and Bleeds option. With the Chain icon checked, change all four Margin fields to 0".

    You're only printing a client proof on letter-size paper, so you do not need bleeds or printer's marks.

9. Click Preview in the list of options.

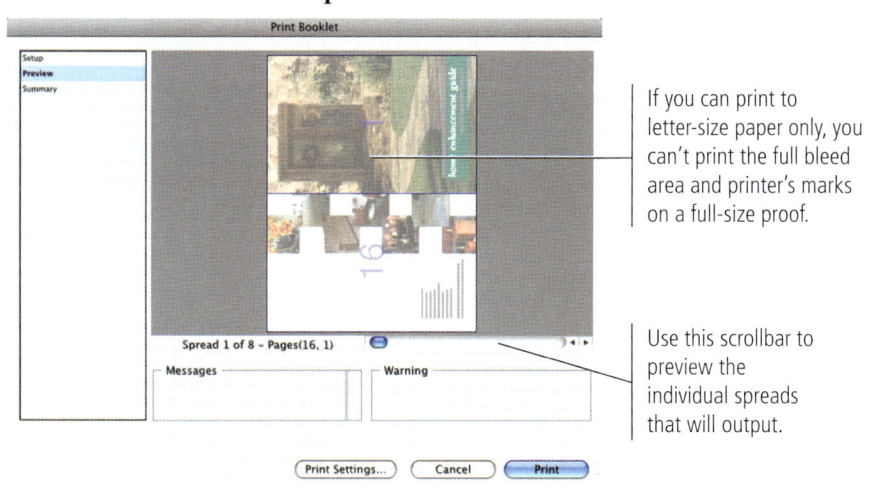

    If you can print to letter-size paper only, you can't print the full bleed area and printer's marks on a full-size proof.

    Use this scrollbar to preview the individual spreads that will output.

10. Click Print.

11. When the file is finished spooling to the printer, continue to the next exercise.

CREATE A PDF WITH PAGE TRANSITIONS

In addition to the printed job, your client requested a low-resolution PDF file that can be posted on the organization's Web site. To add interest to the digital version, you are going to add interactive page transitions that affect the way new pages appear when users navigate through the PDF file.

1. **With booklet_final.indd open, open the Page Transitions panel (Window>Interactive>Page Transitions).**

2. **In the Pages panel, double-click the Page 2-3 spread numbers (below the page icons) to select the entire spread.**

   Remember, there can be a difference between the active and selected pages. Double-clicking the targeted page or spread ensures that the spread you want is the one selected.

3. **Open the Page Transitions panel Options menu and select Choose.**

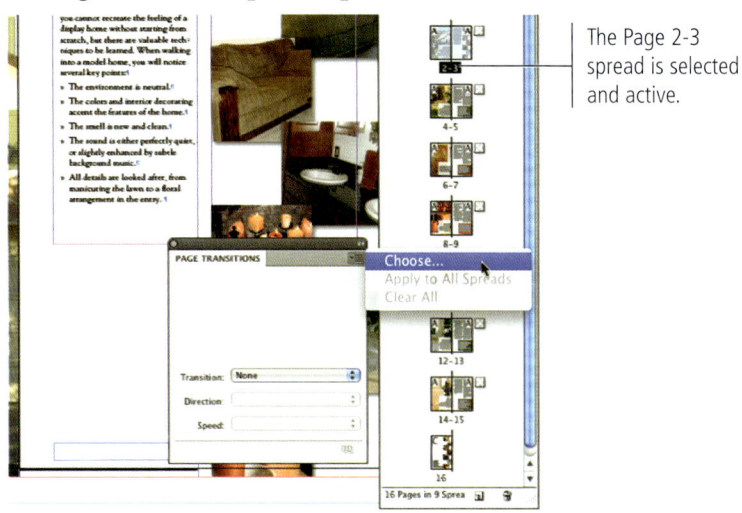

   The Page 2-3 spread is selected and active.

4. **In the resulting Page Transitions dialog box, roll your mouse cursor over the icons to preview the general effect of each.**

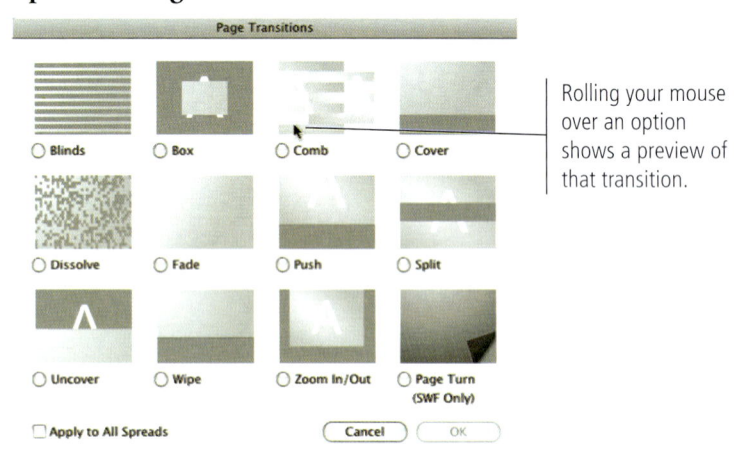

   Rolling your mouse over an option shows a preview of that transition.

316 Project 5: Realtor Collateral Booklet

5. **Make sure the Apply to All Spreads option is unchecked, then activate the Comb radio button and click OK.**

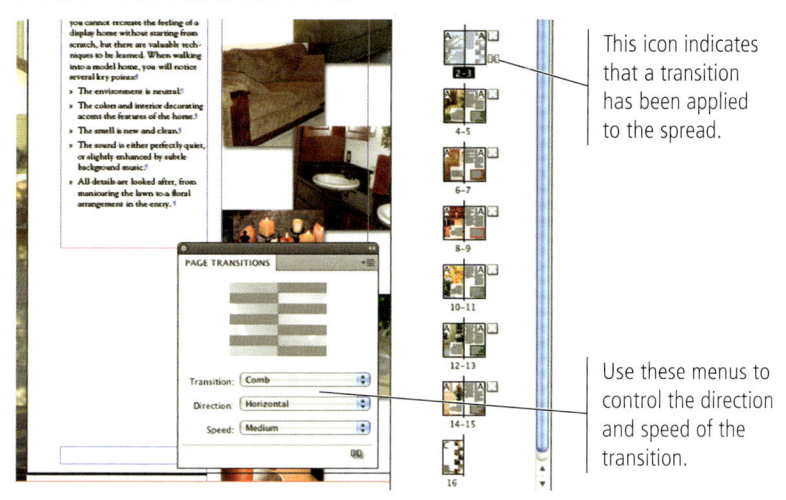

   This icon indicates that a transition has been applied to the spread.

   Use these menus to control the direction and speed of the transition.

6. **Double-click the Page 4-5 spread numbers in the Pages panel. In the Page Transitions panel, choose Wipe in the Transition menu.**

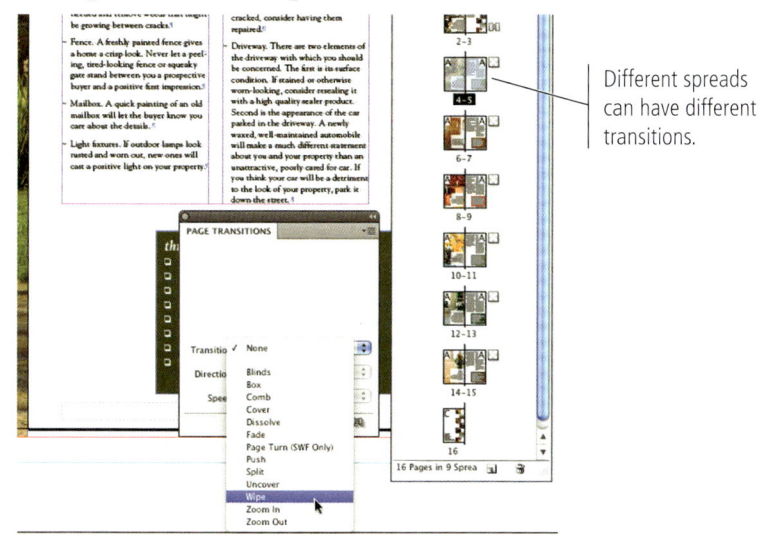

   Different spreads can have different transitions.

7. **With the Page 4-5 spread selected, click the Apply to All Spreads button at the bottom of the Page Transitions panel.**

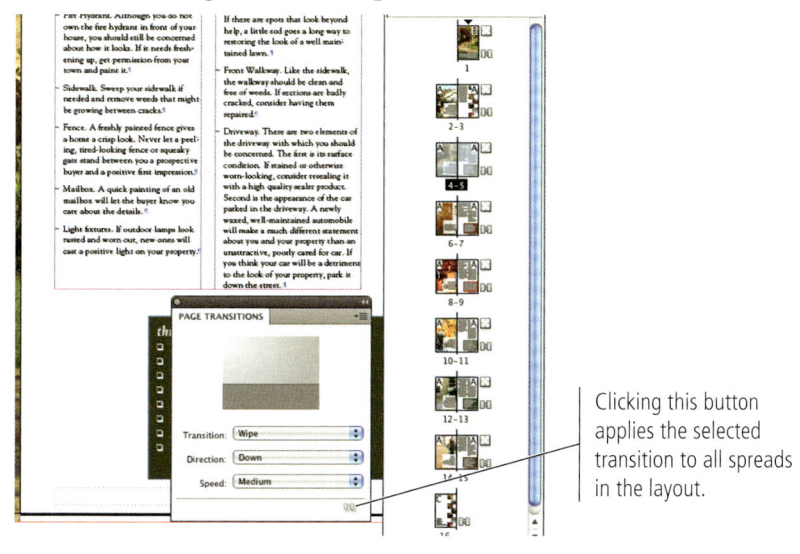

   Clicking this button applies the selected transition to all spreads in the layout.

Project 5: Realtor Collateral Booklet 317

8. **Choose File>Export. Make sure Adobe PDF is selected in the Format menu and click Save.**

9. **In the Export Adobe PDF dialog box, choose Smallest File Size in the Preset menu.**

10. **In the Pages area, make sure the All radio button is selected, and then check the Spreads option.**

    This file is being created for online distribution. Because the file was designed as spreads, it makes sense to export each spread as a single page in the resulting PDF file.

11. **In the Options area, check the View PDF after Exporting option.**

    When the file is created, it will automatically open in Adobe Acrobat (Reader or Pro, depending on which is available on your computer).

12. **In the Include area, check the Interactive Elements option.**

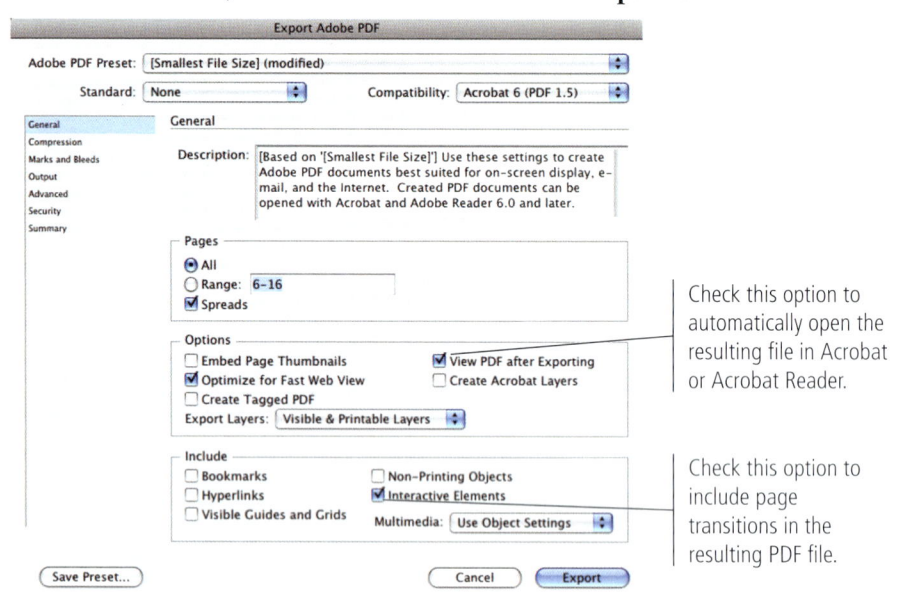

    Check this option to automatically open the resulting file in Acrobat or Acrobat Reader.

    Check this option to include page transitions in the resulting PDF file.

13. **Click Export to create the PDF file.**

14. **When the PDF file opens in Acrobat, press Command/Control-L to display the file in Full-Screen mode.**

Project 5: Realtor Collateral Booklet

15. **Press the Page Down key to navigate through the pages of the layout and watch the interactive page transitions.**

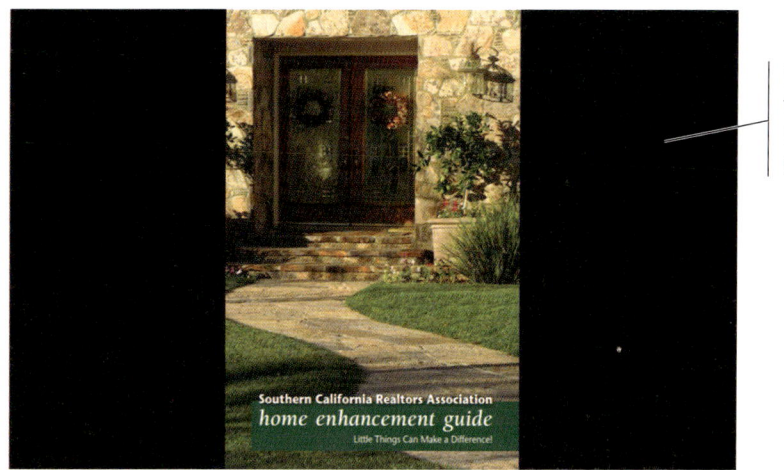

   You have to view the file in Full-Screen mode to see the page transitions.

16. **Press the Escape key to exit Full-Screen mode, close the PDF file, and return to InDesign.**

17. **Continue to the next exercise.**

CREATE VARIATIONS WITH CONDITIONAL TEXT

In this exercise, you create multiple "personalized" versions of the job, which can be output at a local quick-print shop. These versions will include a "Personalized By" message with the name and phone number of a specific realtor who is paying for the extra service. To create these variations, you will use conditional text rather than saving a separate layout file for each agent.

1. **With booklet_final.indd open, navigate to Page 16.**

2. **Create a new text frame in the top-left section of the page. In the new frame, type:**

   Personalized for you by:
   Susan Milton, Agent
   Barrymore Associates
   818-555-4386

3. **Format the text as 14-pt ATC Pine Normal, and apply 0.1" space after the first paragraph.**

4. **Open the Conditional Text panel (Window>Type & Tables>Conditional Text).**

Project 5: Realtor Collateral Booklet 319

5. **Click the New Condition button at the bottom of the panel. In the New Condition dialog box, type** Personalization **in the Name field and click OK.**

   New Condition button

   Use this menu to change the style of indicators from an underline to a highlight.

   Use this menu to change the conditional indicator from the default Wavy style to the Solid or Dashed style.

   Use this menu to change the color of indicators for the specific condition.

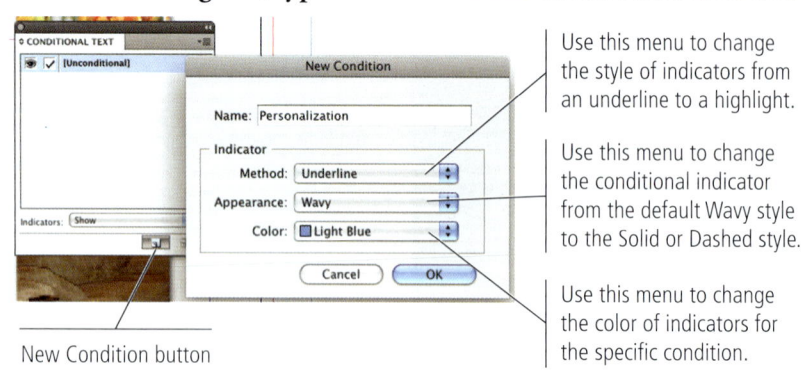

6. **Highlight the first paragraph in the frame. In the Conditional Text panel, click the empty space to the right of the Visibility icon for the Personalization condition.**

   Applying a condition is as simple as selecting the targeted text and checking the appropriate condition in the panel.

   In this case, you created the first line as a condition so you can turn it off if you need to output a non-personalized version of the file.

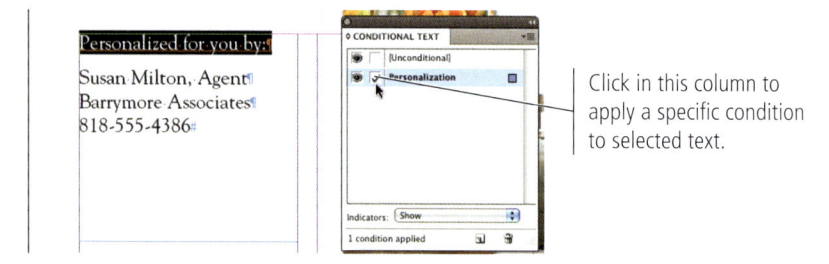

   Click in this column to apply a specific condition to selected text.

7. **Click the New Condition button at the bottom of the Conditional Text panel. In the New Condition dialog box, type** Milton **in the Name field and click OK.**

8. **In the layout, highlight the second through fourth lines in the text frame. Using the Conditional Text panel, apply the Milton condition to the selected text.**

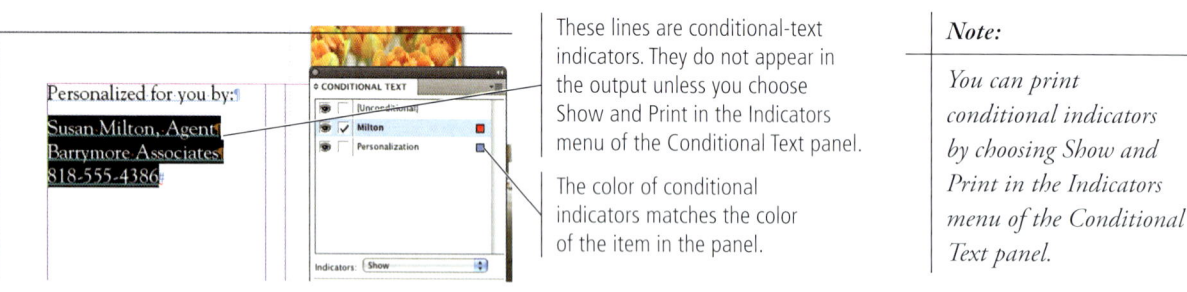

   These lines are conditional-text indicators. They do not appear in the output unless you choose Show and Print in the Indicators menu of the Conditional Text panel.

   The color of conditional indicators matches the color of the item in the panel.

   Note:

   You can print conditional indicators by choosing Show and Print in the Indicators menu of the Conditional Text panel.

9. **In the Conditional Text panel, click the Visibility icon for the Milton condition.**

   Click in this column to show or hide specific conditions.

   This marker identifies hidden conditional text.

Project 5: Realtor Collateral Booklet

10. **Place the insertion point in the empty paragraph where the name and address information appeared (before you hid it). Type:**

   John Dante, Agent
   Wingate Realty
   661-555-7332

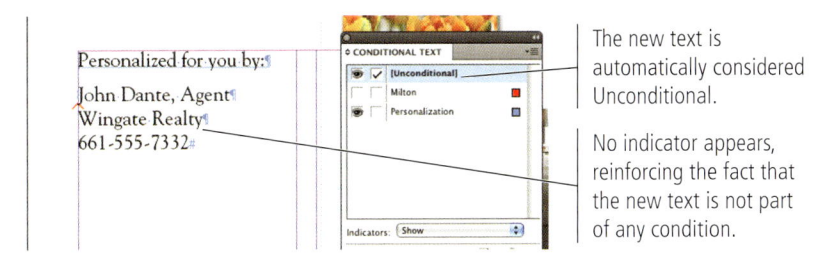

   The new text is automatically considered Unconditional.

   No indicator appears, reinforcing the fact that the new text is not part of any condition.

11. **Click the New Condition button at the bottom of the panel. In the New Condition dialog box, type Dante in the Name field and click OK.**

12. **In the layout, highlight the three lines of new contact information. Using the Conditional Text panel, apply the Dante condition.**

13. **Export the file to PDF, named booklet_dante.pdf, using the High Quality Print preset. Turn off the View PDF after Exporting option, turn on all printer's marks, and use the document bleed settings to export the file.**

   When you have multiple conditions in a file, only the visible conditions will be included in the output. By default, the conditional indicators do not appear on the output.

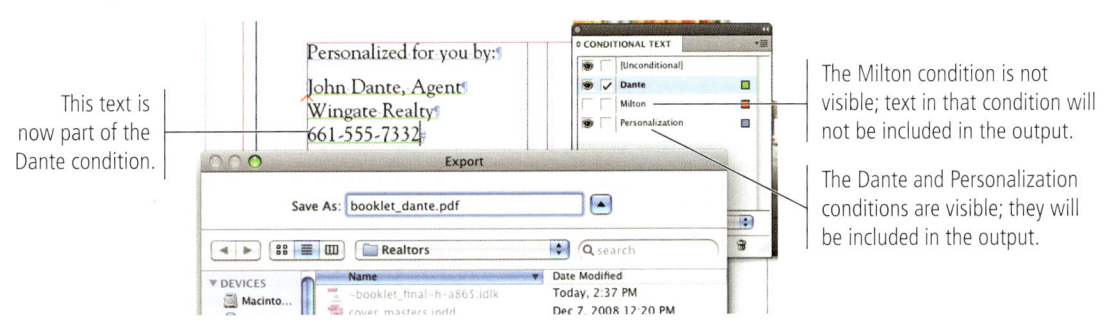

   This text is now part of the Dante condition.

   The Milton condition is not visible; text in that condition will not be included in the output.

   The Dante and Personalization conditions are visible; they will be included in the output.

14. **In the Conditional Text panel, click the Visibility column for the Milton condition to show that condition, and then click the Visibility icon for the Dante condition to hide that condition.**

15. **Export the file to PDF, named booklet_milton.pdf, using the same options as in Step 13.**

   The Dante condition is not visible and will not be included in the output.

   The Milton condition is visible and will be included in the output.

16. **Save the file as booklet_variations.indd and close it.**

Project 5: Realtor Collateral Booklet

Project Review

fill in the blank

1. A(n) _____ can be used to place information such as creation/modification date, file name, or custom text.

2. When _____ is active, InDesign automatically adds pages to accommodate an entire story that is placed in a master text frame.

3. A local formatting override is indicated by _____ next to the style name in the Paragraph Styles panel.

4. A negative first-line indent is called a(n) _____.

5. A(n) _____ is a single line of a paragraph at the end of a column.

6. A(n) _____ is a single line of a paragraph at the top of a column, or a very short (one-word) last line of paragraph.

7. _____ in the Paragraph Style Options dialog box can used to make sure headings stay with following paragraphs.

8. _____ fonts can store more than 65,000 glyphs (characters) in a single font file; the same font file works on both Macintosh and Windows.

9. The _____ provides visual access to individual characters in a font.

10. _____ is the process of arranging pages on a press sheet so, when folded and trimmed, the pages of a job appear in the correct order.

short answer

1. Briefly explain the difference between reader's spreads and printer's spreads.

2. Briefly explain the advantages and disadvantages of nesting text-formatting styles.

3. Briefly explain two scenarios in which conditional text would be useful.

Portfolio Builder Project

Use what you learned in this project to complete the following freeform exercise.
Carefully read the art director and client comments, then create your own design to meet the needs of the project.
Use the space below to sketch ideas; when finished, write a brief explanation of your reasoning behind your final design.

art director comments

Your clients are very happy with the finished Home Enhancement Guide. They would like you to create another collateral booklet that they can provide to prospective home buyers, providing contact information for agents in specific geographic areas.

To complete this project, you should:

❏ Create a 16-page booklet using the same document size as the Home Enhancement Guide.

❏ Design a facing-page layout that is aesthetically pleasing, which clearly presents the necessary information.

❏ Find or create supportive images for each spread that match the overall theme of the project.

client comments

This booklet will list each member agent by general location, including their name and photo, contact information, and their types of property specialties.

We sent you a text file with a short blurb for the inside front page, as well as the realtor information from our database (in the RF_Builders>Realtors folder). We don't have the agents' photos yet; we'll forward them as soon as possible. Just make sure you leave space for them in the layout.

For the covers, use the same layout as the Home Enhancement Guide. On the front cover, use a different picture and change the title to "Buyer's Resource Guide". On the back, replace the checkerboard image with pictures you use in this booklet.

We want the first spread to include only the introductory blurb and some kind of graphics — maybe a montage of different home styles.

One last thing: For now, leave the center spread open. We might want to add something different there, but we haven't figured out what yet.

project justification

_____
_____
_____
_____
_____
_____
_____
_____
_____
_____
_____
_____
_____
_____
_____
_____

Project Summary

Controlling the flow of text in a document — especially for documents with more than one or two pages — is just as important as controlling the appearance of the different type elements. InDesign provides powerful tools that let you control virtually every aspect of document design, from the exact position of individual paragraphs to entire blocks of text to automatic page numbers based on the location of special characters in the layout.

Changing the master page settings for this booklet allowed you to automatically flow a single story across multiple pages. Using the Keep options for the applied styles, you were able to position each element in the appropriate frame on the appropriate spread, which significantly reduced the amount of manual evaluation and adjustment that would have been required without these features.

Using effective master pages also allowed you to place repeating elements to appear on every spread in the layout. Combining that functionality with special characters and variable text elements, you were also able to eliminate a number of unnecessarily repetitive tasks, such as individually applying the gradient feather effect to each picture and manually numbering the pages.

- Save regular pages as master pages
- Load master pages from one file to another
- Use conditional text to create personalized versions
- Control margins and text frames on master pages
- Manage automatic text flow in a facing-page layout
- Define bulleted lists to create visual interest
- Control line, paragraph, and frame breaks
- Create and print imposed printer's spreads
- Use special characters and text variables

project 6

Versioned Brochure

Your client produces a monthly brochure that is mailed to consumers throughout the eastern United States and Canada. The old brochure listed two prices for each product: one in U.S. dollars and one in Canadian dollars. The client now wants to produce two separate versions of the piece — one version with U.S. prices and one with Canadian prices.

This project incorporates the following skills:

❏ Managing color in placed images and layout files

❏ Controlling import options for a variety of image file types

❏ Controlling the language and checking the spelling in layout text

❏ Searching and replacing text and special characters

❏ Searching and changing object attributes

❏ Using layers to create multiple versions of a file

❏ Outputting a color-managed PDF file

Project Meeting

client comments

We print a new brochure every month with a few featured products and sale information. The brochures drive a lot of traffic to our Web store, where we close the sales without needing to maintain a brick-and-mortar storefront.

Every issue of the brochure is printed in five-color — CMYK plus one of the three spot colors in our logo. To ensure brand recognition, we use the same layout in every version, but we cycle through the different spot colors; this issue should use the blue spot color.

We do a lot of business in Canada. We used to print a single version of the brochure with both U.S. and Canadian prices, but that caused a lot of confusion from people who didn't understand why they had to "pay more" for the same product. That's why we decided to print two versions this year; now customers will see only the prices that apply to their country.

After two years, we're starting to broaden our market. Our original name was VermontKids, but we changed it to ToyTrends so the company didn't seem so regional. We included our new logo with the files for this issue.

art director comments

We build each issue of the brochure from a standard template to maintain the brand consistency the client prefers; since they just changed their company logo, you should replace the logo in the template and save a new template so you won't have to make the same changes next month.

The client provided all pieces for the job — a text file with this issue's copy, as well as all product images. As the production artist, your job is to assemble the pieces, check the text and images for errors or technical problems, and create the final printable files. You are ultimately creating two different files: one for U.S. distribution and one for Canada.

project objectives

To complete this project, you will:

❏ Define file color settings

❏ Replace an existing image and save a new template

❏ Place and control a variety of file types, including native Illustrator, native Photoshop, EPS, TIFF, PDF, JPEG, and native InDesign layouts

❏ Place multiple images at one time

❏ Check and correct spelling in the document and linked files

❏ Search and replace basic text and special characters, text formatting, and object attributes

❏ Control paragraph composition options

❏ Create and manage multiple layers

❏ Proof colors and separations on-screen

❏ Export a color-managed PDF file

Stage 1 Controlling Color for Output

You can't accurately reproduce color without a basic understanding of color theory, so we present a very basic introduction to color theory in the following pages. We highly recommend you read this information. Be aware that there are entire, weighty books written about color science; we're providing the condensed version of what you absolutely must know to work effectively with color.

While it's true that color management science can be extremely complex and beyond the needs of most graphic designers, applying color management in InDesign is more intimidating than difficult. We believe this foundational knowledge of color management will make you a more effective and practically grounded designer.

Additive vs. Subtractive Color Models

The most important thing to remember about color theory is that color is light, and light is color. You can easily prove this by walking through your house at midnight; you will notice that what little you can see appears as dark shadows. Without light, you can't see — and without light, there is no color.

The additive color model (RGB) is based on the idea that all colors can be reproduced by combining pure red, green, and blue light in varying intensities. These three colors are considered the additive primaries. Combining any two additive primaries at full strength produces one of the additive secondaries — red and blue light combine to produce magenta, red and green combine to produce yellow, and blue and green combine to produce cyan. Although usually considered a "color," black is the absence of light (and, therefore, of color). White is the sum of all colors, produced when all three additive primaries are combined at full strength.

Printing pigmented inks on a substrate is a very different method of reproducing color. Reproducing color on paper requires subtractive color theory, which is essentially the inverse of additive color theory. Instead of adding red, green, and blue light to create the range of colors, subtractive color begins with a white surface that reflects red, green, and blue light at equal and full strength. To reflect (reproduce) a specific color, you add pigments that subtract or absorb only certain wavelengths from the white light. To reflect only red, for example, the surface must subtract (or absorb) the green and blue light.

Remember that the additive primaries (red, green, and blue) combine to create the additive secondaries (cyan, magenta, and yellow). Those additive secondaries are also called the subtractive primaries because each subtracts one-third of the light spectrum and reflects the other two thirds:

- Cyan absorbs red light, reflecting only blue and green light.
- Magenta absorbs green light, reflecting only red and blue light.
- Yellow absorbs blue light, reflecting only red and green light.

A combination of two subtractive primaries, then, absorbs two-thirds of the light spectrum and reflects only one-third. As an example, a combination of yellow and magenta absorbs both blue and green light, reflecting only red.

Note:

Additive color theory is practically applied when a reproduction method uses light to reproduce color. A television screen or computer monitor is black when turned off. When the power is turned on, light in the monitor illuminates at different intensities to create the range of colors you see.

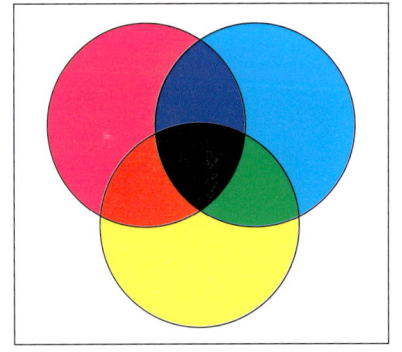

Subtractive color model

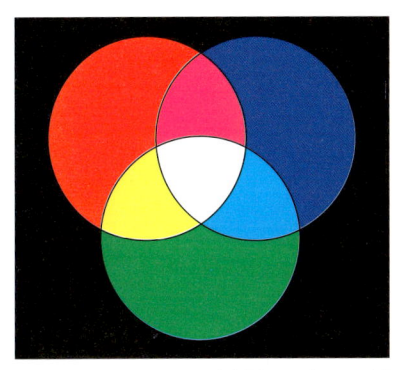

Additive color model

Project 6: Versioned Brochure   327

Color printing is a practical application of subtractive color theory. The pigments in the cyan, magenta, yellow, and black inks are combined to absorb different wavelengths of light. To create the appearance of red, the green and blue light must be subtracted or absorbed, thus reflecting only red. Magenta absorbs green light, and yellow absorbs blue light; combining magenta and yellow inks on white paper reflects only the red light. By combining different amounts of the subtractive primaries, it's possible to produce a large range (or gamut) of colors.

Because white is a combination of all colors, white paper should theoretically reflect equal percentages of all light wavelengths. However, different papers absorb or reflect varying percentages of some wavelengths, thus defining the paper's apparent color. The paper's color affects the appearance of ink color printed on that paper.

Understanding Gamut

Different color models have different ranges or **gamuts** of possible colors. A normal human visual system is capable of distinguishing approximately 16.7 million different colors. Color reproduction systems, however, are far more limited. The RGB model has the largest gamut of the output models. The CMYK gamut is far more limited; many of the brightest and most saturated colors that can be reproduced using light cannot be reproduced using pigmented inks.

This difference in gamut is one of the biggest problems graphic designers face when working with color images. Digital image-capture devices (including scanners and digital cameras) work in the RGB space, which, with its larger gamut, can more closely mirror the range of colors in the original scene. Printing, however, requires images to be first converted or separated into the CMYK color space.

The usual goal in color reproduction is to achieve a color appearance equivalent to the original. Depending on the images, it is likely that at least some colors in the RGB model cannot be reproduced in the more limited gamut of the CMYK color model. These out-of-gamut colors pose a challenge to faithfully reproducing the original image. If the conversion from RGB to CMYK is not carefully controlled, color shift can result in drastic differences between the original and the printed images.

Color Management in Brief

Color management is intended to preserve color predictability and consistency as a file is moved from one color mode to another throughout the reproduction process. Color management can also eliminate ambiguity when a color is only specified by some numbers. For example, you might create a royal purple in the Color Picker; but without color management, that same set of RGB numbers might look more lilac (or even gray) when converted to CMYK for printing. A well-tuned color management system can translate the numbers that define a color in one space to numbers that can better represent that same color in another space.

It's important to have realistic expectations of color management, and to realize that color management isn't a replacement for a thorough understanding of the color-reproduction process. Even at its best, color management can't fix bad scans or

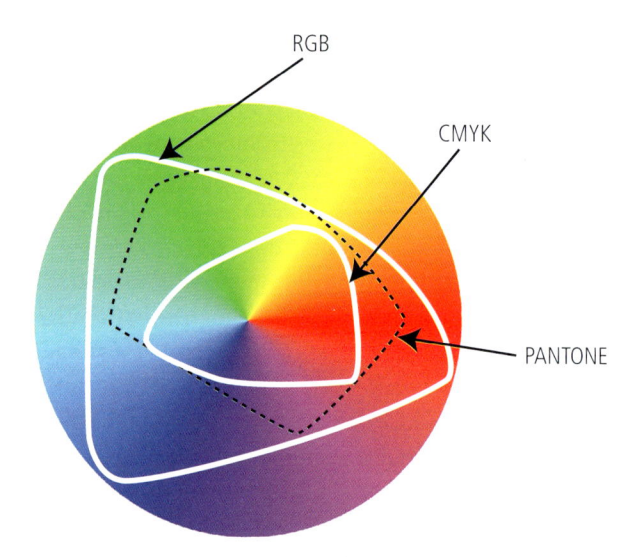

Note:

Color shift can also result when converting from one CMYK profile to another (e.g., a sheetfed press profile to a web press profile), or (though less likely) from one version of RGB to another. Whatever models are being used, color management gives you better control over the conversion process.

bad photos — all it can do is provide consistency and predictability to a process that otherwise rarely has either.

Color management relies on color profiles, which are simply data sets that define the reproduction characteristics of a specific device. A profile is essentially a recipe that contains the ingredients for reproducing a specific color in a given color space. The color recipes in profiles are known as look-up tables (LUTs), which are essentially cross-reference systems for finding matching color values in different color spaces.

Source profiles are the profiles of the devices (scanners, digital cameras, etc.) used to capture an image. Destination profiles are the profiles of output devices. LAB (or L*a*b*, or CIELAB) is a device-independent, theoretical color space that represents the entire visible spectrum. The color management engine uses LAB as an intermediate space to translate colors from one device-dependent space to another.

The mechanics of color-managed conversions are quite simple. Regardless of the specific input and output spaces in question, the same basic process is followed for every pixel in the image:

1. The color-management engine looks up the color values of a pixel in the input-space profile to find a matching set of LAB values.

2. The color-management engine looks up the LAB values in the output-space profile to find the matching set of color values that will display the color of that pixel as accurately as possible in the output space.

Note:

Color profiles are sometimes called "ICC profiles," named after the International Color Consortium (ICC), which developed the standard for creating color profiles.

Note:

Most professional-level devices come with profiles you can install when you install the hardware; a number of generic and industry-specific destination profiles are also built into InDesign.

Color Management in Theory and Practice

INDESIGN FOUNDATIONS

RGB and CMYK are very different entities. The two color models have distinct capabilities, advantages, and limitations. There is no way to exactly reproduce RGB color using the CMYK gamut because many of the colors in the RGB gamut are simply too bright or too saturated. Rather than claiming to produce an exact (impossible) match from your monitor to a printed page, the true goal of color management is to produce the best possible representation of the color using the gamut of the chosen output device.

A theoretically ideal color-managed workflow looks like this:

- Image-capture devices (scanners and digital cameras) are profiled to create a look-up table that defines the device's color-capturing characteristics.
- Images are acquired using a profiled device. The profile of the capturing device is tagged to every image captured.
- You define a destination (CMYK) profile for the calibrated output device that will be used for your final job.
- InDesign translates the document and embedded image profiles to the defined destination profiles.

Two of the "ideal workflow" steps mention a form of the word calibrate, which means to check and correct the device's characteristics. Calibration is an essential element in a color-managed workflow; it is fundamentally important to consistent and predictable output.

Taking this definition a step further, you cannot check or correct the color characteristics of a device without having something to compare the device against. To calibrate a device, a known target — usually a sequence of distinct and varying color patches — is reproduced using the device. The color values of the reproduction are measured and compared to the values of the known target. Precise calibration requires adjusting the device until the reproduction matches the original.

As long as your devices are accurately calibrated to the same target values, the color acquired by your RGB scanner will match the colors displayed on your RGB monitor and the colors printed by your CMYK desktop printer. Of course, most devices (especially consumer-level desktop devices, which are gaining a larger market share in the commercial graphics world) are not accurately calibrated, and very few are calibrated to the same set of known target values.

Keeping in mind these ideals and realities, the true goals of color management are to:

- Compensate for color variations in the different devices
- Accurately translate one color space to another
- Compensate for limitations in the output process
- Better predict the final outcome when a file is reproduced

DEFINE COLOR SETTINGS

InDesign's color management options allow you to integrate InDesign into a color-managed workflow. This includes managing the color profiles of placed images, as well as previewing potential color problems on screen before the job is actually output.

There are two primary purposes for managing color in an InDesign file: previewing colors based on the intended output device before the file is output, and converting colors to the appropriate color space when a file is output (whether to PDF or an imagesetter for commercial printing).

1. **With no file open in InDesign, choose Edit>Color Settings.**

   The Color Settings dialog box defines default working spaces for RGB and CMYK colors, as well as general color management policies.

   The RGB working space defines the default profile for RGB colors and images that do not have embedded profiles.

   The CMYK working space defines the profile for the device or process that will be used to output the job.

2. **Choose North America Prepress 2 in the Settings menu.**

   InDesign includes a number of common option groups, which you can access in the Settings menu. You can also make your own choices and save those settings as a new preset by clicking Save, or you can import settings files created by another user by clicking Load.

   A working space is a specific profile that defines color values in the associated mode. Using Adobe RGB (1998), for example, means new RGB colors in the InDesign file and imported RGB images without embedded profiles will be described by the values in the Adobe RGB (1998) space.

   Note:

   The Adobe RGB (1998) space is a neutral color space that isn't related to a specific monitor's display capabilities. Using this space assumes you are making color decisions on numeric values, not by what you see on your monitor.

   Note:

   The Working Spaces menus identify exactly which version of each space defines color within that space.

3. **In the CMYK menu, choose U.S. Sheetfed Coated v2.**

   There are many CMYK profiles — and each different printer and press has a gamut unique to that individual device. U.S. Sheetfed Coated v2 is a United States industry-standard profile for a common type of printing (sheetfed printing on coated paper). In a truly color-managed workflow, you would actually use a profile for the specific printing press/paper combination being used for the job. (We're using one of the default profiles to show you how the process works.)

4. **In the Color Management Policies, make sure Preserve Embedded Profiles is selected for RGB, and Preserve Numbers (Ignore Linked Profiles) is selected for CMYK.**

   These options tell InDesign what to do when you open existing files, or if you copy elements from one file to another.

   - When an option is turned off, color is not managed for objects or files in that color mode.
   - **Preserve Embedded Profiles** maintains the profile information saved in the file; files with no profile use the current working space.
   - If you choose **Convert to Working Space**, files automatically convert to the working space defined at the top of the Color Settings dialog box.
   - For CMYK colors, you can choose **Preserve Numbers (Ignore Linked Profiles)** to maintain raw CMYK numbers (ink percentages) rather than adjusting the colors based on an embedded profile.

5. **Check all three options under the Color Management Policies menus.**

   The check boxes control InDesign's behavior when you open an existing file or paste an element from a document with a profile other than the defined working space (called a profile mismatch), or when you open a file that does not have an embedded profile (called a missing profile).

6. **If it is not already checked, activate the Advanced Mode check box (below the Settings menu).**

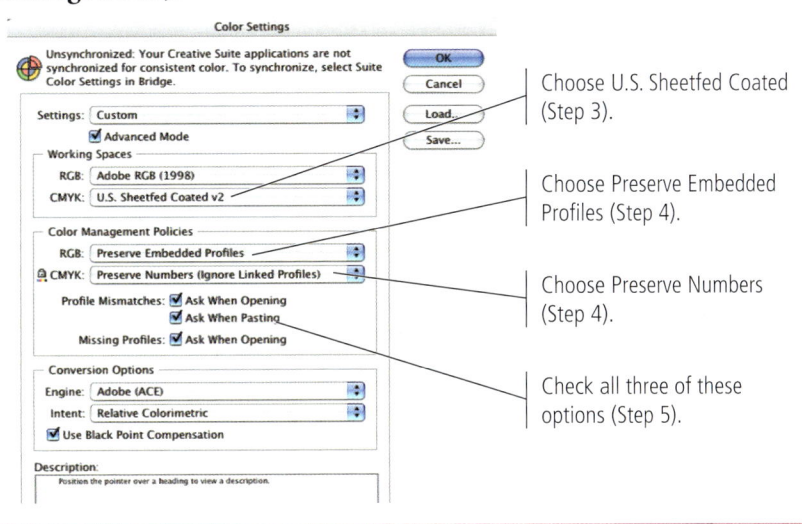

   Choose U.S. Sheetfed Coated (Step 3).

   Choose Preserve Embedded Profiles (Step 4).

   Choose Preserve Numbers (Step 4).

   Check all three of these options (Step 5).

Understanding Rendering Intents

LAB color has the largest gamut, RGB the next largest, and CMYK the smallest. If you need to convert an image from RGB to a more limited CMYK space, you need to tell the CMS (color management system) how to handle any colors that exist outside the CMYK space. You can do this by specifying the **rendering intent** that will be used when you convert colors.

- **Perceptual** presents a visually pleasing representation of the image, preserving visual relationships between colors. All colors in the image — including those available in the destination gamut — are shifted to maintain the proportional relationship within the image.

- **Relative Colorimetric** maintains any colors in both the source and destination profiles. Any source colors outside the destination gamut are shifted to fit into the destination gamut. The Relative Colorimetric method is a good choice, especially when most source colors are in-gamut. This method adjusts for the whiteness of the background media.

- **Absolute Colorimetric** maintains colors in both the source and destination profiles. Any colors outside the destination gamut are shifted to a color within the destination gamut, based on the color's appearance on white paper.

- **Saturation** compares the saturation of colors in the source profile and shifts them to the nearest possible saturated color in the destination profile. Saturation is a good method for images with high levels of saturation, such as pie charts and graphs. The focus is on saturation instead of actual color value, which means this method can produce drastic color shift.

Project 6: Versioned Brochure

The Engine option determines the system and color-matching method for converting between color spaces:

- **Adobe (ACE)** stands for Adobe Color Engine; this is the default, and it is Adobe's recommendation for most users.
- **Apple CMM** (Macintosh only) uses the Apple ColorSync engine and the CMM management system.
- **Microsoft ICM** (Windows only) uses the Microsoft ICM engine and its default color-matching methods.

The **Intent** menu defines how the engine translates source colors outside the gamut of the destination profile.

When the **Use Black Point Compensation** option is selected, the full range of the source space is mapped into the full-color range of the destination space. This method can result in blocked or grayed-out shadows, but it is most useful when the black point of the source is darker than that of the destination.

7. **Click OK to apply your settings.**

8. **Continue to the next stage of the project.**

Assigning and Converting Color Profiles

If you need to change the working RGB or CMYK space in a document, you can use either the Assign Profiles dialog box (Edit>Assign Profiles) or the Convert to Profile dialog box (Edit>Convert to Profile). Although these two dialog boxes have slightly different appearances, most of the functionality is exactly the same.

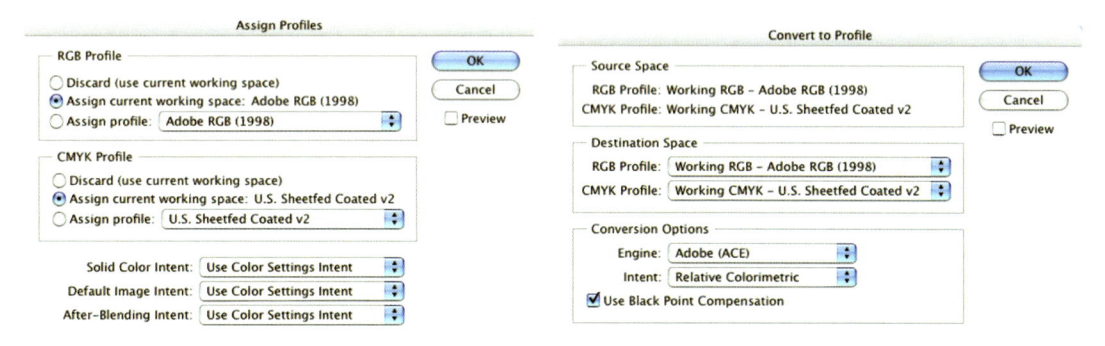

In the Assign Profiles dialog box:

- Discard (Use Current Working Space) removes the current profile from the document. This option is useful if you do not want to color-manage the document. Colors will be defined by the current working space, but the profile is not embedded in the document.
- Assign Current Working Space embeds the working space profile in the document.
- Assign Profile allows you to define a specific profile for the document other than the working space profile. However, colors are not converted to the new space, which can dramatically change the appearance of the colors as displayed on your monitor.

You can also define different rendering intents for solid colors, placed raster images, and transparent elements that result from blending modes, effects, or transparency settings. All three Intent menus default to use the intent defined in the Color Settings dialog box, but you can change any or all menus to a specific intent.

In the Convert to Profile dialog box, the menus can be used to change the RGB and CMYK destination spaces. This is basically the same as using the Assign Profile options in the Assign Profiles dialog box. You can also change the color management engine, rendering intent, and black point compensation options.

Stage 2 Placing and Controlling Images

Adobe InDesign supports a variety of graphics formats. The specific type of graphics you use depends on your ultimate output goal. For print applications such as the brochure you're building in this project, you should use high-resolution raster image files or vector-based graphics files. (Refer to Project 1 for an explanation of resolution requirements for print images.)

Note:

InDesign supports the following graphics file formats: TIFF, PSD, GIF, JPEG, BMP, AI, EPS, DCS, PICT, WMF, EMF, PCX, PNG, Scitex CT, and SWF.

REPLACE A NATIVE ILLUSTRATOR FILE

As part of the Adobe Creative Suite, InDesign supports native Adobe Illustrator files (with the ".ai" extension) that have been saved to be compatible with the PDF format. Illustrator files can include both raster and vector information (including type and embedded fonts), as well as objects on multiple layers in a variety of color modes (including spot colors, which are added to the InDesign Swatches panel).

1. **On your desktop, copy the Toys folder from the WIP folder on your Resource CD to the WIP folder where you are saving your work.**

2. **Open the file toys.indt from the RF_InDesign>Toys folder.**

   The existing template file does not have a defined RGB or CMYK profile. Because you activated the Ask When Opening option in the Color Settings dialog box, InDesign asks how you want to handle color in the file.

Note:

You can also copy objects in Illustrator and paste them into InDesign as a group.

3. **In the Profile or Policy Mismatch dialog box, select the second option (Adjust the document to match current color settings).**

   This option assigns the existing InDesign color settings (which you defined in the previous exercise) to the new file that you are creating by opening the InDesign template file.

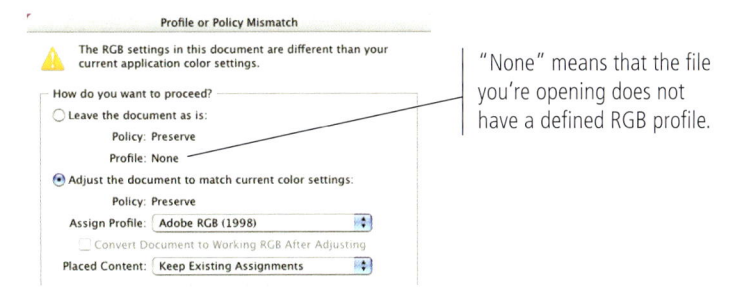

   "None" means that the file you're opening does not have a defined RGB profile.

4. **Leave the remaining options at their default values and click OK.**

   Again, your choice in the Color Settings dialog box was to Ask When Opening if a file was missing a CMYK profile. Because the template file does not have a defined CMYK profile, you see that warning now.

5. **In the second warning message, choose the second radio button (Adjust the document to match current color settings) and click OK.**

   "None" means that the file you're opening does not have a defined CMYK profile.

Project 6: Versioned Brochure

This template contains the layout for a four-page brochure. The layout is designed with a 17 × 11″ page size; the flat size is 8.5 × 11″ when folded in the middle.

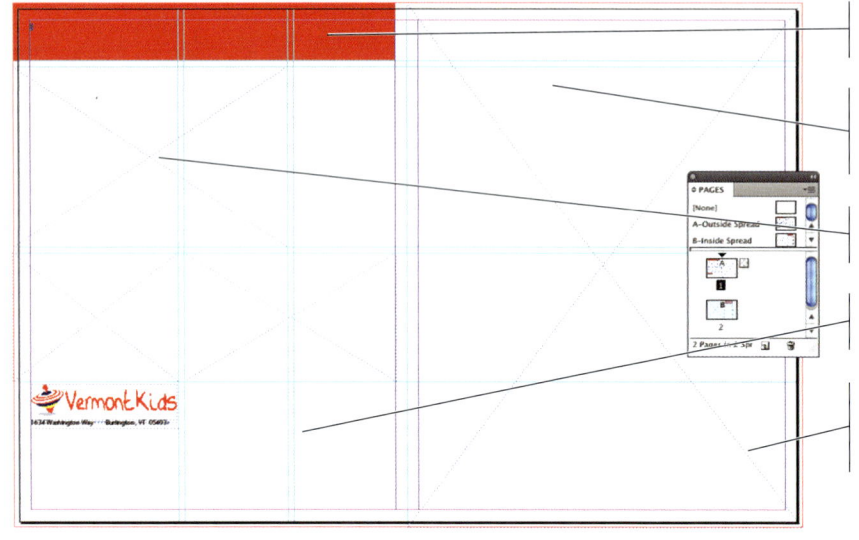

The colored objects will be output in the spot color for that issue.

The layout contains numerous placeholders for different elements of the brochure.

Crossed diagonal lines indicate empty graphics frames.

Frames without diagonal lines are text frames.

Dotted lines indicate that most elements are placed on the master page layouts.

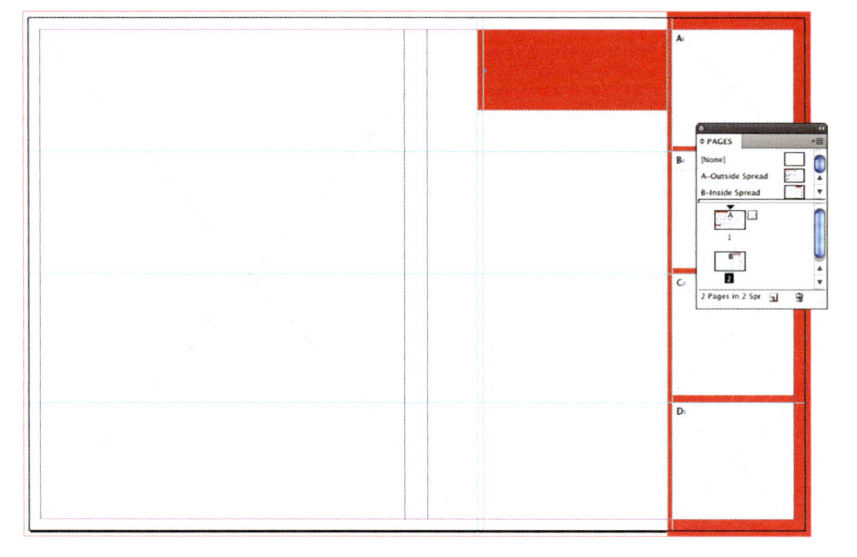

Note:

Although you could design this file as four 8.5 × 11″ pages, this layout is a good example of when a file can be safely built with printer's spreads instead of reader's spreads. On Page 1 of the layout, the back (Page 4) faces the front (Page 1) of the brochure; on Page 2 of the layout, Page 2 of the brochure faces Page 3.

6. **Double-click the A-Outside Spread icon in the master pages section of the Pages panel to show that layout.**

   Your client sent a new logo, which you need to use in the layout and template.

7. **Using the Direct Selection tool, click the logo on the page.**

8. **Open the Transform panel (Window>Object & Layout>Transform).**

   This graphic is scaled to 46.5% proportionally.

   Note:

   Make sure you use the Direct Selection tool to select the logo. If you use the Selection tool, the Transform panel shows the values for the frame instead of the graphic placed in the frame.

9. **With the graphic still selected, choose File>Place.**

10. **Navigate to the file toytrends logo.ai in the RF_InDesign>Toys folder.**

11. **At the bottom of the Place dialog box, check the Replace Selected Item and Show Import Options boxes.**

    When Replace Selected Item is checked, the file you choose replaces the selected item in the layout.

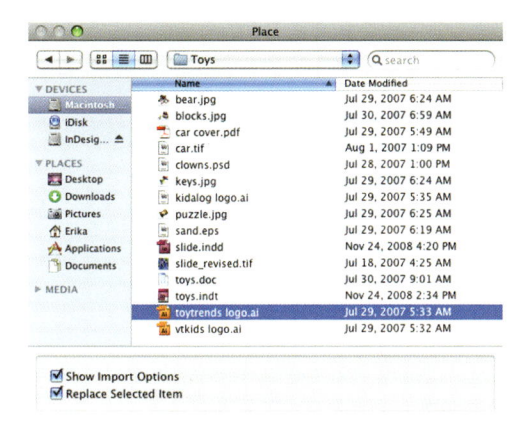

    Note:

    If nothing is selected in the layout, the file you select is simply loaded into the cursor so that you can click to place it.

12. **Click Open.**

    When Show Import Options is checked, the Place [Format] dialog box opens with the options for the relevant file format. (Every file format has different available options.)

    When you place a native Illustrator file, the dialog box shows the Place PDF options because the PDF format is the basis of Illustrator files that can be placed into InDesign. (For an Illustrator file to be placed into InDesign, it must be saved from Illustrator with the Create PDF Compatible File option checked in the Illustrator Options dialog box.)

13. **In the General tab, choose Art in the Crop To menu.**

    The Crop To menu determines what part of the file will import:

    - **Bounding Box** places the file based on the minimum area that encloses the objects on the page.
    - **Art** places the file based on the outermost dimensions of artwork in the file.
    - **Crop** places the file based on the crop area defined in the file. If no crop area is defined, the file is placed based on the defined Artboard dimensions.
    - **Trim** places the file based on trim marks defined in the placed file. If no trim marks are defined, the file is placed based on the defined Artboard size.
    - **Bleed** places the file based on the defined bleed area. If no bleed area is defined, the file is placed based on the defined Artboard size.
    - **Media** places the file based on the physical paper size (including printer's marks) on which the PDF file was created. This option is not relevant for native Illustrator files.

    Note:

    In the General tab, you can also define the specific PDF page or Illustrator Artboard of the file to place.

    When the Transparent Background option is checked, background objects in the layout show through empty areas of the placed file. If this option is not checked, empty areas of the placed file knock out underlying objects.

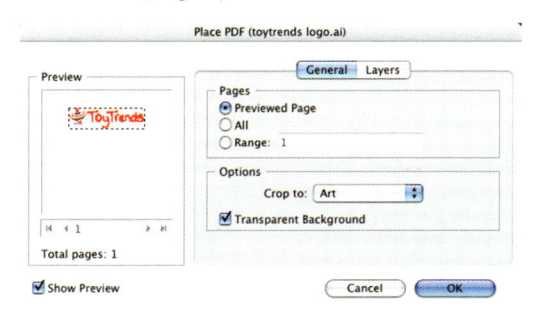

    Note:

    Artwork in the Illustrator file must be entirely within the bounds of the Artboard (page) edge. Anything outside the Artboard edge will not be included when you place the file into InDesign.

Project 6: Versioned Brochure   335

14. **Click the Layers tab to display those options.**

    PDF and native Illustrator files can include multiple layers. You can determine which layers to display in the placed file by toggling the eye icons on or off in the Show Layers list. In the Update Link Options menu, you can determine what happens when/if you update the link to the placed file.

    - **Keep Layer Visibility Overrides** maintains your choices regarding which layers are visible in the InDesign layout.
    - **Use PDF's Layer Visibility** restores the layer status as saved in the placed file.

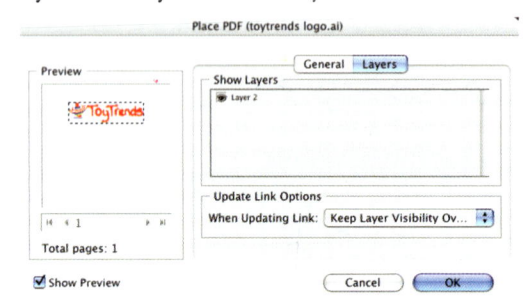

15. **Click OK to place the file.**

    When you replace a selected file, the new file maintains the same transformations that were applied to the original. In this case, the replaced file is also scaled to 46.5%.

16. **Choose File>Save.**

17. **Save the file in your WIP>Toys folder as an InDesign template named `toys_revised.indt`.**

    Because the new logo should be used in all future versions of the catalog mailer, you are resaving the template. In the next exercise, you create a new document from the template for the current issue of the catalog.

18. **Close the template file and continue to the next exercise.**

PLACE A NATIVE PHOTOSHOP FILE

Adobe Photoshop is also part of the Adobe Creative Suite; you can place native Photoshop files (with the extension ".psd") into an InDesign layout. You can control the visibility of Photoshop layers and layer comps, as well as access embedded paths and Alpha channels in the placed file. If a Photoshop file includes spot color channels, the spot colors are added to the InDesign Swatches panel.

1. **Create a new file by opening `toys_revised.indt` from your WIP>Toys folder. Make sure Page 1 of the layout is showing.**

    Because this is a template file, it opens as a new untitled document.

2. **Make sure nothing is selected in the layout, and then choose File>Place. If necessary, navigate to the RF_InDesign>Toys folder.**

    If you continued directly from the previous exercise, the Place dialog box defaults to the last-used location.

Note:

All files for this project are in the RF_InDesign>Toys folder. This is the last time we identify the entire file path for the many images you will place to complete this project.

336 Project 6: Versioned Brochure

3. **In the Place dialog box, select the file** clowns.psd.

4. **Make sure the Show Import Options and Replace Selected Item options are checked.**

   These check boxes default to the last-used settings. If you continued directly from the previous exercise, they should still be selected.

5. **Click Open.**

6. **In the Image Import Options dialog box, click the Image tab and review the options.**

   If the Photoshop file includes clipping path or Alpha channel information, you can activate those options when you place the file.

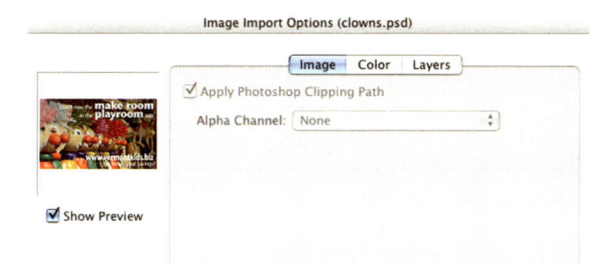

7. **Click the Color tab and review the options.**

   The Profile menu defaults to the profile embedded in the file. If the file was saved without an embedded profile, the menu defaults to Use Document Default. You can use the Profile menu to change the embedded profile (not recommended) or assign a specific profile if one was not embedded.

   The Rendering Intent menu defaults to Use Document Image Intent; you can also choose one of the four built-in options for this specific image.

   Note:

   When you export the finished layout to PDF, you will use the PDF engine to convert the RGB images to CMYK. This profile tells InDesign how the RGB color is described in the file so it can be properly translated to the destination (CMYK) profile.

   Project 6: Versioned Brochure   337

8. **Click the Layers tab and review the options.**

   Photoshop files can include multiple layers and layer comps (saved versions of specific layer position and visibility). You can turn off specific layers by clicking the eye (visibility) icon for that layer. If the file includes layer comps, you can use the Layer Comp menu to determine which comp to place.

   The Update Link Options you see here are the same as those in the Place PDF dialog box.

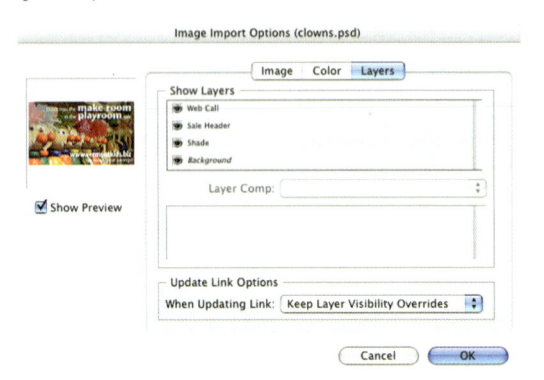

   Note:

   Unless you know what the different layers contain, it is difficult to decide what you want to place, based on the very small preview image.

9. **Click OK.**

   Even though you checked the Replace Selected Item option in the Place dialog box, the image is loaded into the cursor because nothing was selected in the layout (in other words, there is nothing to replace).

   Loaded image cursor

10. **Click the loaded cursor in the middle frame on the left side of the page to place the image (as shown in the following image).**

Reviewing Image Color Settings

INDESIGN FOUNDATIONS

You can review and change the profile associated with a specific image by selecting the image in the layout and choosing Object>Image Color Settings. Keep in mind, however, that just because you can change the profile doesn't mean you should change it. If an image has an embedded profile, you should assume that the embedded profile is the correct one; don't make random profile changes in InDesign.

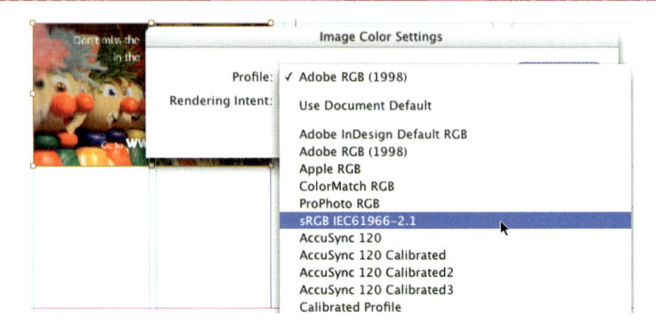

Project 6: Versioned Brochure

11. **With the placed file selected, choose Object>Object Layer Options.**

    This dialog box contains the same options as the Layers tab in the Image Import Options dialog box.

12. **Activate the Preview option, and then click the eye icon for the Web Call layer to turn off that layer. (If necessary, drag the dialog box out of the way so you can see the placed picture as well as the dialog box.)**

    When the Preview option is checked, your changes in the dialog box reflect in the placed image (behind the dialog box). This method makes it easy to experiment with different layer visibility options before finalizing your choices.

    Note:

    You're turning off the Web Call layer because the client changed its company name and set up a new Web address to match the new name.

13. **Click OK to close the Object Layer Options dialog box.**

14. **Create a text frame that extends across the bottom part of clowns image. Apply bottom vertical alignment and inset the edges of the text frame about 1/8″ from the image edges.**

    Add a text frame with Bottom vertical alignment, leaving approximately 1/8″ from the left, bottom, and right edges of the text frame and the edges of the clown image.

15. **In the text frame, type:**

    Go to www.toytrends.biz [line break]
    for more great savings!

    Note:

    To create the line break rather than a paragraph return, press Shift-Return/Enter.

Project 6: Versioned Brochure · 339

16. **Apply right paragraph alignment to the text you just typed. Open the Character Styles panel and apply the Call to Action small text style to the entire paragraph, then apply the Call to Action large text style to only the Web address.**

17. **Save the file as `toys_working.indd` in your WIP>Toys folder and continue to the next exercise.**

Place an EPS File

The EPS (Encapsulated PostScript) format is commonly used for exporting vector graphics from Adobe Illustrator or other vector-based applications. This format uses an adaptation of the PostScript page-description language to produce a "placeable" file for PostScript-based artwork.

Many vector graphics are saved as EPS files, but not all EPS files are vector graphics; the format supports both vector and raster information. Some Photoshop files — specifically, those with embedded clipping paths or spot color channels — also use the EPS format.

When you place an EPS file into InDesign, you can use or ignore an embedded file preview. You can also manage OPI (Open Prepress Interface) image links, as well as embedded clipping paths for Photoshop EPS files. Spot colors in an EPS file are added to the InDesign Swatches panel.

Because InDesign supports native Illustrator and Photoshop files, as well as PDF files, the EPS format is slowly disappearing from the graphics workflow. QuarkXPress, which does not yet support native Illustrator files, still requires the EPS format to read artwork in Adobe Illustrator or Photoshop files that include spot color channels.

Note:

If you print a page with an EPS file to a non-PostScript printer, only the screen-resolution preview prints.

Note:

Photoshop files with spot color information might also be saved using the DCS (Desktop Color Separation) format, which is a modification of the EPS format. DCS files are not particularly common in modern design and print workflows.

1. **With `toys_working.indd` open, select the placed clowns image.**

2. **Choose File>Place and select the file `sand.eps`.**

3. **With the Show Import Options and Replace Selected Item options checked, click Open.**

Project 6: Versioned Brochure

4. **Review the options in the EPS Import Options dialog box.**

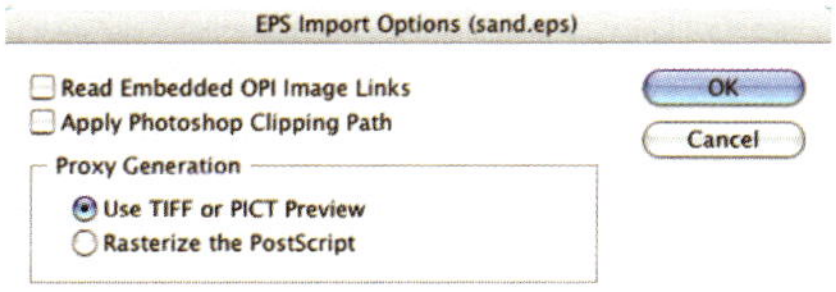

   The **Read Embedded OPI Image Links** option tells InDesign to read links from OPI comments for images included in the graphic. (OPI is a workflow that allows designers to work with low-resolution placement-only images in the layout; when the file is output, high-resolution versions of the images are merged into the output stream, in place of the low-resolution proxies.)

   The **Apply Photoshop Clipping Path** option applies a defined clipping path in a Photoshop EPS file. (If you turn off this option, you can later apply the clipping path by choosing Object>Clipping Path>Options.)

   The **Proxy Generation** options determine how the placed file will be viewed in the layout:

   - **Use TIFF or PICT Preview** shows the preview embedded in the file. If the file has no embedded preview, InDesign generates a low-resolution bitmap after rasterizing the PostScript data.
   - **Rasterize the PostScript** discards the embedded preview.

5. **Activate the Use TIFF or PICT Preview option and click OK to place the file.**

   Because the clowns image was selected and the Replace Selected Item option was checked, the sand image automatically appears in the selected frame.

6. **Choose Edit>Undo Replace.**

   If you accidentally replace a selected item, undoing the placement loads the last-placed image into the cursor.

   Note:

   The Undo command undoes the single last action. In this case, placing the image into the frame — even though it happened automatically — was the last single action.

7. **Click the loaded cursor in the empty frame to the left of the clowns image.**

   This is an easy fix if you accidentally replace an image — simply choose Edit>Undo Replace, and then click to place the loaded image in the correct location.

8. **Save the file and continue to the next exercise.**

Project 6: Versioned Brochure

Controlling Display Performance

By default, files display in the document window using the Typical display performance settings. In the Display Performance pane of the Preferences dialog box, you can change the default view settings (Fast, Typical, or High Quality), as well as change the definition of these view settings.

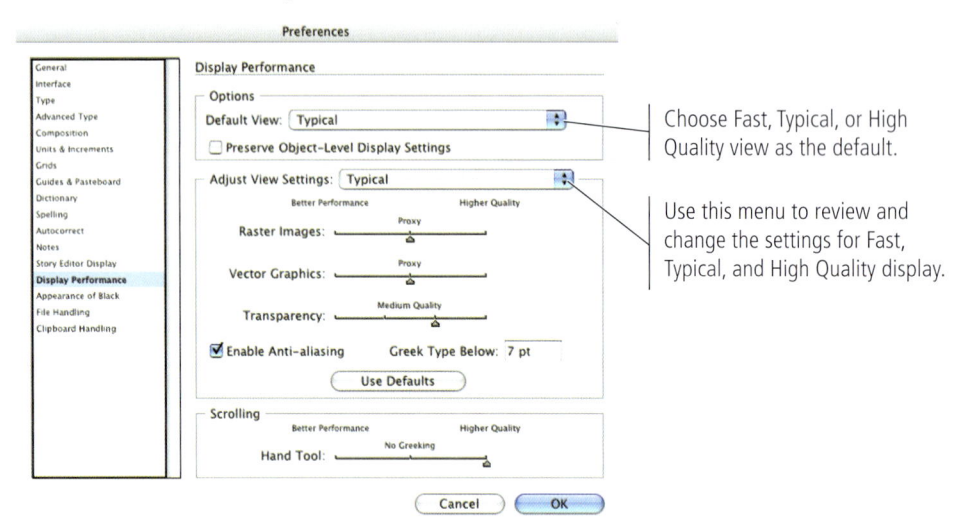

Choose Fast, Typical, or High Quality view as the default.

Use this menu to review and change the settings for Fast, Typical, and High Quality display.

In the Adjust View Settings section, individual sliders control the display of raster images, vector graphics, and objects with transparency. You can change the individual settings for any of the view settings. For example, you may want to view vector graphics at high resolution, even for the Typical view.

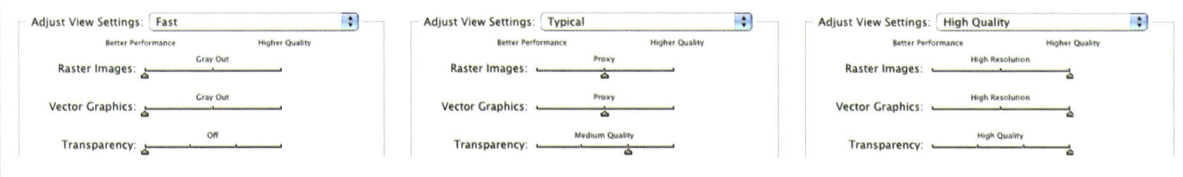

In the layout, you can change the document display performance using the View>Display Performance menu.

If **Allow Object-Level Display Settings** is checked in the View>Display Performance menu, you can also change the preview for a single image in the layout (in the Object>Display Performance menu or using the object's contextual menu).

You can turn object-level display settings on and off using the Allow Object-Level Display Settings toggle. To remove object-level settings, choose **Clear Object-Level Display Settings**. (Object-level display settings are maintained only while the file remains open; if you want to save the file with specific object-level display settings, check the **Preserve Object-Level Display Settings** option in the Display Performance pane of the Preferences dialog box.)

Fast displays gray boxes in place of images and graphics.

Typical shows the low-resolution proxy images.

High Quality shows the full resolution of placed files.

Project 6: Versioned Brochure

Place a TIFF File

The TIFF format is used only for raster images such as those from a scanner or digital camera. These files can be one-color (bitmap or monochrome), grayscale, or continuous-tone images.

1. **With `toys_working.indd` open, make sure the placed sand image is selected in the layout and choose File>Place.**

2. **In the Place dialog box, select the file `car.tif` and uncheck the Replace Selected Item option.**

3. **Make sure the Show Import Options box is checked and click Open.**

   In the Image Import Options dialog box, the Image and Color options for placing TIFF files are the same as the related options for placing native Photoshop files.

   When you place a TIFF file into InDesign, you can access the clipping paths and Alpha channels saved in the files. InDesign does not allow access to the layers in a TIFF file; all layers are flattened in the placed file.

4. **Click OK.**

   Although the placed sand image was selected when you reopened the Place dialog box, the car image is loaded into the cursor because you unchecked the Replace Selected Item option.

5. **Click the loaded cursor in the empty frame above the sand image to place the car file.**

6. **Save the file and continue to the next exercise.**

Project 6: Versioned Brochure

PLACE A PDF FILE

PDF (Portable Document Format) files save layout, graphics, and font information in a single file. The format was created to facilitate cross-platform file-sharing so one file could be transferred to any other computer, and the final layout would print as intended. While originally meant for Internet use, PDF is now the standard in the graphics industry, used for submitting advertisements, artwork, and completed jobs to a service provider.

You can place a PDF file into an InDesign layout, just as you would any other image. You can determine which page to place (if the file contains more than one page), which layers are visible (if the file has more than one layer), and the specific file dimensions (bounding box) to use when placing the file.

1. **With `toys_working.indd` open, choose File>Place.**

2. **In the Place dialog box, select the file `car cover.pdf`.**

3. **Make sure Show Import Options is checked and Replace Selected Item is not checked, and then click Open.**

    The options in the Place PDF dialog box are exactly the same as the options you saw when you placed the native Illustrator file. However, the options in the General tab are typically more important for PDF files than Illustrator files.

    PDF files can contain multiple pages; you can review the various pages using the buttons below the preview image. You can place multiple pages at once by choosing the All option, or you can select specific pages using the Range option.

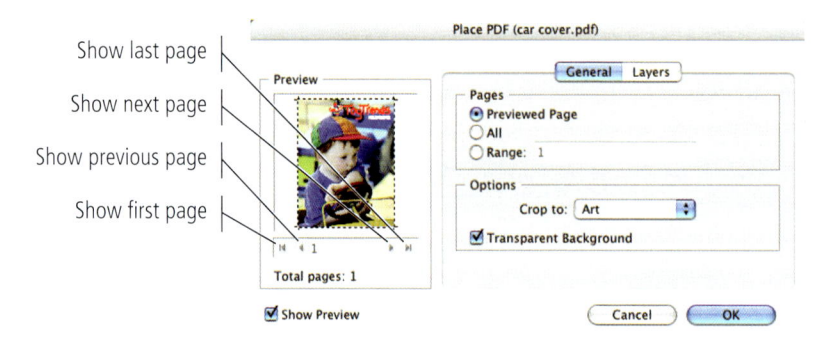

    The Crop To options are also significant when placing PDF files. If the file was created properly, it should include a defined bleed of at least 1/8 inch and trim marks to identify the intended trim size.

4. **Choose Bleed in the Crop To menu and click OK.**

Note:

Before placing a PDF file in an InDesign job, make absolutely sure it was created and optimized for commercial printing. Internet-optimized PDF files do not have sufficient resolution to print cleanly on a high-resolution output device; as such, they could ruin an otherwise perfect InDesign job.

Note:

If you place multiple pages of a PDF file, each page is loaded into the cursor as a separate object.

Note:

Import continuous pages by defining a page range, using a hyphen to separate the first page and the last page in the range. Import non-continuous pages by typing each page number, separated by commas.

Note:

If you place an Illustrator file that contains multiple Artboards, you have the same options for choosing which Artboard (page) to place.

344 Project 6: Versioned Brochure

5. **Click the loaded cursor in the empty frame on the right side of Page 1 to place the loaded file.**

6. **Click the placed image with the Direct Selection tool and look at the Transform panel.**

    This file was created with 1/8″ bleeds on all four sides. In this layout, however, the left bleed allowance is not necessary. When you place the image into the frame, the bleed area on the left side causes the image to appear farther to the right than it should.

    Note:

    Remember, the Selection tool selects the frame; the Direct Selection tool selects the frame content.

    When selected with the Direct Selection tool, you can see the image edge beyond the frame edge.

    The image is placed at X:0, Y:0 (based on the top-left reference point) in relation to the frame.

7. **With the placed file still selected, make sure the top-left reference point is selected, and then change the picture position (within the frame) to X+: −0.125″.**

    The image bounding box now shows the extra bleed allowance, extending beyond the left edge of the graphics frame.

8. **Save the file and continue to the next exercise.**

Project 6: Versioned Brochure

Place an InDesign File

In addition to the different types of image files, you can also place one InDesign layout directly into another InDesign file. As with PDF files, you can determine which page is placed (if the file contains more than one page), which layers are visible (if the file has more than one layer), and the specific file dimensions (bounding box) to use when the file is placed. Placed InDesign pages are managed as individual objects in the file where they are placed.

1. **Copy the file slide.indd from the RF_InDesign>Toys folder to your WIP>Toys folder.**

   You are going to edit this file, so it has to be in a writable location where you can make changes and save the file.

2. **With toys_working.indd open, navigate to Page 2 of the layout.**

3. **Choose File>Place. In the Place dialog box, navigate to the WIP>Toys>slide.indd file.**

4. **With the Show Import Options box checked, click Open.**

5. **In the General tab of the Place InDesign Document dialog box, choose Bleed Bounding Box in the Crop To menu.**

   The options for placing an InDesign file are mostly the same as for placing PDF files; the only exception is the Crop To menu. When you place an InDesign file into another InDesign file, you can place the page(s) based on the defined page, bleed, or slug, as described in the Document Setup dialog box.

6. **Click OK. Read the resulting warning message and click OK.**

   To output properly, image links need to be present and up to date. Images placed in nested InDesign layouts are still images, so the link requirements apply in those files.

7. **Click the loaded cursor in the empty frame on the left side of Page 2 to place the loaded file.**

   When you place one InDesign file into another, the Links panel lists images placed in the InDesign file (indented immediately below the placed InDesign file). You might need to expand the slide.indd item in the panel to see the nested files.

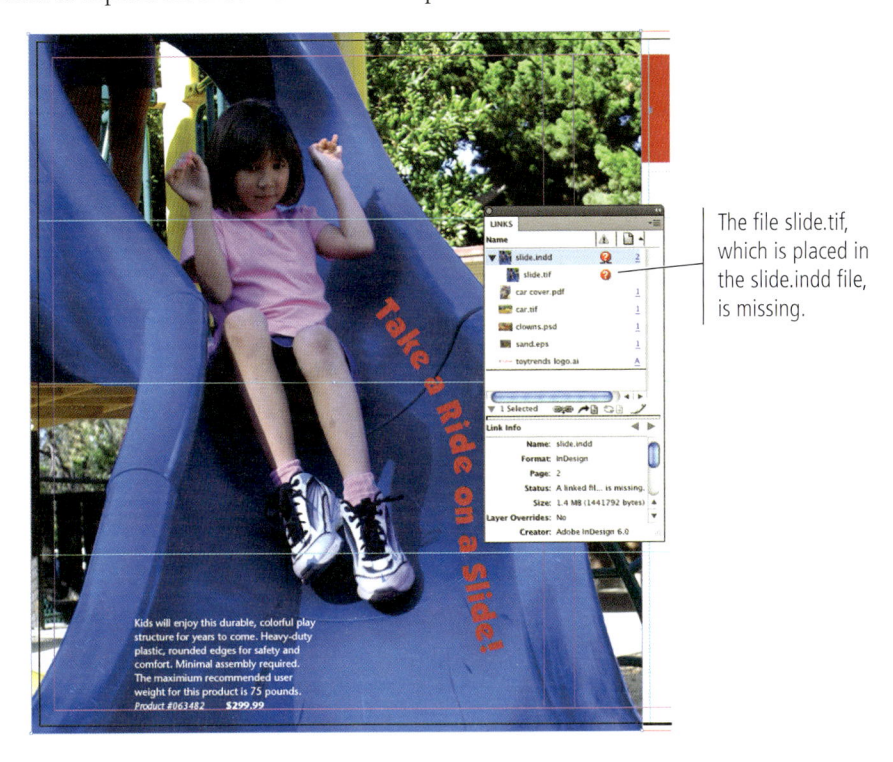

   The file slide.tif, which is placed in the slide.indd file, is missing.

8. **Save the file and continue to the next exercise.**

Edit a Linked File

The InDesign Links panel provides valuable information about the status of placed files. It is more than just an informational tool, however; you can also use the Links panel to navigate to and edit selected images, as well as locate links.

- Relink
- Go to Link
- Update Link
- Edit Original

- The **Relink** button opens a navigation dialog box, where you can locate a missing file or link to a different file.

- The **Go to Link** button selects and centers the file in the document window.

- The **Update Link** button updates modified links. If the selected image is missing, this button opens a navigation dialog box so you can locate the missing file.

- The **Edit Original** button opens the selected file in its native application. When you save the file and return to the InDesign layout, the placed file is automatically updated.

1. **With `toys_working.indd` open, click slide.indd in the Links panel, and then click the Edit Original button.**

   The Edit Original option opens the file selected in the Links panel. Because slide.indd is a placed InDesign file, that document opens in a new document window in front of toys_working.indd.

   When you open any InDesign file, of course, you are first warned if any necessary source file is missing (which you already knew from the Links panel of the toys_working.indd file).

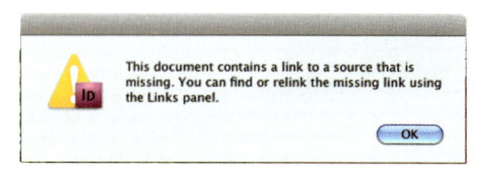

   Note:

   The Edit Original option works for any type of placed file (as long as your computer recognizes the file type), including native Illustrator and Photoshop files, TIFF files, JPEG files, EPS files, and so on.

2. **Click OK to ignore the warning message.**

3. **In the resulting Profile or Policy Mismatch dialog box, choose the Adjust option and click OK.**

   Again, when you open any file, InDesign verifies the file's color based on your choices in the Color Settings dialog box.

   This file (slide.indd) was created with the U.S. Web Coated (SWOP) v2 CMYK working space, as you can see from the profile listed in the Leave Document As Is section. You are working with the U.S. Sheetfed Coated v2 working space, however, so you need to convert this file to the same CMYK working space as the main brochure file.

   Note:

   You can also Control/right-click a specific image in the layout and choose Edit Original from the contextual menu.

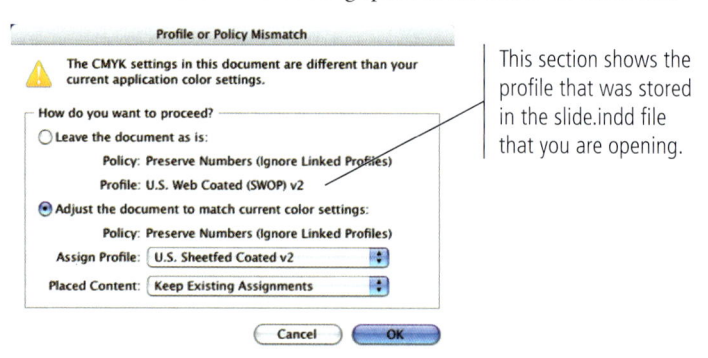

   This section shows the profile that was stored in the slide.indd file that you are opening.

   When the file opens, you see the missing image link in the Links panel — the reason you are editing the file.

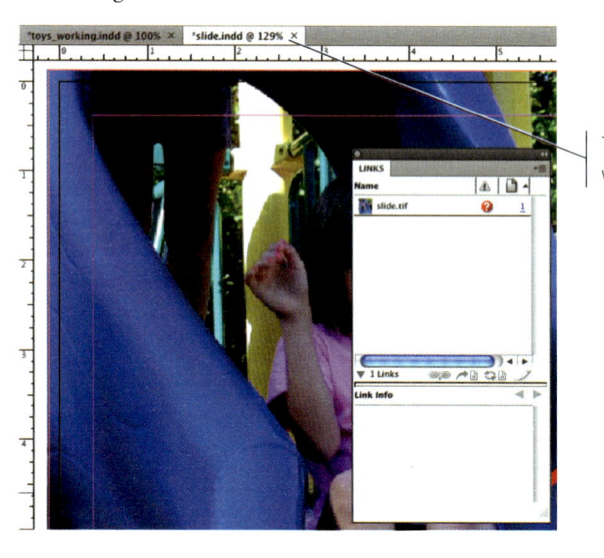

   The document tab shows which file is active.

348   Project 6: Versioned Brochure

4. **In the Links panel for slide.indd, click the missing file to select it, and then click the Relink button at the bottom of the panel.**

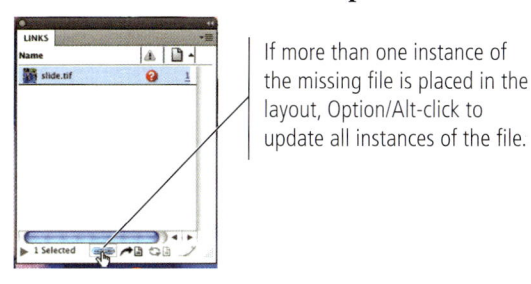

   If more than one instance of the missing file is placed in the layout, Option/Alt-click to update all instances of the file.

5. **Navigate to the file slide_revised.tif in the RF_InDesign>Toys folder and click Open.**

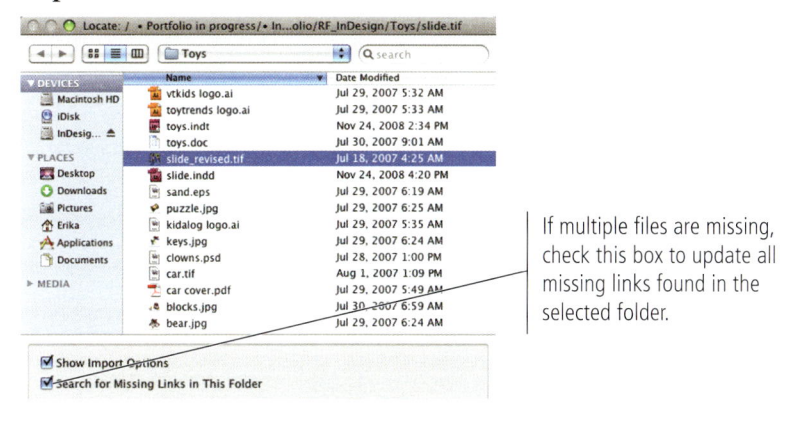

   If multiple files are missing, check this box to update all missing links found in the selected folder.

6. **If the Image Import Options dialog box opens, click OK.**

7. **Save the slide.indd file and close it.**

   When you save and close the slide.indd file, the Links panel for toys_working.indd automatically reflects the new placed file.

   Note:

   If you change a placed file without using the Edit Original option, the Links panel shows a Modified icon. In this case, you have to manually update the link.

8. **Save toys_working.indd and continue to the next exercise.**

Project 6: Versioned Brochure

Place Multiple JPEG Images

The JPEG format is commonly used for raster images, especially images that come from consumer-level digital cameras. Originally used for Web applications only, the JPEG format is now supported by most commercial print design applications (including InDesign).

The JPEG format can be problematic, especially in print jobs, because it applies a lossy compression scheme to reduce the image file size. If a high-resolution JPEG file was saved with a high level of compression, you might notice blockiness or other artifacts (flaws) in the printed image. If you must use JPEG files in your work, save them with the lowest compression possible.

1. **With toys_working.indd open, choose File>Place.**

2. **Navigate to the RF_InDesign>Toys folder and click the file bear.jpg to select it.**

3. **Press Shift and click blocks.jpg to select that file as well.**

4. **Press Command/Control and click keys.jpg and puzzle.jpg.**

   In many cases, you might need to place more than one image from the same location into an InDesign layout. Rather than placing images one at a time, you can streamline the process by loading multiple images into the cursor at once, and then clicking to place each image in the correct location.

5. **With the Show Import Options box checked, click Open.**

   Note:

   Press Shift to select multiple contiguous files in the dialog box.

   Press Command/Control to select multiple non-contiguous files.

6. **Click OK in each of the four Image Import Options dialog boxes.**

   When you place multiple files, you can define different import options for each file. Because you selected four files in the Place dialog box, you see four Image Import Options dialog boxes.

   When the last Import Options dialog box closes, the cursor is loaded with the selected pictures. A number in the cursor shows the number of files that are loaded; the thumbnail and the LP in the Links panel indicate which file will be placed when you click.

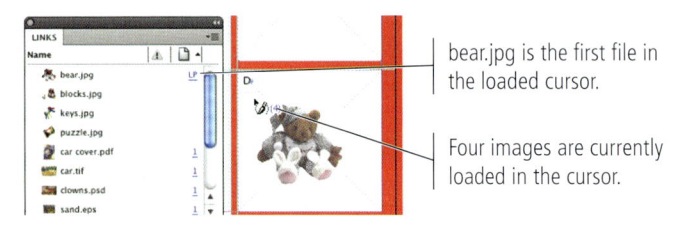

   Note:

   The Import options for JPEG files are the same as those available for TIFF files.

   bear.jpg is the first file in the loaded cursor.

   Four images are currently loaded in the cursor.

350   Project 6: Versioned Brochure

7. **Click the bottom empty frame on the right side of the page to place the bear.jpg file.**

   As soon as you place the bear file, the next loaded image appears in the cursor thumbnail.

8. **Click in the empty frame at the top of the page to place the loaded blocks image.**

9. **Click to place the loaded keys image into the second frame, and then click to place the final loaded image (puzzle) into the third frame.**

   With all four images in place, you might notice two problems. First, the images don't fit perfectly into the available frames. Second, the letters that were in the top-left corner of each frame are missing.

Project 6: Versioned Brochure

10. **Using the Selection tool, click the top image to select it. Control/right-click the selected image and choose Fitting>Fit Content Proportionally from the contextual menu.**

11. **Control/right-click the image again and choose Fitting>Center Content.**

Content Fitting Options

INDESIGN FOUNDATIONS

The Fitting options resize content relative to the containing frame, or resize the containing frame to match the placed content.

- **Fit Content to Frame** resizes content to fit the dimensions of the containing frame, even if that means scaling the content out of proportion (stretched in one direction or another).

- **Fit Frame to Content** resizes the frame to the dimensions of the placed content.

- **Center Content** centers content within its containing frame, but neither the frame nor the content is resized.

- **Fit Content Proportionally** resizes content to fit entirely within its containing frame, maintaining the current aspect ratio of the image. Some empty space might result along one dimension of the frame.

- **Fill Frame Proportionally** resizes content to fill the entire frame while preserving the content's proportions.

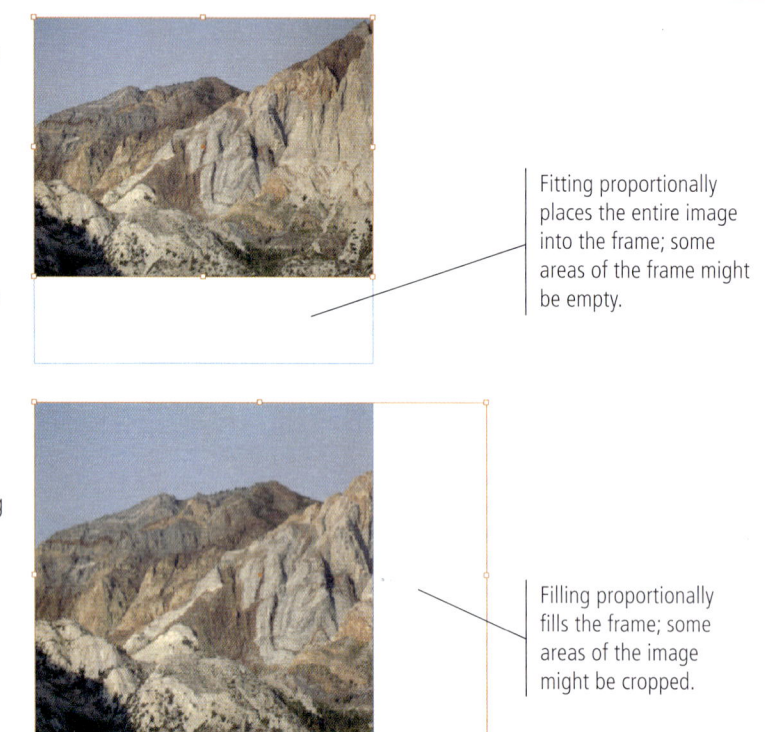

Fitting proportionally places the entire image into the frame; some areas of the frame might be empty.

Filling proportionally fills the frame; some areas of the image might be cropped.

352 Project 6: Versioned Brochure

12. **Repeat Steps 10 and 11 for the remaining three images on the right edge of the page.**

13. **In the Pages panel, Control/right-click the Page 2 icon and choose Override All Master Page Items.**

    When you placed images into the four graphics frames, they were automatically detached from the master layout; the Override All Master Page Items option brings those items to the top of the stacking order, above all items still placed by the master page. The four text frames with the letters were not detached from the master, so they are now behind the placed images.

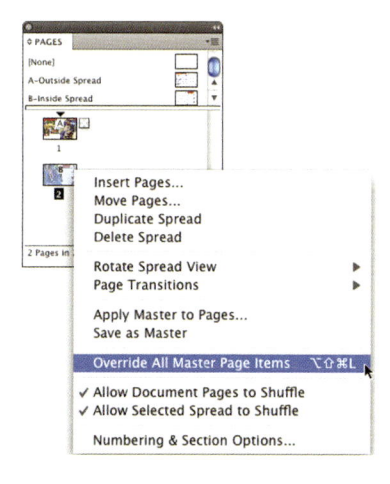

Project 6: Versioned Brochure   353

14. **Using the Selection tool, select the four frames with the placed graphics, as well as the red frame in the background, and choose Object>Arrange>Send to Back.**

    When you overrode the master page for Page 2, the letters became part of the layout page; now, those text frames are back on top of the layers stack.

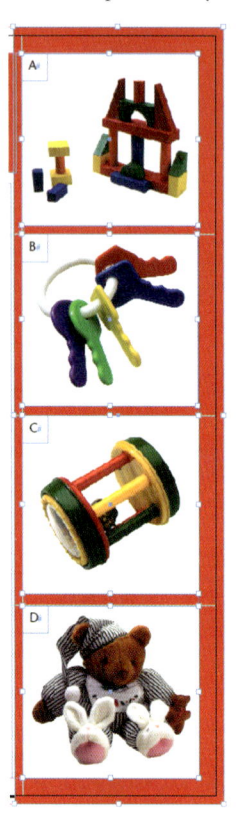

15. **Save the file and continue to the next stage of the project.**

Stage 3 Controlling and Checking Text

As you learned in an earlier project, InDesign gives you extremely tight control over every aspect of the text elements in a layout. You can control the appearance and position of every single character, enabling you to create high-quality typographic elements. This high degree of precision is what separates the amateur from the professional designer.

Some text issues, however, have little to do with typography and more to do with "user malfunction" — common errors introduced by the people who created the text (most often, your clients). Regardless of how knowledgeable or careful you are, some problems will inevitably creep into the text elements of your layouts. Fortunately, InDesign has the tools you need to correct those issues.

PLACE AND CUT TEXT

In an earlier project, you learned about the options for importing a text file. Whenever you work with client-supplied text, we recommend that you maintain text formatting when you import the file, and then make the necessary adjustments once you have reviewed the editorial elements of the imported text.

1. **With toys_working.indd open, choose File>Place.**

2. **Select the file toys.doc, make sure the Show Import Options box is checked, and click Open.**

3. **In the Microsoft Word Import Options dialog box, choose the Preserve Styles and Formatting option.**

4. **Choose Preserve Page Breaks in the Manual Page Breaks menu. Make sure the Import Styles Automatically option is selected, and set both conflict menus to Use InDesign Style Definition.**

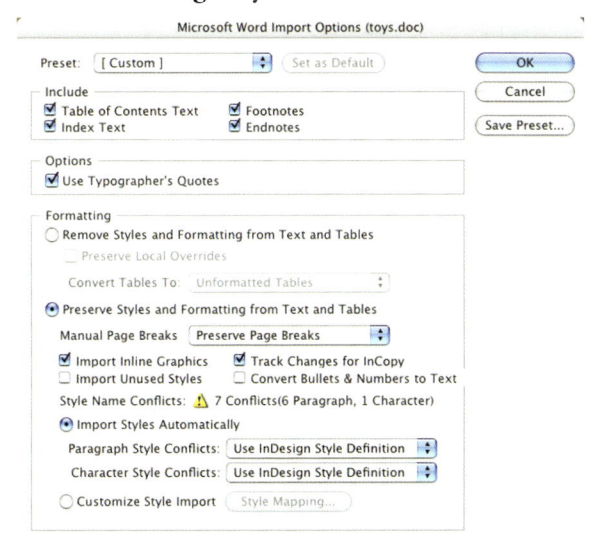

5. **Click OK to import the text into the cursor. If you receive a missing font warning, click OK to dismiss it.**

Project 6: Versioned Brochure 355

6. **Click the loaded text cursor in the empty red frame at the top of Page 2.**

   When the text is placed, it automatically flows from the red frame into the white frame directly below it. Using a responsibly designed InDesign template, coupled with a Microsoft Word template that has the correct style names for this project, the imported text is automatically placed and correctly formatted — almost.

   Despite the best intentions when you set up a file, some items will need to be fixed — especially when dealing with client-supplied text. In this case, the words "Outside Text" are not part of the actual brochure copy. In addition, the client separated every paragraph with an extra return, and placed two spaces after every period in the text (relics of traditional typing techniques, even though most people have never used a manual typewriter). These issues are very common, and they must be fixed.

7. **If hidden characters are not visible, choose Type>Show Hidden Characters.**

8. **Select the text from the beginning of the story to the paragraph return before the words "Inside Text."**

9. **Cut the selected text and navigate to Page 1 of the layout (the "outside" of the brochure).**

10. **In the Pages panel, Control/right-click the Page 1 icon and choose Override All Master Page Items.**

    You can't access the text frames from the master page until you detach the pages from the master.

356 Project 6: Versioned Brochure

11. Place the insertion point in the red frame at the top of the page and paste the text that you cut in Step 9.

12. Delete the words "Outside Text" and the two following paragraph returns from the beginning of the pasted story.

    The frame should begin with the words "In the Fast Lane."

13. On Page 2, delete the words "Inside Text" and the following paragraph returns from the beginning of the story.

14. Save the file and continue to the next exercise.

Find and Change Layout Text

You will often need to search for and replace specific elements in a layout — a word, a phrase, a formatting attribute, or even a specific kind of object. InDesign's Find/Change dialog box allows you to easily locate exactly what you need, whether your layout is two pages or two hundred. For this brochure, you can use the Find/Change dialog box to correct the client's typing errors.

1. **With `toys_working.indd` open, choose Edit>Find/Change.**

2. **Place the insertion point in the Find What field and press the Spacebar twice.**

3. **Press Tab to highlight the Change To field and press the Spacebar once.**

4. **In the Search menu, choose Document.**

   You can use the Search menu to search an entire document, all documents, the selected story, or all text following the insertion point in the selected story (To End of Story).

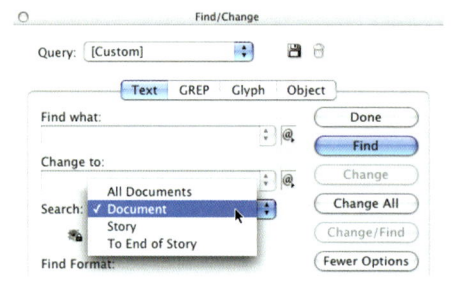

5. **Click Change All. When you see the message that 14 replacements were made, click OK.**

6. **Highlight the content of the Find What field (the two space characters).**

   Because you can't see the space characters in the field, it can be easy to forget about them. If you forget to highlight the space characters, the new content will be added to the space characters instead of replacing them.

7. **Open the menu to the right of the Find What field and choose End of Paragraph.**

   Use this menu to place common special characters in the dialog box fields. When you choose a special character in the menu, the special code for that character is entered into the field.

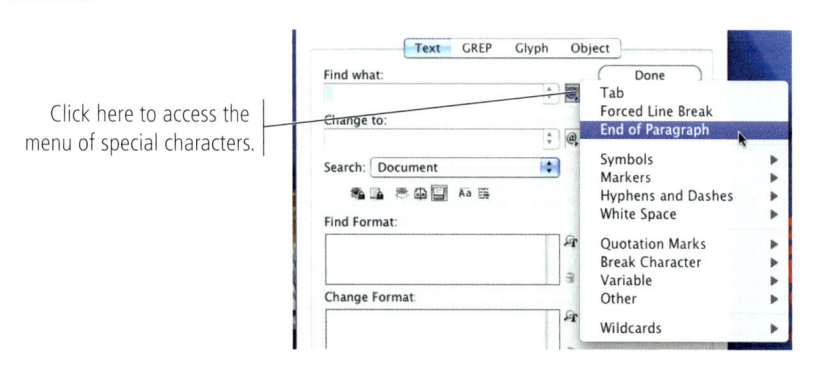

Click here to access the menu of special characters.

Note:

You can also type the special codes directly into a dialog box field. For example, the carat character is accessed by pressing Shift-6.

Project 6: Versioned Brochure

8. **Choose End of Paragraph from the menu again to search for all instances of two consecutive paragraph returns.**

9. **Highlight the Change To field and choose End of Paragraph from the associated menu.**

    You are replacing all instances of two paragraph returns with a single paragraph return.

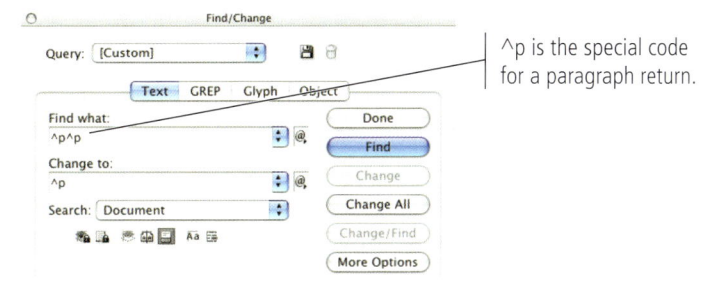

    ^p is the special code for a paragraph return.

10. **Click Change All, and then click OK to close the message box.**

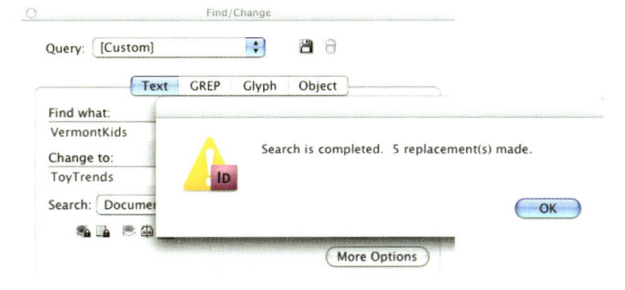

    Note:

    You might need to do the replacement several times to remove all double spaces and paragraph returns from text you receive from clients.

11. **Change all instances of the word "VermontKids" to ToyTrends.**

12. **Click Done to close the Find/Change dialog box.**

13. **On Page 2, place the insertion point in the first paragraph after the paragraph of white copy. Open the Keep options (from the Paragraph panel Options menu) for the paragraph and force the selected paragraph to begin in the next available frame. Click OK.**

    A paragraph of red text is on top of the red frame; you can't see it (except the hidden characters), but it's there.

Project 6: Versioned Brochure 359

Entering Special Characters in Dialog Boxes

You can use special characters in InDesign dialog boxes using the following special codes, called metacharacters. (Note that these metacharacters are case specific; for example, "^n" and "^N" refer to different special characters.)

Character	Code (Metacharacters)
Symbols	
Bullet (•)	^8
Caret (^)	^^
Copyright (©)	^2
Ellipsis (…)	^e
Paragraph	^7
Registered Trademark (®)	^r
Section (§)	^6
Trademark (™)	^d
Dashes and Hyphens	
Em Dash (—)	^_
En Dash (–)	^=
Discretionary hyphen	^-
Nonbreaking hyphen	^~
White Space Characters	
Em space	^m
En space	^>
Third space	^3
Quarter space	^4
Sixth space	^%
Flush space	^f
Hair space	^| (pipe)
Nonbreaking space	^s
Nonbreaking space (fixed width)	^S
Thin space	^<
Figure space	^/
Punctuation space	^.
Quotation Marks	
Double left quotation mark	^{
Double right quotation mark	^}
Single left quotation mark	^[
Single right quotation mark	^]
Straight double quotation mark	^"
Straight single quotation mark	^'
Page Number Characters	
Any page number character	^#
Current page number character	^N
Next page number character	^X
Previous page number character	^V

Character	Code (Metacharacters)
Break Characters	
Paragraph return	^p
Forced line break (soft return)	^n
Column break	^M
Frame break	^R
Page break	^P
Odd page break	^L
Even page break	^E
Discretionary line break	^j
Formatting Options	
Tab character	^t
Right indent tab character	^y
Indent to here character	^i
End nested style here character	^h
Nonjoiner character	^k
Variables	
Running header (paragraph style)	^Y
Running header (character style)	^Z
Custom text	^u
Last page number	^T
Chapter number	^H
Creation date	^S
Modification date	^o
Output date	^D
File name	^l (lowercase L)
Markers	
Section marker	^x
Anchored object marker	^a
Footnote reference marker	^F
Index marker	^I
Wildcards	
Any digit	^9
Any letter	^$
Any character	^?
White space (any space or tab)	^w
Any variable	^v

14. **On Page 1, replace the paragraph return at the end of the first paragraph with a Tab character.**

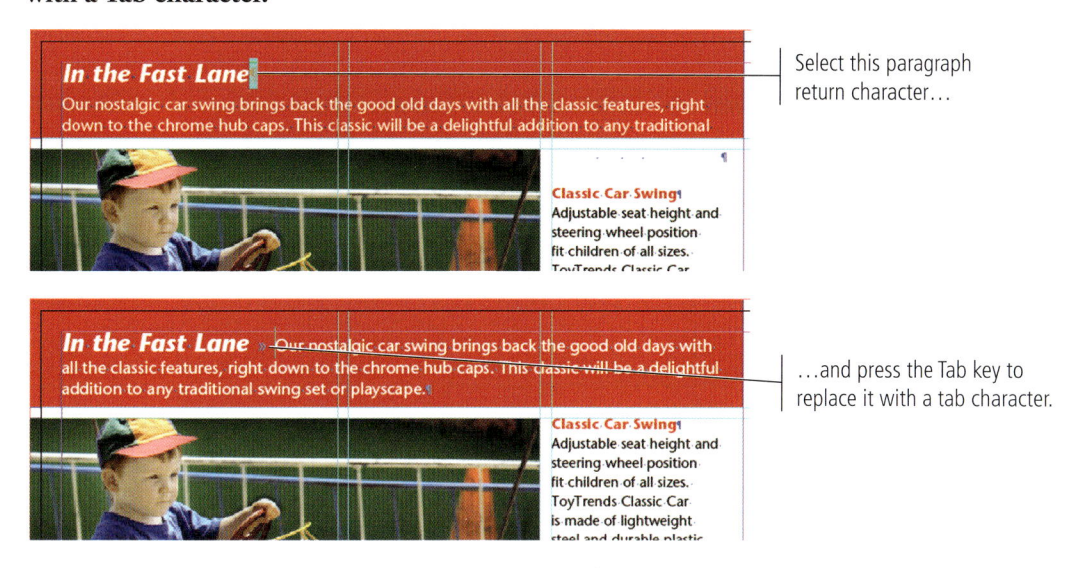

   Select this paragraph return character…

   …and press the Tab key to replace it with a tab character.

15. **Save the file and continue to the next exercise.**

FIND AND CHANGE FORMATTING ATTRIBUTES

In addition to finding and replacing specific text or characters, you can also find and replace formatting attributes for both text and objects. For this project, you need to use the blue spot color as the accent, replacing the red spot color from the template. However, you can't simply delete the red spot color from the Swatches panel because that color is used in the placed logo file. The Find/Change dialog box makes this kind of replacement a relatively simple process.

1. **With toys_working.indd open, choose Edit>Find/Change.**

2. **Highlight the Find What field. Click the associated menu and choose Any Character from the Wildcards submenu.**

   Wildcards allow you to search for formatting attributes, regardless of the actual text. In addition to searching for Any Character, you can also narrow the search to Any Digit, Any Letter, or Any White Space characters.

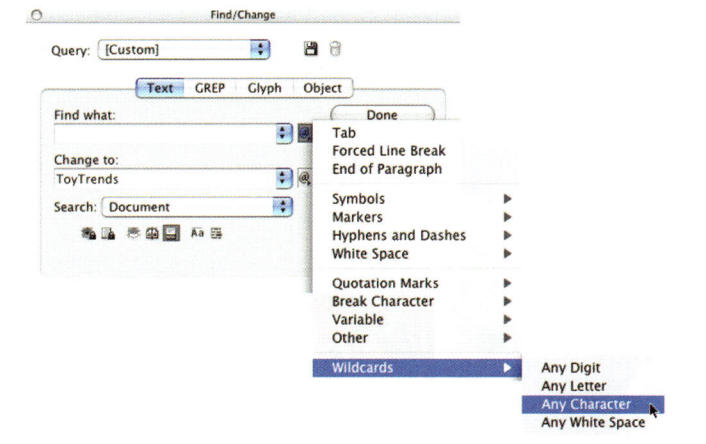

Project 6: Versioned Brochure   361

3. **Delete all characters from the Change To field.**

   You only want to change the formatting, not the text that is formatted. To accomplish this result, you have to delete all characters from the Change To field.

4. **Click the More Options button to show the expanded Find/Change dialog box.**

   When more options are visible, you can find and replace specific formatting attributes of the selected text.

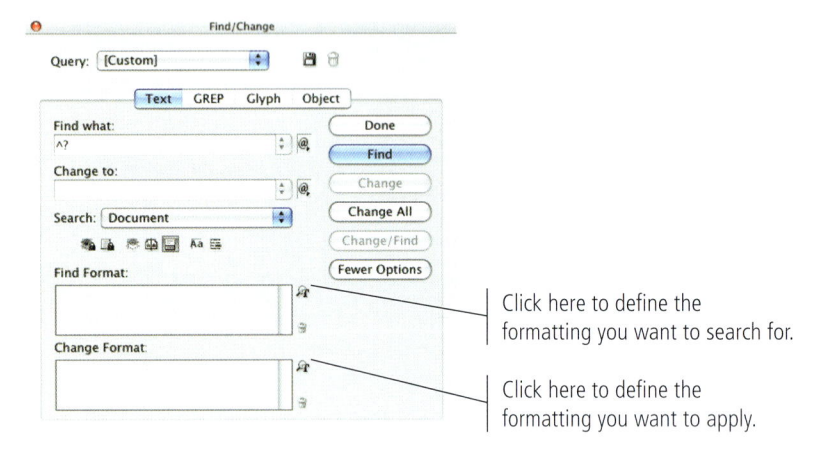

   Click here to define the formatting you want to search for.

   Click here to define the formatting you want to apply.

5. **Click the button for the Find Format field to open the Find Format Settings dialog box.**

   You can search for and replace any character formatting option (or combination of options) that can be applied in the layout.

6. **Show the Character Color options and click the Pantone 186 C swatch.**

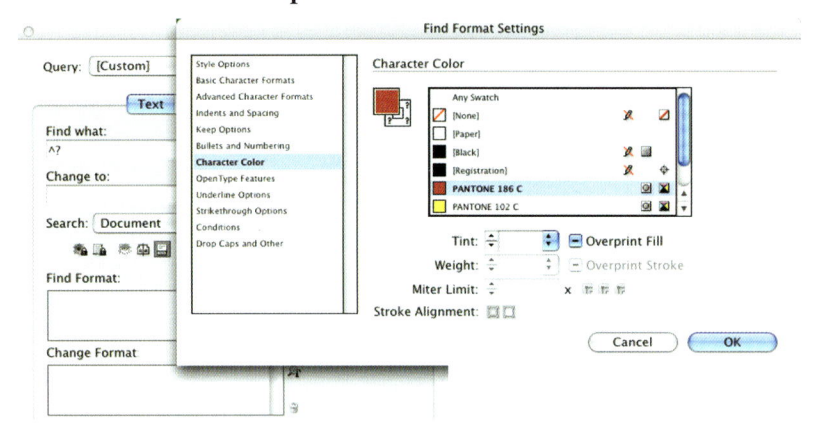

7. **Click OK to return to the Find/Change dialog box.**

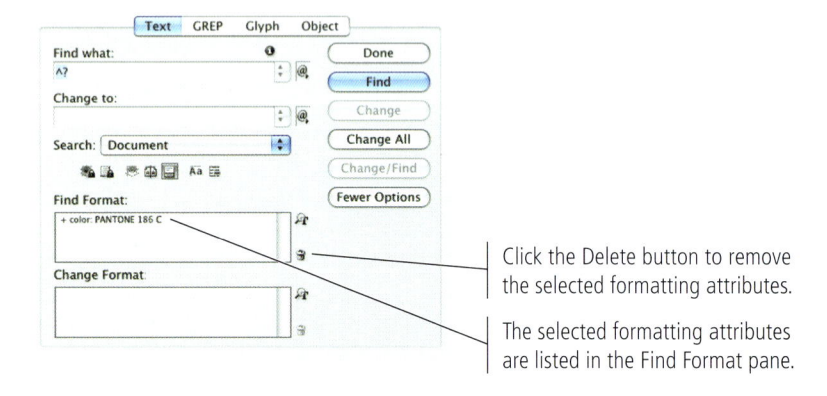

   Click the Delete button to remove the selected formatting attributes.

   The selected formatting attributes are listed in the Find Format pane.

362 Project 6: Versioned Brochure

8. **Click the button for the Change Format field to open the Change Format Settings dialog box.**

9. **Highlight the Character Color options and click the Pantone Blue 072 C swatch. Click OK.**

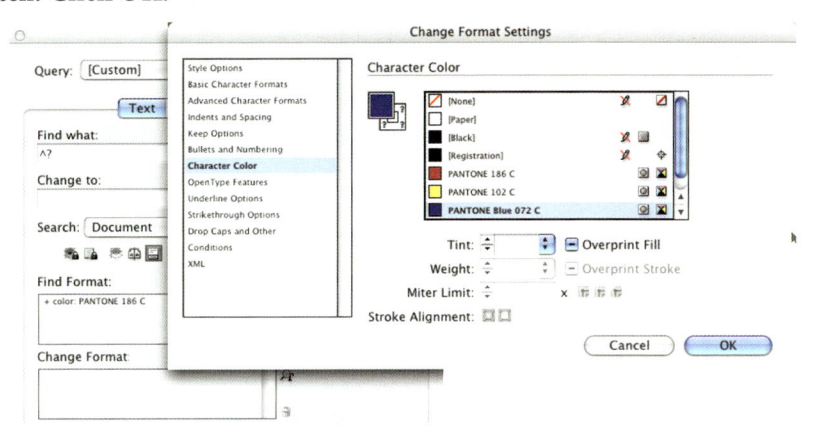

10. **Make sure Document is selected in the Search menu and click Change All. Click OK to close the message about the number of replacements.**

11. **In the Find/Change dialog box, click the Delete button to remove the formatting options from the Find Format and Change Format fields.**

    It can be easy to forget to remove these formatting choices. However, if you leave them in place, your next search will only find the Find What text with the selected formatting. It's a good idea to clear these formatting choices as soon as you're done with them.

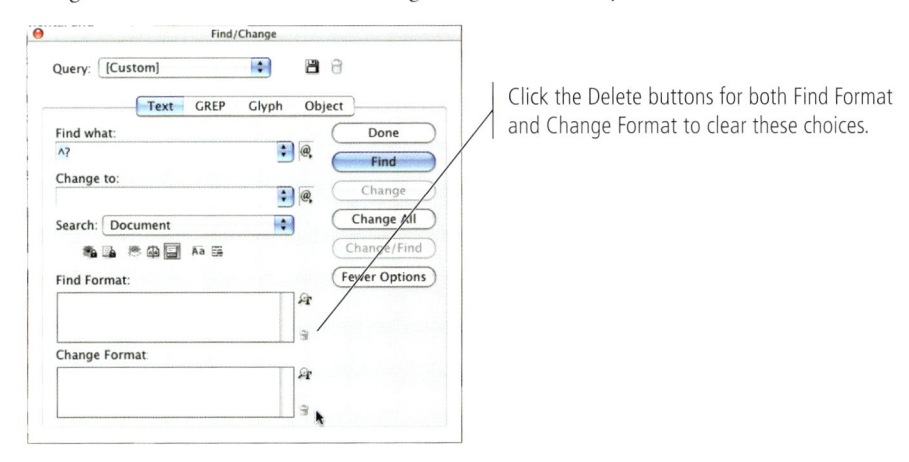

    Click the Delete buttons for both Find Format and Change Format to clear these choices.

12. **Click the Object tab in the Find/Change dialog box.**

    In addition to searching for specific text formatting attributes, you can also find and replace specific object formatting attributes.

13. **Make sure Document is still selected in the Search menu.**

    When you search objects, you can search the current document, all documents, or the current selection.

Project 6: Versioned Brochure

14. **In the Type menu, choose All Frames.**

    This menu allows you to limit your search to specific kinds of frames, or you can search all frames.

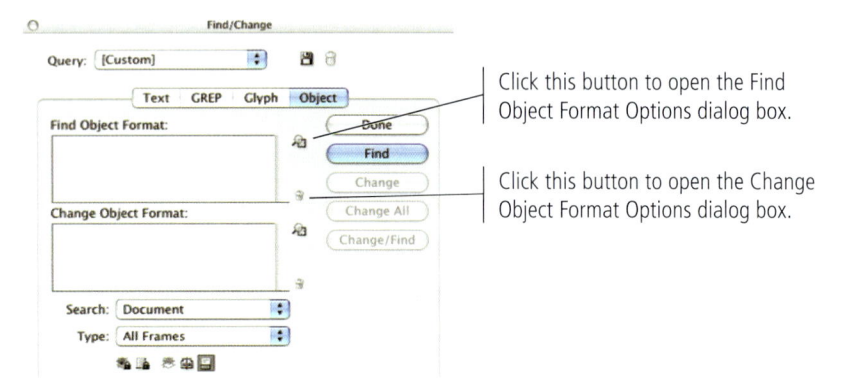

    Click this button to open the Find Object Format Options dialog box.

    Click this button to open the Change Object Format Options dialog box.

15. **Click the button to open the Find Object Format Options dialog box.**

    You can find and change any formatting attributes that can be applied to a frame.

16. **Display the Fill options and click the Pantone 186 C swatch.**

    Note:

    *Selected formatting options are cumulative. If you added the stroke color to the Find options, the search would only identify objects that have a red fill **and** a red stroke. To find **either** of these options, you have to perform two separate searches.*

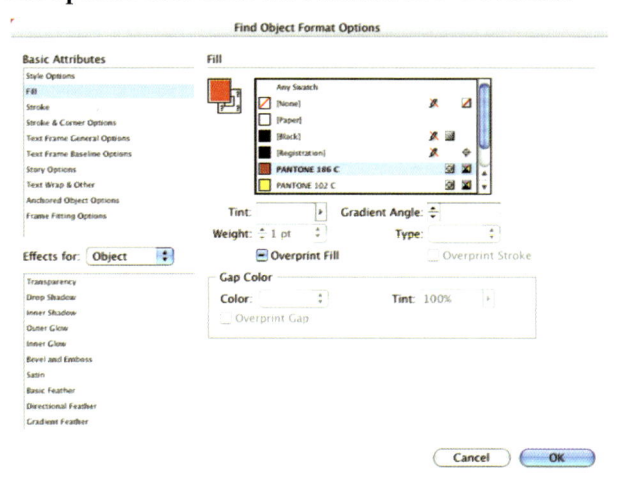

17. **Click OK to return to the Find/Change dialog box.**

18. **Open the Change Object Format Options dialog box and choose the Pantone Blue 072 C swatch in the Fill options.**

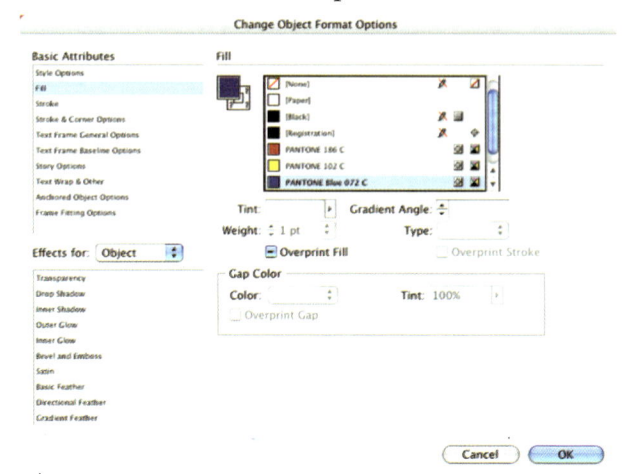

19. **Click OK to return to the Find/Change dialog box, and then click Change All.**

20. **Click OK to dismiss the message about the number of changes.**

21. **Click the Delete buttons for both the Find Object Format and Change Object Format options to clear your choices.**

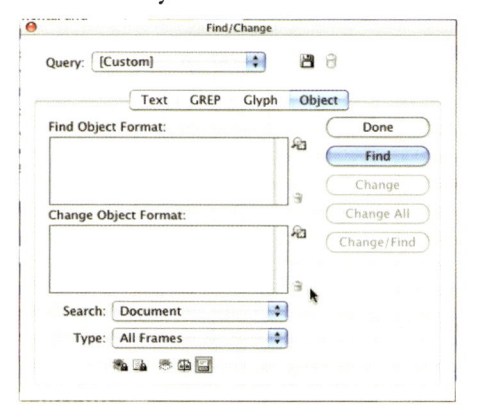

22. **Click Done to close the Find/Change dialog box, and then review the layout.**

    Elements of placed Illustrator, EPS, and PDF files are not affected by the Find/Change function. Placed InDesign files are only affected by the search if those files are also open when you initiate the search. Because the slide.indd file was not already open, the red spot color text in the placed InDesign file was not affected; you now have to open the placed InDesign file and manually change the red text.

Project 6: Versioned Brochure 365

23. **Control/right-click the placed slide.indd file (on page 2) and choose Edit Original from the contextual menu.**

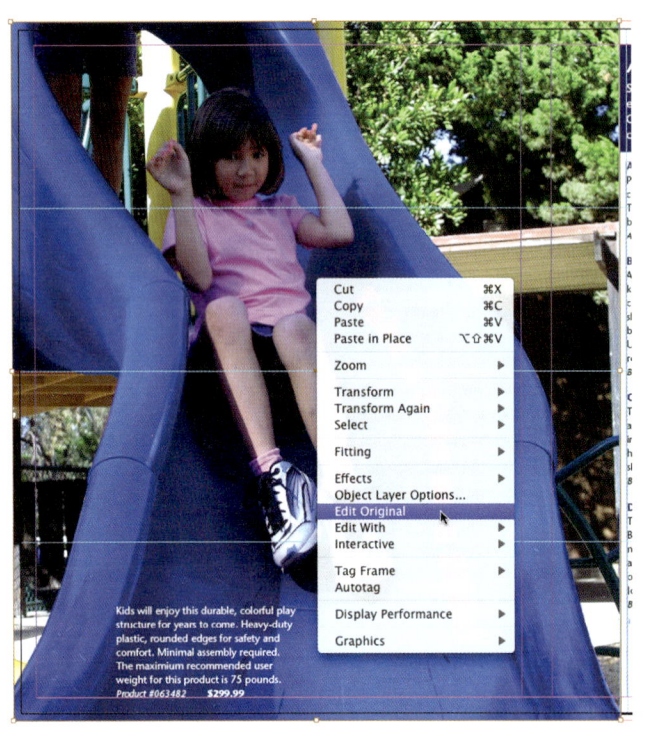

24. **In the linked file, change the red text (along the curved path) to a fill of Paper. Save the slide.indd file and close it.**

    It makes more visual sense to change the red type to white (Paper) rather than placing blue type on a blue image. When you return to the toys_working file, the change will automatically reflect in the placed file.

25. **Save the toys_working.indd file and continue to the next exercise.**

The Find/Change Dialog Box in Depth

INDESIGN FOUNDATIONS

In addition to the tools you use in this project, the Find/Change dialog box has a number of options for narrowing or extending a search beyond the basic options.

The buttons below the Search menu are toggles for specific types of searches:

- When **Include Locked Layers** is active, the search locates text on locked layers; you can't replace text on a locked layer unless you first unlock the layer.

- When **Include Locked Stories** is active, the search locates text that is locked; you can't replace locked text unless you first unlock it.

- When **Include Hidden Layers** is active, the search includes text frames on layers that are not visible.

- When **Include Master Pages** is active, the search includes text frames on master pages.

- When **Include Footnotes** is active, the search identifies instances within footnote text.

- When **Case Sensitive** is active, the search only finds text with the same capitalization as the text in the Find What field. For example, a search for "InDesign" will not identify instances of "Indesign," "indesign," or "INDESIGN."

- When **Whole Word** is active, the search only finds instances where the search text is an entire word (not part of another word). For example, if you search for "old" as a whole word, InDesign will not include the words "gold," "mold," or "embolden."

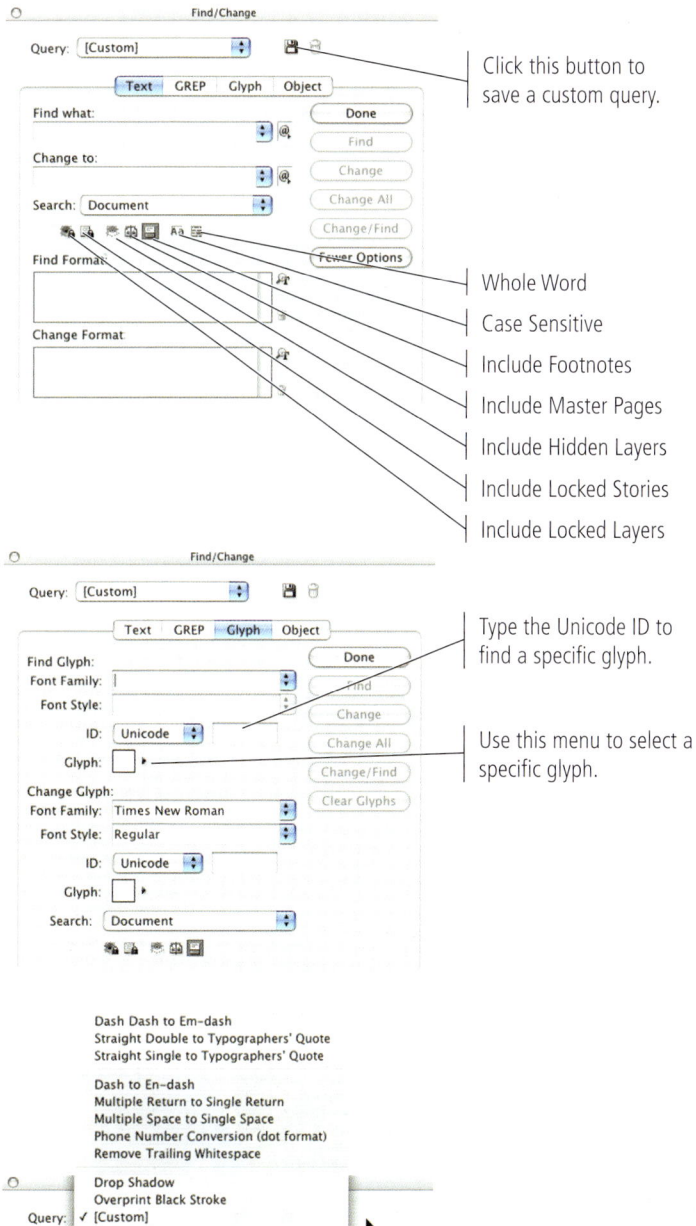

As you have seen, the Text tab allows you to search for and change specific character strings, with or without specific formatting options. The Object tab identifies specific combinations of object formatting attributes, such as fill color or applied object effects.

The GREP tab is used to search with pattern-based search techniques, such as finding phone numbers in one format (e.g., 800.555.1234) and changing them to the same phone number with a different format (e.g., 800/555-1234). Adobe's video-based help system (www.adobe.com) provides some assistance in setting up an advanced query.

The Glyph tab allows you to search for and change glyphs using Unicode or GID/CID values. This is useful for identifying foreign language and pictographic characters, as well as characters from extended sets of OpenType fonts.

You can also save specific searches as queries, and you can call those queries again using the Query menu at the top of the Find/Change dialog box. This option is useful if you commonly make the same modifications, such as changing Multiple Return to Single Return (this particular search and replacement is so common that the query is built into the application).

Click this button to save a custom query.

Whole Word
Case Sensitive
Include Footnotes
Include Master Pages
Include Hidden Layers
Include Locked Stories
Include Locked Layers

Type the Unicode ID to find a specific glyph.

Use this menu to select a specific glyph.

Project 6: Versioned Brochure

Check Document Spelling

In Project 3 you learned about preflighting and how to verify that required elements (graphics and fonts) are available. This simple process prevents potential output disasters such as font replacement or low-resolution preview images in the final print.

Many designers understand these issues and carefully monitor the technical aspects of a job. It is all too common, however, to skip another important check — for spelling errors. Misspellings and typos creep into virtually every job despite numerous rounds of content proofs. These errors can ruin an otherwise perfect print job.

You might not (and probably won't) create the text for most design jobs, and you aren't technically responsible for the words your client supplies. However, you can be a hero if you find and fix typographical errors before a job goes to press; if you don't, you will almost certainly hear about it after it's too late to fix. Remember the cardinal rule of business: the customer is always right. You simply can't brush off a problem by saying, "That's not my job" — at least, not if you want to work with that client in the future.

1. **With toys_working.indd open, open the Dictionary pane of the Preferences dialog box.**

   InDesign checks spelling based on the defined language dictionary — by default, English USA. You can choose a different language dictionary in the Language menu.

   Note:

   Remember, preferences are accessed in the InDesign menu on Macintosh or in the Edit menu on Windows.

2. **Make sure English: USA is selected in the Language menu and click OK.**

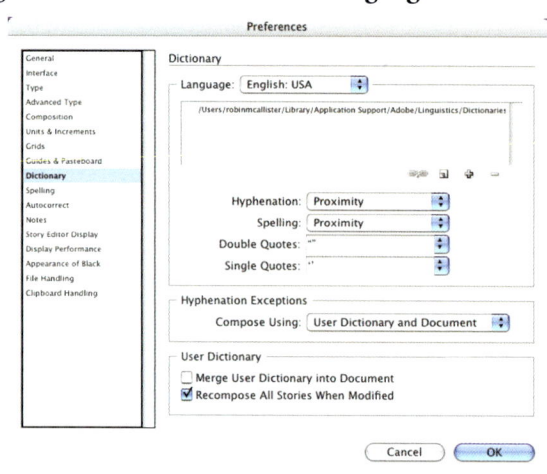

3. **Choose Edit>Spelling>Dictionary.**

   When you check spelling, you are likely to find words that, although spelled correctly, are not in the selected dictionary. Proper names, scientific terms, corporate trademarks, and other custom words are commonly flagged even though they are correct. Rather than flagging these terms every time you recheck the spelling, you can add these words to a custom user dictionary so InDesign will recognize them the next time you check spelling.

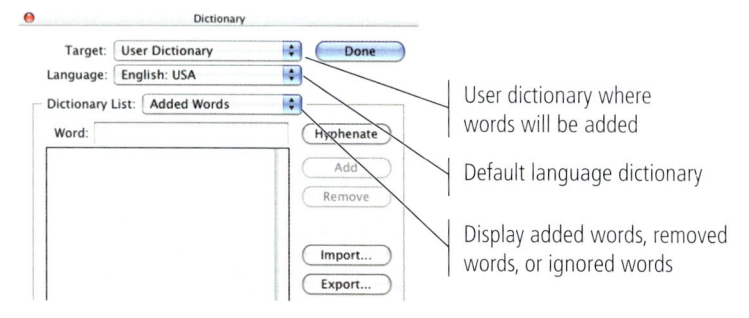

   User dictionary where words will be added

   Default language dictionary

   Display added words, removed words, or ignored words

4. **In the Target menu, choose toys_working.indd.**

    By default, the user dictionary is associated with all documents. You can define custom words for a specific file using the Target menu; when you change the user dictionary for a specific file, words you add for that file will still be flagged in other files.

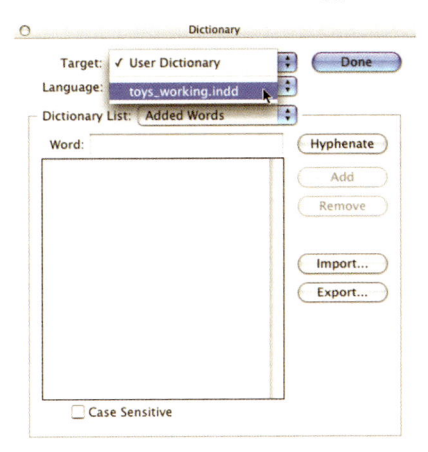

5. **In the Word field, type ToyTrends.**

    Your client's company name is not a real word (even though it is a combination of two real words). If you know certain words will be flagged, you can manually add those words to the user dictionary at any time.

    By adding this word to the file's dictionary (not the language dictionary), you prevent potential errors that might arise if you work on a project that uses the term in a more generic sense. For example, a magazine article about "Toy Trends in Middle America" should result in an error if the first two words are not separated by a space.

6. **Check the Case Sensitive option at the bottom of the dialog box, and then click Add.**

    If Case Sensitive is not checked, InDesign will not distinguish between ToyTrends (which is correct) and toytrends (which is incorrect).

7. **Click Done to close the Dictionary dialog box.**

Project 6: Versioned Brochure 369

8. **With nothing selected in the layout, choose Edit>Spelling>Check Spelling.**

   As soon as you open the Check Spelling dialog box, the first flagged word is highlighted in the layout. The same word appears in the Not in Dictionary field of the Check Spelling dialog box.

   If you are using a shared computer, it is possible that another user might have already added this word to the user dictionary (not the current file's dictionary). In this case, this word will not be flagged for your file; continue to Step 9.

   Use this menu to search the current document or search all documents.

   The flagged word (Burlington) is the name of a city. Although it is not in the dictionary, it is spelled correctly.

   Note:

   If the insertion point is currently placed in a story, the Search menu also includes options to search the selected story or the selected story after the insertion point.

9. **Activate the Case Sensitive option and click Add to add the word "Burlington" to the user dictionary.**

   The layout immediately changes to show the next flagged word — the sole capital letter "B." Many single letters will be flagged when you check spelling.

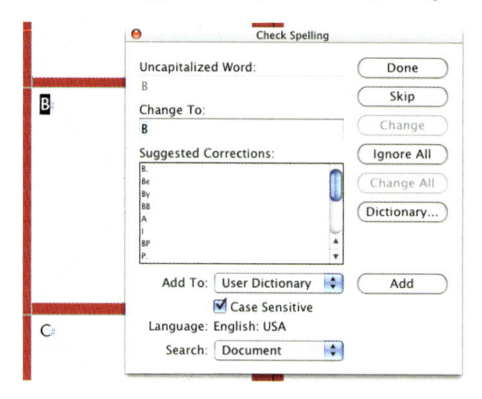

   Note:

   Never simply click Change when checking spelling. Review each flagged word carefully and make the correct choices within the context of the layout.

10. **Click Skip.**

    In context, this single letter is used as an identifier, so it is correct. However, other instances of the single letter B might be errors. Clicking Skip moves to the next flagged word without adding the word to the user dictionary.

370 Project 6: Versioned Brochure

11. **Review the next flagged word (the company's Web address).**

    There seems to be some inconsistency about when Web addresses are flagged on different operating systems, depending on the specific Web address and type (e.g., .biz, .com, .edu, etc.).

    If the Web address is flagged in your file, you don't want to add the Web address to the user dictionary, but you also don't want InDesign to continually flag it as an error.

    Note:

    If you used a paragraph return to separate the two lines of text in this frame, the next suspect after the Web address will be the uncapitalized "for" at the beginning of the sentence. Click Skip to continue to the next suspect.

12. **Click Ignore All, and then review the next flagged word.**

    "KinderKids" is the name of a product line, and it is spelled correctly.

13. **Click the Dictionary button in the Check Spelling dialog box. Choose toys_working.indd in the Target menu and click Add.**

    When you add words in the Check Spelling dialog box, the words are added to the default user dictionary. When you open the Dictionary dialog box from the Check Spelling dialog box, you can choose the file-specific dictionary in the Target menu and click Add to add the word to the dictionary for the selected file only.

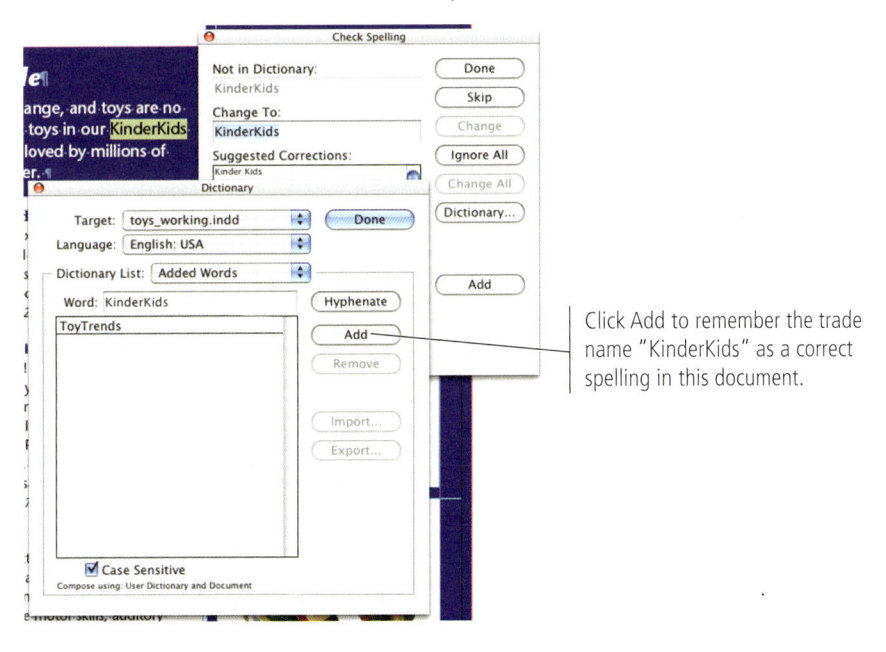

    Click Add to remember the trade name "KinderKids" as a correct spelling in this document.

14. **Click Done to close the Dictionary dialog box and return to the Check Spelling dialog box. Click Skip.**

    When you return to the Check Spelling dialog box, KinderKids still appears in the Word field. You have to click Skip to find the next suspect word.

Project 6: Versioned Brochure | 371

15. **Continue checking the spelling in the document. Make the following choices when prompted:**

and and	Click "and" in the Suggested Corrections list and click Change
Sleepytime	Add to toys_working.indd dictionary
Marvalous	Click "Marvelous" in the Suggested Corrections list and click Change
B	Skip
playscape	Add to toys_working.indd dictionary
ASTM	Skip
37x17x12	Skip

    Note:

    InDesign checks spelling based on the defined language dictionary. In addition to misspellings, however, InDesign also identifies repeated words (such as "the the"), uncapitalized words, and uncapitalized sentences. These options can be turned off in the Spelling pane of the Preferences dialog box.

16. **Click Done to close the Check Spelling dialog box.**

17. **Using the Edit Original function in the Links panel, open slide.indd and check spelling in the zfile. Correct any errors, then save and close the file.**

    As with the Find/Change function, the Check Spelling function only interacts with nested files if those files are already open and the All Documents option is selected in the Search menu.

18. **Save the toys_working.indd file and continue to the next stage of the project.**

Using Dynamic Spelling

INDESIGN FOUNDATIONS

You can turn on dynamic spelling (Edit>Spelling>Dynamic Spelling) to underline potential spelling and capitalization errors in a document without opening the Check Spelling dialog box. You can use the Spelling pane of the Preferences dialog box to assign a different-color underline for each of the four potential problems.

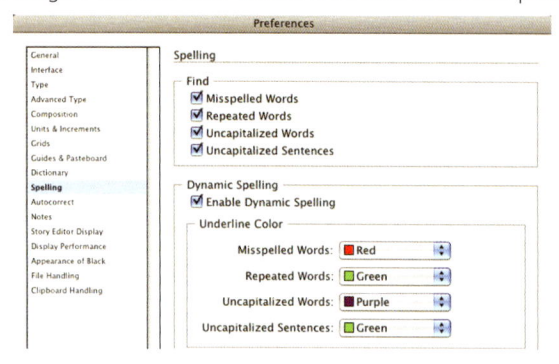

The misspelled word is underlined in red.

The repeated word is underlined in green.

Mideval documents give us many very sophisticated examples of this type of visual communication. Illuminations, or the the beautiful colored illustrations we find in documents that survive from the medieval period, were added by artistically talented monks to embellish the hand-written pages.

If you type directly into InDesign, you can turn on the Autocorrect feature (Edit>Spelling>Autocorrect) to correct misspelled words as you type. Of course, automatic corrections are not always correct; software can't always select the correct word within the context of the layout, and it might produce some very strange results for words that aren't in the active dictionary (technical or corporate terms, for example). To avoid the potential for fixing "errors" that aren't really errors, you can define what misspellings to replace and what spelling should replace those specific errors.

In the Autocorrect pane of the Preferences dialog box, you can click Add to define a specific misspelling, as well as the correct spelling to use. The Autocorrect List is maintained for the specified language dictionary.

Stage 4 Creating Multiple Layers

One of the advantages of using a professional page-layout application is the ability to create and manage complex layouts with a large number of elements. The InDesign Layers utility is a powerful option for controlling the objects that compose your layouts. In addition to managing individual elements, you can also use the Layers utility to create multiple versions of the same layout. This is particularly useful if:

- You are working with multiple overlapping objects on a page. Layers help you manage the stacking order of the objects.

- You are working with multiple versions of the same layout, such as two versions of the same layout in different languages, or several versions with different images in the same position for regional publications.

- You are creating a special die-cut layout using a template created in an illustration application.

Note:

Die-cut documents are cut in an odd, non-rectangular (page) shape or contain an area cut out within the page. The tab on a manila folder and a folded carton are two examples of die-cut jobs.

CREATE A NEW LAYER

When you use layers to create multiple versions of a document, the first step is to determine how many layers you need. Elements that will appear in all versions should exist on one layer. Each element that will change from one version to the next should be placed on its own layer.

This project requires three separate layers: one for the images used on both the U.S. and Canadian brochures; one for the text elements with U.S. prices; and one for the text elements with Canadian prices.

1. **With toys_working.indd open, navigate to Page 1 of the layout.**

2. **Display the Layers panel (Window>Layers).**

   By default, every file has one layer named "Layer 1".

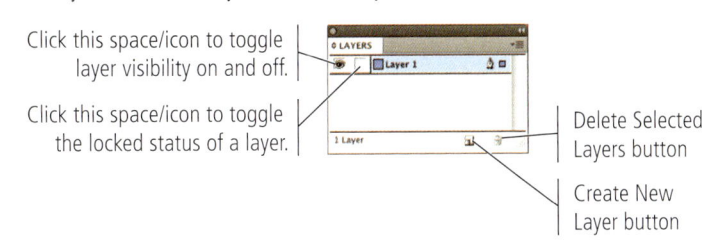

   Click this space/icon to toggle layer visibility on and off.
   Click this space/icon to toggle the locked status of a layer.
   Delete Selected Layers button
   Create New Layer button

   Note:

   Some of the built-in workspaces hide a number of menu options, including certain panels in the Window menu. If Layers is not available in the Window menu, choose the Essentials or Advanced workspace in the Workspace switcher (both of which include all menu commands), or choose Window>Show All Menu Items to reveal the hidden menu commands without changing the overall workspace.

3. **Click the Create New Layer button at the bottom of the Layers panel.**

   New layers are added above the currently selected layer; each new layer is added as Layer [N] (where "N" is a sequential number). In this case, the new layer is "Layer 2" because "Layer 1" already exists.

   The Pen icon indicates the layer where new objects will be created.

4. **In the Layers panel, double-click the Layer 2 name to open the Layer Options dialog box.**

Project 6: Versioned Brochure | 373

5. **Change the Name field to American Prices and review the other options.**

- The **Color** menu determines the color of frame edges and bounding box handles for objects on that layer. You can choose a different color from the menu, or you can choose Custom at the bottom of the menu and define your own color.
- If **Show Layer** is checked, the layer contents are visible in the document window. You can also change this attribute by toggling the eye icon in the Layers panel.
- If **Lock Layer** is checked, you can't select or change objects on that layer.
- If **Print Layer** is checked, the layer will output when you print or export to PDF.
- The **Show Guides** option allows you to create and display different sets of guides for different layers; this is a more versatile option than showing or hiding all guides (which occurs with the View>Grids & Guides>Show/Hide Guides toggle).
- The **Lock Guides** option allows you to lock and unlock guides on specific layers.
- If **Suppress Text Wrap When Layer is Hidden** is checked, text on underlying layers reflows when the layer is hidden.

Controlling Text Wrap on Different Layers

Text wrap attributes of an object affect all text frames that touch that wrap object (unless Ignore Text Wrap in the Text Frame Options dialog box is checked for a specific text frame). The wrap object's position in the stacking order, as well as a layer's position in the layer stack, are both irrelevant.

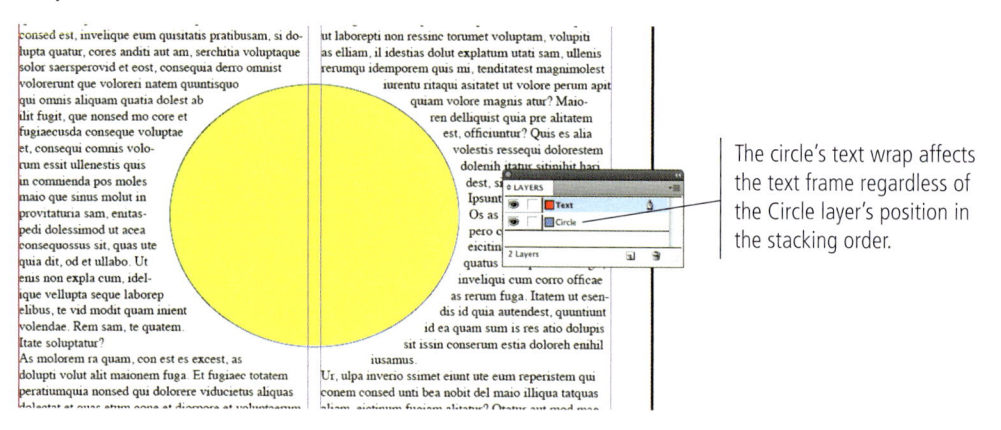

The circle's text wrap affects the text frame regardless of the Circle layer's position in the stacking order.

If Suppress Text Wrap When Layer is Hidden is checked in the Layer Options dialog box, text on other layers reflows when the layer is hidden. The text wrap attributes of objects on the layer are only applied when the layer is visible.

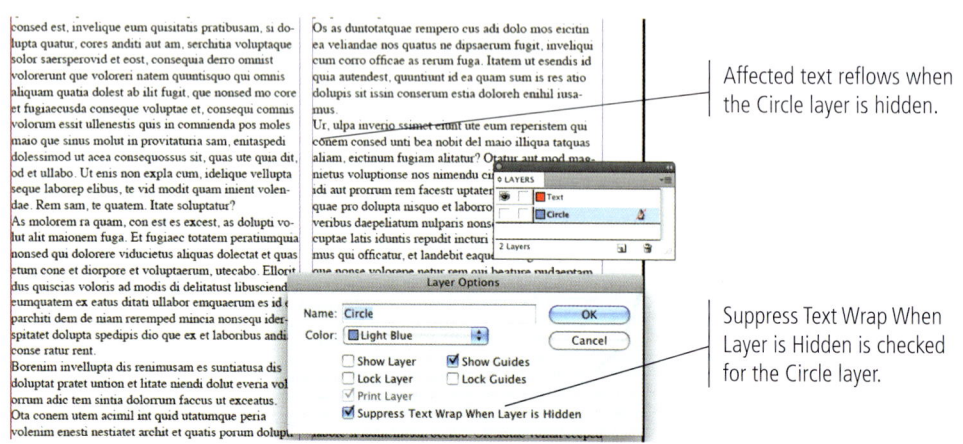

Affected text reflows when the Circle layer is hidden.

Suppress Text Wrap When Layer is Hidden is checked for the Circle layer.

6. **Click OK to close the Layer Options dialog box.**

   The layer shows its new name.

7. **Double-click Layer 1 in the Layers panel. Change the layer name to Common Elements and click OK.**

8. **Save the file and continue to the next exercise.**

Control Objects and Layers

The only variation from one version to the next is the prices, so only text boxes containing prices need to be moved to the variation layer. Rather than creating the Canadian Prices layer immediately, it makes more sense to move the varying elements to the American Prices layer, and then duplicate that layer with the elements already in place.

1. **With toys_working.indd open, navigate to Page 1 of the layout.**

2. **Using the Selection tool, select the text frame that contains the description of the classic car swing.**

   If you remember from the previous exercise, this text frame is actually threaded from the blue text frame at the top of the page.

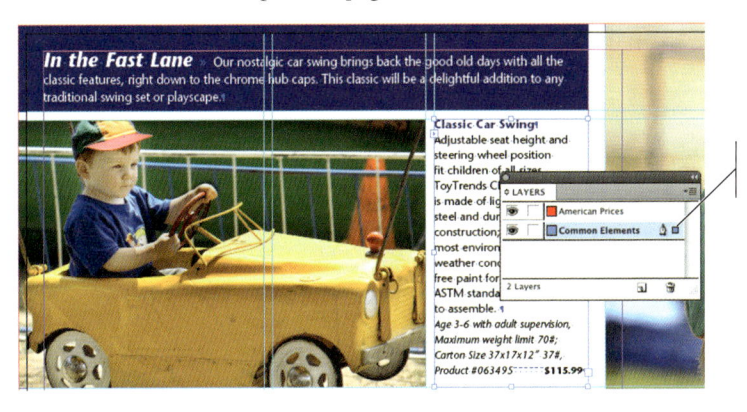

   This icon indicates the location of the selected object(s).

3. **Shift-click the blue text frame at the top of the page to add it to the selection.**

Note:

Although you can thread text from one layer to another, we don't recommend doing so. Whenever possible, place all frames in the same thread on the same layer.

Project 6: Versioned Brochure   375

4. **In the Layers panel, drag the Selected Items icon from the Common Elements layer to the American Prices layer.**

   Drag the Selected Items icon to another layer to move the selected objects from one layer to another.

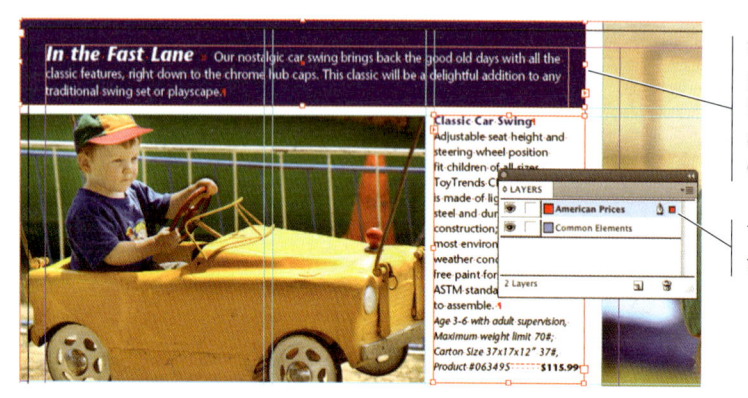

   When you release the mouse button (after dragging the Selected Items icon in the Layers panel), red frame edges and bounding box handles match the color of the American Prices layer.

   The two selected items are now on the American Prices layer.

5. **On Page 2, move the two threaded text frames to the American Prices layer.**

   The last item to move is the description copy for the sliding board, which exists in a separate file. You could accomplish this task using several methods:

   - Move the entire placed slide file and create multiple versions of the slide.indd file to place on each layer in the brochure file.
   - Create multiple layers in the slide.indd file and use the Object Layer Options to control which layers are visible on which layer of the brochure file.
   - Copy the varying text frame from the placed file into the main brochure file.

   Every project will have different requirements. In this case, you're going to use the simplest method — copying the text frame from one file and pasting it into another.

   Note:

   Unfortunately, there is no way to divide the placed InDesign file into its component elements from within the brochure file. If you want those elements to be part of the brochure, you have to copy and paste.

   376 Project 6: Versioned Brochure

6. Control/right-click the placed slide.indd file in the layout and choose Edit Original from the contextual menu.

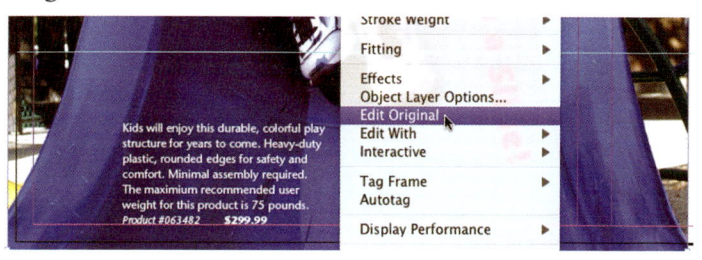

7. In the external file, use the Direct Selection tool to select the text frame and choose Edit>Cut.

8. Save the external file and close it.

The placed file on the Common Elements layer no longer has a description text frame.

9. In the `toys_working.indd` file, make sure the American Prices layer is the target layer and choose Edit>Paste.

10. Move the frame to the same approximate location where it appeared in the original slide.indd file.

11. Save the file and continue to the next exercise.

Project 6: Versioned Brochure

Use a Duplicate Layer to Create Different Versions

Now that all varying text elements are in place on the American Prices layer, it is a simple process to duplicate the layer and create the version for the Canadian prices.

1. **With toys_working.indd open, Control/right-click the American Prices layer and choose Duplicate Layer "American Prices" from the contextual menu.**

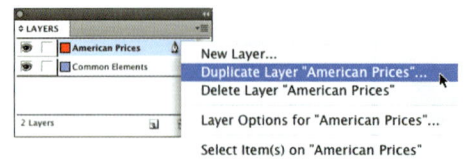

2. **In the resulting dialog box, change the layer name to Canadian Prices.**

3. **Choose a color other than red from the Color menu, and then click OK.**

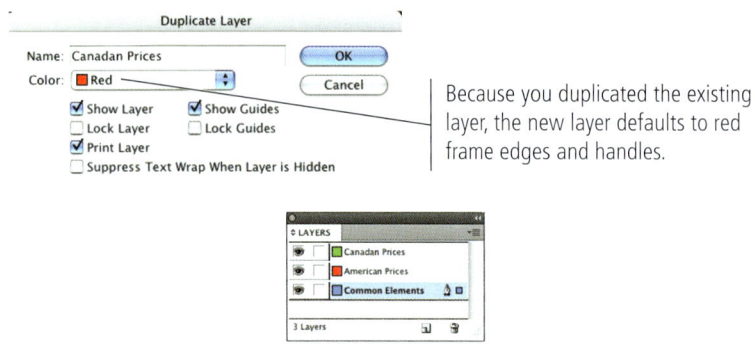

   Because you duplicated the existing layer, the new layer defaults to red frame edges and handles.

   Note:
   Two layers of the same color defeat the purpose of unique layer identifiers. When you duplicate a layer, it's a good idea to change the layer color for the duplicate.

4. **Find and highlight the product price on Page 1 of the layout.**

5. **Change the highlighted price to 139.99.**

   Because the same text frame exists on both prices layers, you can immediately see the problem — with both prices visible, neither is legible.

6. **In the Layers panel, click the eye icon to hide the American Prices layer.**

   Note:
   By default, hidden layers do not print. You learn how to control layer output at the end of this project.

7. **Navigate to Page 2 of the layout.**

Project 6: Versioned Brochure

8. **Find and change each price in the brochure (there are five prices on Page 2):**

Slide	**$359.99**
Blocks	**$29.99**
Keys	**$11.99**
Rattle	**$9.99**
Teddy bear	**$18.99**

9. **Save the file and continue to the next exercise.**

PREVIEW SEPARATIONS

To be entirely confident in your color output, you should also check the separations that will be created when your file is output to an imagesetter. InDesign's Separations Preview panel makes this easy to accomplish from directly within the application workspace.

1. **With `toys_working.indd` open, choose Window>Output>Separations Preview.**

2. **In the View menu of the Separations Preview panel, choose Separations.**

    When Separations is selected in the View menu, all separations in the current file are listed in the panel. You can turn individual separations on and off to preview the different ink separations that will be created:

    - To view a single separation and hide all others, click the name of the separation you want to view. By default, areas of coverage appear in black; you can preview separations in color by toggling off the Show Single Plates in Black command in the panel Options menu.

    - To view more than one separation at the same time, click the empty space to the left of the separation name. When viewing multiple separations, each separation is shown in color.

    - To hide a separation, click the eye icon to the left of the separation name.

    - To view all process plates at once, click the CMYK option at the top of the panel.

3. **Click Pantone 186 C in the Separations Preview panel, and then click the empty space to the left of Pantone 102 C to review where those two colors are used in the layout.**

   The placed logos on Page 1 use both selected Pantone colors.

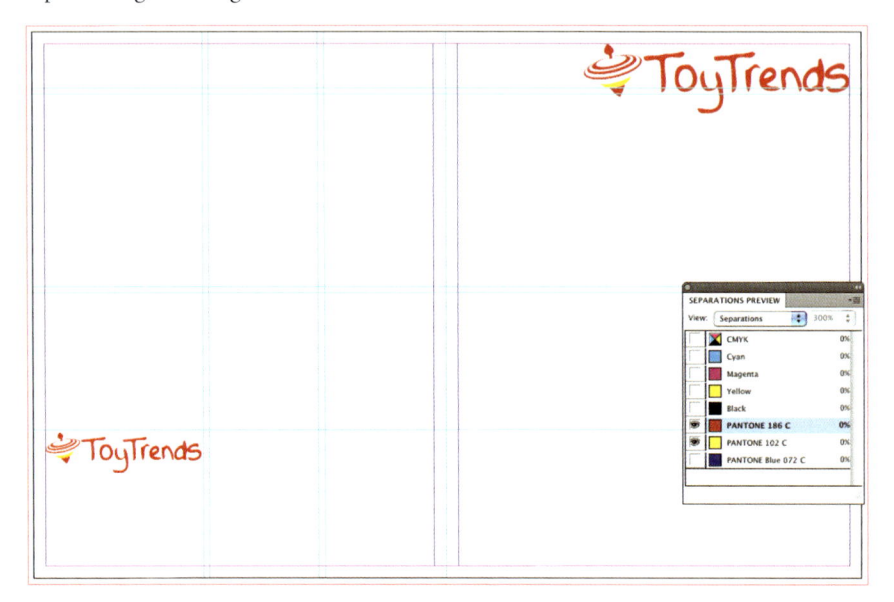

Monitoring Ink Limits

In CMYK color, shades of gray are reproduced using combinations of four printing inks. In theory, a solid black would be printed as 100% of all four inks, and pure white would be 0% of all four inks. This, however, does not take into consideration the limitations of mechanical printing.

Paper's absorption rate, the speed of the printing press, and other mechanical factors limit the amount of ink that can be placed on the same area of a page. If too much ink is applied, the result is a dark blob with no visible detail; heavy layers of ink also result in drying problems, smearing, and a number of other issues.

Total area coverage (also called **total ink coverage**) is the largest percentage of ink that can be safely printed on a single area. This number varies according to the ink/paper/press combination being used for a given job. The Specifications for Web Offset Printing (SWOP) indicates a 300% maximum. Many sheetfed printers require 280% maximum, while the number for newspapers is usually around 240% because the lower-quality paper absorbs more ink.

In the Separations Preview panel, you can choose Ink Limit in the View menu and define the TAC value for the file. You can then preview the layout to find elements that exceed the defined limit; if color is critical, those images should be corrected in Photoshop to be within the defined CMYK working space and ink limits.

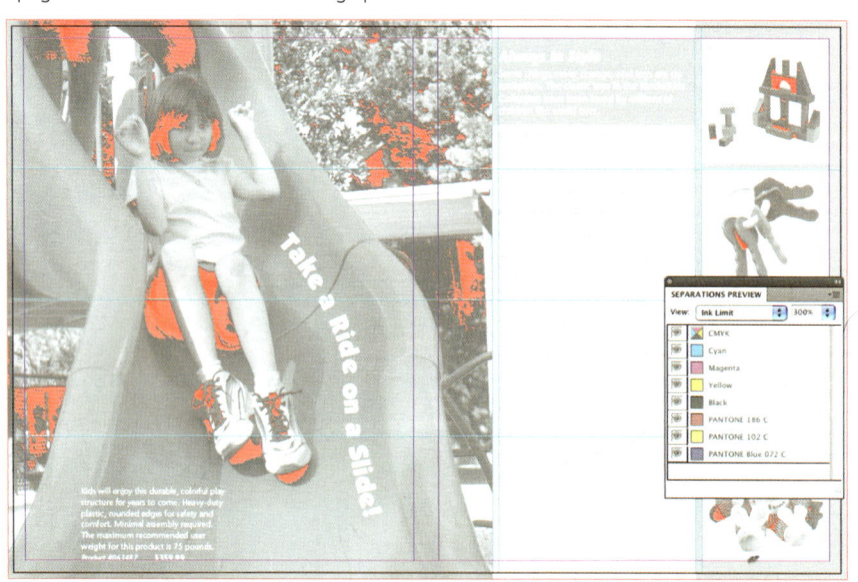

INDESIGN FOUNDATIONS

4. **Click Pantone Blue 072 C in the Separations Preview panel to see where that color is used.**

   As your client stated, the brochure should use a single spot color — for this issue, the blue spot color in the logo. By reviewing the separation, you can see that the blue from the logo is also used for the accent elements on both pages of the layout.

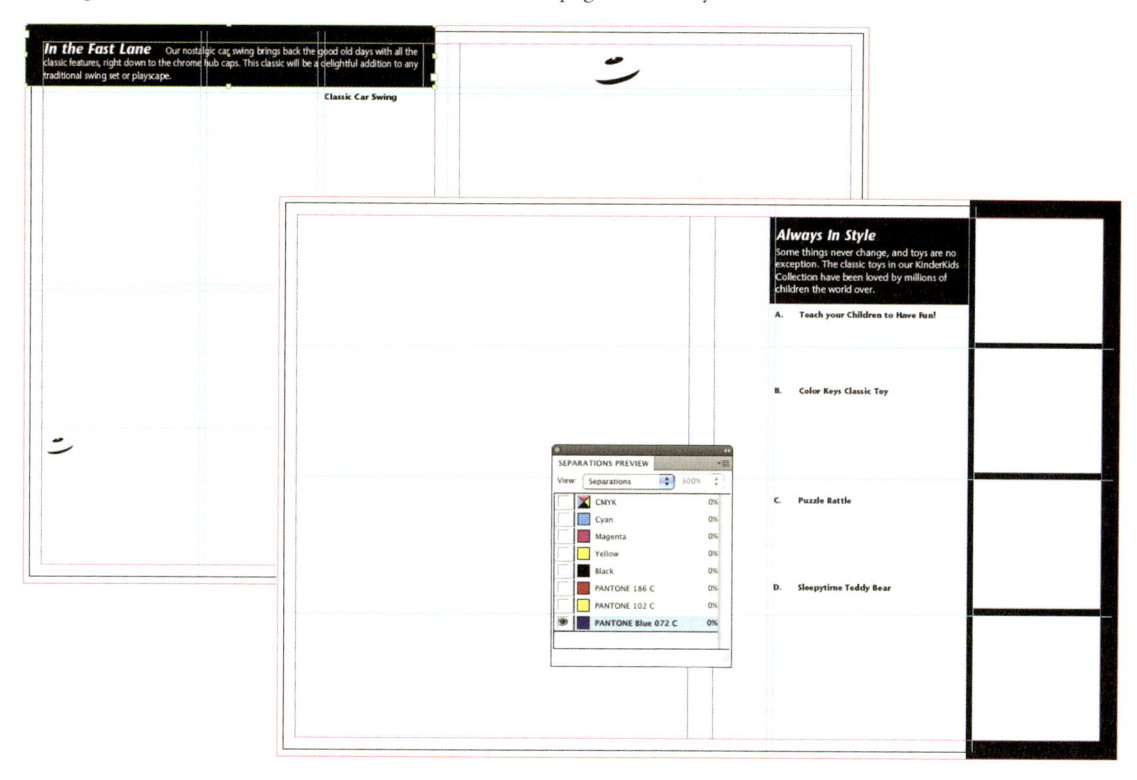

5. **Click the empty space left of CMYK in the Separations Preview panel to view the CMYK separations in addition to the Pantone Blue 072 C separation.**

   You can't simply delete the spot colors because they are used elsewhere in the document. You could convert them for output only, but if you need to output more than once you would have to convert the colors again each time you output the file. In this case, the most efficient option is to convert the unwanted spot colors to process colors before you output the file.

   The red and yellow elements from the two hidden spot separations are not visible.

Project 6: Versioned Brochure   381

6. **In the Swatches panel, Control/right-click Pantone 186 C and choose Swatch Options from the contextual menu.**

7. **Change the Color Type menu to Process and click OK.**

Note:

Be very careful when changing spot colors to process. One reason for using spot colors is to reproduce colors that are outside the CMYK gamut; when spot colors are converted to their nearest possible CMYK equivalents, some (possibly drastic) color shift will occur.

The missing red elements now appear because they are CMYK builds instead of spot colors.

After converting the Pantone 186 C swatch to process color, the separation is removed from the Separations Preview panel.

8. **Repeat Steps 6–7 for the Pantone 102 C swatch.**

All red and yellow elements are now visible.

The Separations Preview panel now shows the correct number of separations for this file.

9. **Save the file and continue to the final exercise.**

382   Project 6: Versioned Brochure

Export Color-Managed PDF Files

The file is now complete and ready for output. To create the two versions of the file, you have to output the same file twice, selecting different layers for each version.

1. **With `toys_working.indd` open, create a final job package (File>Package) with all elements of the job (document, pictures, and fonts).**

   InDesign collects placed files and all necessary pieces for those files in the job's Links folder.

   Note:

   Refer to Project 3 for complete instructions on creating a job package.

2. **Choose File>Export. Navigate to your WIP>Toys folder as the destination and choose Adobe PDF in the Format menu.**

3. **Change the file name to `toys_canadian.pdf` and click Save.**

4. **Choose [High Quality Print] in the Preset menu.**

5. **In the General options, make sure Visible & Printable Layers is selected in the Export Layers menu.**

   When you output a file with layers, you can choose All Layers (including hidden and non-printable layers), Visible Layers (regardless of printable status), or Visible & Printable Layers.

   Use this menu to determine which layers are included.

   Note:

   These options are also available in the Print dialog box.

Project 6: Versioned Brochure 383

6. **In the Marks and Bleed pane, turn on Crop Marks and activate the Use Document Bleed Settings option.**

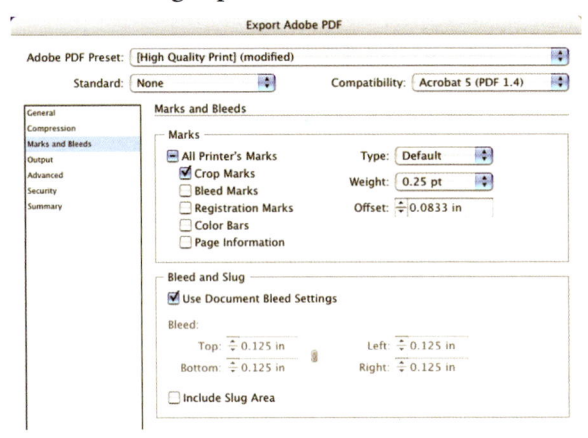

7. **In the Output pane, choose Convert to Destination in the Color Conversion menu.**

    You have several options for converting colors when you output a file:

    - **No Color Conversion** maintains all color data (including placed images) in its current space.
    - **Convert to Destination** converts colors to the profile selected in the Destination menu.
    - **Convert to Destination (Preserve Numbers)** converts colors to the destination profile if the applied profile does not match the defined destination profile. Objects without color profiles are not converted.

    The Destination menu defines the gamut for the output device that will be used. (This menu defaults to the active destination working space.) Color information in the file (and placed images) is converted to the selected Destination profile.

    Note:

    Spot color information is preserved when colors are converted to the destination space.

8. **Choose Include Destination Profile in the Profile Inclusion Policy menu.**

    The **Profile Inclusion Policy** menu determines whether color profiles are embedded in the resulting PDF file. (Different options are available, depending on what you selected in the Color Conversion menu.)

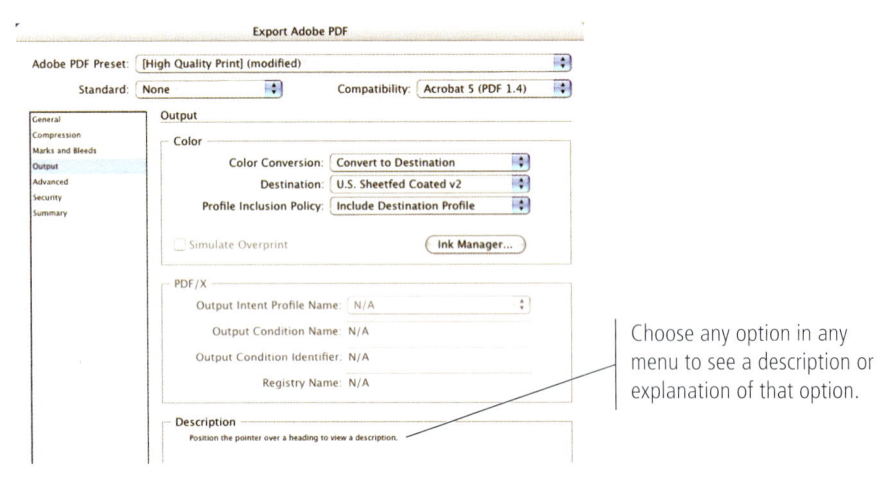

    Choose any option in any menu to see a description or explanation of that option.

9. **Click the Save Preset button. In the Save Preset dialog box, name the preset Toy Brochure PDF and click OK.**

    You're going to export this file twice; creating a preset means you make your export choices only once.

384 Project 6: Versioned Brochure

10. Click Export to create the PDF file.

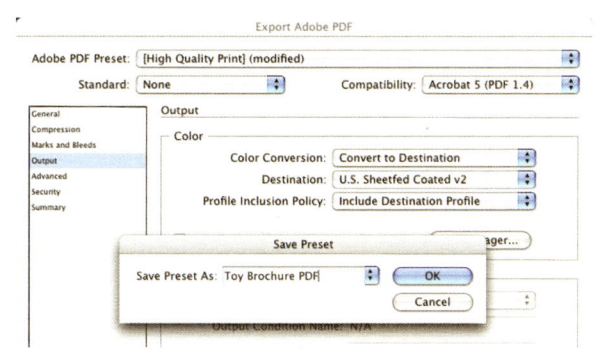

11. When you return to the layout, hide the Canadian Prices layer and show the American Prices layer.

12. Export the file to PDF again, this time with the name **toys_american.pdf**. In the Export Adobe PDF dialog box, make sure the Toy Brochure PDF preset is selected and click Export.

Use this menu to call the preset you just saved.

Note:

When you reopen the Export Adobe PDF dialog box, the Toy Brochure PDF preset is already selected. The menu remembers the last-used settings.

13. Close the toys_working file without saving.

Using the Ink Manager

INDESIGN FOUNDATIONS

The Ink Manager, primarily used by experienced commercial output providers, offers control over specific inks at output time. Changes in this dialog box affect the current output, not how the colors are defined in the document. (You can access this dialog box by clicking the Ink Manager button in the Output pane of the Print or Export Adobe PDF dialog box.)

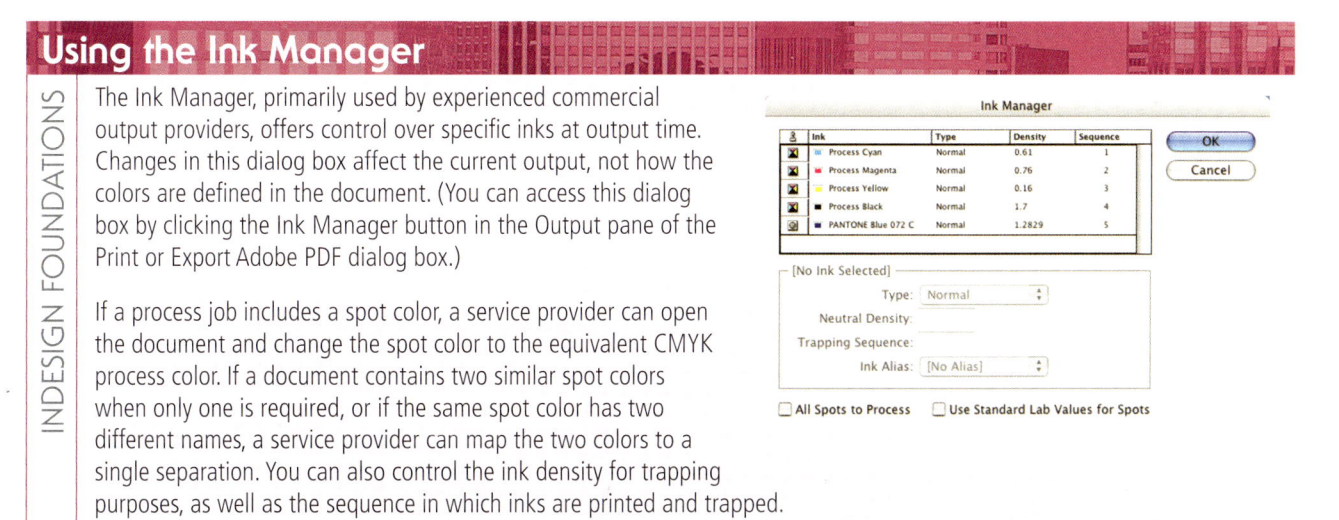

If a process job includes a spot color, a service provider can open the document and change the spot color to the equivalent CMYK process color. If a document contains two similar spot colors when only one is required, or if the same spot color has two different names, a service provider can map the two colors to a single separation. You can also control the ink density for trapping purposes, as well as the sequence in which inks are printed and trapped.

Project 6: Versioned Brochure 385

Understanding Trapping for Color Printing

Although trapping should typically be left to experienced professionals in the output provider's prepress department, if you understand these concepts, you will be better able to prevent potential output problems when you build a layout.

Trapping Theory and Terminology

In process-color printing, the four process colors (Cyan, Magenta, Yellow, and Black) are imaged or separated onto individual printing plates; each color separation is printed on a separate unit of a printing press. When printed on top of each other in varying percentages, the semitransparent inks produce the range of colors in the CMYK gamut. Spot colors are printed using specially formulated inks as additional color separations.

Because printing is a mechanical process, some variation between the different units of the press is possible (if not likely). Paper moves through the units of a press at considerable speed, and some movement from side to side is inevitable. Each printing plate has one or more registration marks (crosshairs) that are used to monitor the alignment of each color. If the units are in register, the cross hairs from each color plate print exactly on top of each other.

Misregistration can cause a noticeable gap of uninked paper between adjacent elements, particularly when these elements are comprised of different ink colors. When a press is out of register, the individual overlapping colors are discernible.

Misregister results in a visible gap between objects.

Misregister

If any misregister occurs, type can become blurry or virtually unreadable. Any time multiple inks are placed on top of each other, you run the risk of misregister.

Trapping is the compensation for misregister of the color plates on a printing press. Trapping minimizes or eliminates these errors by artificially expanding adjacent colors so small areas of color on the edge of each element overlap and print on top of one another. If sufficiently large, this expansion of color, or trap, fills in the undesirable inkless gap between elements. Trapping procedures differ based upon your workflow; most service providers will perform trapping before generating film or plates. The specific amount of trapping to be applied varies, depending on the ink/paper/press combination that will be used for the job.

A **knockout** is an area of background color that is removed so a lighter foreground color is visible. To achieve white (paper-colored) type on a black background, for example, the black background is removed wherever the type overlaps the black. Any time a lighter color appears on top of a darker color, the area of the lighter color is knocked out of the background.

Overprint   Knockout

When a color is set to knock out, anything beneath that color will not be printed. If the black knocks out the Cyan, any misregistration can result in a paper-colored gap where the two objects meet. Setting black to overprint eliminates the possibility of a gap caused by misregistration. (The dashed lines in the graphic are for illustration only.)

Overprint is essentially the opposite of knockout. A darker-color foreground object is printed directly on top of a lighter-color background, which means that slight variation in the units of the press will not be as noticeable, especially if the darker color is entirely contained within the lighter color. Black is commonly set to overprint other colors, as are some special colors that are printed using opaque inks. Black is particularly effective when overprinted since it becomes visually richer when other process colors — especially cyan — are mixed with it.

Understanding Trapping for Color Printing (continued)

A **choke** means that the edge of the background color is expanded into the space in which the foreground color will be printed. A **spread** means that the edge of the foreground color is expanded to overprint the edge of the background color. As a general rule, the lighter object should be trapped into the darker area. This rule helps determine whether you should choke or spread.

- If the background is darker than the foreground object, the lighter color of the foreground object should be spread to overprint the darker background.
- If the foreground color is darker than the background color, the lighter background color is choked so it overprints the darker foreground color.

The foreground circle is spread into the darker background.

The background color is choked into the darker foreground.

If adjacent elements share a large percentage of one or more common colors, trapping between those elements is unnecessary. If both elements contain a lot of magenta, for example, the continuity of the magenta between the two objects will mask any gaps that occur between the other process colors in the two images; this makes trapping unnecessary. The general rule is that if two adjacent elements share one process color that varies by less than 50%, or if two elements share two or more process colors that vary by less than 80%, don't bother with trapping — the continuous layer of the inks common to both elements will effectively mask any gaps.

C: 85
M: 50
Y: 0
K: 0

C: 0
M: 50
Y: 80
K: 0

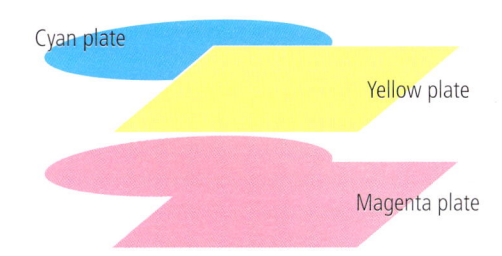

Cyan plate
Yellow plate
Magenta plate

Using the Attributes Panel

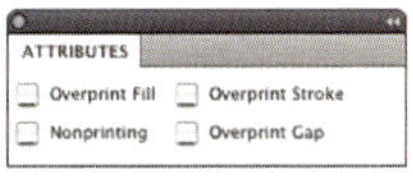

You can overprint strokes or fills of selected paths using the Attributes panel (Window>Attributes). An overprinted stroke or fill doesn't need to be trapped, because overprinting covers any potential gaps between adjacent colors. You can change the overprint attributes of a frame (fill and stroke) by selecting the frame with the Selection tool. You can also set the overprint attributes of frame contents (such as text) by selecting the relevant contents with the Direct Selection tool. The Overprint Gap option is only available if the stroke style has gaps between elements of the stroke (such as dashed lines or double-stroke lines).

Controlling the Appearance and Overprint Attributes of CMYK Black

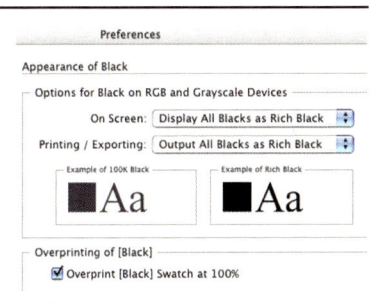

The black inks that are used in process-color printing might not produce a pure opaque black. (You used a rich black in Project 2 to improve the appearance of solid black areas.) On screen or on a desktop inkjet printer, however, 100% black typically looks as black as black can be. This discrepancy can cause problems when you don't get what you expect in the final printed job. To solve the problem, you can change the appearance of black in the Appearance of Black preferences. You can define how blacks appear on-screen and in output.

- **Display All Blacks Accurately** shows 100% CMYK black as dark gray on screen.
- **Display All Blacks As Rich Black** shows 100% CMYK black as pure black (R=0 G=0 B=0) on screen.
- **Output All Blacks Accurately** outputs CMYK blacks based on the actual numbers in the color definition. This allows you to see the difference between pure black and rich black on non-PostScript desktop printers.
- **Output All Blacks As Rich Black** outputs all blacks as pure black (R=0 G=0 B=0) when printing to a non-PostScript desktop printer.

By default, [Black] is set to overprint other colors. If you want to knock out [Black] elements, you have to uncheck the Overprint [Black] Swatch at 100% option.

Project 6: Versioned Brochure   387

Controlling Trapping in InDesign

INDESIGN FOUNDATIONS

InDesign applies trapping using Trap Presets, or defined collections of trapping settings. The Trap Presets panel (Window>Output>Trap Presets) allows you to create, edit, and apply trap presets to specific pages in a layout. If you don't apply a specific trap preset to a page, that page will use the [Default] trap preset.

If you choose Assign Trap Preset in the panel Options menu, you can assign an existing preset to all pages or a specific range of pages. Clicking Done simply closes the dialog box; you have to click the Assign button to change the preset for the selected pages.

Existing trap assignments are listed in this pane.

If you edit the Default trap preset, you open the Modify Trap Preset Options dialog box. If you create a new trap preset, you open the New Trap Preset dialog box. In either case, you have the same choices; the only difference is the availability of the Name field (you can't rename the Default trap preset option).

Trap Width. Different types of paper and inks, as well as different output devices, require different amounts of trapping. The two fields in this section define the amount of overlap that will be created in the traps.

- **Default** defines the trap width for all colors except those with 100% Black. The default value is 0.0035" (1/4 point).
- **Black** defines the distance that other colors will spread into colors with 100% Black. The default is 0.0069" (1/2 point).

Trap Appearance. These menus determine the shape of joins (where two trap edges meet) and ends in trap lines.

- **Join Style** controls the shape of the outside join of two trap segments (Miter, Round, and Bevel).
- **End Style** determines how the ends of lines appear when three different trap lines intersect.

Images. InDesign is able to trap placed raster images; each option handles imported graphics differently.

- **Trap Placement** determines where the trap falls when you trap vector objects to bitmap images. Center creates a trap that straddles the edge between objects and images. Choke causes objects to overlap abutting images. Neutral Density applies the same trapping rules as used elsewhere in the document. Spread causes images to overlap abutting objects.
- **Trap Objects To Images** forces vector objects (e.g., frame strokes) to trap to images using the Trap Placement settings.
- **Trap Images To Images** enables trapping along the edges of two overlapping raster images.
- **Trap Images Internally** enables trapping within an individual raster image. This option should be used with caution for only high-contrast images; it does not produce good results for photographic (continuous-tone) images.
- **Trap 1-Bit Images** enables trapping for 1-bit (bitmap or line art) images.

Trap Thresholds. These values determine when trapping will be applied.

- **Step** specifies the threshold at which a trap is created, or the percentage that adjacent component colors must be different before trapping occurs. Higher Step percentages require greater variance in adjacent colors; lower percentages make the application more sensitive to color differences, resulting in more traps.
- **Black Color** defines the minimum percentage of black ink required before the Black trap-width setting is applied.
- **Black Density** defines a neutral density value at which InDesign treats an ink as black. Any inks with a neutral density at or above this value will use the Black trap-width setting.
- **Sliding Trap** determines when traps start to straddle the centerline of the color edges. The value refers to the proportion of the lighter color's neutral density to that of adjacent darker colors; using the default value (70%), the trap will be applied at the centerline when the lighter color's neutral density is more than 70% of the darker color's neutral density (lighter color's neutral density divided by darker color's neutral density > 0.70).
- **Trap Color Reduction** defines the degree to which components from adjacent colors are used to reduce the trap color. A Trap Color Reduction lower than 100% lightens the color of the trap; Trap Color Reduction of 0% makes a trap with the same neutral density as the darker color.

Project Review

fill in the blank

1. A(n) _____ describes the color reproduction characteristics of a particular input or output device.

2. _____ is the range of possible colors within a specific color model.

3. _____ are the four component colors in process-color output.

4. When importing an Adobe Illustrator file, the Crop To _____ option places the file based on the defined Artboard size.

5. When placing a native Photoshop file, you can check the _____ option in the Place dialog box to be able to control layer visibility before the file is placed.

6. The appearance of all images in a layout is controlled in the _____ menu.

7. When you place a PDF file, the _____ option in the Place PDF dialog box determines which area of the file (trim, bleed, etc.) is imported.

8. When placing images into a layout, press _____ to select multiple, non-contiguous files in the Place dialog box.

9. The _____ lists all files that are placed in a layout, including the location and status of each placed file.

10. The _____ Fitting option scales an image nonproportionally to match the dimensions of the containing object.

short answer

1. Briefly explain the difference between additive and subtractive color.

2. Briefly explain the concept of color management, as it relates to building a layout in InDesign.

3. Briefly explain two scenarios in which layers would be useful.

Project 6: Versioned Brochure

Portfolio Builder Project

Use what you learned in this project to complete the following freeform exercise.
Carefully read the art director and client comments, then create your own design to meet the needs of the project.
Use the space below to sketch ideas; when finished, write a brief explanation of your reasoning behind your final design.

art director comments

Your client, the Miami/Equatorial Travel Agency, wants to create a graphics-rich brochure to promote travel and tourism in Costa Rica.

To complete this project, you should:

❏ Design two versions of the brochure using the client's die-cut template. Make sure to incorporate bleed allowance outside the template edges.

❏ Flip the template horizontally on the second page so the front and back of the piece line up properly.

❏ Create different layers for the English and Spanish versions of the brochure.

❏ Use the die template, images, and text for both languages from the RF_Builders>Travel folder.

client comments

We want this brochure to be unique. Our printer gave us a die-cut template that we'd like to use for this job. The printer's CSR said to just place the file as a template on its own layer in the file, and treat the template lines like page edges.

We want the brochure to focus on images — sunsets, beaches... the kind of images that make someone say, "I want to go there." We've given you some of those, but feel free to find other images that will convey this same message.

There is very little text. The words "Costa Rica" should appear on the front, back, and inside of the piece. Otherwise, we have a blurb about how to contact us, which has to be included in the final piece, and some quotes you can use or not.

Here in Miami, many of our customers are fluent in Spanish. Even though there is very little text for the brochure, we're going to create two versions of the brochure — one in English and one in Spanish.

project justification

_____
_____
_____
_____
_____
_____
_____
_____
_____
_____
_____
_____
_____
_____
_____

Project Summary

As you have seen, placing pictures into an InDesign layout is a relatively easy task, whether you place them one at a time or load multiple images at once and then simply click to place the loaded images into the appropriate spots. InDesign allows you to work with all of the common image formats (including PDF), as well as placing one InDesign layout directly into another. The Links panel is a valuable tool for managing images, from updating file status, to replacing one image with another, to opening an external file in its native application so you can easily make changes in placed files.

Finetuning a layout requires checking for common errors — both technical (such as low-resolution images) and practical (such as spelling errors). You learned in Project 3 how to use InDesign's preflighting tools; the Check Spelling utility is just as important in creating high-quality, professional designs.

The InDesign Layers utility makes it very easy to create versioned documents. Once you have determined which elements will change, you can simply move elements to the appropriate layers and make the necessary changes. This might be as basic as changing some prices, or it might involve entirely new text (for example, a Spanish translation). Regardless of how much content will change, layers are the easiest way to create and manage multiple versions of the same file.

- Place and control a PDF file
- Place and control a TIFF file
- Place and control a layered Photoshop file
- Place and control an EPS file
- Place and control a native Illustrator file
- Place and control a native InDesign file
- Load and place multiple images at one time
- Edit a placed image using the Links panel
- Find and replace elements with specific formatting attributes
- Find and replace text strings, with and without specific formatting attributes
- Check for and correct spelling errors
- Create multiple versions of the layout using layers

Project 6: Versioned Brochure

project 7

National Parks Info Pieces

Your client is the marketing manager for the National Parks Service (NPS). She wants to create a series of collateral pieces that will be used at tourism centers to lure potential visitors. She hired you to produce a one-sheet flyer that will be distributed in print and online, a rack card that can be placed in area hotels, and a postcard that will be given away to park visitors.

This project incorporates the following skills:

❏ Using placeholder objects to design an initial layout concept
❏ Adjusting a layout concept to suit content provided by a client
❏ Creating an XML file using tagged frames and content
❏ Building a layout from imported XML content
❏ Controlling the structure of a layout to merge XML content into tagged frames
❏ Defining hyperlinks to link layout elements to an external Web page
❏ Creating interactive buttons with multiple states
❏ Exporting PDF files without interactive elements for print distribution
❏ Exporting PDF files with interactive elements for digital distribution

Project Meeting

client comments

We want to create several pieces to promote tourism in the national parks. Each piece should include two images, which we'll provide as soon as we decide which ones we want to use. We haven't written any of the content yet, but we can tell you it will include the park name, one paragraph of historical copy, a list of four or five "fun facts" about the park, and directions to the park.

For each park, we want you to create two documents — a flyer and a rack card — with the same content. The flyer will be sent to tourism boards and agencies as a handout; the rack card will be placed in hotels near the park for potential visitors. We also want to create a postcard that we can give away as a souvenir to visitors; this piece will include some (but not all) of the content from the other two pieces.

We'd also like to offer the flyers digitally, both as downloads from our Web site and as attachments to emails. In the digital version, we would like to add buttons that link to the parks' home pages on the NPS Web site and to our basic informational email address.

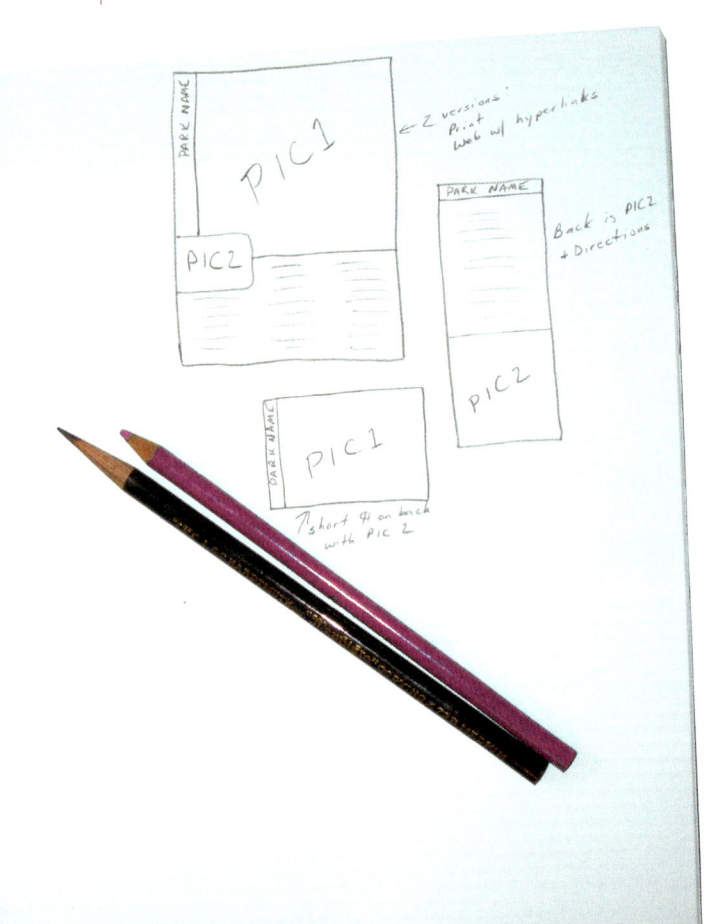

art director comments

The client promised to give us actual content for at least one park by the end of the week. While you're waiting, I want you to start experimenting with a layout. You know all elements that need to be included, so you can use placeholders to play with various options.

There are more than 350 national parks, monuments, and other protected areas in the national park system. When the flyer layout is finalized, save it as a template so you can use it again later when we get the content for the different parks.

Because each piece is going to include the same content, you can use InDesign's XML tools to share the content between the pieces. This way, if the client decides to change something, you can modify only one instance, and then update the XML file in all other documents.

When you create the interactive elements, build them into the flyer file that will be used for print. InDesign makes it easy to control whether those elements will be included in a PDF file, so there is no need to create two versions of that document.

project objectives

To complete this project, you will:

❏ Use text and picture placeholders to design a layout concept

❏ Experiment with glyphs to find suitable bullet characters

❏ Create styles based on formatting in the layout

❏ Redefine styles based on local formatting overrides

❏ Sample colors from a placed image to unify the completed layout

❏ Tag frames and content for XML

❏ Generate a structured XML file from layout content

❏ Create additional layouts from imported XML content

❏ Create hyperlinks and buttons to add user interactivity

❏ Export multiple PDF files for different distribution methods

Stage 1 Experimenting with Layout Options

Many InDesign projects start with little more than an idea. Although templates, master pages, and styles are invaluable tools when implementing a layout, in many cases you simply need to open a blank document and start experimenting. When you have to design a project from scratch, InDesign makes it easy to create and format objects and experiment with different options, and then create masters and styles when you are satisfied with your work.

Use Text Placeholders to Structure a Layout

It's always a good idea to begin a project as soon as possible after getting the assignment. When working with clients, however, you will often find that the idea for a project comes before the actual content — sometimes long before the client has finalized the text or provided the promised images. Rather than waiting until the client's content is ready — which is sometimes the day before a project is due — you can design a layout using placeholders to mark the location of pictures and text frames, and even experiment with the appearance of different elements of the text.

The pieces in this project will include the same basic elements:

- Two images
- The park name
- One paragraph of historical copy about the park
- A short list of "fun facts" about the park
- Directions to the park from major landmarks

The main piece of this project is the so-called "one-sheet," or a single-page flyer printed on one side of the sheet. Because this is the primary piece of the project, you'll create that file first.

1. **Copy the Parks folder from the WIP folder on your Resource CD to the WIP folder where you are saving your work.**

2. **Create a new letter-size file using portrait orientation. Define 1/4" margins on the top and bottom, 3/8" margins on the left and right, and 1/8" bleeds on all four sides. Use non-facing pages and no master text frame.**

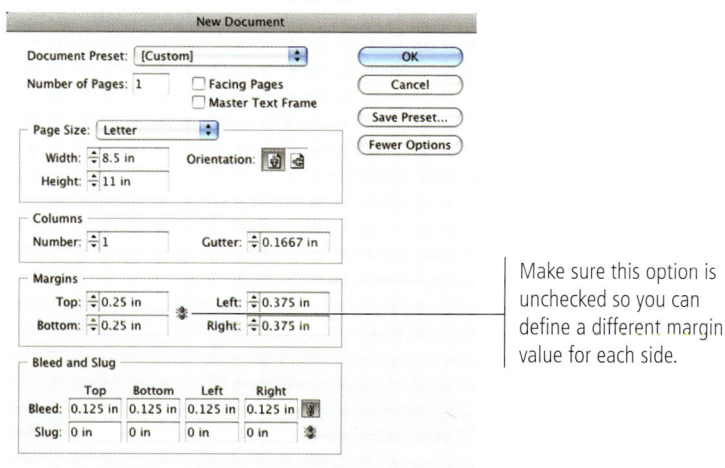

Make sure this option is unchecked so you can define a different margin value for each side.

Project 7: National Parks Info Pieces   395

3. **Create a text frame on the page and rotate it 90° counterclockwise.**

4. **Drag the rotated frame so it snaps to the top and left bleed guides, change the frame height to 0.875", and drag the left (bottom) edge to Y: 6.875".**

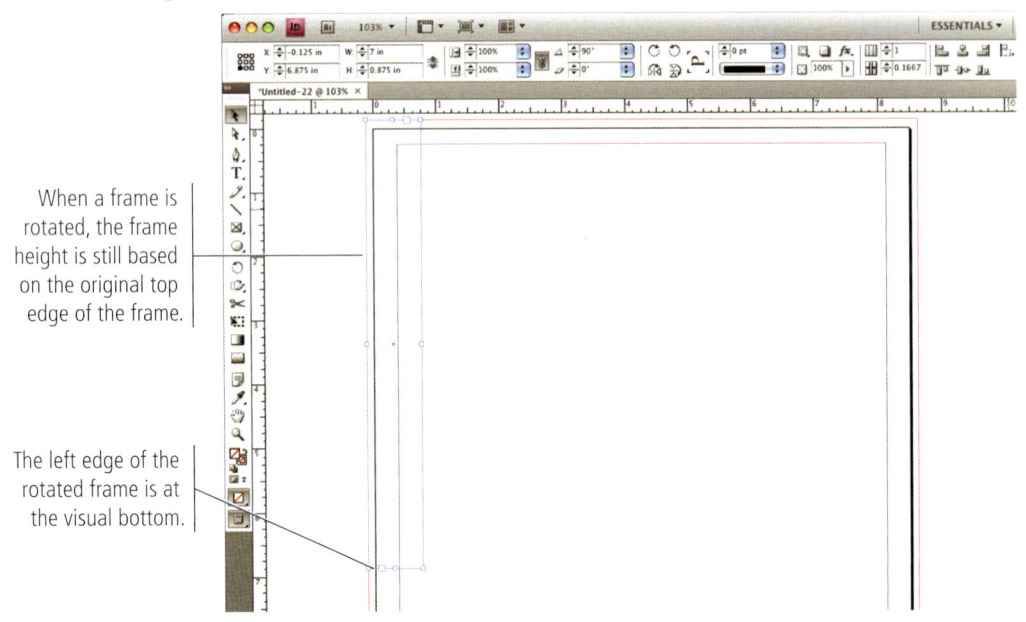

   When a frame is rotated, the frame height is still based on the original top edge of the frame.

   The left edge of the rotated frame is at the visual bottom.

5. **Place the insertion point in the text frame and type Black Canyon of the Gunnison National Park.**

   In some cases, certain text elements will be made clear in the initial project description. Your client stated that the one-sheets should identify the park name, so you can use actual text to plan the appearance of this element.

   When you're working with placeholders, it's a good idea to design around the longest possible content. The words "Black Canyon of the Gunnison" have the most characters of all national parks, so this is a good representation of the possible text that can appear in this area.

6. **Apply right paragraph alignment to the park name paragraph.**

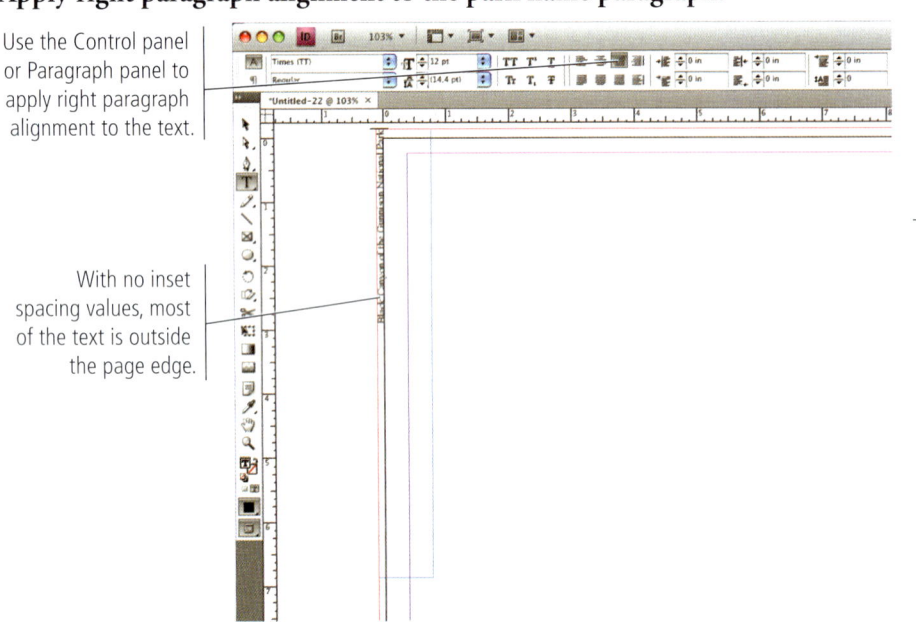

   Use the Control panel or Paragraph panel to apply right paragraph alignment to the text.

   With no inset spacing values, most of the text is outside the page edge.

Note:

It isn't always possible to determine the longest possible content for a particular editorial element. In this case, use your judgment when planning a layout. In other words, don't try to format a main heading with only one or two words of placeholder text.

Note:

A bit of creative thinking might be required to find the longest possible text for a specific element. To identify the longest national park name, we searched the Internet for a list of all parks, formatted the list in a monospace font, and simply looked for the one that extended farthest to the right.

Project 7: National Parks Info Pieces

7. **Control/right-click the text frame and choose Text Frame Options from the contextual menu.**

8. **Change the Align menu to Center.**

9. **Apply 0.375″ inset on the right edge of the frame and 0.125″ inset on the top edge. Click OK to apply the changes.**

    The top inset allows you to center the frame content vertically based on the visible area, excluding the bleed.

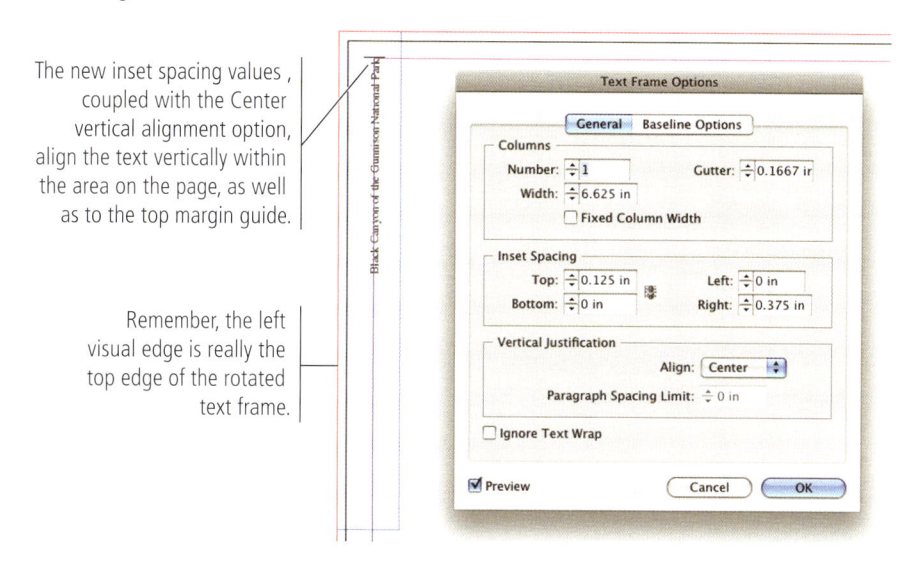

    Note:

    It is unnecessary — and, in fact, poor technical form — to place multiple text frames on top of one another to achieve the text-inset effect.

    The new inset spacing values, coupled with the Center vertical alignment option, align the text vertically within the area on the page, as well as to the top margin guide.

    Remember, the left visual edge is really the top edge of the rotated text frame.

10. **Fill the text frame with the Black swatch, and change the type color in the frame to the Paper swatch.**

11. **Create another text frame with the following dimensions:**

    X: 0.375″   W: 7.75″
    Y: 8″   H: 2.75″

12. **Change the frame to 3 columns with a 0.2″ gutter.**

Project 7: National Parks Info Pieces

13. **Choose Type>Fill with Placeholder Text.**

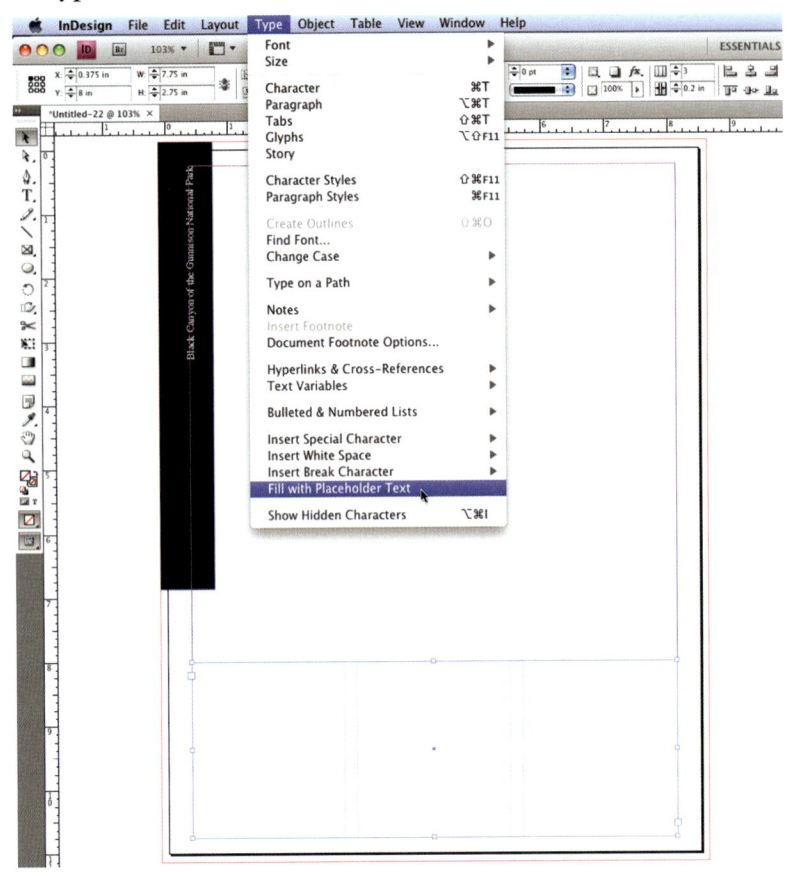

   This command fills the selected text frame with nonsense or lorem text (so called because it is Greek nonsense) using the default text-format settings.

   Lorem placeholder text is valuable for experimenting with the appearance of paragraph text; these random words give you a better idea of what text will look like when real content is placed in the layout.

14. **Save the file as flyer.indd in your WIP>Parks folder and continue to the next exercise.**

Note:

If a text frame is linked to other text frames, the placeholder text fills the entire series of linked text frames.

Note:

The placeholder text is randomly generated, so the exact words in your layout probably do not match what you see in our screen shot. However, the exact words are irrelevant; the important point is that you have placeholder text to work with while you experiment with formatting options.

398 Project 7: National Parks Info Pieces

Experiment with Text Formatting

The best place to begin experimenting is to define the basic font for the layout. Rather than simply selecting the text in a frame and adjusting it locally, you can change the [Basic Paragraph] style to affect the default appearance of all text in the layout.

As you design a layout, it's important to realize that nothing is permanent — including styles — until the job is printed. Of course, some methods for changing a design are better than others. Because changing a style applies the same change to any text formatted with that style, it's better to do as much work as possible with styles.

1. **With `flyer.indd` open, Control/right-click [Basic Paragraph] in the Paragraph Styles panel and choose Edit "[Basic Paragraph]" from the contextual menu.**

2. **In the Basic Character Formats options, change the font to ATC Oak Normal, and change the type size to 9 pt. In the Indents and Spacing options, change the Space After value to 0.0625″. Click OK to apply the change.**

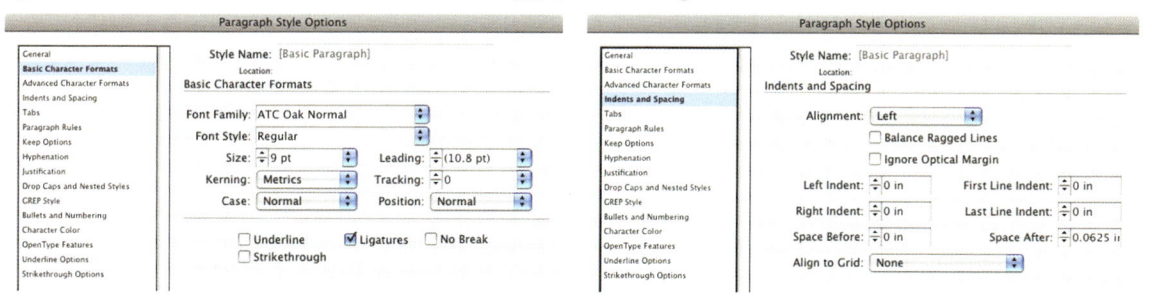

   By changing the default text formatting, the placeholder text no longer fills the frame.

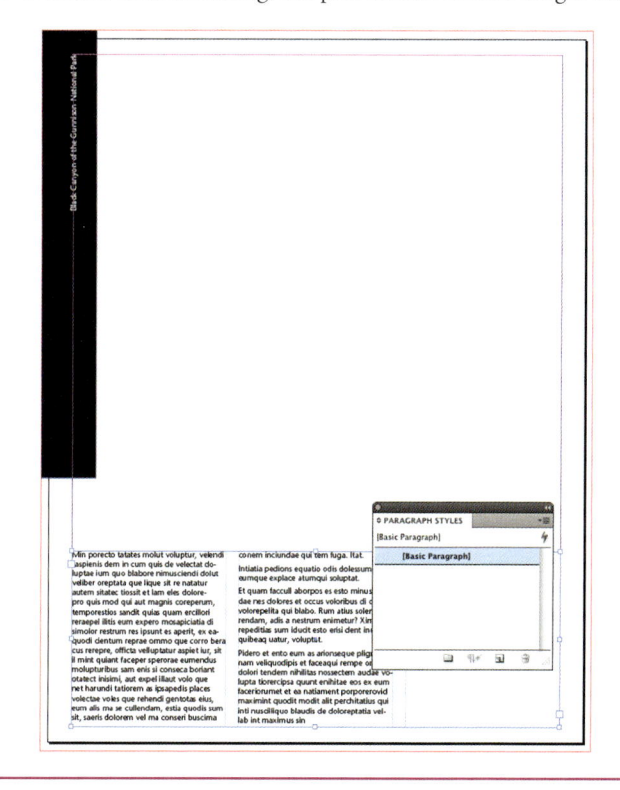

Note:

If you edit the [Basic Paragraph] style with no file open, the adjusted text formatting options become the default settings in all new files.

Project 7: National Parks Info Pieces 399

3. **Highlight the park name (in the rotated frame). Change the font to ATC Oak Bold and apply the All Caps type style.**

4. **Press Command/Control-Shift-period four times to increase the text size to 17 pt.**

   By default, the key command for increasing and decreasing type size changes the size by 2 points. You can change this increment in the Units and Increments pane of the Preferences dialog box.

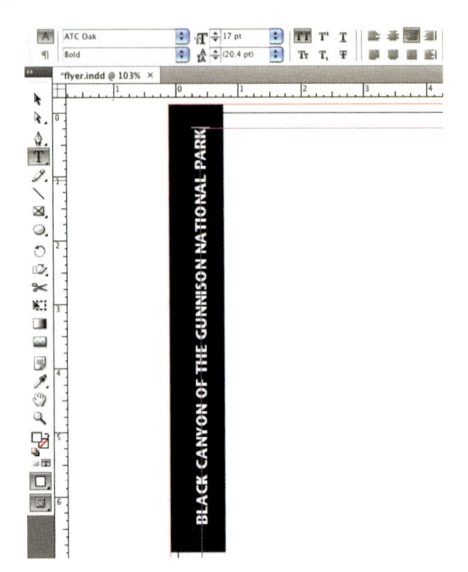

Note:

Add Option/Alt to the basic keyboard shortcut to increase or decrease the type size by five times the defined increment.

Note:

By default, leading is only applied to selected text. To apply leading changes to entire paragraphs, activate the Apply Leading to Entire Paragraphs option in the Type pane of the Preferences dialog box.

Navigating and Selecting Text with Keyboard Shortcuts

Keyboard shortcuts can be helpful, especially in early stages when you are still experimenting with text formatting options.

	Macintosh	Windows
Move left one character*	Left Arrow	Left Arrow
Move right one character*	Right Arrow	Right Arrow
Move up one line*	Up Arrow	Up Arrow
Move down one line*	Down Arrow	Down Arrow
Move left one word*	Command-Left Arrow	Control-Left Arrow
Move right one word*	Command-Right Arrow	Control-Right Arrow
Move to start of line*	Home	Home
Move to end of line*	End	End
Move to previous paragraph*	Command-Up Arrow	Control-Up Arrow
Move to next paragraph*	Command-Down Arrow	Control-Down Arrow
Move to start of story*	Command-Home	Control-Home
Move to end of story*	Command-End	Control-End
Select current line	Command-Shift-\	Control-Shift-\
Select characters from insertion point	Shift-click	Shift-click
Select entire story	Command-A	Control-A
Select previous frame	Command-Option-Page Up	Control-Alt-Page Up
Select next frame	Command-Option-Page Down	Control-Alt-Page Down
Select first frame	Command-Option-Shift-Page Up	Control-Alt-Shift-Page Up
Select last frame	Command-Option-Shift-Page Down	Control-Alt-Shift-Page Down
Delete word in front of insertion point (Story Editor)	Command-Delete	Control-Backspace

* Add Shift to select text between the previous and new location of the insertion point.

5. **If hidden characters are not visible, choose Type>Show Hidden Characters.**

6. **In the three-column text frame, place the insertion point near the end of the first column and press Return/Enter to add a paragraph break.**

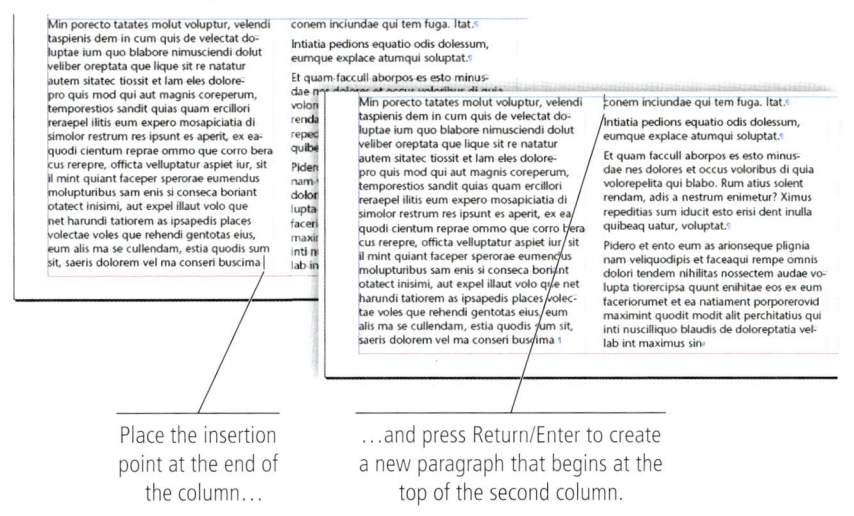

Place the insertion point at the end of the column…

…and press Return/Enter to create a new paragraph that begins at the top of the second column.

7. **Type Did You Know… and press Return Enter.**

   In this case, you know the actual heading that will be used, so you can enter the actual text as the placeholder.

8. **Highlight the new subheading paragraph and change the text to 11-pt ATC Oak Bold.**

   Subheads like this one should typically be related to either the body copy or the main headings. Remember that professional-looking designs do not use 15 different fonts on a page. Try to stick with two or three primary fonts, and use variants of those fonts for emphasis and visual interest. (Of course, rules were made to be broken, but don't break from design conventions unless you have a good reason for doing so.)

9. **In the text after the subheading, break or combine the placeholder text so you have four paragraphs of three lines each. Delete all remaining text.**

   In this experimentation phase of development, these paragraphs represent the "fun facts" that will appear in the final copy. The actual text in these lines (including capitalization) is irrelevant because you are using them for formatting purposes only.

Project 7: National Parks Info Pieces   401

Formatting Text with Keyboard Shortcuts

Keyboard shortcuts can be helpful, especially in early stages when you are still experimenting with text formatting options.

	Macintosh	Windows
Bold type style	Command-Shift-B	Control-Shift-B
Italic type style	Command-Shift-I	Control-Shift-I
Normal type style	Command-Shift-Y	Control-Shift-Y
Underline type style	Command-Shift-U	Control-Shift-U
Strikethrough type style	Command-Shift-/	Control-Shift-/
All Caps type style (on/off)	Command-Shift-K	Control-Shift-K
Small Caps type style (on/off)	Command-Shift-H	Control-Shift-H
Superscript type style	Command-Shift-Plus sign	Control-Shift-Plus sign
Subscript type style	Command-Option-Shift-Plus sign	Control-Alt-Shift-Plus sign
Reset horizontal scale to 100%	Command-Shift-X	Control-Shift-X
Reset vertical scale to 100%	Command-Option-Shift-X	Control-Alt-Shift-X
Align left	Command-Shift-L	Control-Shift-L
Align right	Command-Shift-R	Control-Shift-R
Align center	Command-Shift-C	Control-Shift-C
Justify all lines (all but last line)	Command-Shift-J	Control-Shift-J
Justify all lines (all lines)	Command-Shift-F	Control-Shift-F
Increase point size*	Command-Shift->	Control-Shift->
Decrease point size*	Command-Shift-<	Control-Shift-<
Increase point size by 5 times the defined increment*	Command-Option-Shift->	Control-Alt-Shift-<
Decrease point size by 5 times the defined increment*	Command-Option-Shift-<	Control-Alt-Shift->
Increase leading*	Option-Up Arrow	Alt-Up Arrow
Decrease leading*	Option-Down Arrow	Alt-Down Arrow
Increase leading by 5 times the defined increment*	Command-Option-Up Arrow	Control-Alt-Up Arrow
Decrease leading by 5 times the defined increment*	Command-Option-Down Arrow	Control-Alt-Down Arrow
Auto leading	Command-Option-Shift-A	Control-Alt-Shift-A
Align to grid (on/off)	Command-Option-Shift-G	Control-Alt-Shift-G
Auto-hyphenate (on/off)	Command-Option-Shift-H	Control-Alt-Shift-H
Increase kerning and tracking	Option-Left Arrow	Alt-Left Arrow
Decrease kerning and tracking	Option-Right Arrow	Alt-Right Arrow
Increase kerning and tracking by 5 times	Command-Option-Left Arrow	Control-Alt-Left Arrow
Decrease kerning and tracking by 5 times	Command-Option-Right Arrow	Control-Alt-Right Arrow
Increase kerning between words*	Command-Option-\	Control-Alt-\
Decrease kerning between words*	Command-Option-Delete	Control-Alt-Backspace
Clear all manual kerning and reset tracking to 0	Command-Option-Q	Control-Alt-Q
Increase baseline shift*	Option-Shift-Up Arrow	Alt-Shift-Up Arrow
Decrease baseline shift*	Option-Shift-Down Arrow	Alt-Shift-Down Arrow
Increase baseline shift by 5 times	Command-Option-Shift-Up Arrow	Control-Alt-Shift-Up Arrow
Decrease baseline shift by 5 times	Command-Option-Shift-Down Arrow	Control-Alt-Shift-Down Arrow

*The default increment for type size, leading, and baseline shift is 2 points. The default kerning tracking value is 20/1000 of an em. You can change these values in the Units & Increments pane of the Preferences dialog box.

INDESIGN FOUNDATIONS

10. **Highlight all text in the second column, copy the text, and paste it at the end of the existing story. Change the second subhead to** Directions.

11. **Place the insertion point in the Directions subhead and open the Keep Options dialog box (from the Paragraph panel Options menu). Define the paragraph to start in the next column and click OK.**

12. **Save the file and continue to the next exercise.**

Experiment with Glyphs

The Glyphs panel offers an easy way to review and select specific characters in available fonts. When experimenting with type formatting, the Glyphs panel is an excellent way to search through extended, symbol, and pictographic characters that you can't easily preview in the document layout.

1. With **flyer.indd** open, place the insertion point at the beginning of the first "fun fact" placeholder in the second column of the three-column text frame.

2. Choose Window>Type & Tables>Glyphs.

3. In the menu at the bottom of the Glyphs panel, choose a pictographic font such as Zapf Dingbats or Wingdings.

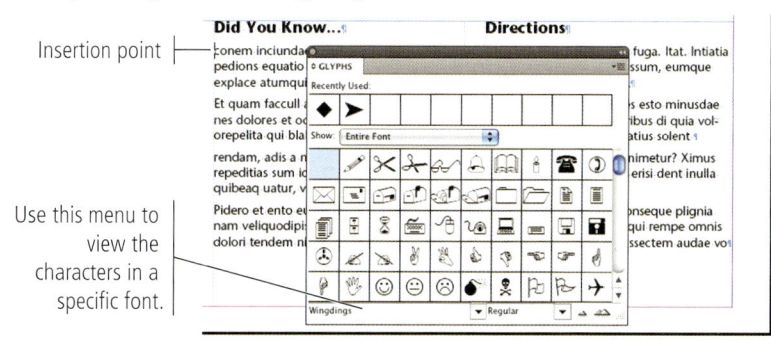

Note:

You can also open the Glyphs panel by choosing Type>Glyphs.

Project 7: National Parks Info Pieces   403

4. **Scroll through the panel and find a character that matches the theme of the document.**

   We found a character in the Wingdings font that looks like a compass crosshair. You can use any character from any font that you feel works with the "outdoors" theme of national parks.

   The important point to remember is that you can use the Glyphs panel to look at all available characters in the selected font; this is an excellent way to explore and experiment when you want to use type characters to create visual interest.

5. **When you find a character you like, double-click that glyph in the panel.**

   Double-clicking inserts the selected character at the location of the insertion point.

   The character is added at the location of the insertion point.

   The character you add into the layout appears in the Recently Used area of the Glyphs panel.

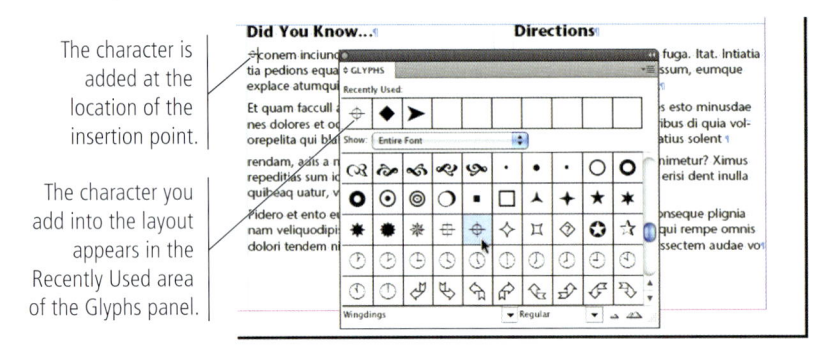

   Note:

   Decorative fonts can be useful for adding visual interest without the need for linked graphics.

6. **Make note of the font that includes the character you selected.**

7. **Select all "fun facts" paragraphs. In the Paragraph panel Options menu, choose Bullets and Numbering.**

   The options you see here are the same options you used to define styles with bullets in Project 5. Anything that can be applied in a style can also be applied as a local formatting option.

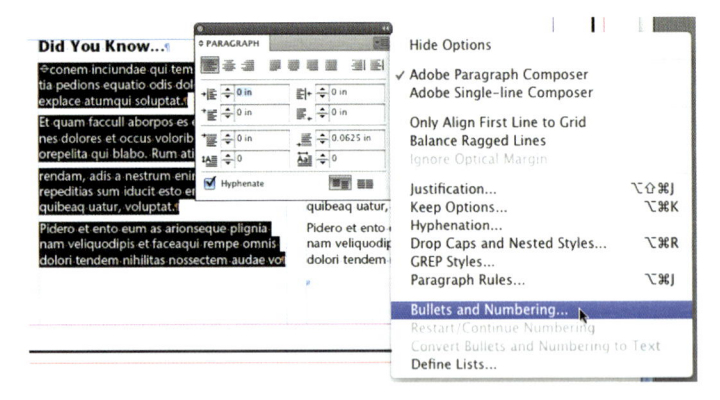

8. **Apply the Bullets list type with a 0.15″ hanging indent and a 0.15″ tab position. (Set the Left indent field to 0.15″ and the First Line Indent field to –0.15″.)**

   Remember, a hanging indent applies a negative first-line indent, typically equivalent to the distance of the overall left indent.

9. **Click the Add button. In the Add Bullets dialog box, select the same font you noted in Step 6. Find and select the character you chose for the bullets and click OK.**

    You could have skipped Steps 2–6, but we believe it's easier to use the Glyphs panel for exploring and experimenting with different characters. Once you know what character you want to use, it's easy to add that character in the formatting of a bulleted list.

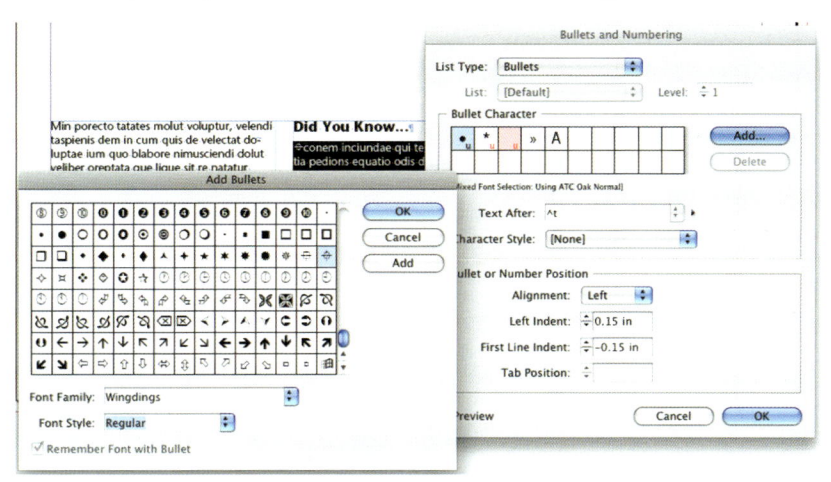

10. **Select the newly added glyph in the Bullet Character area, and then click OK to apply the Bullets list type to the selected paragraphs.**

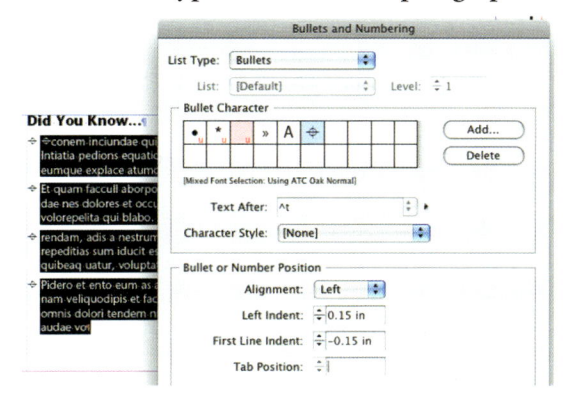

11. **Delete the extra bullet character from the first bulleted paragraph.**

    This is the bullet you added from the Glyphs panel. It is unnecessary now that the same character has been added by the applied bullet formatting.

12. **If adding the bullets results in a fourth line for any of the bulleted paragraphs, delete enough of the text from the bulleted paragraphs so all four bullets fit into the middle column of the frame.**

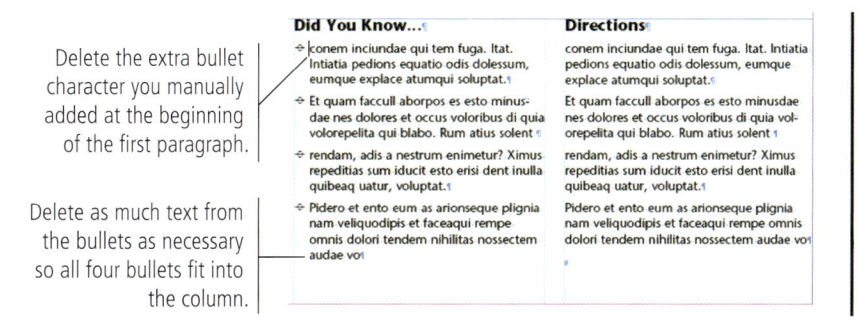

    Delete the extra bullet character you manually added at the beginning of the first paragraph.

    Delete as much text from the bullets as necessary so all four bullets fit into the column.

13. **Save the file and continue to the next exercise.**

Project 7: National Parks Info Pieces

Using OpenType Attributes

The OpenType font format enables you to use the same font files on both Macintosh and Windows computers; it provides storage capacity for more than 65,000 glyphs in a single font. In many cases, these extra glyphs are alternative formatting for other characters (such as ligatures and fractions). You can also use these glyphs for special formatting needs.

OpenType features are treated as a character-formatting attribute. You can apply OpenType features to specific text using the OpenType menu in the Character panel Options menu.

Adobe Garamond is not an OpenType font.

OpenType attributes are bracketed if they are unavailable for the currently selected font.

It's important to understand that OpenType attributes can be applied even if they aren't available for the font you are currently using. For example, you can apply the Fractions attribute to a list of ingredients; as you experiment with different fonts, the Fractions attribute will be applied if it's available in the applied font.

When an OpenType font is used, the Fractions attribute is applied if the font includes the appropriate glyphs.

Warnock Pro is an OpenType font.

It's also important to realize that OpenType attributes change the appearance of glyphs, but do not change the actual text in the layout. When the Fractions attribute replaces "1/2" with "½", the text still includes three characters; the OpenType Fractions attribute has simply altered the glyphs that represent those three characters to display a styled fraction. You can turn off OpenType attributes by toggling off the option in the Characters panel Options menu. With OpenType attributes turned off, the styled characters return to their basic appearance.

Exploring OpenType Fonts in the Glyphs Panel

You can also use the Glyphs panel to explore the different character sets available for a specific font. The Show menu allows you to access different character sets, including extended character sets such as symbols and OpenType alternative character sets. If you select a specific character in the panel, you can also review possible alternatives for the selected character only.

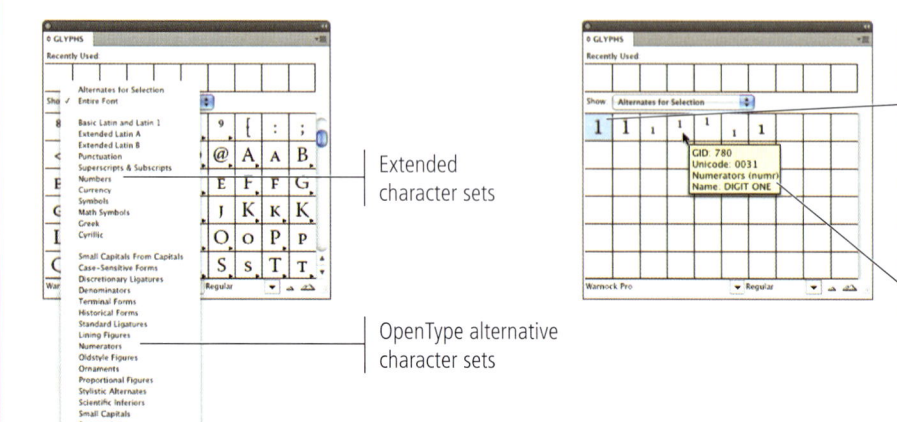

Extended character sets

OpenType alternative character sets

Selecting the "1" glyph and choosing Alternates for Selection shows the different characters that can be applied using OpenType formatting attributes.

Rolling the mouse over a specific glyph shows the alternative set that includes that glyph (in this case, the Numerators set).

Project 7: National Parks Info Pieces

CREATE STYLES FROM EXPERIMENTAL FORMATTING

When you are satisfied — or at least, mostly satisfied — with the appearance of your sample text, it's a good idea to convert that formatting into styles. Styles have the obvious benefit of dynamically changing text by updating the applied style definition. Styles can also be easily applied, they can be imported into other documents, and they can be mapped to different elements in an XML layout (which you do in Stage 2 of this project).

1. **With flyer.indd open, place the insertion point in the paragraph that contains the park name.**

   As you learned in Project 5, a plus sign next to the style name (in the Paragraph Styles panel) indicates that some local formatting has been applied to override the style definition.

   Insertion point

   The current insertion point is formatted with the [Basic Paragraph] style, but some local formatting has been applied to override the style definition.

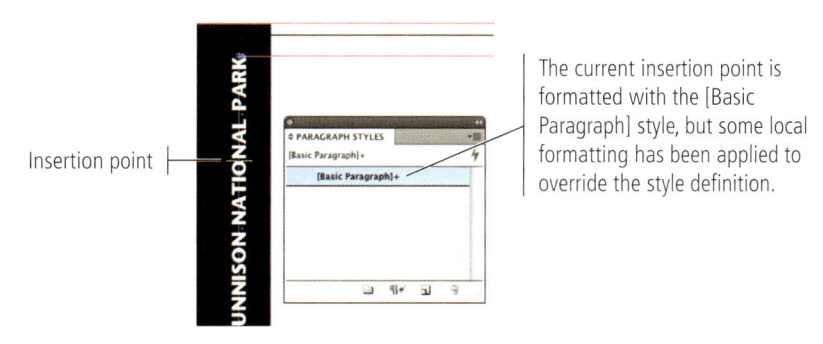

2. **Click the Create New Style button at the bottom of the Paragraph Styles panel.**

   Create New Style button

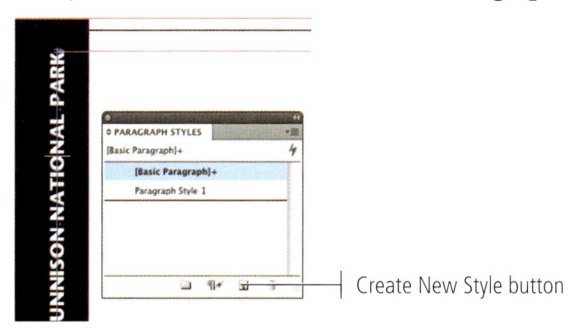

3. **Control/right-click the new style and choose Edit "Paragraph Style 1" from the contextual menu.**

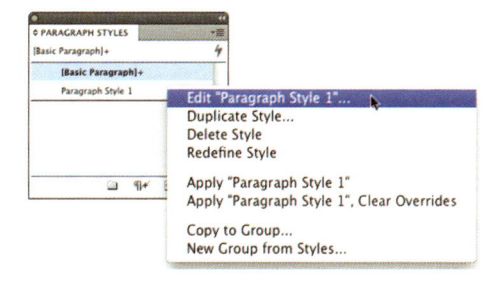

Project 7: National Parks Info Pieces

4. **Name the new style `Park_Name` and click OK.**

   Make sure you use the underscore in the style name; this will be very important in Stage 2.

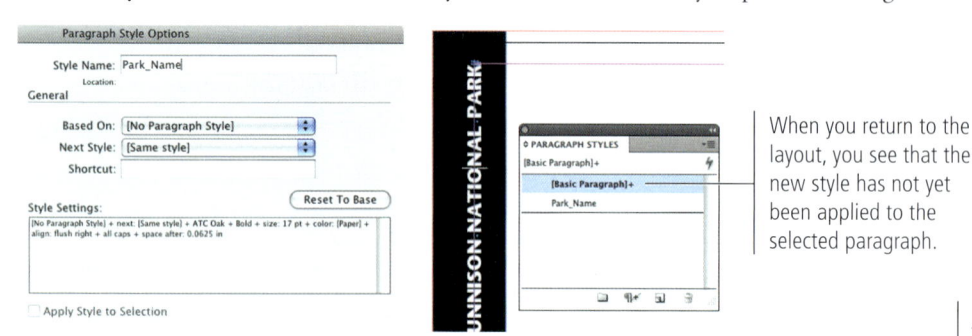

   When you return to the layout, you see that the new style has not yet been applied to the selected paragraph.

   Note:

   If you are building a project that will (or might) be used for XML, it's a good idea to follow XML-based naming conventions, which prohibit spaces in element names.

5. **In the Paragraph Styles panel, click the Park_Name style to apply it to the selected text.**

6. **Place the insertion point in the first paragraph of the three-column frame, then click the Create New Style button at the bottom of the Paragraph Styles panel.**

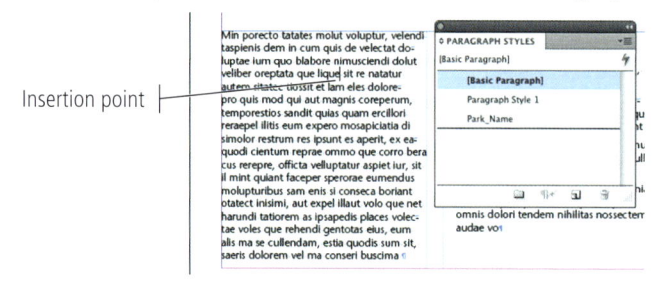

   Insertion point

7. **Double-click the new Paragraph Style 1 to open the Paragraph Style Options dialog box. Change the style name to `Body_Copy` and click OK.**

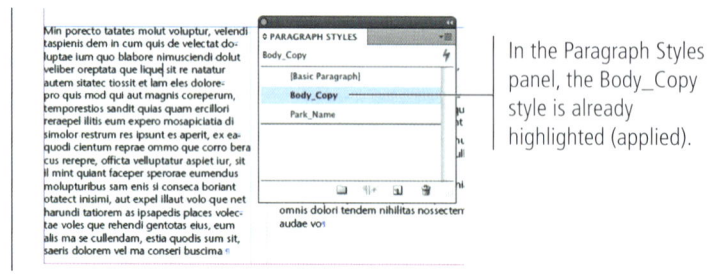

   In the Paragraph Styles panel, the Body_Copy style is already highlighted (applied).

   To apply a style to a paragraph, you simply select the paragraph and click the style name. The first click of double-clicking the style name (to edit the style) applies the style to the selected text.

   This is a very important distinction — Control/right-clicking allows you to edit the style without applying the style. Double-clicking allows you to edit the style and applies the style to the selected text, as well. Each method is useful in different circumstances; be certain that you use the correct method, based on what you are trying to accomplish.

8. **Using the double-click method, define additional styles from the existing formatting. Use the following image as a guide; make sure your style names exactly match what you see in our image:**

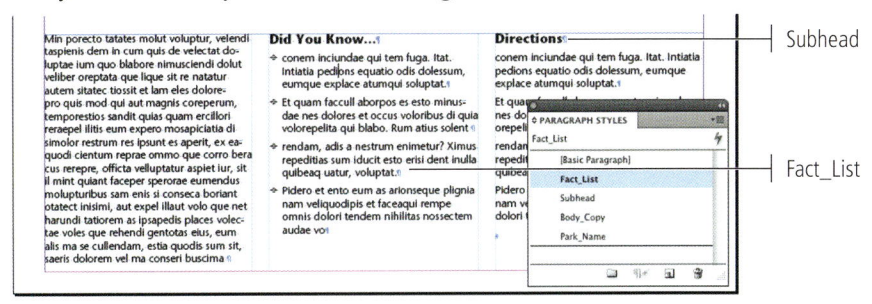

   For the Subhead style, make sure you base it on the "Directions" paragraph because that paragraph has the Keep instruction to force the subhead into the next column. (The "Did You Know…" subhead does not include the Keep formatting.)

9. **Apply the existing Body_Copy style to all the text after the subhead in the right column.**

10. **Save the file and continue to the next exercise.**

Experiment with Graphics Placeholders

To plan image placement, you can simply create and manipulate empty frames. You can even predefine some attributes of the images that will be placed, including applied effects (as you did in Project 5) and content-fitting options.

1. **With flyer.indd open, create a rectangular graphics frame. Align the left edge at X: 0.75″, extend the top and right edges to the bleed guides, and change the frame height to 8″.**

2. **Using the Swatches panel, fill the empty graphics frame with the C=100 M=0 Y=0 K=0 swatch.**

   When designing an initial layout, it can be a good idea to fill empty picture boxes with a color. This serves as a visual cue so you can quickly identify the areas that will be filled with the actual content.

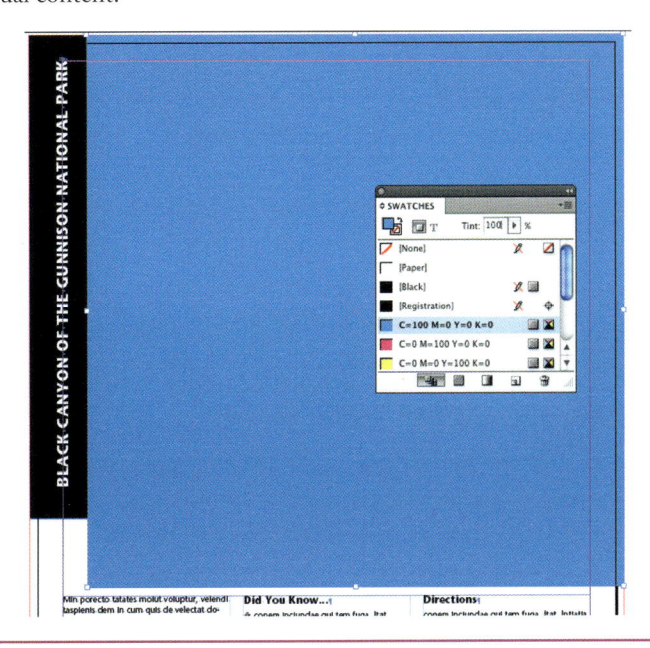

Project 7: National Parks Info Pieces   409

3. **Create another empty graphics frame with the following dimensions:**

   X: –0.125″   W: 3″
   Y: 6.1″   H: 3″

4. **Open the Control panel Options menu and make sure the Dimensions Include Stroke Weight option is not checked.**

   When this option is active, changing the stroke weight changes the physical dimensions of the frame. You want the frame to remain at 3 × 3″, so you must turn off this option before you change the stroke weight.

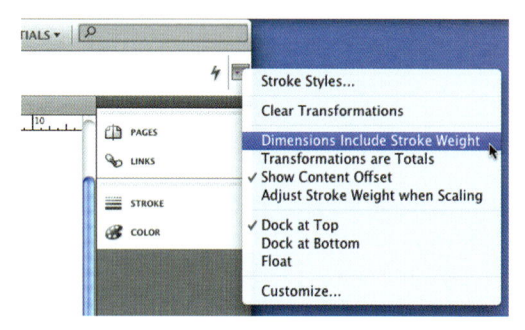

5. **Apply a 5-pt stroke to the frame and change the stroke color to black. Fill the new frame with the C=100 M=0 Y=0 K=0 swatch.**

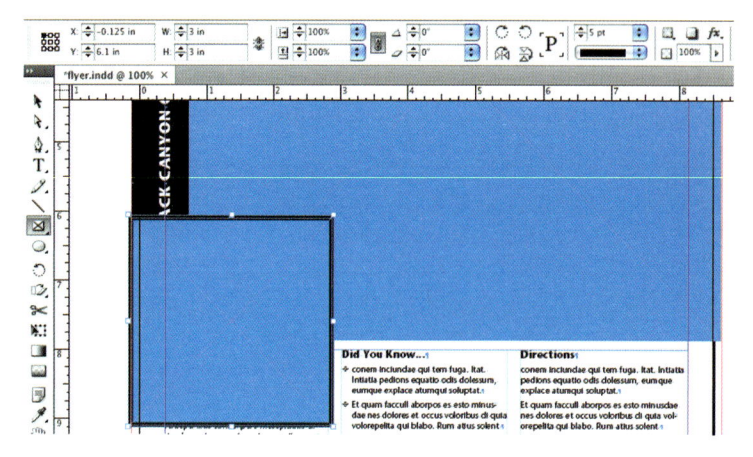

6. **Open the Pathfinder panel (Window>Object & Layout>Pathfinder).**

7. **With the second graphics frame selected, click the Rounded Corner option in the Convert Shape area of the Pathfinder panel.**

   You can use these options to change the shape of any frame at any time. The same options are also available in the Object>Convert Shape menu.

Note:

The icons in the Convert Shape section of the Pathfinder panel indicate the type of shape that will result from the conversion.

Project 7: National Parks Info Pieces

8. **Choose Object>Corner Options. Set the Size field to 0.25″ and click OK.**

   In the Corner Options dialog box, you can change the type of corner effect (the options are the same as those in the Pathfinder panel) and the corner radius of the effect.

   To understand corner radius, imagine the complete circle that would create the same corner effect of the round edge of the rectangle. The radius (the distance from the center to the edge) of that implied circle is the corner radius of the shape.

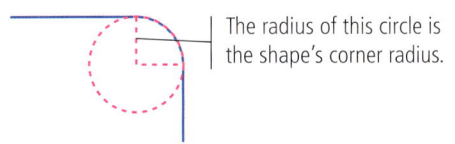

   The radius of this circle is the shape's corner radius.

9. **Using the Text Wrap panel, apply a 0.0625″ text wrap to all four sides of the frame.**

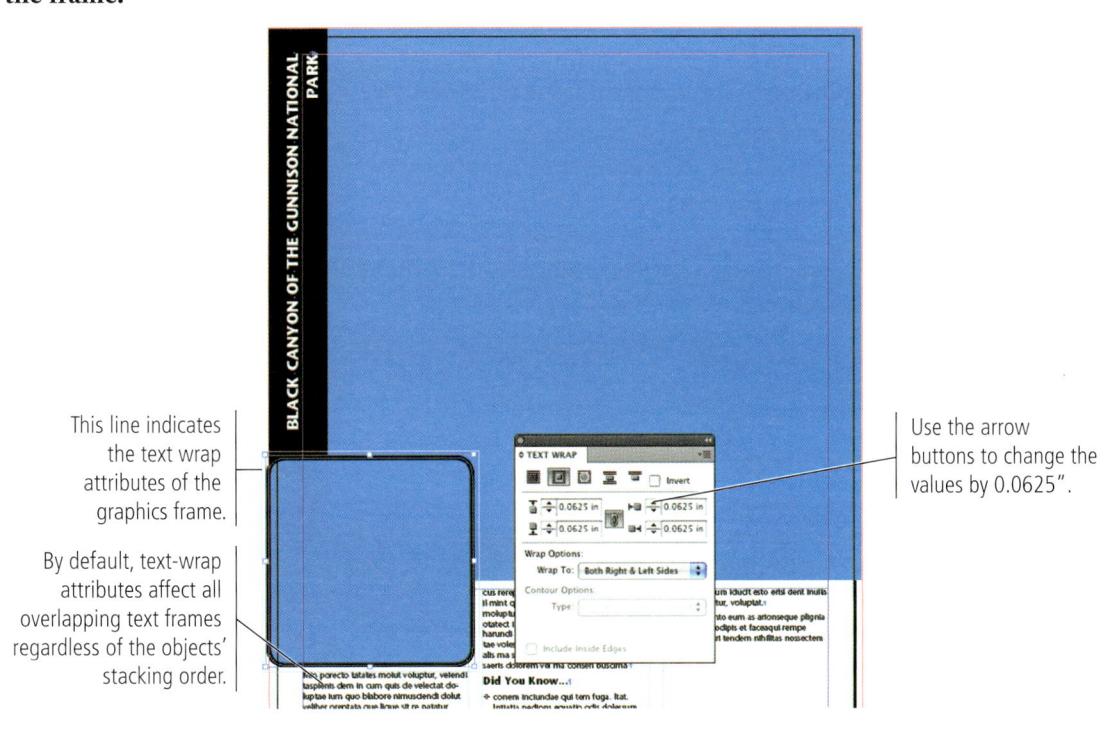

   This line indicates the text wrap attributes of the graphics frame.

   By default, text-wrap attributes affect all overlapping text frames regardless of the objects' stacking order.

   Use the arrow buttons to change the values by 0.0625″.

   Project 7: National Parks Info Pieces

10. **Reformat the Park_Name style to 15.5 pt so the placeholder (the longest possible variant) fits on a single line.**

    You will frequently make this kind of change while designing an initial layout concept.

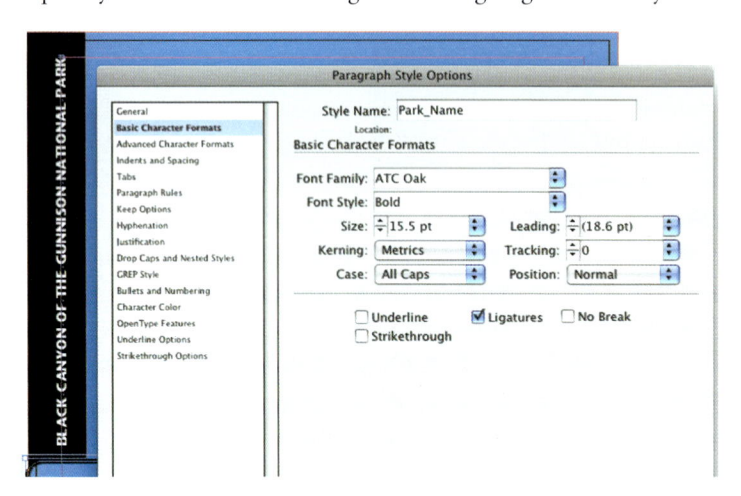

11. **Save the file and continue to the next exercise.**

SAVE THE FINAL TEMPLATE

Now that the layout is finished, you should make the template as user-friendly as possible. The template currently includes a specific park name that might be easy to overlook; it also includes a lot of nonsense text that must be deleted every time you use the template. In this exercise, you modify the template to require as little setup as possible each time you use it to create a new layout.

1. **With flyer.indd open, select the park name text and type Park Name.**

   Changing the text to a generic description can be helpful to designers who later use the template, reminding them to type the actual park name.

2. **Select all text in the three-column frame and delete it.**

   When hidden characters are showing, you can see (if you look closely) that the end-of-story character appears at the location of the insertion point.

   When you formatted the placeholder text in a previous exercise, you applied the Body_Copy style to the text after the second subhead. If the end-of-story character occupied a separate paragraph from the ones you formatted with the Body_Copy style, deleting all the text in the frame applies the [Basic Paragraph] style to the end-of-story character – and thus, as the default for the frame.

   If the end-of-story character was included in a paragraph to which you applied the Body_Copy style, that character maintains the Body_Copy style — thus becoming the default for the frame.

   Formatting of the end-of-story character depends on how you formatted the placeholder text earlier in this project.

   If you did not format the end-of-story character as part of a Body_Copy paragraph, it will carry the [Basic Paragraph] style.

412   Project 7: National Parks Info Pieces

3. **With the insertion point flashing in the empty frame, click the Body_Copy style in the Paragraph Styles panel (if it is not already selected).**

   By applying the style to the insertion point in the empty frame, you define the default formatting options for text you enter into the frame.

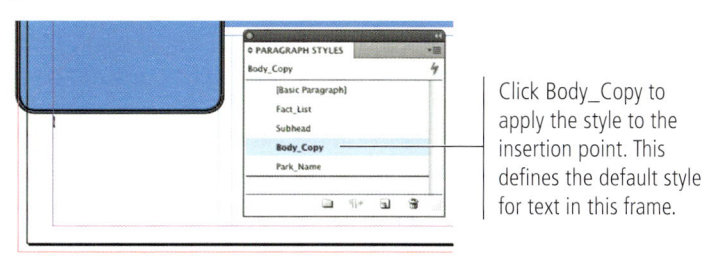

   Click Body_Copy to apply the style to the insertion point. This defines the default style for text in this frame.

   Note:

   Placing text that is already formatted — whether copied from another InDesign text frame or imported from a file that includes formatting — overrides the formatting you applied to the empty frame's insertion point.

4. **Using the Selection tool, Control/right-click the large graphics frame and choose Fitting>Frame Fitting Options from the contextual menu.**

   In this case, you know how much space is available, but you don't yet know the size of the images that will fit the space. You can use the Frame Fitting options to determine what will happen when you place any image into the existing frames.

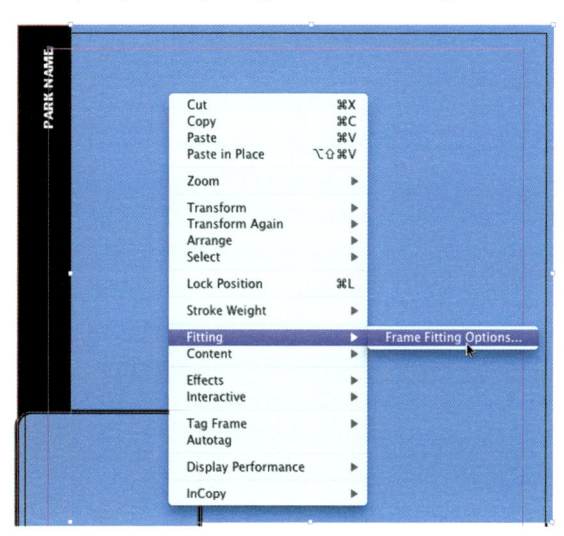

5. **In the Fitting on Empty Frame menu, choose Fill Frame Proportionally and click OK.**

   When an image is placed into this frame, it will fill the entire frame and the aspect ratio of the image will be maintained.

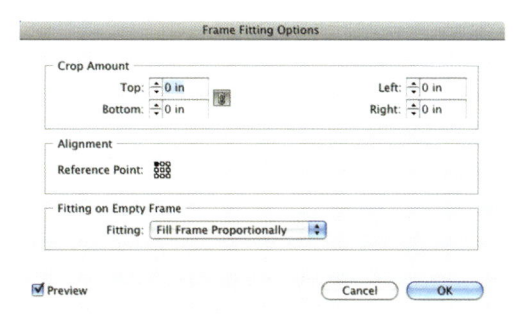

6. **Using the same method as in Steps 4–5, change the Fitting options of the small graphics frame so any placed images will fill the frame proportionally.**

7. **Save the file as a template named flyer.indt in your WIP>Parks folder, close the file, and then continue to the next exercise.**

Project 7: National Parks Info Pieces   413

Adjust the Layout to Supplied Content

InDesign provides all the tools you need to experiment with and plan a basic layout structure. However, the best-laid plans (or planned layouts) always require some adjustment when you place the actual content into the document. Fortunately, nothing in a layout is final until it's printed; until a job leaves your desk, you can change anything in the document.

1. **Open the flyer.indt template file from your WIP>Parks folder to create a new file.**

2. **Click with the Type tool to place the insertion point in the three-column text frame.**

3. **Choose File>Place and navigate to the file bryce.txt in the RF_InDesign> Parks folder. Deselect the Show Import Options check box, select the Replace Selected Item check box, and then click Open.**

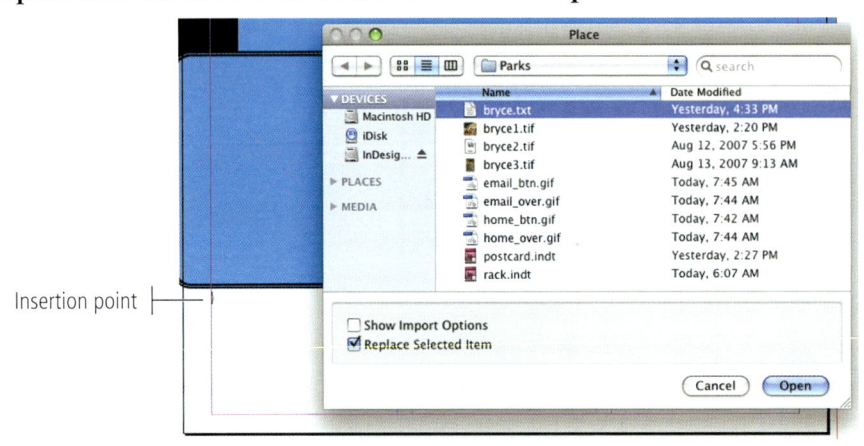

Insertion point

Because the Replace Selected Item option is checked, the text automatically flows into the frame at the location of the insertion point. A text-only file (with the extension ".txt") includes no formatting information; all placed text is formatted with the Body_Copy style, which you defined as the default style for the frame in the previous exercise.

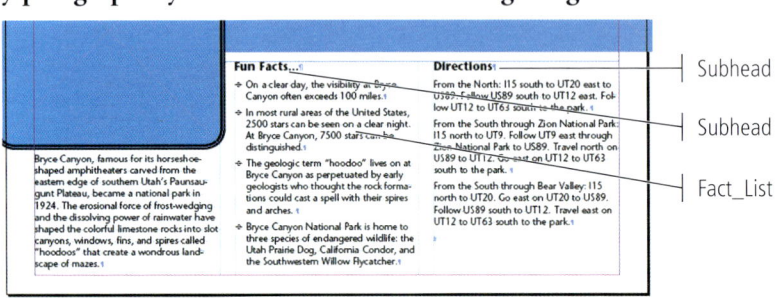

Note:

Nothing is selected, so nothing (other than the insertion point) is replaced. If the Replace Selected Item option is not checked, the imported text loads into the cursor instead of into the selected frame.

4. **Apply paragraph styles as shown in the following image:**

Subhead
Subhead
Fact_List

414   Project 7: National Parks Info Pieces

5. **Deselect everything in the layout.**

6. **Choose File>Place and navigate to the RF_InDesign>Parks folder. Select both `bryce1.tif` and `bryce2.tif` and click Open.**

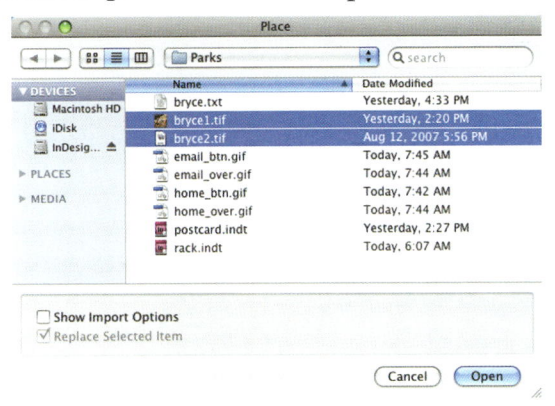

7. **Click to place bryce1.tif in the large graphics frame, and then click to place bryce2.tif in the smaller graphics frame.**

8. **Click the placed bryce1.tif image with the Direct Selection tool and look at the Control or Transform panel.**

   The image is reduced to approximately 98% because you changed the empty frame settings to fill the frame proportionally with whatever image is placed into the frame.

   Be careful when you use this type of setting because an image might need to be enlarged to fill the frame. Remember the rules of effective resolution — enlarging an image's physical dimensions has a proportional negative effect on the image's resolution.

The Control panel shows the dimension and position of the image relative to the frame.

The placed image is selected with the Direct Selection tool.

This line marks the actual edge of the image.

Project 7: National Parks Info Pieces

9. **Select the smaller image and review its scale percentage.**

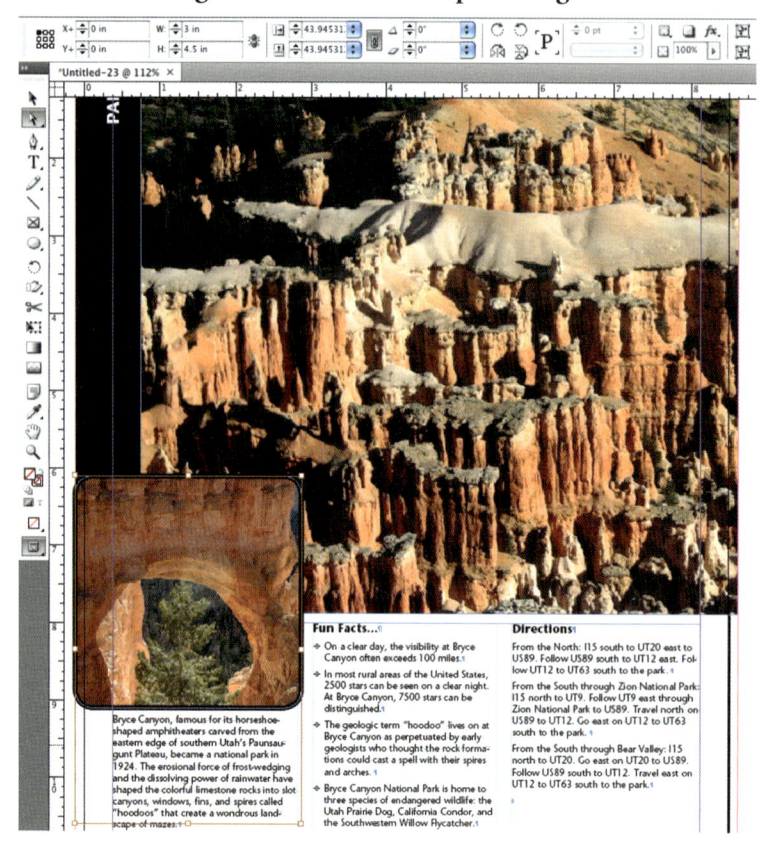

10. **Control/right-click the smaller image and choose Fitting>Center Content in the contextual menu.**

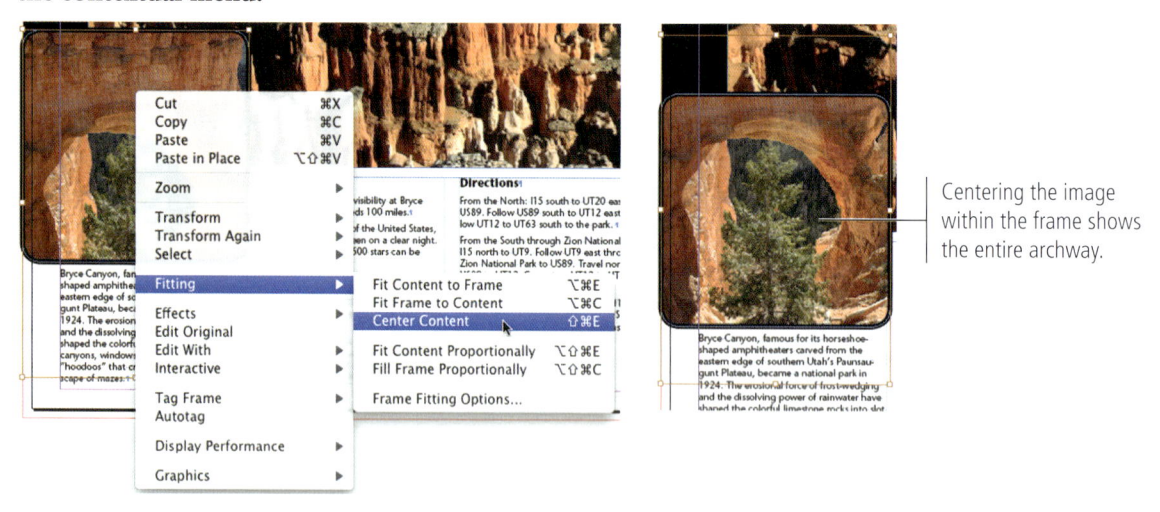

   Centering the image within the frame shows the entire archway.

11. **Save the file as flyer_bryce.indd in your WIP>Parks folder and continue to the next exercise.**

416   Project 7: National Parks Info Pieces

CREATE SWATCHES FROM SAMPLED COLORS

Countless books have been written about the symbolic, cultural, and psychological aspects of color. Color should be selected for a specific reason in relation to the overall document. Although it is not our goal to tell you what colors to select and why, we want you to know how to select them — including sampling colors from images placed into the layout.

1. **With flyer_bryce.indd open, deselect everything in the layout and open the Swatches panel.**

2. **Choose the Eyedropper tool in the Tools panel and make sure the Fill box is active.**

3. **Click the Eyedropper cursor in a dark orange area of the larger image.**

   The Eyedropper tool allows you to select a color from any layout element, including placed images. Selecting a color in this way does not define a swatch in the file. The color only exists for the active attribute (fill or stroke).

   Note:

   *This method of selecting color is called **sampling**.*

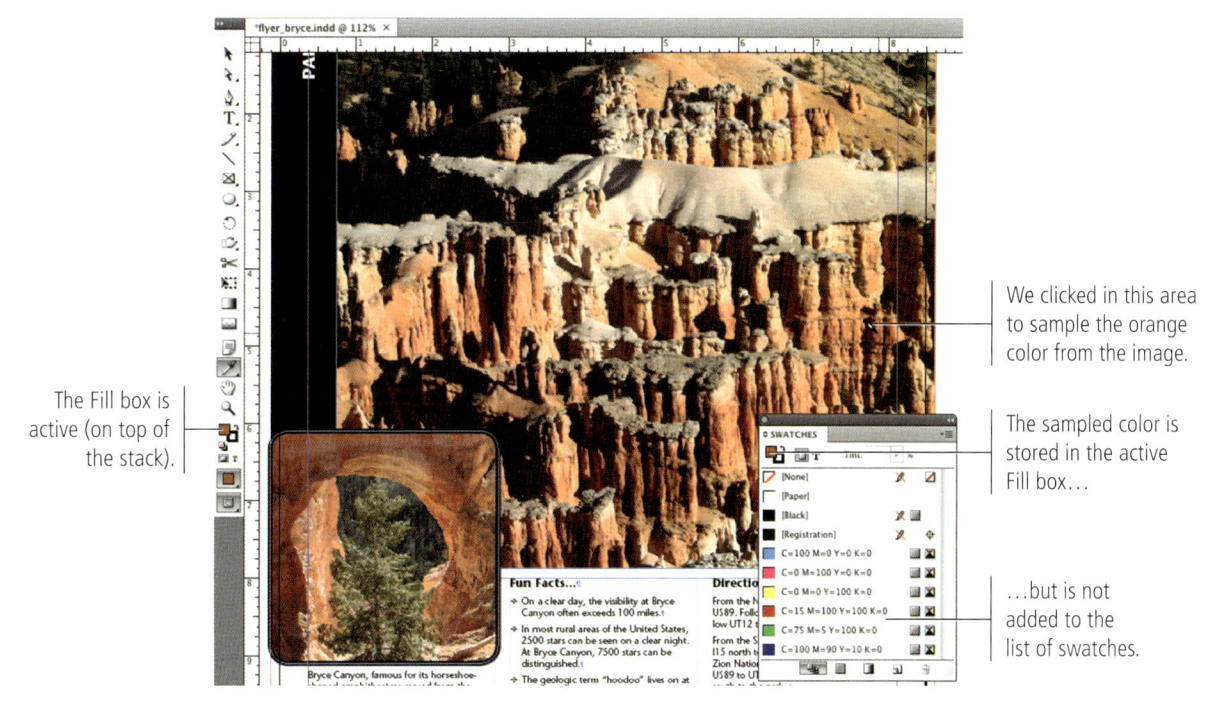

   The Fill box is active (on top of the stack).

   We clicked in this area to sample the orange color from the image.

   The sampled color is stored in the active Fill box…

   …but is not added to the list of swatches.

4. **Click the Create New Swatch button at the bottom of the Swatches panel.**

   The new swatch is created based on the currently active color. Notice, however, that the new swatch is named based on its RGB components. This occurred because the placed image — from which the color was sampled — is in the RGB color mode.

   The new swatch uses the RGB color mode.

   Note:

   If you sample colors from placed images, make sure they are in the correct color mode.

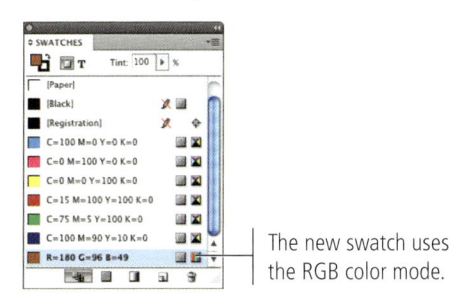

Project 7: National Parks Info Pieces

5. **Double-click the RGB swatch in the Swatches panel to edit the color.**

6. **Choose CMYK in the Color Mode menu of the Swatch Options dialog box.**

   When you change the color mode, notice the difference in the preview swatch. Changing RGB colors to process colors can result in color shift, which might be significant if the original color is far outside the CMYK gamut.

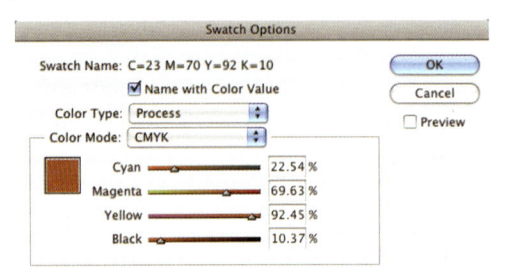

   Note:

   Your color name might be slightly different than ours, depending on the specific location you sampled with the Eyedropper tool.

7. **Click OK to return to the layout.**

8. **Using the Type tool, highlight the Fun Facts heading, and then click the new orange swatch in the Swatches panel.**

   This paragraph is formatted with the Subhead paragraph style. Changing the color of the selected text (instead of changing the style definition) is called local formatting or style override. Of course, local formatting is exactly that — local to the selected text. The other Subhead paragraph ("Directions" in the second frame) remains unchanged.

9. **With the insertion point in the Fun Facts heading, Control/right-click the Subhead style in the Paragraph Styles panel and choose Redefine Style from the contextual menu.**

   You no longer see the plus sign next to the Subhead style because the Subhead style now uses the orange-brown character color. The redefined style formatting also applies to the other subhead.

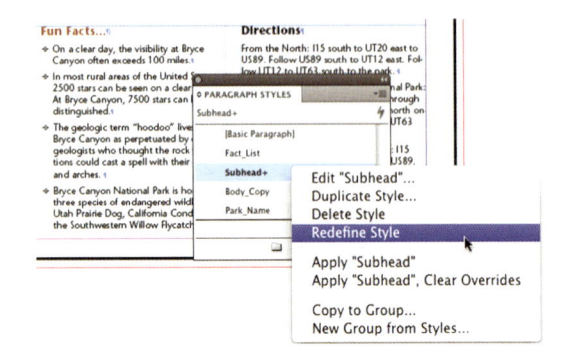

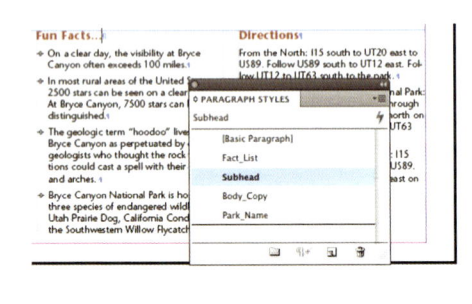

10. **Save the file and continue to the next stage of the project.**

Stage 2 Working with XML

In Projects 5 and 6, you worked with versioning, where the same layout hosts different content for different users. Repurposing content — placing the same content into different layouts — is another common task. InDesign uses XML (Extensible Markup Language) to enable content repurposing.

For many designers, XML is an intimidating concept among the alphabet soup of industry-related acronyms. Despite all the complexities that underlie this programming language, InDesign makes it very easy to implement XML in your layout documents.

As you know, styles define the appearance of content. All paragraphs formatted with the Heading style display the characteristics defined for that style, regardless of the actual content in those headings.

XML, on the other hand, describes the content marked with a specific tag. In other words, the heading is the actual text identified by the Heading tag, regardless of the formatting applied to those words. (This description will make more sense after you complete the following exercises.)

In the following exercises, you create an XML file from the flyer content, and then use that XML file to generate two additional layouts — a rack card and a postcard.

Tag Frames for XML

The first step in creating an XML file is to identify the document content, which is enclosed within tags as shown below:

<Heading>Much Ado About Nothing</Heading>

The first tag, <Heading>, is the opening tag; it identifies the beginning of the content. The second tag, </Heading>, is the closing tag; it identifies the end of the content.

When the XML file is imported into a layout, InDesign places the content from the Heading tag into the appropriate location.

To create the XML file for this project, you first have to define and apply tags for the different elements of the layout.

Note:

When InDesign reads an XML file, it finds the content within tags, and places that content into the appropriate location in the layout.

1. **With flyer_bryce.indd open from your WIP>Parks folder, choose Window>Tags to open the Tags panel.**

   The Tags panel allows you to create and manage XML tags within an InDesign layout. One tag, "Root," exists by default in every file; it is the basic container tag that encloses all other tags in the document.

2. **Using the Selection tool, select the larger image in the layout.**

3. **In the Tags panel, click the Autotag button.**

   The Image tag is automatically created and applied to the selected frame.

4. **If your image is not bordered and overlaid with a purple color, choose View>Structure>Show Tagged Frames.**

   The border and overlay color are for identification purposes. They only appear while you are working in the file; they do not appear when the file is output.

   Autotag button

   New Tag button

   Note:

   You can also click the New Tag button to create a tag; however, this method does not automatically apply the new tag to the selected object.

5. **In the Tags panel, double-click the Image tag to open the Tag Options dialog box.**

6. **Change the Name field to Main_Img and click OK.**

   Because you want to identify two different images, you have to assign a unique tag to each name. If you use the basic Image tag for both images, it will be difficult to control image placement when the XML file is imported into a different InDesign layout.

   Note:

   Tag names cannot include spaces, so you must use the underscore character to separate words in the tag name.

7. **Using the same method, tag the other image frame with a tag named Sub_Img.**

8. **Select the text frame with the park name placeholder and click the Autotag button in the Tags panel.**

   Text frames are automatically tagged with the Story tag. You need to identify two different stories in this job, so you should use a unique tag for each.

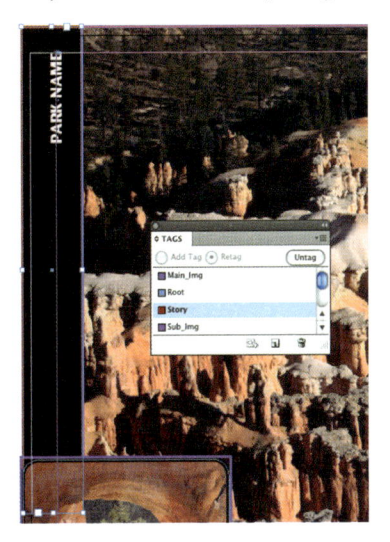

9. **Double-click the Story tag and change the name to Park_Name. Click OK to close the Tag Options dialog box.**

   This is the same name as the paragraph style applied to the text; using the same name for both elements allows you to map the tagged content to styles of the same name (which you do later).

Project 7: National Parks Info Pieces 421

10. **Select the three-column text frame. Create and apply a tag named Main_Text.**

    The file now has four tagged frames, each identified by a unique tag.

    This frame should be tagged with the Main_Text tag.

11. **Save the file and continue to the next exercise.**

REVIEW DOCUMENT STRUCTURE

In addition to tagging frames, you can also tag specific content within frames. Doing so enables you to automatically format XML content in other layouts, and allows you to access specific content when necessary.

1. **With flyer_bryce.indd open, highlight the first paragraph in the three-column text frame (excluding the paragraph return), and then click the New Tag button at the bottom of the Tags panel.**

    The new Tag1 is automatically added and highlighted.

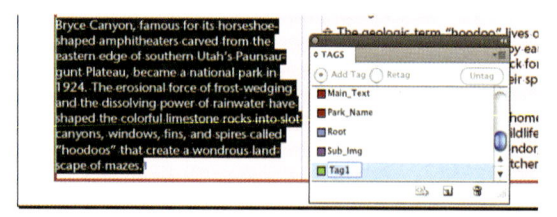

2. **With the tag name highlighted, type Body_Copy and press Return/Enter to finalize the name change.**

    The new tag has been renamed, but it has not yet been applied to the selected text.

3. **With the paragraph still selected in the layout, click the new Body_Copy tag to apply it.**

4. **Click in the paragraph to place the insertion point and remove the text highlighting.**

5. **If you don't see brackets around the paragraph, choose View>Structure> Show Tag Markers.**

    Like the overlay and border on tagged frames, these brackets do not appear in the printed job.

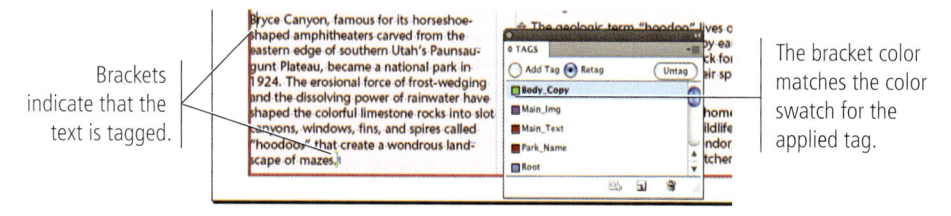

    Brackets indicate that the text is tagged.

    The bracket color matches the color swatch for the applied tag.

422 Project 7: National Parks Info Pieces

6. Highlight the Fun Facts heading (excluding the ending paragraph return). Create and apply a tag named **Subhead**.

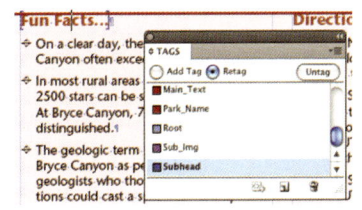

7. Highlight the bulleted paragraphs below the subhead. Create and apply a tag named **Fact_List**.

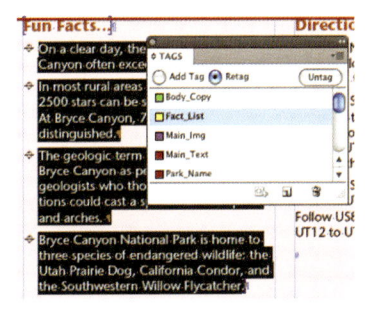

8. Highlight the Directions heading and apply the Subhead tag.

9. Highlight the paragraphs after the Directions heading and apply the Fact_List tag.

10. Save the file and continue to the next exercise.

Review XML Structure and Attributes

XML files allow you to share content across multiple files, using either a structured or an unstructured method. Using the unstructured method (which you utilize to create the postcard in a later exercise), you can simply import the XML into a document, and then drag elements into the layout. Structured repurposing requires more planning, but allows you to merge tagged XML content into tagged frames in another layout.

1. **With flyer_bryce.indd open, choose View>Structure>Show Structure. In the Structure pane, click the arrow to the left of Root to expand the structure.**

   The Structure pane appears in the left side of the document window, showing the hierarchical order of tagged elements in the file. Elements appear in the order they were created; any element with an arrow next to the name can be expanded to show nested elements and associated attributes (we explain those attributes shortly).

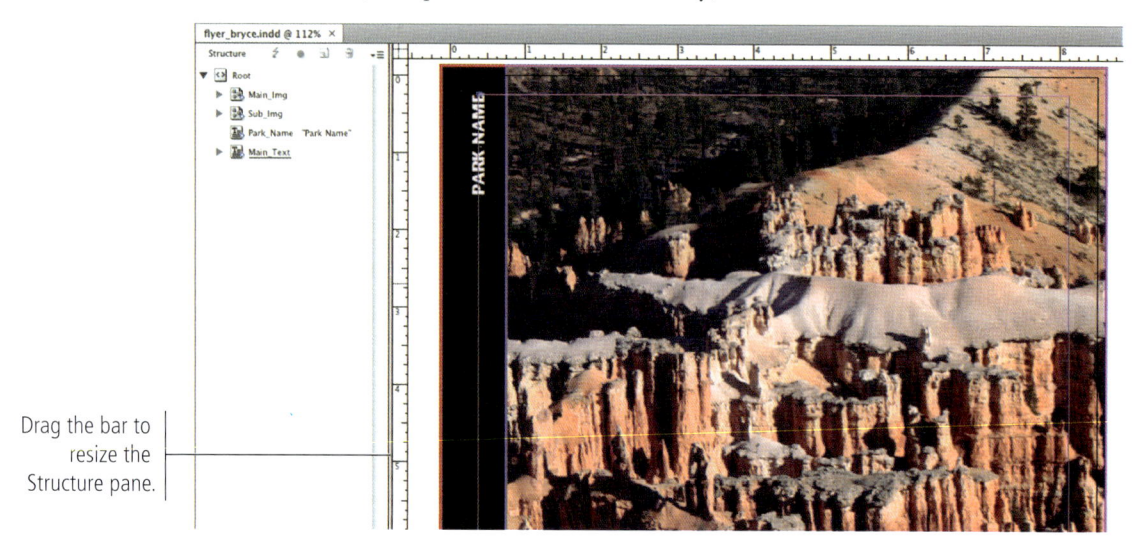

   Drag the bar to resize the Structure pane.

2. **If you don't see the words "Park Name" to the right of the Park_Name element, open the Structure pane Options menu and choose Show Text Snippets.**

   When snippets are visible, the first 32 characters of text in that element display in the pane.

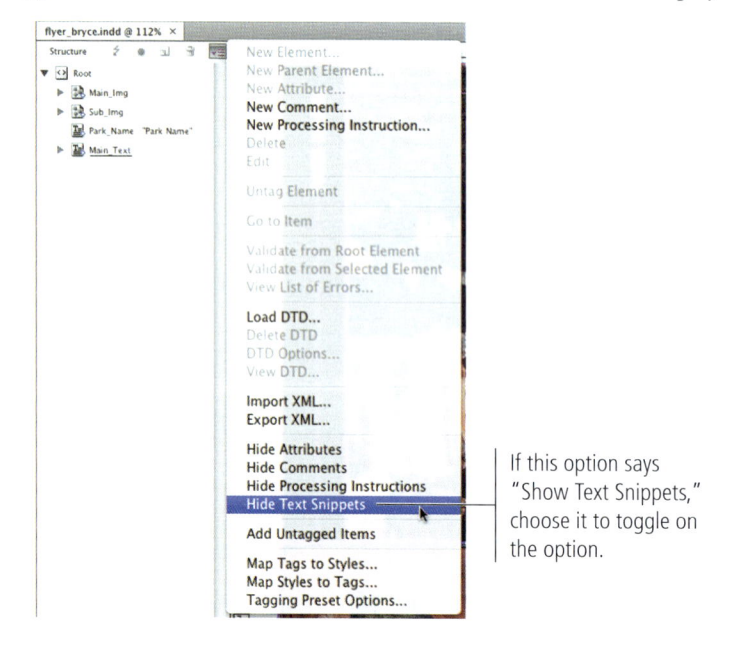

   If this option says "Show Text Snippets," choose it to toggle on the option.

424   Project 7: National Parks Info Pieces

3. **In the Structure pane, click the Main_Img element and drag it to the bottom of the list.**

   XML follows a linear, top-down structure. Although the elements are listed in the order you create them, you should modify the structure to more accurately reflect the order they appear in the layout.

   Like reordering layers in the Layers panel, the tagged element will be placed at the location of the heavy black line.

Identifying Structure Pane Icons

Use the following as a guide to the different icons in the Structure pane:

Icon	Name	Use
	Root element	Every document includes one root element at the top, which can be renamed but not moved or deleted
	Story element	Tagged story (one or more linked frames)
	Text element	Tagged text within a frame
	Graphic element	Tagged frame that includes a placed image; these include an href attribute that defines the path or URL to the linked file
	Unplaced text element	Unplaced text element not yet associated with a page item
	Unplaced graphic element	Unplaced graphic element not yet associated with a page item
	Table element	Table
	Header cell element	Cell in the header row of a table
	Body cell element	Cell within the body of a table
	Footer cell element	Cell in the footer row of a table
	Empty element	An empty frame is associated with this element
•	Attribute	Metadata, such as keywords or location of a linked image (HREF attribute)
	Comment	Comments that appear in the XML file, but not the InDesign document
	Processing instruction	Instruction to trigger an action in applications that can read instructions
	DOCTYPE element	Tells InDesign which DTD file to use when validating the XML file

Project 7: National Parks Info Pieces

4. **Expand all elements by clicking the arrow to the left of each element.**

   The Main_Text element contains additional tagged elements.

   When expanded, the two image elements show the path to the placed image, with the "href" prefix. This path is an attribute of the image element, defining the location of the content placed within the element. This path information tells InDesign which image to use when the file is imported into another layout.

   Note:

   Attributes are identified in the Structure pane by a large bullet character

5. **Save the InDesign file.**

6. **Choose File>Export and navigate to your WIP>Parks folder as the target destination.**

7. **Choose XML in the Format menu and remove flyer_ from the file name. Click Save.**

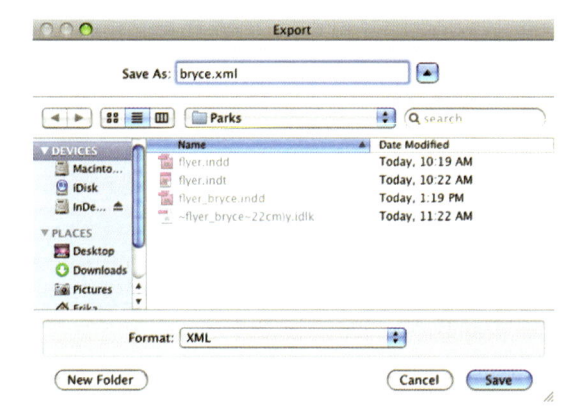

8. **Make sure no boxes are checked in either tab of the Export XML dialog box, and then click Export.**

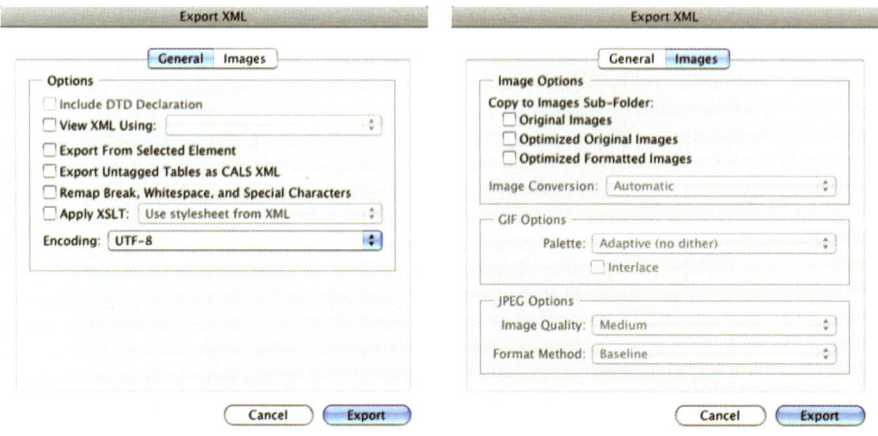

9. **Continue to the next exercise.**

426   Project 7: National Parks Info Pieces

Options for Exporting XML

You can control a number of options when you export an XML file from an InDesign layout. The following options are available in the General tab:

- **Include DTD Declaration** exports a reference to the defined DTD (if any) along with the XML file. This option is only available if a DOCTYPE element is showing in the Structure pane.
- **View XML Using** opens the exported file in the defined browser or editing application.
- **Export From Selected Element** starts exporting from the currently selected element in the Structure pane.
- **Export Untagged Tables As CALS XML** exports untagged tables in CALS XML format. (CALS is an extension of XML, designed by the U.S. Department of Defense Continuous Acquisition and Life-Cycle Support project.)
- **Remap Break, Whitespace, and Special Characters** converts special characters to their XML code equivalents (if equivalents exist).
- **Apply XSLT** applies a style sheet from the XML file or from an external file. (XLST stands for Extensible Stylesheet Language Transformation.)
- **Encoding** defines the encoding mechanism for representing international characters in the XML file.

In the Images tab, you can move images identified in the XML code to a folder created during the export process. (This is similar to the Links folder created when you use the Package utility.)

- **Original Images** copies the original image file into an Images subfolder.
- **Optimized Original Images** optimizes and compresses the original image files, and places copies of the files in an Images subfolder.
- **Optimized Formatted Images** optimizes the original image files that have been transformed in the layout (rotated, scaled, etc.), and places them in an Images subfolder.

If you choose either Optimized option, you can choose the format (GIF or JPEG) to use in the Image Compression menu. You can also define the optimization options for each format in the lower section of the dialog box. The Optimized options are more useful if you are repurposing the XML content into a Web layout; GIF and JPEG are not typically recommended for print layout design.

Place Unstructured XML Content

As we mentioned earlier, you can use either an unstructured or a structured method for applying XML content in a layout. The unstructured method is easiest because you can simply drag the content from the Structure pane and place it in your document.

1. **Open the file postcard.indt from the RF_InDesign>Parks folder to create a new file.**

   This layout includes placeholders for the two images, the park name, and the body copy.

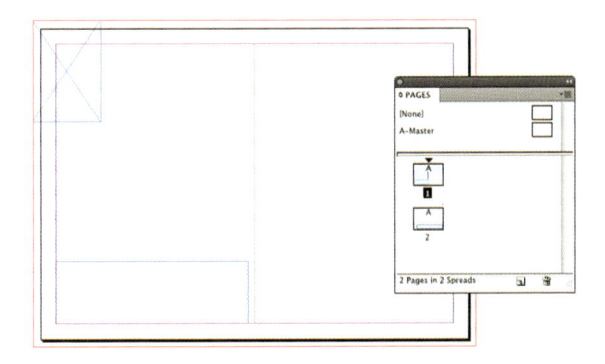

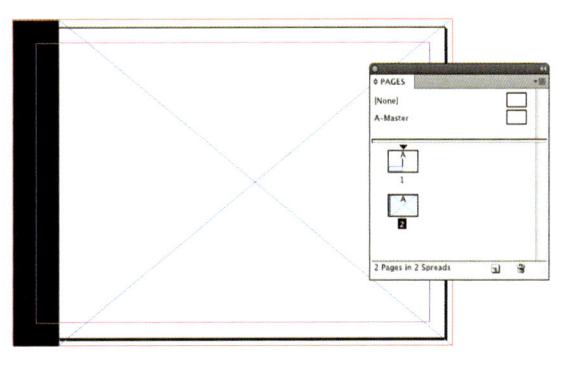

Project 7: National Parks Info Pieces

2. **Open the Structure pane for the postcard layout.**

3. **In the Structure pane Options menu, choose Import XML.**

4. **Navigate to the file bryce.xml in your WIP>Parks folder. Make sure the Show XML Import Options box is checked and click Open.**

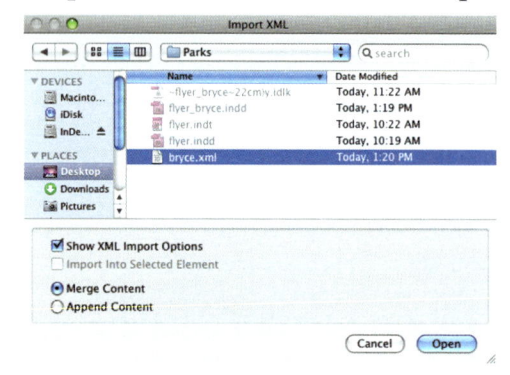

5. **Review the choices in the XML Import Options dialog box.**

   The most important option is the Mode menu:

   - If **Merge Content** is selected, the XML content will be placed into the Root element of the current file. Content in the XML file will be automatically placed into tagged frames in the current layout. If frames in the layout are not tagged, elements from the XML file will be added to the Structure pane.

   - If **Append Content** is selected, the entire XML file will be placed into the Root element of the current document, after any element that already exists in the document.

6. **Make sure Merge Content is selected in the Mode menu and check the Create Link option.**

   The **Create Link** option maintains a dynamic link to the XML file, just as a placed image is linked to the original image file. If content in the XML file changes, you can update the layout to automatically reflect the same changes.

Note:

The Merge Content and Append Content radio buttons are available in the Import XML dialog box because you need to make this choice even if you don't review the other import options.

Project 7: National Parks Info Pieces

7. **Click OK to import the XML file into the postcard document. In the Structure pane, expand all items.**

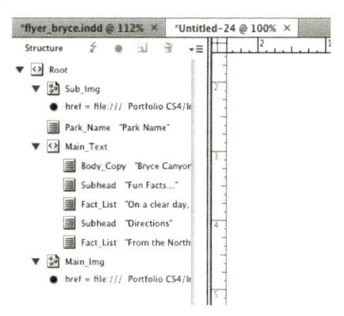

8. **With Page 1 of the postcard showing in the document window, drag the Sub_Img element from the Structure pane onto the empty frame in the top-left corner.**

   Adding content is as easy as dragging it into the layout. If you drag an element into an empty area, a frame is automatically created.

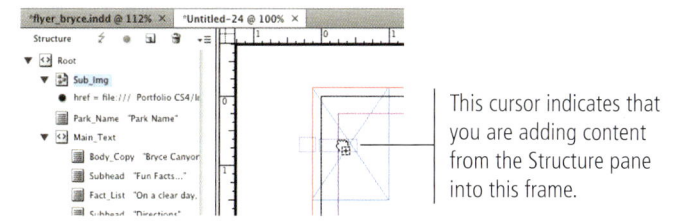

   This cursor indicates that you are adding content from the Structure pane into this frame.

   When you release the mouse button, the frame is automatically tagged with the Sub_Img tag.

   This icon indicates a graphic element that has been placed in the document.

   This icon indicates a graphic element that has not been placed in the document.

Import XML Options

INDESIGN FOUNDATIONS

When importing and placing XML data using the Merge Content option, the XML Import Options dialog box offers the following options:

- **Create Link** links to the XML file so, if the XML file is changed, you can update the XML data in the InDesign document.

- **Apply XSLT** defines a style sheet that transforms XML data from one structure to another.

- **Clone Repeating Text Elements** replicates the formatting applied to tagged placeholder text for repeating content (for example, formatting applied to different elements of an address placeholder).

- **Only Import Elements That Match Existing Structure** filters imported XML content so only elements from the imported XML file with matching elements in the document are imported. When this option is unchecked, all elements in the XML file are imported into the Structure pane.

- **Import Text Elements Into Tables If Tags Match** imports elements into a table if the tags match the tags applied to the placeholder table and its cells.

- **Do Not Import Contents Of Whitespace-only Elements** leaves existing content in place if the matching XML content contains only whitespace (such as a paragraph return character).

- **Delete Elements, Frames, and Content That Do Not Match Imported XML** removes elements from the Structure pane and the document layout if they don't match any elements in the imported XML file.

- **Import CALS Tables As InDesign Tables** imports any CALS tables in the XML file as InDesign tables.

Project 7: National Parks Info Pieces

9. **Drag the Body_Copy element from the Main_Text element to the empty text frame at the bottom of Page 1.**

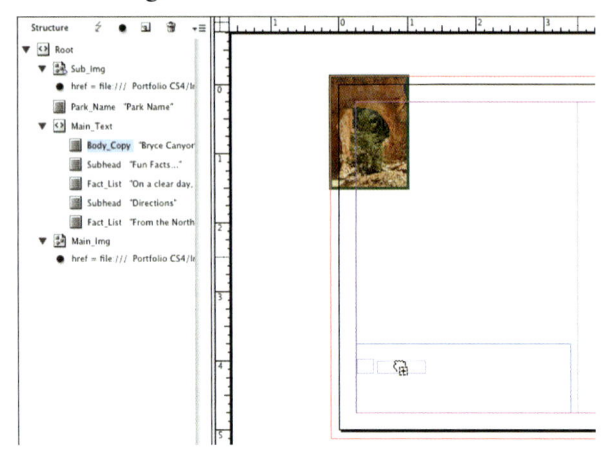

   When you release the mouse button, the content of the selected Body_Copy element is placed into the frame. The paragraph doesn't fit in the assigned space.

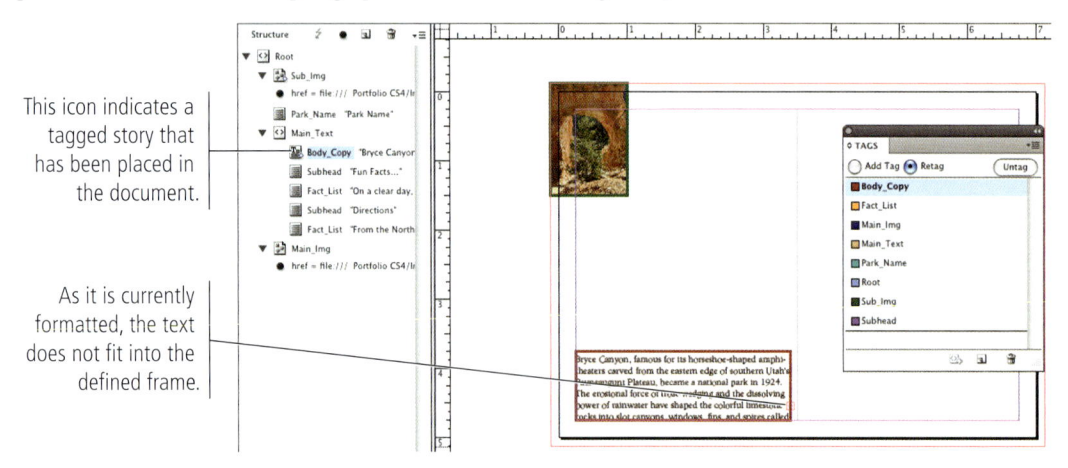

   This icon indicates a tagged story that has been placed in the document.

   As it is currently formatted, the text does not fit into the defined frame.

10. **In the Structure pane Options menu, choose Map Tags to Styles.**

    This dialog box allows you to assign specific styles to specific elements.

430 Project 7: National Parks Info Pieces

11. **Click the Map by Name button at the bottom of the dialog box.**

    Using the same names for tags and styles allows you to easily format different elements with the appropriate style. The Park_Name tag matches the style of the same name, so it is properly mapped to that style. Notice, however, that the Body_Copy tag is not mapped to a style.

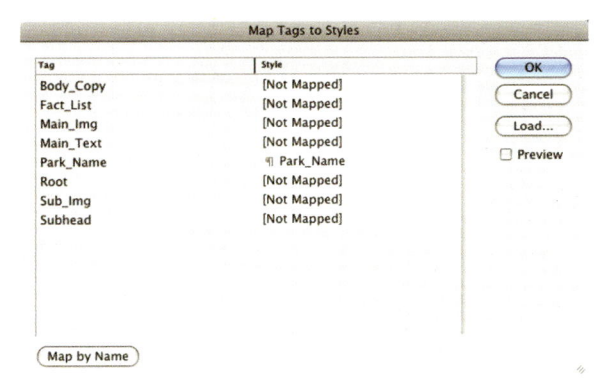

12. **Click the words "[Not Mapped]" to the right of the Body_Copy tag and choose Body Copy from the menu.**

    This menu lists all styles defined in the layout. Paragraph, character, table, cell, and object styles are all listed because all five of these might apply to a specific type of tag.

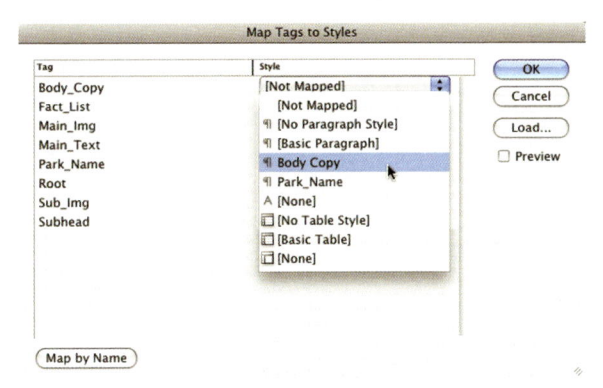

13. **Click OK to apply the defined formatting to the XML tags.**

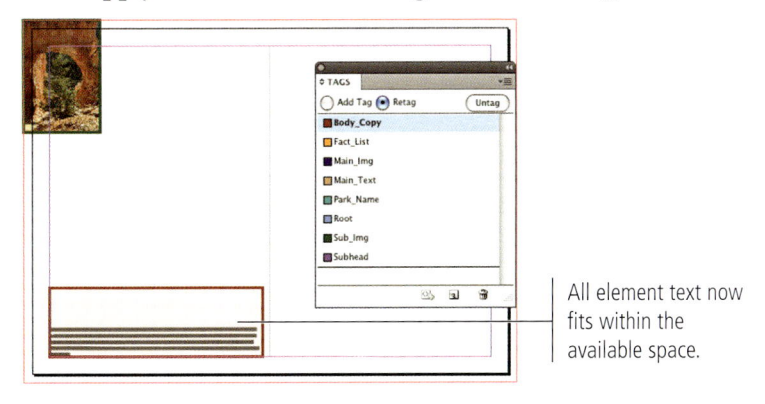

    All element text now fits within the available space.

Project 7: National Parks Info Pieces

14. **On Page 2 of the layout, drag the XML elements into the layout as shown in the following image.**

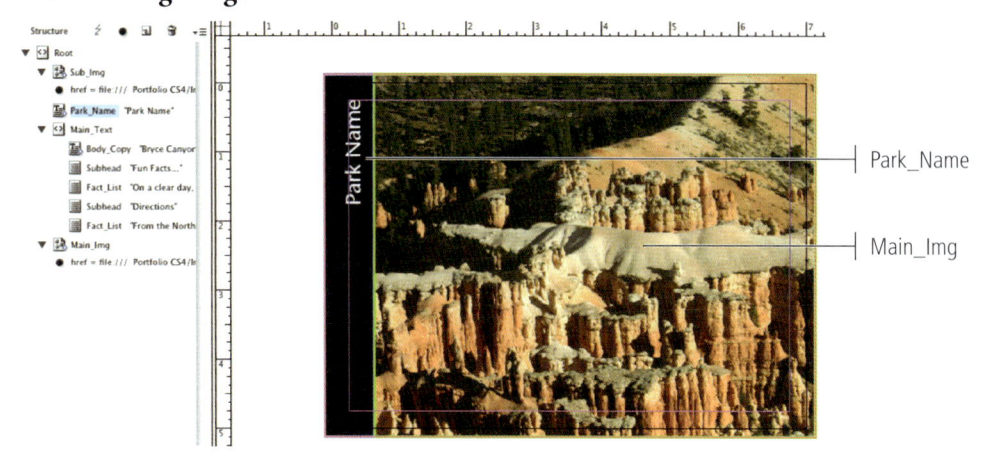

The text element is automatically formatted because you already mapped that tag (Park_Name) to the existing document style (Park_Name).

Remember, XML does not communicate the appearance of the different elements. After mapping the tags to the postcard styles, the Park_Name text is automatically placed with the ATC Oak Normal font with no type styles — as defined by the Park_Name style in the card.indt template file — instead of the ATC Oak Bold font with All Caps style that is used in the flyer.

15. **Save the file as `postcard_bryce.indd` in your WIP>Parks folder.**

16. **Continue to the next exercise.**

UPDATE LINKED XML DATA

When you placed the XML file into the postcard layout, you checked the Create Link option. This means that changes to the XML file can easily be updated in the postcard layout, just as you would update a placed image.

1. **Make sure `flyer_bryce.indd` is open.**

2. **In the page heading, change the words "Park Name" to Bryce Canyon National Park.**

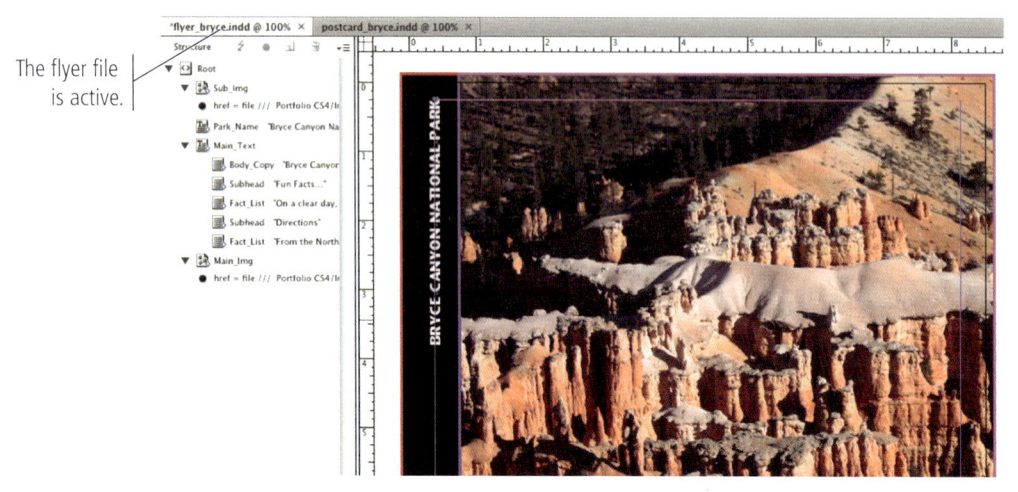

   The flyer file is active.

3. **Save the file.**

432 Project 7: National Parks Info Pieces

4. **Choose File>Export and navigate to the WIP>Parks folder as the target. Make sure XML is selected in the Format menu and the file name is bryce.xml, and then click Save.**

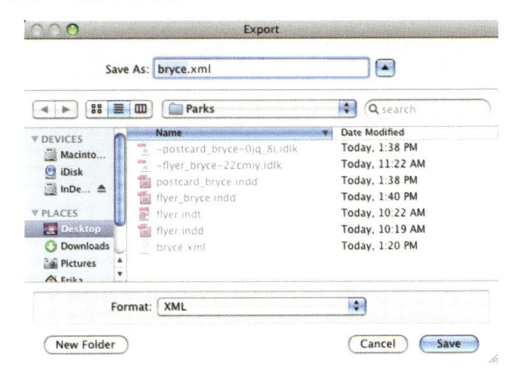

5. **When asked if you want to overwrite the existing file, click Replace/Yes.**

6. **Click Export in the Options dialog box to rewrite the XML file.**

7. **Make postcard_bryce.indd the active file, and then display the Links panel.**

    The XML file is linked to the document, so it appears (appropriately) in the Links panel. The Warning icon indicates that the file was changed since being imported.

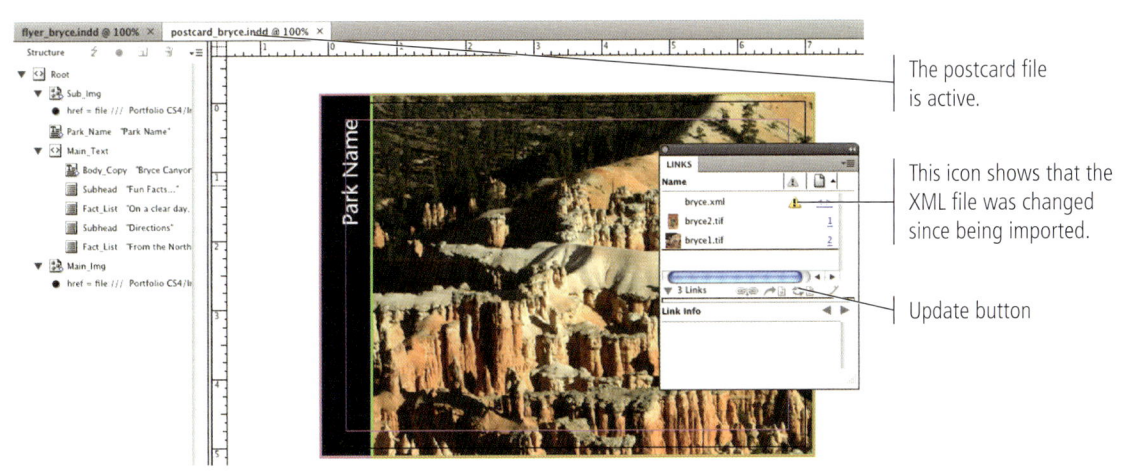

8. **Select bryce.xml in the Links panel and click the Update Link button.**

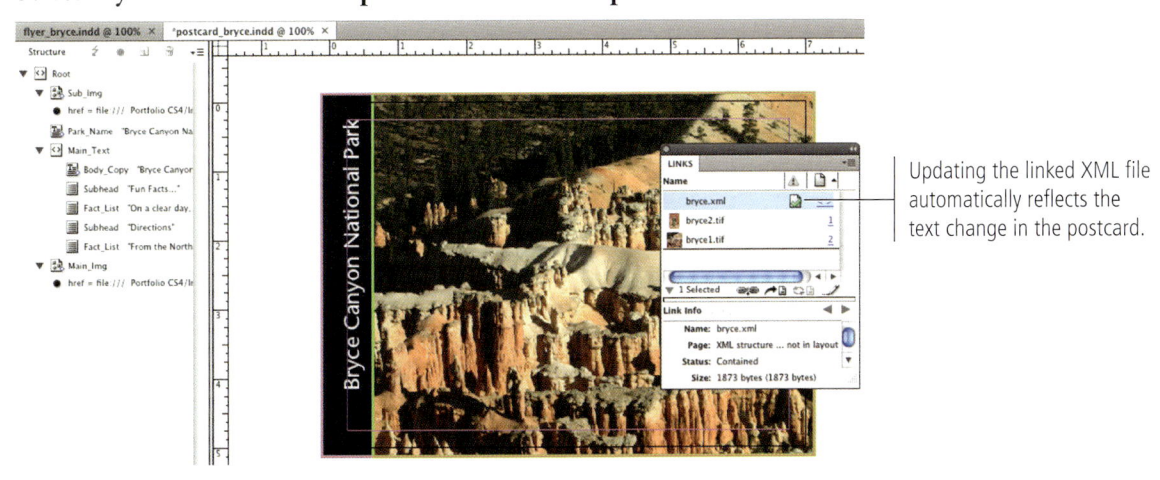

9. **Save the postcard file and close it.**

10. **Continue to the next exercise.**

Project 7: National Parks Info Pieces 433

Import Structured XML

With some advance planning, you can build a layout with tagged frames to automatically contain elements when the XML file is imported. For this process to work correctly, keep the following points in mind:

- The tag names must be exactly the same in the document file as in the XML data. (You can load tags from one InDesign file to another to be sure the names match.)

- You can automatically format imported XML content by mapping tag names to styles. (Style names need to exactly match the tag names.)

- The tagged layout should have the same structure as the data in the XML file. (Remember, the structure in the XML file is based on the order of elements in the Structure pane.)

1. **Create a new file by opening the `rack.indt` template in the RF_InDesign>Parks folder.**

   This layout includes two pages with placeholder frames for all the same elements used in the flyer. To prepare these frames for XML import, you have to tag those frames with the same tag names used in the XML file you want to import.

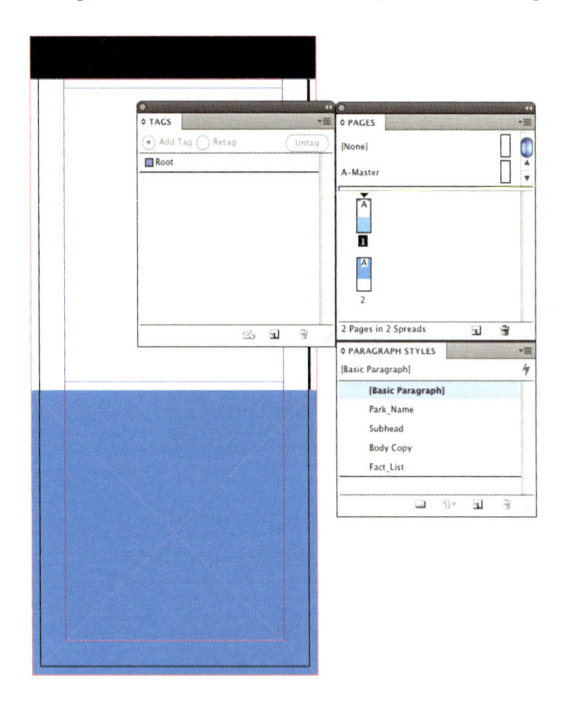

2. **In the Tags panel Options menu, choose Load Tags.**

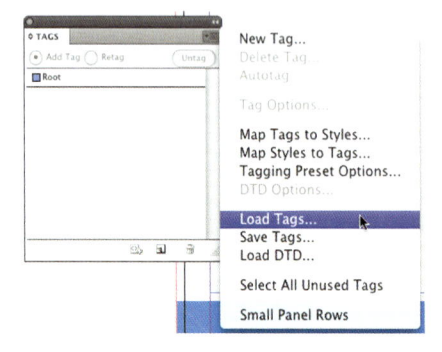

Project 7: National Parks Info Pieces

3. **Navigate to `flyer_bryce.indd` in your WIP>Parks folder and click Open.**

   You used this file to generate the XML file, so its tags match those in the XML file. This method of loading tags ensures that the tags you add in the rack card file exactly match the tags in the flyer (and thus, in the XML file).

4. **Open the Structure pane for the rack card file.**

   Adding tags to the file does not automatically add elements to the structure. Elements aren't added to the structure until you attach the loaded tags to frames in the layout.

5. **Place the Tags panel next to the Paragraph Styles panel and compare the two lists.**

   Remember, for tags to correctly map to styles, the names of the styles must exactly match the names of the tags.

   The space character in the Body Copy style means the style name does not exactly match the tag name (the underscore is missing).

6. **Control/right-click the Body Copy paragraph style and choose Edit "Body Copy" from the contextual menu.**

7. **In the Paragraph Style Options dialog box, change the style name to `Body_Copy` and click OK.**

   The style name now matches the tag name.

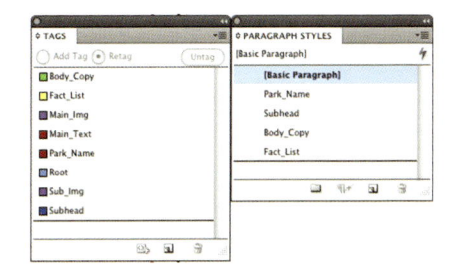

   Note:

   Tag names can't have spaces but style names can, so you will probably see this type of mismatch more than once in on-the-job projects.

Project 7: National Parks Info Pieces 435

8. **Select the black frame at the top of Page 1 in the layout, and then click the Park_Name tag in the Tags panel.**

After tagging the frame, the element is added to the Structure pane.

9. **Using the same method, assign the Main_Text tag to the large text frame, and assign the Sub_Img tag to the cyan graphics frame on Page 1 of the layout.**

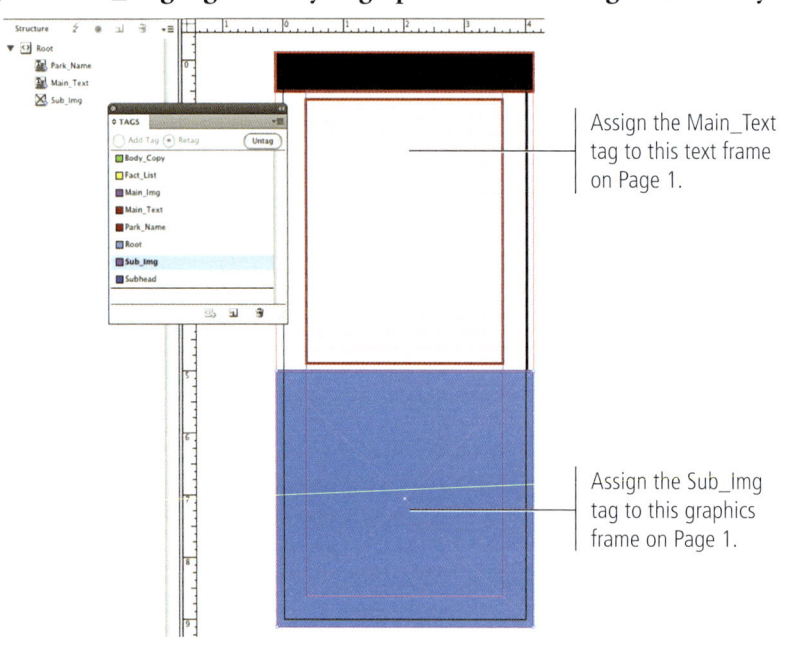

Assign the Main_Text tag to this text frame on Page 1.

Assign the Sub_Img tag to this graphics frame on Page 1.

10. **On Page 2 of the layout, assign the Main_Img tag to the cyan graphics frame.**

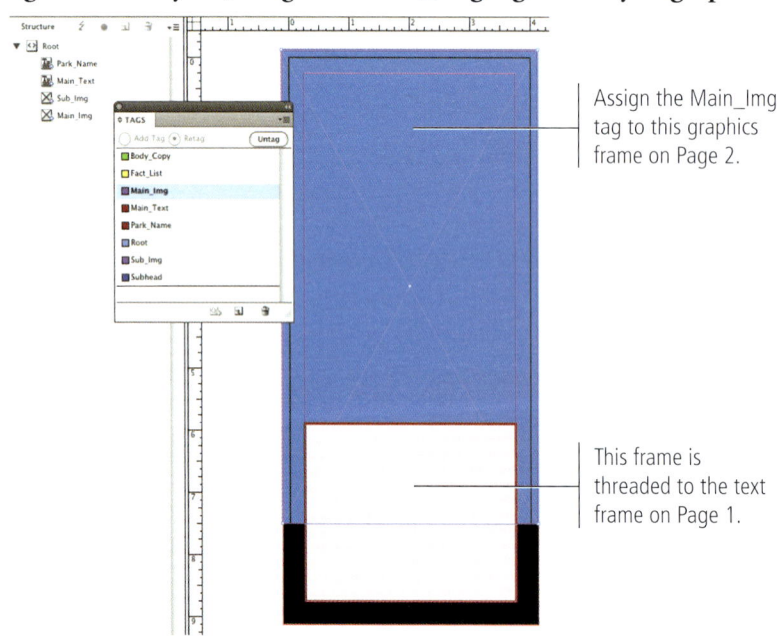

Assign the Main_Img tag to this graphics frame on Page 2.

This frame is threaded to the text frame on Page 1.

Project 7: National Parks Info Pieces

11. **Make sure `flyer_bryce.indd` is open. Choose the 2-Up (side-by-side) document arrangement in the Application/Menu bar.**

    To be sure the XML will import properly, the tagged document structure should exactly match the structure in the XML file. The two Structure panes show that the Sub_Img element is not in the same order; you need to fix this mismatch before importing the XML file.

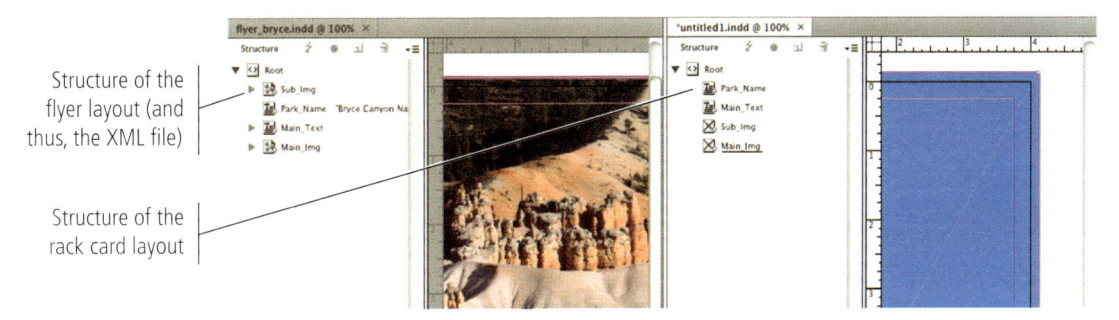

    Structure of the flyer layout (and thus, the XML file)

    Structure of the rack card layout

12. **In the rack card Structure pane, drag the Sub_Img element to the top of the list.**

    Note:

    When you drag to reorder tags in the Structure panel, a heavy black line indicates the potential location of the tag if you release the mouse button.

13. **Return to the single-document arrangement and make the rack card file active.**

14. **With the rack card document active, choose File>Import XML.**

    This is the same as choosing the Import XML option in the Structure pane Options menu.

15. **Navigate to the file `bryce.xml` in your WIP>Parks folder. Make sure Show XML Import Options is checked, Import Into Selected Element is not checked, and then click Open.**

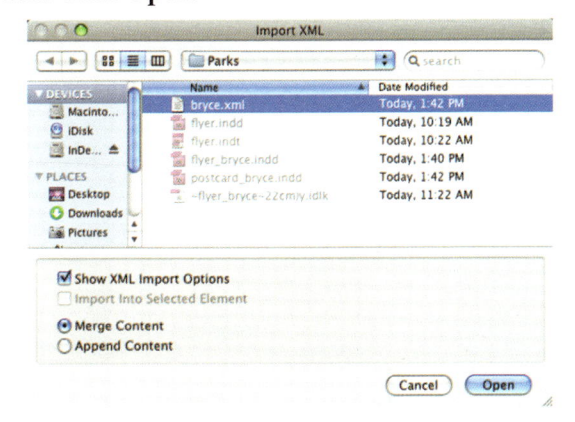

Project 7: National Parks Info Pieces   437

16. In the XML Import Options dialog box, make sure Merge Content is selected in the Mode menu. Check the Create Link option and uncheck all other options.

17. Click OK to import the XML file into the rack card layout and merge the data into the tagged frames.

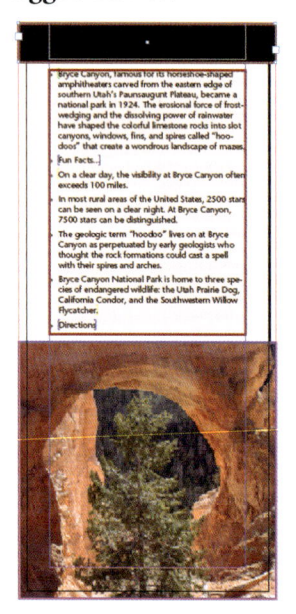

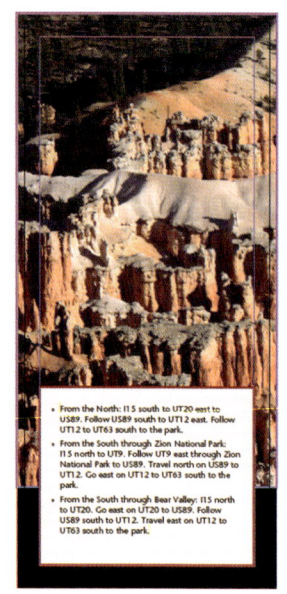

18. In the Structure pane Options menu, choose Map Tags to Styles.

19. In the resulting dialog box, click Map by Name, and then click OK.

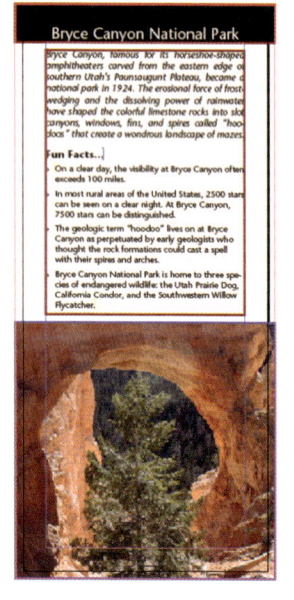

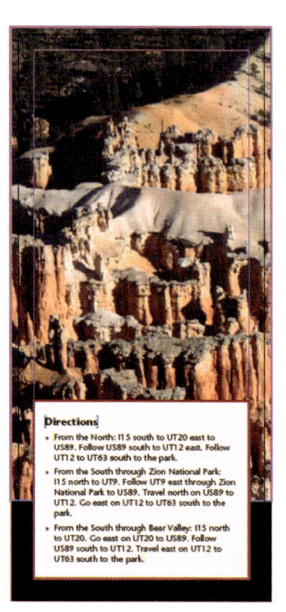

20. **Choose View>Structure>Hide Tagged Frames and Hide Tag Markers to turn off the nonprinting visual indicators.**

21. **Save the rack card file as `rack_bryce.indd` in your WIP>Parks folder, and then close the file.**

    Of course, XML can be far more complex than what you applied in these short documents; in fact, entire books have been written on the subject. The point of this project is to introduce you to the concepts of XML, and show you how InDesign's XML capabilities make it relatively easy to work with XML data. With some careful planning, you can set up multiple files to read the same information and repurpose content into whatever physical format is necessary.

22. **Continue to the next stage of the project.**

Note:

To learn more about the capabilities of XML, we encourage you to explore www.xml.org. This site offers a wealth of information about XML from experts and standards organizations in multiple industries.

Validating Structure with a DTD

INDESIGN FOUNDATIONS

In the previous exercise, you loaded tag names and modified the element structure in the rack card to match the structure in the XML file. Because the XML file was created from another InDesign file, it was easy to compare the tag names and structures in the two files, ensuring the import process would work correctly. In many cases, however, different applications will be involved in the repurposing process, whether generating the XML file or reading the XML file generated from InDesign. When other applications are involved, you need a mechanism to verify that the structure is correct.

A DTD (Document Type Definition) file defines the required structure for an XML document. Using a DTD, you can ensure that the structure in an InDesign file matches the structure in a Web layout file. You can also verify that both layouts match the structure that exists in the XML file being used to transfer content. A DTD file also provides a set of elements and attributes, ensuring consistency of the tag names in different documents.

For example, the DTD file may require the Park_Name element to be a child of a story element (in the case of this project, the story element is named Main_Text). If a document tags a title without tagging the story in which it appears, the DTD file marks the title element as invalid. (The process of comparing a document structure to a specific DTD is called validation.)

You can load a DTD into an InDesign file using the Options menu in the Structure pane or the Tags panel. When you load a DTD, the element names from the DTD appear in the Tags panel so you can tag elements with the correct names. Elements imported with a DTD are locked, so you can't delete or rename them unless you delete the DTD file as well.

If you have loaded a DTD into your InDesign file, you can verify that your layout meets the requirements defined in the DTD. In the Structure pane Options menu, you can validate from the Root element or the selected element.

After validating the file, problems are listed in red in the Structure pane. The bottom section of the Structure pane provides more information about specific errors, including suggestions for fixing them.

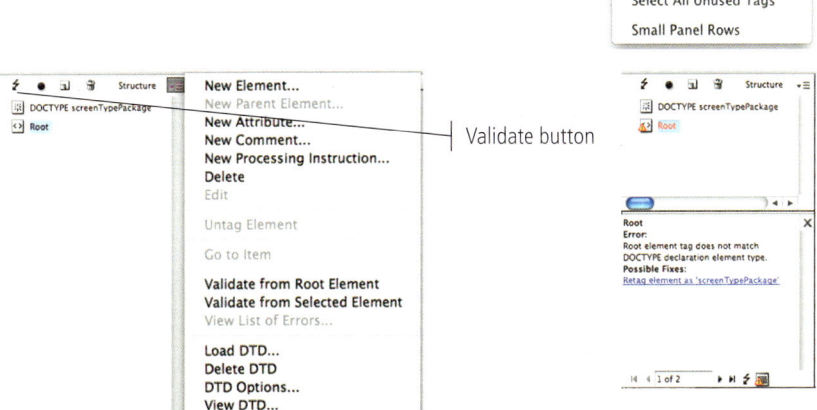

Project 7: National Parks Info Pieces   **439**

Stage 3 Working with Interactive Elements

As we discussed earlier, the PDF format is now an industry standard for transmitting high-resolution files to an output provider. The format was originally created to share files electronically, preserving the appearance of a document regardless of the creating application or platform.

When files are shared on the Internet, they often include interactive elements such as live hyperlinks and buttons that make a digital document more user-friendly. Why force users to retype a Web address, for example, when you could enable them to simply click the text that already appears in the document?

In the final stage of this project, you add interactivity to elements that will appear in the digital version of the PDF flyer file. InDesign includes a number of tools for adding interactive elements — specifically hyperlinks and buttons — that can be useful in digitally distributed PDF files.

Note:

InDesign includes an option to export XHTML for a Web page. However, InDesign is not a Web design application. Just as there are technical requirements for designing print layouts, a number of standards and limitations govern the correct way to design and implement a Web page. We highly recommend using a Web design application such as Adobe Dreamweaver rather than trying to design a Web page layout in InDesign.

DEFINE HYPERLINKS

Hyperlinks are the most basic — and the most common — interactive elements in digital documents. Every hyperlink has two parts — the hyperlink object (which can be text) and the destination. The destination is the document, specific place in the file, or other location that is called by clicking the hyperlink. InDesign's Hyperlinks panel makes it very easy to create and apply hyperlinks to elements of a layout.

1. **With flyer_bryce.indd open, choose View>Structure>Hide Tagged Frames and View>Structure>Hide Tag Markers (if necessary) to hide the non-printing visual indicators.**

2. **Create a new text frame at the top of the smaller image frame.**

3. **In the new frame, type the following:**

   For complete park information, [soft return]
   go to www.nps.gov/brca/.

Although you typed in the frame, the overset text icon appears.

440   Project 7: National Parks Info Pieces

4. **Open the Text Frame Options dialog box for the new frame and check the Ignore Text Wrap option. Click OK to apply the change.**

   By default, text wrap attributes apply to any overlapping object, regardless of stacking order.

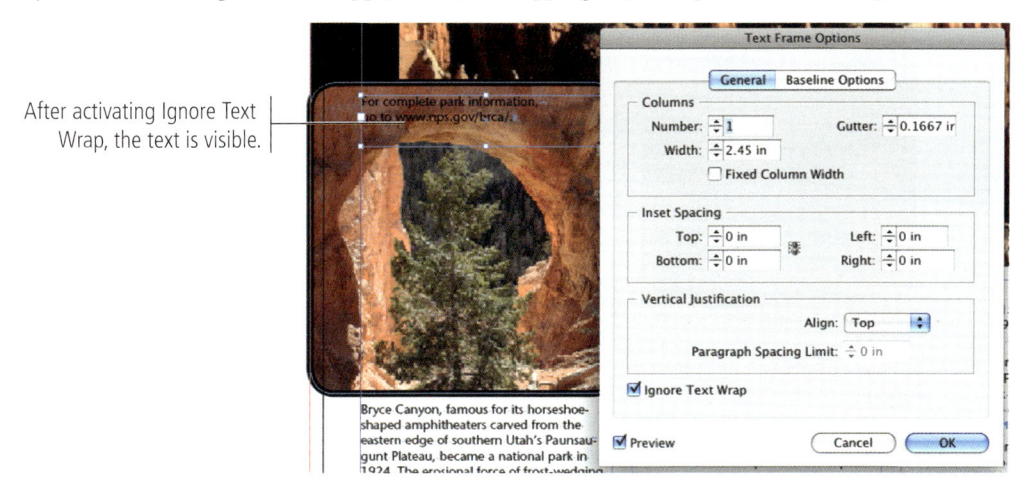

   After activating Ignore Text Wrap, the text is visible.

5. **Select all the text and change it to 10 pt, filled with the Paper swatch.**

6. **Open the Hyperlinks panel (Window>Interactive>Hyperlinks).**

7. **Highlight the Web address you just typed in the text frame (including the final forward slash).**

8. **Choose New Hyperlink from URL in the Hyperlinks panel Options menu.**

   The New Hyperlink dialog box defines the type and destination of the link, as well as the default appearance of the link in the layout. The highlighted text is automatically entered in the Name field.

Project 7: National Parks Info Pieces   441

9. **Click to place the insertion point anywhere in the text of the Web address (removing the highlight).**

    The New Hyperlink from URL option automatically creates a URL destination based on the selected text.

    By default, hyperlinks in the document have a thin black outline.

    Defined destinations are available in this menu.

    After applying the hyperlink destination, the applied hyperlink appears in the panel.

10. **With the new hyperlink selected in the panel, choose Hyperlink Options in the panel Options menu.**

11. **In the Appearance menu, choose Invisible Rectangle.**

    Hyperlinks in an InDesign layout are automatically enclosed in a rectangular shape that marks the hyperlink area. This area can be visible or not, depending on your needs. In this case, the layout will be exported for both print and Web, so you want the hyperlink to be invisible in the layout.

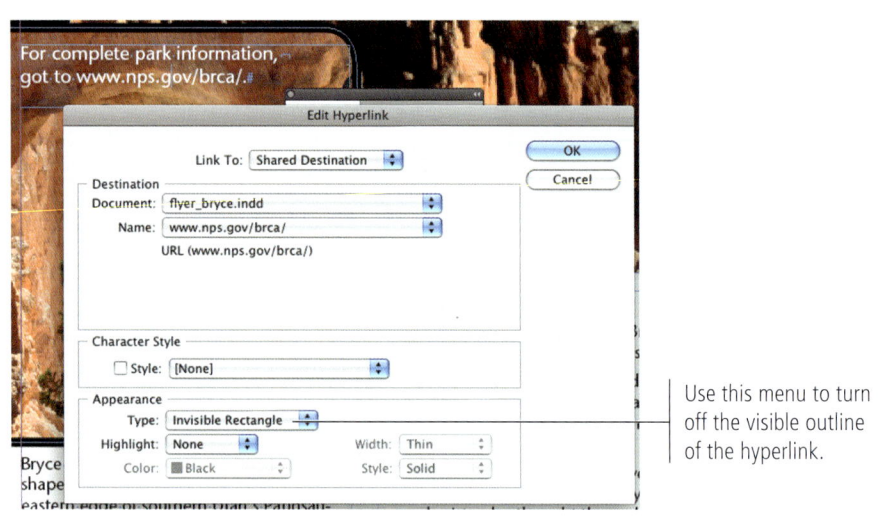

    Note:

    If you use the Invisible Rectangle option, there will be no visual indication that the text is a hyperlink. It will be up to users to accidentally stumble onto the interactivity, which basically defeats the purpose of adding interactivity.

    Use this menu to turn off the visible outline of the hyperlink.

    Note:

    You are only adding this link because not linking the text would seem to be an omission to users who assume that any instance of a Web site should be clickable. In the next exercise, you add hyperlink buttons that clearly provide interactive functionality.

12. **Click OK to close the dialog box.**

13. **Save the file and continue to the next exercise.**

CREATE BUTTON STATES

If you are designing a document for digital distribution, you can incorporate interactive buttons for the user to initiate specific behaviors (such as opening a Web site or sending an email). InDesign buttons are created with the Button tool and managed in the States panel.

1. **With flyer_bryce.indd open, create a small rectangle graphics frame in the empty space in the bottom-right corner of the layout.**

2. **Place the file home_btn.gif (from the RF_InDesign>Parks folder) into the new frame.**

3. **Control/right-click the button in the layout and choose Fitting>Fit Frame to Content.**

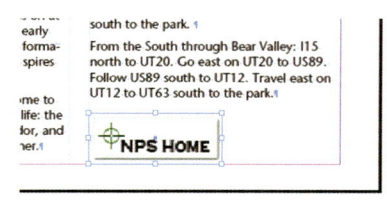

4. **Open the Buttons panel (Window>Interactive>Buttons).**

5. **With the graphics frame from Steps 1–3 selected, click the Convert Object to Button icon at the bottom of the panel.**

   An InDesign button can have up to three states (appearances), based on the position of the user's mouse cursor. The default Up state displays when the cursor is not touching the button.

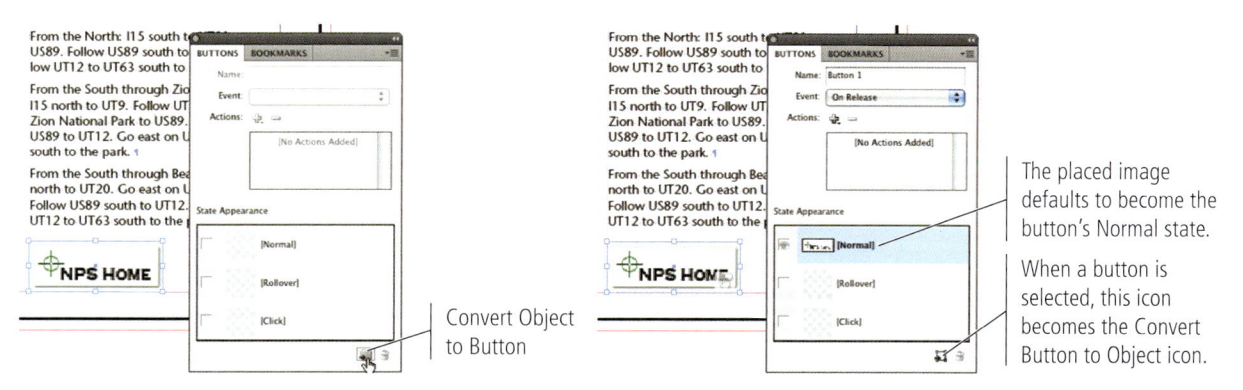

   Convert Object to Button

   The placed image defaults to become the button's Normal state.

   When a button is selected, this icon becomes the Convert Button to Object icon.

6. **In the Buttons panel, click the [Rollover] state to select it.**

7. **Choose File>Place. Navigate to the file `home_over.gif`, make sure the Replace Selected Item option is checked, and click Open.**

   This image (the rollover state) displays when the user's mouse cursor moves over the button.

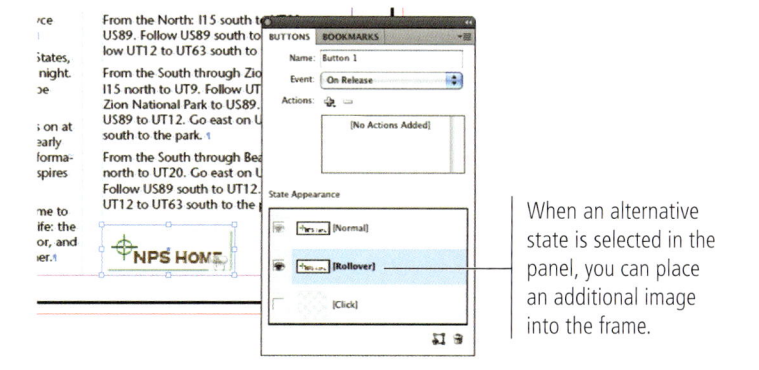

   When an alternative state is selected in the panel, you can place an additional image into the frame.

   Note:

   The images placed into different button states need to be created in another application, such as Adobe Photoshop or Adobe Illustrator.

Project 7: National Parks Info Pieces   443

8. **In the Buttons panel, click the [Click] state to select it.**

9. **Choose File>Place. Navigate to the file home_over.gif and click Open.**

    This image — the click state — displays when the user clicks the button.

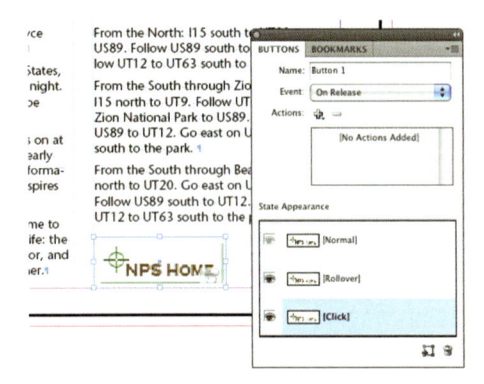

10. **Using the same techniques, create a second button to the right of the existing button. Use the file email_btn.gif in the Up state and use email_over.gif in the Rollover and Click states.**

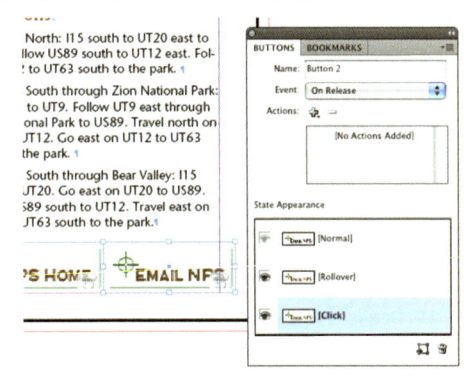

11. **Save the file and continue to the next exercise.**

Define Button Behavior

The two buttons in your file will both cause something to happen when clicked by a user — the "something" that happens is called an action. You can define various behaviors for different events (also called triggers) that cause a behavior (action) to occur, such as when the mouse moves over the button or when the button is clicked.

1. **With flyer_bryce.indd open, select the NPS Home button with the Selection tool.**

2. **Type Link to NPS Home Page in the Name field of the Buttons panel.**

    As with a hyperlink, the button name is used for identification purposes only. In the layout, the button label changes to reflect the new name.

3. **Make sure On Release is selected in the Event menu.**

   InDesign supports six different types of events:

   - The **On Release** event triggers an action when the mouse button is released after clicking.
   - The **On Click** event triggers an action as soon as the mouse button is clicked.
   - The **On Roll Over** event triggers an action when the mouse cursor enters the button area.
   - The **On Roll Out** event triggers an action when the mouse cursor leaves the button area.
   - The **On Focus** event triggers an action when pressing the Tab key highlights the button (called being in focus).
   - The **On Blur** event triggers an action when pressing the Tab key moves the focus to the next button in the tab order.

4. **Click the "+" button in the Buttons panel and choose Go To URL from the Actions menu.**

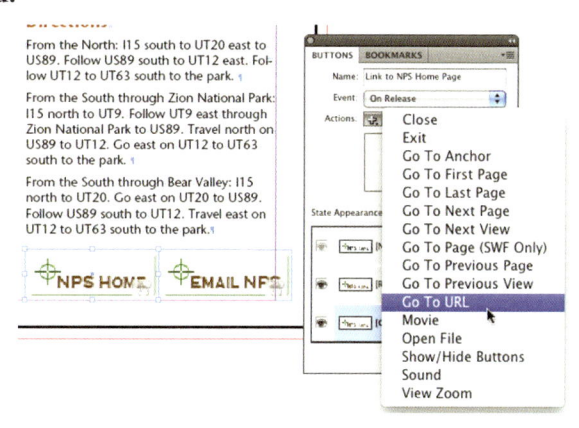

   When the user clicks and then releases the mouse button, an action occurs. The specific action that occurs is defined in this menu:

   - **Close** closes the file.
   - **Exit** quits the application being used to display the file.
   - **Go To Anchor** navigates to the specified bookmark or anchor.
   - **Go To** [First/Last/Next/Previous] Page navigates to the relevant pages in the PDF file.
   - **Go To Previous View** navigates to the most recently viewed page in the PDF file, or returns to the last-used zoom size (similar to the Back button in a browser).
   - **Go To Next View** navigates to a page after going to the previous view (similar to the Forward button in a browser).
   - **Go To URL** opens a specific Web page in the user's default browser.
   - **Movie** allows you to play, pause, stop, or resume a movie file placed in the document.
   - **Open File** opens the specified file in the file's native application (if possible).
   - **Show/Hide Fields** toggles the visibility of specific buttons (fields) in the PDF file.
   - **Sound** allows you to play, pause, stop, or resume a sound file added to the document.
   - **View Zoom** displays the page according to the zoom option you specify.

Note:

You can place QuickTime (.mov) or Microsoft AVI video files, as well as animated Flash files that have been exported to the SWF format, into the layout, just as you would place any other picture. You can also control the properties of placed movie files by choosing Object>Interactive> Movie Options.

Note:

You can place Apple AIFF or Microsoft WAV sound files into a layout. You can also control the properties of placed sound files by choosing Object>Interactive> Sound Options.

5. In the URL field, place the insertion point after the "http://" prefix and type www.nps.gov/, and then press Return/Enter to finalize the URL.

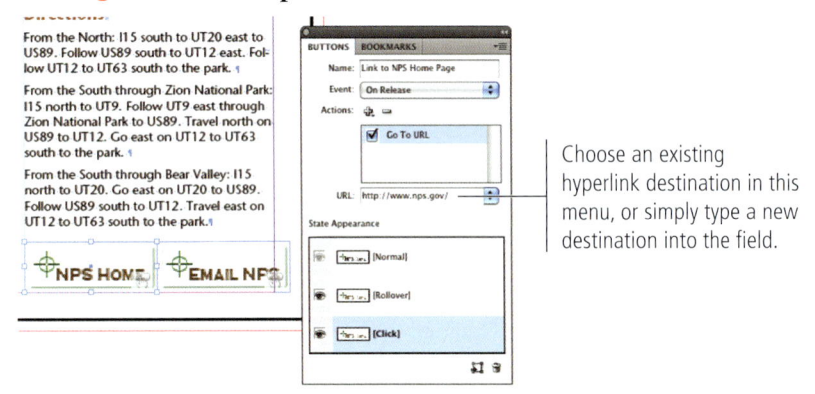

Choose an existing hyperlink destination in this menu, or simply type a new destination into the field.

6. Open the Buttons panel Options menu and choose Visible in PDF but Doesn't Print.

   The default option, Visible in PDF, means (as you might guess) that the button displays in the PDF file. The Visible in PDF but Doesn't Print option is useful if you are going to output directly from the InDesign file instead of creating a separate PDF file for print.

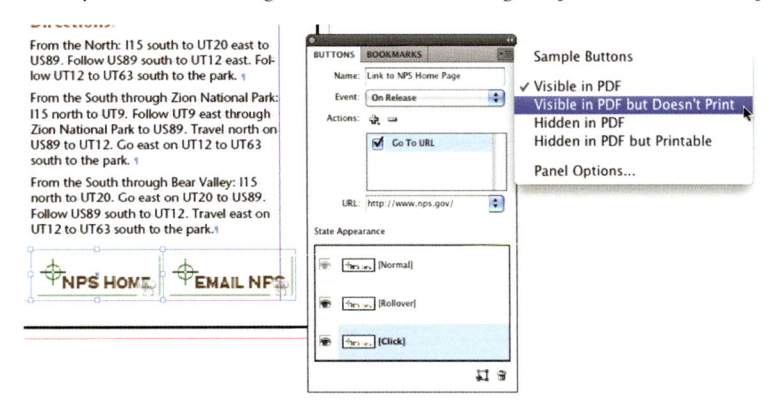

7. Select the second button and change its name to Email NPS Staff.

8. Define an On Release event with the Go To URL behavior. In the URL field, delete the "http://" prefix and type mailto:info@nps.gov, and then press Return/Enter to finalize the URL.

   Note:

   The "mailto:" prefix is the correct code to open a new message that is already targeted to the defined email address.

9. Set the second button to be visible but not to print.

10. Save the file and continue to the next exercise.

446   Project 7: National Parks Info Pieces

Export Multiple PDF Files

Your layout now has two interactive buttons and one hyperlink that is not visually identified in the layout (but it will work if a user clicks the address text). The final step of this project is to output your files to the necessary formats.

1. **With flyer_bryce.indd open, choose File>Export.**

2. **Choose Adobe PDF in the Format menu.**

3. **Navigate to your WIP>Parks folder, change the file name to flyer_bryce_print.pdf, and then click Save.**

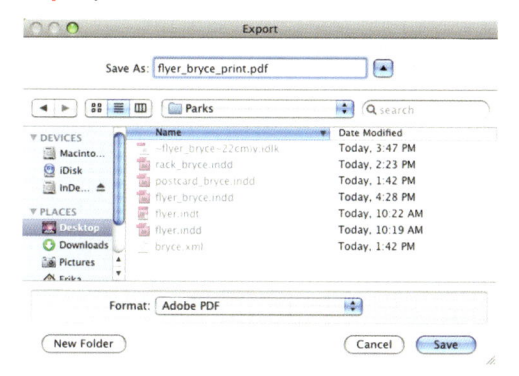

4. **In the Export Adobe PDF dialog box, choose [High Quality Print] in the Adobe PDF Preset menu.**

5. **In the Marks and Bleeds options, add crop marks with a 0.125″ offset and include a 0.125″ bleed.**

6. **Click the Save Preset button and save these settings as Print with Bleed.**

    You need to export two other layouts using the same settings; creating a preset now will save time later.

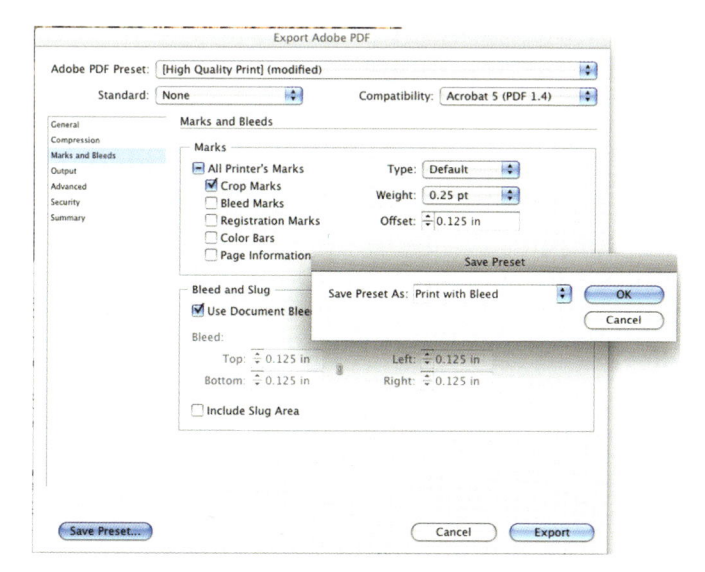

7. **Click OK to close the Save Preset dialog box, and then click Export to create the PDF file for print.**

Project 7: National Parks Info Pieces   447

8. When the export process is complete, choose File>Export again.

9. Change the file name to `flyer_bryce_web.pdf` and click Save.

10. In the Export Adobe PDF dialog box, choose [Smallest File Size] in the Adobe PDF Preset menu.

11. In the General tab, check the Hyperlinks and Interactive Elements options in the Include area.

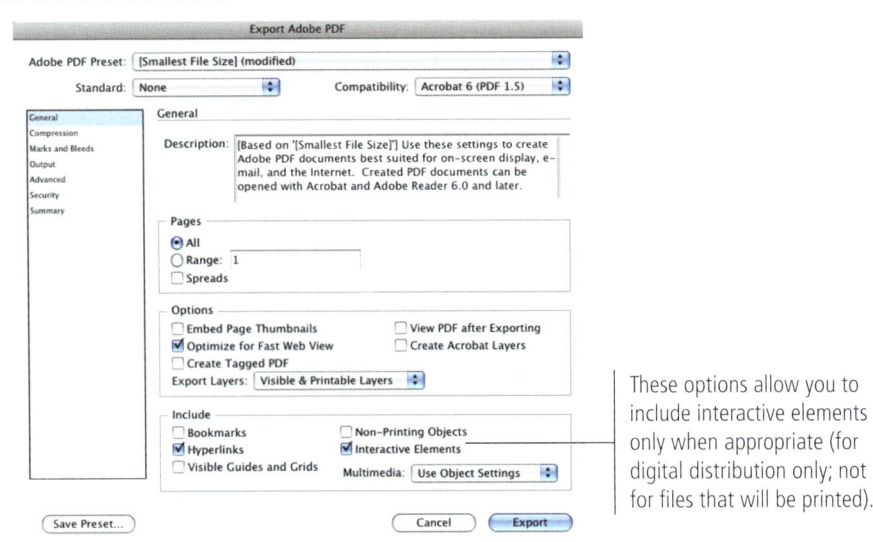

These options allow you to include interactive elements only when appropriate (for digital distribution only; not for files that will be printed).

12. Click Export. When the export process is complete, open both PDF files in Acrobat. Test the buttons and hyperlink in the Web file.

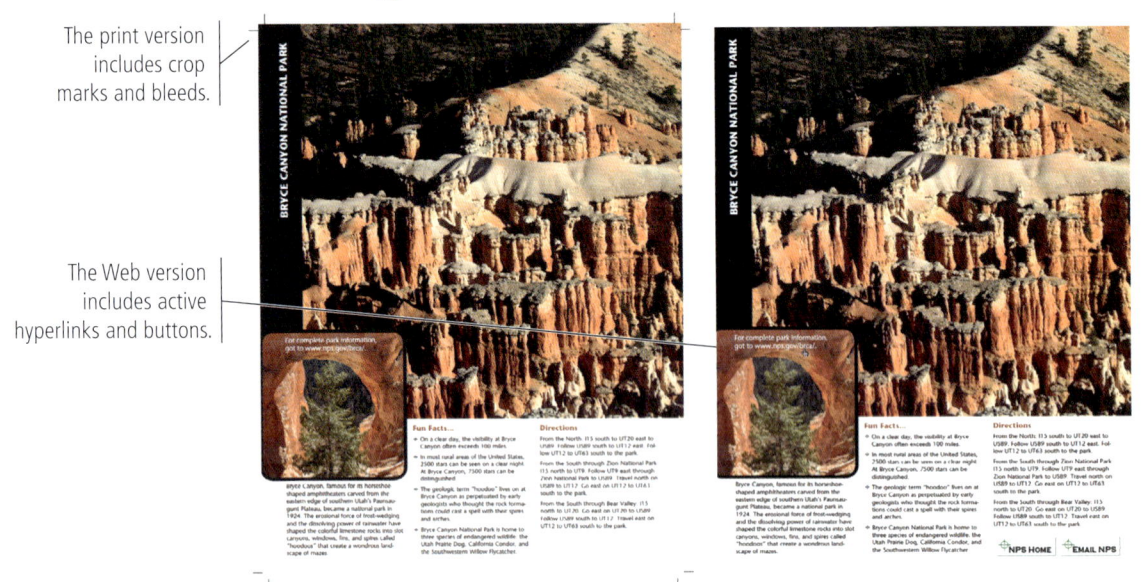

The print version includes crop marks and bleeds.

The Web version includes active hyperlinks and buttons.

13. Close the PDF files and return to InDesign. Save and close the flyer file.

14. Open the postcard and rack card files from your WIP>Parks folder. Export PDF files for print using the Print with Bleed preset.

15. Save and close both InDesign files.

448 Project 7: National Parks Info Pieces

Project Review

fill in the blank

1. You can edit the _____ settings to change the default text formatting for all new text frames.

2. The _____ panel shows every character in the selected font. You can view the entire font, or sort by specific defined sets.

3. A _____ is a negative first-line indent.

4. The _____ format can store thousands of characters in a single font file.

5. You can _____ to edit a paragraph style without applying that style to the selected text.

6. You can change the _____ settings to change the physical appearance of a rounded rectangle.

7. If the _____ option is active, a 50-pt square with a 2-pt stroke would be measured as 54 × 54 pt.

8. In an empty text frame, you can apply a style to the _____ to define the default style for unformatted text that is imported into that frame.

9. You can use the _____ tool to sample colors from placed images.

10. You can use the _____ to review the content and hierarchy of tagged frames.

short answer

1. Briefly explain why styles can be beneficial when experimenting with a page design.

2. Briefly explain two advantages of the OpenType format.

3. Briefly explain two advantages of using XML for repurposing content for different layouts.

Portfolio Builder Project

Use what you learned in this project to complete the following freeform exercise.
Carefully read the art director and client comments, then create your own design to meet the needs of the project.
Use the space below to sketch ideas; when finished, write a brief explanation of your reasoning behind your final design.

art director comments

The client is very pleased with the pieces you have designed to promote tourism in the national parks. Before she presents the project to her director for approval, she would like to have the same pieces for at least one other park.

To complete this project, you should:

❏ Create the flyer, rack card, and postcard layouts for Yosemite National Park. Use the images and text that are provided in the RF_Builders>Parks folder.

❏ Create one additional layout for a letterfold brochure that will include the same content as the other pieces. The inside of the brochure should have only the park name and space for a map of the park.

client comments

These pieces are exactly what I had in mind. I would like to see one additional layout — redesigning our park map brochure to include this same content, but also a large map of the specific park. We already have the maps, but I'll have to find the files for you; for now just leave space on the inside of the brochure.

When I pitch the project to my superiors, I want to be able to show them the pieces for at least two different parks. That way the committee will see how different colors and pictures will affect the individual pieces, but still have a consistent look and feel. I've sent you the text and images for Yosemite for this second set of files.

I'm thinking about combining the flyers for all the parks (when they're done) into a booklet that we might be able to sell. I'm going to include this in my presentation as a potential source of income to justify the cost of the overall project. Having more than one flyer finished will help to explain this part of the project.

project justification

Project Summary

To complete this project, you started with the very basics — defining a new document — and worked all the way through complex content repurposing using XML. You should realize that you have virtually unlimited creative control as you experiment with an initial layout concept, but that creating a unified design sometimes requires minor adjustments based on the actual content that will be placed in the layout.

You used unstructured XML to drag specific types of content into a layout, and you used a more structured approach to automatically place content into tagged frames of a different layout. By maintaining a link to the XML file, you were able to automatically update the placed content to reflect changes in the text. Repurposing the same content in multiple different layouts — both for print and digital distribution — is becoming increasingly common in the design world; using InDesign's XML capabilities makes the process far easier than manually creating each different version.

- Experiment with text formatting based on placeholder text before actual content is ready
- Define frame fitting options for a graphics placeholder frame
- Change the corner style of an existing frame
- Create a swatch based on colors sampled from an image
- Redefine a style based on local formatting overrides
- Create new styles based on existing text formatting
- Create interactive buttons for electronic versions
- Repurpose content using imported XML content

Project 7: National Parks Info Pieces

Multi-Chapter Booklet

Your client, Against The Clock (ATC), publishes books relating to the computer graphics industry. In addition to application-specific books, they are also creating a series of "companion" titles that discuss the concepts underlying the use of digital software — basic design principles, type, color, and so on. You were hired to build an "excerpt" booklet of the companion titles, which ATC will use for marketing purposes.

This project incorporates the following skills:

- ❏ Combining multiple InDesign files into a single book
- ❏ Synchronizing the assets in multiple files to ensure consistency from one piece to the next
- ❏ Building a unified table of contents for the entire book
- ❏ Building an index that covers all chapters of the book
- ❏ Using variable data to build a personalized letter

Project Meeting

client comments

We are launching a new series of books that will complement our application-specific books. We want to use the existing InDesign files to create a sample excerpt booklet that we can use in digital and print advertising.

We sent you the files for the first chapter from two of the books. Unfortunately, the file from the *Color Companion* seems to be one version behind — we can't find the version that was tagged for the book's index. We want the sample booklet to include a representative index, though, so we'd like you to tag a few entries in the *Color Companion* chapter and build a mini-index for the sample. The booklet should also have its own self-cover, title page, and table of contents.

The first set of these booklets will be printed and mailed to 50 clients we selected from our database. We're asking these clients to review the sample chapters and provide quotes that we can use in marketing materials. We provided you with a Microsoft Excel data file that was exported from our database. We also sent you the text for a thank-you letter we want to include with the booklet.

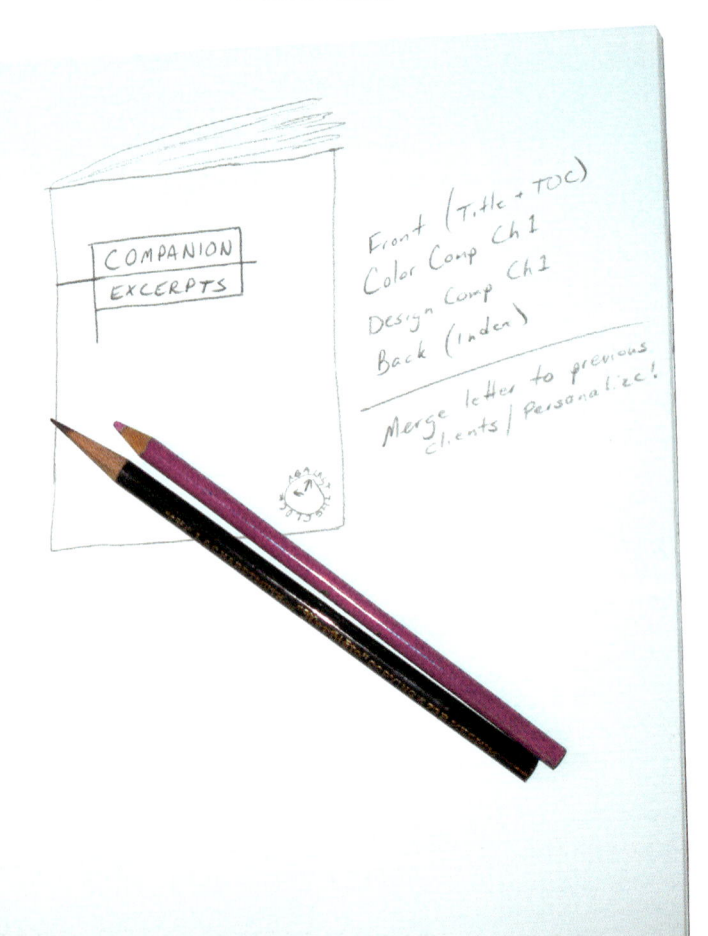

art director comments

Long documents like books (especially non-fiction) require several special elements, including a table of contents and an index. Many publishers spend countless hours manually composing these elements; they literally flip through pages and hand-write every entry in a spreadsheet. Fortunately, InDesign has built-in tools that make this process far easier.

If you consistently use styles, you can build a table of contents based on the styles in the chapters. Unfortunately, the index is a bit more complicated. Although the tools for tagging and compiling an index make the process a bit easier, indexing is still a largely manual process; there is no software smart enough to to decide exactly what to include in the index.

The advantage of using these tools is that you complete the process only once. Using the old methods, changes late in the process — which happen almost every time — meant manually re-compiling the table of contents and index. Using InDesign's built-in tools, you can easily re-compile both elements as often as necessary, and you can format them automatically using other styles.

project objectives

To complete this project, you will:

❏ Create an InDesign book file

❏ Manage different files as chapters of a single book

❏ Control section and page numbering across multiple chapter files

❏ Synchronize assets in all files of the book

❏ Build a table of contents based on styles

❏ Tag index entries in each file of the book

❏ Compile the index for all book chapters at once

❏ Create a variable-data letter addressed to previous ATC clients

Stage 1 Combining Documents into Books

Publication design is a unique subset of graphic design. Attention to detail is critical. You must ensure that subhead formatting in early chapters matches the subhead formatting in later chapters, the captions are all set in the same font, the body copy is the same size throughout the document, and so on. Regardless of whether one or several designers work on the project, consistency is essential from the first page of the book to the last. To make long-document design easier, InDesign includes a special type of book file for combining and managing multiple chapters as a single unit.

Long documents are frequently split into multiple files during the conception and design phases, and then combined at the end of the process to create the final job. This workflow offers several advantages:

- Layouts with numerous images can become very large; dividing these layouts into pieces helps keep the file size smaller.

- If a long document is divided into multiple stand-alone files, several designers can work on different files of the same book without the risk of accidentally overwriting another designer's work.

- If a long document is split into several files, you won't lose the entire job if a single file becomes corrupt.

Note:

When a single design project is composed of several files, it is even more important to maintain consistency from one file to the next. If the font is slightly different from one issue of a newsletter to the next, few people are likely to spot much of a difference. That difference is far more noticeable, however, when two or more files are bound together in the same publication.

Before digital book-building utilities were introduced, multiple files were combined in the prepress department at the output provider. Working with multiple files required extreme care and attention to detail to maintain consistency from one file to the next. InDesign's book-building tools make the process much easier by automating many of the tasks that were previously done manually, including comparing proofs of every page in the document. (Even though the InDesign Book utilities automate much of the process, you must still — and always — pay close attention to the details of your work.)

Build an InDesign Book

An InDesign book is simply a container file into which multiple InDesign files are placed for easier organization and file management. The InDesign Book utility offers several benefits, including:

- synchronizing styles, colors, and other assets to the book's master file;

- monitoring page and section numbering of each individual file in the book, and of the book as a whole;

- easily adding or removing pages, or moving entire chapters, and automatically renumbering pages according to the new order;

- building a table of contents and index from all book files at once; and

- printing or exporting the entire book at once, or outputting only selected chapters.

1. **Copy the Companions folder from the RF_InDesign folder on your Resource CD into the WIP folder where you are saving your work.**

    When you work with book files, you frequently open, save, and close the chapters of the book files; in fact, some operations happen without your direct intervention. For this process to work properly, book chapter files must be unlocked — which means you can't work directly from the Resource CD.

2. **With nothing open in InDesign, choose File>New>Book.**

3. **Navigate to your WIP>Companions folder as the target location.**

   Unlike creating a new file, creating a new book requires you to immediately name and save the book file.

4. **Change the book name to excerpts.indb and click Save.**

   The correct extension is automatically added for you, but if you accidentally remove it, add it to the file name.

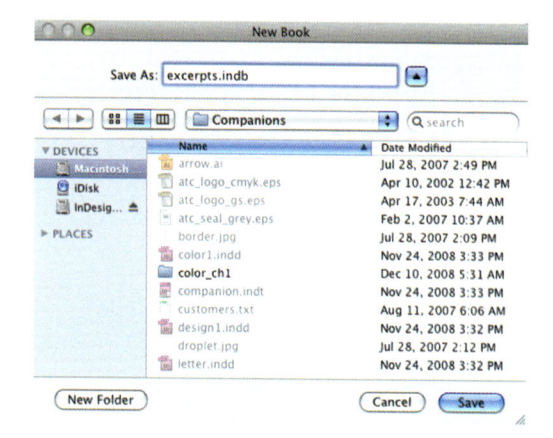

   Clicking Save opens the Book panel; the file name you define is listed in the panel tab.

   By default, the Book panel floats in the workspace; you can drag it anywhere you prefer (including into a specific panel group, whether docked or not).

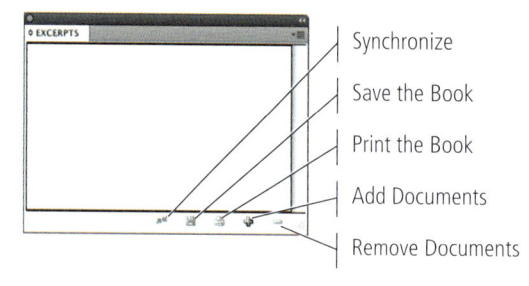

5. **Continue to the next exercise.**

Note:

For the exercises in this project to work properly, the resource files must be in a location where you can save them without choosing Save As. As you move through these steps, make sure you are working with the files in your WIP folder and not the files on your Resource CD.

Note:

You can open a book file the same way you open a regular document file (File>Open).

Note:

You can save a book with a different name by choosing Save Book As from the panel Options menu.

456　Project 8: Multi-Chapter Booklet

ADD BOOK CHAPTERS

Once the book file has been defined, adding chapters is easy. The first chapter you add is (by default) the Style Source chapter, to which other chapters in the book can be synchronized.

1. **With the `excerpts` book file open, click the Add Document button at the bottom of the Book panel.**

2. **Navigate to the file `color1.indd` in your WIP>Companions folder and click Open.**

   Depending on the size of the chapter, it might take a few seconds to process the file.

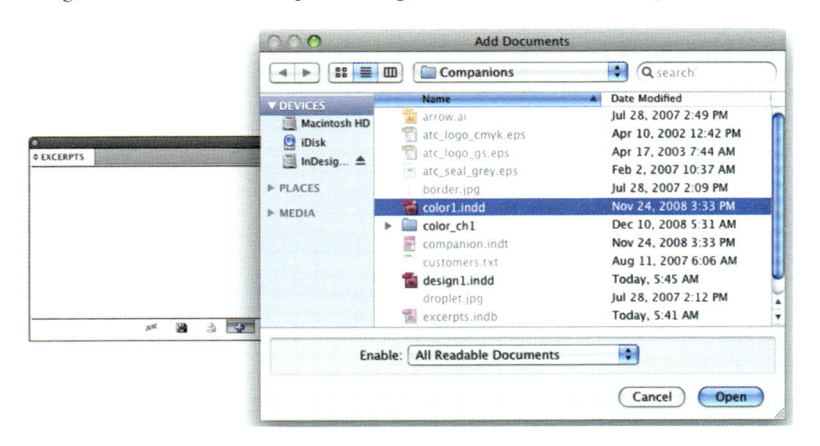

   Note:
   You can change the style source for the book by clicking the empty space to the left of a specific chapter.

   When the process is complete, the file name appears in the Book panel.

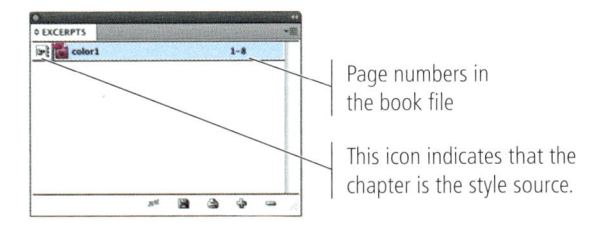

   Page numbers in the book file

   This icon indicates that the chapter is the style source.

   Note:
   You can remove a file from a book by clicking the Remove Documents button at the bottom of the Book panel. Once you remove a chapter from a book, you can't undo the deletion. The file still exists in its original location, however, so you can simply add the file back into the book, if necessary.

3. **Click the Add Documents button again. Navigate to `design1.indd` in your WIP>Companions folder and click Open.**

   New files are automatically added below the previously selected chapter. If no chapter is selected in the panel, new files are added to the end of the book.

   If you haven't changed the section or page numbering options for the files you add, new book chapters are automatically numbered sequentially from one file to the next.

4. **Create a new file by opening `companion.indt` from your WIP>Companions folder.**

   This is the template from which the companion chapters were created. Although the two excerpt chapters are already laid out, you need to create a front matter document that will hold a title page and the table of contents for the combined excerpts.

   Note:
   If you get a Profile or Policy Mismatch warning at any point in this project, select the option to leave the document as is and click OK.

Project 8: Multi-Chapter Booklet   457

5. **In the Pages panel, drag the F-Title Page master page icon onto the Page 1 icon.**

   The front matter document will include the title page and table of contents — both conventional parts of book design, which have been planned for in the existing master-page layouts. By dragging the F-Title Page master onto Page 1, you're applying the existing master page to the first page of the front matter file.

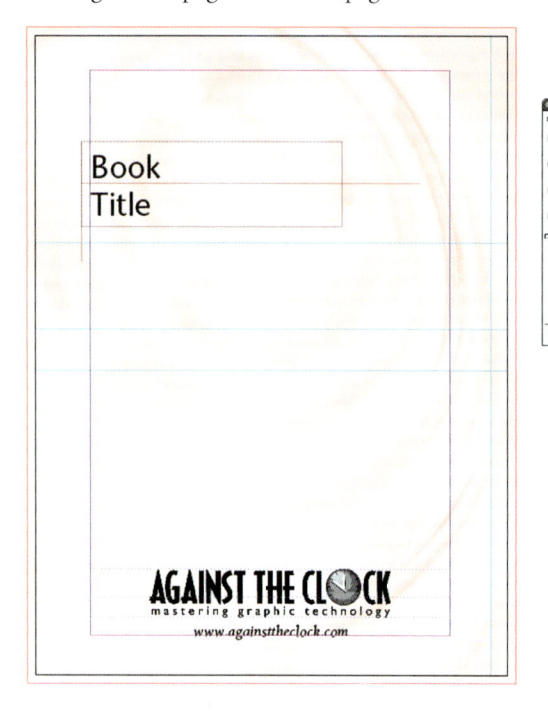

   Scroll through the master page area (if necessary) to find the F-Title Page master at the bottom of the available layouts.

   Drag the F-Title Page master onto the Page 1 icon in the lower section of the Pages panel.

6. **Control/right-click the Page 1 icon and choose Override All Master Page Items from the contextual menu.**

   The text frame for the book title is placed on the master page; to change the text and enter the actual book title, you either have to make the change on the master page or detach the master items on the regular layout page.

7. **Using the Type tool, highlight the text "Book Title" in the text frame and type** Companion Excerpts.

8. **Drag the right-center handle of the text frame until the word "Excerpts" moves to the second line and the right edge of the frame is approximately 1/8″ from the edge of the text.**

9. **Drag the right end of the bisecting line until the end is approximately 1/2″ from the right edge of the text frame.**

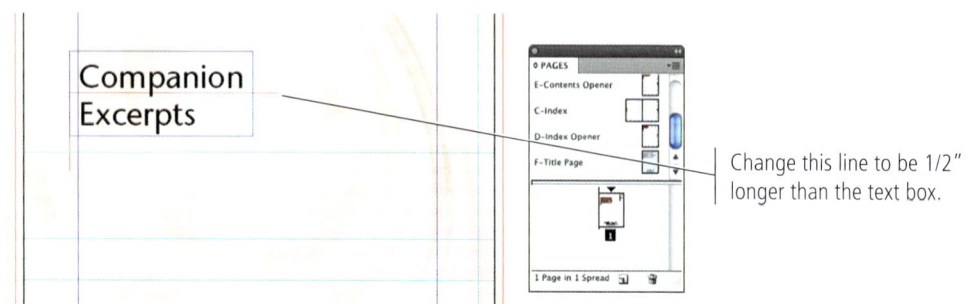

   Change this line to be 1/2″ longer than the text box.

Note:

Front matter typically refers to the information that precedes the main content of a book, including a title page, copyright information, table of contents, acknowledgements, and other important elements.

10. **Save the file as** excerpts front.indd **in your WIP>Companions folder, and then close the file.**

458 Project 8: Multi-Chapter Booklet

11. **In the Excerpts Book panel, click the Add Documents button.**

12. **Navigate to the `excerpts front.indd` file you just created and add it to the book file.**

13. **Click excerpts front in the panel and drag up until a heavy black line appears above color1 in the panel.**

    When you release the mouse button, excerpts front is the first chapter in the book.

    This line indicates the new position of the chapter (when you release the mouse button).

    Color1 is still the style source. The style source does not have to be the first item in the list.

14. **Click the Save the Book button at the bottom of the panel.**

15. **Continue to the next exercise.**

Managing Book Chapters

INDESIGN FOUNDATIONS

When you place a file into a book, the book file acts as a container; this process is very similar to placing an image into a layout. An InDesign layout stores the path to a placed image as a reference. Books use the same methodology, storing references to the files contained within the book.

If the chapter files have been moved since being added to the book, the Book panel shows a missing-link warning icon. When you double-click a missing book chapter, InDesign asks if you want to replace the missing file; clicking Yes opens a navigation dialog box so you can locate the missing file or identify a replacement file. (You can also select a missing file in the panel and choose Replace Document from the Book panel Options menu.)

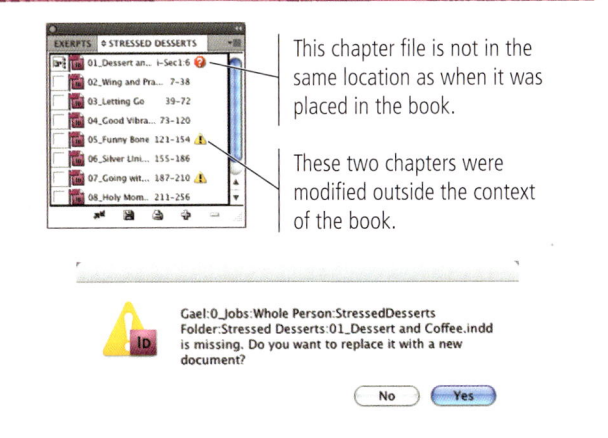

Remember that when you change a placed image using the Edit Original option, changes automatically reflect when you return to the InDesign layout. The same concept applies with book chapters: if you open a chapter using the Book panel, changes automatically reflect in the containing book. When you open a book chapter outside the context of the book, the Book panel displays a modified-link icon for that file.

This chapter file is not in the same location as when it was placed in the book.

These two chapters were modified outside the context of the book.

You can update a modified book chapter by simply double-clicking the file in the panel to open it. When you save the chapter and close it, InDesign updates the book chapter link to reflect the most current version of the file. Once a chapter has been added to a book file, it is best to make changes only within the context of the book.

Project 8: Multi-Chapter Booklet   459

Control Section and Page Numbering

After moving the front matter chapter in front of the color chapter, the page numbers for each chapter automatically change to reflect their new position in the book. The problem, however, is that the second file (color1) begins on Page 2 and the third file (design1) begins on Page 10. Even-numbered pages are left-facing pages, but book design conventions dictate that book chapters begin on right-facing (odd-numbered) pages.

1. **With the excerpts book file open, choose Book Page Numbering Options from the Book panel Options menu.**

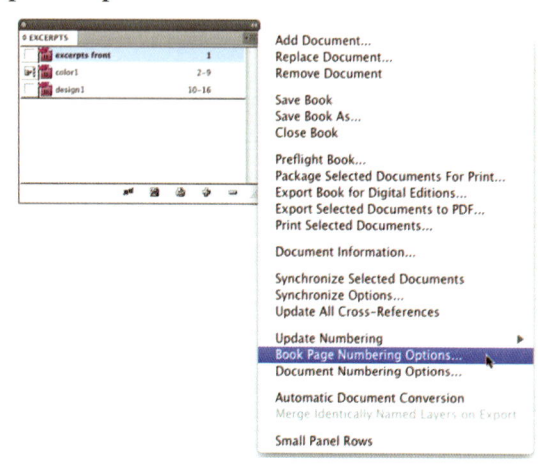

2. **In the Book Page Numbering Options dialog box, choose the Continue on Next Odd Page option.**

   Although some book designs intentionally break from convention and begin chapters on left-facing pages, this is not the norm. Right-facing chapter-starts are so common, in fact, that InDesign's long-document tools include the ability to easily force chapters to begin on the right side of the spread.

   You can use this dialog box to control exactly where new chapter files begin:

   - **Continue from Previous Document**, the default option, allows new chapters to pick up numbering from the end of the previous file. This option allows new chapters to begin on odd- or even-numbered pages.

   - **Continue on Next Odd Page** forces new chapter files to begin on odd-numbered pages. If your layouts use facing pages, this means new chapters will always begin on right-facing pages.

   - **Continue on Next Even Page** forces new chapter files to begin on even-numbered pages. If your layouts use facing pages, this means new chapters will always begin on left-facing pages.

3. **Check the Insert Blank Page option and leave the Automatically Update option checked.**

   The Insert Blank Page option adds a blank page into any file where the defined page order leaves a blank space in the page numbering. When the Automatically Update option is checked (as it is by default), files in the book automatically adjust to reflect additional choices in this dialog box.

4. **Click OK to apply your changes.**

   The second and third files in the book now begin on odd-numbered (right-facing) pages. Blank pages have been added as necessary to fill empty spaces caused by moving the chapters to the appropriate side of the spread.

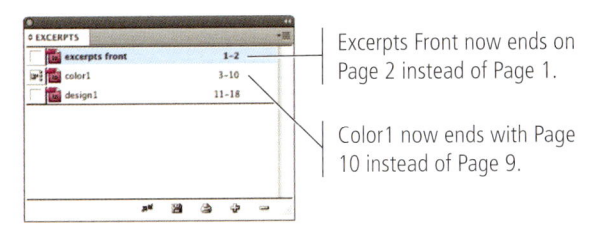

   Excerpts Front now ends on Page 2 instead of Page 1.

   Color1 now ends with Page 10 instead of Page 9.

5. **In the Book panel, click the excerpts front file to select it.**

6. **In the panel Options menu, choose Document Numbering Options.**

   In addition to controlling the page numbering from one file to another, you can also control the page numbering for a specific file. This option is useful if, for example, you want the front matter of a book to be numbered separately from the main body of the document.

   To change document-specific settings such as page numbering and sections, the document must be open. When you choose Document Numbering Options in the Book panel Options menu, the selected file automatically opens so you can make changes.

Understanding Book Page Numbering

INDESIGN FOUNDATIONS

If you had not checked Insert Blank Pages in the Book Page Numbering Options dialog box, each chapter in your book would begin on a right-facing (odd-numbered) page. However, the last page in each file would remain unchanged. The image here shows the original pagination (on the left) in comparison to the renumbered pages; the first page of each file is highlighted in pink. In the middle version — the result of the steps you just took — blank pages are highlighted in yellow.

The third version (on the right) shows what would have happened if you had not selected the Insert Blank Pages option. Although the second and third files would have begun on odd-numbered (right-facing) pages, the blank pages would not have been added to fill the space. This could cause significant problems when the book is imposed into printer's spreads for commercial printing. (Refer to Project 5 for an explanation of printer's spreads.)

Original pagination

Pagination after modifying book numbering (inserting blank pages)

Pagination after modifying book numbering (without inserting blank pages)

Project 8: Multi-Chapter Booklet

7. **In the Document Numbering Options dialog box, choose lowercase Roman numerals in the Style menu.**

   This is another convention in book design and layout — the front matter is numbered separately from the main part of the book, commonly in lowercase Roman numerals.

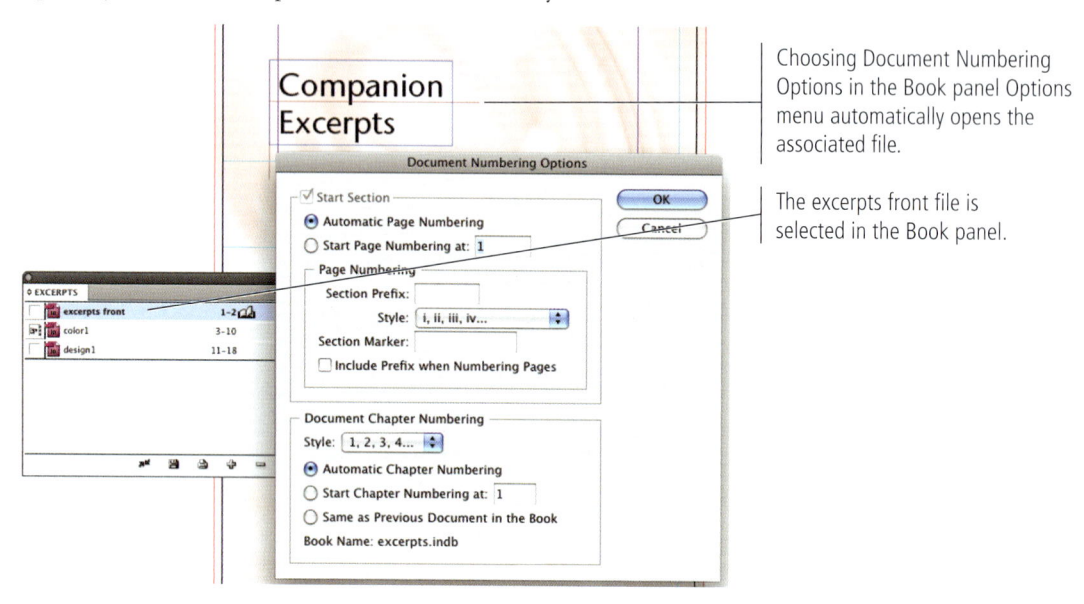

   Choosing Document Numbering Options in the Book panel Options menu automatically opens the associated file.

   The excerpts front file is selected in the Book panel.

8. **Click OK to apply the change, save the open layout, and then close the file.**

   In the Book panel, the excerpts front file reflects the new numbering style. The problem, however, is that the first content chapter still begins on Page 3 (even though this file is still numbered with Arabic numerals).

9. **Double-click color1 in the Book panel.**

   Double-clicking a file in the Book panel automatically opens that file.

10. **Control/right-click the Page 3 icon in the Pages panel and choose Numbering & Section Options.**

    This command opens a dialog box similar to the Document Numbering Options dialog box. The primary difference is that this dialog box provides options for controlling a specific page (Page 3, which you Control/right-clicked to access the dialog box).

    When you use the Document Numbering Options command, InDesign automatically applies your choices, beginning with the first page of the selected file. Using the Numbering & Section Options command, you can change the options for any page in the document.

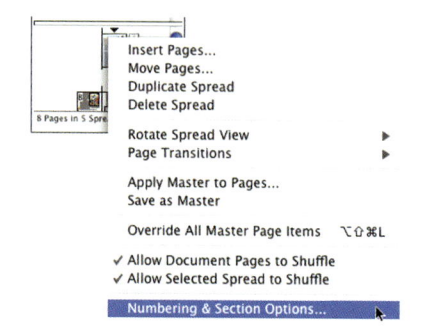

    Note:

    You could also select the page icon in the panel and choose Numbering & Section Options from the Pages panel Options menu.

Project 8: Multi-Chapter Booklet

11. **In the Numbering & Section Options dialog box, choose the Start Page Numbering At option and change the number in the field to 1.**

    InDesign's default behavior — the Automatic Page Numbering option — causes pages to number sequentially from one file to the next in the book. By choosing the Start Page Numbering At option, you can override the default page numbering and determine the exact page number of any file in the book.

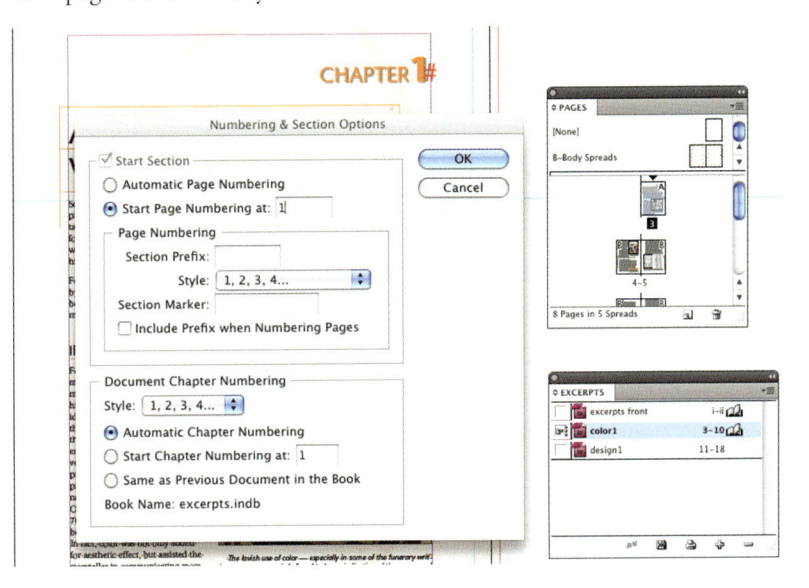

    Note:

    If you are using facing pages, changing an even-numbered page to an odd-numbered page moves the page to the other side of the spread. Remember from earlier chapters that this can cause objects to appear out of position in relation to the page's new position.

    Note:

    The page numbering of a book relies on the Current Page Number marker in the InDesign files. When you use the Current Page Number marker in book chapter files, those markers reflect the correct page number in relation to the entire book.

12. **Click OK to apply the new page number to the first page of the color1 file.**

    Because you haven't changed the numbering options for the design1 file (or any specific page in that file), it is still automatically numbered in sequence with the color1 file.

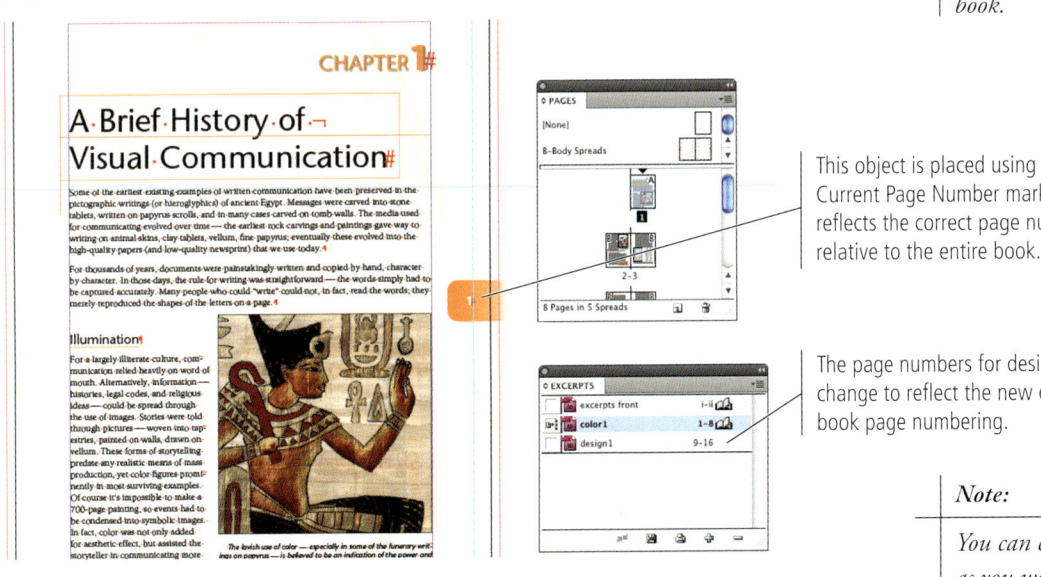

    This object is placed using the Current Page Number marker. It reflects the correct page number relative to the entire book.

    The page numbers for design1 change to reflect the new overall book page numbering.

    Note:

    You can close a book just as you would close any other panel — click the "X" button in the Book panel tab. If you haven't manually saved the book file, you are asked to save before closing the file.

13. **Save the open document (color1) and close it.**

14. **In the Book panel, click the Save the Book button, and then continue to the next exercise.**

Project 8: Multi-Chapter Booklet 463

Section and Chapter Numbering in Depth

Section and Page Numbering in a Single File

Although there are distinct advantages to maintaining long documents in numerous separate files, there are times when you want to work with an entire booklet or other project in a single InDesign file. In this case, it is important to realize that you can change the page and section numbering options for any page in the layout; these options are not restricted to files placed in an InDesign book.

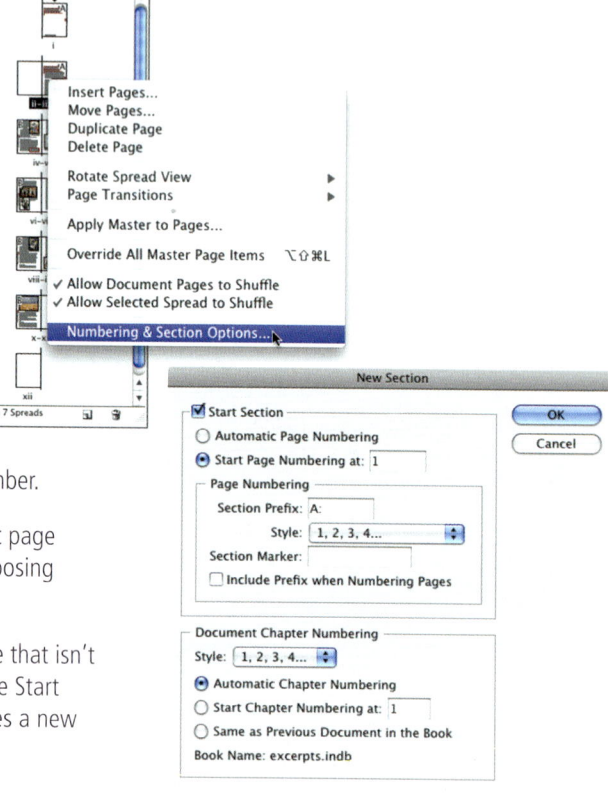

Sections allow you to create different page numbering sequences within a single file. For any section start page, you can restart page numbering at a specific page number, change the style of page numbers in the section, define a section marker for the section, and/or include the section prefix in the page number.

You can change the page and section options for any specific page by Control/right-clicking the page in the Pages panel and choosing Numbering & Section Options from the contextual menu.

When you choose Numbering & Section Options for any page that isn't already a section start, the New Section dialog box opens. The Start Section option is automatically checked, so clicking OK creates a new section for the selected page.

If you choose Numbering & Section Options for an existing section start page, the Numbering & Section Options dialog box opens. The choices in these two dialog boxes are exactly the same; the only differences are the title bar and the choices already selected when you open the dialog box.

When you click OK in the New Section dialog box, the selected page is designated as a section start.

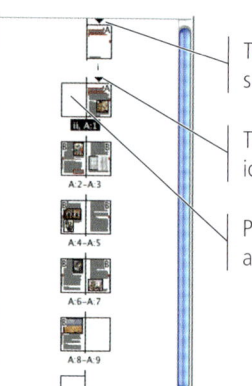

The first page in the file is a section start by default.

The triangle above the page icon indicates a section start.

Pages between two section starts are part of the preceding section.

Adding Section Prefixes

If you use the Page Number markers (Type>Insert Special Character>Markers>Current/Next/Previous Page Number), you can add a section prefix to page numbers in the layout by checking the Include Prefix when Numbering Pages option. Whatever you type in the Section Prefix field is added in front of the page number.

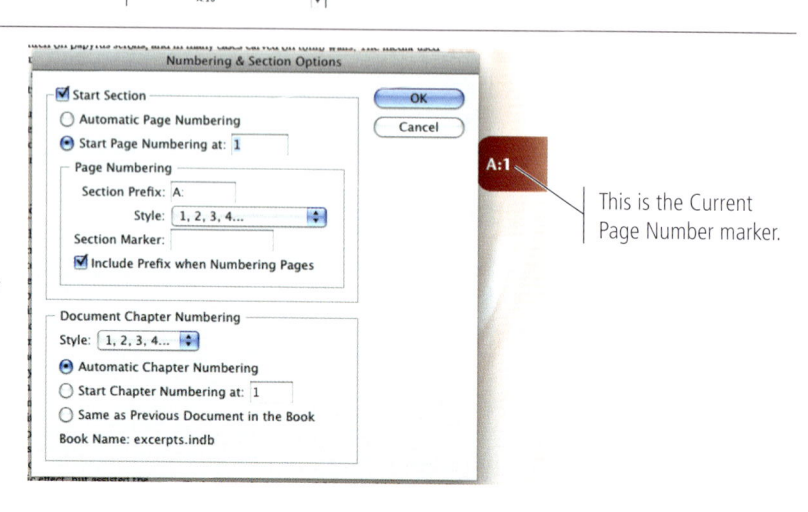

This is the Current Page Number marker.

Section and Chapter Numbering in Depth (continued)

Adding Section Markers

Section markers are a type of variable. You can define the Section Marker text for a specific section, and then place the marker into the layout (Type>Insert Special Character>Markers>Section Marker). The defined Section Marker text for the section where the marker is placed appears at the location of the marker.

The Section Marker character displays the text in the Section Marker field of the Numbering & Section Options dialog box. If a section has no defined Section Marker text, the special character displays nothing. You can also change all instances of the section marker within a section by re-opening the dialog box for the section start page and changing the text in the Section Marker field.

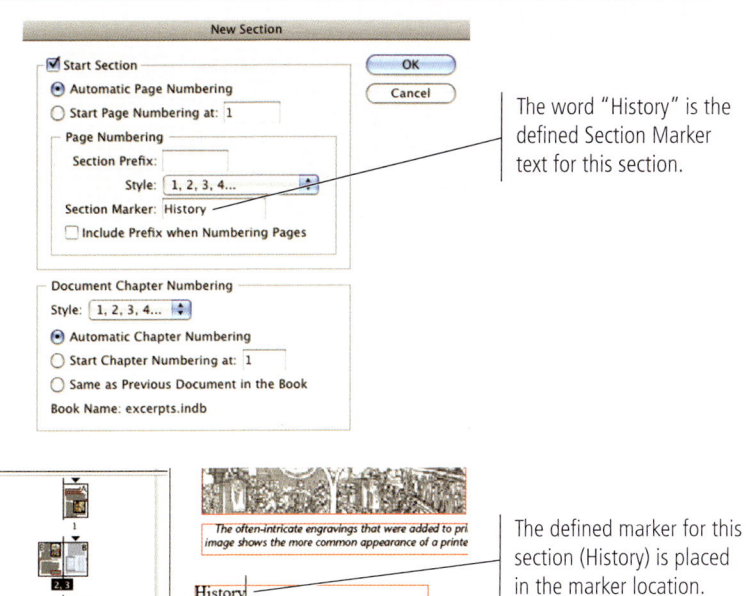

The word "History" is the defined Section Marker text for this section.

The defined marker for this section (History) is placed in the marker location.

Chapter Numbering

When you work with book files, you can also define Document Chapter Numbering options, which is basically section numbering for files. If you define a specific chapter number in the Numbering & Section Options dialog box, you can place the built-in Chapter Number variable (Type> Text Variables>Insert Variable>Chapter Number) in the layout to reflect the current chapter number.

If nothing appears in the Insert Variable submenu, the document was probably created in an earlier version of InDesign. Several predefined variables (including Chapter Number) were added in InDesign CS3. In this case, you can either define your own Chapter Number variable (see Project 5) or load the variables from a file created in InDesign CS3 or CS4.

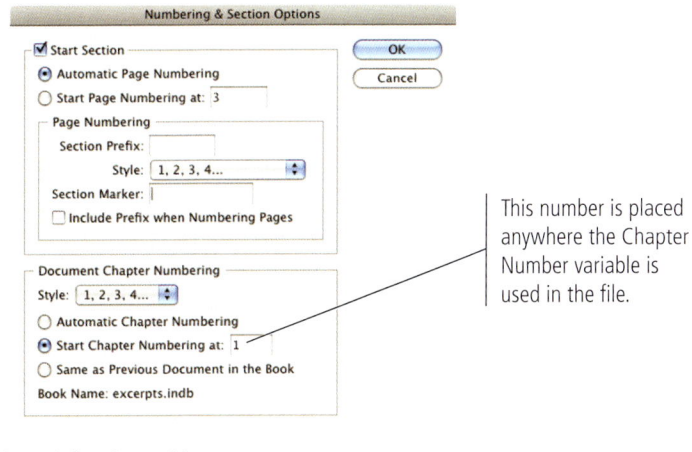

This number is placed anywhere the Chapter Number variable is used in the file.

Project 8: Multi-Chapter Booklet

Synchronize Book Files

An advantage of using styles for text layout is that a style can be changed easily and universally. This is also a disadvantage of using styles, particularly when combining multiple files into a single publication. Layout designers frequently manipulate, tweak, and even cheat to force-fit text into a desired amount of space, to make a runaround work correctly, or to achieve a specific effect. When the files are combined into the final book, these adjustments can cause problems if the variation is noticeable from one chapter to the next.

A primary advantage of using the InDesign book-building functionality is the ability to easily synchronize various assets across multiple chapter files. In the Synchronize Options dialog box, you can choose which types of assets you want to synchronize.

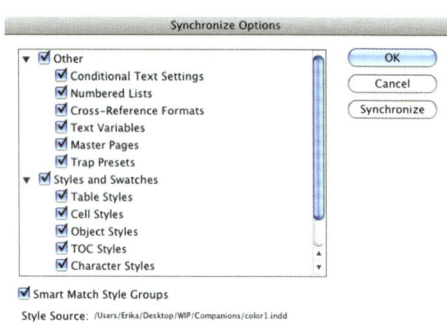

Note:

The tool tip name for the Synchronize button — Synchronize Styles and Swatches with the Style Source — is deceptively non-inclusive. Because you can synchronize far more than just these two elements, we refer to this button as simply "Synchronize."

When a book is synchronized, elements of the Style Source file are added to the other files if they don't already exist in that file. If an element already exists in the other files, the element definition from the Style Source file is applied to the same-named element in the other files. The synchronization process does not affect elements that are not in the Style Source file.

For example, let's say you reduced the leading in the Caption style in a file that is not the Style Source file. When you synchronize the book, the Caption style settings in the Style Source file overwrite the modified Caption style.

Note:

Synchronizing a book does not delete any element from any file, but can override changes you made to a particular file.

1. **With the excerpts book file open, double-click the excerpts front file to open that document.**

2. **Open the Swatches panel, and then open the Swatch Options dialog box for the Companion Color swatch.**

3. **Change the swatch definition to C=70 M=100 Y=0 K=0 and make sure the Name with Color Value option is not checked.**

   This is an instance where there is good reason to break from the color-naming convention based on color definition. The swatch is different in all companion books, but the swatch is named the same in all files of all books. By synchronizing the color in all book files to this new definition, you can change the Companion Color swatch in multiple files at one time.

Note:

If you change a style — to fit text onto a page, for example — synchronizing the book to the master file overwrites the changes, and the text no longer fits in the same way.

Project 8: Multi-Chapter Booklet

4. **Click OK to close the Swatch Options dialog box, save the document and close it, but leave the book file open.**

5. **In the Book panel, click the empty space to the left of the `excerpts front` file to redefine the style source.**

    You can change the style source at any time by clicking in this space.

6. **Click in the empty area at the bottom of the Book panel to deselect all files.**

    If nothing is selected in the Book panel, all chapter files are synchronized. You can also synchronize specific files by selecting them in the Book panel before clicking the Synchronize button. (To select contiguous files, hold down the Shift key and click each file. To select noncontiguous files, hold down the Command/Control key while selecting the desired files.) Of course, synchronizing only certain files defeats the purpose of synchronizing, but the option is available.

7. **In the Book panel Options menu, choose Synchronize Options.**

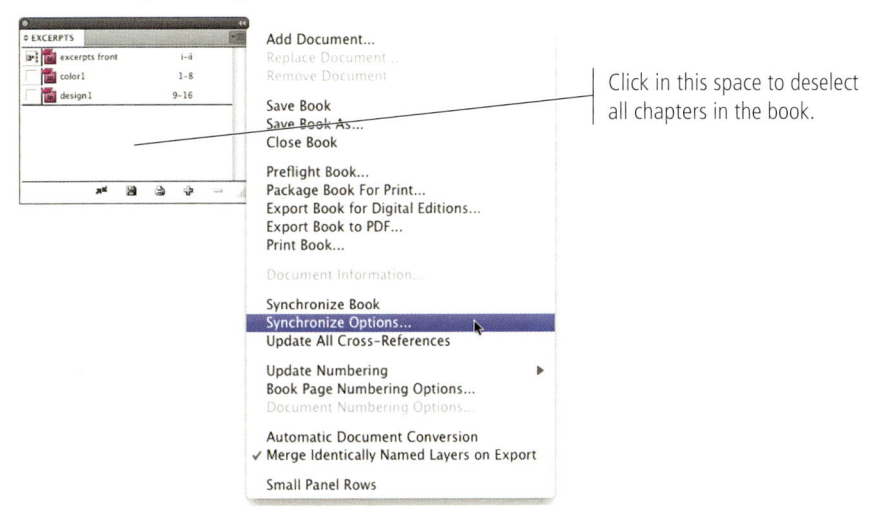

    Click in this space to deselect all chapters in the book.

8. **In the Synchronize Options dialog box, uncheck everything except Character Styles, Paragraph Styles, and Swatches.**

    In this project, your primary concern is consistency of appearance between existing files from the same series of books. The three selected options are sufficient for this project. In other cases where you combine radically different files from a variety of designers, it might be useful — or, in fact, vital — to synchronize the other types of assets as well.

9. **Click OK to close the dialog box.**

Project 8: Multi-Chapter Booklet   467

10. **In the Book panel, click the Synchronize button.**

11. **Click OK in the resulting warning.**

    As we mentioned, synchronizing book files can cause problems. InDesign is smart enough to recognize and warn you about one of the most common and serious problems — overset text.

    > Synchronization will cause some text in color1.indd to become overset.
    >
    > OK

12. **When the process is complete, click OK to dismiss the resulting message.**

    This message warns you of the potential problem we mentioned earlier — documents might have changed.

    > Book excerpts.indb
    >
    > Synchronization completed successfully. Documents may have changed.
    >
    > ☐ Don't show again
    >
    > OK

    When you synchronize book files — especially if you did not create the original files — you should carefully review the pages to be sure the content is still where it belongs.

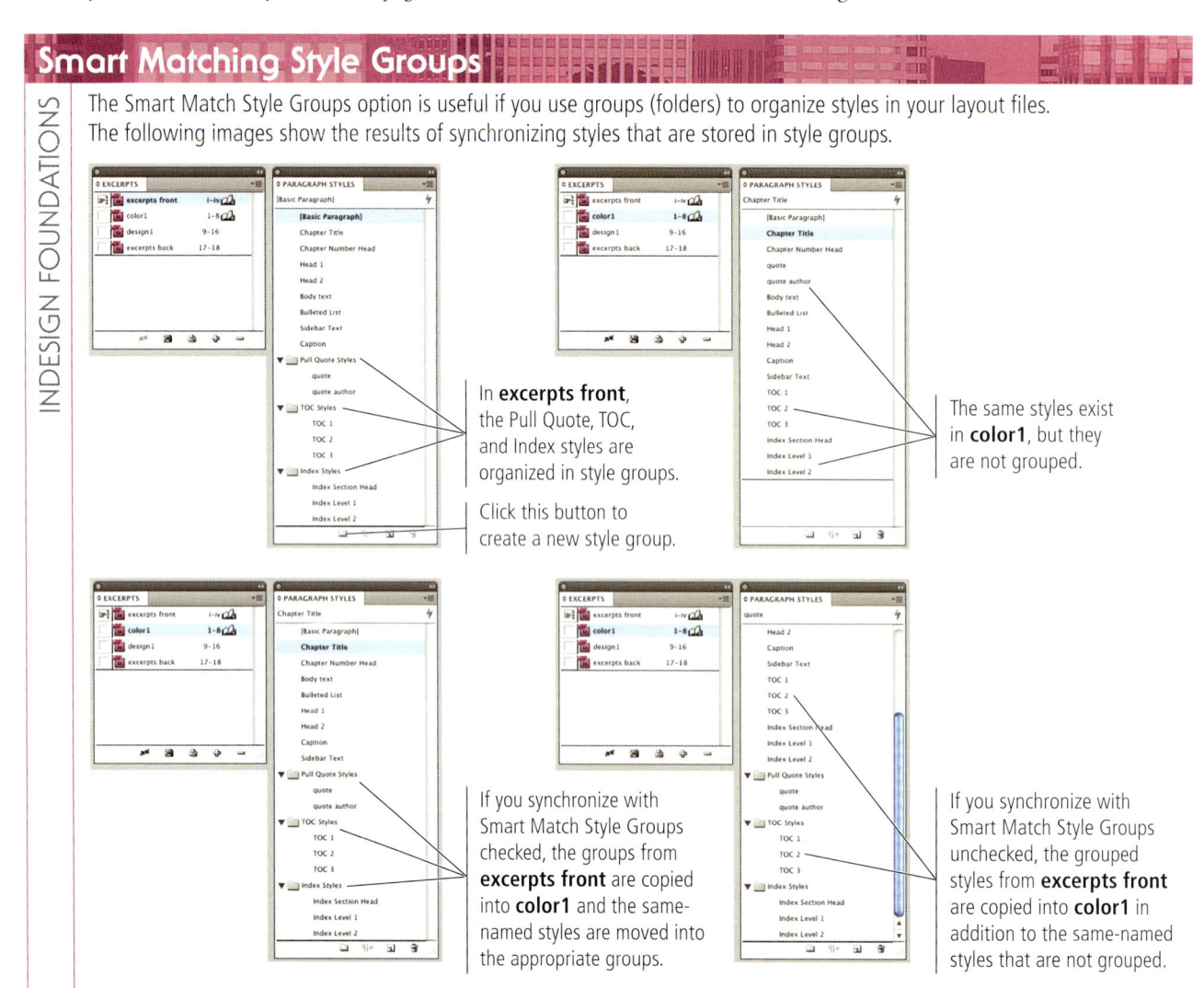

Smart Matching Style Groups

INDESIGN FOUNDATIONS

The Smart Match Style Groups option is useful if you use groups (folders) to organize styles in your layout files. The following images show the results of synchronizing styles that are stored in style groups.

In **excerpts front**, the Pull Quote, TOC, and Index styles are organized in style groups.

Click this button to create a new style group.

The same styles exist in **color1**, but they are not grouped.

If you synchronize with Smart Match Style Groups checked, the groups from **excerpts front** are copied into **color1** and the same-named styles are moved into the appropriate groups.

If you synchronize with Smart Match Style Groups unchecked, the grouped styles from **excerpts front** are copied into **color1** in addition to the same-named styles that are not grouped.

468 Project 8: Multi-Chapter Booklet

13. **Double-click color1 in the Book panel to open that file, and navigate to Page 8.**

    When you synchronize files, you often have no idea what caused the problem — but you still need to fix it. You have several options:

    - Edit the text to fit the overset line in the available space. Of course, this assumes you have permission to edit text, which you usually do not.
    - Add text frames to the chain. This typically assumes you can add pages to a file, which you often can't.
    - Change style definitions to fit text into the available space. If you synchronize again later, your changes will again be overwritten.
    - Adjust local formatting of specific text in the specific file to make the layout work properly.

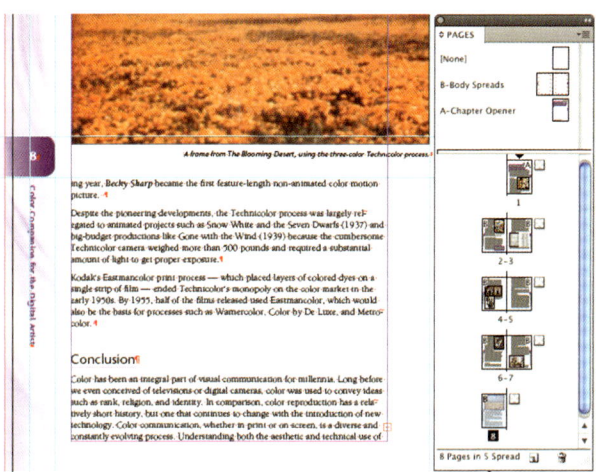

    Note:

    In case you were wondering, the Space Before Paragraph setting for the head 2 style was reduced in the original color1 file to fit the text in eight pages, instead of placing only two lines of text on Page 9 and inserting a blank Page 10.

14. **On Page 7 of the file, place the insertion point in the "In Living Color" head. Change the Space Before Paragraph setting for this paragraph only to 0.1".**

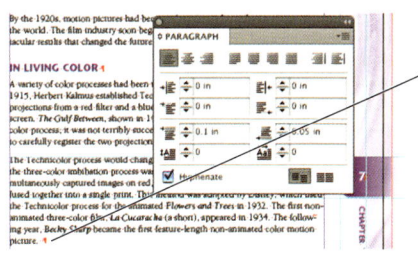

    After changing the Space Before Paragraph setting for the heading, the last two lines of this paragraph again fit on Page 7.

    Note:

    If you absolutely must adjust text in a particular file of a book, we recommend you manipulate the selected text and not the style.

15. **Navigate to Page 8 and review the text.**

    The end-of-story character now shows, and the overset text icon no longer appears in the frame's out port.

16. **Save the document and close it.**

17. **Save the book file and continue to the next stage of the project.**

Project 8: Multi-Chapter Booklet   469

Stage 2 Building a Table of Contents

Before desktop-publishing software automated the document-design process, tables of contents and other lists (figures, tables, etc.) were created manually from page proofs — by turning each page and writing down the appropriate text and page number, and then sorting and typesetting those hard-copy lists into the final document. The process was extremely time-consuming and required precise attention to detail. If the document changed after the lists were completed, the entire piece had to be rechecked, one page at a time.

Fortunately, InDesign includes a Table of Contents feature that automates this process, greatly improving production time and making it easier to maintain accuracy. InDesign tables of contents are based on the paragraph styles used in a layout. If you are conscientious about applying styles when you build a layout, you can easily create a thorough, accurate table of contents based on those styles.

You can define the styles that will be included in the compiled table of contents. For example, a table of contents might include Heading 1, Heading 2, and Heading 3 paragraph styles; any text set in those styles will appear in the list.

You can also determine the styles that will be used to format different elements in the compiled table of contents. Using the same example, TOC1 can be assigned to Heading 1 list items, TOC2 to Heading 2 items, and so on. When you compile the table of contents into the file, it is formatted automatically.

DEFINE A TABLE OF CONTENTS STYLE

A table of contents can be defined and applied in a single process. You can also create and save table of contents styles, which you can apply as needed in the active file, as well as import into and apply in other files. Because of the versatility allowed by styles of all types (paragraph, table, object, etc.), we recommend creating table of contents styles rather than defining a single-case table of contents.

1. **With the excerpts book file open, double-click the excerpts front file in the panel to open that file.**

2. **Drag the E-Contents Opener master page to the right of the Page ii icon.**

   When the new page is added, another blank page is also added because of your choices (Insert Blank Page) in the Book Page Numbering Options dialog box.

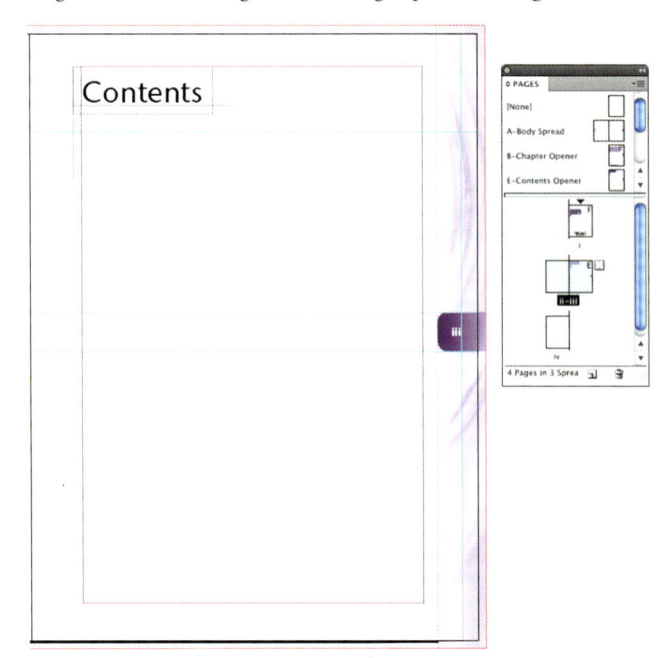

470   Project 8: Multi-Chapter Booklet

3. **Choose Layout>Table of Contents Styles.**

   You probably recognize this dialog box from Project 5; you used it to manage and create text variables. You can create new styles, edit or delete existing styles, or load styles that exist in other files.

4. **Click New. In the resulting New Table of Contents Style dialog box, type Companion Contents in the TOC Style field.**

   The TOC Style field defines the style name. It is basically the same as a paragraph style name (an identifier).

5. **Delete the text from the Title field.**

   The Title field, on the other hand, is actual text that is included at the top of the compiled table of contents. Because the "Contents" title for this layout is built into the master page, you should not include a title in the compiled table of contents.

6. **If necessary, click the More Options button on the right side of the dialog box.**

   When More Options are showing, you can control the appearance of page numbers in the table of contents.

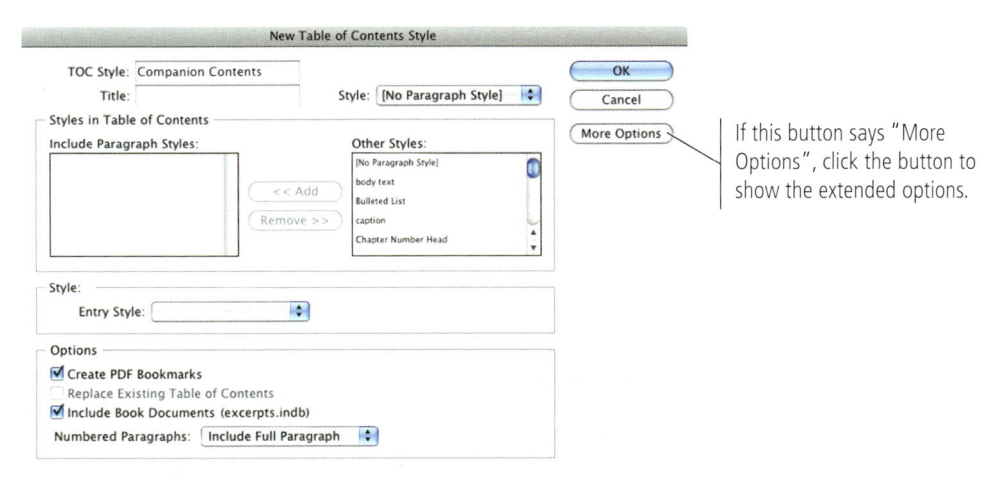

   If this button says "More Options", click the button to show the extended options.

7. **Scroll though the Other Styles list, select Chapter Title, and click the Add button.**

8. **In the middle section of the dialog box, choose TOC 1 in the Entry Style menu.**

Project 8: Multi-Chapter Booklet — 471

9. **Choose After Entry in the Page Number field, and choose TOC Page Number in the associated Style menu. Leave all other options at their default settings.**

   You can define a number of options for each style included in a table of contents:

   - **Entry Style** defines the paragraph style that will be applied to those entries in the compiled list.

   - **Page Number** determines where the page number will be included for each entry (After Entry or Before Entry). You can also choose No Page Number to add the list entry without the associated page number.

   - **Between Entry and Number** defines the character(s) that are placed between the list entry and the associated page number. The default option (^t) is the code for a Tab character. The attached menu includes a number of common special characters, or you can type the code for a specific special character (see Project 6 for details).

   - You can use the Style menus in the right column to define separate character styles for the page number and the character between the entry and page number. If you don't choose a character style in one or both of these menus, that element will be formatted with the paragraph style settings defined for the list entry.

   - If the **Sort Entries in Alphabetical Order** option is checked, the compiled list entries will appear in alphabetical order rather than page-number order.

   - By default, each new style in the Include pane is added one level lower than the previous style. You can use the **Level** menu to change the hierarchy of styles in the list.

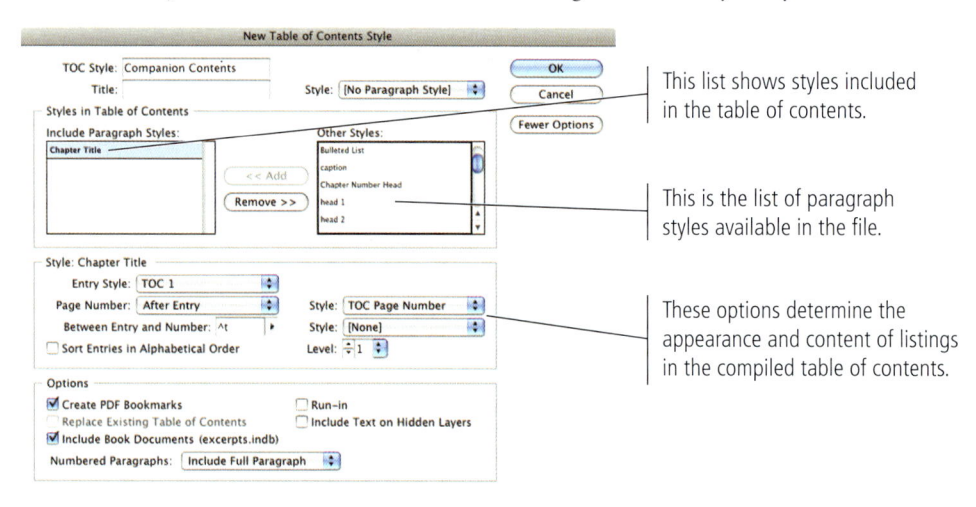

10. **In the Other Styles list, highlight head 1 and click Add. In the Style section of the dialog box, choose TOC 2 in the Entry Style menu. Choose After Entry in the Page Number field, and choose TOC Page Number in the associated Style menu.**

472   Project 8: Multi-Chapter Booklet

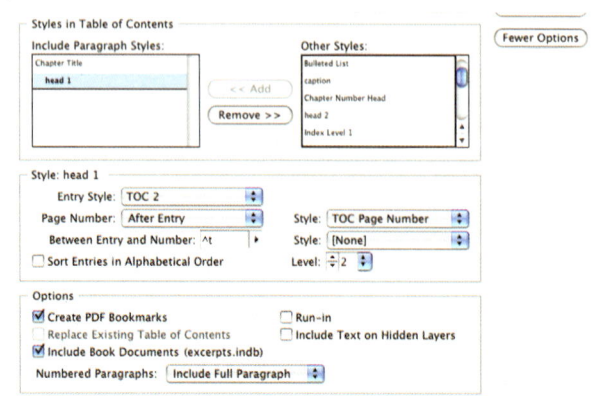

11. **In the Other Styles list, highlight head 2 and click Add. In the Style section of the dialog box, choose TOC 3 in the Entry Style menu. Choose After Entry in the Page Number field, and choose TOC Page Number in the associated Style menu.**

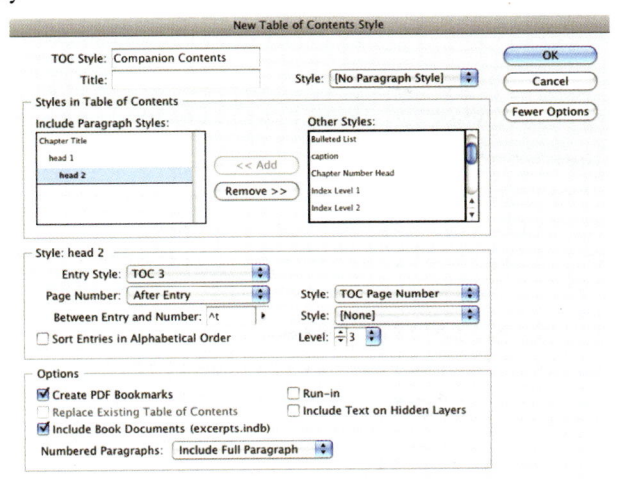

Note:

Different types of projects call for different types of lists. Although called the Table of Contents utility, you can build a list of any editorial element formatted with a paragraph style. For example, some publications call for a separate table of contents for illustrations. If you define and apply a Figure Heading paragraph style, you can create a list of entries formatted with that style.

12. **In the Options area, check the Create PDF Bookmarks and Include Book Documents options.**
    - **Create PDF Bookmarks** tags the table of contents entries to appear in the Bookmarks panel of Adobe Acrobat or Adobe Reader (when the document is exported to PDF).
    - **Replace Existing Table of Contents** is only available if a table of contents has already been built in the open file. This option is more relevant when you build the table of contents than when you define a table of contents style.
    - **Include Book Documents** allows you to build a single table of contents for all files in an InDesign book file. This option is only available if the open file is part of an InDesign book.
    - **Run-in** builds a list in which all entries run into a single paragraph; individual entries are separated by a semicolon.
    - **Include Text on Hidden Layers** adds list entries even if the text is on a hidden layer. This option is unchecked by default, and it should almost always remain that way — unless you have a very specific reason for listing elements that do not actually appear in the document.
    - The **Numbered Paragraphs** menu determines whether the list entry includes the full numbered paragraph (number and text), only the numbers, or only the text.

13. **Click OK to return to the Table of Contents Styles dialog box.**

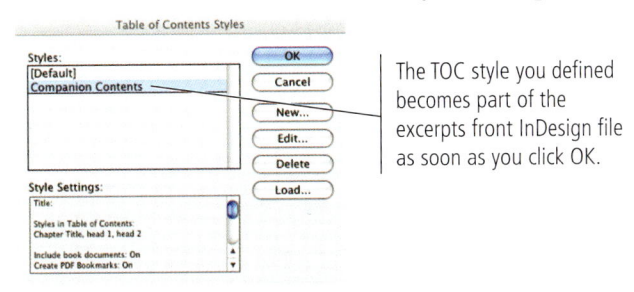

    The TOC style you defined becomes part of the excerpts front InDesign file as soon as you click OK.

14. **Click OK to close the Table of Contents Styles dialog box and return to the document window.**

15. **Save the file and continue to the next exercise.**

Project 8: Multi-Chapter Booklet

Build and Update a Table of Contents

Once a list is defined, whether for a single file or a book, you can build it into the layout very easily. In fact, when you build a table of contents, the compiled list loads into the cursor; you can click to place the loaded list just as you would place any other text element.

1. **With excerpts front.indd open from the excerpts Book panel, choose Layout>Table of Contents.**

   This dialog box has the same options as those available when you defined a TOC style. The only difference is that here you define a one-time table of contents list (although you can click the Save Style button to create a style based on your choices).

2. **Make sure Companion Contents is selected in the TOC Style menu.**

   Because it is the only style in the open file, it should be selected by default.

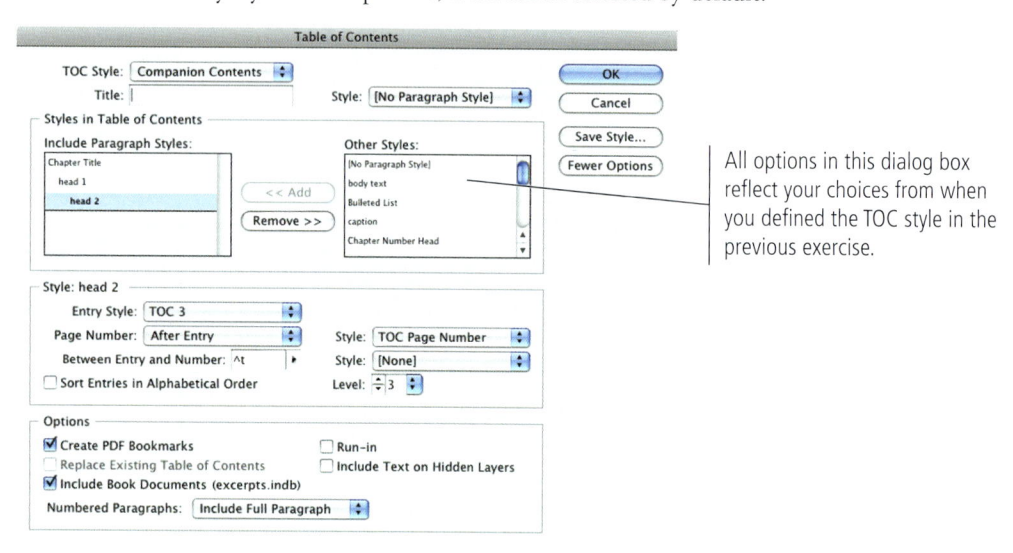

   All options in this dialog box reflect your choices from when you defined the TOC style in the previous exercise.

3. **Click OK.**

   When the list is ready, it loads into the cursor. This process might take a little while to complete, depending on the size of your book, so don't panic or try to force-quit the application after a minute or two. If you're working on a very large book (such as this 500-plus-page Portfolio Series book), now is probably a good time for a coffee break.

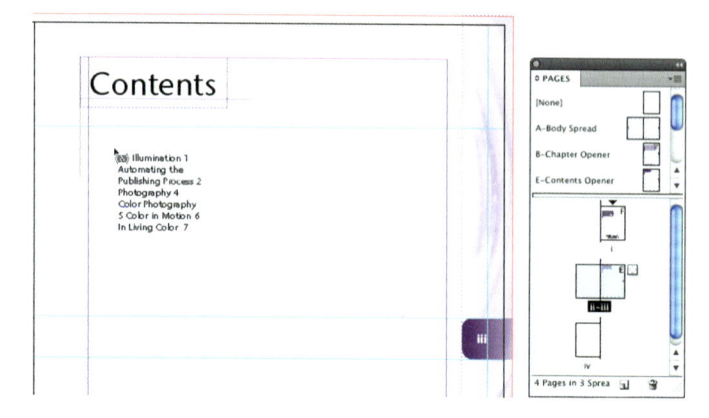

Project 8: Multi-Chapter Booklet

4. **Click the loaded cursor in the middle of Page iii to place the TOC into the text frame on the page.**

   That's all there is to building a table of contents — whether for a single file or for multiple documents combined in an InDesign book file. After a TOC is built into a document, it is a static block of text. The applied styles can be changed as you would any other style, and you can change the text box in which a list is placed. You can change or delete items from the list without affecting the main layout.

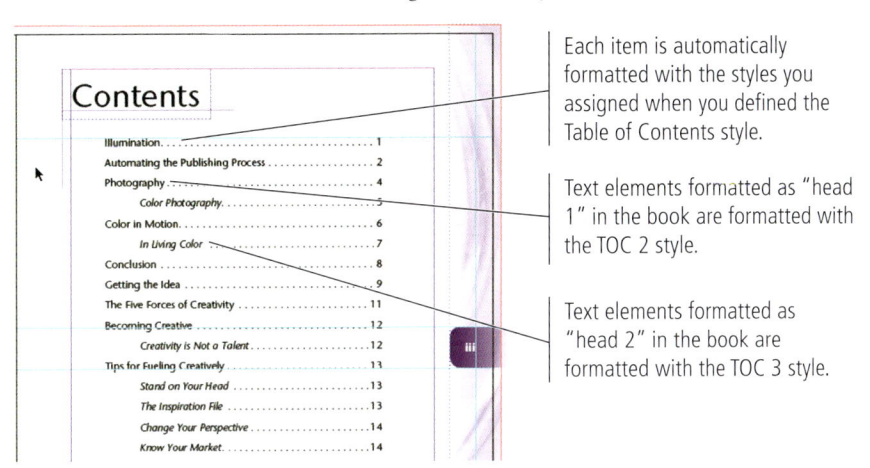

   Each item is automatically formatted with the styles you assigned when you defined the Table of Contents style.

   Text elements formatted as "head 1" in the book are formatted with the TOC 2 style.

   Text elements formatted as "head 2" in the book are formatted with the TOC 3 style.

   Of course, the table of contents InDesign built for this file reveals one potential problem: text that exists on the master page only (i.e., where the layout page hasn't been detached from the master) is not included in the compiled lists. The text frames for each chapter title have not been detached from the master pages, so the chapter titles do not appear in the compiled list.

5. **Double-click `color1` in the Book panel to open the file, and navigate to Page 1. Command/Control-Shift-click the frame containing the document title to detach that frame from the master page.**

6. **Save the file and close it.**

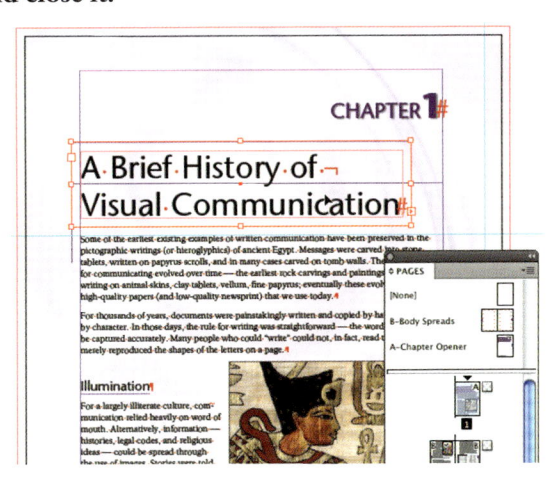

7. **Repeat Steps 5–6 on the first page of the `design1` file to detach the title text frame from the master page.**

Note:

Be careful when building a table of contents for an InDesign book. For a book TOC to function properly, the styles must be consistent in every chapter file. In other words, you shouldn't format second-level headings with "Head 2" in one chapter, "H2" in another chapter, and "Heading 2" in other chapters. If you do, the TOC has to include all three of those styles as separate list items.

Capitalization counts, too; when building a table of contents, "Head 2" is not the same as "head 2."

Project 8: Multi-Chapter Booklet 475

8. **With Page iii of the** `excerpts front` **file showing, place the insertion point anywhere within the current table of contents and then choose Layout>Update Table of Contents.**

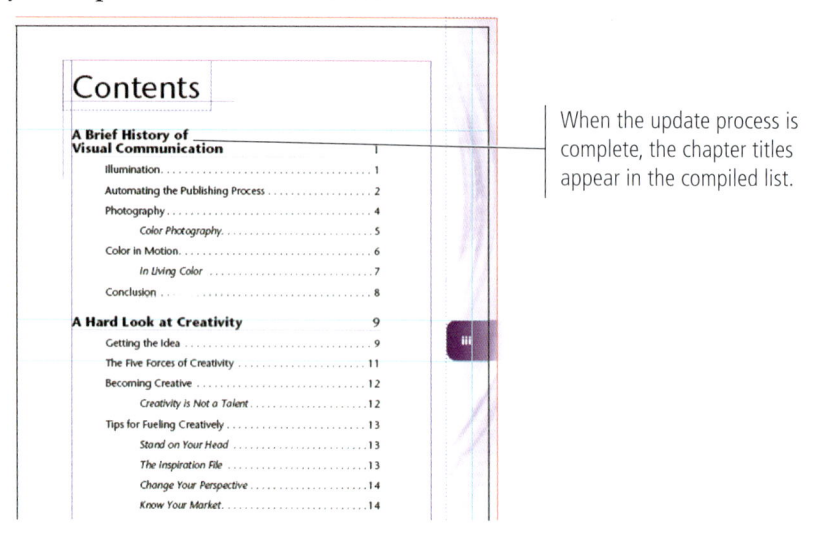

When the update process is complete, the chapter titles appear in the compiled list.

9. **Save your changes and close the document.**

10. **Save the book file and continue to the next stage of the project.**

Stage 3 Building an Index

An index is a map to a publication's contents, providing the reader with an easy reference to specific content. As with tables of contents and other lists, creating an index used to be an extremely time-consuming and labor-intensive process. A professional indexer was hired to read each hard-copy page of a document, write down index entries and page numbers, manually compile the final alphabetized list, and typeset that list into the document. Any changes after the index was finished meant the entire document had to be rechecked manually.

InDesign includes an Index tool that manages and automates part of the indexing process, improving the production workflow and saving considerable time when changes, inevitably, are made.

It's a good idea to plan in advance when you're going to build an index. Several different elements can (and should) be defined before you build your index:

- paragraph styles for index headings (if you decide to use them),
- paragraph styles for up to four levels of index entries,
- character styles for the page numbers of each index entry (if you want them to be formatted differently than the index entry), and
- character styles for cross-references (if you want them to be formatted differently than the index entry).

Of these four elements, the only one that you must define in advance is the character style that will be applied to individual index entries (if you decide to use this option). It is far easier to assign this style as you tag the individual entries, rather than change dozens or hundreds of entries later. The important point is that some advanced planning can make your life easier. You can always change the style definitions later in the process, but creating them in advance will save you time and effort in the long run.

Tag Basic and Reversed Index Topics

1. Double-click `color1` in the `excerpts` Book panel to open that document.

2. Choose Window>Type & Tables>Index to open the Index panel.

   - Go to Selected Marker
   - Update Preview
   - Generate Index
   - Create New Index Entry
   - Delete Selected Entry

   Note:

   Reference mode (the default) is used to add index entries in a layout. Topic mode is used to define a list of topics and review the hierarchy of included topics before compiling the index.

3. On Page 1 of the open document, highlight the word "hieroglyphics" in the middle of the second line of text.

4. Click the Create New Index Entry button at the bottom of the Index panel.

   The New Page Reference dialog box shows the highlighted text in the first Topic Levels field.

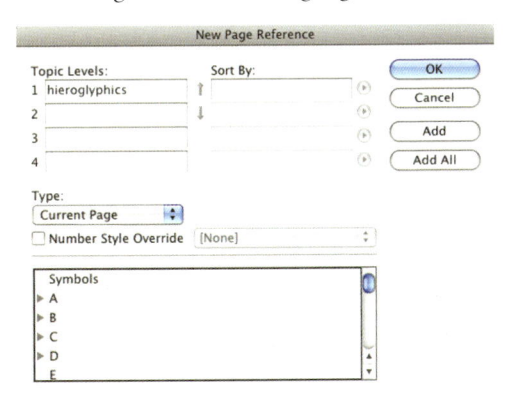

5. Make sure the Type menu is set to Current Page and click OK.

   You can define a number of different types of index entries; the Current Page option adds a reference to the page number where the text is currently highlighted.

   When you close the New Page Reference dialog box, you see that the highlighted text is preceded by a large carat character. This nonprinting character is an index marker — it indicates the location of a tagged reference, but it will not appear in the output job.

Project 8: Multi-Chapter Booklet   477

6. **In the Index panel, click the arrow to the left of the "H", and then click the arrow to the left of the word "hieroglyphics".**

   You can see that the topic was added using the text in the Topic Levels field, and the reference was added with the Current Page number of the highlighted text.

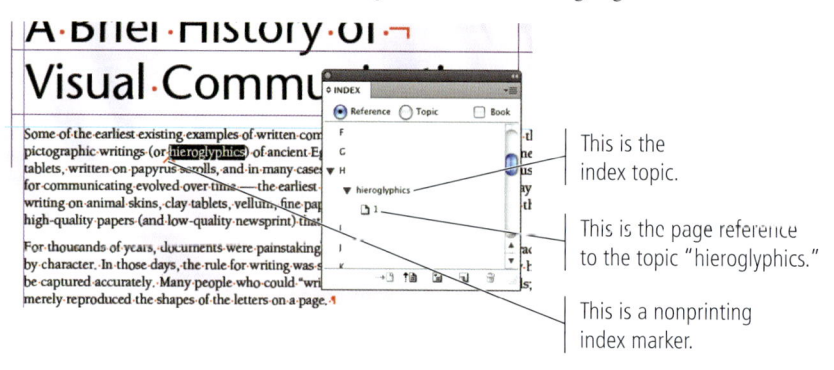

   This is the index topic.

   This is the page reference to the topic "hieroglyphics."

   This is a nonprinting index marker.

7. **Click the arrow to collapse the "H" section of the Index panel.**

8. **Highlight the word "papyrus" in the next line and press Command-Option-Shift-[(Macintosh) or Control-Alt-Shift-[(Windows).**

   Using this key command, you can add a new Current Page reference without opening the New Page Reference dialog box.

9. **In the Index panel, expand the "P" list and the "papyrus" topic.**

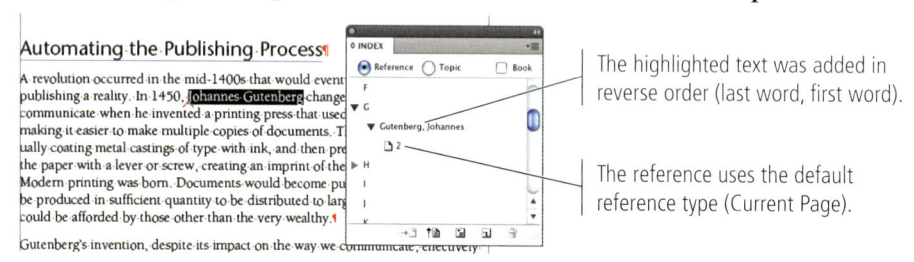

   Note:

   If text is highlighted, Command-Option-Shift-[(Macintosh) or Control-Alt-Shift-[(Windows) adds the highlighted text to the topic list and places an index marker for the selected text, without opening the New Page References dialog box.

10. **Create new Current Page references to "rock carvings", "clay tablets", and "vellum" in the same paragraph.**

11. **On Page 2 of the document, highlight the words "Johannes Gutenberg" in the second line of the first paragraph after the "Automating…" heading.**

12. **Press Command-Option-Shift-] or Control-Alt-Shift-] to add a reversed topic reference to this name.**

13. **In the Index panel, expand the "G" list and the nested index topic.**

    The highlighted text was added in reverse order (last word, first word).

    The reference uses the default reference type (Current Page).

478   Project 8: Multi-Chapter Booklet

Changing Topic Sort Order

INDESIGN FOUNDATIONS

The Sort By field allows you to change the alphabetical order of an index topic in the built index. When the index is built, the entries will appear in the list based on the Sort By text, but the entry text will still be the text defined in the Topic Levels field.

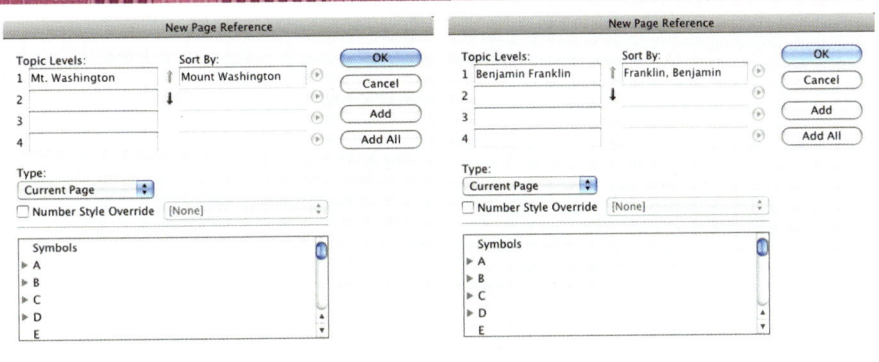

This option is particularly useful for indexing abbreviations and proper names. In the examples shown here, the abbreviated text "Mt." will be alphabetized according to the full word "Mount". The name "Benjamin Franklin" will appear in the index under F instead of B —alphabetized by last name but appearing in the text in standard first name/last name order.

Reversing Index Entries

In addition to changing the sort order of a name, you can also change the actual order of the highlighted words when you add an entry to the index. When text is selected, pressing Command-Option-Shift-] (Macintosh) or Control-Alt-Shift-] (Windows) adds a reversed index entry without opening the New Page Reference dialog box. Using this key command, the highlighted text is added as an entry with the format "last word, comma, all other words".

If the text "Benjamin Franklin" is highlighted, for example, using this key command will add a reference to the term "Franklin, Benjamin." In this case, the added topic will appear in the built index with the reversed text instead of simply re-alphabetized based on the reversed Sort By text.

If more than two words are highlighted when you add a reversed index reference, only the last highlighted word will be placed before the comma. If you add a reversed entry for the text "Martin Luther King", for example, the index topic will be "King, Martin Luther".

In a situation such as this, compound nouns that are not hyphenated can cause problems. If you highlight the text "Martin Luther King Jr." and add a reversed index entry, the index topic will be "Jr., Martin Luther King". However, very few people would look for this reference in the "J" section of an index, and the point of an index is to be useable.

To prevent this type of reference, you can change the text to a nonbreaking space between two words in the selection. With the nonbreaking space between "King" and "Jr.", the reversed index entry would be "King Jr., Martin Luther".

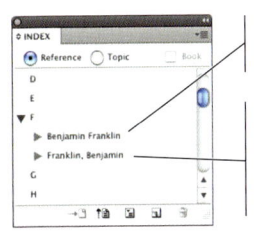

This entry was added with the text reversed in the Sort By field.

This entry was added by highlighting the text and pressing Command-Option-Shift-] (Macintosh) or Control-Alt-Shift-] (Windows).

This entry was added in reverse without changing the highlighted text.

^S is the special code for a nonbreaking space. InDesign properly translates this code when it builds an index.

To create this entry, we replaced the standard space between "King" and "Jr." with a nonbreaking space.

Project 8: Multi-Chapter Booklet   479

14. On Page 4 of the layout, highlight the words "William Henry Fox Talbot" in the first line of the second paragraph.

15. **Press Command-Option-Shift-] or Control-Alt-Shift-] to add a reversed topic reference to this name. Review the entry in the Index panel.**

    Only the last word of the highlighted text is placed before the comma in the index topic.

    In this case, the index topic is technically correct because some people might look for the last name "Talbot" to find information about this person. Others, however, might look for his full last name "Fox Talbot", so you should add another index entry for the same text.

16. **In the text, highlight the space character between the words "Fox" and "Talbot". Choose Type>Insert White Space>Nonbreaking Space.**

17. **Highlight the entire name again and press Command-Option-Shift-] or Control-Alt-Shift-] to add a reversed topic reference to this name. Review the entry in the Index panel.**

    ^S is the special code for a nonbreaking space. InDesign properly translates this code when it builds an index.

    Nonbreaking space character

    Note:

    The key command for a nonbreaking space is Command-Option-X/ Control-Alt-X.

18. **Scan the text of the document and add Current Page index entries to all people mentioned in the chapter. Add all names in reverse order, using nonbreaking spaces as necessary to keep compound last names together.**

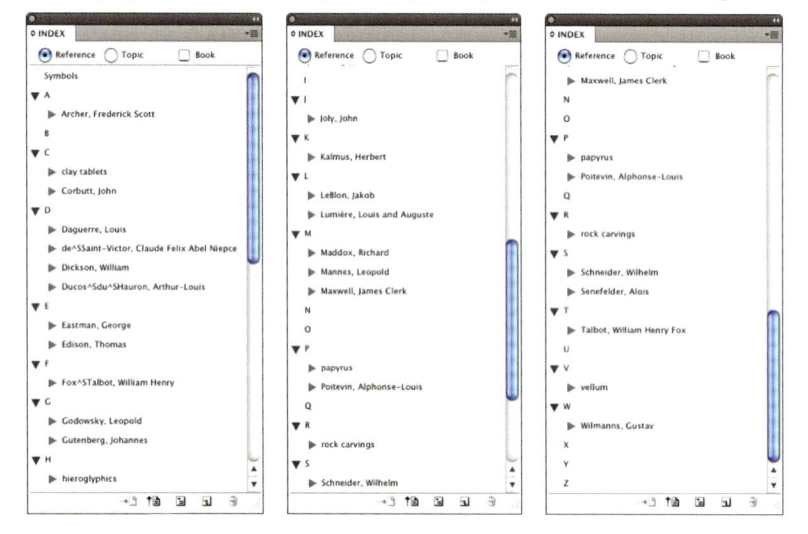

19. **Save the document and continue to the next exercise.**

ADD MULTIPLE PAGE REFERENCES

In some cases, you need to add multiple references to a specific index topic. Rather than searching through the text to find every instance of the topic, you can use the Add All button in the New Page Reference dialog box.

1. **With the color1 file open from the excerpts Book panel, navigate to Page 3 of the layout.**

2. **Highlight the word "Printing" in the first line of the page and click the Create New Index Entry button at the bottom of the Index panel.**

3. **In the New Page Reference dialog box, click the Add All button.**

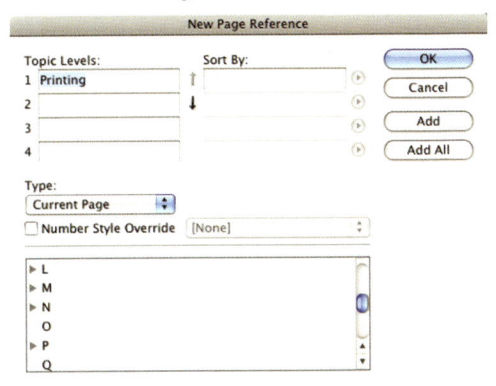

4. **Click Done to close the New Page Reference dialog box.**

5. **In the Index panel, expand the "Printing" topic in the "P" list.**

    When creating an index, topics are case-sensitive. "Printing" is not the same as "printing". The word "Printing" is capitalized only once in the layout, so the Add All function added only one reference to the topic "Printing".

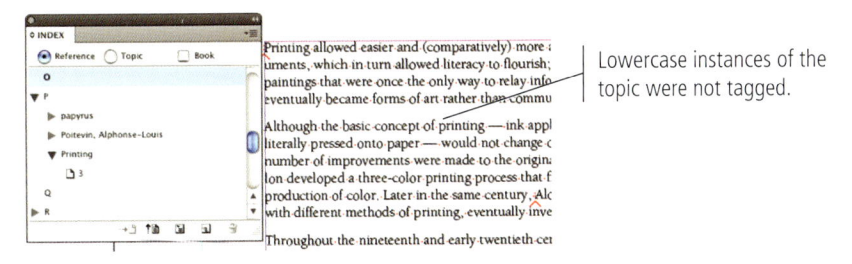

    Lowercase instances of the topic were not tagged.

6. **Highlight the word "printing" in the first line of the second paragraph and click the Create New Index Entry button.**

7. **In the New Page Reference dialog box, click the Add All button and then click Done.**

8. **Review the new topic and references in the Index panel.**

   Your index now includes two references to the same term, one capitalized and one lowercase. This is not good practice, so you need to combine the two terms.

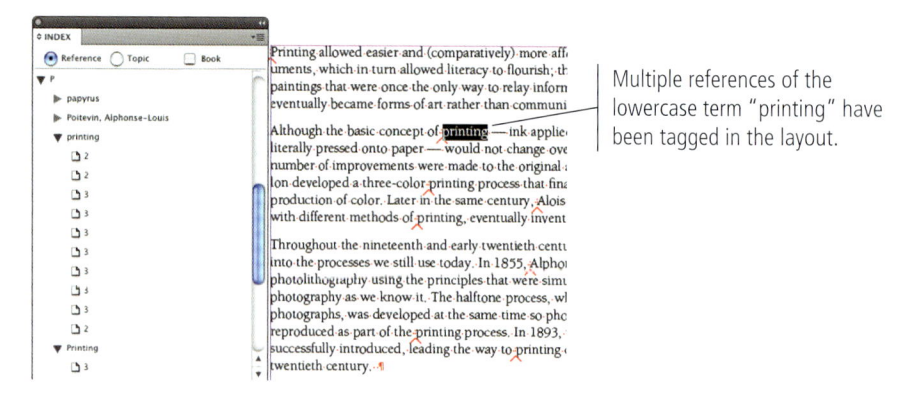

   Multiple references of the lowercase term "printing" have been tagged in the layout.

9. **In the Index panel, double-click the capitalized "Printing" topic.**

   Double-clicking a term in the panel opens the Topic Options dialog box.

10. **In the pane at the bottom of the dialog box, expand the "P" list.**

    This pane shows all topics currently used in the document or book. In this case, you are working with an InDesign book; topics defined in the other book files (such as "Perspective") are also included in the topic list.

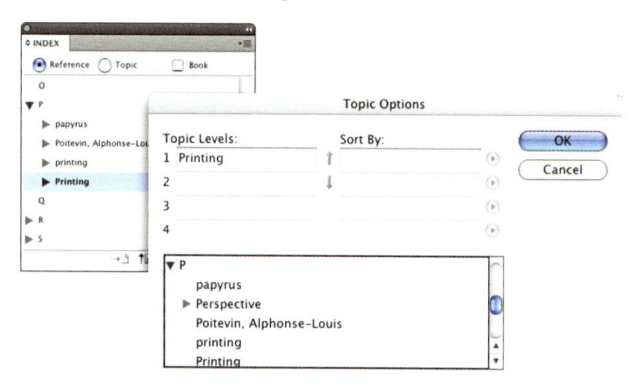

11. **Double-click "printing" in the topic list.**

    Double-clicking an existing topic changes the text in the Topic Levels field.

    After double-clicking the lowercase "printing" in the topic list, the topic you are editing (the capitalized version) changes to reflect the topic you selected from the list.

    This method of choosing an existing topic also works in the New Page Reference dialog box. When you double-click a topic in the list at the bottom of the dialog box, text in the Topic Levels field changes to reflect the topic you double-click. The index marker will be placed at the location of the highlighted text, but the reference will be added for whatever was shown in the Topic Levels field.

482   Project 8: Multi-Chapter Booklet

12. **Click OK to close the dialog box, and then review the "P" list in the Index panel.**

    Your index now includes a single reference to the term "printing." The page reference for the previously capitalized term has been merged into the references for the lowercase term.

13. **Save the file and continue to the next exercise.**

ADD PAGE-RANGE REFERENCES

Index references are not limited to single page numbers. You can use the Type menu in the New Page Reference dialog box to define a number of reference types.

- **Current Page** includes a single-page reference for the index entry.

- **To Next Style Change** creates a page-range reference that starts at the location of the insertion point and ends at the first point where a different paragraph style has been applied in the text.

- **To Next Use of Style** creates a page-range reference that starts at the location of the insertion point and ends at the first instance in the story where a specific paragraph style has been applied in the text. When you choose this option, you can select the style that will end the range.

- **To End of Story** creates a page-range reference that starts at the location of the insertion point and ends at the last page of the current story.

- **To End of Document** creates a page-range reference that starts at the location of the insertion point and ends at the last page of the current document.

- **To End of Section** creates a page-range reference that starts at the location of the insertion point and ends at the last page of the current section.

- **For Next # of Paragraphs** creates a page-range reference that starts at the location of the insertion point and ends after the defined number of paragraphs. You can define the specific number of paragraphs to include in the reference.

- **For Next # of Pages** creates a page-range reference that starts at the location of the insertion point and ends after the defined number of pages. You can define the specific number of pages to include in the reference.

- **Suppress Page Range** creates a topic reference with no associated page number.

1. **With the `color1` file open from the `excerpts` Book panel, navigate to Page 1 of the layout.**

2. **Highlight the word "History" in the chapter title and click the Create New Index Entry button in the Index panel.**

3. **In the New Page Reference dialog box, change the capital "H" in the first Topic Levels field to a lowercase "h".**

Project 8: Multi-Chapter Booklet 483

4. **Choose To End of Document in the Type menu and click the Add button.**

5. **Click Done to close the dialog box, and then review the new topic and reference in the Index panel.**

   The page-range reference has been added to the index. The document ends on Page 8, so the reference extends from Pages 1–8.

6. **Highlight the word "Illumination" in the heading on Page 1 and click the Create New Index Entry button.**

7. **In the Type menu, choose To Next Use of Style. In the related Style menu, choose head 1.**

   This heading is formatted with the head 1 style. You are adding a reference that spans all text between this heading and the next instance of the head 1 style.

8. **Click Add, and then click Done to close the dialog box.**

9. **Review the new topic and reference in the Index panel.**

   The new reference points to the current page only, instead of to the true next instance of the head 1 style.

   This problem highlights an apparent bug in the software, or at least something that does not work intuitively. When you highlight text formatted with the same style defined in the To Next Use of Style menu, InDesign identifies the highlighted text as the next use of the style — the reference points to the location of the highlighted text only. Solving this problem requires a workaround.

484   Project 8: Multi-Chapter Booklet

10. **In the Index panel, click the "1" reference to the "Illumination" topic and click the panel's Delete button.**

11. **In the resulting message, click Yes to confirm the deletion.**

12. **In the document, highlight the word "For" at the beginning of the paragraph after the Illumination heading.**

13. **Click the Create New Index Entry button in the Index panel.**

14. **In the lower half of the dialog box, expand the "I" list of topics and double-click the word "Illumination" in the list of topics.**

    As in the Topic Options dialog box, this method changes the current text in the Topic Levels field to the topic you double-click in the list.

    In Step 10 you deleted the reference to this topic, but you did not delete the topic itself.

    Note:

    If you use this workaround technique, you can simply type to replace the text in the Topic Levels field with the topic you want to reference. For this technique to work correctly, you can — but don't have to — select from the existing topics.

15. **In the Type menu, choose To Next Use of Style. In the related Style menu, choose head 1.**

16. **Click Add, and then click Done to close the dialog box.**

17. **Review the new topic and reference in the Index panel.**

    The new reference shows the correct range between the selected text and the next instance of the head 1 paragraph style (on Page 2 of the document).

    Note:

    You can delete an entire topic from the index by selecting it in the panel and clicking the Delete button. If you delete a term from the index, all references to that term are also deleted.

18. **Save the file and continue to the next exercise.**

Project 8: Multi-Chapter Booklet 485

ADD MULTIPLE-LEVEL REFERENCES

You might have noticed that the New Page Reference dialog box includes four fields in the Topic Levels area. These fields allow you to created multi-level or nested index entries. You can create up to four levels of nested index entries, depending on the complexity a particular project requires.

1. With the **color1** file open through the **excerpts** Book panel, navigate to Page 4 of the layout.

2. Highlight the words "daguerreotype method" in the second line of the first paragraph. Click the Create New Index Entry button in the Index panel.

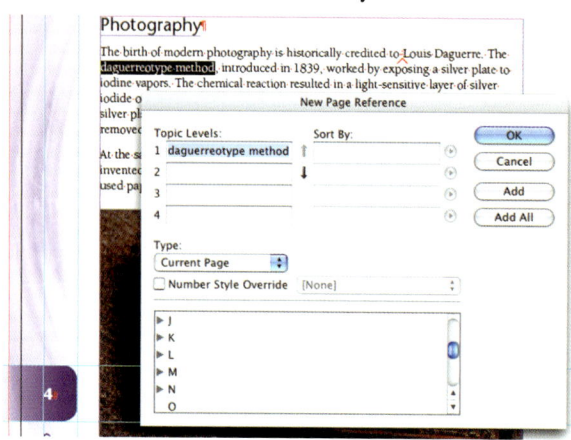

3. In the New Page Reference dialog box, click the down-arrow button in the Topic Levels area.

   This button moves the selected term down one level to become a second-level index term. Of course, when you add a second-level term, you also need to define the parent term for that nested entry.

Adding Cross-References in an Index

INDESIGN FOUNDATIONS

A cross-referenced item refers the reader to another index entry. For example, the index entry for "CIELAB" might say, "See LAB color." If you choose to create an entry as a cross-reference, you need to also define the type of notation. The Referenced field defines the topic to which a cross-reference will point; you can type in the field or drag an existing topic into the field from the list at the bottom of the dialog box.

- **See [also]** allows InDesign to choose the appropriate cross-reference method — "See" if the topic has no page references of its own, or "See also" if the topic includes page numbers.

- **See** refers the reader to another topic or topics; the entry has no page number, only text listing the cross-referenced topic. For example, if the index entry is "Dogs", the cross-reference might be "See Canine".

- **See also** directs attention to the current topic, as well as other information elsewhere in the index. For example, an index item called "Dogs" may have its own list of page numbers, and then a cross-reference to "See also Pets".

- **See herein** and **See also herein** refer the reader to entries within the current index entry. For example, if the main (Level 1) index entry is "Dogs", you might want to direct the index to a subentry (Level 2 or Level 3 item) that might not be expected under this heading, such as "See herein Wolf."

- **[Custom Cross-Reference]** allows you to define the text that will be used as the cross-reference, such as "Go to" or some similar text.

Project 8: Multi-Chapter Booklet

4. **Click the first Topic Levels field and type photographs.**

   You can select an existing topic as the first level or type a new term in the field.

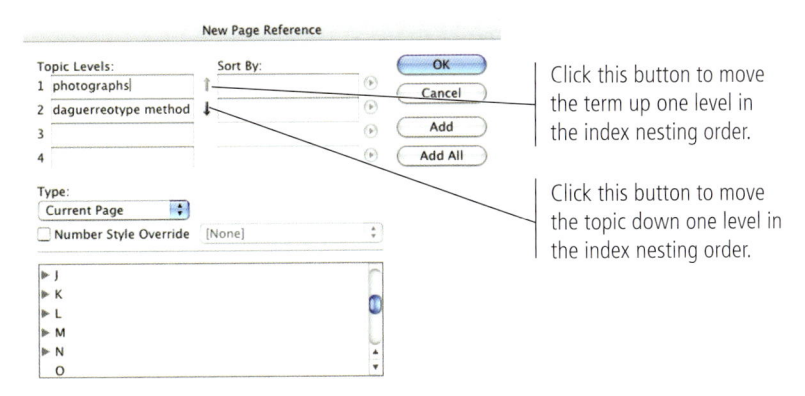

   Click this button to move the term up one level in the index nesting order.

   Click this button to move the topic down one level in the index nesting order.

5. **Click OK to add the term and reference to the index.**

6. **In the Index panel, expand the "photographs" entry in the "P" list.**

7. **Within the "photographs" entry, expand the "daguerreotype method" entry.**

   This second-level term will be listed under the new first-level "photographs" term.

   This is the page number reference for the second-level "daguerreotype method" entry.

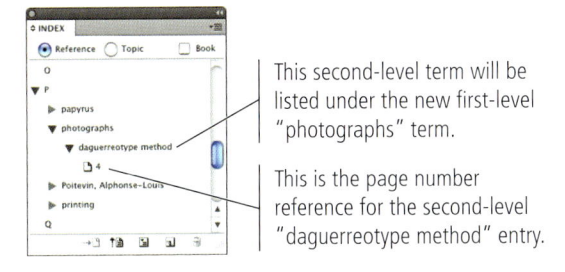

8. **Save the color1 file and close it.**

9. **Save the book file and continue to the next exercise.**

BUILD THE BOOK'S INDEX

Building an index into a document is very similar to building a table of contents. Once the index has been generated, it is loaded into the cursor so you can place it in the layout. When you are working with a book file, you can build the index into an existing chapter file, or you can add a separate back matter file to hold the index.

Note:

Back matter is anything that comes after the primary chapters of a document, such as appendices and an index.

1. **Open the file companion.indt from the WIP>Companions folder.**

2. **Drag the D-Index Opener master page onto the Page 1 icon.**

3. **Save the file as excerpts back.indd in your WIP>Companions folder and close the file.**

4. **In the excerpts Book panel, make sure nothing is selected in the panel and click the Add Document button. Navigate to the file excerpts back.indd file in your WIP>Companions folder and click Open.**

5. **Open the Synchronize Options dialog box from the Book panel Options menu.**

6. **Deselect everything but the Swatches check box and click OK.**

Project 8: Multi-Chapter Booklet

7. **Make sure no files are selected in the Book panel and click the Synchronize button at the bottom of the panel.**

8. **Double-click the `excerpts back` file in the Book panel to open the file.**

9. **At the bottom of the Index panel, click the Generate Index button.**

10. **Delete the word "Index" from the Title field.**

    In the Generate Index dialog box, the Title and Title Style options are the same as the related options for building a table of contents. Because the master page you're using already includes the title "Index", you should not include a title in the built index.

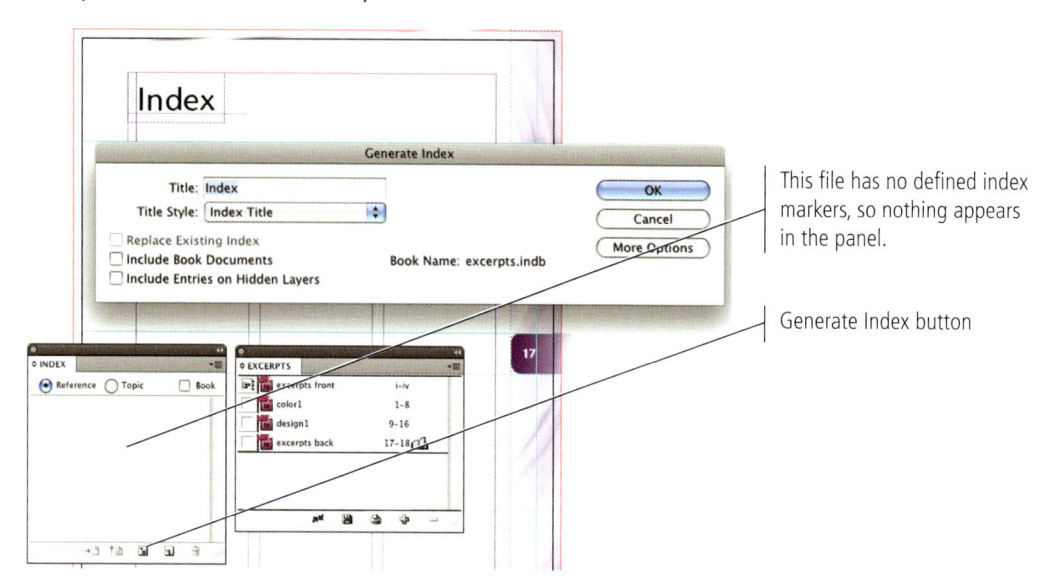

    This file has no defined index markers, so nothing appears in the panel.

    Generate Index button

11. **Select the Include Book Documents option.**

    Even though there are no index references in this back-matter file, it is part of the book with files that have index markers.

12. **Click the More Options button in the Generate Index dialog box (if necessary).**

13. **Review the available options. Click the Following Topic menu and choose Em Space as the character that will appear between the entry text and the associated references.**

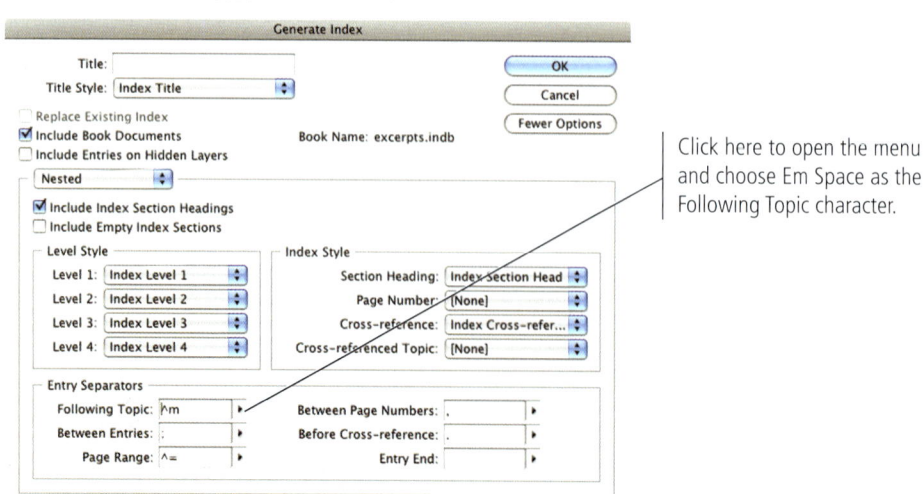

    Click here to open the menu and choose Em Space as the Following Topic character.

488 Project 8: Multi-Chapter Booklet

14. **Click OK to generate the index. Click the loaded cursor in the three-column text frame to place the index.**

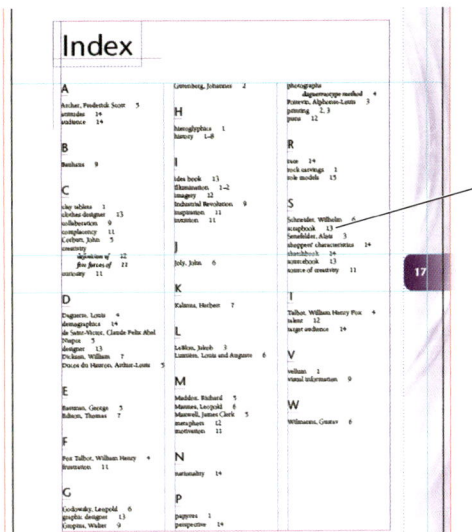

   Some of these entries are from the second chapter (the file from the Design Companion); these tags were already created in the file provided by the publisher.

   Note:

   Your index might be slightly different than our example, depending on which names you added in the previous exercise.

15. **Save the file and close it.**

16. **Save the book file and continue to the next stage of the project.**

Options for Generating an Index

INDESIGN FOUNDATIONS

When you generate an index, you have a number of options for automatically formatting the compiled list. In many cases, the default settings will work perfectly well, but you can change any or all of the following options as necessary:

- The **Nested** or **Run-in** menu determines how individual entries in the index are placed. Nested creates each entry on its own line. Run-In forces all index entries to run together in the same paragraph.

- If **Include Index Section Headings** is checked, alphabetical headings (A, B, C, etc.) are added to the index.

- If **Include Empty Index Sections** is checked, all letter headings are added to the built index, even if that letter has no associated terms.

- The **Level Style** menu defines paragraph styles used to format different levels of index entries. If you don't choose different styles in these menus, the default options (Index Level 1, etc.) are created and applied to the headings. (If you define your own style named "Index Level 1," your settings are applied in the built index.)

- The **Section Heading** menu defines paragraph styles used to format the section headings in the index. If you don't choose a different style, the default Index Section Head is created and applied to the headings. (If you define your own style named "Index Section Head," your settings are applied in the built index.)

- The **Page Number** menu defines the character style applied to page numbers in the generated index.

- The **Cross-Reference** menu defines the character style applied to the cross-references in the index (for example, the "See also" part of "See also LAB color").

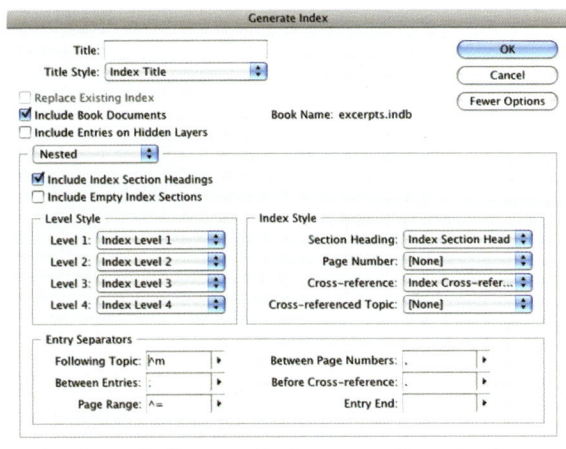

- The **Cross-Reference Topic** menu defines the character style applied to the text of a cross-reference (for example, the "LAB color" part of "See also LAB color").

- The **Entry Separators** area defines the characters used in specific parts of the index:
  - **Following Topic** is used between the entry text and the entry page references.
  - **Between Page Numbers** is used between individual page references.
  - **Between Entries** is used between entries in a run-in index.
  - **Before Cross-reference** is used before the text of a cross-reference.
  - **Page Range** separates numbers in a page range.
  - **Entry End** is added at the end of individual entries.

Project 8: Multi-Chapter Booklet   489

Stage 4 Exporting Book Files

Another advantage of combining multiple files is the ability to output those files all at once — choosing print or export settings once, instead of opening each file and changing the print or export settings individually. Using the Book panel, you can output all chapter files at once, or you can output specific selected chapters.

Export PDF Files for Print and Digital Distribution

Your client asked for two separate files — one that can be printed at high quality and one that can be posted on the company's Web site and sent via email. Because you're working with a single file for the entire book, you can easily create these two output files in a few steps.

1. **With the `excerpts` Book panel open, click the empty area at the bottom of the panel to deselect all files in the book.**

2. **Choose Export Book to PDF in the panel Options menu.**

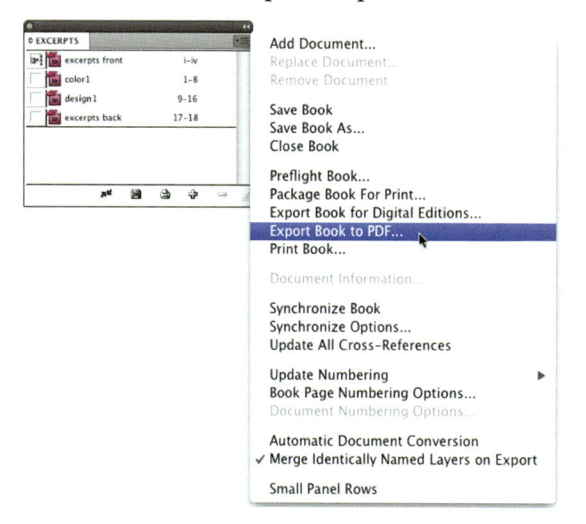

   Note:

   If any files are selected, the menu option changes to Export Selected Documents to PDF.

3. **Navigate to your WIP>Companions folder as the target and change the file name to `excerpts print.pdf`.**

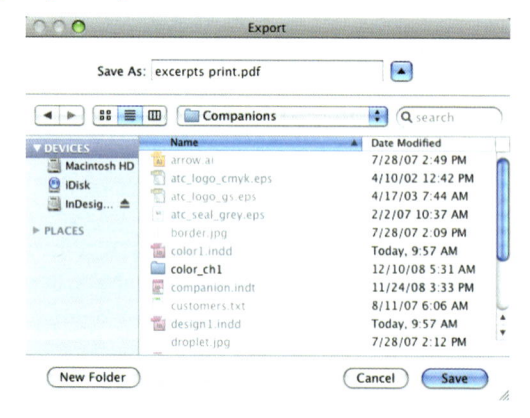

4. **Click Save.**

5. **In the Export Adobe PDF dialog box, choose [High Quality Print] in the Adobe PDF Preset menu.**

490   Project 8: Multi-Chapter Booklet

6. **In the Marks and Bleeds options, check the Crop Marks option. Change the Offset field to 0.125 in, and change all four Bleed fields to 0.125 in.**

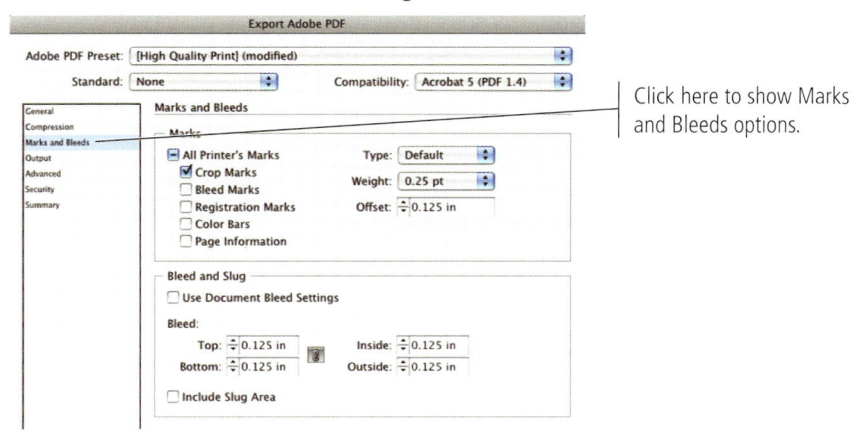

   Click here to show Marks and Bleeds options.

7. **Click Export.**

8. **In the Book panel Options menu, choose Export Book to PDF again.**

9. **Name the second file `excerpts digital.pdf` and click Save.**

10. **Choose [Smallest File Size] in the Adobe PDF Preset menu.**

11. **In the Compression options, change both Image Quality menus to Medium.**

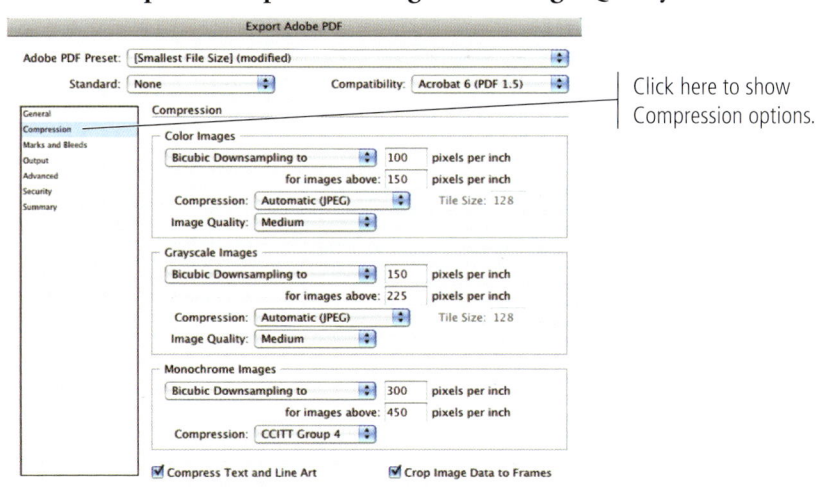

    Click here to show Compression options.

    Note:

    In Project 5 you used the Print Booklet command to output a booklet as printer's spreads for proofing purposes. In most commercial printing workflows, however, the output provider will create the necessary printer's spreads from the individual pages in your exported PDF file. Always consult with your output provider about what you need to supply to efficiently achieve the best possible result.

12. **Click Export. If you get a warning about transparency settings, click OK to dismiss the warning.**

    Using the Book utility, you now have two complete PDF files for different purposes — created in only a few easy steps.

13. **Save the book file and then close it.**

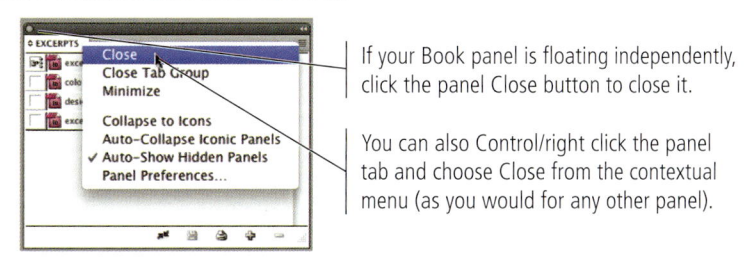

    If your Book panel is floating independently, click the panel Close button to close it.

    You can also Control/right click the panel tab and choose Close from the contextual menu (as you would for any other panel).

14. **Continue to the next stage of the project.**

Project 8: Multi-Chapter Booklet 491

Stage 5 Merging Data into an InDesign Layout

For the final stage of this project, you need to create a thank-you note from the publisher to previous clients. This note will be included with the printed copies of the Excerpts booklet when the sample is mailed to the clients. Your client provided a Microsoft Excel file with the client mailing addresses; it also identifies which book each client purchased.

Data merge is a fairly sophisticated utility in most word-processing applications; it allows you to combine text with information stored in a database (such as a Microsoft Excel file). For example, data merge allows you to write one letter, click a few buttons, and print or export 147 copies of the letter, each with a different mailing address. InDesign's Data Merge capabilities can be used for this type of personal letter generation, but — with a bit of advanced planning — it can also be used for more sophisticated database-driven layouts such as catalogs with graphics.

Personalized printing uses data to produce items such as catalogs that specifically target your interests. Other applications for personalized printing include newspaper inserts for a specific region. A national company might create a single weekly sale advertisement with one page that varies according to the local distribution; why, for example, would a company want to advertise snow shovels in southern California?

InDesign's Data Merge feature makes it fairly simple to create a layout incorporating variable data. Once the data source file has been established, you can create any layout you want, add the data, and create multiple versions of a finished layout in one action.

Note:

Variable database printing is currently one of the hottest topics in the graphic design and printing industries. Marketing specialists have spent millions to determine that you are far more likely to open a piece of mail with your name on it than one addressed to "Resident."

The Data Source File

INDESIGN FOUNDATIONS

If you have a contact manager anywhere on your computer, you are familiar with the idea of a simple database. A database is made up of **fields** that contain information. Each field has a **field name**, which is usually descriptive text that defines the contents of the field. Each listing in a database is called a **record**; each record contains every field in the database (even if a particular field contains no information for a given record).

In the following example, Name, Address, and Telephone are all fields. The first line of the file contains the field names "Name," "Address," and "Telephone Number." Each record appears on a separate line.

Name	Address	Telephone Number
James Smith	123 Anywhere St., Someplace, MI 99999	800-555-0000
Susan Jones	3208 Street Ct., Small Town, ID 55555	800-555-8888

InDesign's Data Merge feature does not interact directly with a database application. Data must first be exported from a database into a tab- or comma-delimited ASCII text file.

In the text file, the information in each field (called a **text string**) is separated by the delimiter (comma or tab), which tells the software that the next text string belongs in the next field. Records are separated by a paragraph return, so each record begins on a new line.

If a particular text string requires one of the delimiter characters — for example, a comma within an address — that string is surrounded by double quotation marks in the text file.

A comma contained within quotation marks is treated as a text character, not as a delimiter.

The first line of the text file should list the field names. If your database application does not export field names as the first line of the text-only file, you need to open the file in a text editor and add the field name line at the beginning.

Project 8: Multi-Chapter Booklet

Create the Merged Document and Load the Source Data

The target document for a data merge needs to include placeholders, or locations where the data will appear after the data merge is complete. Once you have established the data source for the InDesign file, you can easily create these placeholders anywhere in the document.

1. **Open the file letter.indd from your WIP>Companions folder.**

   Your client wrote this letter using her InDesign letterhead template. She used all capital letters to indicate where she wants database information to be added in the letter text.

2. **Choose Window>Automation>Data Merge to open the Data Merge panel.**

   Before you define a data source, the Data Merge panel provides instructions for its use.

3. **Open the Data Merge panel Options menu and choose Select Data Source.**

4. **Navigate to the file customers.txt in your WIP>Companions folder and click Open.**

   When the file is processed, the available fields (defined by the first line in the data file) are listed in the Data Merge panel.

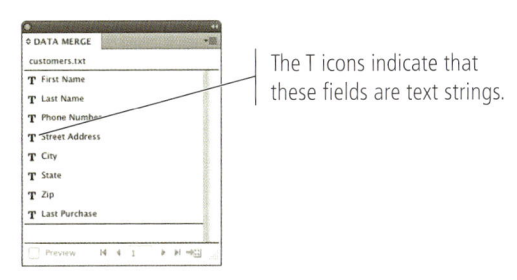

   The T icons indicate that these fields are text strings.

Project 8: Multi-Chapter Booklet 493

5. **In the document, turn on hidden characters (Type>Show Hidden Characters).**

6. **Highlight the first line in the letter (excluding the paragraph return character), and then double-click the First Name item in the Data Merge panel.**

Highlight this line of placeholder text (excluding the paragraph return character).

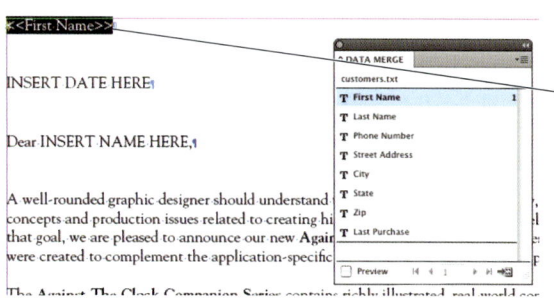

Double-clicking an item in the Data Merge panel replaces the highlighted text with a placeholder for that data field.

Cleaning Up Data

INDESIGN FOUNDATIONS

Placeholders are comprised of the field name enclosed within double brackets, such as <<Name>>, inserted anywhere in the target document.

<<Name>>
<<Address>>

Dear <<Name>>,

Congratulations! We are writing to inform you that your house at <<Address>> has been selected for a free facelift!

Once data from the source file has been merged into the document, it looks like this:

James Smith
123 Anywhere St., Someplace, MI 99999

Dear James Smith,

Congratulations! We are writing to inform you that your house at 123 Anywhere St., Someplace, MI 99999 has been selected for a free facelift!

The same document is reproduced for every record in the text file, personalizing each copy of the letter for the intended recipient.

Notice that the address is entirely on one line of text, and that the "Dear" line includes the person's whole name — not a tremendous improvement over "Dear Occupant."

You should make sure your data includes the exact information you need. The previous example would benefit greatly from a different arrangement:

First_Name, Last_Name, Street_Address, City, State, Zip

James, Smith, "123 Anywhere St.", Someplace, MI, 99999

Susan, Jones, "3208 Street Ct.", Small Town, ID, 55555

The target file can then appear much more personal. Placeholders can be positioned with text characters (including spaces) in between to make the document more personal:

<<First_Name>> <<Last_Name>>
<<Street Address>>
<<City>, <<State>> <<Zip>>

Dear <<First_Name>>,

Congratulations! We are writing to inform you that your house at <<Street_Address>> has been selected for a free facelift!

Once data from the source file has been merged into this version, it looks like this:

James Smith
123 Anywhere St.
Someplace, MI 99999

Dear James,

Congratulations! We are writing to inform you that your house at 123 Anywhere St. has been selected for a free facelift!

7. **Press the Right Arrow key or click to place the insertion point after the placeholder.**

8. **Press the Spacebar, and then double-click the Last Name item in the Data Merge panel.**

   > Note:
   >
   > Like a text variable, a placeholder is treated as a single character in the layout.

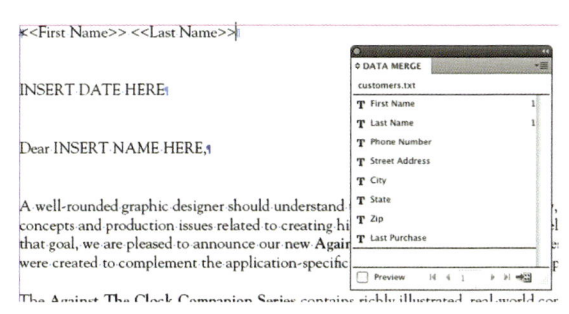

9. **Press Return/Enter to start a new paragraph in the document, and then double-click the Street Address item in the Data Merge panel.**

10. **Press Return/Enter again. Add the City, State, and Zip fields on the third line, separated by the appropriate punctuation and spaces.**

11. **Highlight the All Caps text in the salutation line, and then replace it with the First Name data field placeholder.**

    > Note:
    >
    > If your database file includes a title field, you could address the letter as "Dear <<title>> <<last name>>", which would result in Dear Mr. Smith instead of the less-formal Dear Jim.

12. **In the third paragraph of the letter, replace the All Caps text with the Last Purchase data field placeholder.**

    > Note:
    >
    > Highlighting a few letters in any field name (in the document) automatically highlights the entire field name, including the brackets.

13. **With the Last Purchase placeholder selected, change the font to ATC Pine Italic.**

    After placeholders have been entered in the document, you can apply text and paragraph formatting as you would for any other text element.

    > Note:
    >
    > If you were going to re-use this letter, you might consider using a type variable for the date instead of typing an actual date.

14. **Highlight the text "INSERT DATE HERE" and type today's date.**

15. **Save the file and continue to the next exercise.**

Project 8: Multi-Chapter Booklet 495

Incorporating Images in a Data Merge

A data source file is not limited to text; you can also incorporate images in the data source file to create variable images in a layout. If you want to incorporate graphics or images in your data merge, your data source file must include a field that contains the full path to the image, beginning with the drive name where the image resides (called an **absolute path**). In the field names, the name of the image field should start with the "@" symbol (for example, "@image").

The absolute path for an image tells the Data Merge processor where to find the necessary file. On a Macintosh, the components in the path name are separated by colons:

Hard Drive:Pictures:image.tif   Mac:Catalog Files:Pictures:sweater.tif

On a Windows computer, the path name begins with the drive letter:

C:\My Documents\Pictures\image.tif   D:\Vector files\graph.eps

The only spaces in the path name are those that exist in the name of a file or folder; no spaces should separate any of the backslash or colon characters.

Creating and Controlling Image Placeholders

When a data source includes an image field, the Data Merge panel shows a small picture icon for that field. You can attach an image placeholder to any graphics frame by selecting the frame in the layout and double-clicking the image item in the Data Merge panel.

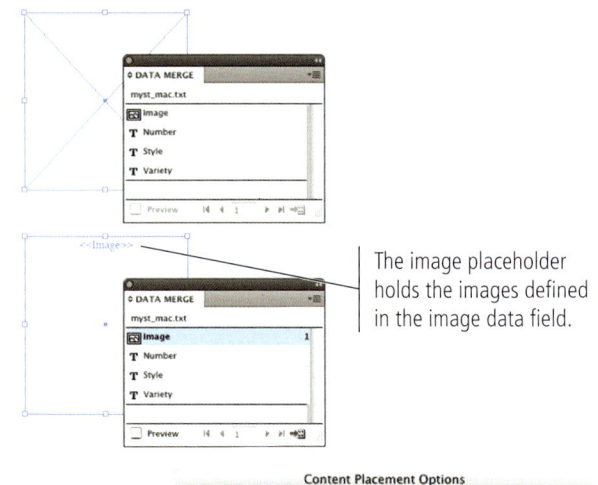

When you use images from a data source file, you can choose Content Placement Options in the Data Merge panel Options menu to predetermine the appearance of the image in relation to the placeholder frame.

- The **Fitting** menu includes the same options that are available for fitting placed images in a graphics frame.
- If **Center in Frame** is checked, the image is centered within the placeholder frame after the Fitting option has been applied.
- The **Link Images** check box, active by default, links the data source images to the layout that's created when you generate the merged document. If this option is not checked, the images are embedded in the resulting file. (Embedding images drastically increases file size; as a general rule, you should leave the Link Images box checked.)

The image placeholder holds the images defined in the image data field.

You can preview variable images just as you preview text. If an image path is incorrect or a file is not in the path defined in the data, you will see a warning when you try to preview that record.

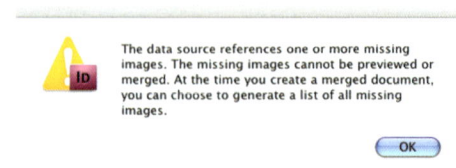

496   Project 8: Multi-Chapter Booklet

COMPLETE THE MERGED DOCUMENT

Once you have created your target document and formatted all the elements, you can preview the data and create the merged document. InDesign uses the data source file and the target layout to create a third document — the merged file. This third file is not linked to the data source; any changes you make to the data are not applied to the merged document. If you change the data file, you have to repeat the merge of the original layout file with the changed data.

1. **With letter.indd open from your WIP>Companions folder, activate the Preview check box at the bottom of the Data Merge panel.**

   You can preview your document at any time by activating the Preview check box in the Data Merge panel. The arrows to the left and right of the record number allow you to move through each record in the merged document.

   When Preview is turned on, the actual data from the source file replaces the placeholder elements.

   Check this box to preview the actual data in the layout.

   Preview First Record

   Preview Previous Record

   Preview Next Record

   Preview Last Record

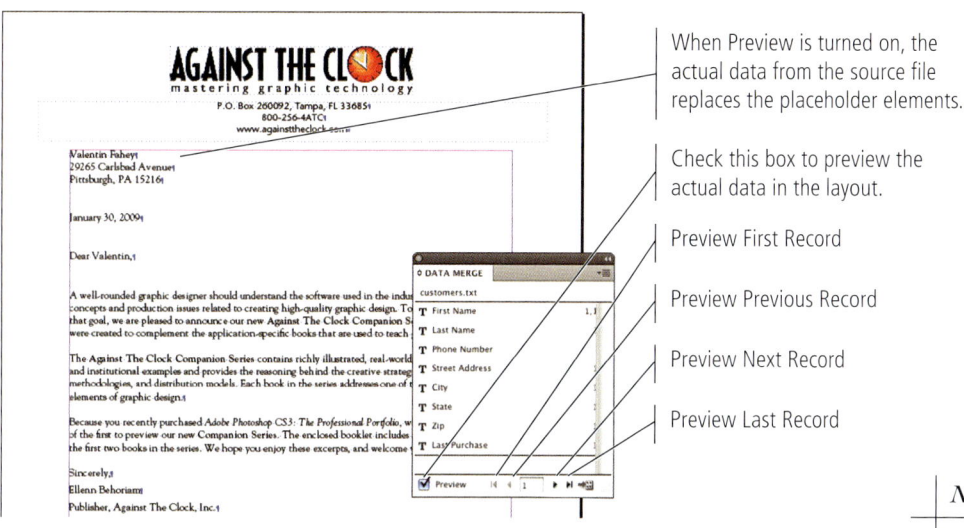

2. **Choose Export to PDF in the Data Merge panel Options menu.**

   In the Create Merged Document dialog box, you can define specific options for your merged document. The Records tab determines which records (all, one specific record, or a specific range) will be included in the merged document.

   The two check boxes at the bottom of the dialog box provide feedback after you create the data merge. Checked by default, these important options allow you to make sure all your data is available and fits into the spaces you defined.

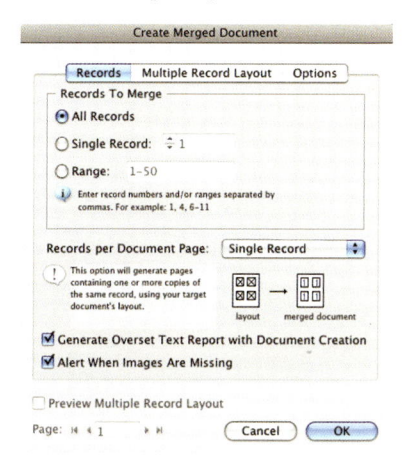

   Note:

   If you choose Create Merged Document, the merge process results in an InDesign file with the necessary number of copies. The Export to PDF option skips this intermediary step.

   Note:

   The Records per Document Page option allows you to place multiple records on a single page in the merged document. This option can be useful for creating catalog listings, multiple labels, or other projects with more than one database record on a single page.

3. **Click OK in the Create Merged Document dialog box.**

Project 8: Multi-Chapter Booklet — 497

4. **Choose the [High Quality Print] preset in the Export Adobe PDF dialog box and click Export.**

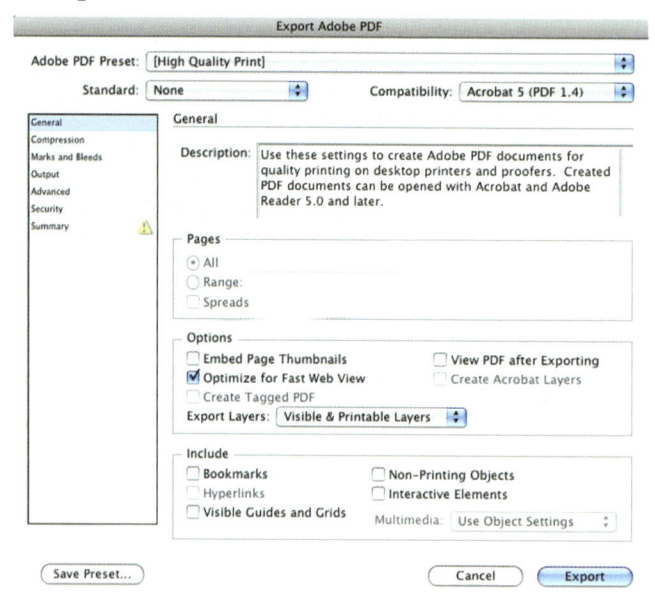

5. **In the resulting dialog box, navigate to your WIP>Companions folder as the target location, and then click Save.**

6. **When you see the message that the data merge resulted in no overset text, click OK.**

Managing Empty Data Fields

When you merge data, you should be aware that one or more fields for a specific record might be empty. For example, a specific record might not include a company name. If your target document includes a company name placeholder, the merged document might end up with an empty line where that placeholder appears.

In the example shown below, the record for James Smith doesn't include a company name. In the merged document, the line is blank.

In the Options tab of the Create Merged Document dialog box, the Remove Blank Lines for Empty Fields option solves this potential problem. (The same option is available in the Content Placement Options dialog box, which you can access in the Data Merge panel Options menu.) In the merged document, placeholders are ignored for fields that have no content.

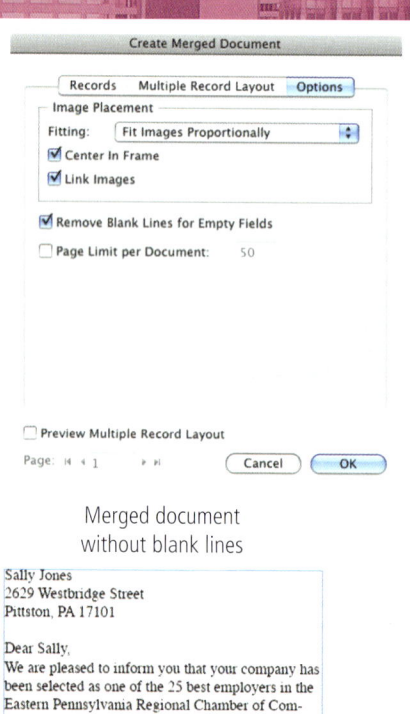

Placeholders in original document

Merged document with blank lines

Merged document without blank lines

498 Project 8: Multi-Chapter Booklet

7. **On your desktop, find and double-click the `letter.pdf` file (in your WIP>Companions folder) to open it in Adobe Acrobat or Adobe Reader.**

Because there were 50 records in the data source file, the new document has 50 pages (one page for each record/letter).

8. **Close the PDF file, return to InDesign, and then save and close the letter.indd file.**

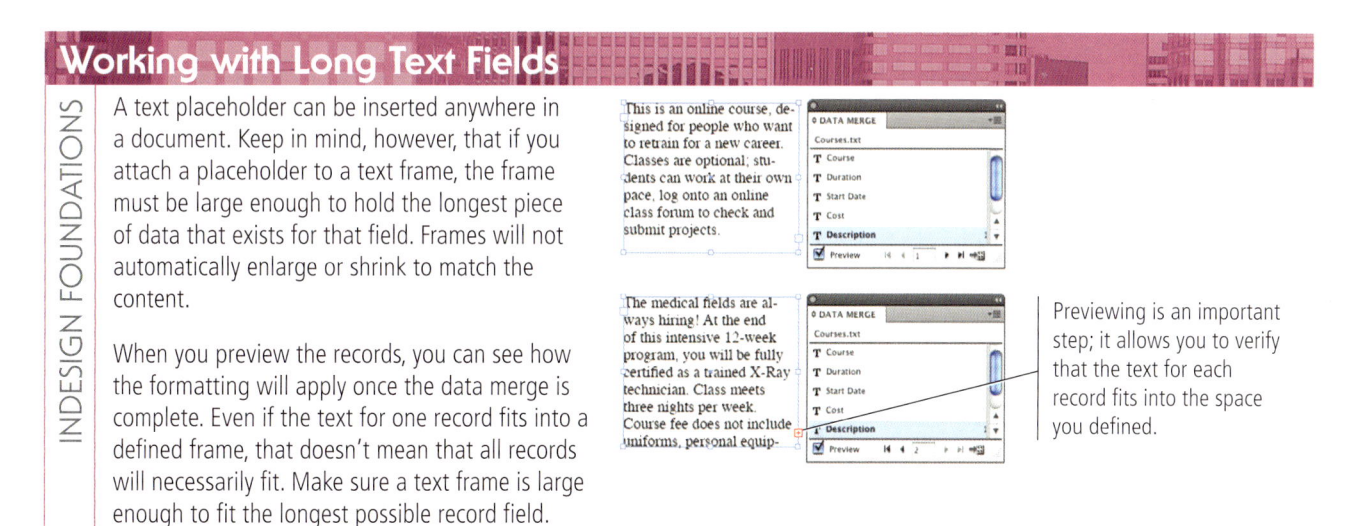

Working with Long Text Fields

INDESIGN FOUNDATIONS

A text placeholder can be inserted anywhere in a document. Keep in mind, however, that if you attach a placeholder to a text frame, the frame must be large enough to hold the longest piece of data that exists for that field. Frames will not automatically enlarge or shrink to match the content.

When you preview the records, you can see how the formatting will apply once the data merge is complete. Even if the text for one record fits into a defined frame, that doesn't mean that all records will necessarily fit. Make sure a text frame is large enough to fit the longest possible record field.

Previewing is an important step; it allows you to verify that the text for each record fits into the space you defined.

Project 8: Multi-Chapter Booklet 499

Merging Multiple Records on a Single Page

INDESIGN FOUNDATIONS

You can merge more than one record onto a single page by selecting Multiple Records in the Records per Document Page menu. When this option is selected, the Multiple Record Layout tab determines how records are placed and separated in the merged document.

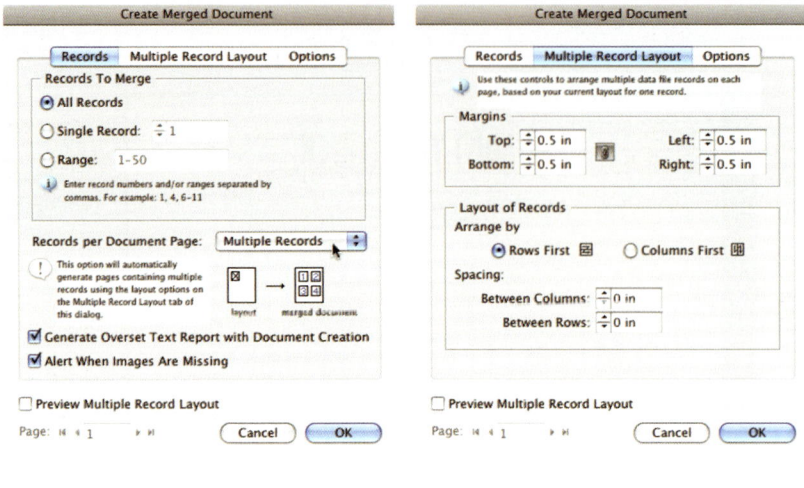

Half an inch is added between each record in the merged document.

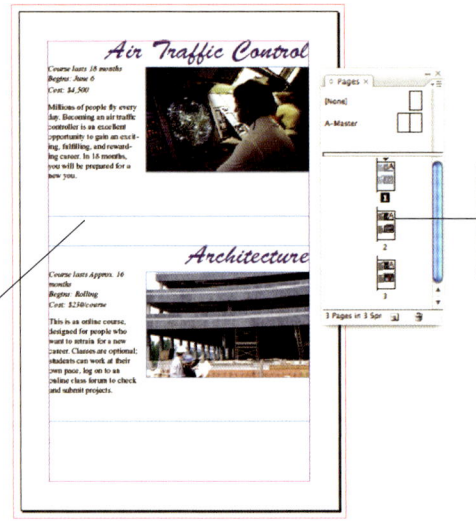

The merged document has three pages because two records fit onto each page.

500   Project 8: Multi-Chapter Booklet

Project Review

fill in the blank

1. The _____ is used to organize and manage multiple chapter files in a book.

2. If a chapter file shows a _____ icon, it has been edited outside the context of the InDesign book.

3. Book chapters typically begin on _____-numbered, _____-facing pages.

4. _____, typically including a title page and table of contents, is the content preceding the main body of a book.

5. _____, typically containing indexes and appendices, appears after the primary content of a book.

6. The _____ option can be used to renumber any specific page in a document.

7. You can change the _____ of an index entry to rearrange its alphabetical position in the compiled index.

8. Clicking the _____ button in the New Page Reference dialog box is case-sensitive. "Printing" will not be tagged if the topic is "printing".

9. A(n) _____ is useful for tagging references to people based on their last names without changing the text in the document.

10. You can delete a(n) _____ without deleting its parent topic from the Index panel. The reverse is not true; deleting a parent topic deletes all _____ for that topic.

short answer

1. Describe three conventions that relate to and govern long-document design.

2. Briefly explain the concept of synchronization, including potential problems that might arise from it.

3. Briefly explain two advantages and two disadvantages of the InDesign indexing functionality.

Project 8: Multi-Chapter Booklet

Portfolio Builder Project

Use what you learned in this project to complete the following freeform exercise.
Carefully read the art director and client comments, then create your own design to meet the needs of the project.
Use the space below to sketch ideas; when finished, write a brief explanation of your reasoning behind your final design.

art director comments

Every professional designer needs a portfolio of their work. If you've completed the projects in this book, you should now have a number of different examples to show off your skills using InDesign CS4.

The eight projects in this book were specifically designed to include a broad range of *types* of projects; your portfolio should use the same principle.

client comments

Using the following suggestions, gather your best work and create printed and digital versions of your portfolio:

❏ Include as many different types of work as possible — one-page layouts, folding brochures, multi-page booklets, etc.

❏ Print clean copies of each finished piece that you want to include.

❏ For each example in your portfolio, write a brief (one or two paragraph) synopsis of the project. Explain the purpose of the piece, as well as your role in the creative and production process.

❏ Design a personal promotion brochure — create a layout that highlights your technical skills and reflects your personal style.

❏ Create a PDF version of your portfolio so you can send your portfolio via email, post it on job sites, and keep it with you on a CD at all times — you never know when you might meet a potential employer.

project justification

Project Summary

As you completed the exercises in this project, you learned to use InDesign tools to define special formatting, combine multiple files, build tables of contents and indexes, and merge variable data into a page layout.

You discovered the importance of consistency in long-document design. You learned how to combine multiple chapter files into a single book, as well as how to synchronize those files so related elements are consistent from page to page and chapter to chapter. This book-building functionality works equally well for combining single-page documents or lengthy chapters with many pages.

You also learned how to automate (as much as possible) building tables of contents and indexes — two processes that used to require days of manual checking and rechecking if even a single page in the layout changed. You now understand the interaction between styles and tables of contents. You learned that effectively implementing styles throughout a long document makes it relatively easy to compile a thorough table of contents that includes every heading from Page 1 to the final page in the document.

You also discovered that software is not "smart" enough to identify which terms are important in a document, so the process of tagging index entries remains manual. However, the ability to store index markers in a document means compiling and recompiling the final index is far simpler than building and compiling the list by hand.

These skills are relatively rare in the graphics marketplace. Your ability to master them makes you much more marketable as a professional graphic designer.

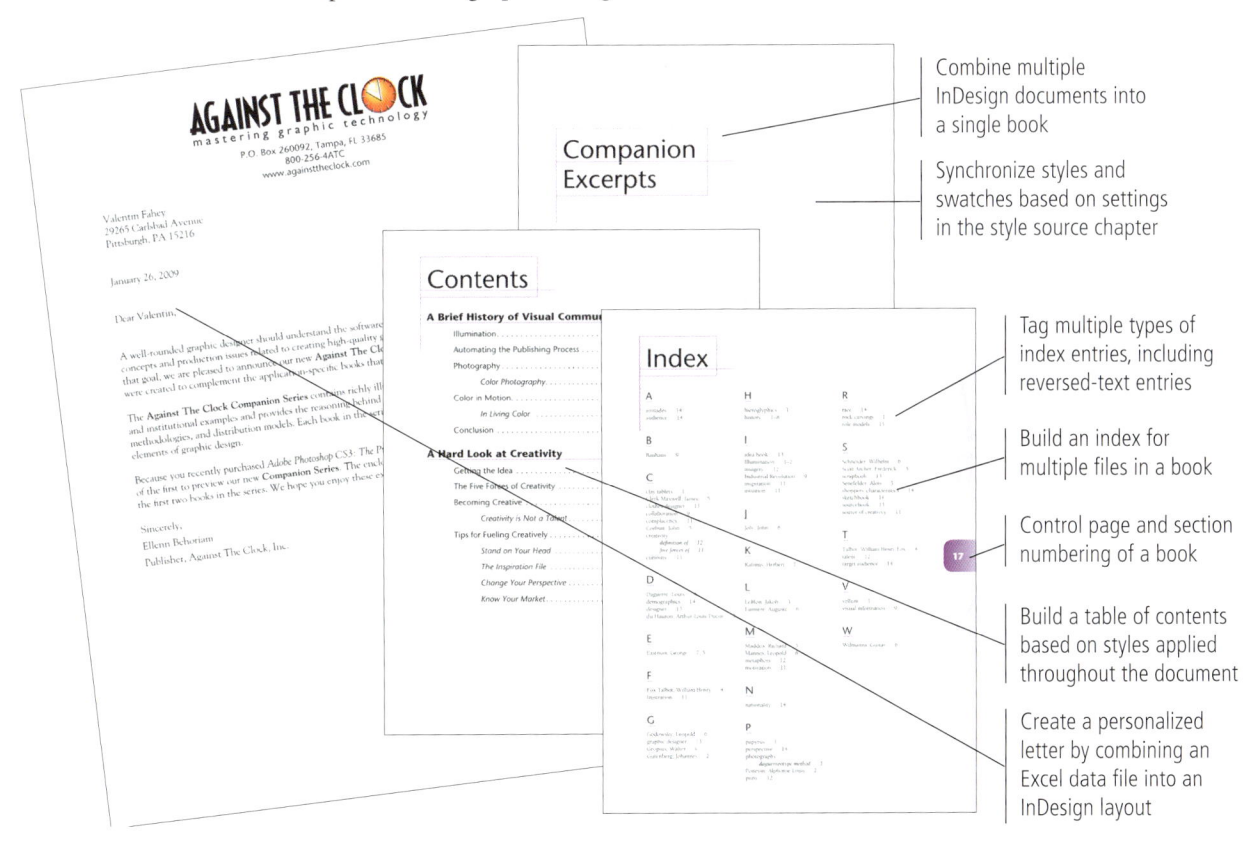

- Combine multiple InDesign documents into a single book
- Synchronize styles and swatches based on settings in the style source chapter
- Tag multiple types of index entries, including reversed-text entries
- Build an index for multiple files in a book
- Control page and section numbering of a book
- Build a table of contents based on styles applied throughout the document
- Create a personalized letter by combining an Excel data file into an InDesign layout

Index

A

accordion folds   208
actions   447
actual size   19
Add   61
Add All   483
Add Anchor Point tool   45
Add Bullets dialog box   294, 405
Add Document   457
additive primaries   327
additive secondaries   327
add pages to   284
adjust stroke weight when scaling   40, 60
adjust view settings   342
Adobe Illustrator   37, 333–336, 340, 344
Adobe Paragraph Composer   306
Adobe PDF Preset   138
Adobe Photoshop   72, 193, 196, 336–340, 343, 443
Adobe Single-line Composer   306
advanced character formats   225
Advanced Type preferences   119
after first _ letters   304
align objects   44
align-on-decimal tab   238
Align panel   44, 241
align stroke   56
all caps   119
Allow Document Pages to Shuffle   216
Allow Master Item Overrides   213, 218
Allow Master Overrides on Selection   155
Allow Object-Level Display Settings   16, 342
Allow Selected Spreads to Shuffle   216
all printer's marks   87
Alpha channel   110, 176, 244, 246, 336, 343
alternating pattern   184, 185
anchored object marker   360
anchored objects   129–131, 240
anchored placeholders   131
anchor points   45–48, 66, 133, 247
Appearance of Black preferences   387
Append Content   430
Application bar   2, 10, 13, 19, 20, 80
Application frame   2, 3, 13
Apply Leading to Entire Paragraph   119
Apply Master to Page   155, 264
Apply Photoshop Clipping Path   245, 341
Apply to All Spreads   317
Apply XSLT   427, 429
Arrange Documents panel   20
Arrange menu   49, 251, 310, 354
arrowheads   56, 240
ASCII characters   297

Ask When Opening   333
Assign Profiles   332
Assign Trap Presets dialog box   388
Attributes panel   213, 240
Auto-Collapse Iconic Panels   4
Autocorrect preferences   372
auto-flow text   284–286
Automatically Adjust to Fit Marks and Bleeds   315
Automatically Update   460
automatic page numbers   274–277
Auto Rename   166, 171, 222
Autotag   419, 422

B

back matter   487
barrel folds   208
based on   290. *See also* parent-child relationships
baseline   240
baseline grid   123
baseline shift   119
Basic Feather effect   108
Basic Graphics Frame style   239, 243–244, 248
Basic Paragraph style   249, 399
before last _ letters   304
behaviors   444–446
between entry and number   474
Bevel and Emboss effect   108
Bézier curves   47, 49, 56, 109
bitmapping   35
bleed   28, 30, 68, 82, 195, 259, 272, 345
bleed between pages   313
bleed guides   96
Bleed screen mode   81
bleed/trim hazard   196
blending mode   104
booklet type   313
Book Page Numbering Options dialog box   460, 461, 470
Book panel   457, 459–463, 467, 474, 477, 487, 488
books   455–469
bounding box   38, 176, 374
Bring to Front   49, 310
bullet character list   294, 405
bullet or numbering position   295
Bullets and Numbering options   225, 294, 404
Buttons panel   443–446

C

calibration   329
cap options   56
case sensitive   367, 369, 370
CCITT compression   139

Cell Options dialog box   181–183, 186–187
Cell Styles panel   190
Center Content   352, 416
Center in Frame   496
chain icon   26, 30, 39, 174
change case   119
chapter numbering   465
Chapter Number variable   282, 465
character color   225
Character panel   118, 119, 120, 225
character styles   165, 225
Check Spelling   370
choke   387
CIELAB. *See* LAB color
Clear Attributes   190
Clear Object-Level Display Settings   342
Clear Overrides   168, 174, 180, 190, 250, 291
Clear Transformations   40
clip complex regions   136
clip contents to cell   183
clipping paths   109–113, 244, 245, 343
clone repeating text elements   429
cloning   53, 213
Close Tab Group   7
CMYK   67, 69, 70, 82, 93, 95, 97, 136, 193, 195, 198, 328, 329, 330, 331, 332, 337, 379, 382, 385, 386, 418
color
   management   328–332
   mode   65, 69
   profiles. See profiles
   shift   198, 328
   swatches   84
   theory   327
Color blending mode   104
Color Burn blending mode   104
Color Dodge blending mode   104
Color panel   49–50, 65, 78, 80, 84
Color Picker   328
color-separated proofs   86
Color Settings dialog box   330–332, 333
color space not allowed   197
column break character   275, 276
column guides   152
columns   153, 154, 172, 259
column strokes   184
common colors   387
composite CMYK   87
composite proofs   85
compound paths   59
compression   139, 427
conditional text   196, 319–324
conflict with existing style   222
consolidate all   20
Content Placement Options dialog box   498
continue from previous document   460

Index

continue on next even page   460
continue on next odd page   460
contour options   246
Control panel   39, 40, 41, 43, 44, 50, 56, 61, 63, 73, 76, 79, 98, 99, 107, 112, 113, 118, 122, 149, 154, 163, 172, 180, 181, 210, 226, 243, 415
Convert All Strokes to Outlines   136
Convert All Text to Outlines   136
Convert Bullets & Numbering to Text   171
Convert Clipping Path to Frame   111
Convert Direction Point tool   47, 48
Convert Object to Button   443
Convert Rows   189
Convert Shape   61, 412
Convert to Destination   384
Convert to Destination (Preserve Numbers)   384
Convert to Profile   332
Convert to Working Space   331
Convert Variable to Text   278
Copy Fonts   200
Copy Linked Graphics   200
corner effects   240
corner options   413
corner points   48
corner radius   412
Create Acrobat Layers   138
Create Link   428, 429, 432, 438
Create Merged Document   497
Create New Index Entry   477, 484, 485
Create New Layer   373
Create New Style   233, 239, 407
Create New Swatch   417
Create Outlines   65
Create PDF Bookmarks   473
Create Tagged PDF   138
creation date variable   282
creep   313, 314
crop to   335, 344, 346
cross-references   196, 486, 489
current page number marker   274, 276, 277
Customize Control Panel   120
customize style import   171
custom text   279
cutting   209

D

Darken blending mode   104
databases   492
Data Merge   492–503
data sources   492
date format   282
DCS format   340
Default Fill and Stroke button   38, 41
Delete Elements   431
Delete Empty Pages   284

Delete Master Spread   262
Delete Page/Spread   216
Delete Paragraph Style dialog box   287
delimited text   492
density   385
destination space   329, 332
Detach All Objects from Master   155
Detach Selection from Master   155
Detect Edges   110, 176
device-independent color   329
DICColor   69
Dictionary dialog box   305, 368, 371
Dictionary preferences   368
die cutting   34, 373
Difference blending mode   104
dimensions include stroke weight   40, 410
Directional Feather effect   108
Direct Selection tool   40, 42, 45, 46, 47, 53, 55, 57, 66, 68, 73, 101, 103, 109, 111, 112, 154, 163, 247, 334, 345, 377, 415
discretionary hyphen   274, 276
discretionary line break   275
Display Performance preferences   16, 342
distribute objects   44
document bleed settings   87
document numbering   463, 462
Document Setup dialog box   152, 346
document tabs   13, 19, 21
do not import contents of whitespace-only elements   429
dots per inch (dpi)   36
double-parallel folds   208
downsampling   139
drop caps   225, 234
Drop Shadow effect   107, 112
drop zone   3, 7
DTD   439
Duplicate   53, 54
Duplicate Layer   378
Duplicate Page/Spread   216
dynamic spelling   196, 372

E

Edit Original   347, 348, 349, 377
effective resolution   139, 415
Effects dialog box   105
Effects panel   101, 103–107, 240
em   119
embedded paths   336
embedded profiles   330
Embed Fonts   68
Embed Page Thumbnails   138
Emboss effect   108
em dash   274, 276
em space   275, 276, 277
en dash   235, 274, 276

en space   275, 276
encoding   427
end cap   240
End Nested Style Here character   274
End of Document   483
End of Section   483
End of Story   483
entire pasteboard   19
entry separators   489
entry style   472
EPS format   67–71, 84, 136, 340–341
EPS Import Options dialog box   341
even page break   275
events, button   445
exclude overlap   61
Exclusion blending mode   104
Export Adobe PDF dialog box   138–140, 318, 385, 447, 448, 490–491, 498
Export dialog box   67–71, 137, 426
Export EPS dialog box   70
Export From Selected Element   427
Export Layers   138
Export to PDF   497
Export Untagged Tables As CALS XML   427
Export XML dialog box   426–427
extended ASCII characters   297
Eyedropper tool   127, 311, 417

F

face trim   314
facing pages   30, 32, 207, 259, 264, 268
fast display   16, 342
fields   492
figure space   275
file name variable   282
fill   49, 55, 59, 101, 184, 240, 311
Fill Frame Proportionally   352, 413
Fill with Placeholder Text   398
Find/Change dialog box   358–367
Find Font dialog box   149
Find Format Settings dialog box   362
Find Object Format Options dialog box   364
Fit Content Proportionally   75, 83, 352
Fit Content to Frame   352
Fit Frame to Content   179, 187, 352, 443
Fit Page in Window   14, 15, 19
Fit Spread in Window   19
fitting   498. *See also* frame fitting options
Fitting on Empty Frame   413
fixed column width   172
flat   312
flattener presets   136
Flattener Preview panel   137
flattening   136, 195
floating panels   8, 9

506

Index

Float in Window 19
flush space 275
Focoltone 69
folding 207, 209
folding dummy 312
folding guides 209–212
following topic 488
fonts 64, 118, 147, 149, 191
   licensing 200
   metrics 119
   variations 64
font types not allowed 196
footer rows 189
footnote number marker 274
footnote reference marker 360
footnotes 367
forced line break 236, 275, 276
Formatting Affects Text button 65
for next # of pages 483
for next # of paragraphs 483
FPO images 195
frame break character 116–118, 275, 276
frame content 102
frame fitting options 75, 240, 413
front matter 458

G

gamut 67, 101, 328, 329, 331
ganging 31, 312
gap attributes 56, 240
gate-fold documents 208
Generate Index 488
GIF format 427
global light 107
glyphs 118, 120, 297
Glyphs panel 297, 403–405, 406
Go to Link 150, 347
gradient and mesh resolution 136
Gradient Feather tool 100, 105, 108
Gradient panel 97–99, 99
gradients
   angle 99
   effect 105
   feathering 105, 108
   swatches 94, 98, 99
Gradient tool 100
graphics frame 163, 176, 411
graphics placeholder 409–412
greeked text 115
GREP 367
Grids & Guides 123, 212
Grids preferences 123
gripper margin 28
groups 54, 55, 66
Guides & Pasteboard preferences 43
gutter 152, 153, 172, 259

H

hair space 275
halftone dots 36
handles 47, 48, 133
Hand tool 15, 19
hanging indent 295
hanging punctuation 126
Hard Light blending mode 104
header rows 189
hidden characters 117, 126
hidden layers 367, 378
Hide Frame Edges 51, 185, 187
Hide/Show Master Items 155
Hide Tagged Frames 439, 440
Hide Tag Markers 439, 440
Hide Text Threads 273
high quality display 16, 342
horizontal scaling 119, 121
Hue blending mode 104
hyperlinks 440–442
Hyperlinks panel 441
hyphenation 225, 303–305
hyphenation zone 304
hyphen limit 304

I

ICC profiles 196. *See* profiles
iconized panels 4, 7, 9
Ignore Optical Margin 127
Ignore Text Wrap 172, 441
Illustrator Options dialog box 335
image color settings 338
Image Import Options dialog box 245, 246, 337, 343, 350
image placeholders 496
image resolution 194. *See also* resolution
Import CALS Tables As InDesign Tables 429
Import Inline Graphics 171
Import Into Selected Element 437
Import Options dialog box 285
Import Styles Automatically 166, 171, 219, 285
Import Text Elements Into Tables If Tags Match 429
Import Unused Styles 171
Import XML dialog box 428, 437
imposition 31, 259, 312, 314
Include Book Documents 473, 488
Include DTD Declaration 427
Include Empty Index Sections 489
Include Footnotes 367
Include Index Section Headings 489
Include Inside Edges 110, 113
Include Master Pages 367
Include Text on Hidden Layers 473
indents 124, 225
indent to here character 274, 276

indexes 476–489
index marker 360
Index panel 477, 478, 483, 484, 488
ink limits 380
Ink Manager 385
inks 327
inline graphics. *See* anchored objects
Inner Bevel effect 108
Inner Glow effect 107
Inner Shadow effect 107
in port 114
Insert Blank Pages 460, 461
insertion point 62, 63, 76, 79, 114, 116, 124, 125, 177, 288, 292, 293, 407
Insert Pages 216, 217
Insert Special Character 276, 279
Insert Table 177
Insert Variables 279, 280
inset. *See* text inset
Inset Frame 113
intent. *See* rendering intent
interactive elements 196, 318, 440–451
Interface preferences 71, 102
intersect 61
invert 113
island spread 216
Item Information dialog box 252

J

join options 56
JPEG compression 139
JPEG format 350, 427
jump object 176
jump to next column 176
justification 225

K

Keep Layer Visibility Overrides 336
Keep options 183, 225, 298–303, 359
kerning 119
keyboard shortcuts 6, 11, 400, 402
knockout 59, 308, 386

L

LAB color 93, 97, 195, 329, 331
language 368
last page number variable 282
Layer Options dialog box 373–374
layers 338, 373–391
Layers panel 373, 376, 378
layer visibility overrides 196
leader character 238
leading 119, 121
letterfold documents 208
level 472
level style 489
library files 251–256
Library panel 252

507

Index

ligatures   119
Lighten blending mode   104
limit to master text frames   284
line art   35
line art and text resolution   136
line screen   36, 194
line segments   48
lines per inch (lpi). *See* line screen
Line tool   51, 52, 214
linked graphics   191
Link Images   496
Links panel   147, 150, 151, 347–349, 350, 433
list type   294, 405
live area   31, 196
Load All Text Styles   222
loaded cursor   71, 76, 114, 167, 220, 338, 341, 347, 350, 351
Load Master Pages   155, 263
Load Object Styles   248
Load Styles   222
local formatting   165
local formatting overrides   290, 306–308
locked layers   367
locked stories   367
Lock Guides   212, 374
Lock Layer   374
look-up tables   329
Lorem text   398
Luminosity blending mode   104

M

make compound path   60
manual page breaks   171
Map by Name   431, 438
Map Tags to Styles   430, 438
margin guides   270
margins   26, 28, 30, 152, 154, 209, 259
Margins and Columns dialog box   152, 270
Marks and Bleed options   87, 140, 315, 384
Master Options dialog box   155, 262
master pages   148, 152, 154, 155, 158, 260–262, 266–271, 367
master text frame   209, 259, 270
Menu bar   1, 2, 3, 10, 13, 19–21, 80
menus   1, 11
Merge Cells   182
Merge Content   428, 438
metacharacters   360
Microsoft Excel   177, 180, 492
Microsoft Word   165, 166, 168, 171, 180, 217, 219, 222, 224, 237, 356
minimum stroke weight   196
minimum type size   196

mismatched color names   94–95
misregistration   386
missing files   150, 193, 349, 459
missing fonts   147, 148, 149, 166, 194, 196, 219, 285
miter limit   240
mixed Ink swatches   94
modification date variable   278, 282
modified files   150, 193, 459
Modify Trap Preset Options dialog box   388
Move Pages   216
multiple record layout   500
multiple-up   31
Multiply blending mode   104

N

nameplate   148
name with color value   94
navigating text   400
nested line styles   232
nested styles   190, 225, 227, 231–236. *See also* parent-child relationships
nested tools   6
New Book   456
New Color Swatch   69, 94–95
New Condition   320, 321
New Document   25–28, 29, 31, 32, 33
New Gradient Swatch   97
New Hyperlink from URL   441
New Library Item   252
New Master   155
New Nested Style   234
New Page Reference   477, 479, 481, 483
New Section   464
New Table of Contents Style   471
New Text Variable   279, 280
New Workspace   10
next page number marker   274
next style change   483
next use of style   483
no color conversion   384
nonbreaking hyphen   274, 276
nonbreaking space (fixed width)   275
nonbreaking spaces   275, 276, 479, 480
None swatch   59, 93, 96
non-facing pages   207
non-joiner character   274
nonprinting attribute   213, 240
non-proportional scaling of placed object   196
non-proportional type scaling   196
Normal screen mode   81
Normal style   168
no text wrap   176
numbered paragraphs   475
Numbering & Section options   216, 462, 463, 464

O

object knocks out drop shadow   107
object layer options   339
Object Style Options dialog box   239–240
object styles   239–242, 248, 251
Object Styles panel   241, 242, 244, 248, 250
odd page break   275
offset [rule]   229
only import elements that match existing structure   429
opacity   101
Open dialog box   12, 18, 159
OpenType fonts   120, 225, 297, 406
OPI   195, 340
optical margin alignment   126–128, 240
optimized formatted images   427
optimized original images   427
optimize for fast Web view   138
original images   427
orphans   247, 302
Outer Bevel effect   108
Outer Glow effect   107
out-of-gamut colors   328
out port   114, 115, 116, 167, 178
output date variable   282
Overlay blending mode   104
overprint   195, 386
override all master page items   155, 160, 161, 218, 353, 356, 458
override automatic hyphenation   305
overset text   114, 115, 178, 194, 196, 468

P

Package dialog box   199
packaging   191–203
page break   275, 276
page description language (PDL)   85
page geometry   209
page numbering   457, 460, 464
page-number references   489
page-range references   483–485
Page Size menu   29
Pages panel   17, 137, 148, 153, 155–159, 210, 216, 217, 263–267, 458
page transitions   216, 316–319
panel dock   2, 3
panels
  Align panel   44, 241
  Arrange Documents panel   20
  Attributes panel   213, 240
  Book panel   457, 459–463, 467, 475, 477, 487, 488
  Buttons panel   443, 445, 446
  Cell Styles panel   190
  Character panel   118, 119, 120, 225

Index

Color panel 49–50, 65, 78, 80, 84
Control panel 39, 40, 41, 43, 44, 50, 56, 61, 63, 73, 76, 79, 98, 99, 107, 112, 113, 118, 122, 149, 154, 163, 172, 180, 181, 210, 226, 243, 415
Effects panel 101, 103–107, 240
Flattener Preview panel 137
Glyphs panel 297, 403–405, 406
Hyperlinks panel 441
Index panel 477, 478, 483, 484, 488
Layers panel 373, 376, 378
Library panel 252
Links panel 147, 150, 151, 347–349, 350, 433
Object Styles panel 241, 242, 244, 248, 250
Pages panel 17, 137, 148, 153, 155–159, 210, 216, 217, 263–267, 458
Paragraph panel 119, 122–127, 225
Paragraph Styles panel 168–172, 221, 222, 223, 226, 233, 240, 249, 263, 287, 407, 408, 413, 435
Pathfinder panel 59–62, 410, 411
Preflight panel 191, 192, 195, 197
Separations Preview panel 379–382
Story panel 126, 127, 240
Stroke panel 56, 99, 185, 214, 240
Swatches panel 68, 93–96, 97, 98, 99, 115, 135, 157, 185, 198, 225, 240, 263, 336, 340, 382, 409, 417
Table panel 181, 183, 184
Table Styles panel 190
Tabs panel 225, 237, 238
Tags panel 419–422, 434, 439
Text Wrap panel 175, 176, 188, 231, 240, 246, 411
Tools panel 5, 6
Transform panel 41, 98, 163, 334, 345, 415
Trap Presets panel 388
Pantone Matching System 69
paper size 86
Paper swatch 93, 115, 157, 195, 397, 441
paper thickness 207
paragraph alignment 124, 135, 180
paragraph formatting 79, 124
Paragraph panel 119, 122–127, 225
paragraph return character 275, 276
paragraph rules 225, 227
paragraph spacing limit 175
Paragraph Style Options dialog box 226–229, 234, 287, 289, 294, 303
paragraph styles 165, 225, 240
Paragraph Styles panel 168–172, 221, 222, 223, 226, 233, 240, 249, 263, 287, 407, 408, 413, 435

parent-child relationships 227, 290–293
parent style 290
Paste in Place 58
Pathfinder panel 59–62, 410, 411
path options 61
patient-user mode 73
PDF format 85, 136–140, 147, 312, 318–319, 344–345, 346, 383–385, 440, 447, 490–492
PDF/X 138
Pen tool 45–49, 48, 51, 56, 109, 132
perfect binding 313
Photoshop Path 176
picas 25
Pillow Emboss effect 108
pixels per inch (ppi) 36
placed graphics 150
Place dialog box 71, 74, 75, 103, 163, 166, 170, 178, 219, 245, 246, 335, 344, 346
placeholders 395–398
Place InDesign Document dialog box 346
Place PDF dialog box 335, 338, 344
Polygon tool 56, 57
PostScript 68, 85, 86
PostScript fonts 120
PPD 86
preferences 12
 Advanced Type 119
 Appearance of Black 387
 Autocorrect 372
 Dictionary 368
 Display Performance 16, 342
 Grids 123
 Guides & Pasteboard 43
 Interface 71, 102
 Type 119, 284
 Units & Increments 27, 29, 211, 271
preflighting 191–203
Preflight panel 191, 192, 195, 197
Preflight Profiles dialog box 192, 195
Preserve Embedded Profiles 331
Preserve Facing-Page Spreads 284
Preserve Numbers (Ignore Linked Profiles) 331
Preserve Object-Level Display Settings 342
Preserve Styles and Formatting 166, 219, 285
presets 32, 33
prevent manual positioning 129, 240
Preview screen mode 80
previous page number marker 274
print blank printer spreads 313
Print Booklet dialog box 313–315
Print dialog box 85–90, 136, 213, 314, 383

printer's marks 87
printer's spreads 312, 461
printing 328, 386
Printing Instructions dialog box 200
printing plates 67
print layer 374
print nonprinting objects 213
process color 67, 94, 95, 157, 193, 198, 381, 382, 385
profile inclusion policy 384
Profile or Policy Mismatch 333, 348, 457
profiles 196, 328, 329, 337
proxy generation 341
pull quote 231–236
punctuation space 275

Q

QuarkXPress 340
quarter space 275
quick apply 40
quotation marks 274, 276

R

range kerning. *See* tracking
raster image processor (RIP) 85
raster images 35, 36, 45
Rasterize the PostScript 341
raster/vector balance 136
Read Embedded OPI Image Links 341
reader's spread 312
records 492
records per document page 497, 500
Rectangle tool 38, 41
recto pages 264
Redefine InDesign Style 171
Redefine Style 307, 308, 418
Redefine Style When Changing All 149
reference point 39, 72
Registration color 93, 195
registration marks 85
Release Compound Paths 60
Relink 150, 199, 347, 349
Remap Break 427
Remember Font with Bullet 295
Remove All Local Overrides 155, 269
Remove Blank Lines for Empty Fields 498
Remove Documents 457
Remove Selected Local Overrides 155, 269
rendering intent 331, 332, 337
repeating footers 189
repeating headers 189
Replace Document 461
Replace Existing Table of Contents 475
Replace Selected Item 74, 82, 103, 109, 128, 163, 166, 170, 178, 335, 337, 338, 341, 343, 414, 443

509

Index

Replace With   223
Reset To Base   291
resolution   36, 139, 194, 196
resolution independence   35
Restrict to Frame   113
reversed topic reference   479, 480
RGB color   67, 93, 95, 97, 136, 193, 195, 327–332, 337, 417
right indent tab   274, 276
roll folds   208
Rotate Text   181
Rotate View   17, 216
row height   181, 183
row strokes   184
rulers   26, 210, 211
ruler units   27, 29, 271
ruler units origin   211
Run-in   473
run length encoding   139
running header variable   282

S

saddle stitching   313
same as clipping   176
sampling   311, 417
Satin effect   108
Saturation blending mode   104
Save As dialog box   28, 159, 161, 216
Save as Master   155, 261
Save Preset   32, 140, 384, 447
Save the Book   459
Scale tool   58
scaling   154, 163
Screen blending mode   104
screen ruling   36
search for missing links   151
section heading   489
section marker   274, 360, 465
section numbering   457, 460, 464
section prefix   464
Select All   76, 115, 156
Select Data Source   493
Selected Items icon   376
selecting text   63, 400
Selection tool   41, 42, 43, 49, 52, 53, 54, 66, 81, 112, 113, 114, 129, 134, 154, 160, 175, 187, 213, 249, 334, 345, 419
Select Next Object Below   83
Select Unused Masters   155
self mailer   154
semi-automatic text flow   220
Send to Back   250, 251, 273, 354
separations   67, 87
Separations Preview panel   379–382
Show All Menu Items   11, 53, 58, 98, 373
Show Baseline Grid   123

Show Content Offset   40
Show Frame Edges   134, 187, 265, 273
Show Guides   265, 374
Show Hidden Characters   76, 117, 277, 356, 401, 494
Show Import Options   166, 170, 178, 219, 245, 246, 285, 335, 337, 343, 344, 346, 350
Show Layers   336, 374
Show Rulers   26
Show Single Plates in Black   379
Show Structure   424
Show Tagged Frames   420
Show Tag Markers   422
Show Text Snippets   424
Show Text Threads   116, 273
Show Thumbnails on Place   102
Show XML Import Options   437
sidebars   173
signature size   313
sixth space   275
size   118
skew   119
slugs   30, 195, 212–215, 259, 281
small caps   119
Smart Guides   38, 42, 43, 44, 47, 53, 57, 66, 210
Smart Match Style Groups   468
Smart Text Reflow   284, 286
smooth points   47
Snap Above Frame   237
Soft Light blending mode   104
soft return   236
sort by   479
Sort Entries in Alphabetical Order   472
source profiles   329
space before paragraph   79, 124
space between pages   313
special characters   274–275, 360, 427
spelling   305, 368–373
spine   211
spot color   69, 70, 84, 94, 104, 157, 193, 195, 198, 336, 340, 381, 382, 385, 386
spots per inch (spi)   36
spread flattening   216
spreads   30, 207, 210, 387
stacking order   49
star inset   57
start page numbering at   463
start section   464
states, button   442–444
step and repeat   54
stop color   97
Story options   240
Story panel   126, 127, 240
story tag   421
strikethrough   119, 225

stroke   50, 55, 80, 96, 101, 184, 240
Stroke & Corner options   240
stroke drawing order   186
Stroke panel   56, 99, 185, 214, 240
stroke style   40, 56
stroke weight   50, 51, 55, 96
Structure pane   424–425, 428, 429, 430, 435, 437, 439
styles   147, 149, 165–176, 253
   conflicts   166, 171, 222
   editing   226–229
   importing   219–221, 222–224
   overrides   196
Style Source file   457, 466
subscript   119
subtract   60, 61
subtractive primaries   327
superscript   119
Suppress Page Range   483
Suppress Text Wrap When Layer is Hidden   374
Swap Fill and Stroke button   39
Swatches panel   68, 93–96, 97, 98, 99, 115, 135, 157, 185, 198, 225, 240, 263, 336, 340, 382, 409, 417
Swatch options   198, 382, 418
symmetrical points   48
synchronization   466–470
Synchronize options   467, 487

T

tab characters   177, 237–239
tab leader   238
table cells   179–180, 184
Table of Contents   470–476
Table of Contents Styles   471
Table options   184, 185–191
Table panel   181, 183, 184
tables   177–188
Table Setup   184, 185
Table Styles panel   190
Tabs panel   225, 237, 238
Tag options   420, 421
Tags panel   419–422, 434, 439
templates   147–164, 207–216, 412–413
text
   auto-flow   284–286
   frames   62–66, 113–115, 147, 167, 172, 178, 180, 183, 184, 215, 421
   inset   172, 174, 181, 182, 183, 272, 397
   orientation   181, 183
   snippets   424
   string   492
   threads   113–116, 126, 217–218, 273
   variables   278–283, 465
   wrap   175, 374, 441

510

Index

Text Frame Baseline Options 240
Text Frame General Options 240
Text Frame Options 152, 153, 156, 172–176, 240, 270, 272, 399, 441
Text Variables dialog box 279, 280
Text Wrap panel 175, 176, 188, 231, 240, 246, 411
thin space 275, 276
third space 275
threshold 113
TIFF format 343
tint swatch 94
to end of document 484
tolerance 113
to next use of style 484, 485
tools
    Add Anchor Point tool 45
    Convert Direction Point tool 47, 48
    Direct Selection tool 40, 42, 45, 46, 47, 53, 55, 57, 66, 68, 73, 101, 103, 109, 111, 112, 154, 163, 247, 334, 345, 377, 415
    Eyedropper tool 127, 311, 417
    Gradient Feather tool 100, 105, 108
    Gradient tool 100
    Hand tool 15, 19
    Line tool 51, 52, 214
    Pen tool 45–49, 51, 56, 109, 132
    Polygon tool 56, 57
    Rectangle tool 38, 41
    Scale tool 58
    Selection tool 41, 42, 43, 49, 52, 53, 54, 66, 81, 112, 113, 114, 129, 134, 154, 160, 175, 187, 213, 249, 334, 345, 419
    Type on a Path tool 133
    Type tool 62, 76, 79, 113–116, 149, 156, 179
    Zoom tool 14, 15, 19
Tools panel 5, 6
tool tips 6
topic levels 477, 479, 485, 486, 487
total area coverage 95, 380

total ink coverage 95, 380
Toyo 69
track changes 171
tracking 119
transformations are totals 40
Transform panel 41, 98, 163, 334, 345, 415
transparency 101–106, 136–143, 195, 196, 216, 244
transparency blend space 136
Transparency Flattener 68
Transparency Flattener presets 136, 140
transparent background 335
trapping 195, 386–388
Trap Presets panel 388
TrueType fonts 120
TruMatch 69
type on a path 132–136
Type preferences 119, 284
type scaling 196
type size 64
Type tool 62, 76, 79, 113–116, 149, 156, 179
typical display 16, 342

U

underline 119, 225
Undo 341
Unicode fonts 297
Units & Increments preferences 27, 29, 211, 271
Update Graphic Links 200
Update Link 338, 347, 433
Update Table of Contents 477
Use Black Point Compensation 332
Use Document Bleed Settings 140
Use Global Light 107
Use InDesign Style Definition 171
Use PDF's Layer Visibility 336
user interface 1–6
user-modified path 176, 247
Use TIFF or PICT Preview 341

V

vector graphics 35, 45
verso pages 264
vertical alignment 181, 182, 183
vertical justification 175, 176
vertical scale 119, 121
View menu 19, 51
view PDF after exporting 138, 318
view percentage 13
view XML using 427
visible in PDF but doesn't print 446
visible & printable layers 383

W

white space 274–275
whole word 367
widows 302
wildcards 360, 361
Window menu 2, 7, 18, 49
words with at least _ letters 304
working space 330, 332, 348
workspaces 2, 40
Workspace switcher 10, 11
Wrap Around Bounding Box 176
Wrap Around Object Shape 176, 246

X

XML 419–439
XML Import options 428, 438

Z

zero point crosshairs 212
z-fold documents 208
ZIP compression 139
Zoom Level field 13, 19
Zoom tool 14, 15, 19

511

Project Portfolio Design Awards

The **Against The Clock Project Portfolio Design Awards** are your chance to gain recognition for your creative and technical design skills. Prizes range from your work being displayed in the Against The Clock Web Gallery, to cash prizes, to having your design published in an upcoming ATC book.

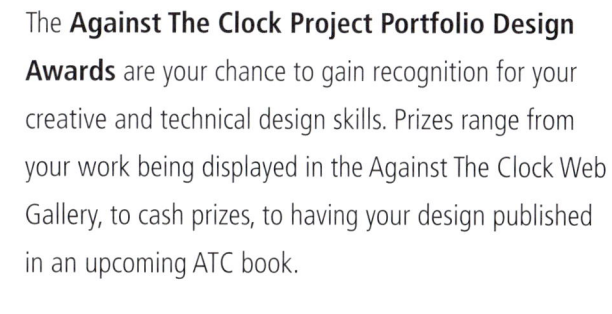

The **Project Portfolio Design Awards** are designed to test both your creative talents and technical skills. Submit your Portfolio Builder project from any of the Professional Portfolio Series books for your chance to win. Entries will be judged on design quality, originality, understanding of client needs, and technical skills.

Go to **www.againsttheclock.com/contest.html** for complete contest details and rules, and to download the official contest entry form.

AGAINST THE CLOCK
mastering graphic technology

Use our portfolio to build yours.

The Against The Clock Professional Portfolio Series walks you step-by-step through the tools and techniques of graphic design professionals.

Order online at www.againsttheclock.com
Use code **PFS409** for a 10% discount

Go to **www.againsttheclock.com** to enter our monthly drawing for a free book of your choice.

AGAINST THE CLOCK
mastering graphic technology